SOCIAL PSYCHOLOGY

SOCIAL PSYCHOLOGY
A SOCIOLOGICAL PERSPECTIVE

Christine M. Von Der Haar

Indiana University

PEARSON
Prentice Hall

Upper Saddle River, New Jersey 07458

Library of Congress Cataloging-in-Publication Data

Von Der Haar, Christine M.
   Social psychology: a sociological perspective / Christine M. Von Der Haar.—1st ed.
     p. cm.
   ISBN 0-13-080983-7
   1. Social psychology.   2. Sociology.   I. Title.

HM1033.V66 2005
302–dc22
                                       2004057641

Editorial Director: Leah Jewell
AVP/Publisher: Nancy Roberts
Editorial Assistant: Lee Peterson
Director of Manufacturing and Production: Barbara Kittle
Senior Marketing Manager: Marissa Feliberty
Marketing Assistant: Jennifer Lang
Production Editor: Joan Stone
Prepress and Manufacturing Manager: Nick Sklitsis
Manufacturing Buyer: Mary Ann Gloriande
Creative Design Director: Leslie Osher
Senior Art Director: Anne Bonanno Nieglos
Interior and Cover Design: GGS Book Services/Brian Molloy

Director, Image Resource Center: Melinda Reo
Manager, Rights and Permissions: Zina Arabia
Manager, Visual Research: Beth Brenzel
Image Permission Coordinator: LaShonda Morris
Photo Researcher: Diana Gongora
Composition: Lithokraft
Printer/Binder: Courier Companies, Inc.
Cover Printer: The Lehigh Press, Inc.
Typeface: 10/12 Janson Text
Cover Photo: Gerald Bustamante/
   Stock Illustration Source, Inc.

Acknowledgments for photographs, illustrations, tables, and text from other sources and reproduced, with permission, in this textbook appear on page 469.

Pearson Education LTD.
Pearson Education Singapore, Pte. Ltd
Pearson Education, Canada, Ltd
Pearson Education-Japan
Pearson Education Australia PTY, Limited

Pearson Education North Asia Ltd
Pearson Educación de Mexico, S.A. de C.V.
Pearson Education Malaysia, Pte. Ltd
Pearson Education, Upper Saddle River, NJ

10 9 8 7 6 5 4 3 2 1

ISBN: 0-13-080983-7

In loving memory of my father,
Gerard A. Von Der Haar, M.D.

Brief Contents

Contents

Boxes

Social psychology is a subject that is bound to capture and hold the attention of students for generations to come. Its focus on human behavior stirs the imagination about social life. It addresses fascinating questions that are relevant to our lives. For example, we all have an interest in questions about the development of the self, such as Who am I? and Why do I identify with certain groups? We also have questions about other people. Are leaders born, or do certain situations create them? Why would someone risk her own life to save a stranger? Why do people smoke when they know that doing so causes cancer?

In some cases, we want to understand how other people influence us. For example, we might wonder how a salesperson persuaded us to buy a product that we did not need and could not afford. Or we might want to know why we participated with other members of our fraternity in hazing rituals that could injure or even cause the deaths of pledges.

Social psychology offers answers for questions that arise in our personal lives every day. It also helps us make sense of an increasingly complicated world. News stories that take us far from home make us aware of complicated issues that can profoundly affect our lives. Many of the questions that these stories raise stump not only the reporters but also our leaders. Consider some of the questions that wars raise. What are the rules of war? What is a war crime? Are we all capable of committing one?

The 2003 *Columbia* disaster, which resulted in the deaths of seven astronauts, led us to ask what caused this tragic accident. Was it equipment failure or human error? Investigators concluded that a flaw in the decision-making process, known as *groupthink*, contributed to this accident. What can NASA do to prevent this from happening in the future?

Finally, what can social psychology teach us about Al Qaeda? Like NASA, it is a huge organization composed of many small groups. How does it operate? What kind of power does its leader exercise? How do groups within Al Qaeda make decisions? And how does this organization recruit and train followers?

We all want answers to these kinds of questions. This book goes beyond simple answers and provides full explanations of human behavior based on scientific research. As an introduction to the scientific study of human behavior, it covers the full range of questions that social psychologists have posed since the latter part of the nineteenth century. One story has been chosen to illustrate the main theme of each chapter. The first chapter begins with an incident that took place in New York City in 1999. It involves the story of Amadou Diallo, a 22-year-old immigrant from the African nation of Guinea, who met an untimely death in the vestibule of his own apartment building. His story tragically illustrates how socially constructed views of the world influence the thoughts, feelings, and behaviors of human beings. As one of the most important lessons of social psychology, this idea recurs throughout the book.

GOALS

The main purpose of this text is to help students understand the world in which they live. Three specific goals were considered in the pursuit of that objective. First, the book was written to provide relevant and interesting examples of how human beings are influenced by other people. This approach is designed to impress students with the relevance that social psychology has for their own lives. Creating this connection to real life should also stimulate interest and motivate students to apply the lessons learned in class to observations of their daily interactions.

The second goal of this book is to encourage students to develop critical thinking skills. The importance of this goal cannot be underestimated. In a world where the media so heavily shape public perceptions, a danger exists that people may become passive consumers of information. Students are therefore encouraged throughout the book to question the experts, to separate fact from opinion, to evaluate the evidence, to question the research methods, to look for flaws in reasoning—in short, to ask the right questions.

Finally, the third goal of this textbook is to show how sociologists have contributed to the field of social psychology. From Auguste Comte's nineteenth-century definition of social psychology to George Homans's twentieth-century explanation of how people balance the costs and rewards of their relationships, the tremendous influence of sociologists cannot be ignored. Among these stands the greatest contribution of all—George Herbert Mead's theory of symbolic interactionism. In recognition of that, one entire chapter is devoted to an explanation of his ideas and to the theories that evolved from them.

FEATURES

This book is designed to appeal to students who want to see and understand the relevance of college courses to their own lives. Social psychology is ideally suited to meet that expectation. To make the most of this natural advantage, the book incorporates a number of special features.

News Stories

One of the special features of this book is the use of news stories to illustrate the theme of a chapter, a concept, or a theory. Current or popular news stories offer a number of instructional advantages. First, they are interesting. They pique our curiosity and often raise questions that have no pat answers. Second, they supply students with examples that are already somewhat familiar. As a result, readers have already processed important information about an event, process, or actor in a particular situation. Third, news stories are a natural vehicle

for classroom discussions. Although students may not be prepared to analyze a particular story in terms of a social psychological theory, many feel knowledgeable enough to express an opinion about it. Classroom discussions that involve many students generate the kind of excitement that makes learning fun. They allow students to ask questions, suggest ideas, and propose solutions to problems. Ultimately, they also reveal the important lesson that the story is designed to tell. In some cases, news stories deal with controversial issues that can serve as topics for a classroom debate.

Self-Tests

Many of the chapters include self-tests that will help students recognize the relevance of social psychology to their own lives. These self-tests are instruments designed and used by social psychologists in their research. For example, Table 10.1 includes a questionnaire that was designed by Arnold Buss and Mark Perry to measure aggression. Students will quickly recognize how this instrument measures aggression in people's thoughts, feelings, and behaviors. Presenting methodology in this way makes research interesting, appealing, and relevant to students' lives. These kinds of self-tests also involve students in an exercise that will help them understand and remember the concepts being studied. When students apply Rosenberg's Self-Esteem Scale or Rubin's Measurements of "Loving" versus "Liking" to themselves, they are more likely to understand and remember the concepts being studied.

Boxes

A variety of boxes appear in each chapter. Many of these are designed to help students recognize how they can apply social psychology to their own lives. Some of them include excerpts from the writings of well-known social theorists such as Georg Simmel or Sigmund Freud. Other excerpts illustrate the raw data of qualitative research—verbatim quotations from subjects who provide insights into a research question. Excerpts also come from the Bible, *The New York Times*, Abraham Lincoln, and Martin Luther King, Jr. All of these boxes show the relevance of social psychology to everyday life.

Pedagogical Features

This book also includes a number of pedagogical features.

- *Figures, tables, and graphs* are designed to aid comprehension of theoretical models and to graphically summarize research findings.
- *Key concepts* are highlighted throughout each chapter, are listed at the end of the chapter as a study guide, and are defined in the Glossary at the back of the book.
- *Chapter summaries* review the most important ideas presented in each chapter.
- *Critical review questions* actively engage students with the material they have read.

SUPPLEMENTS

The ancillary materials that accompany *Social Psychology* are part of a complete learning package and have been carefully created to enhance the topics discussed in the text.

Instructor's Resource Manual with Tests

For each chapter in the text, this valuable resource provides a detailed outline, summary, list of objectives, discussion questions, and classroom activities. In addition, more than five hundred test questions in multiple-choice and short answer formats are available for each chapter; the answers to all questions are page-referenced to the text.

TestGEN-EQ

This computerized software allows instructors to create their own personalized exams, to edit any or all of the existing test questions, and to add new questions. Other special features of this program include random generation of test questions, creation of alternate versions of the same test, scrambling question sequence, and test preview before printing.

 **OneSearch with Research Navigator™: Sociology**

This guide focuses on using **Research Navigator™**—Prentice Hall's own gateway to databases—including *The New York Times* Search-by-Subject Archive, *ContentSelect™* Academic Journal Database powered by EBSCO, *The Financial Times*, and the "Best of the Web" Link Library. It also includes extensive appendices on documenting online sources and on avoiding plagiarism. This guide, along with the Research Navigator™ access code, is free to students when packaged with *Social Psychology*.

ACKNOWLEDGMENTS

This book represents the combined efforts of a remarkably talented, hardworking, and understanding team of people. Words cannot express my appreciation for the Prentice Hall professionals who played vital roles in producing this book. I can honestly say that nothing brought me more pleasure in writing this book than the relationships that developed through this collaborative process.

Nancy Roberts, Publisher for Anthropology, has my deepest respect and admiration. As the guiding force for this book, she has served as a model for excellence every step of the way. I am very fortunate for having the opportunity to work with Nancy. And I sincerely appreciate all of her support and encouragement.

Sharon Chambliss, who also worked on this book from the very beginning, deserves my sincere gratitude. Her expertise, encouragement, and delightful sense of humor lightened my load and made working a joy. Her understanding after the death of my father lifted my spirits and will forever remind me of the extraordinary value of human compassion.

Joan Stone, my production editor, has been a priceless asset. Standing out from her many talents are her tremendous organizational skills, her attention to detail, and especially her ability to solve problems. Working with Joan on a daily basis kept me focused and on track. It was a pleasure, and I owe her a debt of gratitude.

I would also like to thank Bruce Emmer. I truly value his conscientious editing, which was reflected in insightful questions and thoughtful comments. I would also like to extend my appreciation to Diana Gongora and Diane Kraut. Only through the efforts of these folks can a book be complete.

Mary Larson also deserves recognition for encouraging me to write this book. Her advice at the start of this project continues to guide me.

Although the final responsibility for the contents of this book rests with me, I would like to extend my sincere appreciation to the sociologists who reviewed the manuscript: Barbara Chesney, University of Toledo; Joline Jones, Worcester State College; Tom Petee, Auburn University; Cherylon Robinson, The University of Texas at San Antonio; Barbara Trepagnier, Texas State University, San Marcos; Diana Tumminia, Cal. State, Sacramento; and Clovis White, Oberlin College.

Finally, I would like to thank my family for their support and encouragement. My sisters, who provided the initial support for undertaking this project, have not wavered in their enthusiasm. And I want to express my deep gratitude to my parents who provided, among many other important things, a fine education.

Christine M. Von Der Haar

Christine Von Der Haar did her undergraduate work at Indiana University, where she majored in psychology and biology. She returned to I.U. for graduate work, earning masters degrees from the School of Education and the School of Journalism and a Ph.D. from the Department of Sociology.

Dr. Von Der Haar taught her first social psychology class more than twenty years ago. Today, she also teaches courses on Media and Society, Social Theory, and Introduction to Sociology. Her interest in writing college textbooks began at Baruch College in New York City when a colleague asked her to write a study guide for statistics. This fascination with statistics and survey research led to a position as Manager of Surveys for the CBS News/*New York Times* poll. In this position, she collaborated with the finest public opinion researchers in the business as well as with reporters and producers covering political campaigns and elections. She saw firsthand how the newsroom of a major network operates. When she returned to teaching at Indiana University, Dr. Von Der Haar discovered how much students appreciated this particular experience.

Dr. Von Der Haar's students describe what they like about her courses in one word—enthusiasm. For her this means a love of her subject and a curiosity about what students think. She has been nominated for several teaching awards and recently received the Trustees Teaching Award.

ONE

The Scientific Foundations of Social Psychology

In the early morning hours of February 4, 1999, Amadou Diallo, a 22-year-old immigrant from the African nation of Guinea, stood in the vestibule of his Bronx apartment when four men dressed in street clothes stepped out of a car and fired forty-one shots in his direction. A coroner's report would later suggest that most of the bullets had hit him after he had fallen to the ground and was dead or dying. Nineteen bullets had riddled his body (Dwyer 1999).

What went through this young man's mind during the last moments of his life? Did he think these men were about to rob him? That might explain why he pulled a wallet from his pants pocket. We will never know. What we do know is that the four men who shot him to death were New York City policemen assigned to the city's "street crimes unit" (Page 2000). They were looking for a serial rapist when they confronted Diallo in front of his apartment. In a split second, Diallo, an innocent, unarmed man, died in a hail of bullets. The four policemen who killed him were subsequently indicted for murder.

According to the tearful testimony of police officer Sean Carroll, the policemen began to fire after Carroll shouted "Gun!" in response to Diallo's reaching into his pocket. Only five people actually saw what happened—the four officers and a woman who testified that Carroll had shouted "Gun!" This became the defense for the actions of the four policemen, whose lawyers argued that they had made a tragic, but reasonable, mistake (Roane 2000).

On March 3, 2000, after twenty-three hours of deliberation, twelve jurors found the four police officers not guilty of all charges filed against them in this case. Based on interviews with jurors later, it appeared that their decision was linked to the judge's instructions to them. He had reminded them that the police officers had a right to shoot if they honestly believed that Diallo was pulling a gun out of his pocket—they had the right to defend themselves (Jackson 2000). Many questions remained unanswered. For example, why was it necessary to shoot forty-one times? Would the officers' reactions have been different if Diallo were white? Ultimately, these questions did not matter. And the jury claimed that the prosecutors failed to prove their case. The prosecution's argument, which varied little from the defense's, left jurors with too much reasonable doubt to convict any of the policemen (Page 2000).

W hat does the tragic death of Amadou Diallo teach us? There are perhaps no comforting lessons. But it does illustrate how human beings interact on the basis of shared meanings. Language and other symbols provide a shared **definition of a situation** that allows us to perceive and interpret the world in a common way. In this case, the result was tragic. Shouting "Gun!" defined the situation for the police officers as life-threatening. Inaccurate as it was, this definition guided the actions of the officers. Carroll's mistaken perception led to the death of Amadou Diallo. William and Dorothy Thomas captured this particular aspect of social life brilliantly when they wrote, "If men define situations as real, they are real in their consequences" (1928, 572). These New York City policemen were acting in a world they had defined, not the "real" world.

Controversy surrounded the acquittal of the four police officers in this case. In defense of the prosecutors, the Bronx district attorney, Robert T. Johnson, argued that they had presented a strong case, and he addressed many of the troubling questions that remained. He understood the situation only too well. Drawing on his own personal experience, he offered these insightful words of advice:

> "I've been in the Bronx since I was 16," he said. "I have a 19-year-old son who lives here. I know that when I get stopped, and I have a couple of times, I have to say my license is in my back pocket; the registration is in the glove compartment. That kind of fear that some people have has to be addressed. And even if it's not a policy thing, it's an attitudinal thing.
>
> "Your mind," he said, "must be open to innocent interpretations of people's conduct." (Waldman 2000)

THE FOCUS OF SOCIAL PSYCHOLOGY

Long before anyone even thought of the discipline now known as social psychology, political philosophers were seeking an answer to the question *What is the social nature of man?* (Allport 1985, 3). This ancient question, which continues to capture the imagination today, summarizes the key problem of modern social psychology. Understanding the social nature of humans would answer many questions and solve many problems. For example, what causes individuals to explode in fits of rage, as we have too often witnessed in the halls and on the playgrounds of American schools? Do depictions of violence in the media cause aggression in human beings? Or do these media depictions simply reflect human aggression without revealing its real cause?

Understanding the relationship between the individual and society is difficult. August Comte (1798–1857), an early social psychologist, expressed the problem best when he asked, "How can the individual be at once cause and consequence of society?" (Allport 1985, 8). Indeed, individuals are born into a preexisting society. They do not determine the social position they occupy at birth or many of the interactions that their position in society (the social structure) will determine. They may choose some of the roles they will play, but not all of them. From birth, society exerts a tremendous influence on the development of an individual. It shapes an individual's understanding of reality.

Social psychology is the scientific study of the relationship between the individual and society. To be more precise, Gordon Allport (1985, 5) defined it as

> an attempt to understand and explain how the thought, feeling, and behavior of individuals are influenced by the actual, imagined, or implied presence of other human beings. The term "implied presence" refers to the many activities the individual carries out because of his position (role) in a complex social structure and his membership in a cultural group.

As this definition suggests, the field of social psychology covers many aspects of human behavior. Social psychologists have classified the behaviors they study into three basic areas: (1) the influence of social factors on the individual, (2) social interaction between and among individuals, and (3) group processes (see Table 1.1). Research in each of these general areas of interest covers a range of specific topics.

Research that seeks to understand how social factors influence an individual includes topics such as person perception, self-perception, stereotyping, learning, attribution, and self-presentation. Social psychologists who focus on these topics examine how an individual processes information about the world. They might want to know how people form attitudes or how they judge other people. Everyday observations of human behavior provide a ready source of questions for the topics in this area. For example, how can we tell if someone is lying to us? Why do we tend to blame a driver involved in an automobile accident rather than bad weather or mechanical failure? Which is more important, the first or the last impression that we make?

Social psychologists who study social interaction between and among individuals examine topics such as interpersonal relationships, aggression, altruism, attitudes and attitude change, and communication. Researchers might ask, why do we fall in love? What causes domestic violence? Why would someone donate a kidney to a complete stranger?

The third general area of interest in social psychology, group processes, includes topics such as power and leadership, conformity, cooperation versus competition, group decision making, and organizational culture. Social psychologists interested in these topics focus on various aspects of groups—roles, statuses, norms, and values. Studies

TABLE 1.1 Subdivisions within Social Psychology

Area of Interest	Subjects
Influence of social factors on the individual	Person perception
	Self-perception
	Stereotyping
	Learning
	Attribution
	Self-presentation
Social interaction between and among individuals	Interpersonal relationships
	Aggression
	Altruism
	Attitudes and attitude change
	Communication
Group processes	Power and leadership
	Conformity
	Cooperation versus competition
	Group decision making
	Organizational culture

Studies in the field of social psychology seek to understand how other people influence our thoughts, feelings, and behaviors.

of group processes address questions such as these: Why do people obey the orders of cruel leaders? How do juries make decisions about the guilt or innocence of a defendant? How does our culture shape the way we view the world?

Classifying specific subjects within each of these three general areas of interest is not always easy. In many cases, human behavior involves a number of social psychological processes. As a result, there is considerable overlap between these general areas of interest. Consider, for example, the question *Why do we fall in love?* Although that falls into the general area of social interaction between and among individuals, it also involves perception, which falls into the general area of how social factors influence an individual.

THE ROOTS OF SOCIAL PSYCHOLOGY

In tracing the development of social psychology, Gordon Allport (1985) found it difficult to identify one person as its founder because no definitive history of this discipline existed. The candidates he considered included many of the world's greatest scholars and philosophers: Plato, Aristotle, Hobbes, and Hegel. Choosing one man as the father of social psychology posed many problems for Allport. Ultimately, he argued that a Frenchman by the name of August Comte deserved recognition as the founder of social psychology as a scientific field of inquiry.

Comte's intellectual interests and scholarly contributions reflect the impact of the social disorder surrounding him, as well as the influence of an emerging academic emphasis on scientific approaches to studying problems. In seeking to explain the evolution of human society, Comte abandoned traditional explanations that were rooted in religious beliefs and philosophical notions. Instead he adopted a systematic approach and argued that we must use reasoning and observation in our search for knowledge (Coser 1977; Babbie 1995). Other nineteenth-century social thinkers accepted Comte's new method for studying society, and it soon became the model for the developing social sciences.

The first laboratory designed for the scientific study of human behavior was established in 1879. But the first experiment, which was conducted by Norman Triplett, did not take place until 1897.

Auguste Comte, who advocated the scientific study of society, is recognized as the founder of social psychology.

Even though critics faulted Triplett's experimental design, it was the first experiment to involve social psychological variables (Allport 1985).

Although the origin of modern social psychology can be traced to Europe, Allport claimed that the expansion of this field of scientific inquiry was an American phenomenon. In 1902, one of the most influential books in the field of social psychology was written by an American named Charles Horton Cooley. Bearing the title *Human Nature and the Social Order*, Cooley's book presented the idea that "self and society are twin-born" (Coser 1977, 305). This idea—that there is an inseparable link between self and society— remained the major theme of Cooley's work. And it is the most important contribution he made to the field of social psychology

The first book to carry the title *Social Psychology* was written by Edward Ross, an American sociologist, in 1908. Later that year, another book on social psychology was published, written by William McDougall, an English psychologist. These books reflected the fundamental differences between sociology and psychology. Ross focused on groups, crowds, and interpersonal processes, while McDougall emphasized instincts and innate drives. Although many social sciences examine the topics of social psychology, sociology and psychology have clearly played the greatest role in its development. Floyd Allport's 1924 social psychology textbook provided complete coverage of the field, from old subjects like the impact of an audience on the performance of individuals to new ones such as how facial expressions convey human emotions. It promoted experimental research and was a driving force in the continued growth of the discipline.

In 1934, one of the most influential books ever written on the topic of the self was published: *Mind, Self, and Society*, based on the thoughts and insights of George Herbert Mead. Mead defined social psychology as the study of "the activity or behavior of the individual as it lies within the social process" (Coser 1977, 334). The influence of Mead's contemporaries is evident throughout the book: William James's ideas on the subjective and objective aspects of the self, John Dewey's belief that the mind emerges through social interactions, and Charles Horton Cooley's theory on self-hood—how a person can be both the subject who perceives the world and the object that is being perceived. For Mead, the development of the self was concurrent with an individual's ability to take social roles. Arguing that the self begins to develop once a child's language skills are established, he stressed the importance of symbolic meanings. Built on these key concepts, his theory came to be known as **symbolic interactionism.** Mead's sociological approach to understanding the development of the self was fundamentally at odds with Sigmund Freud's psychological approach, which emphasized the role of drives and instincts (1930/1962).

During the 1930s, a number of other social psychologists made significant contributions to understanding the relationship between the individual and society. Richard La Piere (1934) examined the inconsistencies between attitudes and behavior in a field study that focused on racial prejudice and discrimination. Muzafer Sherif (1936) conducted research on social norms and how they influenced conformity. And Kurt Lewin (1939), a German immigrant who was affected by the rise of Adolf Hitler, collaborated with Ronald Lippitt and Ralph White to study different styles of leadership (autocratic, democratic, and laissez-faire). In the area of methodology, George Gallup made a major contribution to survey research with the establishment of the Gallup Poll in 1935. In 1943, William Foote Whyte promoted the advancement of another method known as field research with the publication of *Street Corner Society*. In contrast to the quantitative approaches of experiments and surveys, Whyte's qualitative study of an Italian slum stressed the importance of studying human behavior in a natural setting, and it involved participant observation.

These early years marked a period of tremendous growth for social psychology. And the reasons were to be found in social circumstances. In his assessment of the development of social psychology, Allport (1985) argued that social psychology began to flourish after World War I, fueled by questions that arose from troubling events—the spread of communism, the Great Depression, the rise of Hitler, World War II, the Holocaust, and race riots. Through research undertaken to understand the social problems associated with these events, social psychologists gained keen insights into a wide range of social phenomena, including propaganda, public opinion, rumor, attitudes and values, power and leadership, prejudice, and race relations. Steeped in a tradition of free inquiry, as well as a philosophy and ethics of democracy, Allport maintained that America provided the ideal environment for the growth of social psychology.

This growth continued in the years following World War II. The decade of the 1950s is remembered in particular for its focus on groups. George Homans's book *The Human Group* was published in 1950. The first of its kind, the book described and analyzed the structure and processes of groups. At about the same time, Robert Bales (1950, 1953) developed a method for studying the interaction of group members and identified two distinct types of leadership roles that emerged in small groups. Gordon Allport's book *The Nature of Prejudice* (1954) provided an in-depth analysis of prejudice and stereotyping. The work of three other prominent social psychologists came out of the 1950s: Leon Festinger (1957) launched his theory of cognitive dissonance; Fritz Heider, in *The Psychology of Interpersonal Relations* (1958), introduced attribution theory; and *The Social Psychology of Groups*, by John Thibaut and Harold Kelley (1959b), proposed a theory of social exchange and interpersonal relations.

Thus the roots of modern social psychology were firmly established by the early 1960s. Over the course of the next forty years, social psychologists would build on the theories and research of the early pioneers. They would continue to ask questions such as *How is the performance of an individual influenced by the presence of others?* And they would make scientific advances in the methods used to study human behavior.

RESEARCH METHODS IN SOCIAL PSYCHOLOGY

> When the smoke cleared, the drumming stopped and the police broke formation around 6:30 a.m., some eight hours after the burning, looting and youth-gone-wild marauding of Woodstock '99 had begun, an older state trooper walked toward a vendor who was offering free coffee. "Remember Woodstock," the officer said, wearily, to the bedraggled teen-agers sitting nearby. "The first one."
>
> Then he dropped his hammy fist onto the coffee counter and proclaimed, sarcastically, more wearily, "Peace." (Strauss 1999)

On July 26, 1999, a three-day concert, which was designed to resemble the celebrated 1969 Woodstock counterculture music festival, literally went up in flames. The next day, the *New York Times's* quotation of the day read, "There was looting and lots of damage—but not to anyone's tents. As riots go, it was a very friendly riot." But the facts seemed to indicate otherwise. Seven people were arrested for their involvement in the incident on charges ranging from rioting to criminal mischief. Police investigated at least six rape allegations. And ten concertgoers were hospitalized for injuries. The incident also resulted in significant property damage. After setting a dozen bonfires, youths tore down several 50-foot-tall light towers and torched a row of cargo containers. Rioters also threw propane gas tanks into the fires. In the end, fires destroyed four refrigeration trucks (*Los Angeles Times* 1999).

How did this all start? Why did things get so out of control? Even though the Red Hot Chili Peppers were on stage when the trouble began, observers blamed Limp Bizkit, a rap-rock group from Florida, for inciting the riot. When concertgoers began to tear down towers and scaffolding near the stage a day earlier, the frontman for the band shouted, "There are no rules." Problems in the mosh pit escalated when the group sang "Break Stuff" (Bouchner 1999).

In the weeks following this riot, many people tried to explain what had happened. One witness told a *Los Angeles Times* reporter, "Many of those seen tossing wood onto the fires said that they were taking revenge against the high costs for basic supplies such as food and water. Although free water was available, getting to it often required a lengthy walk" (*Los Angeles Times* 1999).

In fact, the prices were outrageous: A small bottle of water cost $4. But others present at the concert disputed this explanation, arguing that it was an afterthought. Neil Strauss (1999), a *New York Times* reporter, wrote:

> During the riot, they didn't chant "rip-off" or "free water": they chanted "Woodstock," "U.S.A." and "Canada," showing the world that they were rioting solely because they could, because security fled the site the minute trouble started and left them alone for over an hour.

Theory and Research in Social Psychology

As the Woodstock '99 riot illustrated, people want to understand human behavior, and they develop a **theory,** a general explanation of the relationships among a set of variables, to explain what they observe. Like the promoters of future concerts, we believe that our theories can help us anticipate future behavior. But how much confidence do others have in our theories? Everyone had a theory for the Woodstock riot, but no one seemed to agree.

Riots that erupted at the 1999 Woodstock festival raised many questions about group behavior.

In contrast to the way that casual observers develop theories, social psychologists take a **scientific approach.** They develop theories in a systematic way, building on an accumulated body of theory and research findings. These scientific theories allow them to process, organize, and make sense out of vast amounts of information (Shaw and Costanzo 1970). Theories allow them to see the patterns in a puzzle and form a meaningful picture. Ultimately, theories help researchers recognize relationships that are not evident in isolated observations and understand their implications.

Developing a theory is thus an important step in the scientific approach that social psychologists take to find answers about human behavior. Although it is often one of the first steps taken to investigate a research question, it is actually better to think of it as just one in a repeating cycle of steps. As Figure 1.1 shows, theory and research operate hand in hand, one mutually directing and refining the other.

Concepts and Variables

To explain what they observe, scientists must think in abstract ways. They must develop a general understanding or idea that they can apply to particular instances or occurrences of human behavior.

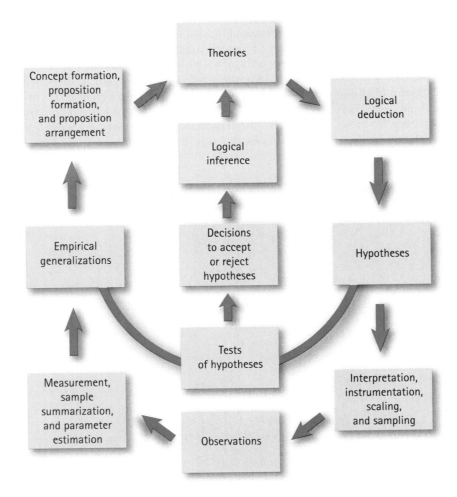

FIGURE 1.1

The Theory–Research Cycle

Source: Adapted from Wallace 1971, 18.

For example, suppose a researcher sees one child deliberately push another child onto the floor in his observations of preschool children at play. Later he notices a child hitting another child with a ruler. In thinking about his observations, he might call this kind of behavior *aggression*. General ideas like aggression, which can be applied to specific examples, are called **concepts.** They are the "basic building blocks of theory" (J. H. Turner 1978, 2).

Some concepts capture the essence of an observation readily. Consider what we mean by "book." It is easy to understand what we mean by "book" because we can point to many examples. Some of the concepts that social psychologists use are like this. "Age" and "gender" are not likely to cause much confusion, but consider a more complex concept like "gender ideology." As we shall see, the meaning of a concept is not always self-evident. The researcher must clearly define what the concept means.

All research involves special concepts called **variables.** These kinds of concepts vary over space and time and consist of a set of attributes. For example, the variability of the concept "gender" is clearly designated by the attributes of "male" and "female." The attributes of other variables are not always so clear. For instance, consider again the concept "aggression." Is it a variable? Yes, it is. It varies over space and time and consists of a set of attributes—"aggressive" or "not aggressive." Using the variables "gender" and "aggression," a social psychologist could develop a theory to explain why males tend to be more aggressive than females.

Hypotheses and the Operationalization of Variables

Once a social psychologist has defined a research problem and has chosen a theory that seems to fit, the next step is to formulate a **hypothesis**—a tentative statement that is designed to test a prediction about the relationship between variables. In some cases, researchers form hypotheses on the basis of hunches. This method resembles the kind of speculation that appeared in the stories of

reporters who covered the riot at Woodstock '99. Other researchers might base their hypotheses on existing data. Most researchers, however, derive their hypotheses from well-developed theories. This offers several benefits. First, the accumulated body of knowledge developed by other social psychologists provides a solid foundation for new research. Second, it allows a researcher to link new findings to other established explanations, which contributes to the advancement of the entire field of social psychology.

Before a researcher can test a hypothesis, she must translate it into specific terms. The translation of abstract concepts into concrete, measurable variables is called **operationalization.** In some cases, this is easy. For example, if you were interested in testing the hypothesis that the number of crimes committed at concerts varies with the number of policemen on duty, you might operationalize "number of policemen" as any value starting with zero. And you could define "crimes" according to the definitions used by the FBI and then simply count them. Operationalizing hypotheses is not always so easy, however. For example, try to translate the hypothesis *Love ensures a stable marriage.* How would you define "love"? How could you measure it? And what exactly do you mean by "stable marriage"?

These examples show that operationalizing hypotheses can be difficult. They also point out the fundamental difference between theories and hypotheses. The hypotheses in the examples state only the relationship between variables: crimes committed at concerts and number of policemen on duty; love and stable marriage. Unlike theories, these statements do not explain why these relationships exist.

Choosing a Research Method

To test their hypotheses, researchers select a particular research method. Choosing among the various methods requires thoughtful consideration of a number of questions.

What Is the Ultimate Goal of This Study?
Social psychologists use a variety of methods to

test their theories. These include surveys, experiments, and observational studies. The particular method that a researcher selects depends on many things (see Box 1.1). One of the first questions he should consider is *What is the ultimate goal, or primary purpose, of this study?* One researcher might want to describe the voting decisions of the electorate. Another might want to explain why people join groups that promote hate crimes. Someone else might want to predict when riots are most likely to occur.

Description, explanation, and prediction are common goals of scientific research. The exploration of a topic, particularly when the research question involves a subject that has received little or no attention, is another typical goal. Although a particular study might seek to achieve one or more of these goals, researchers should identify the most important goal. By doing so, they put themselves in the best position to determine the direction of the research. It will help them make decisions about what they should observe, how they should make the observations, and how they should interpret what they have observed (Babbie 1995).

How Well Does This Study Measure What It Claims to Measure? When social psychologists select a research method, they anticipate all of the steps involved in research, including the final one—the review of findings by other social scientists. In evaluating the significance and value of any study, one of the most important questions they will consider is *How well does this study measure what it claims to measure?* To determine the answer to this question, they will focus on two aspects of the methods used: **internal validity** and **reliability.** Internal validity refers to the fit between a theoretical concept and the researcher's empirical measurement of that concept. Consider, for example, IQ. In judging the internal validity of research on human intelligence, we would ask, *Do IQ tests really measure human intelligence, or do they measure something else?* If they measure what we think they are measuring, then internal validity is high. If not, it is low.

Reliability refers to consistency in measurements. To say that a study or research instrument is reliable means that if another researcher repeated our study or used the same instrument that we did, she would obtain the same results. A bathroom scale illustrates how a research instrument might provide faulty measurements. Suppose you fixed the scale so that the reading was 5 pounds off. This scale would provide a reliable measure of any

---

BOX 1.1   **CHOOSING A RESEARCH METHOD: ASKING THE RIGHT QUESTIONS**

Researchers consider many factors in deciding which research method is the most appropriate for their study. The following questions illustrate some of the things you should consider.

1. What is the primary purpose of your study—description, explanation, prediction, or exploration?
2. Is this method compatible with the theoretical perspective you have chosen to study this particular topic? How will you gather data? How will you analyze the data? How do you plan to interpret the observations you make?
3. To what group or population do you want to generalize the results of this study? Will this method prevent you from generalizing the findings beyond the subjects in this particular study? What can the results of this study tell you about the way people behave in real-life settings?
4. Which method is best for measuring the concepts specified in your theory?
5. How easy will it be to replicate this study?
6. Can you make adjustments in the research design once you have begun, or will you have to stick with your original design?
7. How much money can you spend on this research project?
8. How long will the study take?

weight change. But the reading would be wrong every time someone stepped on the scale. That is, it would not be valid.

In considering the significance and value of a study, researchers must also ask, *Can the results of this study be generalized beyond the subjects in this particular study to the population under consideration?* Researchers use the term **external validity** to refer to this aspect of a study's final results. Methods that produce findings that can be generalized to the population are considered high in external validity.

What Are the Strengths and Weaknesses of Different Research Methods? When it comes to choosing a research method, researchers essentially weigh the strengths and weaknesses of each one. In addition to the concerns discussed so far, researchers must consider some practical matters. They must determine the cost and time involved in conducting a study. In some cases, this might depend on the flexibility of the method chosen. As we shall see, each research method has its own unique characteristics (see Table 1.2). Recognizing these from the outset helps researchers choose the method most appropriate for a particular research

problem. Ultimately, the method a researcher chooses depends on the problem to be studied. No method is perfect, and no method is, in and of itself, the best method. The variety of methods available to social psychologists allows them to view social behavior from many different perspectives. In some cases, researchers are able to use more than one research method. This strategy, which is called **triangulation,** helps researchers test their findings. It is particularly helpful in determining whether the research method itself influenced the results (Babbie 1995).

Survey Research

Are blacks in your community treated less fairly than whites in dealings with police? Are there any individual students at your school who you think are potentially violent enough to provoke a dangerous situation? Do you think it is possible nowadays for someone in the United States to start out poor and become rich by working hard? Pollsters have been asking Americans about their opinions on topics like these for more than seventy years (Gallup 1999, 2000a). Questions like these tend to

		Surveys	Laboratory Experiments	Field Experiments	Naturalistic Observation
Type of Research	Quantitative Qualitative	Quantitative	Quantitative	Quantitative	Qualitative
Primary Purpose of Research	Description Explanation Prediction Exploration	Description Explanation Exploration	Explanation Prediction	Explanation Prediction	Explanation Exploration
Methodological Strengths and Weaknesses	External validity Internal validity Reliability Flexibility	Strength Weakness Strength Weakness	Weakness Strength Strength Weakness	Strength Strength Weakness Strength	Weakness Strength Weakness Strength
Practical Considerations	Cost Time	Weakness Strength	Strength Strength	Weakness Weakness	Weakness Weakness

TABLE 1.2 ASSESSING RESEARCH METHOD STRENGTHS AND WEAKNESSES

generate a great deal of interest. They address problems that concern us, and they lead us to wonder what other people think. **Survey research** is designed to tell us that and much more.

Social psychologists use survey research to describe, explain, and explore human behavior. In the social sciences, it is used more frequently than any other method (Williamson et al. 1982; Babbie 1995). The basic procedure involves three distinct steps: (1) selecting a representative sample of respondents, (2) designing a questionnaire, and (3) gathering the data.

The Sample. Survey researchers are acutely aware of problems associated with selecting a **sample.** Most are familiar with a classic example that taught pollsters a lesson about the importance of a representative sample. In 1936, *Literary Digest* conducted a survey to predict who would win the presidential election. Based on more than two million responses, it predicted that Alf Landon would beat Franklin Delano Roosevelt by a margin of 57 to 43 percent. The actual election results proved the newsmagazine wrong. Roosevelt won by a landslide with 61 percent of the vote.

How could a survey based on two million responses go so wrong? *Literary Digest* had failed to poll a representative sample of American voters. The magazine had drawn respondents' names from two sources: telephone directories and automobile registration lists. In 1936, this did not provide a representative cross section of Americans who planned to vote. It failed to include people who could not afford telephones or automobiles— the very ones who voted in droves for Roosevelt and his New Deal recovery program.

Today, survey research methods are used to predict election results on the basis of interviews with as few as one thousand Americans (Babbie 1995). And in contrast to the *Literary Digest* poll, pollsters can now predict the winner to within a few percentage points. They are able to do this because they now use scientific sampling methods, which are based on mathematical probabilities. By knowing the chance of choosing each person in a target population, researchers can design a representative sample that will accurately reflect the views of the surveyed population.

Survey research is not always designed to measure the attitudes, beliefs, and experiences of a national population. Social psychologists might limit their study to teenagers, parents, or students. In these cases, the **population** would refer to the total group of people of interest. Drawing a representative sample from these populations requires the same chance procedure, so that the researcher can generalize the results of the survey to the population under consideration.

Probability sampling methods provide researchers with representative samples, but that does not guarantee that the final sample will be unbiased. Suppose, for instance, that only 30 percent of the persons in the sample responded to the survey. This low response rate means that the sample no longer fairly represents the entire population but rather only its most motivated or most cooperative members. It therefore prevents researchers from claiming that their results reflect the views of that population.

The Questionnaire. The second step in survey research involves the design of a measurement instrument—a questionnaire. Creating an instrument that fairly measures what it claims to measure requires that researchers pay close attention to the wording of questions. Consider a few examples:

Do you agree that gun control laws are unconstitutional?

Should marijuana and heroin be legalized?

How much confidence do you have in military leaders?

How much confidence do you have in the military?

The first question will lead respondents to give more positive responses than negative ones. To avoid this problem, researchers should word questions in a neutral, impartial fashion. And the possible response choices must be balanced. The second question is double-barreled. People hold different attitudes about marijuana and heroin. Asking about both drugs in a single question will cause confusion and produce unreliable results. The problem with the third and fourth questions might stump you. It lies in how respondents interpret the word *confidence*. Research shows that respondents can define this term in four different ways: (1) trust, (2) capability, (3) attention to the common good, or (4) following a respondent's self-interest (Smith 1981; Smith 1987). Questions should never contain language that could produce different interpretations.

Social psychologists who conduct survey research are well aware of these kinds of question-wording problems (Babbie 1995; Schuman and Presser 1995). In fact, social scientists have conducted experiments on question-wording effects since the early 1940s. These studies identified a number of other factors that could affect the validity of measurements. A particularly troubling finding was that researchers can overestimate what respondents know or understand. If questions are designed so that respondents can answer anyway, they are likely to do so to avoid looking stupid. Unfortunately, this means that the results will not be valid. Getting honest answers also becomes a problem with sensitive questions or issues. Finally, researchers should examine the order of questions in an interview to determine if one question might bias another.

Gathering Data. Social psychologists use three methods to collect survey data: self-administered questionnaires, face-to-face interviews, and telephone surveys. Each has its own advantages and disadvantages (Babbie 1995). Overall, self-administered questionnaires tend to cost less than other methods and allow researchers to ask sensitive questions. Face-to-face interviews achieve higher response rates than self-administered questionnaires, which might require several follow-ups if they are sent through the mail. They also allow interviewers to probe for more information if necessary, and they reduce the number of "don't know" and "no answer" responses to questions.

Telephone surveys cut costs and save money. In some cases, this method allows respondents to answer more honestly, especially when their answers are not considered socially desirable. However, it is also easier for respondents to end an interview by simply hanging up the phone.

Strengths and Weaknesses of Survey Research. Survey research allows social psychologists to study attitudes and behaviors that are not necessarily public or easy to study (Williamson et al. 1982). It is appropriate for studying a broad

Survey research is ideal for gathering information on a broad range of issues. Researchers must, however, pay close attention to how they select respondents. Survey findings cannot be generalized to the population if the sample is not representative.

range of topics and problems. And it enables researchers to gather a great deal of information on large populations. In addition to questions that address the central topic of a study, surveys also include variables such as gender, race, age, education, income, and social class. These data allow researchers to analyze more complex relationships that might explain differences in respondents' attitudes and beliefs.

Researchers must be careful, however, in drawing conclusions from survey data. The results of surveys show the relationships or associations between and among variables. Researchers may even show that a correlation exists between two variables. For example, one could show that there is a correlation between the amount of alcohol that students consume and their grade point averages. Suppose in this case that the results showed that students who drink a lot of alcohol tend to have low grades. These two variables would be negatively correlated. That is, as the value of one variable increases, the value of the other one decreases.

Knowing how these two variables are related provides valuable information. However, it fails to tell us which variable had an effect on the other one. That is, does the consumption of alcohol cause poor grades, or do poor grades cause students to consume more alcohol? Survey data that show a correlation between two variables cannot answer that question.

A correlation between variables can mean several different things (see Figure 1.2):

1. Variable X may cause an effect in variable Y.
2. Variable Y may cause an effect in variable X.
3. A third, unspecified variable, Z, may cause an effect in both variable X and variable Y.

In his book *How to Lie with Statistics,* Darrell Huff (1954) illustrated the problem with claiming cause and effect on the basis of survey data that are correlated. The example he chose is one that has recently been resurrected in public service announcements that are designed to discourage young people from smoking. According to Huff,

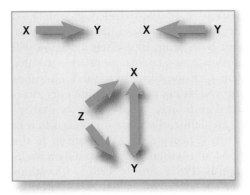

Example

What does the relationship between smoking and grades tell us about cause and effect?

• Does smoking cause students to get low grades?

Smoking ➡ **Low grades**

• Do low grades cause students to smoke?

Smoking ⬅ **Low grades**

• Does an extroverted personality influence both low grades and smoking?

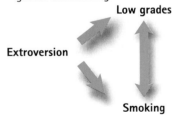

Extroversion   **Low grades**

     Smoking

FIGURE 1.2

Cause-and-Effect Relationships

someone conducted a study to determine whether individuals who smoked made lower grades in college than those who did not smoke. The sample was drawn properly, and the results showed that a significant correlation existed between smoking and low grades—more smoking was associated with lower grades. He criticized the researcher's conclusion that smoking caused bad grades by pointing out that the lower grades might actually cause students to smoke more. He further observed that a third variable, a student's personality, could cause an effect in each of the observed variables. He therefore argued that sociable students might be more likely to smoke and to get bad grades. And he pointed out that another study had actually shown a correlation between extroversion and low grades.

Survey research is appropriate for the study of many topics. It allows researchers to gather data on a large population and to analyze relationships among many different variables. It is particularly useful for tracking trends in attitudes and beliefs. However, it does not allow researchers to study human behavior in depth, and it does not allow researchers to examine cause-and-effect relationships between variables. To establish cause-and-effect relationships, a researcher must have some control over the variables. As we shall see, experiments are the best way to achieve this kind of control.

Experimental Research

Social psychologists began to conduct experiments toward the end of the nineteenth century. The first problem they sought to address concerned the effect that people's presence had on an individual's behavior. They asked, "What change in an individual's normal solitary performance occurs when other people are present?" (Allport 1985, 46). Norman Triplett, who had earlier observed that a cyclist's racing speed was about 20 percent faster when he was "paced by a visible multicycle," in 1897 conducted the first experiment to answer this question. The design was simple. Using children between the ages of 10 and 12, he measured the time it took them to wind fishing reels alone compared to the time it took when they were in a group situation. The results of this experiment led Triplett to conclude that performance was enhanced by the presence of others. Today, social psychologists conduct **experimental research**

either in a laboratory or in the field. Researchers who seek a tightly controlled situation will choose a laboratory setting, while those who want to approximate the conditions of a natural setting will conduct their experiment in the field. Each method has its own distinct advantages and disadvantages.

The Experimental Method. Experiments are ideal for testing hypotheses, that is, for investigating the relationship between two variables. The researcher manipulates one of these variables, the **independent variable**, and measures its effect on the other variable, the **dependent variable**. The aim of the experiment is to establish a cause-and-effect relationship between the two. However, before making this claim, the researcher must show that no other factor, no **extraneous variable**, influenced the dependent variable.

Tightly controlled experiments provide the best method for isolating the effects of an independent variable. To understand how this is accomplished, let's consider an ideal experiment (see Figure 1.3). It would begin with the random assignment of subjects to one of the two conditions created by the researcher. These are typically called the **experimental group** and the **control group.** The goal is to make these groups identical in every way except one—the introduction of the independent variable. This will occur only in the experimental group.

Experimenters use **pretesting** and **posttesting** to determine whether the introduction of the independent variable has an effect on the dependent variable. During the first part of the experiment, the dependent variable is measured—the subjects in both groups are pretested. Then the independent variable is introduced into the experimental group. The last step—the posttest—involves remeasuring the dependent variable. If the results of the pretest differ from those of the posttest, the researcher will conclude that the independent variable caused the change. By using experimental and control groups, the researcher isolates the specific effects of the independent variable. If the posttest shows that the experimental

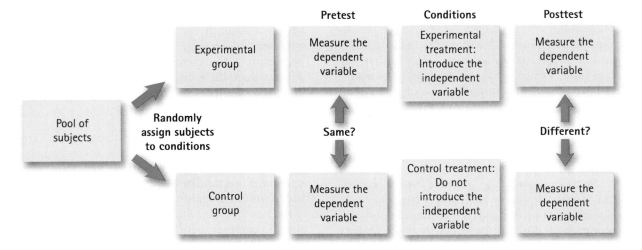

FIGURE 1.3

An Ideal Experiment

group differs from the control group in terms of the dependent variable, the researcher can attribute the difference to the effects of the independent variable. He will then either confirm or reject his hypothesis.

To illustrate, suppose that a researcher wants to see if ads that encourage wearing seat belts have an effect on people's attitudes toward automobile safety. She begins by randomly assigning her subjects to the experimental or the control group. She then measures the attitudes of subjects in both groups. Every day for the next two weeks, the experimental group watches ads that encourage drivers to wear their seat belts. Subjects in the control group do not see any ads. After these two weeks, the researcher measures the attitudes of the subjects again and compares the results.

By using an experimental group and a control group, she can conclude that differences between them are due to the different experimental conditions. In this case, she can say that the independent variable (seat belt ads) produced the effects observed, not some other variables. Based on this comparison, the researcher will either confirm or reject the hypothesis she is testing.

The **random assignment** of subjects to either the experimental or the control group is crucial in experimental research. It ensures that any differences between the groups are due only to chance. And the laws of probability guarantee that particular traits of the subjects—such as intelligence, gender, age, and ethnicity—will occur in a representative way in each group. The procedure for random assignment is relatively simple. You can flip a coin, pull names from a hat, or use a table of random numbers.

Laboratory versus Field Experiments. Researchers consider a number of factors in determining which particular experimental method is appropriate for their research question. **Laboratory experiments** offer the advantage of a highly controlled situation. They allow researchers to create different experimental treatments, to isolate the effects of variables, and to take precise measurements. This kind of control is ideal for establishing cause-and-effect relationships. Unfortunately, the artificial conditions created in a laboratory can seem unnatural to participants in the experiment. These kinds of experiments may not provide the kind of real-life experience that subjects would feel outside the laboratory. They lack what social psychologists call **mundane realism** (Aronson, Brewer, and Carlsmith 1985). The results of a laboratory experiment may not, therefore, tell us anything about the way people behave in the real world. To offset the effects of an artificial situation, researchers try to increase **experimental realism.** In other words, they try to design a believable experiment, one that fully involves the subject.

Field experiments, which are conducted in natural settings, are more likely than laboratory experiments to approximate the everyday experiences of subjects—to have mundane realism. In fact, they have been conducted in a number of settings that are difficult to create in a laboratory, such as prisons, schools, factories, and organizations. The mundane realism of field experiments makes it easier for researchers to argue that their results can be generalized to the population. And it makes them particularly well suited for studying consumer behavior, groups and organizations, and the effects of mass communication. Despite these advantages, however, field experiments also have a unique set of problems. Since researchers cannot

tightly control the experimental conditions, as they can in a laboratory, it is more difficult to establish cause-and-effect relationships. Researchers may also have difficulty in determining the appropriate setting for a field experiment. Even when that has been decided, researchers must still gain the permission of the appropriate authorities to conduct the experiment in that setting. Convincing large organizations, schools, or law enforcement agencies to open up their doors to a field experiment can be a challenge, especially if these authorities might feel threatened by the results.

To illustrate some of the problems involved in experimentation, consider a classic example. From the late 1920s to the early 1930s, researchers conducted a series of experiments at the Hawthorne, Illinois, plant of the Western Electric Company (Roethlisberger and Dickson 1939; Mayo 1966). The management of the company wanted to know how different levels of lighting affected employee productivity. When their initial studies showed that productivity rose regardless of how lighting conditions changed, the company asked Elton Mayo to investigate. Mayo and his team of researchers tested over a dozen different working conditions, including variations in lighting, coffee

Researchers conduct field experiments in natural locations like schools to reduce the negative effects of artificial settings.

breaks, lunch hours, and methods of payments. They discovered that every new change led to increased productivity. Surprised by these findings, Mayo and his team eventually restored the original working conditions. To their amazement, productivity rose yet again. Ultimately, the researchers realized that the variable that had caused increased productivity was the attention employees in the experiment had received—not the independent variables the researchers had specified.

This study is remembered not for the validity of its findings but rather for the methodological problems that face researchers. It showed why control groups are necessary, and it stressed the importance of clearly specifying independent and dependent variables. Above all, it taught researchers to be aware of effects that an experiment may itself produce. Today, that phenomenon is known as the **Hawthorne effect.**

Strengths and Weaknesses of Experimental Methods. The primary advantage of a laboratory experiment is the control that it provides. For researchers to establish a cause-and-effect relationship between variables, they must isolate the effects of the independent variable. The tightly controlled conditions of laboratory experiments allow experimenters to do this. By exposing subjects to experiences that are carefully designed to be comparable, experimenters minimize the influence of extraneous variables and thereby maximize internal validity. The major disadvantage of a laboratory experiment is its artificial nature. What do the results of an experiment tell us about the way people behave in the world outside of a laboratory? Perhaps nothing. Subjects may act quite differently in a real-life situation. If the subjects in a laboratory experiment do not fairly represent the population, external validity becomes a serious problem. Laboratory experiments are, however, relatively easy to repeat. In contrast to other methods, they often investigate narrow topics and do not require large investments of time or money. By repeating experiments, researchers can determine whether their findings are reliable, and this may give them a better assessment of the degree to which they can generalize their findings (Babbie 1995).

Researchers may choose to conduct field experiments to avoid problems associated with the artificial nature of a laboratory. Since researchers observe subjects in real-life situations, it is easier to generalize their findings to the population. In many cases, field experiments are the only way to investigate a research question. Consider research on natural disasters or human tragedies. Experimenters could not ethically manipulate these kinds of conditions. Although the random assignment of subjects to different conditions is a problem in field experiments, researchers may discover that chance factors operated in a way that allows them to make this assumption about the composition of their groups. The realistic nature of field experiments increases internal validity and usually reduces bias associated with suspicions about the purpose of a study.

Naturalistic Observation

Some topics in social psychology require an approach that will allow researchers to see the world through the eyes of their subjects—to gain a deeper understanding of their attitudes, beliefs, values, and motives. Robert Park, an early-twentieth-century sociologist, recognized that researchers had to put themselves in the position of their subjects to gain this subjective perspective. To accomplish this, he gave students the following advice:

> "Go and sit in the lounges of the luxury hotels and on the doorsteps of the flophouses; sit on the Gold Coast settees and on the slum shakedowns; sit in Orchestra Hall and in the Star and Garter Burlesk. In short, gentlemen, go get the seats of your pants dirty in real research." (Quoted in McKinney 1966, 71)

Park's approach, which stressed the importance of studying human behavior as it occurred naturally, resembles what we do when we try to figure out why people behave in certain ways. We do this every day—avoiding "crazy" drivers on the way to work, watching a parent discipline a child, or even eavesdropping on a lover's quarrel. Most of the time, the behavior that puzzles us is ordinary. But sometimes it is not. Consider the riot at Woodstock '99.

Social psychologists recognized the value of studying and understanding human behavior as it occurs naturally and developed an approach known as **naturalistic observation** or **field research** to help them enter the worlds of their subjects. William Thomas and Florian Znaniecki were two of the earliest social psychologists to take this approach in their classic study of Polish peasants in Europe and America (1918). The theoretical foundation of this study, which emphasized how perceptions of reality influence human behavior, was ideally suited for this method. Understanding

subjective perceptions that may depart substantially from objective reality was critical for Thomas, who believed, as noted earlier, "If men define situations as real, they are real in their consequences" (Thomas and Thomas 1928, 572).

Social psychologists use a number of qualitative methods to measure subjective perceptions, including direct observation and **participant observation.** These methods are particularly well suited for getting a sense of how people understand their own worlds—where they fit, the roles they play, and the norms that govern their lives. Relationships, groups, organizations, and even communities are therefore often the focus of field research (Lofland 1984). Whereas the earliest in-depth studies of human behavior focused on the lives of adults, recent studies have examined the daily lives of children (see Table 1.3).

TABLE 1.3 **NOTEWORTHY EXAMPLES OF NATURALISTIC OBSERVATION**

Researcher	Date	Topic	Publication
William I. Thomas and Florian Znaniecki	1918	Polish peasants	*The Polish Peasant in Europe and America*
William F. Whyte	1943	Italian American working-class men	*Street Corner Society*
Howard S. Becker, Blanche Geer, Everett C. Hughes, and Anselm L. Strauss	1961	Student culture in medical school	*Boys in White*
Herbert Gans	1962	Italian American neighborhoods in Boston	*Urban Villagers*
Elliot Liebow	1967	African American men	*Talley's Corner*
Carol B. Stack	1974	African American families	*All Our Kin*
Arlie R. Hochschild	1989/2003	Working mothers	*The Second Shift*
Donna Eder, Catherine Colleen Evans, and Stephen Parker	1995	Gender and adolescent culture	*School Talk*
William A. Corsaro	1997	Childhood	*The Sociology of Childhood*
Barrie Thorne	1993	Girls and boys in school	*Gender Play*

William Foote Whyte's study of an Italian slum, a classic example of participant observation, illustrates the value of stepping into the shoes of the people being studied. Viewed from his subjects' perspective, the slum no longer conformed to Whyte's own upper-middle-class expectations. Once he lived and participated in the life of the slum that he called Cornerville, he saw a very different world. "The middle-class person looks upon the slum district as a formidable mass of confusion, a social chaos," he observed. "The insider finds in Cornerville a highly organized and integrated social system" (Whyte 1943, xvi).

Whyte's conclusions were based on an analysis of the notes he took during the two years he lived in Cornerville. Notes like his, which contain detailed qualitative descriptions of events and statements made by the people observed, are called **ethnographies** (Williamson et al. 1982). These descriptions constitute the raw data of participant observation. Unlike the kinds of data gathered in experiments and surveys, ethnographies provide rich details of social life, which help us understand how other people think, feel, and behave.

Gaining the perspective of the people who lived in Cornerville was a remarkable achievement for Whyte, since his own background was so different from theirs. When a researcher resembles his subjects, gaining their perspectives may be easier. But it still requires a great deal of time and effort. In their four-year study of medical students, Howard Becker and his team (1961) participated as fully as possible in the lives of their subjects. They attended classes with them, watched over their shoulders as they worked in labs, ate meals with them, and discussed various aspects of their medical training. Based on their observations during the first few weeks of medical school, Becker and his colleagues described the perspective of first-year medical students as idealistic. Summarized in a way that reflects how these students might express it, the researchers wrote (1961, 94):

1. We want to learn everything, as we will need it when we become physicians.
2. There is a tremendous amount to learn.
3. We have to work very hard—that is, many hours.

What would you conclude about social life in this neighborhood? William Whyte's research showed that you cannot judge a book by its cover.

4. If our present hours of work are not enough for us to get everything, we'll do whatever we can to increase them—but how?

Within a short time, medical students began to feel the strain. Becker's team captured these feelings in their field notes (1961, 97):

As we left physiology lecture this afternoon, there were general expressions from the students of lack of comprehension and anger. Fred Brown said in a loud voice, "I'm getting near my excitation point. . . . I'm going to boil over." (The lecture had been on excitation points in muscle.) There was general laughter at this by the students going down the stairs. Bob Simpson said, "I am beginning to think it's true. You haven't got time to think about anything in your first year; you just learn it." Fred agreed with this. He said, "It's only Monday, and I'm behind all ready." Al Jones who was also there said, "Well, it's just the tradition to load all this stuff on us."

Eventually, these medical students realized that they could not learn everything. And they developed a group perspective that solved the problem. The solutions for getting through school involved a number of strategies including ways to determine what to study, how to figure out what their teachers wanted them to know, and the most efficient ways of studying.

The insight that Becker and his team gained by participating as fully as possible in the lives of their subjects illustrates the unique strength of naturalistic observation. Compared to survey and experimental measurements, which critics may fault for failing to measure what they claim to measure, conversations and detailed descriptions of events and interactions speak for themselves. And they often convey deep meanings, which can get lost in abstract conceptualizations. Consider, for example, how Arlie Hochschild (1989/2003, 41–42) used the words of her subject, Nancy Holt, to describe how gender ideology became rooted in her early experience:

My mom was wonderful, a real aristocrat, but she was also terribly depressed being a housewife. My dad treated her like a doormat. She didn't have any self-confidence. And growing up, I can remember her being really depressed. I grew up bound and determined not be to like her and not to marry a man like my father. As long as Evan doesn't do the housework, I feel it means he's going to be like my father—coming home, putting his feet up, and hollering at my mom to serve him. That's my biggest fear. I've had *bad* dreams about that.

In contrast to survey researchers and experimenters who define concepts, field researchers commonly use detailed descriptions like Hochschild's to illustrate what they mean (Babbie 1995). This example shows why naturalistic observation is recognized for producing measurements with high internal validity.

Conducting Naturalistic Observation and Field Research. The studies of Whyte, Becker, and Hochschild reveal the deep insights that naturalistic observation can offer. But their studies do not provide clear blueprints for conducting this kind of research. Field researchers often make their intentions clear in the description of their methodology. Consider what Becker and his team (1961, 17) wrote:

In one sense, our study had no design. That is, we had no well-worked-out set of hypotheses to be tested, no data-gathering instruments purposely designed to secure information relevant to these hypotheses, no set of analytic procedures specified in advance. Insofar as the term "design" implies these features of elaborate prior planning, our study had none.

This description highlights some of the fundamental differences between quantitative and qualitative research approaches. Recall the order of steps taken in quantitative approaches like experiments and surveys (see Figure 1.1). In these studies, social psychologists typically begin with a theory. They then translate that theory into a testable hypothesis. After that, researchers begin to collect data. Because these data are quantitative, researchers can then analyze them in a relatively short time.

In contrast, field research does not typically begin with a theory. In fact, this qualitative approach is often used as a means for theory generation (Glaser and Strauss 1967; Hammersley and Atkinson 1990). Fieldworkers usually enter the research cycle at the point of observation. Although they might have some general notions about what they are studying, they rely on their initial observations to guide them further—to formulate questions and tentative hypotheses (Williamson et al. 1982). This method allows investigators to move back and forth between data collection and analysis (Williamson et al. 1982; Babbie 1995). As they proceed, fieldworkers analyze their notes, looking for evidence that either supports or fails to support

their hunches. This kind of flexibility, which allows researchers to make adjustments at any point, is a major strength of naturalistic observation.

The subjective nature of field research is woven into the way that researchers gather and analyze their data. In contrast to experiments and surveys, which require a relatively short time to complete, observational studies make heavy demands on a researcher's time and attention. The value of taking good field notes and keeping up-to-date records cannot be overestimated. Because field researchers do not start with a theory or testable hypotheses, they cannot determine which observations will ultimately be important (Williamson et al. 1982). Fieldworkers should never rely on memory; they must keep detailed and complete notes. In addition to empirical

---

BOX 1.2   BIASES OF AMATEUR SOCIAL PSYCHOLOGISTS

As the tragic death of Amadou Diallo demonstrated, human beings cannot always believe what they "see." Our perceptions are subject to a number of biases, which cause them to depart from objective reality. To illustrate the effect of these biases, consider a famous experiment conducted at a psychology congress in Göttingen, Germany, with a crowd of presumably trained observers.

> Not far from the hall in which the Congress was sitting there was a public fete with a masked ball. Suddenly the door of the hall was thrown open and a clown rushed in madly pursued by a Negro, revolver in hand. They stopped in the middle of the room fighting: the clown fell, the Negro leapt upon him, fired, and then both rushed out of the hall. The whole incident hardly lasted twenty seconds.
>
> The President asked those present to write immediately a report since there was sure to be a judicial inquiry. Forty reports were sent in. Only one had less than 20% of mistakes in regard to the principal facts; fourteen had 20% to 40% of mistakes; twelve from 40% to 50%; thirteen more than 50%. Moreover in twenty-four accounts 10% of the details were pure inventions and this proportion was exceeded in ten accounts and diminished in six. Briefly a quarter of the accounts were false.

> It goes without saying that the whole scene had been arranged and even photographed in advance. The ten false reports may then be relegated to the category of tales and legends; twenty-four accounts are half legendary, and six have a value approximating to exact evidence. (van Gennep 1910, 158–159)

How can we explain the high percentage of mistakes made in this experiment? In considering this question, Walter Lippman (1922/1991) argued that we would be exhausted if we had to see things in fresh detail every time we turned around. In referring to this particular experiment, he asserted that the observers had relied on images of brawls that they had acquired during their lives. Stereotyping—seeing things as types and generalities—saved them both time and effort.

The Göttingen experiment was intentionally designed to show that even trained observers make mistakes. And it suggests that ordinary people are even more likely to do so. Scientific approaches to studying human behavior help us avoid biases in our observations and analysis. Earl Babbie (1995) identified the most common kinds of errors that people make in their "casual inquiries" and suggested a number of ways that scientific approaches could prevent them. Let us consider each one.

observations, field notes should include interpretations (Babbie 1995).

Strengths and Weaknesses of Naturalistic Observation. Although researchers may not have an exact blueprint for their study or know exactly how they are going to proceed, they are likely to anticipate some of the problems they will face (see Box 1.2). The first major problem that researchers are likely to encounter is gaining access to the group they want to study. Suppose that you want to study a satanic cult, organized crime, or the IRA. Groups like these, which may be involved in questionable activities, are not likely to welcome strangers with open arms. Even when groups have nothing to hide, researchers might still have to get past the **gatekeepers**—individuals who have the power to let you in or keep you out.

Gaining access to a group does not mean that subjects will automatically accept or trust a researcher. In some cases, the ascribed characteristics of researchers—gender, race, or age—can cast them in certain roles that prevent them from gaining the acceptance and trust of the people they wish to study (see Box 1.3) (Hammersley and Atkinson 1990). If subjects are suspicious for any reason, they may not behave naturally, which defeats the whole purpose of field research.

Raymond Gold (1969) identified four roles that fieldworkers take in conducting research: complete observer, observer as participant, participant as observer, and complete participant. Researchers determine which of these roles to play on the basis of two considerations. First, they must decide how involved they plan to become in the activity of their subjects. Second, they must consider

- *Inaccurate observation:* The Göttingen experiment illustrated how people make mistakes in their casual observations of human behavior. A scientific approach to making observations improves the accuracy of what we see because it is a deliberate activity undertaken with care.
- *Overgeneralization:* This kind of bias explains how stereotypes evolve. If we believe that a particular pattern exists, we are likely to formulate an explanation for it. In so doing, we are likely to pay attention to information that confirms the pattern and ignore information that does not. To avoid this kind of bias, scientists conduct studies over and over again.
- *Selective observation:* The error occurs when we selectively focus on evidence that fits the pattern that we believe exists and ignore details that do not. A scientific approach involves a predetermined set of observations that we must make regardless of whether we see a pattern forming.
- *Made-up information:* When something happens that contradicts our expectations or conclusions, we often make up information to restore consistency or to eliminate our confusion. Scientists also tend to do this when their results do not turn out the way they expected. That usually involves consideration of assumptions about things that are not observed. To avoid this kind of error, scientists make more observations to test their assumptions.

- *Illogical reasoning:* When we make observations, we do not always use logical reasoning. For example, a person might identify "the exception that proves the rule" (Babbie 1995, 23). Scientists use logic consciously in their studies to avoid this kind of bias.
- *Ego involvement in understanding:* This kind of bias occurs when our understanding of something is influenced by our own personal needs. Scientists can also get too personally involved in a study and lose their objectivity. Colleagues can reduce this problem by evaluating a study from a more objective position.
- *Mystification:* When an observation seems to defy a scientific explanation, we often explain it in terms of the supernatural. This conclusion can stop further exploration. Scientists are less prone to attribute the unknowable to the supernatural and persist in trying to understand what they observe.

Babbie's list provides a useful way for recognizing the most common errors that people make in their casual observations. And it shows how we can reduce these errors by taking a scientific approach to the study of social psychology.

BOX 1.3 GAINING ACCEPTANCE IN NATURALISTIC OBSERVATION

Conducting field research might seem easy, since we all do something similar when we try to figure out the people around us. But in fact, it places heavy demands on researchers and requires special abilities and skills. Consider something that we as amateur social psychologists take for granted—our acceptance as a member in a particular group. Field researchers cannot take this for granted and must figure out how to enter the lives of their subjects and gain their trust. Sometimes this is difficult, if not impossible. Suppose that a researcher wants to study an adolescent gang, the police, or schoolchildren. The ascribed characteristics of researchers—gender, race, or age—can cast them in certain roles that prevent them from gaining the acceptance and trust of the people they wish to study (Hammersley and Atkinson 1990).

In his ethnographic research in preschools, William Corsaro (1997) recognized that his physical size could hinder him from gaining entry into the world of children. If children viewed him as an adult, which his size would naturally lead them to do, they might be less likely to draw him into their activities. To gain their acceptance, Corsaro entered free-play areas, sat down, and waited for them to react to him. Although this "reactive" method took time, the children in Corsaro's studies did eventually accept him as a "big kid." Corsaro (1981, 117) described the process by which this occurred in his field notes (Betty and Jenny are 4-year-old girls, and Bill is the adult researcher):

BETTY: You can't play with us!
BILL: Why?
BETTY: Cause you're too big.
BILL: I'll sit down. (*sits down*)
JENNY: You're still too big.
BETTY: Yeah, you're "Big Bill"!
BILL: Can I just watch?
JENNY: OK, but don't touch nuthin!
BETTY: You just watch, OK?
BILL: OK.
JENNY: OK, Big Bill?
BILL: OK.

(Later Big Bill got to play.)

---

the extent to which they will conceal their true intentions (Williamson et al. 1982). As a complete participant or complete observer, researchers hide their true identities. A complete observer does not become involved with her subjects but remains concealed, perhaps behind a one-way mirror. The complete participant, on the other hand, becomes fully involved both behaviorally and emotionally. Researchers who assume the role of participants as observers become fully involved emotionally, but they downplay their roles as researchers. Finally, those who take the role of observer as participant do not hide anything but are completely open about their research. Which of these roles a researcher takes depends ultimately on the situation and what he wants to know.

Apart from particular challenges facing field researchers, there are a number of methodological weaknesses (Williamson et al. 1982). Field research is not appropriate for studying large populations. In fact, many studies involve only one participant observer, who conducts a case study—an analysis of a single case. Case studies do not provide data that are representative of a population, so researchers cannot make generalizations from their findings. In other words, they are low in external validity. The subjective nature of naturalistic observation also makes this method susceptible to a number of biases. For one thing the presence of a researcher may itself influence how subjects behave. And a researcher's own values, attitudes, and assumptions can influence what she sees and what she chooses to analyze. Finally, since researchers find it difficult to describe how they designed a study, others will have a hard time replicating it (Williamson et al. 1982).

Field research is labor-intensive. And it poses many problems and challenges for field researchers. However, the rich details of social life—conversations and behaviors that occur spontaneously in natural settings—give field researchers what they want, a view of the world from the subject's perspective.

Ethics in Research

Richard Curtin, a Defense Department budget analyst living in Falls Church, [Virginia,] does not usually open his daughter Allison's mail, but in the fall of 1998 she was away at college and the envelope was large and thick.

He pulled out a 25-page questionnaire from a researcher at Virginia Commonwealth University who was studying twins, like Allison and her brother Kevin. Curtin read the questions. The more he saw, the less he liked. His daughter was being asked, among other things, if her father had ever suffered from depression or had abnormal genitalia. This seemed to him an invasion of his privacy.

Curtin complained to the Virginia Commonwealth researcher, who wrote back that there was nothing to worry about because the study was voluntary and names were kept confidential. Curtin also got nowhere when he wrote to VCU officials.

So he contacted federal regulators. As a result of his complaint and at least one other, most of VCU's medical research has been shut down. About 1,100 out of 1,500 VCU research projects have been halted while the Richmond university responds to demands from two federal agencies to improve its procedures for protecting research subjects' privacy and safety. (Mathews 2000)

In its investigation of Curtin's complaint, the federal Office for the Protection from Research Risks (OPRR) told VCU that the researcher in charge of this study had violated Curtin's rights by failing to obtain his consent before sending a questionnaire to his daughter that asked for personal information about him. Unfortunately, the incident at Virginia Commonwealth University is not an isolated case. Federal investigators have taken disciplinary action against a number of other universities for violating guidelines that were established to protect human subjects from harm. Although most of these violations involved medical research, the behavioral and social sciences have

also been affected. The University of Illinois at Chicago (UIC) shut down over sixteen hundred research projects after inspectors from OPRR found fault with the university's procedures for protecting human subjects (Pankratz 2000).

Concern for the protection of human subjects dates back to the 1950s. In the aftermath of World War II, the Nuremberg trials revealed unimaginable details of various experiments that had been conducted by the Nazis. These atrocities involved unwilling human subjects in dangerous and degrading procedures that often resulted in death. In the United States, the Tuskegee Syphilis Study was one of the most unethical experiments ever conducted. This forty-year project, conducted by the U.S. Public Health Service, was designed to study the long-term effects of syphilis. Even after penicillin became available to treat this life-threatening disease, it was withheld from the subjects, 399 African American men in Tuskegee, Alabama. In the social sciences, Stanley Milgram's experiment on obedience (1974) became a classic example of research that posed psychological harm to human subjects. His experiment, which was designed to understand why people follow orders that can harm other human beings, involved deception. Believing that they were participating in a learning experiment, subjects were instructed to deliver an electric shock to a learner (seated in a separate room) whenever he failed to correctly match a pair of words. Even though no shock was actually delivered to the learner, subjects were led to believe that it was. Hearing the learner screaming, pounding on the wall, and pleading to end the experiment did not stop many subjects from delivering what they believed to be high-voltage shocks. The subjects in this experiment were visibly upset by their own actions. Some of them even experienced psychological problems following the experiment.

These kinds of experiments raised serious concerns about human subjects and led to the establishment of ethical guidelines for conducting scientific research. In the United States, these guidelines became known as the **Common Rule** (Meyers 2000). They provide that subjects who volunteer to take part in a clinical experiment must be fully informed about the experiment. To ensure that ethical guidelines are followed, universities and research institutions that receive federal funding must establish a committee to review all research that uses human subjects. Known as an **institutional review board** (IRB), this committee is responsible for ensuring that subjects' rights are protected.

When social psychologists design research, they must consider the ethical dilemmas that their procedures could create. Suppose that a social psychologist wants to study adolescent gangs. Is he obligated to reveal his true identity as a researcher? What, if anything, must he tell his subjects about his research? What if he witnesses a serious crime? Must he keep what he observes a secret?

To identify the problems that a particular study poses, researchers and institutional review boards ask a number of questions:

> Could this research cause harm to the participants?
>
> Does this research violate a participant's right to privacy?
>
> What measures will be taken to protect the identity of participants?
>
> Does this study involve deception? If so, how do the researchers justify it? And how do they plan to help participants deal with the fact that they have been misled?

Surveys, experiments, and naturalistic observation pose unique ethical dilemmas. Let us now consider some of the most common problems researchers must solve.

Informed Consent. Obtaining a subject's consent indicates that he has voluntarily agreed to participate in a study. Researchers also have an obligation to tell the subjects as much as possible about the study, especially any risks that it might involve. This was the idea behind the Common Rule. Today, this practice is known as obtaining **informed consent.** As the historical examples in Nazi Germany and Tuskegee, Alabama, showed, violating this guideline in medical research is clearly unethical. But is obtaining informed consent necessary in social psychological research? The results of experiments and surveys that require informed consent may not be based on a representative sample of the population studied. People who volunteer for experiments and surveys differ in significant ways from those who do not volunteer, which means that a researcher cannot generalize the results of the study to all people (Babbie 1995). The findings of naturalistic observation can also be affected if researchers must obtain the informed consent of participants. If researchers must identify themselves and reveal the purpose of their study, they defeat the primary purpose of naturalistic observation—to understand human behavior as it occurs naturally. Social psychologists must decide whether obtaining informed consent is necessary. If they feel justified in violating this guideline, they must make sure that the study will not harm their subjects.

Privacy. Social psychologists can protect the privacy of subjects in two ways. The first method involves **anonymity,** which means that the information that subjects provide in a study cannot reveal their identity in any way. This might seem to pose a problem for survey research, which requires researchers to follow up with respondents to ensure a representative sample. But survey researchers have devised ways to conduct follow-ups that do not require respondents to link their answers to their identities. Another way to protect a participant's privacy is to guarantee **confidentiality.** In this case, the researcher promises participants that any information they provide will be kept private. It does not guarantee, however, that the information cannot be traced back to a respondent. This can pose a serious problem for researchers if a court of law orders them to hand over information that they have collected. This kind of information is not considered "privileged communication" as is the case with priests and attorneys (Babbie 1995). To avoid problems with confidentiality, researchers should remove names from questionnaires as soon as possible and substitute identification numbers. A file that links names to these identification numbers can be used if researchers need to update or correct information, but that should be kept in a secure place.

Honesty. How much should researchers tell their subjects about a study? As the problems with obtaining informed consent showed, being completely honest with subjects can contaminate the results of a study. On the other hand, deceiving subjects can also harm them, as Milgram's obedience experiment showed. Misleading subjects about the purpose of research is fairly common in laboratory experiments. And in most cases, this will not harm a subject. But researchers must consider this issue carefully. Ultimately, they are obligated to inform participants about the real purposes of the study. Researchers refer to this part of the study as **debriefing.** Lying to people is wrong. And some social psychologists believe that it is always unethical to use deception in research. Others, however, argue that it can be justified in some cases when there is a compelling reason (Babbie 1995).

SUMMARY

1. Society exerts a powerful influence on individuals from the moment of birth. It shapes our understanding of reality and influences our perceptions of ourselves and others, our attitudes, our feelings, and our tendencies to behave in certain ways.

2. Social psychology is the scientific study of the relationship between the individual and society. Social psychologists seek to explain how our thoughts, feelings, and behaviors are influenced by other human beings. The field of social psychology encompasses three basic areas: the influence of social factors on individuals, social interactions between and among individuals, and group processes.

3. Although social psychology originated in Europe, it flourished in the United States, prompted by interest in the social problems of the twentieth century, including race relations, war, and the spread of communism.

4. George Herbert Mead's theory of symbolic interaction is one of the most influential theories in sociological social psychology. According to Mead, the self develops along with an individual's ability to take social roles.

5. Social psychologists develop theories systematically by considering past research findings. These theories help researchers process, organize, and make sense of vast amounts of information.

6. Researchers use various research methods to test their theories. The basic ones include surveys, experiments, and naturalistic observation. In determining which method is appropriate for a particular research problem, researchers consider the primary goal of their study. Description, explanation, prediction, and exploration are common goals of scientific research. The selection of a research method is also based on a consideration of its strengths and weaknesses.

7. Social psychologists ask a number of questions when they evaluate the methodology of a particular study. How well does the study measure what it claims to measure? Would another study yield the same results? And can the results of the study be generalized to the population? These questions provide valuable information about a study's internal validity, reliability, and external validity.

8. Survey research is useful for collecting data on large populations. Carefully worded survey questions provide researchers with data that can be analyzed to show relationships among many different variables. And because randomly chosen subjects provide a representative sample, the results of survey research can be generalized to the population. Survey research does not, however, allow researchers to determine cause and effect or to study human behavior in depth.

9. Experiments are ideal for investigating the relationship between two variables under tightly controlled conditions. Laboratory experiments allow

researchers to establish a cause-and-effect relationship between two variables. This is the main advantage. The major disadvantage of laboratory experiments is their artificial nature. To avoid this problem, researchers may choose to conduct field experiments instead. If experiments are conducted on a nonrepresentative sample of subjects, the results cannot be generalized to the population.

10. Naturalistic observation is often used to generate theories, ordinarily starting with observation and then proceeding to data analysis. This methodology is not appropriate for studying large groups, and the focus on small groups means that the

results cannot be generalized to the population. Nonetheless, naturalistic observation is superior to other methods at providing deep insights into human behavior.

11. Social psychologists must consider the possibility of ethical dilemmas when they design research. They must do nothing that would harm a subject physically, psychologically, or emotionally. Steps must also be taken to safeguard the privacy of subjects. And once the research is complete, researchers should debrief subjects by disclosing the real purpose of the study. Failure to comply with ethical guidelines can result in the loss of funding from agencies that sponsor research.

KEY TERMS

Definition of a situation   4
Social psychology   4
Symbolic interactionism   7
Theory   9
Scientific approach   10
Concept   11
Variable   11
Hypothesis   11
Operationalization   11
Internal validity   12
Reliability   12
External validity   13
Triangulation   13
Survey research   14

Sample   14
Population   14
Experimental research   17
Independent variable   17
Dependent variable   17
Extraneous variable   17
Experimental group   17
Control group   17
Pretesting   17
Posttesting   17
Random assignment   18
Laboratory experiment   18
Mundane realism   19
Experimental realism   19

Field experiment   19
Hawthorne effect   20
Naturalistic observation or field
  research   21
Participant observation   21
Ethnography   22
Gatekeeper   25
Common Rule   27
Institutional review board   28
Informed consent   28
Anonymity   28
Confidentiality   28
Debriefing   29

CRITICAL REVIEW QUESTIONS

1. Identify human behavior that involves more than one kind of social psychological process. Describe how your example overlaps two general areas of interest in the field of social psychology.
2. The development of social psychology is considered an American phenomenon. In fact, many social psychological theories grew out of the research conducted on the social problems that arose in the United States in the twentieth

century. Identify a twenty-first-century social problem that is suited for social psychological analysis. Clearly define the problem, and then describe how you would design a research project to investigate it.

3. Examine the results of two recent public opinion surveys. Focus on items that seem to ask similar questions. How might the exact wording of these questions affect the observed results?

TWO

Primary Socialization

When the Cold War ended, the world was horrified to learn how innocent children had suffered. In a *New York Times* article, Walter Goodman referred to them as "nobody's children" (1990). They were "the unwanted human legacy of the deposed Ceaucescu regime" (Kenny 1990). Millions of Romanians had suffered under the brutal twenty-four-year dictatorship of Nicolae Ceaucescu, but the consequences were particularly grave for women and children. In an effort to increase Romania's population from 22 million to 30 million, Ceaucescu had banned all forms of contraception and ordered Romanian women of childbearing age to have at least four children. Abandoned by parents who were unable to care for them, thousands of Romanian children were confined to institutions, where they remained isolated from the world, receiving little or no human attention.

After Ceaucescu's regime collapsed, Westerners discovered these children, living in subhuman conditions. Journalists who visited the state-run institutions where the orphans lived described them as "asylums," "baby warehouses," and "concentration camp–like orphanages" (Ward 1990). Barbara Bascom, an American pediatrician who took up the plight of these innocent victims, described the conditions as appalling, saying: "When you walk into one of these orphanages you see rows of babies in iron cribs and you see them rocking themselves very quietly, providing their own stimulation" (Kenny 1990).

Goodman (1990) described the pictures that journalists had taken of Romanian orphans as "wrenching: puny infants, some with their hands bound, attracting flies.

Naked children jammed into filthy prisonlike areas. Sickly looking boys and girls waiting to die." Some of the worst pictures showed "frightened children being pushed two and three at a time into a stagnant pool of black water, which was supposed to be a bath." In a report for CBS News, Peter Van Sant (1991) described comparably disturbing scenes: "Thousands had been left starving in little more than death camps. Some were without clothing, living amid their own excrement." According to Goodman (1990), the children in these orphanages suffered from many serious medical problems, but they were turned away from a nearby pediatric hospital because they were "nobody's children."

Social psychologists have long sought to understand the effects of early childhood deprivation (Davis 1940; Bowlby 1951; Provence and Lipton 1962; Dennis 1973; Freud and Burlingham 1973). But the relatively small number of cases that approximated the kind of early deprivation suffered by Romanian orphans left many questions unanswered. One of the first cases studied involved a girl named Anna Harris, who was hidden in her grandfather's attic for the first six years of her life because she was illegitimate (Davis 1940, 1947). When she was discovered, Anna showed no signs of intelligence; she could not walk and was unable to communicate. Efforts to help Anna catch up proved largely unsuccessful. Eventually she was able to walk and to understand simple commands. She could identify a few colors, build with blocks, and talk in phrases. But she never attained a mental level much beyond that of a 2-year-old. Researchers were not sure if Anna's early childhood deprivation prevented her from achieving a higher level of mental development. Her mother reportedly had the intelligence of a child between 7 and 12 years, making it impossible to rule out a congenital deficiency in Anna.

Isabelle, a child who had suffered a similar kind of deprivation, provided an interesting case for purposes of comparison (Davis 1940, 1947). She was discovered about nine months after Anna,

at the age of about $6\frac{1}{2}$ years. She, too, had been isolated from the outside world because she was illegitimate. However, in contrast to Anna's nearly complete isolation, Isabelle did have contact with her mother, who was deaf and mute. Although this isolation prevented her from learning how to speak, Isabelle did communicate with her mother through a system of gestures. At first, researchers were not sure that Isabelle could hear. And they described her behavior as typical of a 6-month-old child. The specialists who worked with Isabelle eventually determined that her mental level was about $2\frac{1}{2}$ years. They believed she was feebleminded and were not optimistic about further advancement. Nonetheless, specialists made an intensive effort to help Isabelle catch up. And her progress was remarkable. By the time she was $8\frac{1}{2}$ years old, Isabelle had reached a normal mental level.

Both Anna and Isabelle showed the short-term effects of early childhood deprivation. Without the rich environment and stimulation found in normal homes, they failed to achieve the typical milestones of early childhood (see Table 2.1). Whereas this damage remained permanent in Anna, Isabelle did not suffer serious long-term effects. What made the difference? Researchers have long sought to answer this question, and it still stirs debate today. Some theorists believe that early experience has a long-lasting impact on a child that is difficult to reverse. Others disagree, arguing that the effects of deprivation in early childhood can be overcome.

Social psychologists cannot devise an ethical experiment to determine the effects of early childhood deprivation. But the tragic plight of Romanian orphans provided a natural experiment. Researchers who examined the development of Romanian orphans observed the kinds of effects reported in earlier studies (Kaler and Freeman 1994; Mainemer, Gilman, and Ames 1998). Michael Rutter and his colleagues (1998), who examined subjects at the time of their adoption, reported what many others saw: The orphans suffered from malnutrition and infections and showed signs of retarded development.

TABLE 2.1   EARLY CHILDHOOD DEVELOPMENT: THE FIRST TWO YEARS

Age	Language	Motor Skills	Emotions
0–1 month	Small throaty sounds, often turning into cooing by the end of the first month.	Sucks, pulls closed fists to mouth, turns head.	Pleasure, surprise, disgust, distress
1–4 months	More vowel-like sounds ("ooh-ooh" and "ahh-ahh"). Whimpers, squeals, chuckles, gurgles.	Kicks, reaches, grasps.	Joy, anger
4–8 months	Begins to make sounds like "m" and "b." Makes new sounds by changing shape of mouth.	Swipes at dangling objects, clenches rattle and puts in mouth, bangs objects. Rolls over in both directions. Supports weight on legs.	
8–12 months	Starts to imitate a broader range of sounds. May say "ma-ma" and "da-da." Adds gestures to words: Waves when saying "bye-bye" or shakes head while saying "no."	Puts objects into containers and then takes them out. May hold crayon and scribble. Likes to turn pages. Is fascinated by doors swinging back and forth. Can retrieve object from a hidden location.	Sadness, fear
12–18 months	May say two to eight words by 12 months. Gestures become more important; uses them to complete an idea. Begins to follow simple commands. Starts to use words to express needs: "up" to be held.	Walks. Picks up small objects with thumb and index finger. Turns containers over to dump contents. Throws balls. Drinks from a cup. Sorts shapes and drops them into matching holes.	Tender affection
18–24 months	Vocabulary explodes. "No" is chief word. May refer to self by name. Learns by the end of the second year that everything has a name. May use words to express feelings or ideas. Uses facial expressions to communicate feelings. Vocabulary may contain two hundred words by the end of the second year.	Mental representation, as evidenced by solutions to sensorimotor problems. Engages in make-believe play.	Shame, pride

Sources: Goleman 1984; Berk 2000; *Newsweek* 2000.

Over the course of their study, Rutter and his colleagues (1998) conducted follow-up examinations, reassessing when they turned 4 children who had been adopted between birth and 2 years of age. The degree to which these children had caught up, both physically and cognitively, was impressive. But even more important, they discovered something that promised to offer some answers to the question about long-term effects. The progress made by individual children varied by the age at which they had been adopted. Children adopted after the age of 6 months did not show the same kind of progress as children adopted before they had reached 6 months. As measured by IQ scores, Romanian orphans adopted before 6 months of age resembled British children who had also been adopted before the age of 6 months. But the IQ scores of Romanian orphans adopted after 6 months of institutionalization lagged behind their British counterparts who did not suffer from early deprivation. This finding suggests that recovery from early childhood deprivation is related to the period of time during which deprivation occurs.

Modern technology provides some additional insight into the effects produced by early childhood deprivation. Using positron emission tomography (PET), medical researchers discovered that the electrical and chemical activity in the brains of Romanian orphans differed from that of normal children (Chugani et al. 1998). What does this suggest about early childhood deprivation? Consider the case of Julianna, a Romanian orphan who had been adopted by American parents in 1991 (*Good Morning America* 1997). Julianna's adoptive parents expected her to have some developmental problems because she had spent her early life in an orphanage where children were routinely tied down and rarely picked up or touched. But they had been optimistic and believed that time, love, and medical attention would help her. Unfortunately, five years after her adoption, Julianna still failed to show signs of normal progress. She was unable to speak in sentences, to interact with other children, or to do simple things like cutting and pasting.

Positron emission tomography suggested an explanation. In the brain of a normal child, a PET scan shows the same degree of activity in the right and left sides, indicated by a red glow. Pictures of Julianna's brain showed an abnormality. While activity on the left side was fine, the right side showed lower activity—not as much red. The brains of other children who have suffered early childhood deprivation show patterns similar to Julianna's, lending support to researchers' beliefs that a child's early experiences play a critical role in hardwiring the brain for thought, emotion, and behavior.

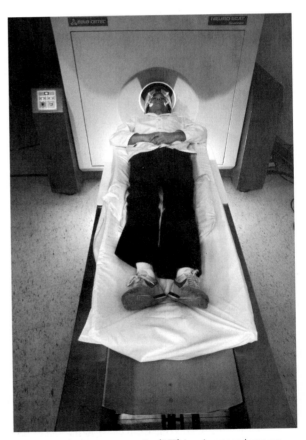

Positron emission tomography (PET) has increased our understanding of the damage caused by social isolation during early childhood development.

PET allows scientists to see how a baby's brain develops. Using this new technology, they have already measured the brain activity of infants from the moment of birth and have discovered that the primitive structures of the brain that control respiration, reflexes, and heartbeat are already wired at birth. The neural circuits in higher regions of the cortex, however, are undeveloped. And most of the connections that an infant's neurons will make will be determined by early experiences (*Newsweek* 1997; *Time* 1997).

While scientists have just begun to understand how experiences after birth hardwire the brain, they do know that these experiences exert a dramatic and precise impact (*Newsweek* 1997; *Time* 1997). Different parts of the brain are wired at different ages. Creating these connections is natural and does not require parents to engage a child in structured activities like using flashcards. Nor are expensive toys required. Pots and pans, blocks, beads, playing peekaboo, and talking to babies—the kinds of stimulation that commonly occur in most households—will provide sufficient stimulation for proper brain development. When children are isolated or deprived of sensory experiences, however, their brains do not get hardwired—and that can result in irreversible damage.

THEORETICAL APPROACHES TO CHILD DEVELOPMENT AND SOCIALIZATION

Social psychology seeks to understand how the thoughts, feelings, and behaviors of individuals are influenced by other human beings. The tragic fate of Romanian orphans shows us something else—the adverse effects of social isolation. Deprived of the love and attention of nurturing caregivers, these children showed signs of retarded motor skills, impairments in cognitive and language skills, and emotional damage. No one captured their plight better than Walter Goodman, who called these sickly-looking boys and girls "nobody's children." They were not learning how to become members of society but were rather just

waiting to die. These children showed the world in the starkest way what can go wrong during the most critical period of human development. We will now turn our attention to what should have gone right. Among a number of other questions, we will ask, How do human beings come to understand their social world? How do they interpret their experiences with the environment and other members of society? And how do they learn their place in society, its rules, and the roles that they must play?

Interest in how children develop and in how they should be trained for life in a particular society can be traced to at least the sixteenth century, when childhood was first recognized as a distinct stage in the life cycle. The puritanical belief in original sin promoted a harsh authoritarian approach to disciplining children. The adage "Spare the rod and spoil the child" reflects the philosophy of Thomas Hobbes (1651/1904), who believed that children were inherently selfish, self-centered creatures who must be controlled by society. But the philosophies of Jean-Jacques Rousseau (1762/1955) and John Locke (1693/1913) encouraged the more humane treatment of children. Rousseau's "inherently good" child popularized images of children as "sweet, innocent lambs" (Rotundo 1993, 255). From his perspective, children have an innate moral sense that is often steered in the wrong direction by society. And Locke's view of the child's mind as a *tabula rasa*, or "blank slate," suggested that parents bore heavy responsibility for the formation of their child's character. Each of these views influenced child-rearing practices and shaped ideas about the process called **socialization**.

The range and diversity of socialization theories reflect the complex nature of this process. They must explain not only how individuals come to understand the world that surrounds them but also how individuals come to understand themselves. Victor Gecas (1992) captured the complex nature of socialization by defining it as two interconnected processes. He described the first process as one "through which individuals learn the values, norms, motives, beliefs, and roles of the groups or society with which they are associated."

The other parallel process refers to the way that "individuals develop and change in terms of personality and self-concept or identity" (Snow and Oliver 1995, 579).

In this chapter, we will examine a number of theories that seek to explain how human beings become members of society. Ranging from classic theories to modern ones, they will include some of the most hotly debated theories of the twentieth century: Freud's psychoanalytic theory, Piaget's theory of cognitive development, and Watson's theory of behaviorism. Recognizing the key differences among these theories will help us understand, compare, and evaluate them. These differences often reflect important assumptions that theorists make about human beings, society, and biological and social processes. As we examine each theory, we will consider four basic questions:

1. Does this theory stress the influence of nature or nurture?

2. Are children actively involved in the developmental or socialization process, or are they passive recipients of social or biological influences?

3. Does development or socialization proceed in stages, or is it continuous?

4. What overall pattern or worldview do the main assumptions of this theory suggest?

Nature versus Nurture

To assess where you stand on the nature-versus-nurture debate, consider a criminal case that involves a defendant who is accused of brutally murdering an innocent victim. What do you think caused him to kill another human being? Was he biologically programmed to commit this heinous act, or did he learn to behave this way? This example illustrates a debate that dates back to the middle of the nineteenth century: Are human beings the products of heredity (nature) or learning (nurture)?

Charles Darwin's theory of evolution, which proposed that inherited factors determined the

behavior of animals, led many people in the late nineteenth and early twentieth centuries to favor the "nature" position (Robertson 1987). They believed that human beings, like other animals, were the product of their genes. Psychologists even compiled lists of human instincts to explain various behaviors, including warfare and acquisitiveness. But this instinct theory of human behavior did not remain popular. During most of the twentieth century, the debate favored the "nurture" position. Ivan Pavlov's research on classical conditioning (1927), which influenced the development of behaviorism, played a significant role in changing opinions in this debate.

Today, most social scientists have adopted a middle position on the issue, arguing that nature and nurture both contribute to human development. Recognizing that the process of socialization involves a complicated interplay between biological and environmental factors, the focus has now turned to understanding how these two separate factors interact as they influence the course of a child's development.

Active versus Passive Participant Models

Another issue that theories of socialization consider is whether children play a passive or an active role in the developmental process. Do children actively participate in this process, or does society determine who they will be? Many early theories of socialization, which were heavily influenced by behaviorism, viewed the process as a one-way street where a passive child was shaped by rewards and punishments (Corsaro 1997). However, by the middle of the twentieth century, Jean Piaget's theory of cognitive development began to revolutionize ideas about children, including the notion that they are curious, active explorers of their environments. Today, many social scientists view the process of socialization as one that involves reciprocal interaction between the individual and the environment (Corsaro 1997; Kaplan 2000; Shaffer 2000). They believe that human beings actively participate in the creation of their environments.

Continuous Process Theories versus Stage Theories

Another way to classify theories of socialization is on the basis of their assumptions about how development proceeds. Continuous process theories view development as progressing in smooth, small steps toward greater learning. These theories also tend to view the nature of learning as quantitative or additive—children learn more and more. Stage theories, in contrast, view development as a series of stages that are qualitatively different. As children move from one stage to the next, they experience abrupt changes that make them fundamentally different from the way they used to be.

Overall Patterns or Worldviews

The assumptions that different theories make concerning the three issues just addressed tend to reflect an overall pattern or worldview (Shaffer 2000; Overton 1984). Two patterns characterize early developmental theories (Overton 1984). The mechanistic model views human beings like machines, which are made up of parts (behaviors) that can be taken apart. According to this model, individuals are passive participants who respond to external influences. Change is gradual as individuals acquire or lose certain patterns of behavior. The second pattern, the organismic model, thinks of human beings as living organisms who cannot be understood as a collection of parts. As active participants in the developmental process, individuals change in response to internal forces (instincts or maturation). This model suggests that human development proceeds through a sequence of stages. Recently, a new model has emerged (Lerner 1986). Known as the contextual model, this worldview suggests that development is a product of the interplay between individuals and the environment. According to this perspective, human beings are active participants in this process. While certain aspects of development are seen as universal, other aspects are viewed as products of particular cultures, times, or individuals.

COGNITIVE DEVELOPMENT

Two theories dominated ideas about cognitive development in the twentieth century: Jean Piaget's theory of cognitive development and Lev Vygotsky's socioculture theory. Both men, who were born at the end of the nineteenth century, sought to understand the role of language in cognitive development. They wanted to know, "Do children first master ideas and then translate them into words? Or does the capacity for language open new cognitive doors, enabling children to think in more advanced ways?" (Berk 2000, 221).

In *The Language and Thought of the Child*, Piaget (1926) claimed that language played a relatively unimportant role in shaping a young child's thinking (Berk 2000). Instead, he stressed the importance of children acting directly on the physical world, which led them to modify the way they thought so that it fit external reality better. He later explained (1967, 11) how thought evolved before language:

> Intelligence actually appears well before language, that is to say, well before internal thought, which presupposes the use of verbal signs (internalized language). It is an entirely practical intelligence based on the manipulation of objects; in place of words and concepts it uses percepts and movements organized into "action schemata." For example, to grab a stick in order to draw up a remote object is an act of intelligence (and a fairly late developing one at that: about eighteen months). Here, an instrument, the means to an end, is coordinated with a pre-established goal.

Vygotsky disagreed with Piaget, arguing that cognitive development takes place through a child's interaction with parents, teachers, and other significant people. In *Thought and Language* (1934/1962), he claimed that the acquisition of language was the most significant achievement in a child's development. It provided the primary way for human beings to exchange social meanings and was critical for cognitive change.

What do you think? Before you decide, let us examine each of these theories more closely. We will begin with Piaget's theory of cognitive development.

PIAGET'S THEORY OF COGNITIVE DEVELOPMENT

Jean Piaget was born in Neuchatel, Switzerland, in 1896. He was by all accounts a gifted child who published his first scientific article at the age of 10—a description of a partly albino sparrow. During his adolescence, Piaget combined his biological interest with epistemology, the branch of philosophy that seeks to understand the foundation of knowledge. The impact of these early research interests is evident in Piaget's theory of mental development. For example, his proposal that the mind builds cognitive structures to help individuals adapt to the world—to help them organize and make sense of their experiences—reflects the conclusions he had drawn about mollusks that inhabited the lakes of Switzerland.

According to Piaget, the process of adapting to the external world involves active learning. From infancy through adolescence, children interpret their experiences in terms of cognitive structures that exist at a given time. This development proceeds through a sequence of four invariant stages: sensorimotor, preoperational, concrete operational, and formal operational. The transition from one stage to the next is not gradual but is marked by a fundamental change in the way children process information. As children progress through these stages, their cognitive structures grow more sophisticated, and their thinking becomes more abstract and more logical.

Basic Concepts in Cognitive Development Theory

Piaget used five key concepts to explain how cognitive development occurs: schema, assimilation, accommodation, equilibrium, and equilibration. A **schema** is a cognitive structure that changes from one stage to the next. Individuals use schemas to identify and process information. You might therefore think of a schema as a concept or category. Another way to think of it is in terms of an index file. Each card in the file would represent a schema. As children grow, the number of cards in the index file increases, and the new cards become more and more refined to take into account changing classifications of what an individual experiences (Wadsworth 1979). Consider a child who is just beginning to learn how to identify different animals. Initially his index file contains only a few cards—perhaps only those for family pets, such as *dog* or *cat*. As the child develops, more cards are needed to account for what he sees in the world. During a trip to the zoo, a child might mistakenly refer to a tiger as a dog. Since he has never seen a tiger before, the child may try to fit it into an existing schema. Eventually, he will recognize the differences between tigers and dogs and create a separate card (schema) for *tiger* in the index file.

Through organization and adaptation, the cognitive structures that a child uses to understand and interpret external reality grow and develop into those he will use as an adult. As children develop more and more schemas, they rearrange and organize them into more complex cognitive structures. These ever-evolving structures in turn facilitate the process of adaptation.

Piaget described two processes involved in adaptation: assimilation and accommodation. **Assimilation** refers to the cognitive process that occurs when an individual uses an existing schema to classify a new stimulus. The child who puts a tiger into the existing category of *dog* illustrates this process. When a child cannot assimilate new information into an existing schema, he can either modify the existing schema or create a new schema—a process called **accommodation**. This process allows the child to reorganize or modify information so that it fits reality better. Assimilation influences the growth of schemas, but it does not produce any change.

Every time we interact with the environment, we use our existing schemas to interpret our experiences. If necessary, we refine our schemas to fit our experience better. Assimilation and accommodation operate together in this way to create increasingly more adequate schemas for understanding the world. Piaget referred to the balance between these two processes as **equilibrium**, suggesting that this is a steady, comfortable state. Disequilibrium occurs during periods of rapid cognitive change when children are unable to fit new information into current schemas. The discomfort of disequilibrium motivates them to make their cognitive structures more adequate—to accommodate. Once they have accomplished that, they shift back toward assimilation. This fluctuation, which Piaget called **equilibration**, results in increasingly adequate cognitive structures.

Stages of Cognitive Development

As noted earlier, Piaget described four invariant stages of cognitive development (see Table 2.2). Each stage builds on the previous one. Therefore, children must advance in order and cannot skip a stage. Movement from one stage to the next also involves an abrupt change in a child's manner of thinking. It is not only more advanced than that in the previous stage, but it is also qualitatively different. Progression through these stages moves from the simple to the complex and from the pure egocentrism of an infant to the social perspective of an adult.

Sensorimotor Stage (First 2 Years). Although Piaget recognized that infants do not know enough about their world to explore it in a meaningful way, he nevertheless believed that their intellectual development was already under way at birth. He based this claim on the idea that sensorimotor behaviors lay the foundation for later cognitive development. The basic reflexes present at birth—sucking, grasping, crying, and the movement of different parts of the body—constitute the rudiments of sensorimotor intelligence. During the first month of life, infants assimilate new information through their reflex system. By the end of the first month, they are already showing signs of accommodation. The progress that infants make from this point until the end of the sensorimotor stage is extraordinary—from simple reflex behaviors to the internal representation of thought (see

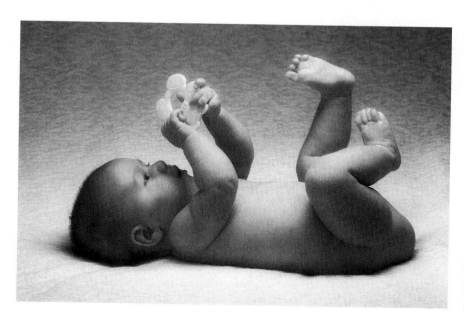

During the sensorimotor stage of development, babies explore the world through their senses and physical movements.

TABLE 2.2	PIAGET'S STAGES OF COGNITIVE DEVELOPMENT	
Stage	**Characteristics of the Stage**	**Major Change of the Stage**
Sensorimotor (0–2 Years)		Development proceeds from reflex activity to representation and sensorimotor solutions to problems.
Substage 1 (0–1 month)	Reflex activity only No differentiation	
Substage 2 (1–4 months)	Hand-mouth coordination Differentiation via sucking reflex	
Substage 3 (4–8 months)	Hand-eye coordination Repetition of unusual events	
Substage 4 (8–12 months)	Coordination of two schemas Object permanence attained	
Substage 5 (12–18 months)	New means through experimentation—child follows sequential displacements	
Substage 6 (18–24 months)	Internal representation New means through mental combinations	
Preoperational (2–7 Years)	Problems are solved through representation and language development (2–4 years). Thought and language are both egocentric. Conservation problems cannot be solved.	Development proceeds from sensorimotor representation to prelogical thought and solutions to problems.
Concrete Operational (7–11 Years)	Reversibility is attained. Conservation problems can be solved; logical operations are developed and applied to concrete problems. Complex verbal problems and hypothetical problems cannot be solved.	Development proceeds from prelogical thought to logical solutions to concrete problems.
Formal Operations (12–15 Years)	Individual logically solves all types of problems and thinks scientifically. Individual solves complex verbal and hypothetical problems. Cognitive structures have matured.	Development proceeds from logical solutions to concrete problems to logical solutions to all classes of problems.

Source: Adapted from Wadsworth 1979, 126–127.

Table 2.2). The wide range of learning that occurs during the first two years of life led Piaget to divide this period into six substages.

One of the most important developments during the sensorimotor stage involves the concept of object permanence. Piaget noted that babies at the beginning of substage 3 (about 4 months old) will not look for a toy with which they have been playing if it rolls out of sight. Babies at this stage of development do not realize that an object exists if they cannot see it. By substage 4 (about 8 months old), babies grasp the idea of object permanence. At this point, they will look for toys that disappear from view. The phenomenon of object permanence explains why babies are so delighted by the game of peekaboo.

By the end of the sensorimotor stage, children are able to keep a mental picture of an object in their mind. Representational thought, the ability to let one thing stand for another, allows them to solve some problems in their head. And it marks a dramatic change in the way they play. They begin to participate in make-believe play, such as pretending to drive a car. From this point, development increasingly involves concepts and symbols rather than senses and motor skills.

Preoperational Stage (Ages 2–7 Years). The preoperational stage of cognitive development is marked by a dramatic increase in mental representation or symbolic activity, especially language. This new development allows children to think in words—to separate thought from action (Berk 2000). Beginning with "one-word sentences," children gradually build an extensive vocabulary. Most children have mastered the spoken language by the time they reach 4 years of age (Wadsworth 1979).

Piaget (1967, 17) described the impact of language on the intellectual life of a child as follows:

> [Language] has three consequences essential to mental development: (1) the possibility of verbal exchange with other persons, which heralds the onset of the socialization of action; (2) the internalization of words, i.e., the appearance of thought itself, supported by internal language and a system of signs; (3) last and most important, the internalization of action of such which from now on, rather than being purely perceptual and motor as it has been heretofore, can represent itself intuitively by means of pictures and "mental experiments."

According to Piaget, mental representation makes processing information more efficient than it was in the sensorimotor stage, since a child's thinking is no longer tied to an action. Another significant outcome of symbolic activity is a child's ability to carry on internal conversations—to communicate with himself or herself.

Despite the dramatic changes associated with a child's ability to communicate symbolically, Piaget did not believe that cognitive development depended on language. In fact, he argued just the opposite—that "the development of sensorimotor schemata is seen as a prerequisite to language development (as in blind children)" (quoted in Wadsworth 1979, 74). According to Piaget (1926), a child's development during the sensorimotor stage produces schemata of their experience, which they later labeled with words.

Concrete Operational Stage (Ages 7–11 Years). In his description of the preoperational stage of cognitive development, Piaget considered not only what children are able to do but also what they cannot do (Beilin 1992). As his choice of the term *preoperational* suggests, he compared children in the second stage of cognitive development to children in the third stage, which he called the concrete operational. By preoperational Piaget meant that children in the second stage do not understand logical operations that are typical of arithmetic, measurement, and hierarchical classification. Children in the preoperational stage think in rigid ways, focusing on only one aspect of reality at a time.

To illustrate that preoperational children do not understand logical rules, Piaget developed a number of experiments that involved what he called conservation problems. **Conservation** refers to that idea that the amount of an object stays the same even when its appearance changes (see Figure 2.1). A simple experiment illustrates the conservation of liquid. To begin, an experimenter presents a child with two containers of equal size and shape that are filled with liquid. She then asks the child to compare the containers and tell her if they contain the same amount of liquid.

Conservation Task	Original Presentation	Transformation
Number	Are there the same number of pennies in each row?	Now are there the same number of pennies in each row, or does one row have more?
Length	Is each of these sticks just as long as the other?	Now are the two sticks of equal length, or is one longer?
Mass	Is there the same amount of clay in each ball?	Now does each piece have the same amount of clay, or does one have more?
Liquid	Is there the same amount of water in each glass?	Now is there the same amount of water in each glass, or does one have more?
Weight	Does each of these two balls of clay weigh the same amount?	Now (without placing them back on the scale to confirm what is correct for the child) do the two pieces of clay weigh the same, or does one weigh more?

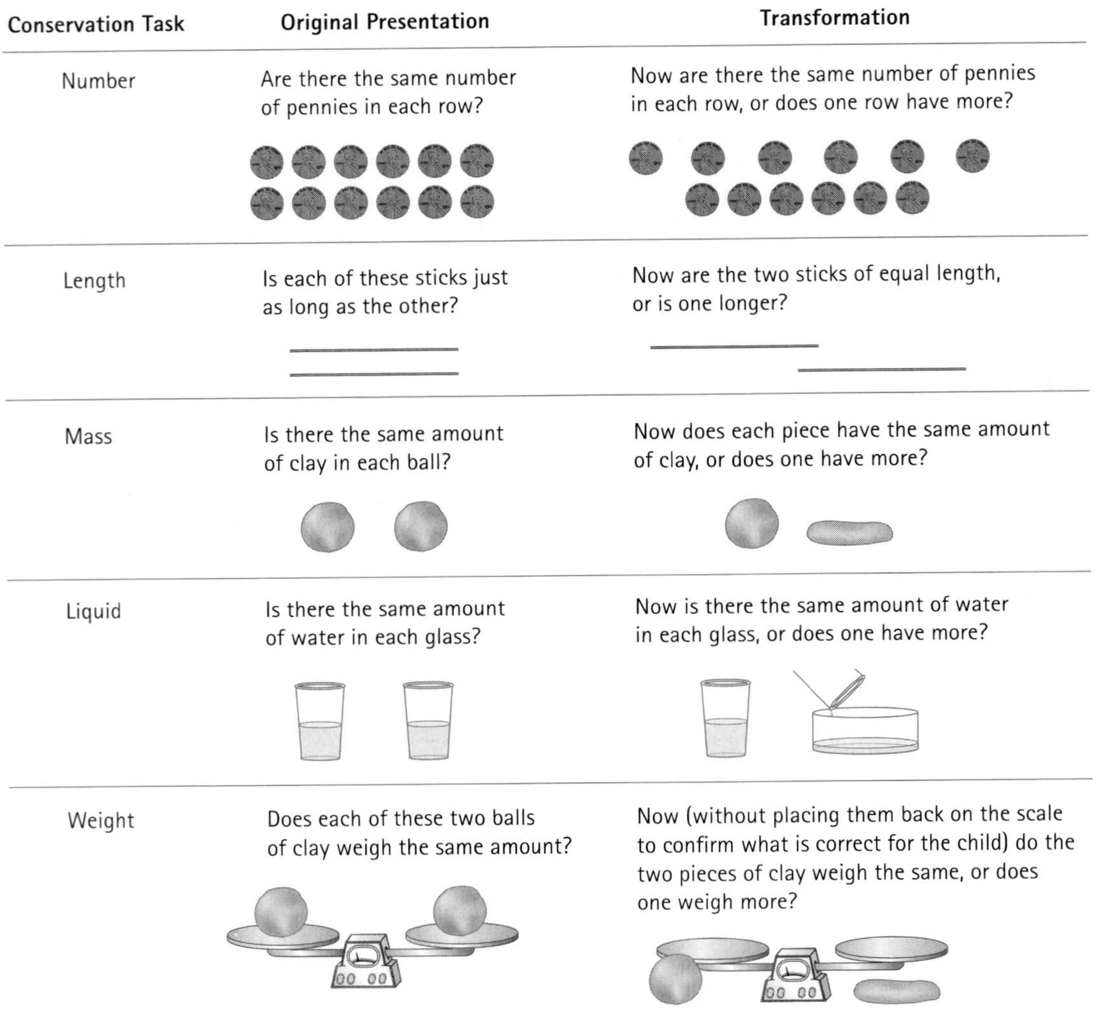

FIGURE 2.1

Some Piagetian Conservation Tasks

Children at the preoperational stage cannot yet conserve. These tasks are mastered gradually over the concrete operational stage. Children in Western nations typically acquire conservation of number, length, mass, and liquid sometime between 6 and 7 years and weight between 8 and 10 years.
Source: Berk 2000, 242.

Once the child agrees that they do contain equal amounts, she then pours the liquid from one container into a short, wide container. Although this changes the appearance of the liquid, the amount has not changed. The child is then asked to compare the containers of liquid once more and to indicate whether the amount of liquid is the same. A typical preoperational child will say that the amount of liquid is now different—usually, that the short, wide container has less liquid. This reasoning is based on the height of the two containers. When the experimenter pours the liquid back into the original container, a preoperational child will then say that both containers again contain the same amount of liquid. This kind of reasoning is not logical and shows how children in the preoperational stage focus on perceptual aspects of the problem (Wadsworth 1979).

Children in the concrete operational stage grasp the notion of conservation. Unlike preoperational children, they realize that the amount of liquid does not change even though its appearance does. They may explain what has happened by saying that even though the water in the shallow container is shorter, it is also wider. And they might add that if you pour the water back into the original containers, you will see the same amounts. This shows that children understand the operation of **reversibility**.

Two other logical operations characterize this stage of development. **Hierarchical classification** refers to a child's ability to sort and classify objects into classes and subclasses. Many activities at this age involve this kind of logic, including many board and card games. **Seriation** involves the ability to order items along a quantitative dimension such as height or weight. Teachers often ask children to perform this kind of task when they ask them to line up in order of height from shortest to tallest.

In contrast to the egocentric preoperational child, the concrete operational child has the ability to assume the viewpoints of others. Language at this age is social and communicative (Wadsworth 1979). Although children in this stage do use logic, they can only solve problems that involve "concrete" objects and events. They have not yet reached the highest level of thinking, which involves hypothetical problems, word problems, and abstract operations.

Formal Operational Stage (Age 12 Years and Older). Consider the following problem (Piaget 1950, 149): "Edith is fairer than Susan. Edith is darker than Lilly. Who is the darkest of the three?" Children who have not yet entered the stage of

formal operations have difficulty solving this problem. The ability to use reasoning and logic to solve hypothetical word problems like this characterizes the final stage of cognitive development, the formal operational stage. Although children use logic in the stage of concrete operations, their problem-solving abilities involve tangible, concrete problems in the present (Wadsworth 1979). In contrast, children in the stage of formal operations consider the past, present, and future, and they can deal with hypothetical problems. Consider another typical problem that Piaget used to show how children in the last stage of cognitive development differ from those in the previous stage. He would ask children to complete the following statement: "If coal is white, snow is _____." Children in the stage of concrete operations will insist that coal is black. They are bound by reality—the concrete. Children in the final stage of cognitive development, however, can think abstractly. They understand the hypothetical nature of this problem and will say, "Snow is black."

Thinking in the stage of formal operations involves scientific reasoning, hypothesis building (and testing), and an understanding of causation (Wadsworth 1979). Children in this stage become capable of hypothetico-deductive reasoning (Berk 2000). Thus when they try to solve a problem, they begin with a general theory of all the variables that might produce an outcome and then deduce from it specific hypotheses about what might occur. This kind of problem solving proceeds from many possibilities to reality. Children who are still in the concrete operational stage cannot think beyond reality and cannot solve problems that require abstract thinking.

Piaget demonstrated the kind of scientific reasoning used by children in the stage of formal operations with a problem involving a pendulum (Inhelder and Piaget 1958; Wadsworth 1979; Berk 2000). He would give a child several strings of varying lengths, a number of objects of different weights to attach to the strings, and a bar from which to hang the objects. Then he would ask, What will cause the pendulum to swing faster or slower through its arc? Children in the stage of concrete operations usually adjust the weight of the pendulum. They do not attempt to solve the problem in a systematic way, nor do they try to separate the effects of each variable. But children in the stage of formal operations do consider the effects of each variable and will systematically test different hypotheses by varying one factor at a time while holding the others constant.

Children in the last stage of cognitive development are capable of introspection—they are "able to think about their own thoughts and feelings as if they were objects" (Wadsworth 1979, 110). The ability to think abstractly, combined with the physical changes of adolescence, influences perceptions of oneself and others (Berk 2000). One of the distorted images characteristic of adolescence is called the **imaginary audience**—a teenager's feeling that he or she is the focus of everyone else's attention (Elkind and Bowen 1979). This explains why they are especially self-conscious at this age. Another distortion is called the **personal fable** (Berk 2000). Given their feeling that others are focusing on them, teenagers often develop an exaggerated sense of self-importance. This may explain why teenagers often feel that no one else could possibly understand how they feel (Elkind 1994). And it might account for teenagers' feelings of invulnerability, which often lead to risky behavior.

Not all individuals reach the stage of formal operations. In fact, studies have shown that no more than half of Americans do (Elkind 1962; Kohlberg and Mayer 1972; Kuhn et al. 1977). Even college students stumble with abstract thinking (Keating 1979). To demonstrate this, just ask several of your classmates to solve one of Piaget's problems.

Evaluation of Piaget's Theory

Piaget's theory of cognitive development was not particularly popular in the United States when it first appeared in the 1920s (Lerner 1986; Thomas 2000). By the late 1950s, however, Piaget's revolutionary ideas had begun to receive attention and acceptance. Throughout the 1960s, his ideas dominated the field of developmental psychology (see Figure 2.2). As one of the most important developmental theories of the twentieth century, Piaget's ideas have been scrutinized and tested again and again. Educators have found his description of different levels of cognitive development particularly interesting and have used them to determine the sequence of skills appropriate for different grade levels, particularly in mathematics and physical sciences (Shaffer 2000). Perhaps the most important contribution Piaget made to understanding how children think was his idea that children are curious beings who actively seek and acquire information through their exploration of the environment. He also pointed out that children do not think like adults but perceive and organize their worlds in qualitatively different ways.

While these ideas continue to influence theories today, other aspects of Piaget's theory have not weathered so well. At the center of today's debate is the issue of whether cognitive development proceeds through a universal and invariant sequence of stages (Berk 2000; Shaffer 2000). Piaget's belief that children are independent learners largely ignored the influence of cultural and social experiences. Although he recognized that a child's social context could influence the rate of cognitive development, Piaget paid little attention to the social factors that might have some impact. Instead he focused on nonsocial factors such as conservation, mathematics, time, number, and space (Zimmerman 1983; Thomas 2000).

Critics also note that Piaget's method for evaluating cognitive abilities fails to provide valid measurements. Modern studies show that Piaget underestimated children's cognitive abilities and social understandings and overestimated those of adolescents and adults (Berk 2000; Shaffer 2000). Researchers now acknowledge the importance of social interaction in cognitive development and have shown that children's performance on Piagetian problems can improve when they receive assistance from a teacher (Shaffer 2000).

Despite these weaknesses, critics still recognize Piaget's theory as a classic (Kaplan 2000).

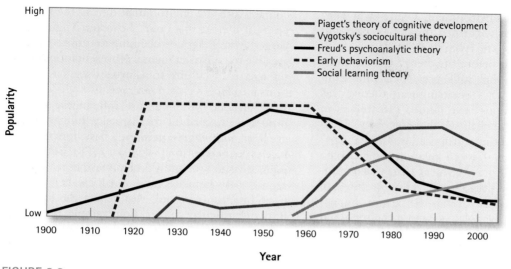

FIGURE 2.2

Trends in the Popularity of Theories

Source: Thomas 2000, 518–523.

Though some argue that it has limited explanatory power, they still recognize its value as a model for understanding developmental changes (Shaffer 2000).

VYGOTSKY'S SOCIOCULTURAL THEORY

Piaget's theory of cognitive development gained wide acceptance by the middle of the twentieth century. Regarded then as the dominant theory of cognitive development, it withstood the debates that ensued among other prominent theories, including behaviorism and psychoanalytic theory (Kozulin 1999). These debates did not, however, involve Vygotsky's sociocultural theory of cognitive development. Vygotsky, a Russian psychologist, had written a few articles that were published in English during his short life (1896–1934), but they had little impact on Western psychology before the 1960s. Even Vygotsky's Russian colleagues knew little about his research because his writings

were banned from the mid-1930s through the mid-1950s for political reasons. Thus even though Vygotsky was a contemporary of Piaget, Freud, and Watson, his theory has just recently begun to gain recognition in social psychology.

Although his contemporaries knew little about his work, Vygotsky was familiar with theirs. And his invisible participation in their debates is reflected in his writings. While Vygotsky considered the ideas of early behaviorists, particularly those of Ivan Pavlov, another Russian psychologist, Vygotsky quickly progressed to more complicated explanations of human behavior and soon came to focus on a sociocultural theory that involved language, thought, and human development. Once Vygotsky's ideas began to spread to the West in the 1960s, a number of them were accepted instantly, particularly his ideas about the social origin of individual behavior and the link between thought and behavior (Kozulin 1999). Rejecting the idea that cognitive development proceeds in an individualistic manner through adaptations to the environment, Vygotsky favored the idea of a socially formed mind (Wertsch and Tulviste 1992; Rogoff, 1998; Berk 2000).

Vygotsky died before his theory gained much recognition. Although this prevented him from fully developing his sociocultural theory, his provocative questions have guided researchers in new directions. We shall see that Vygotsky's ideas challenge many of those proposed by Piaget, especially when it came to the relationship between thought and language. We will also see that a number of Vygotsky's ideas closely resemble those of George Herbert Mead (1863–1931), a prominent American social psychologist whose theory about the self is fully explored in Chapter 4. For now, let us consider how Vygotsky's theory differs from Piaget's. To begin, recall what these two men wanted to know about the role of language in human development: "Do children first master ideas and then translate them into words? Or does the capacity for language open new cognitive doors, enabling children to think in more advanced ways?" (Berk 2000, 221).

Culture and Cognitive Development

Piaget claimed that language played a relatively small role in shaping the cognitive development of young children. The most important factor was a child's interaction with the physical world, which modified the way he thought so that it fit external reality better. Thus, he argued, intelligence precedes language—that is, intelligence comes before internal thought, which presupposes verbal signs (internalized language). Vygotsky disagreed, arguing that cognitive development takes place through a child's social interactions with parents, teachers, and other significant persons in a specific sociocultural context (Shaffer 2000).

To understand the key differences between these two arguments, let us begin at a point where the two men actually agree—infancy. Vygotsky viewed infancy much like Piaget, claiming that babies are born with a number of basic functions—perceptions, sensation, and memory. And he believed that these functions develop through direct contact with the environment during the first two years of life. At this point, however, Vygotsky diverged from Piaget by claiming that once children are able to construct mental representations (about the age of 2), culture transforms these basic functions into *higher mental functions*.

Consider how culture influences memory processes. According to Vygotsky, human beings are born with *natural memory*, a basic function that resembles perception (Vygotsky 1978). But natural memory is not the only kind humans use. Vygotsky argued that human beings progress beyond this basic function with aids that reflect the influence of their particular culture. For example, preliterate cultures may use notched sticks or knots to facilitate memory processes, while more advanced cultures have developed writing as an aid. Aids like these involve artificial stimuli called *signs* to transform basic biological functions into higher mental functions. Vygotsky (1978) argued that these kinds of socially created transformations, which teach children how to think, are the products of specific conditions of social development and are absent even in the highest species of animals. As he saw it, culture shapes an individual's beliefs and values as well as the way the person thinks. Cognitive development was therefore not universal but in fact varied from culture to culture. This notion of a socially formed mind departs radically from Piaget's individualistic view that the course of cognitive development is the same in all human beings.

Social Interaction

Zone of Proximal Development. One of the most significant discoveries that Vygotsky made in studying how children learn involved what he called the **zone of proximal development**—the difference between what a child can do independently and what the child can do with some assistance from a "teacher." To understand this concept, consider a question that Vygotsky posed: Are two children, who are the same age chronologically and at the same age in terms of what they can do, the same age mentally?

To answer this question, Vygotsky analyzed the social interaction that took place when a child attempted to solve a problem with the assistance of a "teacher." He concluded that the "actual developmental level" of a child's mental functions—as measured by a battery of tests—provided a poor indication of what the child was capable of doing. These tests, which measured a child's ability to solve problems independently, focused on the end products of development. They did not measure the child's "level of potential development," which could be determined only by watching a child solve problems with the assistance of an adult or more capable peer (Vygotsky 1978). Thus he concluded that even though children might be the same age chronologically and at the same stage in terms of what they can do independently, they are not the same age mentally.

Vygotsky's research led him to argue that children develop higher mental processes through activities that involve the cooperative assistance of an adult or a more capable peer. These "teachers" may provide help in many different ways. For example, they might model an activity, give verbal instructions, ask leading questions, or initiate a solution and then ask a "pupil" to complete it (Vygotsky 1978). Because psychologists focused on the individual instead of the teacher-pupil interaction, no one prior to Vygotsky had even considered the possibility of measuring the level of potential cognitive development in this way.

This discovery led Vygotsky to emphasize the importance of teaching based on a child's potential, not on what the child could do alone. He believed that children should be viewed as active participants in the learning process. He also recognized that collaborative learning was most effective when the teacher kept the lesson within a child's zone of proximal development (Berk 2000).

Private Speech. Vygotsky's focus on social interaction explains why he stressed the role that language played in shaping the cognitive development of children. For him, it did open new cognitive doors for children, enabling them to think in more advanced ways (Berk 2000). According to

Vygotsky (1978), the most significant moment in intellectual development occurred when speech and practical activity converged. To illustrate this point, he referred to an experiment that involved a $4\frac{1}{2}$-year-old girl who was asked to get candy from a cupboard with a stool and a stick. The notes of his collaborator, R. E. Levina, described what they observed:

> (Stands on a stool, quietly looking, feeling along a shelf with stick.) "On the stool." (Glances at experimenter. Puts stick in other hand.) "Is that really the candy?" (Hesitates.) "I can get it from that other stool, stand and get it." (Gets second stool.) "No, that doesn't get it. I could use the stick." (Takes stick, knocks at the candy.) "It will move now." (Knocks candy.) "It moved, I couldn't get it with the stool, but the, but the stick worked." (Vygotsky 1978, 25)

It is not unusual to see children speaking to themselves as the little girl did in this experiment. Children often do it when they play, and it is especially noticeable when they are trying to solve a problem. Piaget referred to this behavior as *egocentric speech*, suggesting that children in this stage are not able to imagine the situation from the perspective of others. Vygotsky took an entirely different position. He argued that children speak when they act because these two behaviors are part of one complex psychological function that is aimed at solving a problem. By uniting perception, speech, and action, a child is able to internalize the visual field. Speech not only helps children manipulate objects but also controls their behavior—as the candy example illustrates. Vygotsky (1978, 26) argued, therefore, that "with the help of speech, children, unlike apes, acquire the capacity to be both the subjects and objects of their own behavior."

Vygotsky viewed speech directed at oneself as a transitional form between external and internal speech. He claimed that children use language to devise a plan and to guide their own behavior. And he noticed that children increase their use of self-directed speech when a task becomes more complicated and when an adult is unavailable to provide assistance. As children get older, the frequency of self-directed speech declines and takes the form of internal speech—the kind of conversations that we carry on with ourselves throughout the day as we think and try to solve problems. Research over the past thirty years lends support to Vygotsky's explanation of self-directed speech (Berk 2000). As a result, the term **private speech** has now replaced what Piaget originally referred to as egocentric speech.

It is important to understand how external knowledge and abilities in children become internalized (Vygotsky 1978). Vygotsky's theory suggests that social interaction plays a major role in what children learn and in what they eventually internalize. First they interact with others; then they interact with themselves, using private speech.

Intersubjectivity and Scaffolding. Vygotsky did not completely explain how internalization occurred. However, building on his ideas, researchers today propose that two processes are involved: intersubjectivity and scaffolding (Berk 2000; Shaffer 2000). **Intersubjectivity** refers to the process by which two individuals, who undertake a joint task from two different perspectives and understandings, arrive at a common understanding (Newson and Newson 1975). By adjusting to the perspective of the other person, participants involved in a joint task create a way to share information and ideas. One of the most important aspects of intersubjectivity is the idea that children and adults jointly contribute to the products of social interaction. By managing the shared tasks together, both participants play a role in creating the zone of proximal development (Berk 2000).

Scaffolding refers to the adjustments that "teachers" make in the kind of assistance they provide to "pupils" over the course of a particular period of instructional interaction (Bruner 1983; Wood 1989). If a pupil does not know where to begin in solving a problem, a teacher might start with direct instruction and then tailor further directions to fit the pupil's unique abilities (Berk 2000; Shaffer 2000). Scaffolding resembles the

descriptions that Vygotsky (1978) gave of the ways that teachers provide assistance: modeling an activity, giving verbal instructions, asking leading questions, or initiating a solution and then asking a pupil to complete it. It is also consistent with his idea that collaborative learning is most effective when the teacher keeps a lesson within a child's zone of proximal development (Berk 2000).

The Role of Play in Children's Development

Although Vygotsky did not consider play a predominant feature of childhood, he did believe that it had an enormous influence on a child's development. Using the zone of proximal development to explain the function play served, he claimed that children act older when they play. In contrast to their everyday behavior, when they act without considering how they ought to behave, children become particularly aware of the rules during play. To illustrate his point, Vygotsky wrote, "The fact that two sisters decided to play sisters induces

Learning is highly effective when a teacher keeps a lesson close to a student's present performance level. This is often accomplished by making adjustments over the instructional period—a process called scaffolding.

them to acquire rules of behavior. Only actions that fit these rules are acceptable to the play situation" (1978, 95). One of the most important results produced by this kind of playing is the girls' realization that their relationship to one another is different from their relationships with other people. As children participate in various forms of play, they begin to understand social norms and expectations. By playing various roles, they also recognize differences in the relationships that exist among different members of society.

Creating imaginary situations helps children develop the ability to think in abstract ways. Thus, for example, when they substitute a stick for a horse during play, they change the meaning that is usually attached to the stick (Vygotsky 1978). It is difficult for young children to separate thought (the meaning of a word) from an object, but they gradually develop this ability through play. Eventually, they behave according to rules that are determined by ideas, not by objects.

Play for children under the age of 3 differs from that of older children. Young children do not separate fantasy from reality; for them play is a serious game. Although even adolescents regard play as a serious game, it has evolved into a new form. For school-age children, play refers primarily to athletic games that emphasize rules. Though it has a less significant influence on children's development at this point, play nevertheless helps children set goals and continues to prepare them for social life.

Evaluation of Vygotsky's Sociocultural Theory

As noted, although Vygotsky was a contemporary of Piaget in the 1920s, his sociocultural theory remained virtually unknown until the 1960s (see Figure 2.2). After an initial positive reception in the Soviet Union, Vygotsky's writings were banned for two decades and remained unavailable to Western scholars until the 1960s. Vygotsky spent only ten years developing his ideas before he died of tuberculosis. His theory is therefore not as complete as Piaget's. It has nonetheless sparked great interest in recent years by offering a new perspective on how children develop cognitive skills. In contrast

to Piaget, who stressed cognitive development as a universal process that involves an invariant sequence of stages, Vygotsky proposed that children's social interactions and cultural experiences produce wide variations in cognitive skills. His idea of a socially formed mind has attracted a great deal of attention. And his emphasis on collaborative learning has led researchers to reconsider the function that peers play as agents of socialization (Shaffer 2000).

Despite the recent enthusiasm for Vygotsky's theory, critics have cited a number of weaknesses. First, they note that while Vygotsky indicated that cultural lines of development join with natural ones to form a single developmental path, he failed to adequately explain the natural line (Wertsche and Tulviste 1992; Berk 2000). By suggesting that social and cultural processes determine individual processes, Vygotsky failed to explain how individuals introduce innovation and creativity into the social world.

Second, they have questioned the emphasis that Vygotsky placed on language (Rogoff 1990, 1998; Rogoff et al. 1993; Berk 2000; Shaffer 2000). According to Barbara Rogoff, the kind of verbal instruction described by Vygotsky is not necessarily the most effective way for all children to learn. Cross-cultural differences suggest why. Although verbal instruction may be the ideal way for American children to learn academic concepts, it seems less effective for Mayan children who must learn how to weave baskets. For them, observation and practice seem better.

FREUD'S PSYCHOANALYTIC THEORY

Sigmund Freud (1856–1939) developed his theory of personality development during the same period of time that Piaget and Vygotsky were developing their theories. And by the middle of the twentieth century, Freud was stirring debates about the effects of early childhood experiences. In contrast to popular American theories like behaviorism, which stressed observable human behavior, this European theory focused on people's inner thoughts and feelings. Freud, a Viennese physician, based his theory on the case histories of patients who suffered from various nervous conditions—hallucinations, fears, and paralyses. When examinations of these patients showed that these symptoms were not caused by tissue damage, he began to explore the work of a French psychologist, Jean Charcot, who was conducting experiments with hypnosis. Charcot had discovered that he could use hypnosis to produce physical symptoms in his subjects—numbness of the skin, paralysis, or even deafness. The procedure was simple. He would put them into a hypnotic state and tell them that they would experience a particular symptom when they awoke but that they would not remember the cause of it. Indeed, when they awoke, they did not know the cause, nor did they remember that Charcot had suggested the ailment while they were under a hypnotic spell. Charcot discovered that he could use this technique to rid patients of the symptoms that had originally brought them to him (Freud 1910; Thomas 2000).

Freud spent a year in Paris studying Charcot's methods, seeking to understand how hypnosis worked and what relationship, if any, it had to the puzzling cases he had seen in his own practice. He concluded that the cause of his patients' symptoms involved a connection between the mind and the body. Believing that this could explain why his patients' emotional problems subsided when they talked about distressing early childhood experiences, Freud sought to understand the structure and function of the mind and personality (Freud 1910; Thomas 2000).

The Structure of the Mind

Focusing on how the mind was structured, Freud proposed three levels of awareness: the conscious, the preconscious, and the unconscious. According to him, we experience the **conscious** level as immediate awareness. It is the most visible part of the mind and yet the smallest. The **preconscious** level contains memories that can be readily accessed and transferred to the conscious level. The **unconscious** level, however, contains ideas and motivations that are beyond our awareness. Although they influence our behavior, they are repressed (forced out of awareness) because they are unacceptable to the conscious mind. Freud discovered, however, that the unconscious may reveal itself in a number of ways—for example, through dreams and slips of the tongue. In seeking to help his patients discover the unconscious motivations underlying their behavior, Freud used a number of methods, including hypnosis, free association, and dream analysis (see Box 2.1). Based on his analysis of patients' childhood memories, Freud concluded that the development of one's personality involves a struggle between the individual and society.

Viewing human nature much as Thomas Hobbes did, Freud believed that human beings are born with basic drives that seek satisfaction—such as those for sex and aggression. And he argued that these impulses create conflict because they pose a threat to social order. Ultimately, society restrains these natural drives by channeling them into socially acceptable outlets. Freud believed that parents play a critical role in shaping a child's personality during the first few years of life as the socialization process gets under way.

The Structure of the Personality

According to Freud, the personality consists of three parts—the id, the ego, and the superego. Each of these parts develops and becomes integrated through five stages of development (see Table 2.3). The **id** is the source of biological drives and desires that demands immediate and continual satisfaction. Present at birth, it constitutes the major part of an infant's personality and will remain a part of the individual's personality for life.

The **ego** is the conscious, rational part of the personality, which emerges when a child discovers that the id cannot always be satisfied immediately. At this point in development, the child will seek a realistic way to satisfy a basic biological need. For example, in contrast to an infant who cries when she is hungry, an older child might attempt to satiate this need by grabbing a cookie off the countertop.

BOX 2.1   FREUD'S INTERPRETATION OF DREAMS

In *The Interpretation of Dreams*, . . . Freud proposes the radical idea that the purpose of dreams is to express primitive sexual and aggressive wishes. These desires, he wrote, are rooted in our childhood experiences but are too anxiety-provoking to break the surface of our consciousness.

But in the 1960s, scientists dismissed Freud, claiming that dreams were a series of baseless, irrational responses, unworthy of interpretation and analysis. They cited research showing dreams to be controlled by the pons—the part of the brain stem involved in automatic tasks such as breathing.

Nevertheless, new technology suggests Freud was on to something after all, and even critics admit that the findings are significant.

With the use of new scanning techniques—positron emission tomography (PET) together with functional magnetic resonance imaging (MRI)—Allen Braun, M.D., of the National Institute on Deafness and other Communication Disorders (NIC-CD), has discovered that the regions of the brain which control emotion and motivation are highly active during REM sleep, the phase in which dreaming most often occurs.

On this basis, many now feel it is time to take a fresh look at Freud.

In the following passages, Freud—in his own words—explores and celebrates the strangeness and purpose of dreams, and shares his own twisted reveries.

Excerpts from The Interpretation of Dreams
by Sigmund Freud

I am indebted not to a patient but to an intelligent jurist of my acquaintance for the following dream, which again was told me with the intention of restraining me from rashly generalizing my theory of wishful dreams. "*My dream,*" says my informant, "*is that I am arriving at my house with a lady on my arm. A closed carriage is waiting there, a man comes up to me, identifies himself as a police agent, and invites me to follow him. I ask only for time to put my affairs in order.*"—Do you believe that it is perhaps a wish of mine to be arrested?"—"*Certainly not, I have to admit.*" "Do you know what you were being arrested for?"—"*Yes, I believe it was for infanticide.*"—"Infanticide? But you know that this is a crime that only a mother can

commit against her newborn child?"—"*That is so.*"—"And what were the circumstances of your dream? What happened the evening before?"—"*I would rather not tell you, it is a delicate matter.*"—"I need it, however, or we must forgo the interpretation of the dream."—"*Well then, listen. I spent the night not at home but with a lady who means a lot to me. When we woke in the morning we again did something together. Then I went back to sleep and dreamed what I told you.*"—"Is the lady married?"—"*Yes.*"—"And you don't want to have a child by her?"—"*No, no, that could give us away.*"—"So you don't practice normal coitus?"—"*I take care to withdraw before ejaculating.*"—"May I assume you had performed this feat several times that night, and after repeating it in the morning you were a little uncertain whether or not you had succeeded?"—"*That may well be so.*"—"Then your dream is a wish-fulfilment. You received from it a reassurance that you have not begotten a child, or, what is almost the same thing, that you had killed a child. I can easily demonstrate the connecting links to you. You will recall that a few days ago we were talking about the distress of marriage, and of the inconsistency which permits coitus in ways which avoid pregnancy, although once ovum and semen have met and formed a foetus, any kind of interference is punished as a crime. In connection with this we also considered the medieval dispute over the point in time when the concept of murder becomes admissible. You are also sure to know Lenau's ghastly poem in which infanticide and contraception are equated."—"*Remarkably enough, I happened to think of Lenau only this morning.*"—"That too is an echo of your dream. And now I shall demonstrate to you a little subsidiary wish-fulfilment in your dream. You are arriving at your house with the lady on your arm: you are therefore taking her home, instead of spending the night at her house, as you did in reality. That the wish-fulfilment forming the core of the dream should conceal itself in such an unpleasant form has perhaps more than one cause. From my essay on the aetiology of anxiety neurosis you could learn that I claim that coitus interruptus is one of the causal factors in the creation of neurotic anxiety. It would accord with this if, after several acts of coitus of this kind, you were left with a feeling of unease which then became an element in the composition of your dream." (Freud 1899/1999)

Source: Psychology Today 2000, 50–52.

TABLE 2.3	FREUD'S PSYCHOSEXUAL STAGES OF DEVELOPMENT	

Psychosexual Stage	Age	Description
Oral	0–1 year	Infants derive pleasure during the first stage of development through oral stimulation—sucking, chewing, and biting. Feeding times are important. Fixation at this stage can result from weaning an infant too early or abruptly. This may cause thumb sucking and fingernail biting in childhood and overeating and smoking in adulthood.
Anal	1–3 years	The sex drive is satisfied through pleasure associated with holding and releasing urine and feces. Toilet training involves conflict between children and parents. Difficulties can produce a number of results: extreme orderliness, cleanliness, and stinginess or disorder, messiness, and cruelty.
Phallic	3–6 years	Stimulating the genitals produces pleasure. Children develop a desire for the opposite-sex parent (Oedipus complex in boys; Electra complex in girls). Children resolve this conflict by internalizing the traits and moral standards of the same-sex parent. The superego develops during this stage. A number of sexual problems are associated with this stage, including confusion about gender identity.
Latency	6–11 years	Following the conflicts of the phallic stage, sexual urges lie dormant. During the latency stage, children focus on same-sex friends and schoolwork. The superego develops during this stage. Fixation at this stage can cause individuals to feel uncomfortable around members of the opposite sex.
Genital	12 years and older	At puberty, adolescents turn their attention to the opposite sex, experiencing adult sexual urges for the first time. Individuals enter adulthood during this stage.

The third part of the personality, the **superego**, develops between the ages of 3 and 6. Through interactions with their parents, children internalize the moral values of their parents and learn to conform to society's expectations—they develop a conscience. Once the superego has emerged, children recognize when they have violated a social norm and will experience guilt or shame for failing to live up to certain expectations. The ego plays a central role in balancing the demands of the id and the superego. It must balance the demands for gratification that come from the id with the forces of the superego, which require a chosen behavior to fit society's moral expectations.

Stages of Psychosexual Development

Freud believed that the sex drive was the most important instinct and that it shifted its attachment to different parts of the body as a child developed. The five stages of Freud's psychosexual theory correspond to these regions. Table 2.3 summarizes the development that takes place in each of these stages.

The most controversial part of Freud's theory was his explanation of how children acquire their gender identity. He believed that this occurred during the phallic stage, a time when children begin to sexually desire the parent of the opposite sex. According to Freud, anxiety develops when children begin to fear that the same-sex parent will punish them for having these kinds of desires. He called this anxiety the **Oedipus complex** in boys and the **Electra complex** in girls. Gender identity formed when children resolved these conflicts and came to identify with the same-sex parent.

Freud believed that parents played a critical role in the formation of a child's personality at each stage of development. If children experienced difficulties with their parents as they proceeded through these stages, they could become fixated at that stage and show signs of it for the remainder of their lives. Thus, for example, a child who is punished during toilet training for having accidents could become an "anal-retentive" adult—stingy and obsessed with orderliness or messy and cruel.

Evaluation of Freud's Psychoanalytic Theory

Sigmund Freud's *Interpretation of Dreams* was published in 1899. Freud considered this book his most important work, but early sales were disappointing—only 351 copies were sold in the first six years in print (Tolson 1999). Interest in Freud's theory grew in the United States during the 1920s and the 1930s when his publications were first translated from German into English (Thomas 2000). His ideas infiltrated Americans' everyday language—unconscious motives, ego, repression, projection. Slips of the tongue took on new meanings. Psychoanalytic therapy became the primary treatment for neuroses by the 1940s, and books on child-rearing practices reflected the heavy influence of Freud's ideas. The popularity of psychoanalytic theory peaked in the 1950s (see Figure 2.2).

Freud's theory continues to influence culture, but it finds little support as a theory of personality development. Critics cite a number of serious weaknesses. First, most agree that Freud placed far too much emphasis on the influence of sexual drives. Though he deserves credit for recognizing that children have sexual feelings, he never studied children directly. His theory was instead based on his analysis of emotionally disturbed patients who

suffered from problems associated with sexual repression. It is therefore impossible to generalize his findings to a normal population. Second, Freud did not consider the influence that social or cultural variables could have on the development of personality. Ironically, his focus on sexuality was probably a result of the Victorian attitudes that prevailed at the time he developed his theory. It is likely that his patients' problems stemmed from the idea that sexuality was sinful and unhealthy (Thomas 2000). Finally, Freud's concepts are difficult to measure, and his theory lacks empirical evidence.

Freud's concept of the unconscious, nonetheless, remains one of the most important ideas of the twentieth century. Freud deserves credit for two other major contributions: for recognizing the importance of early childhood experiences within the family and for considering the role of emotions in human development (Shaffer 2000).

BEHAVIORISM

The theories presented so far have focused on a person's mental state to explain his or her behavior. These theories were not always dominant in the United States. In fact, before Piaget's theory revolutionized ideas about child development in the mid-twentieth century, many psychologists focused on the environment as the most important factor influencing behavior. This approach, which is called **behaviorism**, originated at the turn of the twentieth century in the research of Edward L. Thorndike (1898) and Ivan P. Pavlov (1910), who had independently discovered the role of reinforcement in learning (Shaw and Costanzo 1970).

John B. Watson (1925), who is recognized as the father of behaviorism, viewed the infant as John Locke had—as a blank slate whose development depended on his unique experiences. Watson did not believe that children progressed through a series of stages, as others argued; he saw child development as a continuous process that was influenced by the individual's environment. And he built on the idea that human development involved learned associations between external stimuli and observable responses that he called **habits** (Shaffer 2000). Distinguishing behaviorism from other theories of human development, Watson (1913) believed that explanations of human behavior should be based not on unconscious motives or cognitive processes that were not observable but rather on observations of overt behavior.

Watson (1925, 82) captured the essence of early learning theories in a famous challenge:

> Give me a dozen healthy infants, well formed, and my own specified world to bring them up in and I'll guarantee to take any one at random and train him to become any type of specialist I might select— doctor, lawyer, artist, merchant, chief, and yes, even beggar man and thief, regardless of his talents, penchants, tendencies, abilities, vocations, and race of his ancestors. There is no such thing as an inheritance of capacity, talent, temperament, mental constitution, and behavioral characteristics.

From one perspective this might sound like a good idea. Ultimately, it seems, you could use the basic principles of learning theory to scientifically engineer a perfect society. But in 1932, Aldous Huxley suggested why it might be a bad idea in his novel *Brave New World*. Families did not exist in this fictional utopian society. Human beings were created in test tubes and raised in institutions. From the moment of birth, infants were *conditioned* to accept their place in society. Cloning predetermined their talents and abilities, and scientific methods were used to define who they were—to give them an identity. In this society, human beings did not think. They had no freedom. From the moment of birth, they were programmed to accept the ways of this society—its values and norms.

Classical Conditioning

The method used to socialize children in *Brave New World* is called **classical conditioning**. Ivan Pavlov, a Russian physiologist, was the first to demonstrate this learning process. While conducting research on the digestive processes of dogs, Pavlov noticed that a dog would salivate not only when meat was put in its mouth but also at the mere sight of the meat. He also noticed that the dog would salivate when it saw the bowl or the experimenter or heard the sound of the experimenter's footsteps.

These observations led Pavlov to conduct his famous experiments (see Figure 2.3). He would begin an experiment by placing some meat on a dog's tongue. Doing this caused the dog to salivate. Over the course of several trials, Pavlov then rang a bell at the same time he gave the meat to the dog. After these trials, he noticed that the sound of the bell alone caused the dog to salivate. Pavlov explained that an unconditioned stimulus (meat) elicits an unconditioned response (salivation) prior to conditioning. A neutral stimulus (the bell) can then be paired with the unconditioned stimulus to produce a learned response— a conditioned response (salivation). This association caused the bell to become a conditioned stimulus.

How does classical conditioning operate in human beings? Consider the following sequence of events. Whenever Jimmy visits the dentist, he finds out that he has a cavity. Getting it filled always involves some kind of pain. After a few visits, Jimmy's mother notices that he begins to cry as soon as he sees the dentist. Even though Jimmy liked the dentist on the first visit, the sight of him soon became associated with pain. Now the sight of the dentist alone causes Jimmy to cry. As this example illustrates, the pairing of a neutral stimulus (the dentist) with an unconditioned stimulus (a drill) produces a learned response (crying).

Jimmy might begin to cry when he sees people who resemble his dentist. This reaction is called stimulus generalization. Over time, however, he can learn to distinguish the difference between similar people and the dentist, a process called **discrimination**. It is possible for Jimmy's response to the dentist to change. If he does not need to have cavities filled every time he visits the dentist, he will probably stop crying when he sees the dentist—a process called **extinction**.

Prior to Classical Conditioning

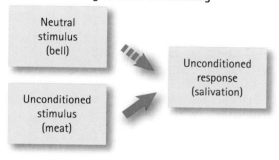

During Classical Conditioning

After Classical Conditioning

FIGURE 2.3

Classical Conditioning

Operant Conditioning

The era of stimulus-response psychology originated in Pavlov's research (Thomas 2000). American behaviorists ignored concepts like the mind to explain human behavior and focused instead on how different stimuli produced various kinds of responses. They quickly realized, however, that it was often difficult to identify the stimulus that produced the responses they observed. And they conceded that unidentified stimuli were involved in the learning process.

B. F. Skinner (1938) offered a solution to this problem by proposing another kind of conditioning, which he called **operant conditioning**. Skinner noted that a variety of behaviors occur in the absence of any observable stimulus. For example, babies reach for objects and make babbling sounds. Skinner was not interested in identifying the stimulus that initiated responses like these. Instead, he focused on the consequences of the behavior.

Operant conditioning results when an individual's behavior is followed by something that either increases or decreases the likelihood that the behavior will be repeated. An individual's behavior is thus shaped by the consequences that follow it. Suppose that a child offers you a bite of her cookie. You smile, say thank you, and give her a kiss. It is likely that this child will offer food to you again. During this interaction with the child, you have provided a reward that reinforces a particular behavior; you have thereby increased the likelihood of it happening again.

During the early years of socialization, parents are the most important sources of reinforcement. And they have the ability to shape not only children's behavior but their attitudes as well. Consider another example. Let's say that a little boy's parents want to teach him to resolve conflict without violence. An opportunity to express their feelings about this issue arises while they view a television program that shows teenagers fighting at school. Suppose the child comments on what he has just seen by saying, "Kids need to talk about their problems instead of fighting." Parents can reinforce this attitude by expressing their approval in some way—perhaps a smile or a hug.

In the 1940s, Skinner wrote a novel about a fictional society that he titled *Walden Two* (1948). In contrast to Huxley, who used his book to show the down side of using scientific methods to create the perfect society, Skinner used his novel to promote their use. He firmly believed that "behavioral engineering" could be used to improve people's lives—to save students and teachers time, to make homes better social environments, to improve people's satisfaction with their jobs, to help psychotic and retarded people live better lives, and to create a better society. His book remains controversial to

"I think I should warn you that the flip side of our generous bonus-incentive program is capital punishment."

this day. He is nevertheless regarded as one of the most influential research psychologists of the twentieth century (Thomas 2000).

Social Learning Theory

At 7 p.m. on October 6, 1993, a happy-go-lucky kid named Austin Messner parked himself in front of the family television set to watch another episode of *Beavis & Butt-head.* Later that night, the precocious 5-year-old boy in Moraine, Ohio (near Dayton), got up from his bed and walked to the kitchen area of his trailer home. He was not looking for cookies and milk to help him sleep. He was searching for his father's cigarette lighter.

Then, following the lead of his animated friends on MTV, Austin set his bed on fire and burned the home to the ground. His 2-year-old sister, Jessica, was tragically killed. (Ho 1994)

The story of Austin Messner raises an important question: Can children learn new behaviors by simply observing and imitating models? According to social learning theorists, they can. Albert Bandura (1977, 1986, 1992), a prominent

social learning theorist, was one of the first to express this view. Agreeing that learning can occur through operant conditioning as Skinner showed in his experiments with animals, Bandura argued that learning would be both laborious and dangerous if it occurred only in this way. He also found it difficult to imagine the socialization process in this way. Teaching the language, customs, norms, and other cultural practices through operant conditioning would not be feasible. And in contrast to Skinner, who ignored cognitive processes, Bandura argued that human beings think about their behavior and its consequences.

Bandura described four interrelated steps that are involved in observational learning (see Table 2.4). First, we pay attention to a model's behavior. Second, we store the information in memory. Third, we must now be able to reproduce the model's behavior. Fourth, before we imitate an act, we consider the consequences that accompanied the model's behavior.

In contrast to early learning theories, which viewed children as passive products of the socialization process, Bandura (1986, 1989) regards children as active, cognitive beings who play a role in their own development. Human development, he contends, is a process of continuous reciprocal interaction between a child and the environment. Children are not simply shaped by their environments. They play a role in the developmental process by producing changes in the environment through their behavior.

Evaluation of Behaviorism

Early Theories. From 1913 to 1930, behaviorism and the measurement of intelligence were the primary concerns of American psychologists (Thomas 2000). Different versions of behaviorism, including Skinner's operant conditioning model, dominated the field from 1930 to 1952. The popularity of behaviorism began to decline by the mid-1950s and today exerts little influence as a theory of development (see Figure 2.2). Although concepts such as "unconditioned stimulus" and

"conditioned response" are easy to define and measure in laboratory experiments, critics argue that they do not provide an adequate explanation of human behavior. The mechanical view of learning theories, which ignores thinking and subjective experiences, fails to identify the difference between animals and human beings (Kaplan 2000).

Social Learning Theory. From the late 1930s to the present, social learning models have gained increasing popularity as explanations of human behavior (Thomas 2000). With their emphasis on the impact of observational learning and imitation, they are valuable for understanding a wide range of behaviors, from altruism to aggression (Kaplan 2000). But critics fault social learning theory for lacking a developmental framework (Cairns 1979, 1998). And they argue that the concept of imitation does not consider age differences between individual observers, which are important in explaining developmental differences for different age groups.

TABLE 2.4   BANDURA'S STEPS IN OBSERVATIONAL LEARNING

Step	Features
1. We pay attention to a model's behavior.	Individuals are more likely to learn the behaviors of the people surrounding them, since they have the opportunity to observe them repeatedly. Within this group, members who possess appealing characteristics are more likely to serve as models.
2. We store the information in memory.	Visual images of modeled behavior are one type of representation involved in observational learning. Another kind is language, which plays an important role in this step by providing an efficient way to store complex behaviors.
3. We must be able to reproduce the model's behavior.	Physical limitations may prevent some individuals from achieving this. For example, although a child can learn how to drive a car through observation, she may be too short to reach the mechanisms that operate the vehicle.
4. Before we imitate an act, we consider the consequences that had accompanied the model's behavior.	In anticipation of similar consequences, we are more likely to imitate behaviors that led to rewards than those that resulted in punishment.

Source: Based on Bandura 1977.

BRONFENBRENNER'S ECOLOGICAL THEORY

Urie Bronfenbrenner's ecological theory provides a modern explanation of how an individual's environment influences the process of socialization. Bronfenbrenner (1993, 22) describes the environmental influences that shape an individual as "a set of nested structures, each inside the next, like a set of Russian dolls." Surrounded by four different environmental systems, developing human beings are shaped by the influences of immediate settings like the small intimate circle of one's family, as well as the larger contexts within which settings like these are embedded (see Figure 2.4). According to Bronfenbrenner, each of these environmental systems is linked to and influences the others. Human beings are affected by this ecological system, but they have an impact on it as well.

Bronfenbrenner called the innermost structure in his model a **microsystem** and defined it as "a pattern of activities, roles, and interpersonal relations experienced by the developing person in a given setting with particular physical and material characteristics" (1979, 22). Activities include what people are doing within a given microsystem. Roles refer to the expectations associated with the positions that particular people hold in society, such as parent, teacher, coach, minister, doctor, or friend. And interpersonal relations describe the way that people act toward and in response to one another (Thomas 2000). Bronfenbrenner claims that a child's development is influenced by her perception and interpretation of these factors, not by some objective measure of them.

Microsystems are located in a variety of settings where face-to-face interactions occur: at home, in school, and wherever peer groups interact. The family initially exerts the strongest influence on children. Eventually children enter other microsystems, which are linked to and mutually influence one another.

Bronfenbrenner used the term **mesosystem** to refer to the interrelationships among two or more settings that influence the development of a child. As the double-pointed arrows in Figure 2.4 indicate, these settings are linked and mutually influence one another. Consider the mesosystem that involves the relationship between a child's parents and the school. This model suggests that a child's academic performance depends not only on the quality of instruction provided by teachers but also on the parents' encouragement and involvement.

A child's neighborhood could involve a number of microsystems: home, school, peer groups, and neighbors (Thomas 2000). R. Murray Thomas (2000, 409) offered William Julius Wilson's interpretation of a neighborhood's influence to illustrate how mesosystems operate:

> In poor neighborhoods in which most of the adults are working perceptive youngsters are more likely to observe individuals regularly going to and from work, see a clear connection between education and meaningful employment, be aware of the presence of many intact families, notice a significant number of nonwelfare families, and recognize that many individuals in their neighborhoods are not involved in drug trafficking.
>
> However, in the new-urban-poverty neighborhoods with a paucity of regularly employed families, the chances of children interacting on a sustained basis with people who are employed or with families that have a steady bread-winner are slim. . . . Youths are more likely to see joblessness as normative and perceive a weak relationship between schooling and postschool employment. This environment is not conducive for development of the cognitive, linguistic, and other educational and job-related skills necessary for the world of work in the mainstream economy. (Wilson 1995, 538)

The **exosystem** in Bronfenbrenner's model refers to the interrelationships between two or more settings that affect a child, even if the child is not an active participant in those settings. Consider how a parent's work can exert an impact on a child: The stress or anxiety that parents experience at work can easily influence parent-child interactions at home. Similarly, a child's performance in school can be affected by decisions made by a school board—such as a plan to mainstream

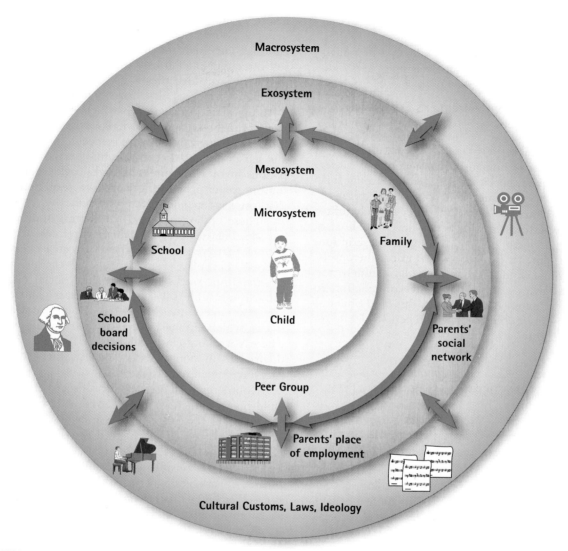

FIGURE 2.4

Nested Systems of Children's Environmental Experiences

Sources: Adapted from Bronfenbrenner 1979; Shaffer 2000.

children with learning disabilities or to close certain neighborhood schools (Shaffer 2000; Thomas 2000).

Microsystems, mesosystems, and exosystems are all embedded in the most remote source of influence—the **macrosystem**. Bronfenbrenner described this outermost circle in his model as a *cultural milieu*—the broad ideology, customs, and laws of a child's culture, subculture, or social class (Shaffer 2000; Thomas 2000). He also included time as a dimension in his model, pointing out that the effects of environmental influences can differ, depending on the age of the child, and that environmental influences change over time.

Evaluation of Bronfenbrenner's Ecological Theory

Bronfenbrenner's ecological theory offers a broader view of human development than earlier environmental theories. Unlike early learning theorists, Bronfenbrenner does not view children as entirely passive but claims that they actively influence the settings in which they develop. He also provides a clearer and more complete description of environmental influences that affect the development of a child. Although this allows him to account for the social, political, and economic forces that affect human development, this kind of complexity poses problems for researchers who want to test his theory.

SOCIAL STRUCTURE AND PERSONALITY THEORIES

Social structure and personality theories focus on the process of socialization as a key concept for understanding the effects of society on the individual (Corsaro and Eder 1995). Social psychologists who take this approach to understanding human behavior examine how particular features of the social structure influence interpersonal processes in different socialization contexts (Gecas 1981; Elkin and Handel 1984).

Melvin Kohn (1959, 1969) was one of the first researchers to examine the effect of the social structure on child-rearing practices. Focusing on the link between parental occupation and the values that parents stressed in raising their children, Kohn found significant social class differences (Kohn 1959; Kohn and Schooler 1983). When Kohn asked parents to identify the most important characteristics that children should have, working-class parents stressed good manners,

neatness, honesty, obedience to authority, and being a good student. Middle-class parents, in contrast, stressed independence, responsibility, self-direction, and curiosity.

Kohn explained these differences in terms of specific experiences that parents have at work. Working-class occupations, which tend to be closely supervised and involve repetitive tasks such as assembly line work, involve respect for authority and self-discipline. By contrast, middle-class occupations involve self-direction and provide opportunities to perform a variety of tasks—experiences that foster independence and creativity.

These findings suggest that parents of different social classes prepare their children for occupations that are suited for their own social class. Schools may play a similar role by channeling children into tracks linked to their social class (Bowles and Gintis 1976). Middle-class children are thus likely to follow college preparatory tracks, which emphasize creativity and initiative, whereas working-class children are likely to find themselves in nonacademic tracks, which stress rote learning and discipline.

Kohn's research on the effect of social class on child-rearing practices has received wide support. However, his research does not show how parents' values are passed on to children through the socialization process (Corsaro and Eder 1995). We must therefore consider the possibility that the influence of variables may run in the opposite direction—that individuals who value independence seek out occupations that offer more freedom (Cherlin 1999). It is also possible that a third variable such as intelligence has a bearing on both an individual's values and the type of occupation the individual selects.

INTERPRETIVE APPROACHES TO SOCIALIZATION

Reflecting the influence of both Piaget and Vygotsky, interpretive approaches to socialization view children as active participants in a process of social and collective development. While this relatively new theory about childhood socialization views a child's acquisition of adult skills and knowledge as an important part of the developmental process, it criticizes traditional theories for failing to recognize the important role that children themselves play. Through interaction with their peers, children develop their own **peer culture**—a stable set of activities or routines, values, and concerns (Corsaro 1992). The experiences that are involved in the production of peer cultures play a critical role in transforming childhood knowledge and practices into the knowledge and skills necessary for participation in the adult world (Corsaro 1992).

In their study of nursery school children, William Corsaro and Thomas Rizzo (1988) identified a number of **cultural routines** that children collectively produce—teasing, fighting, defending play groups, and mocking adults. As taken-for-granted patterns of behavior, these routines provide a sense of belonging to children and other members of a social group. Within these routines, sociocultural knowledge is created, considered, and interpreted. And as children play together and participate in these kinds of behaviors, they realize that some children have more power than others—that a status hierarchy exists (Corsaro 1979).

Children begin to participate in cultural routines almost from the moment of birth. Even though infants have not yet developed the ability to communicate or interact socially, others treat them as if they were socially competent. Eventually they do become socially competent and become active participants in cultural routines (Corsaro 1997). To illustrate how babies participate in cultural routines, William Corsaro (1997) considered a common type of mother-infant interaction—the game of peekaboo. Citing a study conducted by Bruner and Sherwood (1976), Corsaro noted four sequential kinds of interactions. The routine starts by establishing shared attention. A mother may do this by talking to the baby or through eye contact. She will then disappear—by covering her face with a blanket or her hands. Shortly thereafter, the mother will reappear by uncovering her face. The last part of this routine involves reestablishing contact. The mother might end the routine with "Boo!" or "There's the baby." The baby will then usually respond by laughing.

This routine teaches children not only the basic rules of the game but also a range of variations (Bruner and Sherwood 1976; Corsaro 1997). The predictable rules provide children with a sense of security. However, they also learn that departures from the rules are possible and even rewarding. Eventually children become active participants in the game of peekaboo and even create their own versions.

Children's participation in cultural routines is central to the interpretive approach to childhood socialization (Corsaro 1992). These routines are collective processes that have cognitive and behavioral components. According to Corsaro (1985, 1988) cultural routines provide children with a way to reproduce and deal with the confusions, fears, and conflicts that may result from adult-child interactions. The nature of the socialization process is transformed when children realize they can produce their own social worlds without the assistance of adults (Corsaro 1992). At this point, the asymmetrical adult-child relationship loses its dominance, and other children become important players in the socialization process.

William Corsaro's ethnographic research in nursery schools shows how children influence the process of socialization. To illustrate how it happens, Corsaro (1992) describes how children actively resist adult rules. The rule involved in one case banned children from bringing personal possessions to school. Adults had implemented this rule to prevent disputes that would arise when children refused to share their possessions. To evade the rule, children brought in small objects, which they could hide in their pockets. Favorite items included tiny model cars, candy, chewing gum, and small toy animals. Children would carefully reveal their personal treasures to others when they thought it was safe. Candy was a favorite kind of forbidden item because children could get rid of it—eat it—even when teachers were close by.

Teachers often overlooked violations of this rule. In fact, they recognized that because the children were forbidden to bring these kinds of things to school, they voluntarily shared them with others. Allowing children to break the rules actually produced the kind of behavior teachers desired. This example shows not only how children develop their own unique peer cultures but also how that influences the maintenance of adult rules.

In contrast to passive participant models of socialization, the interpretive approach views development as a creative process of production and reproduction. Children do not simply internalize the adult world; they actively contribute to it. Socialization proceeds in this manner as children develop stronger cognitive abilities and language skills and as they experience changes in their social worlds.

Table 2.5 provides a valuable tool for comparing and evaluating the theories presented in this chapter. In reviewing each theory in the table, consider how it answers the questions posed at the beginning of the chapter.

AGENTS OF SOCIALIZATION

The process of socialization begins at birth and involves many **agents of socialization**—people, groups, and institutions who influence the growth and development of new members of society. The primary agents of socialization include the family, schools, and the mass media. Acting as loving parents, dedicated teachers, friends, and sources of information, agents of socialization have enormous influence on the thoughts, feelings, and behaviors of new members of society.

The Family

The family has served as the most important agent of socialization since the beginning of recorded history. It is within this small, intimate group that infants grow and develop. They form their first emotional attachments to family members, who take care of their physical needs and usually provide love, security, and comfort. As the tragic plight of the Romanian orphans showed, institutions cannot provide the kind of loving attention that children need to survive.

Schools

Outside of the family, the school serves as the next most important agent of socialization. The first schools were established several thousand years

School serves as an important agent of socialization.

TABLE 2.5 THEORIES OF CHILD DEVELOPMENT AND SOCIALIZATION

Theory	Nature versus Nurture	Active versus Passive Participant	Continuous Process versus Stages	Overall Pattern
Piaget's Theory of Cognitive Development	**Nature and nurture** Hereditary and environmental factors influence development.	**Active** Children actively explore the world, seeking to make sense of their experiences.	**Stages** Four qualitatively distinct, invariant cognitive stages: 1. Sensorimotor 2. Preoperational 3. Concrete operational 4. Formal operational	Organismic
Vygotsky's Sociocultural Theory	**Nurture** Social interactions and cultural experiences shape cognitive processes.	**Active** Children actively seek and acquire knowledge through social interaction.	**Continuous process** Children gradually develop ways of thinking through social interaction.	Contextual
Psychoanalytic Theories Psychosexual theory (Freud)	**Nature and nurture** Personality is a product of the struggle between nature (biological drives) and nurture (expectations of society).	**Active and passive** Children are active beings with biological drives and needs, but they are also molded by early experiences with parents and later by experiences with other significant persons.	**Stages** Freud's theory has five stages: 1. Oral 2. Anal 3. Phallic 4. Latency 5. Genital	Organismic
Learning Theories Classical conditioning Operant conditioning Social learning theory	**Nurture** The environment plays the most important role in learning.	**Passive** Early theorists insisted that children were passive—shaped by the environment. However, contemporary social learning theorists, especially Bandura, argue that children also influence the environment.	**Continuous process** Learning occurs in a gradual, additive manner.	Mechanistic
Bronfenbrenner's Ecological Theory	**Nurture** Environmental contexts influence development.	**Active and passive** Individuals are affected by the environment, but they also have an impact on it.	**Both** Development proceeds gradually in an additive manner, but personal or environmental events can cause abrupt qualitative changes (e.g., puberty or a family crisis).	Contextual
Interpretive Theories of Socialization	**Nurture** Society and culture influence the way children construct their worlds.	**Active** Children actively participate in their culture and contribute to the creation of the adult world.	**Both** The interpretive model extends the notion of stages. From this perspective, children enter into a social nexus, which is involved in a productive-reproductive process of socialization.	Contextual

BOX 2.2   THE SCHOOL AS AN AGENT OF SOCIALIZATION

As an important agent of socialization, schools teach children many kinds of lessons. Traditionally that has included the three Rs—reading, writing, and arithmetic. These subjects involve certain kinds of language which serve as vehicles of thought. In early American schools, society's rules were taught along with the rules of language. Nothing illustrates this better than *The American Spelling Book*, originally published in 1788.

Table XXII

Words not exceeding three syllables, divided.

Lesson I

THE wick-ed flee when no man pur-su-eth; but the right-e-ous are as bold as a li-on.

Vir-tue ex-alt-eth a na-tion; but sin is a re-proach to a-ny peo-ple.

The law of the wise is a foun-tain of life to de-part from the snares of death.

Wealth got-ten by de-ceit, is soon wast-ed; but he that gath-er-eth by la-bor, shall in-crease in rich-es.

II

I-dle-ness will bring thee to pov-er-ty; but by in-dus-try and pru-dence thou shalt be fill-ed with bread.

Wealth mak-eth ma-ny friends; but the poor are for-got-ten by their neigh-bors.

A pru-dent man fore-seeth the e-vil, and hid-eth him-self; but the thought-less pass on and are pun-ish-ed.

III

Train up a child in the way he should go, and when he is old he will not de-part from it.

Where there is no wood the fire go-eth out, and where there is no tat-ler the strife ceas-eth.

A word fit-ly spok-en is like ap-ples of gold in pic-tures of sil-ver.

He that cov-er-eth his sins shall not pros-per, but he that con-fess-eth and for-sak-eth them shall find mer-cy.

IV

The rod and re-proof give wis-dom; but a child left to him-self bring-eth his pa-rents to shame.

Cor-rect thy son, and he will give thee rest; yea, he will give de-light to thy soul.

A man's pride shall bring him low; but hon-or shall up-hold the hum-ble in spir-it.

The eye that mock-eth at his fath-er, and scorn-eth to o-bey his moth-er, the ra-vens of the val-ley shall pick it out, and the young ea-gles shall eat it.

V

By the bless-ing of the up-right, the cit-y is ex-alt-ed, but it is o-ver-thrown by the mouth of the wick-ed.

Where no coun-sel is, the peo-ple fall; but in the midst of coun-sel-lors there is safe-ty.

The wis-dom of the pru-dent is to un-der-stand his way, but the fol-ly of fools is de-ceit.

A wise man fear-eth and de-part-eth from evil, but the fool rag-eth and is con-fi-dent.

Be not hast-y in thy spir-it to be an-gry; for an-ger rest-eth in the bo-som of fools.

Source: Webster 1788/1824, 64–65)

---

ago for members of society's small elite class (Vago 1999). Entrusted with the responsibility for passing on the culture of their entire society, this select group received training in grammar, rhetoric, logic, arithmetic, geometry, astronomy, and music (Box 2.2). Traditional societies did not need a separate educational institution to prepare the masses for adult roles. But complex, modern societies do have this need and have established systems of formal education to teach specialized skills to the masses.

Mass Media

The term **mass media** refers to all of the ways used to spread cultural knowledge to large audiences

| BOX 2.3 | PRINCE WILLIAM: A PRODUCT OF PRIMARY SOCIALIZATION |

On June 11, 2000, an article written by the historian Andrew Roberts appeared in the *London Sunday Telegraph*, comparing the character and upbringing of Prince William, heir to the British throne, to his father, Prince Charles. Here's how it began:

> As Prince William attains his majority on June 21, those responsible for his upbringing—including of course Prince Charles—can allow themselves a large measure of self-congratulation.
>
> For despite the ghastliness of his parents' public confessions of adultery, then their divorce and his mother's tragic death, Prince William has grown into a well-adjusted, mature, eminently sensible young man.
>
> For all his interest in "techno" music and motorbikes, he is no angry teenage rebel, as he might so easily have become. Instead, we have a king-in-waiting who is well-mannered, charming and seems eminently ready to embark on the next stage of his life.

With the good looks of a movie star and the charisma of his mother, it is not surprising that Prince William's birthday made international news. However, as Roberts's introduction suggests, his eighteenth birthday had special significance. Under the Regency Acts, Prince William could now sit on the throne alone in his own right. Law and tradition recognized that he had reached the end of childhood—for him a period of socialization that included preparation for assuming the role of a king.

Few individuals are prepared for this particular role. All of us, however, do pass through childhood in preparation for the next stage of life. This process, which is called primary socialization, transforms individuals into members of society (Berger and Luckmann 1966). Socialization after childhood does not match the impact of early life experiences. It does not play a significant role in the development of an individual's self-concept. Nor, therefore, does it have the same influence over an individual's attitudes and behaviors. However, individuals do continue to grow and develop for the rest of their lives.

(Ryan and Wentworth 1999). Books, magazines, and newspapers were the primary forms of mass media in the nineteenth century. Today, the mass media also include television, radio, recorded music, and the Internet. We take these various forms of mass media for granted, and yet they act as powerful agents of socialization. However, determining exactly how the media influence the thoughts, feelings, and behaviors of individuals is difficult. Researchers must consider a number of variables—an individual's psychological makeup, social status, age, and so on. Nonetheless, it is fair to say that the mass media are a powerful agent of socialization.

Parents take most of the responsibility for primary socialization. They ultimately make decisions about how much influence the other agents of socialization exert on their children. They have a long and difficult job in preparing their children for adulthood. It usually takes about eighteen years. At that point, individuals make the transition into adulthood (see Box 2.3).

In the next chapter, we will examine adult development. In contrast to early childhood development, social psychologists have paid less attention to how individuals develop over the course of their adult lives (Dion 1985). Yet adults have much to learn. They must accomplish new tasks and learn adult roles. Progression through life also requires people to make many adjustments—to these adult roles and to the transitions that mark turning points in their lives. This process is not easy. But one thing is clear: Successful childhood socialization provides a solid foundation for the challenges awaiting us in adulthood.

SUMMARY

1. Socialization refers to the process whereby individuals learn the values, norms, motives, beliefs, and roles of their society or group, as well as the process by which they develop and change in terms of personality and self-concept or identity.

2. Four basic questions help us understand the key differences between theories of childhood socialization: (a) Does this theory stress the influence of nature or nurture? (b) Are children actively involved in the developmental or socialization process, or are they passive recipients of social or biological influences? (c) Does development or socialization proceed in stages, or is it continuous? (d) What overall pattern or worldview do the main assumptions of this theory suggest?

3. Jean Piaget and Lev Vygotsky dominated ideas about cognitive development in the twentieth century. Both sought to understand the role of language in cognitive development.

4. According to Piaget, the process of adapting to the external world involves active learning. From infancy through adolescence, children interpret their experiences in terms of cognitive structures that exist at a given time. This development proceeds through a sequence of four invariant stages: sensorimotor, preoperational, concrete operational, and formal operational.

5. Vygotsky rejected Piaget's argument that cognitive development proceeds in an individualistic manner through adaptations to the environment and instead favored the idea of a socially formed mind. Vygotsky's sociocultural theory focuses on the roles of language and thought in human development.

6. Freud developed psychoanalytic theory during the same period of time that Piaget and Vygotsky developed their theories. According to Freud's theory, the personality consists of the id, the ego, and the superego. These parts develop and become integrated through five stages of development. Although his theory of personality development has little support today, his concept of the unconscious remains one of the most important ideas of the twentieth century. Freud made two

other noteworthy contributions: his recognition of the importance of early childhood experiences within the family and his insight into the role that emotions play in human development.

7. Behaviorism provides another explanation for the process of socialization. From 1913 to 1930, behaviorism and the measurement of intelligence were the focus of American psychologists. Different versions of behaviorism, including Skinner's operant conditioning model, dominated the field from 1930 to 1952. From the 1930s to the present, social learning models have gained popularity as explanations of human behavior.

8. Bronfenbrenner's ecological theory provides a modern explanation of how an individual's environment influences the process of socialization. According to this theory, developing human beings are shaped by the influences of immediate settings like the family, as well as the larger contexts in which those settings are embedded.

9. Social psychologists who adopt the perspective of social structure and personality theories examine how particular features of the social structure influence interpersonal processes in different socialization contexts. Kohn's research on the effect of social class on child-rearing practices provides a good example. His findings suggest that parents of different social classes prepare their children for occupations that are suited for their own social class. Schools may play a similar role by channeling children into tracks linked to their social class.

10. Interpretive approaches to socialization reflect the influence of both Piaget and Vygotsky. They view a child's acquisition of adult skills and knowledge as an important part of the developmental process but stress the role that children themselves play in the process.

11. The process of socialization begins at birth and involves many agents of socialization—people, groups, and institutions who influence the growth and development of new members of society. The primary agents of socialization are the family, schools, and the mass media.

KEY TERMS

Socialization 37
Schema 40
Assimilation 40
Accommodation 40
Equilibrium 41
Equilibration 41
Conservation 43
Reversibility 45
Hierarchichal classification 45
Seriation 45
Imaginary audience 46
Personal fable 46
Zone of proximal development 48

Private speech 50
Intersubjectivity 50
Scaffolding 50
Conscious 52
Preconscious 52
Unconscious 52
Id 52
Ego 52
Superego 54
Oedipus complex 55
Electra complex 55
Behaviorism 55
Habits 56

Classical conditioning 56
Discrimination 56
Extinction 56
Operant conditioning 57
Microsystem 60
Mesosystem 60
Exosystem 60
Macrosystem 61
Peer culture 63
Cultural routines 63
Agents of socialization 64
Mass media 66

CRITICAL REVIEW QUESTIONS

1. Language (symbols or signs) plays an important role in many theories of childhood socialization presented in this chapter. In your opinion, which comes first, language or thought?
2. Which of the theories presented in this chapter provides the best explanation for prejudice? What about aggression and altruism?
3. Analyze a children's book, television program, or film and identify the lessons (social norms) or values that it tries to teach.

THREE

Socialization
and
the Life Course

In 1990, at the age of 70, Stuart Campbell sat down with researchers from the University of California at Berkeley to discuss the details of a remarkable longitudinal study. This project, the Oakland Growth Study (OGS), began in the fall of 1931 and was designed to last only through the participants' senior high school years. But follow-up studies had been conducted, providing researchers with a rich data base containing the life histories of many of the original study members.

Stuart had a personal interest in this study. He was one of the original 215 study members. When it began, he was 11 years old. Since then Stuart had passed through all of the significant stages of adult development. In fact, he had lived through most of the twentieth century—the Great Depression, World War II, the turbulent 60s, and the end of the Cold War. What could these researchers learn from his life history? John Clausen (1995), the primary investigator, believed that Stuart's life provided insight into the factors that influence adult development.

In his book *American Lives,* Clausen (1995) presents the life stories of many of the subjects who participated with Stuart in the Oakland Growth Study. One of the primary purposes of Clausen's analysis of these lives was to understand the factors that contributed to what he called "lives well lived." Clausen described a number of lives that fit this description, but he believed that Stuart's life represented it best. By all accounts, Stuart had achieved the American dream when he met with Clausen in 1990 for a final interview about his life. But few would have predicted such a successful outcome in 1931. His early childhood was far from ideal. In 1926 when he was only 6 years old, Stuart's mother died. Shortly thereafter, his father abandoned the family. Stuart's maternal grandmother, an immigrant from Scotland, took full responsibility for Stuart and two younger siblings.

Getting by was difficult. Their only steady source of income came from a small trust fund that Stuart's grandfather had set up for his wife before he died. Even with this, the family barely lived above the subsistence level. Eventually, Stuart and his brother had paper routes, which enabled them to contribute some money to household expenses.

The tragic circumstances of Stuart's early childhood could readily explain a troubled life. But as his OGS records showed, Stuart's life had progressed along a normal course with few problems and in fact with many remarkable achievements. Why did things turn out so well for him? One possible explanation lies in the influence of this particular time in American history. Many children who grew up during the 1930s were expected to take on adult responsibilities at a young age. They would be called "children of the Great Depression" (Elder 1974; Elder, Modell, and Parke 1993). And research would show that this historical influence did operate in their favor.

Stuart recognized that these hard times had a positive influence on the course of his life. Looking back on his life during one particular OGS interview, he expressed this in a regret about how he had raised his children.

> He felt that his children, like most other suburban children, had had insufficient life experience. They did not struggle for anything, were never deprived of anything, had not had to work for anything. Everything had been handed to them sometimes whether they wanted it or not. (Clausen 1995, 112).

Linking this concern to the positive effect that his own deprivation had on him, Stuart claimed that "his early experience of getting what he wanted for himself, by himself, contributed to his self-esteem, as well as the respect of others for him" (Clausen 1995, 112).

Although the deprivation in his early life clearly motivated Stuart to get what he wanted, he had something else going for him. He was also a gifted child. In fact, Stuart had shown great academic promise from his earliest school years. And his OGS file showed that

staff members consistently rated him as being very intelligent. Curiously, his grandmother regarded Stuart as a child with average abilities. And yet, she expected him to bring home A's. As the oldest child in his family, she also expected Stuart to take on more responsibility than his siblings. Fortunately, Stuart was fully capable of meeting these kinds of expectations. And as the OGS files suggested, this explained why he was mature for his age and was viewed by his peers as a natural leader.

The information contained in Stuart's OGS file also showed that he set high standards for himself. Although he decided to attend a technical high school, Stuart dreamed of going to the best schools, always planned to attend college, and never lost sight of his career goals. In fact, Stuart had already decided to become a physician by the time he entered college.

Stuart's early adulthood was filled with great accomplishments, major transitions, and adjustments to a variety of adult roles. An early marriage shortly after he entered medical school did, to his regret, end in divorce. But by the age of 27, Stuart had served as a medical officer in World War II, had remarried, was earning good money, and had become a parent.

Stuart's journey through the middle and later adulthood stages of life proceeded for the most part without much difficulty. He accomplished the major tasks of adult development with ease. The transitions from one stage of life to the next and his adjustment to adult roles were smooth. Despite the tragic loss of his parents in early childhood, Stuart never lost a sense of his direction. When Stuart met with Clausen in 1990 for the last interview about his life, he said that he felt he had led a meaningful life.

In summarizing his analysis of Stuart Campbell's life history, Clausen (1995, 112) described some of the things that people reflect on when they look back on their lives in old age:

> An enduring, dependable relationship with his wife and strong family ties have been of central importance to him, as has his role as a doctor. Being a doctor and a strong family man, a man who assumes civic

responsibility, a man who can be counted on, are the major components of Stuart's sense of identity.

Stuart Campbell's life was only one of the many that Clausen examined in his analysis of the factors that shape the course of people's lives. In searching for an explanation for what he called "lives well lived," Clausen concluded that the experiences of one's early life have a clear impact on the life course. Drawing the main conclusion of his study, Clausen (1995, 16) wrote:

> An adolescent's competence by the end of the high school years and the antecedents that gave rise to it strongly influence the direction that the life course will take, the ease of major transitions, and the person's success in performing the major roles that will be enacted over much of the life course."

One day we will all have a story to tell about our lives. Above all else, this autobiography will tell us who we are. From beginning to end, it will contain details about the people, events, and experiences that influenced us. Social psychologists who study the life course believe that like Stuart Campbell, we will reflect on the important decisions that we made at turning points in our lives. We are likely to evaluate our occupational choices and family roles. We all hope that our lives will turn out well, as Stuart Campbell's did. But some of us may be disappointed. Understanding all of the factors that influenced us over the course of our lives is difficult. In this chapter, we will consider what social psychologists have learned so far.

ADULT DEVELOPMENT

All of us pass through childhood and adolescence in preparation for adulthood. During this early period of **primary socialization**, we learn the ways of our society from parents and other key actors who take responsibility for various aspects of our cognitive, emotional, and physical development. By the time we reach 18, this long process of becoming a member of society is complete. Society now views us as adults who are equipped with the "knowledge, skills, and dispositions" necessary to be productive members of society (Brim 1966, 3; Dion 1985).

But entry into adulthood does not end the socialization process. Human beings continue to grow and develop for the rest of their lives. The transition from childhood into early adulthood marks the onset of **adult socialization**. Like primary socialization, this process still involves learning. But adult development presents a new set of tasks that involve transitions and adaptations to adult roles (Brim 1966; Dion 1985). The unique feature of adult socialization is its emphasis on the process of learning these adult roles.

The roles that Stuart Campbell played changed over the course of his life. They did not evolve in isolation but in tandem with the relationships that his roles defined. And this all occurred within changing social contexts. Theories of adult socialization do not explain the complex relationships among these variables. To understand this, we must consider theories and perspectives on the **life course**. These will help us understand "the mutual relationship between changing times and places, and changing lives and development" (Elder 2003, 58; Settersten 1999; Elder and Johnson 2003).

Studies of the life course span a number of disciplines and have given rise to an assortment of concepts and theories (Clausen 1986; Elder and O'Rand 1995; Heinz and Marshall 2003). The list of terms that refer to the course of an individual's life shows this wide interdisciplinary interest: *life span, life cycle, stages of life, career, aging,* and *life course* (Cain 1964; Marshall and Mueller 2003). Leonard Cain (1964, 278) provided one of the earliest definitions of the life course, describing it simply as "successive statuses individuals are called upon to occupy in various cultures and walks of life as a result of aging." Today, life course theorists view the life course as a more complex concept. Glen Elder and Angela O'Rand (1995, 453), leading experts in the field, define it as

> the age-graded life patterns embedded in social institutions and subject to historical change. The life course consists of interlocking trajectories or pathways across the life span that are marked by sequences of events and social transitions. Instead of the once prominent single-career studies, life course theory relates multiple careers or trajectories and centers on their coordination.

INFLUENCES ON THE LIFE COURSE

Disciplinary approaches to the study of the life course vary, but they all consider a similar set of important influences on human development: biology, psychology, and sociocultural factors. These approaches also recognize the important role that history plays in shaping the life course (Clausen 1986). How do these influences affect us? Let us consider each one.

Biology

Human development across the life course involves biological processes that influence our thoughts, feelings, and behaviors. How we view ourselves, our attraction to the opposite sex, and the way we feel about getting older are all influenced by biology. Signs of these influences appear early in the prenatal period of development (Craig and Baucum 2002). They reveal themselves later in the physical and mental changes associated with the timing of puberty, menopause, and signs of aging such as gray hair. Hereditary factors influence how we look and feel as we age over the life course. Our genes may predispose us to a healthy, long life or to one that is chronically plagued with illness and an early death. We can make efforts to exercise and control our weight. And many people color their hair when it starts to turn gray. But genes play a large role in how we look at age 20, 30, 40, 50, and so on.

Biology also influences human attributes that may be related to the decisions that individuals make at certain points in their lives (Clausen 1986). Consider how physical attractiveness, height, or strength leads individuals to pursue certain careers or to engage in particular activities. John Clausen (1986, 4) summarized it well:

> The groups we belong to as well as our ability to perform in various social roles will be influenced by our sex, our appearance, our temperament, and our intelligence, and all of these depend to a significant degree on our genetic constitution and our early physiological development.

Biological factors limit what individuals are capable of doing at certain points in their lives. But that is not where these factors exert the greatest influence. That lies in the way individuals behave and how they make decisions based on the meaning they assign to biological factors (Eisenstadt 1956; Elder 1975). When some people recognize the first signs of aging, they become depressed with thoughts of old age and mortality. Other people may view these changes as outward signs of maturity that should bring them respect.

Sociocultural Factors

From birth to death, the life course is a "progression through time" (Clausen 1986, 2; Riley 1979). Chronological age is one way to mark how far we have progressed in life. Researchers might use it as an indicator of a person's stage of adult development. For example, it might place a person in early adulthood (20s–30s), middle adulthood (40s–50s), or later adulthood (over 60 or 65 years) (Craig and Baucum 2002). At the same time, researchers recognize that chronological age is not the perfect measure for identifying the stage of a particular individual's development. In studies of the life course, sociocultural aspects of age are far more important.

In fact, Cain (1964) recognized the importance of the sociocultural aspect of age in his early definition of the life course. For him, progression through the life course could be described as moving through a succession of **age statuses**. These statuses constituted a system that all cultures develop "to give order and predictability to the course followed by individuals" (278).

We feel the effects of our culture over the entire course of our lives. For Ruth Benedict (1934), nothing exceeded the strength of culture's influence on a person's life. Describing how it influenced the entire process of human development, she wrote:

> The life history of the individual is first and foremost an accommodation to the patterns and standards traditionally handed down in his community. From the moment of his birth, the customs into which he is born shape his experience and behavior. By the time he can talk, he is a little creature of his culture, and by the time he is grown and able to take part in its activities, its habits are his habits, its beliefs his beliefs, its impossibilities his impossibilities" (2–3).

Cain described the role of culture in the life course in a similar way, claiming that progression through time involves the process of socialization (Marshall and Mueller 2003). This process helps people move in and out of age statuses. He also noted that this process involved **rites of passage** or the formal ceremonies that signified these transitions. These kinds of cultural rituals alleviate the stress that transitions into adult roles often produce. And many of them are religious ceremonies, including weddings, baptisms, confirmations, bar and bat mitzvahs, and funerals. Graduations and retirement parties are also rites of passage that signify some kind of role transition (see Box 3.1).

Age norms represent another important cultural influence on the life course. In the United States, an individual's birth date is linked to certain rights, privileges, or duties by law (Clausen 1986). The drinking age in many states is 21. State laws similarly determine the age at which a person can get a driver's license, vote, or get married without a parent's consent. Even a child's admission to public school is based on age.

Bernice Neugarten (1970) referred to this kind of cultural influence as "socially defined time." Emphasizing the connection between age and roles, she wrote:

BOX 3.1 | RITES OF PASSAGE

Marriage is a major transition in the life course because it involves a separation from a person's family of origin and usually the establishment of a new home for both spouses. Wedding ceremonies ease the stress and conflicts of this transition. Arnold van Gennep describes the rites of passage ceremony that transforms members of the Vai of Liberia from single to marital status.

> Among the Vai of Liberia the separation of the sexes is reinforced by the fact that a girl sometimes does not leave the *sande* except to marry. The *sande* is a sacred place in the forest to which all girls are taken before or around the age of ten, and where they remain till after their first menses. . . . They are considered dead, as are the old women who come to instruct them in domestic and sexual behavior. Their annual coming-out celebration is a rebirth. Often, however, a girl's parents affiance her while she is in the *sande*, and in that case she does not leave it on the annual holiday but must remain there until her first menses. The girl's parents are immediately informed when these occur, and they notify her betrothed, who sends gifts to the *sande*. The girl is rubbed with perfumed oil, adorned with jewels, and so forth, and her parents come and fetch her at the entrance to the sacred forest.
>
> After a ceremonial meal the girl's mother takes her to the hut of her betrothed. Coitus is consummated while the two families and their friends eat a meal together; when the act is terminated, the husband comes out of the hut and participates in the meal. The ceremony is the same if the betrothal occurs after the departure from the *sande*. Thus among the Vai the period of betrothal merges with the initiation period, and the first menses are important for departure from the *sande* only if the girl is already betrothed. Physiological puberty is a legal prerequisite for marriage among the Vai, as among many other peoples. Moreover, the sexual separation of the betrothed pair is here guaranteed by the sacred nature of the *sande*.

Source: van Gennep 1910/1960, 138–139.

A bar mitzvah marks the passage of a 13-year-old Jewish boy into adulthood. This religious ceremony signifies his assumption of the moral and religious duties of an adult.

Every society has a system of social expectations regarding age-appropriate behavior. The individual passes through a socially regulated cycle from birth to death . . . a succession of socially delineated age-status, each with its recognized rights, duties, and obligations. . . . This normative pattern is adhered to, more or less consistently, by most persons. (71–72)

The process by which individuals learn age-appropriate norms is an important component of adult socialization (Dion 1985). Neugarten (1969) argued that people expect certain events to take place at specific times in their life span. If these events do not occur on time, people may feel that they are either ahead or behind schedule. And that may influence the way individuals judge the event. One study showed how marrying earlier or later than expected affected the life outcomes of women (Elder and Rockwell 1976). Interviews conducted with the women in this study when they were middle-aged indicated that those who had married early or late would prefer for their own daughters to marry on time (Dion 1985).

Historical Time

Historical periods or circumstances represent another important dimension of time that life course

theorists consider when they study people's lives (Clausen 1986). Historical conditions such as wars or economic depressions shape the lives of people living during particular eras in unique ways (Riley 1973; Brim and Ryff 1980; Dion 1985; Clausen 1986, 1995). In describing how a particular historical period influenced the lives of members in the Oakland Growth Study, John Clausen (1995, 9) wrote:

The lives of our study members span a period of enormous change in America. Automobiles were just becoming common on the streets of the United States in the 1920s. Radios began to appear as broadcasting stations were established in the major cities. Women's hair was bobbed and sexual mores flouted in the flapper age as skirts went up and inhibitions went down in the mid- and late 1920s. Then came the stock market crash of 1929 and the most prolonged economic depression the country had ever experienced. In Europe, fascism emerged as a sequel to the social and economic ills left by World War I, and its rise to power was assisted by the depression. The threat of war replaced unemployment as a primary concern in the United States. These changes were experienced, if often only dimly recognized, by the oldest group of our study members, born between 1920 and 1922, and they had powerful effects on their parents and those of the younger group of study members, the latter born in 1928 or 1929.

To measure the effect of a particular historical period on the life course, researchers separate their subjects into **cohorts**. Life course theorists view the concept of cohorts as central to their research and carefully distinguish it from the term *generation*, which is commonly used in conjunction with kinship (Uhlenberg and Miner 1995; Marshall and Mueller 2003). Sticking with its original conceptualization by demographers, life course theorists use the term *cohort* to specify all people who were born in a particular period of time (Clausen 1986). Clausen defined it specifically as "a group that moves along together through the life course and thus experiences historical events at about the same age" (8).

In his study *Children of the Great Depression*, Glen Elder (1974) examined the lives and historical context of two birth cohorts (see Box 3.2). Members of the Oakland study were born in 1920 and 1921. The Berkeley study included people born in 1928 and 1929. As Elder points out, members of both cohorts experienced the Great Depression, World War II, and the prosperous postwar era. The key difference between these two cohorts was the point in their lives when they had these experiences. Did that make a difference? His analysis of these two cohorts showed that it did (Elder, Modell, and Parke 1993). People who experienced the Depression as teenagers (the 1920–1921 cohort) had a stronger sense of direction, were more self-confident, and achieved more in their lifetime than people who experienced it as young children (the 1928–1929 cohort).

The term *cohort* commonly refers to people who were born in the same period of time or who experience a common event (Maddox and Wiley 1976; Marshall 1983; Marshall and Mueller 2003). But it is also used to convey the idea that people born in certain historical times experience reality in a distinctive way (Clausen 1986; Marshall and Mueller 2003). In discussing "the problem of generations," Karl Mannheim (1952) argued that certain periods of time have a unique *Zeitgeist* or "spirit of the time." He meant that

people who live during certain times think in ways that reflect that time's unique influence. This idea is similar to the way that popular culture sorts cohorts by certain experiences (Marshall and Mueller 2003). The "baby boom generation," the "beat generation," and "Generation x" are examples. Clausen (1986) offered another way of thinking about this. He said that "cohorts . . . experience somewhat different cultures or subcultures" (8).

LIFE COURSE THEORIES AND PERSPECTIVES

Theories of the life course vary in their disciplinary approaches and in the scope of what they attempt to explain. Among current theories, Glen Elder's life course paradigm is one of the best (Marshall and Mueller 2003). His theory is defined by five main principles (Elder 1995, 1998; Elder and Johnson 2003), as listed by Marshall and Mueller (2003, 9–11):

- Human development and aging are lifelong processes.
- The life course of individuals is embedded in and shaped by the historical times and places they experience over their lifetime.
- The antecedents and consequences of life transitions and events vary according to their timing in a person's life.
- Lives are lived interdependently and social-historical influences are expressed through this network of relationships.
- Individuals construct their own life course through the choices and actions they take within the opportunities and constraints of history and social circumstances.

Elder's theory attempts to give a complete explanation of the life course. It incorporates the key concepts recognized by life course researchers today. And it is widely respected.

Understanding the life course also takes the form of general perspectives that offer different

BOX 3.2	CHILDREN OF THE GREAT DEPRESSION

We have come to see that the biographies of men and women, the kinds of individuals they have become, cannot be understood without reference to the historical structures in which the milieux of their everyday life are organized. Historical transformations carry meanings not only for individual ways of life, but for the very character—the limits and possibilities of the human being.

—C. Wright Mills, *The Sociological Imagination* (1959, 158)

On October 24, 1929, an event occurred that would leave an indelible mark on the lives of American men and women whose families would struggle to make ends meet for years to come. It was called Black Tuesday, the day the New York stock market crashed. And it marked the beginning of the Great Depression (1929–1941).

Will Rogers found some humor in this economic disaster, saying: "We are the first nation in the history of the world to go to the poor house in an automobile" (Bowen 1969a, 23). But for most Americans, the Great Depression brought devastating consequences. By 1933, industrial output had plummeted to less than half of what it had been in 1929. Unemployment had risen to a record high of 25 percent of the labor force. And family incomes fell to levels that amounted to around half of what they had been in 1929. The immediate effect of Black Tuesday was linked to tales of suicides. "The president of Union Cigar, stunned when his company's stock plummeted from $113.50 to four dollars in a day, fell or jumped to his death from the ledge of a New York hotel" (Bowen 1969a, 128). Tales like this failed to mention that the suicide rate was actually higher in the months preceding the stock market crash than after it.

What kind of long-term effect did the Great Depression have? In his book *Children of the Great Depression* (1974),

Glen Elder wrote, "From little more than intuition and self-reflection, hard times during the Depression have been linked to an extraordinary work commitment, a self-conscious desire for security, and an inability to partake of pleasure or leisure without guilt feelings" (277). This might have remained a conclusion based on anecdotal stories from the generation of individuals who lived through these tough times. But it did not, thanks to the foresight of Herbert Stolz and Harold E. Jones, who set up the Oakland Growth Study in 1931. This study was originally established to study adolescents as they made the transition through puberty. But additional funding allowed researchers to conduct follow-up interviews with the participants over the course of their lives. The data from this longitudinal study allowed Glen Elder to examine how historical, sociological, and psychological influences shaped the course of the lives of children who had lived through the Great Depression.

One of the most important findings in Elder's analysis of the effects of the Great Depression showed how this hardship shaped people's values. Men and women alike placed great value on the "centrality of the family and the importance of children in marriage" (1974, 282). Other important values revolved around work. The economic hardship of the Depression impressed this generation with the importance of getting a job. It also instilled them with an ethic of hard work and taught them the importance of job security.

Elder's study provides keen insight into the factors that influence the life course. It stands as one of the best studies ever conducted on the effects of the Great Depression. And it leaves no doubt that historical circumstances have a significant impact on the life course.

ways of viewing the life course (Clausen 1986). Clausen identified five perspectives that contain concepts and principles that any life course theory must consider. Let us briefly review each of these perspectives.

The *developmental perspective* focuses on how individuals grow over a period of time. Growth is viewed as a process that involves the unlocking of an individual's potentials through a process of

development. This perspective focuses on normal development, but it also seeks to understand the factors that account for differences in the rate or quality of growth. The weakness of this perspective lies in its inability to explain growth after one has reached maturity.

The *socialization perspective* focuses on how individuals learn the ways of their society. According to this view, socialization is a lifelong process that involves the internalization of shared expectations. Through this process, people "acquire the knowledge, skills, and dispositions that make them more or less able members of their society" (Brim 1966, 3). Early socialization is intense and prepares children for adulthood by providing them with knowledge about their physical world and social environment. Children learn what society expects of them in terms of behavior, attitudes, and values. And they come to recognize and understand the wide variety of roles that people play. When people enter adulthood, the process of socialization changes. Now it focuses on the demands that other people in society make on them. These demands will influence a person's attitudes, interests, and goals in a variety of ways (Clausen 1986).

The *adaptational perspective* on the life course is closely associated with the process of adult socialization. From this perspective, adult development involves a series of adaptations to the changing circumstances of life. Many of these adjustments involve transitions into important adult roles— worker, spouse, and parent. The way that we cope with the demands of these roles varies over the course of our lives as we age physically, emotionally, and mentally.

The concept of "socially defined time" is central to the *timing-of-events perspective*. All societies have age norms that dictate when people ought to accomplish certain tasks. Finishing school, getting married, and having children are some of the most important tasks in life. And being on time is important. If we are either too early or too late, we will feel the pressure. People who do not adhere to the socially defined timing of important life events can experience great stress when they get off schedule.

Finally, the *normative-crisis perspective* views adult development as a sequence of tasks that must be accomplished in a particular order. Theories that adopt this perspective see the life course as a series of stages where people face tasks that pose a "crisis." An individual's success or failure in dealing with the crisis at a particular stage influences further development. The challenges that we face as adults primarily involve interpersonal relationships, our identity, and accepting our own life stories (Clausen 1986).

STAGE THEORIES OF ADULT DEVELOPMENT

Stage theories are based on the idea that development proceeds in a fixed sequence from one stage to the next. Movement to a higher level indicates that an individual has mastered the skills of the lower one. For example, children babble before they talk. A number of researchers have developed theories that define the stages of adult development by intellectual development, individual needs, and social expectations (Craig and Baucum 2002). Based on their research findings, they propose that certain "crises" or conflicts arise during particular stages in adult development. These theories offer descriptions of the kinds of concerns that trouble adults at particular points in the course of their lives. And they suggest some interesting insights into adult development. But do they suggest universal principles for adult development? Not necessarily. Nonetheless, many of them do show similar patterns in this development. Let us take a look at the similarities and differences in these theories.

Erikson's Theory of Psychosocial Stages

Sigmund Freud drew a number of followers who modified various aspects of his psychoanalytic theory. Among these neo-Freudians, Erik Erikson (1902–1994) became the most famous with his theory of psychosocial stages. Although he accepted many aspects of Freud's psychosexual theory, he also differed in a number of important ways. For example, as the name of Erikson's theory suggests, he believed that sociocultural influences were more important than sexual drives. For Erikson (1995), the mind was more than drives and instincts. He therefore rejected Freud's view of children as passive beings who are driven by biological urges. Instead, he believed that children are active explorers who interact with and adapt to the environment (Berk 2000). He also viewed human growth and development within the communal environment—within a circle of significant social encounters. And he stressed the hopeful and active part of the person.

These fundamental differences carried over into Erikson's ideas about the relationship between the id and the ego. In contrast to Freud, who stressed the id, Erikson focused on the ego and proposed that it did not simply balance the demands of the id and the superego. In his theory, which covered the entire life span, the ego played an important role at each stage of human development. As the rational part of the personality, it helped individuals resolve specific kinds of conflicts that characterized different stages in human development.

The Eight Stages of Life. Erikson's psychosocial conception of the life cycle was originally based on the insights that Freud gained into the impact of the early stages of life. However, in contrast to Freud's focus on what can go wrong in each stage of development, Erikson (1995, 595) asked, "What should have gone and can go right?" Focusing on the development of human potentials, he proposed that the life cycle had eight developmental stages. The key characteristics of these stages included a specific crisis (or turning point), a psychosocial strength, and a radius of significant relations (see

Table 3.1). Erikson chose the term *crisis* to refer to a turning point rather than a threat of catastrophe. Characteristic of each of his eight stages of life, *crisis* suggested a period of increased vulnerability as well as heightened potential. The following description summarizes each stage.

1. *Infancy (trust versus mistrust).* If parents provide adequate and consistent care, infants will develop a sense of trust. If parents are anxious, angry, or fail to meet a child's needs, children may feel rejected and develop a sense of mistrust for others that may be carried through later stages. The mother, who is a child's first "world," is the most significant person in the radius of significant relations. The positive outcome of resolving the crisis faced at this stage (the psychosocial strength) is hope.

2. *Early childhood (autonomy versus shame or doubt).* As 2- and 3-year-olds improve their motor and mental skills, they start to develop a sense of autonomy. Parents who do not allow children to do things on their own and at their own pace may cause them to feel shame or to doubt their own abilities. These children may fail to develop self-confidence. Both parents play an important role during this stage of development. Guided properly, children can develop the determination (will) to exercise their free choice as well as self-control.

TABLE 3.1	ERIKSON'S PSYCHOSOCIAL STAGES OF HUMAN DEVELOPMENT	
Psychosocial Crises	**Psychosocial Strength**	**Radius of Significant Relations**
1. Trust versus mistrust	Hope	Maternal person
2. Autonomy versus shame or doubt	Will	Parental persons
3. Initiative versus guilt	Purpose	Basic family
4. Industry versus inferiority	Competence	Neighborhood, school
5. Identity versus identity diffusion	Fidelity	Peer groups and outgroups; models of leadership
6. Intimacy versus isolation	Love	Partners in friendship, sex, competition, cooperation
7. Generativity versus stagnation	Care	Divided labor and shared household
8. Integrity versus despair	Wisdom	"Humankind," "my kind"

Source: Adapted from Erikson 1995, 601.

3. *Play age (initiative versus guilt).* During the preschool years, children can move independently and vigorously. They begin to understand their expected role in the adult world, and they play out roles worthy of imitation. Children want to learn new things at this age, and thus learning becomes intrusive. Whether this leads a child to develop initiative or a sense of guilt depends on the response of parents. Through example, they can show the child the difference between play and adult "reality" or "purposefulness." Children who manage this turning point well will develop a sense of initiative. If, however, parents punish a child for expressing new ideas or desires, the child will develop a sense of guilt. The family constitutes the radius of significant relations for this stage. Purpose is the psychosocial strength.

4. *School age (industry versus inferiority).* Children learn important social and academic skills during the middle years of childhood. At this age, children compare themselves to their peers to assess their accomplishments. The danger of this turning point lies in the possibility that children can develop a sense of inadequacy or inferiority if comparisons to peers constantly make them feel that they have failed or fallen short. Parents and teachers who recognize and value a child's achievements help the child develop a sense of industry. A child's neighborhood and school form the radius of significant relations during this stage. The positive outcome of resolving the conflict at this stage is competence.

5. *Adolescence (identity versus identity confusion).* This stage is marked by the end of childhood and the onset of puberty. Adolescents now seek to discover "who they are." To integrate various components of their identity, they try to fit their talents and skills to the occupational prototypes of their culture. Erikson (1995, 606) also claimed that "'falling in love' . . . can be an attempt to arrive at a self-definition by seeing oneself reflected anew in an idealized as well as eroticized other." To cope with their regressive insecurities, adolescents form cliques and stereotype themselves, their ideals, and their "enemies." Adolescents who do not gain a sense of identity at this point may develop role confusion. The radius of significant relations for this stage includes peer groups, outgroups, and models of leadership.

6. *Young adulthood (intimacy versus isolation).* During young adulthood, individuals seek love and companionship. Forming intimate relationships, which involves sacrifices and compromises, requires young adults to turn the focus away from themselves toward others. An integrated identity makes that possible. The danger of this stage is the development of isolation, which results from the failure to achieve intimate relationships. Love, the psychosocial strength of this stage, explains why most people date and marry during this period. Partners in friendship constitute the radius of significant relations.

7. *Maturity (generativity versus stagnation).* Maturity is characterized by the need to be needed. Middle-aged individuals express this need through their efforts to guide the next generation. The concept of generativity refers to procreativity, productivity, and creativity. The positive outcome of the crisis experienced in this stage is the psychosocial strength of caring. Individuals who are self-centered at this stage do not feel enriched but experience a sense of stagnation or boredom. One's spouse and children play important roles during this stage.

8. *Old age (integrity versus despair).* Old age is a period of reflection. As people examine their lives, they will feel either satisfaction or disappointment. Those who view their lives as meaningful and fulfilled will feel a sense of integrity. If, however, they see in their lives missed opportunities and unrealized goals, they may fall into despair. Wisdom is the psychosocial strength of this stage. All of human kind is the radius of significant relations.

Providing guidance to the next generation is a characteristic displayed by middle-aged individuals during Erikson's stage of maturity.

Culture and History. In contrast to Freud, Erikson stressed both culture and history. He would therefore argue that identity formation is different for an American than for an Indonesian. Each culture exerts its own unique influence on the development of a child. Erikson also recognized the importance of the historical period in an individual's development. For example, Americans who grew up in the 1930s during the Great Depression faced different challenges than children growing up today. Reflecting his emphasis on the relationship between the individual and society, Erikson (1995, 609) concluded that "psychosocial strength . . . depends on a total process which regulates individual life cycles, the sequence of generations, and the structure of society simultaneously, for all three have evolved together." Faith, willpower, purposefulness, efficiency, devotion, affection, responsibility, and wisdom are all products of an individual's progression through the life cycle.

Evaluation of Erikson's Psychosocial Theory. Erikson's psychosocial theory began to influence ideas about child development after a comprehensive description of it was published in 1959 (Thomas 2000). Although it is rooted in psychoanalytic

theory, its emphasis on the sociocultural determinants of personality rather than sexual drives makes it a more plausible theory. Erikson's description of the crises that individuals face at different points in the life cycle is another appealing feature. Many of the weaknesses of psychosocial theory reflect those of psychoanalytic theory. Critics therefore argue that Erikson is not specific enough about the causes of development (Shaffer 2000). For example, he does not clearly explain what kinds of experiences help children develop self-confidence. And like psychoanalytic theory, it is not easy to test experimentally.

Havighurst's Model of Developmental Tasks

Robert Havighurst (1953, 1972) proposed another early model of adult development that focused on developmental tasks (Dion 1985). According to Havighurst (1953, 2):

> A developmental task . . . arises at or about a certain period in the life of the individual, successful achievement of which leads to . . . happiness and to success with later tasks, while failure leads to unhappiness . . . , disapproval by the society and difficulty with later tasks.

Havighurst's developmental task reflects Erik Erikson's theoretical influence (Dion 1985). But it also refers to societal expectations associated with specific role-related tasks faced in adulthood (see Table 3.2). These tasks are key events that most people experience during certain age-related phases in their lives (Brim and Ryff 1980). For

| TABLE 3.2 | HAVIGHURST'S MODEL OF DEVELOPMENTAL TASKS |

Developmental Tasks of Early Adulthood

Selecting a mate

Learning to live with a marriage partner

Starting a family

Rearing children

Managing a home

Getting started in an occupation

Taking on civic responsibility

Finding a congenial social group

Developmental Tasks of Middle Adulthood

Achieving adult civic and social responsibility

Establishing and maintaining an economic standard of living

Developing adult leisure-time activities

Assisting teenage children to become responsible and happy adults

Relating oneself to one's spouse as a person

Accepting and adjusting to the physiological changes of middle age

Adjusting to aging parents

Developmental Tasks of Later Maturity

Adjusting to decreasing physical strength and health

Adjusting to retirement and reduced income

Adjusting to death of spouse

Establishing an explicit affiliation with one's age group

Meeting social and civic obligations

Establishing satisfactory physical living arrangements

Source: Havighurst 1953.

example, the transition from childhood to adulthood usually occurs when a person leaves school and finds a job. Accomplishing this task is a sign that a person has established economic independence from his or her parents. Getting married and starting a family are two other important tasks of early adulthood. The tasks of middle adulthood involve career advancement, family responsibilities, and adjusting to the aging process. In older adulthood, people must deal with tasks that involve retirement, declining health, and the death of a spouse.

Havighurst's model suggests that adult socialization presents individuals with developmental tasks that require them to meet "the demands of expected role-related events" and to adjust to role transitions (Dion 1985, 124–125). The most important roles that individuals learn as adults involve work and family life. Accomplishing the tasks of one of these roles can be difficult. The real challenge is juggling a multitude of role responsibilities simultaneously.

Since Havighurst first proposed this model in the 1950s, American society has experienced significant social changes. And that has prompted critics to ask whether his theory can still explain adult development. Overall, the answer is yes (Craig and Baucum 2002). Although not everyone will accomplish the tasks that he linked to different periods of adulthood, many people will. In some cases, the timing of accomplishing these tasks will depart from Havighurst's model. Higher rates of divorce also suggest that more people today will have to adjust to the role of an ex-spouse. And parents may have to raise their children without the help of a partner. If anything, this suggests the strength of Havighurst's model—the emphasis placed on learning the developmental tasks of particular adult roles.

Levinson's Theory: Seasons of Life

When Daniel Levinson set out to study adult life in the late 1960s, he pointed out that until then, researchers had focused most of their efforts on childhood development. And he noted distinct periods of this development: infancy, early childhood, middle childhood, pubescence, early adolescence, and late adolescence. He argued that the study of adult-hood required a similar developmental approach, and he designed a study that revealed a number of interesting patterns.

The subjects in Levinson's 1969 study of adult development were forty men born between 1923 and 1934. Viewed in terms of historical time, that meant that by the time Levinson collected data on these subjects, they had experienced a number of significant social changes, including the Great Depression, World War II, the Korean War, the prosperous period of the conformist 1950s, and the turbulence of the 1960s. Recognizing the importance of a man's occupation, Levinson selected men from four occupational subgroups, which he believed represented the diversity of work in the United States: novelists, university biologists, business executives, and hourly industrial workers. This sample turned out to be diverse in other important respects, with men coming from different social classes; racial, ethnic, and religious backgrounds; educational levels; and marital statuses. To illustrate particular concepts in adult development, Levinson also included analyses of the lives of historical figures such as Mahatma Gandhi, Martin Luther King Jr., and John Milton.

Levinson's theoretical perspective was rooted in the theories of Freud, Jung, and Erikson. This approach allowed him to consider the influences of both nature and nurture on adult development. Specific influences included biology, psychology, history, culture, and social institutions. As set forth in his book *The Seasons of a Man's Life* (1978), Levinson proposed that individuals progress through a sequence of developmental *eras* that constitute the *life structure* (see Figure 3.1).

Designating the life structure as the pivotal concept in his theory, Levinson pointed out that a man's life contained many components: his occupation, marriage, family, and various social roles. For Levinson (1978, 41), life structure referred to "the underlying pattern or design of a person's life at a given time." And it evolved as one progressed through a particular sequence of periods. Although individuals go through these periods in the same order, their experiences differ significantly.

According to Levinson, that explains the unique character of individual lives.

Levinson did not view his theory of adult development as a model for the "normal" path that people should take. It was, rather, a way to identify the developmental tasks that confront adults as they move through successive periods in life. Mastering these tasks presents different challenges for different individuals. And moving from one period to the next is not a simple matter. Levinson described the transition as "a basic change in the fabric of one's life," and he claimed that it took four to five years to move from one period to the next.

The periods in Levinson's theory of adult development begin with the Early Adult Transition, which occurs between the ages of 17 and 22, plus or minus two years (see Figure 3.1). During this transition, individuals modify or end existing relationships with important people, groups, and institutions. Conceptions of the self are also reconsidered and changed. This is a time when men imagine themselves in the adult world and begin to make choices about their futures. From about 22 to 28 years of age, men develop the first adult life structure. As young adults who have separated from their families of origin, they now consider important choices about occupations, marriage and family, friendships, values, and lifestyle. This period can be confusing and difficult as men consider choices that have lifelong consequences.

The second transition (Age 30 Transition) in a man's life occurs between the ages of 28 and 32. During this time, men recognize the importance of choices made during the first adult life structure and may feel an urgency to make necessary changes before it is too late. Men's experiences during this transition vary. Some men make simple modifications without feeling a sense of crisis. Others have problems with the developmental tasks of this period and may experience a severe crisis. When a man reaches the age of 33, he has completed the period of early adulthood.

By the end of the Age 30 Transition, the second life structure has formed. It will remain in place during the period of Settling Down, which extends from ages 33 to 40. Men become

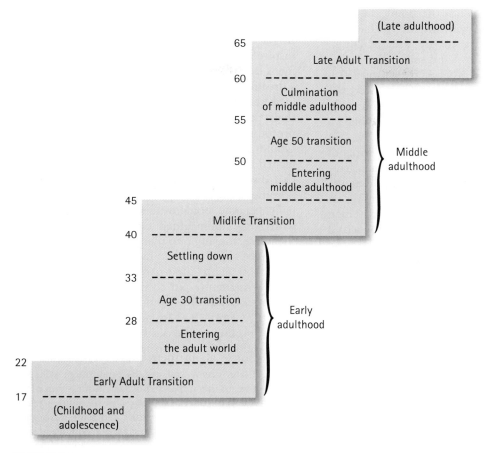

FIGURE 3.1

Levinson's Seasons of Life

Source: From *The Seasons of a Man's Life* by Daniel Levinson, copyright © 1978 by Daniel J. Levinson. Used by permission of Alfred A. Knopf, a division of Random House, Inc. and SII/Sterling Lord: Literistic, Inc.

full-fledged adults during this period by advancing in their jobs and personal lives according to an established timetable. Levinson (1978, 59) used the expression "making it" to convey the idea that during this period, one strives to "build a better life for oneself and to be affirmed by the tribe." Using the imagery of the ladder to express the essence of the Settling Down period, Levinson wrote:

> By "ladder" we refer to all dimensions of advancement—increases in social rank, income, power, fame, creativity, quality of family life, social contribution—as these are important for the man and his world. The ladder has both objective and subjective aspects: it reflects the realities of the external social world, but it is defined by the person in terms of his own meanings and strivings.

Early adulthood ends in a man's late thirties. At this point, men experience the Midlife Transition, which lasts from about 40 to 45 years of age. This transition, like earlier ones, causes men to ask questions about their lives. At this point, they may ask: "What have I done with my life? What do I really get from and give to my wife, children, friends, work, community—and self? What is it I truly want for myself and others?" (Levinson 1978, 60). Men continue to ask questions after the Midlife Transition ends. But their attention shifts to new developmental tasks as they begin to build a new life structure.

According to Levinson, the life structures of men in their mid-forties vary greatly. If men have experienced failures in childhood or early adulthood, they may not be capable of developing an adequate life structure at this point. Some men form life structures that are adequate for the world but inadequate for themselves personally. Because the life structures of these men lack a personal connection, their lives are often devoid of meaning or excitement. But other men experience great satisfaction during middle adulthood. Men who have formed deep attachments to others and have a strong sense of self can feel relieved from the pressures of earlier periods. For them, this period may be the best time of their lives.

Criticisms of Levinson's Theory. Critics cite a number of problems with Levinson's theory of the life cycle. For one thing, even his case studies show discrepancies between the sequences and timing that he describes (Clausen 1986). And longitudinal studies that are based on larger samples show that only a small proportion of men conform to his model of the life cycle. His original study was also faulted because he did not include women. In fact, even Levinson found that regrettable.

He did, however, respond to that criticism. In *The Seasons of a Woman's Life* (1996), Levinson analyzed the adult development of forty-five women: fifteen homemakers, fifteen businesswomen, and fifteen academics. Some of his findings fit the model that he proposed for men, including the transition that occurs around the age of 30 when people reevaluate their careers and lifestyles. But women's experiences also differed significantly from men's.

Gould's Theory of Transformations

Roger Gould (1978), an American psychiatrist, was inspired to delve into theories of adult development by a personal experience that he described as a dream colliding with reality. He and his wife had expected to feel great joy when they moved into their first home. Instead, they both experienced profound depression. This unexpected reaction led Gould to consider the underlying meaning attached to this significant life event. He recognized that owning a home was a childhood dream that becomes a myth about adulthood. When adults finally become homeowners, reality sets in along with some unimagined emotional reactions. In their case, moving into their first home destroyed a protective illusion that had connected them to childhood and to their parents. It resurrected and then permanently put to rest the false childhood assumption that they would live in the same community as family and friends. Their sadness was a way of mourning the death of these expectations.

Gould (1978, 11) wrote:

> As I later discovered, my disappointment at having to give up this rather minor false assumption of my childhood is part of a process of shedding a whole network of assumptions, rules, fantasies, irrationalities and rigidities that tie us to our childhood consciousness. This network of assumptions allows us to believe, on a nonrational, emotional level, that we've never really left the safe world provided by omnipotent parents. The act of taking a step into an adult life—our moving into our new house—exposed this second, unsuspected emotional reality: a childhood consciousness coexisted alongside our rational, adult view of reality.

Like Erikson's psychosocial theory, Gould's explanation of the phases of adult life is rooted in psychoanalytic theory (Gould, 1972; Clausen 1986). Guided by questions that arose from his own experience, Gould examined the assumptions, myths, and worldviews of adults at different phases in life. As a supervisor of psychiatric residents, he became familiar with the life stories of about 125 people over a period of five years. This experience helped him recognize patterns in age-related concerns. Teenagers expressed concerns about establishing their independence from parents. People in their twenties focused on their new roles as spouses, parents, and workers. Once they reached their thirties, individuals began to talk about "being stuck and mired down" (Gould 1978, 13). And they seemed confused about the important issues of their lives. People in their late thirties and early forties were preoccupied with questions about the past and the future. What had their lives been? And what could they still be? These questions were accompanied by strong feelings of dissatisfaction and an urgent desire to find answers.

Gould's research on the phases of adult life included subjects between the ages of 16 and 60. An analysis of the life histories of these subjects showed clear patterns in the kinds of experiences they had at certain stages. Recognizing progression through these different phases as a sign of growth, Gould viewed the process as one of discarding childish illusions and false assumptions.

Gould (1978) identified a number of false assumptions of childhood that individuals must challenge in order to grow, including the following:

Ages 16–22: "I'll always belong to my parents and believe in their world" (43).

Ages 22–28: "Doing things my parents' way, with willpower and perseverance, will bring results. But if I become too frustrated, confused or tired, or am simply unable to cope, they will step in and show me the right way" (71).

Ages 28–34: "Life is simple and controllable. There are no significant coexisting contradictory forces within me" (153).

Ages 35–45: "There is no evil or death in the world. The sinister has been destroyed" (217).

Individuals challenge the first false assumption of childhood between the ages of 16 and 22. Parental influence tends to feel particularly strong during this phase as people try to establish their independence. Young adults, whose sense of self is still fragile, are not fully prepared to question parental authority. And that often makes them sensitive to criticism. One young man in Gould's study said that his parents' harsh words "feel like dumdum bullets that expand inside me and tear me up" (1978, 45). At the same time, young adults begin to see the imperfections in their parents and start to move toward their own perceptions of the world.

From 22 to 28 years of age, individuals challenge the second false assumption of childhood. Although doing things our parents' way can bring results, young adults must now take full responsibility for their own life decisions. Jobs, marriage, and children become new responsibilities. The self-centeredness of the previous phase disappears as young adults turn their attention to other people and things. Even the way that we think changes during this period. Gould (1978, 73) claimed that "thinking must become critical, analytical, sequential, experimental and goal-oriented. Instead of flashes of insight, we must learn to value perseverance, will-power and common sense and tolerate being wrong in order to learn how to be right." Succeeding in the tasks presented to us during this phase builds self-confidence and contributes to a sense of being an adult. We no longer feel that we are appendages of our parents.

During the third phase of adult development, from age 28 to 34, people have usually lived away from their parents' home for eight to ten years. They are now prepared to challenge the third false assumption of childhood: "Life is simple and controllable. There are no significant coexisting contradictory forces within me." Looking deep inside themselves, people discover desires, talents, and strengths that they suppressed during their early twenties. For Gould, this kind of discovery amounts to a spiritual awakening. The desire to "make it" in the world, which was the primary focus of the early twenties, recedes as people begin to experience a wide range of new feelings.

To illustrate the kind of change that occurs during this phase of adult development, Gould

(1978) recounted a number of real-life stories. Let us consider two examples:

> Terry, 29, will soon become a partner in a prestigious law firm. Yet he begins to think more and more about devoting himself to public service or running for office. He is considering a leave of absence that will jeopardize the position he has been working toward for several years.
>
> Beryle, an independent 30-year-old woman who enjoys her single life as a stewardess and prides herself on her good spirits, feels a sudden urgency to marry and have a family, even though it will change her successful life. (156)

The third phase of adult development is a period of turbulence, questioning, and disillusionment. It is a time when people reexamine the rigid rules of their early twenties and adopt a new approach to realizing their dreams. People replace the belief that their dreams will come true if they do what is expected of them. Now they believe, "I will get what I can reasonably expect to get based on what I have done. Dreams don't come true by wishful contracts" (Gould 1978, 160). As people gain a more realistic sense of their own power, they let go of the idea that magic plays some role in their achievements. During this phase, people recognize their interests, values, and other parts of themselves that will continue to develop for the rest of their lives.

As people enter the last phase in Gould's theory, the decade between 35 and 45, they view time as the "ultimate limitation in life." This is a vulnerable period for people who must now confront their own immortality. They feel the pressure of time with a sense of urgency. Gould (1978) captured it well when he wrote, "Whatever we must do must be done now" (217).

Gould (1978) argued that "to achieve an adult sense of freedom, we must pass through periods of passivity, rage, depression and despair as we experience the repugnance of death, the hoax of life and the evil within and around us." At this point, people confront the last major false assumption of childhood: "There is no evil or death in the world. The sinister has been destroyed" (217).

According to Gould, people achieve an independent adult consciousness by progressing through a series of conflicts that initiate various phases of separation from childhood. As people resolve the conflicts that characterize a specific phase in adult development, they undergo a transformation—a reformulation of their self-definition. This occurs as people confront the false assumptions of their childhood, overcome their fears, and then make life-altering changes. The phases that Gould describes differ from the stages proposed by Erikson and Levinson, but they still suggest that adults continue to grow and develop by facing a series of crises (Clausen 1986).

The stage theories described to this point view the life course as a process of development that unfolds in a set order. Progression from one stage to the next depends to a large extent on completing the tasks presented in the previous stage. Although these theories see progression over the life course as occurring in social contexts, these contexts do not define the stages. Nor do they determine their order (Clausen 1986). Next, we will turn to theories that emphasize the social context within which the life course unfolds. Instead of focusing on the stages of adult development, these theories focus on the social roles that people occupy at different points in their lives.

THE PROCESS OF ADULT SOCIALIZATION

> All the world's a stage,
> And all the men and women merely players.
> They have their exits and their entrances,
> And one man in his time plays many parts,
> His acts being seven ages.
> At first the infant,
> Mewling and puking in the nurse's arms.
> Then the whining school boy with his satchel
> And shining morning face, creeping like snail
> Unwillingly to school. And then the lover,
> Sighing like furnace, with a woeful ballad
> Made to his mistress' eyebrow. Then a
> soldier,

Full of strange oaths, and bearded like the
pard,
Jealous in honor, sudden and quick in quarrel,
Seeking the bubble reputation
Even in the cannon's mouth. And then the
justice,
In fair round belly with good capon lined,
With eyes severe and beard of formal cut,
Full of wise saws and modern instances;
And so he plays his part. The sixth age shifts
Into the lean and slippered pantaloon,
With spectacles on nose and pouch on side;
His youthful hose well saved, a world too
wide
For his shrunk shank; and his big manly voice
Turning again toward childish treble, pipes
And whistles in his sound. Last scene of all
That ends this strange eventful history,
Is second childishness and mere oblivion;
Sans teeth, sans eyes, sans taste, sans
everything.

—William Shakespeare, *As You Like It*

In these memorable lines from *As You Like It*,
William Shakespeare traces the life course through
seven ages. These ages are linked to the central
roles that people play over the course of their lives.
And the actors' exits and entrances represent significant transitions from one role to the next. Sociological theories take a similar view of the life
course—as structured social roles that we occupy
at certain times in our lives (Clausen 1986). These
roles are defined by a set of expectations, responsibilities, and privileges. They prescribe how people
in certain categories should behave in their relationships with others.

Sociological perspectives recognize that periods of our lives are linked to the ages when we
enter and exit certain roles. But people do not
move through roles in an invariant sequence. And
some people skip some roles altogether. For example, most people marry and have children, but
some remain single. Other people have children
but never marry, and not all people who marry
have children.

The beginning and end of our lives are characterized by roles that do not entail major duties or
responsibilities. Infants are totally dependent on
caretakers. In many cases, so are the elderly as they
prepare for their final exit. But between these two
extremes, people play many important social roles.

Learning these roles and adapting to their
unique requirements occur through the process of
adult socialization. Adjustment to new roles could
explain much of the change in adulthood behavior
(Becker 1964; Dion 1985). And an individual's
commitment to various roles could account for behavioral stability. At the same time, adults may experience strain or conflict from having to assume
multiple roles simultaneously (Dion 1985).

THE ROLES AND CONTEXTS OF ADULT SOCIALIZATION

The most important roles that individuals learn as
adults involve two social contexts—work and family. When Stuart Campbell reflected on his life in
1990, he indicated that he wanted to be remembered as a good doctor, a good husband and father,
and a good citizen. These roles gave his life meaning and constituted key components in his sense of
identity. In fact, these roles and the adjustments
they required all played an important role in
Stuart's adult development.

Many people define adulthood in terms of
these roles. The occupational role has long signified entrance into adulthood for men. It was the
first sign that they had established economic independence from their parents. It was also the first
step toward two other roles associated with adult
status—spouse and parent. Family roles have always signaled a woman's entrance into adulthood
(Clausen 1986). Today, occupational roles also signal women's entry into adulthood.

Juggling occupational and family roles is difficult for men and women in the twenty-first century. But it is particularly challenging for women,
who continue to take primary responsibility for
raising children and housekeeping (Hochschild

BOX 3.3	WOMEN'S CONFLICTING ROLES

Nancy Holt arrives home from work, her son, Joey, on one hand and a bag of groceries in the other. As she puts down the groceries and opens the front door, she sees a spill of mail on the hall floor, Joey's half-eaten piece of cinnamon toast on the hall table, and the phone machine's winking red light: a still-life reminder of the morning's frantic rush to distribute the family to the world outside. Nancy, for seven years a social worker, is a short, lithe blond woman of thirty who talks and moves rapidly. She scoops the mail onto the hall table and heads for the kitchen, un-buttoning her coat as she goes. Joey sticks close behind her, intently explaining to her how dump trucks dump things. Joey is a fat-cheeked, lively four-year-old who chuckles easily at things that please him.

Having parked their red station wagon, Evan, her husband, comes in and hangs up his coat. He has picked her up at work and they've arrived home together. Apparently unready to face the kitchen commotion but not quite en-titled to relax with the newspaper in the living room, he slowly studies the mail. Also thirty, Evan, a warehouse fur-niture salesman, has thinning pale blond hair, a stocky build, and a tendency to lean on one foot. In this matter there is something both affable and hesitant.

From the beginning, Nancy describes herself as an "ar-dent feminist," an egalitarian (she wants a similar balance of spheres and equal power). Nancy began her marriage hoping that she and Evan would base their identities in both their parenthood and their careers, but clearly tilted toward parenthood. Evan felt it was fine for Nancy to have a career, if she could handle the family too.

As I observe in their home on this evening, I notice a small ripple on the surface of family waters. From the commotion of the kitchen, Nancy calls, "Eva-an, will you *please* set the table?" The word *please* is thick with irritation. Scurrying between refrigerator, sink, and oven, with Joey at her feet, Nancy wants Evan to help; she has asked him, but reluctantly. She seems to resent having to ask. (Later she tells me, "I *hate* to ask: why should I ask? It's begging.") Evan looks up from the mail and flashes an irritated glance toward the kitchen, stung, perhaps, to be asked in a way so barren of appreciation and respect. He begins setting out knives and forks, asks if he will need spoons, then answers the doorbell. A neighbor's child. No, Joey can't play right now. The mo-ment of irritation has passed.

Later as I interview Nancy and Evan separately, they describe their family life as unusually happy—except for Joey's "problem." Joey has great difficulty getting to sleep. They start trying to put him to bed at 8:00. Evan tries but Joey rebuffs him; Nancy has better luck. By 8:30 they have him *on* the bed but not *in* it; he crawls and bounds play-fully. After 9:00 he still calls out for water and toys, and sneaks out of bed to switch on the light. This continues past 9:30, then 10:00 and 10:30. At about 11:00 Joey com-plains that his bed is "scary," that he can only go to sleep in his parents' bedroom. Worn down, Nancy accepts this proposition. And it is part of their current arrangement that putting Joey to bed is "Nancy's job." Nancy and Evan can't get into bed until midnight or later, when Evan is tired and Nancy exhausted. She used to enjoy their love-making, Nancy tells me, but now sex seems like "more work." The Holts consider their fatigue and impoverished sex life as results of Joey's Problem.

Source: Hochschild 1989/2003, 35–36.

1989/2003) (see Box 3.3). Let us consider how people learn these different roles through the process of adult socialization.

Family Roles

Most of us spend about a quarter of our lives in the family created by our parents—the **family of ori-entation**. But we will spend the rest of our lives as adults in the families we create—the **family of procreation**. This family provides an important context for adult socialization. Our most impor-tant and enduring relationships are formed here as we carry out the tasks and responsibilities of fam-ily life. Some of these activities define specific fam-ily roles. Others require the cooperation of family members. Taken altogether, the experiences of family life teach us a great deal about how the world operates. Studies also show that people believe that family roles are very important in determining their sense of self—who they are (Beroff, Douvan, and Julka 1981; Whitbourne 1986; Whitbourne and Ebmeyer 1990; Van Manen and Whitbourne 1997). How do we learn the roles of spouse and parent? What kinds of changes are required of us as we enter and exit these roles? And how important will these roles be when we assess our lives in the end?

Marital Roles

Our expectations of marriage are heavily influenced by the way our parents interacted (Clausen 1986). Did they treat each other with respect and kindness? How did they express differences of opinion? Did they enjoy doing things together, or did they seem to live separate lives? If our parents treated each other as friends who enjoyed spending time together, if they made efforts to meet each other's needs, and if they showed mutual affection, we are likely to seek that kind of marital relationship. On the other hand, if we view our parents' marriage as unhappy, we might not even consider marriage. Whatever we learned from our parents, forming an intimate relationship with a person of the opposite sex is an important task that faces us in early adulthood development. But it is not all that easy.

Moving from the status of a single person to wife or husband involves all kinds of adjustments that can cause stress and conflict. An engagement period can ease the tension for people who plan to marry. It also allows friends and family members to make adjustments to new relationships that are based on these new roles (son-in-law, daughter-in-law, and so on). Showers and parties for the bachelor and bachelorette also prepare young adults for these new roles. But the wedding ceremony is the most important rite of passage for this significant life event.

In the United States, this ceremony marks the beginning of a couple's transition into the new roles that they will play as married persons. It usually begins with the recitation of vows or promises between the bride and groom. Then they exchange wedding rings, which serve as visible symbols of their new marital status. Before it is over, the bride and groom will sign a wedding license to make their union legal. Adjustment to the new roles will continue as spouses negotiate their duties and responsibilities over the course of their marriage. In cases of divorce or death, individuals will exit their roles as husband or wife. These kinds of transitions also require adjustments that usually involve stress and strain.

Parental Roles

Some childhood behaviors and experiences suggest that preparation for parental roles begins early. For example, young children often adopt the roles of mommy or daddy when they play house. Children also observe how older siblings care for younger ones. And teenagers might baby-sit for family or friends (Benokraitis 2005).

This does not suggest that the duties and responsibilities of parenthood are either simple or easy. And men and women rarely feel prepared for these new roles. In fact, we are often reminded that we receive more training to become a licensed driver than to become a parent. Pediatricians and older family members provide helpful advice with the first baby. From that point, though, parents often learn through trial and error. They also learn from one another as they try to determine what their proper roles are (Stamp 1994). But this process presents new challenges at every turn as children proceed through their own stages of development.

The family context has been described as a series of phases that present unique tasks or challenges to the adults (see Table 3.3) (Duvall 1971; Clausen 1986). These phases usually begin before the birth of the first child when young married people imagine themselves as parents. After the birth of the first child, the family cycle then proceeds through a series of child-rearing stages that ends when the last child leaves home—the empty nest. The last stage in the family cycle occurs when one spouse dies, leaving the other in widowhood.

TABLE 3.3	**STAGES IN THE FAMILY LIFE CYCLE**

Life as a pair

Life with children in the home

    Youngest child under 6 (preschool)

    Youngest child 6–12 (preadolescent)

    Youngest child 13–20 (adolescent)

    Youngest child over 20 (unlaunched)

Empty nest—couple with no children at home

Life without a spouse—widowhood

Source: Clausen 1986, 130.

At each stage in the family life cycle, adults face unique tasks and responsibilities. Havighurst's model of developmental tasks provides a general idea of what spouses and parents are expected to do at different stages (see Table 3.2). Clausen (1995) provides a more specific list for parents whose responsibilities include the early socialization of their children (see Table 3.4). The influence of historical time is reflected in changes in the specific duties and responsibilities of mothers and fathers (see Box 3.4).

The requirements of family life are demanding. Men and women must juggle many roles simultaneously. This can be particularly stressful for adults in

TABLE 3.4	**TASKS OF EARLY CHILDHOOD SOCIALIZATION IN THE FAMILY**

Parental Aim or Activity	Child's Task or Achievement
Provision of nurturance and physical care	Acceptance of nurturance (development of trust)
Training and channeling of physiological needs in toilet training, weaning, provision of solid foods, etc.	Control of the expression of biological impulses; learning acceptable channels and times of gratification.
Teaching and skill training in language, perceptual skills, physical skills, self-care skills in order to facilitate care, ensure safety, etc.	Learning to recognize objects and cues; language learning; learning to walk, negotiate obstacles, dress, feed self, etc.
Orienting the child to the immediate world of kin, neighborhood, community, and society and to the child's own feelings.	Developing a cognitive map of one's social world; learning to fit behavior to situational demands.
Transmitting cultural and subcultural goals and values and motivating the child to accept them for his or her own.	Developing a sense of right and wrong; developing goals and criteria for choices; investment of effort for the common good.
Promoting interpersonal skills, motives, and modes of feeling and behaving in relation to others.	Learning to take the perspective of another person; responding selectively to the expectations of others.
Guiding, correcting, helping the child formulate his or her own goals and plan activities.	Achieving a measure of self-regulation and criteria for evaluating one's own performance.

Source: Clausen 1995, 152.

BOX 3.4	HISTORICAL DIFFERENCES IN ADULT TRANSITIONS

The transition from adolescence into adulthood has never been easy. But how does it compare to earlier times? In fact, the transition from adolescence into adulthood in the late twentieth century was described as a longer and more difficult process when compared to earlier historical times (Modell, Furstenberg, and Hershberg 1976). Researchers cannot accurately evaluate the sequence of transitions that young adults took a century earlier—from finishing school, taking a job, and establishing independence from parents to marrying and having a family (Clausen 1986). But census data do show that these transitions took longer than and varied more between people who made earlier versus later transitions.

The transition from school to the labor force happened quickly in 1880, just as it does today. However, in 1880, many people left school in early adolescence (12–14 years of age). Although they then went to work, they did not leave their parents' home. Instead, they remained with their parents and contributed to the household income. Only a small percentage of men married before the age of 20. In fact, the average age at which men married was 27. For women it was 23. The gap in these ages reflects significant gender differences in the sequence of transitions and the relative importance assigned to different adult roles. Before they could marry, men had to show that they could provide for their families. For them, entrance into adulthood was signified by the transition into an occupational role. In contrast, women were not expected to enter the labor force to provide for their families. They were expected to marry and raise a family. For women, marriage was a sign of their transition into adulthood.

Today, the transition from adolescence to adulthood is accomplished more quickly, and it seems that the schedule

for completing this transition is clearer than it was a century ago (Clausen 1986). But that does not make it any easier. The timing of marriage and children depends largely on a couple's educational and occupational aspirations. And it is not unusual for people to delay entry into family roles until they have finished school and firmly established their careers.

Parental roles have also changed over time. During colonial times, fathers played the dominant parental role (Demos 1986). Although mothers did take responsibility for infants and children under the age of 3, fathers showed a keen interest in them (Rotundo 1993). After this early childhood period, fathers took on a wider range of supervisory responsibilities, including the teaching of moral values. And they expected their wives to defer to them on matters of child rearing. The father's role began to change during the eighteenth century when patriarchal authority began to decline (Wood 1991). Sons and daughters alike established independence from their fathers by leaving home and by declaring the right to choose their own spouses. Fathers recognized that they could not control their children by threats of disinheritance. Children no longer had to rely on inherited land to marry. The Industrial Revolution helped young people achieve economic independence from their parents by offering new kinds of work. As men's working roles separated them from the household, women came to assume primary responsibility for raising children. Today, changes in the workplace have again affected the roles that parents play. Many mothers work outside the home, and some fathers choose to stay at home to care for the children.

---

middle age, who must take care of children and perhaps elderly parents. As we shall see, this juggling act also often includes occupational roles.

Occupational Roles

When researchers spoke with Stuart Campbell in 1982, they asked him a number of questions about his medical career. They were particularly interested in how important it had been in determining

his sense of self. His answer said it all: "It's very important that I'm a doctor. You kind of wonder after a while, what was I like before I was a doctor? Because you're always playing this role" (Clausen 1995, 102).

Being a doctor was a central part of Stuart's identity. Although he had considered other specialties when he reached middle age, Stuart never questioned his dedication to medicine. He saw himself as a successful and well-respected physician. And he recognized how this had contributed to his positive self-esteem. Nothing, however, captured the value that Stuart placed on this aspect of his life (who he was) better than his hope that he would be remembered as a good doctor.

Preparation for occupational roles begins early. From a young age, children are asked, "What do you want to be when you grow up?" Children offer many different answers to this question. Decisions about some occupations are made early. Individuals who want to become physicians usually decide by the time they enter college. They will spend four years in medical school before they even begin training for a specialty. Lawyers tend to make their occupational choice later than physicians (Clausen 1986). After they graduate from college, they will spend only three years in law school (Lortie 1959). Regardless of the career people choose, occupational roles require some training.

Researchers have studied a number of professions to understand how people are socialized into certain occupational roles. Howard Becker and his associates (1961) shadowed medical students as they progressed through four years of medical school. They discovered how these men and women adapted to the demanding study of medicine in the first few months of school by altering their idealistic notions of what it meant to be a doctor. Succeeding in medical school required a more realistic approach. As they reached the end of their training, however, their idealistic notions of this role had returned. This comprehensive study of how medical students become doctors provided insight into the way that individuals make transitions and adapt to adult roles.

In contrast to professions like medicine or law, some occupations do not require an extended period of training. Nonetheless, entry into these occupational roles requires some degree of socialization. Journalism provides a useful example. The most important lesson that journalists must learn is to identify a "newsworthy" story. Every day, they must sort out all of the information that

TABLE 3.5	THE SOCIALIZATION OF AMERICAN JOURNALISTS

In his book *Deciding What's News,* Herbert Gans identified a set of values that journalists adopt in the process of being socialized into this occupational role. These values, which underlie what is known as the news perspective, guide the way that journalists decide what stories to cover—what news is. Consider the eight values listed below. How similar are they to your own values? What role do these values play in constructing a particular version of social reality?

Individualism: Admiring people who succeed by doing things their own way, even against all odds.

Moderatism: Rejecting extreme behavior and supporting moderate views.

Social order: Desiring peace and order.

Leadership: Expecting leaders to meet high standards. Showing little tolerance for leaders who are weak, dishonest, or immoral.

Ethnocentrism: Judging other countries on the basis of how well they live up to American standards.

Altruistic democracy: Expecting the government to operate in the public interest.

Responsible capitalism: Supporting fair competition in business without undue profits or taking advantage of workers.

Small-town pastoralism: Preferring small towns over large urban areas. Viewing life in small towns as innocent and wholesome.

Source: Gans 1980, 42–55.

flows past them and recognize what is worthy of a headline. Decisions about the selection and construction of stories are based on what is called the "news perspective," and James Potter (1998, 116) claims that "learning to be a journalist means being socialized into this news perspective." In essence, that means that journalists must adopt the values that form the foundation of this news perspective (Gans 1980; Shoemaker and Reese 1996) (see Table 3.5). Succeeding in the field of journalism ultimately depends on the degree to which journalists construct stories that reflect these values. They must also learn the norms that prescribe how journalists should behave. Fabricating stories or quotations, staging events, and missing deadlines are grounds for dismissal in most media organizations.

No matter what occupations people pursue, success in these roles is measured by occupational advancement over the life course. And at certain stages in life, people assess where they stand. Are they on schedule for a promotion? Are they making enough money? Would they find more rewards in another occupation? The answers to these kinds of questions provide a measure of occupational success and the self-esteem attached to that. In many cases, occupational roles also provide a sense of identity for people.

RESOCIALIZATION

No discussion of adult socialization and the life course would be complete without examining **resocialization,** the process whereby individuals unlearn old attitudes, values, and behaviors and replace them with new ones. It also involves a transformation of an individual's identity or sense of self. In essence, resocialization erases everything that a person learned in primary socialization. Few people undergo this kind of radical resocialization. In fact, the course of normal adult development rests heavily on the solid foundation established in primary socialization.

Erving Goffman (1961) sought to understand the process by which the self underwent a radical change after primary socialization through studies of mental patients, prisoners, members of religious orders, and others who live in *total institutions.* According to Goffman, these kinds of establishments are "the forcing houses for changing persons" (12). Describing them as social hybrids—part residential, part formal organization—he defined total institutions as places of residence and work where a large number of similar individuals lead regimented lives in isolation from the wider society for an extended period of time. Jails, penitentiaries, prisoner-of-war camps, concentration camps, army barracks, boarding schools, mental hospitals, monasteries, abbeys, convents, and cloisters fit Goffman's concept.

Soldiers undergo the process of resocialization during basic training. To erase their civilian identities, all personal possessions are taken away from them.

BOX 3.5	RESOCIALIZATION OF A MILITARY CADET

In many total institutions, the privilege of having visitors or of visiting away from the establishment is completely withheld at first, ensuring a deep initial break with past roles and an appreciation of role dispossession. A report on cadet life in a military academy provides an illustration:

> This clean break with the past must be achieved in a relatively short period. For two months, therefore, the swab is not allowed to leave the base or to engage in social intercourse with non-cadets. This complete isolation helps to produce a unified group of swabs, rather than a heterogeneous collection of persons of high and low status. Uniforms are issued on the first day, and discussions of wealth and family background are taboo. Although the pay of the cadet is very low, he is not permitted to receive money from home. The role of the cadet must supersede other roles the individual has been accustomed to play. There are few clues left which will reveal social status in the outside world. (Dornbusch 1955, 317)

Source: Goffman 1961, 15.

The basic training of newly inducted members of the military provides an excellent example of resocialization. This training is intentionally designed to change a civilian's identity into that of a soldier. To accomplish transformations like this, total institutions follow similar steps. First, individuals are isolated from the outside world and confined to the institution (see Box 3.5). Then they undergo a process of stripping or mortification. This begins with admission procedures that may require them to undress, bathe, receive a haircut, and put on a uniform. Prisoners tend to undergo an even harsher form of mortification, involving fingerprinting, searching, and disinfecting. The institution is also likely to confiscate all personal possessions at this point. This is a particularly powerful way to take away a person's identity because we invest much of our sense of self in our possessions. If this effect is achieved by taking away physical possessions, total institutions often take away something even more important—a person's name. All of these things are done with one goal in mind: to erase an individual's past identity.

The second major step in the resocialization process involves the reconstruction of the individual's self. The goal of this step is to indoctrinate individuals with a new set of beliefs about the world and to provide them with a new conception of self. Learning to obey the "house rules" may involve a system of rewards or privileges (Goffman 1961). Goffman describes how the cooperation of mental patients is obtained through a system of control. In return for following the rules, attendants can give patients privileges such as better jobs, more privacy, or a little reward such as coffee on the ward. Privileges can also be suspended as a punishment for failing to obey the rules.

This chapter has focused on adult socialization and the life course. We have seen how adult development involves transitions and adaptations into adult roles. This process is built on the foundation established by primary socialization. This aspect of the socialization process focuses on how individuals come to understand the world that surrounds them. In the next chapter, we will explore the second interconnected process of socialization that Gecas (1992) described: how individuals come to understand themselves.

SUMMARY

1. Entry into adulthood does not end the socialization process. In fact, this transition marks the beginning of adult socialization, which emphasizes the learning of adult roles.

2. Studies of the life course span a number of disciplines and have given rise to an assortment of concepts and theories, all of which treat biology, psychology, sociocultural factors, and history as important influences on human development.

3. Glen Elder's life course paradigm is one of the best explanations of the life course, though more general perspectives offer different approaches.

4. A number of stage theories also seek to explain adult development. These theories offer descriptions of the concerns that trouble adults at particular points in the course of their lives. The most important theories are Erikson's theory of psychosocial stages, Havighurst's model of developmental tasks, Levinson's "seasons of life" theory, and Gould's theory of transformation.

5. Resocialization refers to the process by which individuals unlearn old attitudes, values, and behaviors and replace them with new ones. It also involves a transformation of the individual's identity or sense of self.

KEY TERMS

Primary socialization   73
Adult socialization   73
Life course   73
Age statuses   74

Rites of passage   75
Age norms   75
Cohort   77
Family of orientation   90

Family of procreation   90
Resocialization   95

CRITICAL REVIEW QUESTIONS

1. What lessons have your parents or grandparents taught you about progress over the life course? How do their experiences resemble or differ from what you might expect based on the theories presented in this chapter?

2. What historical events in your life have influenced or will influence your development over the life course?

3. Describe the expectations attached to adult roles that people take in the family.

FOUR

The Self

February 13, 1960   15¢

On January 20, 1923, in Willow Corners, Wisconsin, Hattie Dorsett gave birth to a tiny 5-pound $1\frac{1}{2}$-ounce baby girl. Her husband, Willard, named the child Sybil Isabel. Disliking that name, Hattie chose instead to call her daughter Peggy Louisiana, which was often shortened to Peggy Lou, Peggy Ann, or simply Peggy. As the remarkable life story of Sybil Isabel Dorsett would show, these names took on far more significance than her mother's use of them would ever suggest. Peggy Lou and Peggy Ann came to represent two of an additional fourteen alternate selves that would occupy Sybil's body at different times and places over the next forty-two years of her life. When Sybil awoke from these experiences—which she called blank spells—two questions would haunt her: *Where am I?* and *How much time has passed?* Curiously, she never thought to ask, *Who am I?*

In many respects, Sybil's life began only after many years of psychoanalysis with Dr. Cornelia B. Wilbur. By June 1945, when Sybil first met the doctor at the age of 22, her condition had grown so bad that authorities at the teachers' college she attended required her to see a psychiatrist before they would allow her to resume her studies.

As far back as grade school, Sybil recognized that she had a problem with time and memory.

People she had never seen before would insist that they knew her. She would go to a picnic and have a vague sense of having been there before. A dress that she had not bought would be hanging in her closet. She would begin a painting and return to the studio to find that it had been completed by someone else—in a style not hers. Sleep was a nightmare. She just couldn't be sure about sleep. Often it seemed as if she were sleeping by day as well as by night. Often, too, there was no dividing line between the time of going to bed at night and waking up in the morning. Many were the occasions of waking up without going to sleep, of going to sleep to wake up not the next morning, but at some unrecognizable time. (Schreiber 1973, 57)

Sybil kept her problem a secret. However, Dr. Wilbur eventually did discover that much of Sybil's life was mysteriously unaccounted for, at least to Sybil, the waking self. But it could be pieced together from the perspective of the other selves, who, the doctor hypothesized, emerged to cope with some traumatic experience in her early childhood.

Relying heavily on Vicky, an alternate self who served as Sybil's memory trace, Dr. Wilbur began to unravel the details of her patient's troubled childhood. One clue was Sybil's inability to remember two years of her childhood—from the third grade, when her beloved paternal grandmother died, until the fifth grade, when she "awoke" in a bewildered state in Miss Henderson's classroom. Blanking out at the edge of her grandmother's grave, Sybil had no memory of the next two years. But Vicky did. According to Vicky, Peggy Lou (another alternate self) had taken over at the grave in order to deal with the anger that Sybil could not express.

This dissociation went entirely unnoticed by her family. Following Vicky's suggestion, Peggy Lou answered to Sybil's name. In fact, all of Sybil's alternate selves did so, masking for those around her what was actually happening inside her head. Her parents did notice, however, some changes in Sybil's behavior. Peggy Lou, in contrast to Sybil, was an active child, the kind who would talk back to her parents, even walk on the furniture in a rage. These traits made Peggy Lou a lot like Hattie.

In 1957, Dr. Wilbur discovered why the death of Sybil's grandmother had been so traumatic. She had been Sybil's escape from Hattie—an abusive mother who had inflicted terrifying physical and sexual abuse on Sybil from 6 months of age. Hattie's secret rituals were nothing less than sadistic torture.

> A favorite ritual . . . was to separate Sybil's legs with a long wooden spoon, tie her feet to the spoon with dish towels, and then string her to the end of a light bulb cord, suspended from the ceiling. The child was left to swing in space while the mother proceeded to the water faucet to wait for the water to get cold. After

muttering, "Well, it's not going to get any colder," she would fill the adult-sized enema bag to capacity and return with it to her daughter. As the child swung in space, the mother would insert the enema tip into the child's urethra and fill the bladder with cold water. "I did it," Hattie would scream triumphantly when her mission was accomplished. "I did it." The scream was followed by laughter, which went on and on. (Schreiber 1973, 209)

Dr. Wilbur believed that Sybil had been normal at birth and had fought back until she was about $2\frac{1}{2}$. At that point, she could fight no more. Realizing that no one would rescue her from her mother, she sought refuge within herself. Ultimately, Sybil's escape came in the form of multiple selves, who defended her against her worst nightmares.

In searching for a way to integrate all of Sybil's multiple selves, Dr. Wilbur eventually realized that none of them had ever grown up. Despite an IQ of 170, Sybil never felt like an intelligent adult around her parents. She had never been able to grow up in their eyes. Through the use of hypnosis, Dr. Wilbur was able to age Sybil's alternate selves to match her chronological age. This turned out to be the key to fusing them into one whole self. "On September 2, 1965, Dr. Wilbur recorded in her daily analysis notes on the Dorsett case: 'All personalities one'" (Schreiber 1973, 436). After thirty-nine years of disintegration, Sybil was finally whole again; she had regained control over time.

Sybil's case is relatively rare. Few people develop multiple selves to deal with the kind of abuse that she suffered. (At the time Sybil began treatment with Dr. Wilbur, only eleven cases of multiple personality had been reported in the medical literature, and only one of them—a woman by the name of Eve—was still alive.) Yet Sybil's story gives us insight into what the self is, how it develops, and the important role that child care plays in its development.

THE CONCEPT OF THE SELF

The term *self* is used in conversation daily but its meaning is not always clear (Charon 2004). Most people understand what Shakespeare meant when he wrote: "To thine own self be true." But what exactly did he mean? Many of the different views of the self that exist in philosophy and the social sciences have contributed to current thinking.

William James

William James (1842–1910), a psychologist and philosopher at the University of Chicago, was the first American to write about the concept of the self (1992). In fact, in seeking answers to the questions that Sybil's case raised, Dr. Wilbur had consulted his *Principles of Psychology* (1890), which included a discussion of alternating personality and the history of two well-known cases. Most of James's text, however, was devoted not to this aberration but rather to the nature and development of the self.

The vocabulary surrounding this concept was relatively new. Terms such as *self-made man, self-interest, self-expression,* and *self-esteem* were products of social changes that occurred primarily during the nineteenth century. Marked by the transition from an agricultural society to an industrial one, this period ushered in the concept of individuality as the focus of American life shifted from dependence to independence, from ascribed status to achieved status, and from the community to the individual (Wood and Zurcher 1988; Rotundo 1993).

During this transition, American ideas about the nature of the self were influenced by two Enlightenment philosophers—John Locke and Jean-Jacques Rousseau. Locke regarded the individual not as an inner being but as a public actor, social and outward-facing, engaged in relationships with social institutions—the state, the law, and the economy. Rousseau, in contrast, conceptualized the self as inward-facing, as a spiritual and emotional entity. According to Rousseau, the self was a

"secular version of the soul: the innermost core of the person" (Rotundo 1993, 279).

Although James's ideas about the self were original and focused on its psychological nature, his concept did incorporate both an outward and an inward aspect of the self, which he called the *I* and the *Me.* In explaining what he meant by the self, he wrote:

> Whatever I may be thinking of, I am always at the same time more or less aware of *myself,* of my *personal existence.* At the same time it is I who am aware; so that the total self of me, being as it were duplex, partly known and partly knower, partly object and partly subject, must have two aspects discriminated in it, of which for shortness we may call one the *Me* and the other the *I.* (James 1992, 174)

James further explained that the **Me** was the known aspect of the self and included material items (one's body, clothes, immediate family, and home), emotions that these might arouse (pride, self-esteem, or personal despair), and acts that they prompt (e.g., self-preservation). The **I** was the *thinker.* Finding it more difficult to conceptualize, he wrote that the I was the conscious part of the self and the Me was only one of the things of which it was conscious.

George Herbert Mead: The Social Self

William James provided the building blocks for George Herbert Mead's theory of symbolic interactionism (1934), which, in contrast to behaviorist theories, emphasized the role of thinking in human behavior. Adopting John Dewey's ideas about the mind as a process of adjusting and thinking about intended actions, Mead (1863–1931) saw the mind as emerging through social interaction (Dewey 1922; Stryker 2002). Inward thinking, according to both men, was the defining trait of humanity.

Borrowing James's use of the personal pronouns *I* and *Me* to distinguish two aspects of the self, Mead explained the relationship between the two as the self in process—an ongoing interplay involving a particular act. As the subject, the I

© 1992 United Feature Syndicate, Inc.

© PEANUTS reprinted by permission of United Feature Syndicate, Inc.

would initiate social action and respond to objects in a situation. It was the impulsive, spontaneous part of the self. The Me, in contrast, represented the self as the object. It was the experience an individual had of imagining herself as the object in a situation. While the I propelled an act, the Me entered the process to give it direction or guidance (Meltzer 1972). When an individual became aware of her initial response to an act, the Me would then come into play.

Consider a police officer in the process of stopping a speeding motorist. The officer asks the driver to pull out her license. She begins to argue but reconsiders and searches for her wallet. As she begins to protest, she imagines the officer's likely reaction and decides that complying with him would be the best way to avoid trouble. The I, which spontaneously began to plead her innocence, was intercepted by the emergence of the Me. When the motorist imagined the officer's attitudes toward her protests, she was taking herself into account as an object. She became a Me. In fact, at that moment, she might even, in her own mind, address herself as such, saying, *He'll write me a huge ticket if I fight this.* The I and the Me alternate continually during social interaction—between action and reflection—giving humans control over their behavior.

The self in process also takes place in our internal conversations, involving again the interplay between the I and the Me. For instance, imagine that you agreed to baby-sit for your uncle on Saturday night. Then your roommate calls to say that he was just given free tickets to the NCAA playoffs—that same night. *What should I do?* you ask

yourself. *If I back out of my commitment to baby-sit, my uncle will think I am irresponsible, and he will never trust me again. But this might be my only chance to see my college team win an NCAA championship. I graduate from college this year. Surely my uncle will understand why this is so important to me. But he did ask me a month ago, since he needed a firm commitment. Maybe Mom will agree to babysit for me.*

This internal dialogue between the I and the Me shows how a college student imagines himself when faced with a dilemma. He imagines how his uncle will react if he backs out on him. Then he imagines how he will feel if he misses an NCAA championship game. The I and the Me continue to converse in this way as he seeks a solution to his dilemma.

Development of the Self

According to Mead, the development of the self requires individuals to take the role of the other, an ability that is acquired in three stages: the preparatory stage, the play stage, and the game stage.

Preparatory Stage. During the earliest stage of the self, the **preparatory stage**, a child simply imitates the behavior of others. Imagine, for example, a baby just learning to play patty-cake with his mother or the way babies learn to wave goodbye. Imitations like these are initially performed without any understanding of the underlying intentions. The actions lack meaning and carry no symbolic understanding. It is only when the child realizes that he is separate and distinct from others that his self emerges.

During the preparatory stage (top left), children imitate the actions of others toward objects without understanding the meaning of their actions. During the play stage (lower left), children take the role of a particular person. By playing this role, children are able to imagine the world from the unique perspective of that person. During the game stage (above), children take on the roles of many other people simultaneously. The self achieves a unitary stance that allows the child to act in an organized and consistent manner.

Play Stage. Children enter the second stage, the **play stage**, as they acquire language and other symbols. Equipped with words to identify and label objects, children no longer act toward objects in meaningless imitation but with shared understandings about these objects with others (see Box 4.1). The child now recognizes her own self

and may point this out by saying, "Molly wants to play house." As other people point the child out to herself, she acquires the ability to see herself as a social object. Names (*Molly*), pronouns (*you, she*), and adjectives (*funny, sad, pretty*) come to identify Me.

During this stage, children model themselves on important people, such as parents, whom Mead

| BOX 4.1 | HELEN KELLER |

In 1892, accompanied by W. E. B. Du Bois (a student of his in the late 1880s), William James visited 12-year-old Helen Keller at her school in Boston. Following this visit, he would continue to correspond with her. In the following selection, taken from her autobiography, Helen Keller describes her transition from simply imitating meaningless hand games to the first stages of what Mead would call the play stage.

The most important day I remember in all my life is the one on which my teacher, Anne Mansfield Sullivan, came to me. I am filled with wonder when I consider the immeasurable contrasts between the two lives which it connects. It was the third of March, 1887, three months before I was seven years old.

On the afternoon of that eventful day, I stood on the porch, dumb, expectant. I guessed vaguely from my mother's signs and from the hurrying to and fro in the house that something unusual was about to happen, so I went to the door and waited on the steps. The afternoon sun penetrated the mass honeysuckle that covered the porch, and fell on my upturned face. My fingers lingered almost unconsciously on the familiar leaves and blossoms which had just come forth to greet the sweet southern spring. I did not know what the future held of marvel or surprise for me. Anger and bitterness had preyed upon me continually for weeks and a deep languor had succeeded this passionate struggle.

Have you ever been at sea in a dense fog, when it seemed as if a tangible white darkness shut you in, and the great ship, tense and anxious, groped her way toward the shore with plummet and sounding line, and you waited with beating heart for something to happen? I was like that ship before my education began, only I was without compass or sounding line, and had no way of knowing how near the harbor was. "Light! Was the wordless cry of my soul, and the light of love shone on me in that very hour.

I felt approaching footsteps. I stretched out my hand as I supposed to my mother. Some one took it, and I was caught up and held close in the arms of her who had come to reveal all things to me, and, more than all things else, to love me.

The morning after my teacher came she led me into her room and gave me a doll. The little blind children at the Perkins Institution had sent it and Laura Bridgman had dressed it; but I did not know this until afterward. When I had played with it a little while, Miss Sullivan slowly spelled into my hand the word "d-o-l-l." I was at once interested in this finger play and tried to imitate it. When I finally succeeded in making the letters correctly I was flushed with childish pleasure and pride. Running downstairs to my mother I held up my hand and made the letters for doll. I did not know that I was spelling a word or even that words existed; I was simply making my fingers go in monkey-like imitation. In the days that followed I learned to spell in this uncomprehending way a great many words, among them *pin, hat, cup* and a few verbs like *sit, stand* and *walk*. But my teacher had been with me several weeks before I understood that everything has a name.

called **significant others**. As the concept suggests, these are people the child seeks to impress, whose acceptance the child values, or with whom the child identifies. By taking the roles of these people, by playing mommy or daddy, the child imagines the world from their perspectives.

Mead's designation of the second stage as the play stage indicates that children take the role of significant others one at a time. Not yet able to view themselves from the perspectives of many others simultaneously, the child flits from one role to the next. "A child plays at being a mother, at being a teacher, at being a policeman"—taking the perspective of just one particular other each time (Mead 1934, 150).

Game Stage. Over time, children learn to take the roles of many others simultaneously. To use the metaphor of baseball, they have progressed from playing catch (which involves just one other player) to a major league game (which involves many other players as well as complicated rules). Mead fittingly called this third stage the **game stage**.

As a child realizes that living in groups requires him to know his position as well as how that

One day, while I was playing with my new doll, Miss Sullivan put my big rag doll into my lap also, spelled "d-o-l-l" and tried to make me understand that "d-o-l-l" applied to both. Earlier in the day we had a tussle over the words "m-u-g" and "w-a-t-e-r." Miss Sullivan had tried to impress it upon me that "m-u-g" is *mug* and that "w-a-t-e-r" is *water*, but I persisted in confounding the two. In despair she had dropped the subject for the time, only to renew it at the first opportunity. I became impatient at her repeated attempts and, seizing the new doll, I dashed it upon the floor. I was keenly delighted when I felt the fragments of the broken doll at my feet. Neither sorrow nor regret followed my passionate outburst. I had not loved the doll. In the still, dark world in which I lived there was no strong sentiment or tenderness. I felt my teacher sweep the fragments to one side of the hearth, and I had a sense of satisfaction that the cause of my discomfort was removed. She brought me my hat, and I knew I was going out into the warm sunshine. This thought, if a wordless sensation may be called a thought, made me hop and skip with pleasure.

We walked down the path to the well house, attracted by the fragrance of the honeysuckle with which it was covered. Someone was drawing water and my teacher placed my hand under the spout. As the cool stream gushed over one hand she spelled into the other the word *water*, first slowly, then rapidly. I stood still, my whole attention fixed upon the motions of her fingers. Suddenly I felt a misty consciousness as of something forgotten— a thrill of returning thought; and somehow the mystery of language was revealed to me. I knew then that

"w-a-t-e-r" meant the wonderful cool something that was flowing over my hand. That living word awakened my soul, gave it light, hope, joy, set it free! There were barriers still, it is true, but barriers that could in time be swept away.

I left the well house eager to learn. Everything had a name and each name gave birth to a new thought. As we returned to the house every object which I touched seemed to quiver with life. That was because I saw everything with the strange, new sight that had come to me. On entering the door I remembered the doll I had broken. I felt my way to the hearth and picked up the pieces. I tried vainly to put them together. Then my eyes filled with tears; for I realized what I had done, and for the first time I felt repentance and sorrow.

I learned a great many new words that day. I do not remember what they all were; but I do know that *mother, father, sister, teacher* were among them—words that were to make the world blossom for me, "like Aaron's rod, with flowers." It would have been difficult to find a happier child than I was as I lay in my crib at the close of that eventful day and lived over the joys it had brought me, and for the first time longed for a new day to come.

Source: Keller 1902/1980, 20–24.

---

fits with respect to many other positions, he recognizes the need to develop a group perspective. At this point, the self incorporates all one's significant others into one **generalized other**. In contrast to the segmented self in the play stage, the self now achieves a unitary stance toward others. The child no longer darts from role to role, changing dramatically each time. Instead, he must be prepared to take the roles of everyone else in the game. And he must understand the relationships among these different roles.

The development of the generalized other represents an individual's internalization of society's

rules. From this generalized standpoint, the individual can behave in an organized and consistent manner. Mead used the game of baseball to make the point:

> The play antedates the game. For in a game there is a regulated procedure, and rules. The child must not only take the role of the other, as he does in the play, but he must assume the various roles of all the participants in the game, and govern his action accordingly. If he plays first base, it is as the one to whom the ball will be thrown from the field or from the catcher. Their organized reactions to him he has embedded in his own playing of the different

positions, and this organized reaction becomes what I have called the "generalized other" that accompanies and controls his conduct. And it is this generalized other in his experience which provides him with a self. (Mead 1925, 269)

Multiple Selves versus Multiple Personality

Mead recognized that in everyday experience, an individual may not mean much of what she says or does, saying that those who know us well may even comment that "she is not herself." By the same token, we may leave a job interview regretting what we did not say about ourselves. Both Mead and James saw that we maintain many relationships with different people, indicating that we are one thing to one person and another thing to someone else. We exchange recipes with our mother but ideas about the upcoming election with our professor.

Elaborating on what this meant for the nature of the self, William James wrote:

> Properly speaking, a man has as many social selves as there are individuals who recognize him and carry an image of him in their mind. To wound any one of these images is to wound him. But as the individuals who carry the images fall naturally into classes, we may practically say that he has as many different social selves as there are distinct groups of persons about whose opinion he cares. He generally shows a different side of himself to each of these different groups. Many a youth who is demure enough before his parents and teachers, swears and swaggers like a pirate among his "tough" young friends. We do not show ourselves to our children as to our club-companions, to our customers as to the laborers we employ, to our own masters and employers as to our intimate friends. From this there results what practically is a division of the man into several selves; and this may be a discordant splitting, as where one is afraid to let one set of his acquaintances know him as he is elsewhere; or it may be a perfectly harmonious division of labor, as where one tender to his children is stern to the soldiers or prisoners under his command. (James 1992, 177)

Though James and later Mead considered the existence of **multiple selves** normal, both men

distinguished this notion from the condition suffered by Sybil, which Mead (1934) dubbed **multiple personality**. Mead explained the illness as the emergence of separate Me's and I's that produce different selves, which cause the personality to split. No unified self can exist in this condition.

IMPORTANCE OF THE SELF-CONCEPT: WHO AM I?

"*Who am I?* She asked herself. *Who is she?* Dr. Wilbur likewise asked. For although Sybil was not yet a whole person, she was no longer a mere waking self" (Schreiber 1973, 430). Sybil's inability to integrate her multiple personalities had impaired her ability to participate in society. From the time she was forced to leave college until she became whole in 1965, she was not able to hold a full-time job. Her personal life had suffered as well. Relationships with men had been a lifelong problem. When she finally did fall in love with a man at the age of 41, Sybil turned his marriage proposal down, haunted by fears and self-doubt. Would the man she loved one day ask in bewilderment: *Who is she?* She refused to marry until she was able to provide the answer to *Who am I?*

Unaware of any continuity of herself from role to role and from one situation to another, Sybil could not make sense of the present, let alone make plans for the future. As much as she longed for children of her own, her anxiety over motherhood prevented her from realizing this desire. Crippled by the gaps in her memory, she could not see herself as a whole object. Her **self-concept** was incomplete.

In search of who she was, particularly after experiencing blank spells, Sybil would find reassurance by rummaging through her wallet and checking pieces of her ID—her Social Security card, health insurance card, driver's license, library card. These items gave her comfort and some reassurance about who she was.

Most people have no need to check their own identity in this way. Yet even you might be stumped by the question *Who am I?* To find some answers, take the **Twenty Statements Test**: Number the lines on a sheet of paper from 1 to 20, and fill in each line with an answer to the question *Who am I?*

Self-Identities

The Twenty Statements Test was developed by Manford Kuhn (1960) to measure an individual's conception of his or her own self. Take a look at your list again. Symbolic interaction theorists call the descriptions on your list **self-identities**.

As we explore this concept further, consider the hypothetical example in Table 4.1. All of the items on Renee Martin's list give us a good idea of who she believes she is; they constitute her self-identities. Compare your own list to Renee's. In what ways is your list similar to hers? Notice that Renee included race, memberships in groups, roles that have been socially assigned to her, personal characteristics, and clues to her behaviors (African American, member of a softball team, student, competitive, vegetarian). Each of these represents a distinct kind of self-identity.

Symbolic interactionists tend to divide self-identities into two broad categories: **role identities** (which reflect a sociological interest) and **dispositional identities** (which reflect a psychological interest). Each of these categories is then further divided. Role identities include *social categories, group memberships,* and *social roles.* Dispositional identities include *characteristics* and *behavioral tendencies* (see Figure 4.1).

Self-Identities and Social Change

The multidimensional concept of self-identities reflects the complicated process involved in the development of unique personal identities. Composed of both role and dispositional identities, it provides researchers with an ideal tool for studying how social change influences the way individuals define who they are (Zurcher 1977; Snow and Phillips 1982; Wood and Zurcher 1988). Consider how you have incorporated ideas about your gender role into how you define yourself. In what way do you and members of your generation differ from your great-grandparents?

As you might guess, the roles men and women play today have changed dramatically from those of earlier generations. Chances are that your great-grandmother saw herself defined primarily in terms of her roles as wife and mother. Few women considered a career. Men, by contrast, defined themselves almost entirely by their occupational role and their ability to support their families. This suggests that the way we view ourselves

TABLE 4.1	EXAMPLE: RENEE MARTIN'S SELF-IDENTITIES	
1. Renee Martin	11.	intelligent
2. African American	12.	funny
3. female	13.	sister
4. generous	14.	gardener
5. member of softball team	15.	friend
6. Baptist	16.	environmentalist
7. vegetarian	17.	aunt
8. student	18.	liberal
9. competitive	19.	democrat
10. music lover	20.	Rhodes scholar

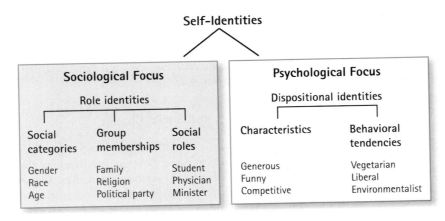

FIGURE 4.1

Self-Identities

is inextricably linked to the nature of our society (see Box 4.2).

In an effort to demonstrate how the transformation from an industrial to a postindustrial society influenced conceptions of the self, Wood and Zurcher (1988) compared diary entries for three periods of time: 1818–1860, 1911–1939, and 1949–1972 (see Box 4.3). This comparison showed that individuals in the early nineteenth century were preoccupied with their own moral and spiritual development, the glorification of God, secular duty, hard work, temperance and moderation, and the rejection of worldly comforts and sensual experience. This pattern of themes and ideas is consistent with the **Protestant ethic**, a concept described by Max Weber (1930) to

---

BOX 4.2   TRANSFORMATIONS IN MASCULINITY

Focusing on the changing definition of American manhood from colonial America to the twentieth century, historian E. Anthony Rotundo linked three distinct male identities to fundamental changes in society. According to Rotundo, the social world of colonial New England created a male identity that was inseparable from his duties to the community. Referring to this conception of self as *communal manhood*, Rotundo described the identity of men as shaped more by the social status of their families than by their own individual achievements. Manhood was also understood in terms of its contrast to womanhood. Men were considered superior to women in every way. "Men were seen as the more virtuous sex. They were credited with greater reason, which enabled them to moderate passions like ambition, defiance, and envy more effectively than women could" (Rotundo 1993, 3).

Communal manhood, which persisted through the first decades of the nineteenth century, was replaced by a self-made manhood, which began to develop in the late eighteenth century. Shaped by political and economic changes, a man's identity now became linked to his personal achievements rather than the status of his paternal family. Manhood thus rested heavily on a man's occupational role.

During the late nineteenth century, another definition of manhood appeared, which Rotundo called *passionate manhood*. Built on the existing beliefs about self-made manhood, the most dramatic change was a new emphasis on male passions. As, Rotundo (1993, 6) noted:

> In the closing years of the [nineteenth] century, ambition and combativeness became virtues for men; competitiveness and aggression were exalted as ends in themselves. Toughness was now admired, while tenderness was a cause for scorn. Even sexual desire, an especially worrisome male passion in the nineteenth century, slowly gathered legitimacy.

| BOX 4.3 | CONCEPTIONS OF THE SELF: DIARY EXCERPTS |

Time Period 1 (1818–1860)

Cambridge, October 22, 1843 . . . What am I doing to prepare myself for the life struggle upon which I am soon to enter? What have I learned which will aid me in the severe conflicts through which a lawyer must pass, and by which he is to be proved before he can reach the higher walks of his profession? What training of the faculties have I submitted to, to give them that vigor which is needed to grapple successfully [with] the difficulties of the most trying profession known among men? What have I done to give me that refined and correct taste which is required for success even in the lowest literary efforts? Alas, to all these and a thousand similar questions which might be asked, I have but one answer. Nothing, nothing, absolutely nothing. But it is not yet too late. From henceforth let me bend up my best energies to the great work of fitting myself to act well my part in the drama of life. Let not another sun set upon a day which has not added something to my stock of the instruments or my power and skill in using them.

I belong to one law club and one debating club where questions upon miscellaneous subjects are discussed. Let me never utter a sentence in either which has not been well weighed, and found worthy of utterance. In brief, let me in all things work, with a will, and thus may my year at Cambridge be one of joy and usefulness.

From the diary of Rutherford B. Hayes

Time Period 2 (1911–1939)

April 17, [1914] . . . Myself, you see, stands for my better judgement, for my permanent self, and Me is my unstable self, the part that is continually changing. Myself is the part of me that sees its way out of my "self-to-me" arguments, as for instance the one above about cleverness; and Me is that part that writes things in diaries in angular words, angular phrases and angular thoughts.

Like this:—Myself is inside, and Me is trying to sort of fit around the outside only it can't very well because it's so

angular, you see, and can do no more than touch myself and feel that myself is there.

Myself laughs, sometimes mockingly and sometimes indulgently but encouragingly withal, at my poor attempts to express Myself. I do not mind its laughing, for some day I hope to become one with Myself.

What in the world makes me write these things to-night? (and that, by the way, was Me again. Myself knows perfectly well that I can't help it.)

From the diary of Wanda Gag

Time Period 3 (1949–1972)

September 21, [1970]—I woke up even before the alarm went off. It's only five minutes after five and I doubt that anyone else on this block is up, but I am so wide awake I can barely stand it. Frankly, I think I'm scared witless inside about going back to school but in my head I know it's going to be all right because I have Joel and my new super straight friends and they'll help me. Besides I'm much stronger than I used to be. I know I am.

I used to think I would get another diary after you are filled, or even that I would keep a diary or journal through my whole life. But now I don't really think I will. Diaries are great when you're young. In fact, you saved my sanity a hundred, thousand, million times. But I think when a person gets older she should be able to discuss her problems and thoughts with other people, instead of just with another part of herself as you have been to me. Don't you agree? I hope so, for your are my dearest friend and I shall thank you always for sharing my tears and heartaches and my struggles and strifes, and my joys and happinesses. It's all been good in its own special way, I guess.

See ya.

From the diary of a young woman

NOTE: The writer of the 1970 excerpt died of a drug overdose three weeks after writing the last entry in her diary.

Source: Wood and Zurcher 1988, 72, 78–79, 81.

describe the traits associated with the rise of capitalism in the West.

In contrast, diaries from the second period lacked a dominant philosophy like the Protestant ethic and saw self-improvement more as an end in itself than as a means to salvation. These diaries also showed the writers' interests in their own personalities and reflections about feelings, fears, and wishes.

Entries from the later twentieth-century diaries suggest that these writers possessed a casual but intimate awareness of the self. In contrast to nineteenth-century diarists, these individuals did not reflect on the whole of their lives but focused instead on personal experiences, impressions, and their emotions.

The pattern discovered in Wood and Zurcher's analysis—a shift in emphasis from role identities to dispositional identities—clearly shows how individuals' self-perceptions are linked to the specific nature of their own societies.

In another study, Zurcher (1977) used the Twenty Statements Test to study how conceptions of self had changed for college students from the 1960s through the early 1980s. His results showed that students in the 1960s were more likely than students from the other periods to define themselves in terms of role identities rather than dispositional identities.

Return to the answers you provided for the Twenty Statements Test. Use Figure 4.1 to help you classify your responses as either role identities or dispositional identities. In what directions do you think students in the twenty-first century are headed?

Identity Salience

As you review your answers to the Twenty Statements Test, consider one more question: Which of your identities is most important to you? Starting with that answer, rank your remaining self-identities in descending order of importance. Social psychologists have discovered that some identities are central to us, while others are less important and may even change (Rosenberg 1979; Stryker 2002). For example, whereas gender identity is central to who we think we are, a temporary identity such as college roommate is not.

Sheldon Stryker (2002) distinguishes identities by both their relative importance, which he called **identity salience**, and the degree to which people commit themselves to their identities. According to Stryker, identities can be ranked in a hierarchy of salience. Identities located at the top of the hierarchy, such as mother, are important to an individual all of the time, while less salient identities, such as gardener, are important only part of the time.

While *salience* specifies the level of importance attached to an identity in many situations, Stryker proposes that *commitment* emphasizes the value placed on an identity in relation to particular people. So, for example, when Billy Crystal is surrounded by an audience, his identity as a comedian is very important to him. But when he is surrounded by his wife and children, his identity as a family member is important.

Self-Esteem

How would you rate your popularity with other students? What about your intelligence or attractiveness? If you are like most people, you have not only wondered about these kinds of things but also recognize that questions like these tend to make us feel good or bad. Doubts about our own self-worth may nag at us, causing us to seek some kind of reassurance. So it was with the wicked stepmother of Snow White, who frequently stood before her "magic mirror," asking; "Looking-glass upon the wall, who is fairest of us all?" As we learn, the queen's irrational insecurity about her beauty ultimately led to her own self-destruction. The fairy tale teaches us something well recognized by social psychologists today: that feelings of inadequacy can lead to jealousy, hatred, and the loss of loving relationships.

Social psychologists call our feelings of worth **self-esteem**. This concept is so important that for many years social psychologists considered it almost synonymous with the self-concept (Gecas and Burke 1995). Self-esteem is, however, only one part of the self. In contrast to self-identities, which include beliefs and cognitions about the self, self-esteem involves our feelings and is therefore an affective component.

But how does self-esteem develop? And what bearing does it have on our lives? According to Charles Horton Cooley (1864–1929), we find answers to questions about our self-worth reflected in the attitudes and reactions of others toward us. Acting as a "looking-glass," other people provide us with an image of ourselves. Cooley (1902/1970) describes the **looking-glass self** as follows:

As we see our face, figure, and dress in the glass, and are interested in them because they are ours, and pleased or otherwise with them according as they do or do not answer to what we should like them to be; so in imagination we perceive in another's mind some thought of our appearance, manners, aims, deeds, character, friends, and so on, and are variously affected by it. (184)

This process, which occurs in our mind's eye, involves three main elements. First, we imagine how we appear to others. Then we imagine how they judge our appearance. Finally, we experience some kind of emotion, such as pride or mortification. Consider how a high school basketball player might see himself when he wins the game for his team by making an impossible basket in the last second of the game. The first thing he would imagine would be the reaction of the crowd—perhaps their awe as the ball glides through the hoop. Then he would imagine how they judge his performance—"It was extraordinary, he is a star." Finally, as he leaves the arena, he would feel some kind of emotion. He might beam with pride over his accomplishment.

Of course, we can also imagine the same player later at a school dance. Now he might see himself as a nerd in the eyes of the cheerleader he wants to impress. Imagining that she must be laughing on the inside at his awkward attempt to dance, he might now feel like he is going to die of embarrassment. As this suggests, people may view one part of the self positively but another more negatively. A Rhodes scholar who has a great deal of self-confidence in her intellectual abilities might still feel the effects of low self-esteem due to a weight problem.

According to many social psychologists, high self-esteem is associated with positive consequences for individuals, such as success, popularity, and the ability to develop and maintain loving relationships. Rooted in the explanation behind this expectation is the popular idea that we must love ourselves before we can love others. In fact, according to Dion and Dion (1988), people with higher self-esteem experience romantic love more

What does this teenage girl see in the mirror? Cooley used the concept of the looking glass to explain how self-esteem develops.

often and enjoy more satisfying relationships. One of the reasons offered for this finding is the idea that loving others requires self-disclosure—sharing who we are and how we feel with someone else. People with higher self-esteem are more likely to do this.

Social psychologists have found that low self-esteem is associated with negative consequences such as depression, failure, and poor interpersonal relationships. In this case, low self-esteem may actually involve what is known as a **self-fulfilling prophecy** (Merton 1948). Consider the child whose teacher has told him that he is stupid. In response to her expectations, the child develops low self-esteem and expects to do poorly. As a test approaches, the child actually reduces the amount of time spent on studying. He figures, *What difference would effort make if my problem lies in my ability?* As a result, he does in fact fail the test, which in turn simply reinforces his low self-esteem. Morris Rosenberg (1965) developed one of the best instruments for measuring self-esteem. As shown in Box 4.4, Rosenberg's Self-Esteem Scale attempts to measure the extent to which individuals believe themselves to be capable, worthy, and successful.

Self-Efficacy

Suppose that you just failed your midterm in statistics. How would you now view your chances of passing the course? Unlike the student in the previous example, whose low self-esteem contributed to a cycle of failure, you might approach the rest of the semester optimistically, eager to meet the challenge, fully believing that success is under your control. If so, you are a person with high **self-efficacy**.

Congruent with a Western emphasis on values such as mastery, self-reliance, and achievement, people with high self-efficacy think of themselves as competent and effective—as causal factors in what happens to them (Gecas 1989). They are not discouraged by failure. Believing that they will be successful, they tend to put forth greater effort and show greater determination. As a result, they actually enhance the likelihood of their success.

In contrast, people with low self-efficacy tend to undermine their chances of success. By attributing the causes of their failures to factors beyond their control, such as luck, they feel powerless—unable to influence what happens to them. They are quickly discouraged by failure and tend to give up without even trying.

Julian Rotter (1966) called the inclination to attribute the causes of events to either oneself or to the environment **locus of control**. According to his theory, some people believe that they control what happens to them, good or bad.

Because they locate the causes of what happens to them and other people in factors such as ability and effort, Rotter identified them as *internals*. In contrast, other people may believe that the causes of events are controlled by factors outside themselves or others, such as luck, opportunity, or other people. Rotter referred to these kinds of people as *externals* (see Box 4.5).

Early experiences with success and failure shape individuals' beliefs about their self-efficacy. As the primary caretakers, parents initially exert the most influence on the development of self-efficacy in children. Parental responsiveness, such as support and encouragement, expectations for high achievement, and the use of reason as opposed to force in controlling children, are all related to the development of self-efficacy (Gecas 1989).

The effects of early childhood socialization in the development of self-efficacy are particularly evident in the differences between boys and girls. Block (1983) summarized her review of the literature on these differences, as follows:

> The self-images of males, in contrast to those of females, include stronger feelings of being able to control (or to manipulate) the external world. . . . Males describe themselves as more powerful, ambitious, energetic, and as perceiving themselves as having more control over external events than females. . . . The self-descriptions of males, more than those of females, include concepts of agency . . . , efficacy . . . , and instrumentality—all reflections of a self-concept in which potency and mastery are important components. In contrast, females describe themselves as more concerned for others. . . . The self-concepts of females emphasize interpersonal relations and communion . . . and do not emphasize competition and mastery. (1339–1340)

Although these gender differences carry over into adulthood, research shows that they diminish with increasing age (Bengtson, Reedy, and Gordon 1985).

The concept of self-efficacy is central to the theories of both Karl Marx and George Herbert

BOX 4.4	MEASURING SELF-ESTEEM: ROSENBERG'S SCALE

Morris Rosenberg developed one of the best instruments for measuring self-esteem. Rosenberg's Self-Esteem Scale attempts to measure the extent to which individuals believe themselves to be capable, worthy, and successful.

	Strongly Agree	Agree	Disagree	Strongly Disagree
1. I feel that I am a person of worth, at least on an equal basis with others.	☐	☐	☐	☐
2. I feel I have a number of good qualities.	☐	☐	☐	☐
3. All in all, I am inclined to feel that I am a failure.	☐	☐	☐	☐
4. I am able to do things as well as most other people.	☐	☐	☐	☐
5. I feel I do not have much to be proud of.	☐	☐	☐	☐
6. I take a positive attitude toward myself.	☐	☐	☐	☐
7. I wish I could have more respect for myself.	☐	☐	☐	☐
8. At times I think I am no good at all.	☐	☐	☐	☐
9. On the whole, I am satisfied with myself.	☐	☐	☐	☐
10. I certainly feel useless at times.	☐	☐	☐	☐

SCORING

Sum your score for all items as indicated here. The higher your score, the higher your self-esteem.

Items 1, 2, 4, 6, and 9:

Strongly agree	= 4
Agree	= 3
Disagree	= 2
Strongly disagree	= 1

Items 3, 5, 7, 8, and 10:

Strongly agree	= 1
Agree	= 2
Disagree	= 3
Strongly disagree	= 4

Source: Rosenberg 1965, 305–307.

BOX 4.5	ROTTER'S INTERNAL–EXTERNAL LOCUS-OF-CONTROL SCALE

When you try to figure out why things happen to you or to other people, where do you tend to locate the causes of an outcome? Do you believe that you control your own fate, or does luck or opportunity? Julian Rotter developed this scale to differentiate internals from externals. Take the test yourself. You can determine whether you tend toward internal or external control by summing your choices in each column.

I more strongly believe that	or that
Promotions are earned through hard work and persistence.	Making a lot of money is largely a matter of getting the right breaks.
In my experience I have noticed that there is usually a direct connection between how hard I study and the grades I get.	Many times the reactions of teachers seem haphazard to me.
The number of divorces indicates that more and more people are not trying to make their marriages work.	Marriage is largely a gamble.
When I am right I can convince others.	It is silly to think that one can really change another person's basic attitudes.
In our society a man's future earning power is dependent upon his ability.	Getting promoted is really a matter of being a little luckier than the next guy.
If one knows how to deal with people they are really quite easily led.	I have little influence over the way other people behave.
In my case the grades I make are the result of my own efforts; luck has little or nothing to do with it.	Sometimes I feel that I have little to do with the grades I get.
People like me can change the course of world affairs if we make ourselves heard.	It is only wishful thinking to believe that one can really influence what happens in society at large.
I am the master of my fate.	A great deal that happens to me is probably a matter of chance.
Getting along with people is a skill that must be practiced.	It is almost impossible to figure out how to please some people.

Source: Rotter 1971, 42. Reprinted with permission from *Psychology Today* Magazine, Copyright © (1971) Sussex Publishers, Inc.

Mead (Gecas 1989). Arguing that a person's work played a central role in the development of the self, Marx focused on the effects produced by removing a worker's control over his labor and its products. When that control exists outside the individual—for example, in a machine—the worker will experience "alienation," a condition characterized by powerlessness in which a person's self-efficacy is destroyed.

The role of self-efficacy in the development of the self is also evident in Mead's theory of symbolic interaction, which stresses an active and creative self. As the spontaneous and creative part of the self, the I plays an important role in creating the world of an actor. The sense of freedom and initiative, which Mead attached to the I, suggests that actors cause things to happen. They shape their world even as they are shaped by it. This notion is clearly evident in the theories of modern symbolic interactionists, such as Erving Goffman (1959), who describes the way people intentionally manage the impressions they make in everyday life.

SOCIAL COMPARISON THEORY

As the theories presented so far suggest, the way we view ourselves develops largely through our interactions with others. In fact, we would be unable to develop a sense of self without these interactions. They define our roles, provide us with clues about our abilities and skills, and serve as a mirror to view our attractiveness and social skills.

Comparing Ourselves to Others: Behaviors, Abilities, Expertise, and Opinions

Interacting with others also involves social comparison. As described by Leon Festinger (1954), people compare themselves to others out of their need to evaluate their own behavior, abilities, expertise, and opinions. Do I hold "politically correct" opinions? Are my mathematical abilities strong enough for an engineering career? Did I express the appropriate emotion when my girlfriend tripped on the stairs?

According to Festinger, the ease with which we find answers to these kinds of questions varies with the physical evidence available. For example, if you believe that two United States senators are women and forty-eight are men, you can verify the correctness of your belief by consulting a reference book or the Senate's Web site. However, if you hold the opinion that female sports journalists should be allowed in men's locker rooms after a game, it will be more difficult to assess the correctness of your opinion. In this case, physical reality does not provide a measuring stick to evaluate your

opinion. Instead, we must rely on **social reality**, a subjective determination of how other people view the world, including their opinions, beliefs, and attitudes. When others share our view of the world, we feel more confident that our own opinions and beliefs are right.

We do not, however, compare ourselves to just anyone. According to Festinger's **social comparison theory**, we choose people who share similar characteristics. Suppose you want to determine your ability as a figure skater. Unless you are competing in the nationals for a spot on the Olympic team, you know that you don't skate as well as Tara Lipinski or Michelle Kwan. At the same time, you may not think of yourself as a beginner. Perhaps you have even won several titles. Festinger suggests that the people you are most likely to consider in your comparison will be skaters similar to yourself in age, gender, and experience.

When it comes to opinions, we may focus on other relevant characteristics. For instance, consider your opinion about the rights of female sports journalists again. Suppose that after a heated debate on this issue with your close friends, you learn that a Gallup poll was recently conducted about this controversy. According to Festinger, you will seek this poll out to evaluate your opinion against those of other Americans. Let's say that in contrast to your own opinion, you discover that 60 percent of Americans feel that women should be barred from the locker room. You will not necessarily conclude that you hold the wrong opinion—especially if you consider yourself to be liberal in this matter. In fact, Festinger would expect you to take one further step in your comparison—to locate the cross-tabulation showing opinions by political ideology.

Recognizing Our Emotions: Determining How We Feel

Imagine yourself in a forest when a grizzly bear suddenly confronts you. How would you describe your most likely reaction? Would you say that you saw the bear, became terrified, and ran like crazy?

If so, you fit William James's description of our "natural way" of thinking about emotions—that a mental perception of some fact triggers an emotion that in turn prompts a bodily response. "Common-sense says, we lose our fortune, are sorry and weep; we meet a bear, are frightened and run; we are insulted by a rival, are angry and strike" (James 1992, 352).

But James did not accept this sequence as accurate. On the contrary, he proposed that bodily responses follow from the mental perception of a fact and that perceptions of our feelings come last in this sequence. We do not run from the bear because we are frightened; we are frightened because we run. Likewise, "we feel sorry because we cry, angry because we strike, afraid because we tremble" (352). Our behavior becomes a clue for the label we attach to our emotion.

Although you might find this hypothesis difficult to accept, Schacter and Singer (1962) devised an experiment to test one variation of it. Conceptualizing emotion as consisting of two parts—physiological arousal and a cognitive label—they hypothesized that the label we assign to our emotion does not necessarily come from our own behavior but from cues given by other people.

Schacter and Singer led subjects to believe that they were taking part in an experiment on the effect of a "vitamin" called Suproxin. Researchers told subjects that they had been injected with Suproxin when in fact they had received epinephrine, which causes a high state of physiological arousal—an increased heart rate and flushing of the face. One group of subjects was made aware of the drug's effects, but another was not.

Once they had been injected, subjects were then taken to a room where they joined another subject—in reality, a confederate. As they waited for the Suproxin to take effect, the confederate began to behave in one of two ways. In one condition, he acted euphorically, wadding paper up to practice basketball shots in a wastebasket, making and flying paper airplanes, and playing with a hula hoop. In another condition, the confederate acted as if he were angry, ripping the paper up and stomping around the room.

After a while, the researcher returned and asked subjects to complete a questionnaire describing their mood. The results showed that subjects who had been informed about the drug's effects were not influenced by the confederate's behavior. They attributed their physiological arousal to the drug and did not rely on the confederate's behavior to label their emotions. Subjects who had not been informed about the drug's effects, however, were affected by the confederate's behavior. Those who waited with the confederate who acted euphorically reported feelings of happiness, and those who waited with the angry confederate reported feeling angry.

Understanding our emotions can be difficult and confusing. The results of Schacter and Singer's experiment suggest why. Physiological arousal causes people to search for an explanation of what they are feeling. If a reasonable explanation exists, people will accept that. But if one does not exist, people will look for clues in their environment to explain their arousal. As Schacter and Singer's experiment shows, the label we attach to our physiological state can mislead us.

PRESENTATION OF SELF IN EVERYDAY LIFE: IMPRESSION MANAGEMENT

> All the world's a stage,
> And all the men and women merely players.
> —William Shakespeare, *As You Like It*

William Shakespeare stored a brilliant insight into human behavior in these two simple lines. Our everyday lives involve acts, which are based on specific roles and are intricately bound to the roles of fellow players. As a stage, the world is designed to provide us with cues—for what we say and to whom we speak. These are the human interactions that take place every day of our lives in a variety of settings.

How would you define the situation depicted in this photo? Which of Goffman's elements of impression management provide clues?

The Dramaturgical School of Thought: Playing Our Roles

Erving Goffman (1959) borrowed Shakespeare's metaphor to explain the process people use in real life to define a situation so that they themselves will know how to act. Known as the **dramaturgical school of thought**, Goffman's theory proposes that people seek to acquire information about those with whom they interact for the practical purpose of being able to predict their present and future behavior.

For example, imagine that you have been invited to a presidential inaugural ball. If this is your first invitation to the White House, you will probably be very concerned about the impression you make. Let us say that upon your arrival, a man stops you at the door and asks to see your invitation. Based on your assessment of his appearance and his manners, you may conclude that this actor is the doorman, not a senator or foreign dignitary. You quickly comply and proceed through the front door. Once inside, you continue to seek

information about others (their general socioeconomic status, their conceptions of self, and their attitudes toward others). You clearly do not want to mistake the speaker of the House for a waiter. But what clues will tell you whether you are speaking with someone of equal or unequal status with yourself? Again you rely on appearance and manners to determine which roles men and women are playing. According to Goffman, this information will help you predict how these people will behave not only tonight but in the future as well, which you know is important to your career.

As you move through the receiving line toward the president and first lady, you become anxious. How should you address the president? Should you extend your hand or wait for him to do so? What if you mistake the first lady for the president's mother—an irreversible faux pas? Fortunately, the clues are apparent. The stage has been set and the actors have mastered the parts they are supposed to play.

We all want others to see us in certain ways. Goffman called our attempt to control the way we present ourselves to others **impression manage-ment**. And he identified a number of elements that operate in this process.

Elements in Impression Management

As this example suggests, we can rely on a number of clues to help us define a situation and predict how people will act.

Front. Some of the most important clues in a situation are elements of what Goffman calls the *front—setting, appearance,* and *manner.*

The *setting* is the geographical location. It includes furniture, décor, the physical layout, scenery, and any items that we would consider props used for staging performances. Take, for example, a courtroom. This setting consists of the judge's bench located in the front of a room and elevated to a position above all others to indicate his superior status. Directly next to the judge is the witness stand, and along one side of the courtroom a jury box—seats for twelve jurors in two rows of six. Facing the judge's bench are tables for lawyers and their clients. The prosecution faces the judge on the right side of the courtroom; the defense sits to the left. Behind these major players are seats for the audience.

Props also help us define a situation. In a courtroom, these would include the gavel (used to quiet the players when the action gets out of hand); the equipment used by the court stenographer; law books; and, of course, the evidence—perhaps a murder weapon, photographs of the crime scene, bloody shoes worn by the defendant, and possibly correspondence revealing a motive for a murder.

As our inaugural ball example showed, the appearance of others helps us determine their roles and shapes our own behavior accordingly. *Appearance* constitutes part of what Goffman calls the *personal front* and includes personal items belonging to particular actors. This would include insignia of office or rank and clothing. In our courtroom example, addressing the judge as "your honor," a title befitting his position, defines his status as one deserving deference and social distance. And his attire, a black robe, clearly distinguishes him from other actors in the courtroom. Similarly, a bailiff's uniform, badge, and gun signify his role as an officer of the court with the authority to enforce the law if necessary.

Manner, which is also part of personal front, refers to an actor's disposition or style of performance. An arrogant defense lawyer may try to give the impression that his client has been wrongfully accused of a crime. And he might try to control how the jury perceives his client by aggressively protesting remarks made by the prosecution. The judge, however, may respond by warning the attorney that he will be held in contempt of the court if he does not obey the judge's rulings. The attorney may then take on an apologetic manner, signaling a retreat and willingness to comply with the judge's requests.

Perhaps the most important performance in any courtroom is that given by the defendant. In trying to manage the impression he gives to jurors, he will most likely cut his hair short and appear clean-shaven to avoid a sinister look. In addition, he will probably wear a pressed suit, clean shirt, and tie—not gold chains, jeans, and a leather jacket. He will, moreover, sit quietly and attentively next to his lawyer, assume an innocent expression, and appear harmless.

Regions. The courtroom represents what Goffman calls the *front region,* or the place where the performance is given. The *back region* or *backstage* is, in contrast, the place where the performer can relax, drop his front, and abandon the lines of his script. Backstage (behind bars), a defendant may step out of character and reveal his true disposition as a cold-blooded murderer, cursing and making threats against his victim's family. Similarly, a judge—once in his own quarters behind a closed door—might express anger toward the behavior of attorneys, calling them arrogant and contentious. As these examples suggest, the back region is a place "where the impression fostered by the performance is knowingly contradicted as a matter of course" (Goffman 1959, 112).

Goffman (1959) offered a number of examples to illustrate the distinction between front region and back region. One of these includes the performances given at a funeral home.

> If the bereaved are to be given the illusion that the dead one is really in a deep tranquil sleep, then the undertaker must be able to keep the bereaved from the workroom where the corpses are drained, stuffed, and painted in preparation for their final performance. (114)

This particular example suggests that maintaining boundaries between the front region and back region is a relatively simple matter. But that may not be the case, as Goffman's example of radio and television broadcasting work shows.

> In these situations, back region tends to be defined as all places where the camera is not focused at the moment or all places out of range of "live" microphones. Thus an announcer may hold the sponsor's product up at arm's length in front of the camera while he holds his nose with his other hand, his face being out of the picture, as a way of joking with his teammates. Professionals, of course, tell many exemplary tales of how persons who thought they were backstage were in fact on the air and how this backstage conduct discredited the definition of the situation being maintained on air. (119)

Gaffes, Boners, and Faux Pas. One such incident, which occurred in the final hours of ABC's coverage of the 1996 presidential election, became national news for over a week. Thinking that the cameras and microphones had been turned off, David Brinkley committed a nationally broadcast faux pas when he expressed his true feelings about President Clinton. In criticizing the president's acceptance speech, Brinkley proclaimed that Americans could expect four more years of "goddamned nonsense" from Clinton, who did not have a "creative bone in his body."

Brinkley's colleagues, realizing that they were actually still on the air, looked horrified. He had made a thoughtless remark that served to destroy his own team's image—what Goffman called a *gaffe* or *boner*. To make matters worse, Clinton was scheduled to appear on ABC the following Sunday in a special interview with Brinkley to commemorate the commentator's retirement from broadcast news. Coming at the end of an otherwise stellar career as a dignified and impartial journalist, Brinkley's remark garnered much media attention. How could he repair the damage he had done?

Brinkley made a convincing apology to President Clinton at the outset of the Sunday interview:

> Now, before we begin, I'm reminded of something I wrote years ago. It may be impossible to be objective, I said, but we must always be fair. Well, after a long day, election day, and seven hours on the set, what I said at the end of our election night coverage was both impolite and unfair, and I'm sorry. I regret it.

Allowing Brinkley to save face, President Clinton nodded, smiled, and then said:

> Well, thank you. Let me just say I accept that. I've said a lot of things myself late at night when I was tired, and you had really been through a rough day. And I always believe you have to judge people on their whole work, and if you get judged on your whole work, you come out way ahead. And besides that, one person loved it. The vice president was very happy when you said I was boring.

By allowing Brinkley to save face, President Clinton was perceived as the winner. Goffman would say that he "saved the show."

In terms of understanding the focus of this chapter—the concept of the self—Clinton did something else rather remarkable. As his comments suggest, he put himself in Brinkley's shoes (took the role of the other) to gain an understanding of the journalist's perspective, attitudes, and behaviors.

SUMMARY

1. William James was the first American to write about the concept of the self. His concept included an outward and inward aspect of the self, which he called the *I* and the *Me*, respectively.

2. George Herbert Mead developed the theory of symbolic interaction. According to Mead, the development of the self rests on an individual's ability to take roles. His theory proposes that the self is formed in three stages—the preparatory stage, the play stage, and the game stage.

3. Manford Kuhn developed an instrument called the Twenty Statements Test to measure an individual's self-concept. This instrument reveals two broad categories of our self-identities: role identities and dispositional identities.

4. Self-esteem involves feelings of worth. Charles Horton Cooley provided the widely accepted concept of the looking-glass self. Self-efficacy refers to a person's sense of competence. It is influenced by an individual's beliefs about the causes of his or her own successes or failures.

5. Leon Festinger claimed that social interaction involves comparisons intended to evaluate our own behaviors, abilities, expertise, and opinions. We tend to compare ourselves to people similar to ourselves.

6. Determining our feelings can be difficult and confusing. William James suggested that our behavior provides a clue for the label that we attach to our emotional reactions. Research shows that people may also look for clues in the environment.

7. Goffman's dramaturgical school of thought is based on the idea that human interaction involves social roles that help us define how we ought to act in certain situations. Elements that serve as important clues for defining a situation include the setting, appearance, and manner. Goffman also distinguishes the front region, where a performance is given, from the back region, where actors can abandon their scripts.

KEY TERMS

Me   101

I   101

Preparatory stage   102

Play stage   103

Significant others   104

Game stage   104

Generalized other   105

Multiple selves   106

Multiple personality   106

Self-concept   106

Twenty Statements Test   107

Self-identities   107

Role identities   107

Dispositional identities   107

Protestant ethic   108

Identity salience   110

Self-esteem   110

Looking-glass self   110

Self-fulfilling prophecy   111

Self-efficacy   112

Locus of control   112

Social reality   115

Social comparison theory   115

Dramaturgical school of thought   117

Impression management   118

CRITICAL REVIEW QUESTIONS

1. In what way does George Herbert Mead's theory of symbolic interaction resemble Lev Vygotsky's sociocultural theory, discussed in Chapter 2?

2. In the United States, individuality and freedom are important values. Other societies restrict personal freedom and place greater value on the group rather than the individual. How would the restriction on personal freedom and a deemphasis of individuality influence how people in other societies might respond to the Twenty Statements Test?

3. Suppose you are invited to interview for two jobs. One of them is with a top-ten advertising agency in New York. The other is with an investment bank on Wall Street. How could you use Goffman's theory of impression management to prepare for these two interviews?

FIVE

Person Perception

In April 1996, after the longest and most expensive manhunt in U.S. history, the FBI descended on a tiny, isolated mountain cabin outside of Lincoln, Montana, to arrest a man they believed to be a serial killer—the notorious "Unabomber." If their suspicions were correct, they would finally end a madman's reign of terror, which had killed three innocent victims and maimed twenty-eight. If the feds were wrong, they risked harsh public judgment for a sloppy investigation that might be perceived as having led to the false arrest of an eccentric, middle-aged hippie seeking a utopian life in the secluded Montana wilderness.

For eighteen years, an eighty-man task force composed of agents from the Federal Bureau of Investigation; the Bureau of Alcohol, Tobacco and Firearms; and the United States Postal Service had been gathering clues, which they hoped would ultimately identify and stop the Unabomber (so named because the bomber's original targets were universities and airlines). The first clue to his identity came in November 1979 after a bomb exploded aboard American Airlines Flight 444 out of Chicago. Based on an examination of the debris, investigators concluded that the triggering device was an altimeter, set to explode when the cabin pressure reached a certain point.

Examining evidence recovered from earlier bombings on college campuses in the Chicago area, investigators discovered a possible pattern that could point to the identity of the bomber—the use of wooden boxes and materials commonly found in households, including sink traps, pipes, lamp cords, furniture parts, recycled screws, and match heads. This ingenious use of materials, which had at first led federal investigators to dub their suspect the "junkyard bomber," caused them to conclude that although the terrorist was not an explosives expert, he was clever, intelligent, and sophisticated.

By 1985, the FBI had begun to build a behavioral profile. After a bomb exploded in a computer room at the University of California at Berkeley, blowing off the fingers of an aspiring astronaut and engineering graduate student, the Unabomber sent a letter to the *San Francisco Examiner* claiming responsibility and identifying himself as a member of a terrorist group called the Freedom Club (FC). A clearer picture began to emerge: he was anticommunist, antileftist, antiscience, and antitechnology. From this point in time, investigators would find the initials FC engraved in virtually all his bombs.

Using a sophisticated computer system borrowed from the Pentagon, federal investigators analyzed school lists, driver's license registries, and records of people who had checked certain books out of libraries in California and the Midwest, searching for a person who would match certain incriminating characteristics. Based on their analysis, they expected the Unabomber to be an intelligent, well-educated, middle-aged Caucasian—an ideal neighbor who kept to himself, someone who would not be missed for weeks at a time by anyone.

On April 3, 1996, as they prepared to make their move on a crude cabin in the Montana wilderness, and under the pressure of CBS News, which threatened to break the story, the federal agents were still not absolutely certain they had their man. But their confidence had recently been bolstered by the fears of someone who probably knew their suspect better than anyone else—his own brother, David Kaczynski.

In August 1995, in response to the Unabomber's threat to blow up an American airliner, the *Washington Post* and the *New York Times* published part of the madman's "manifesto." They hoped that a reader would recognize a clue to the man's identity. David Kaczynski became troubled after reading the manifesto; it resembled the angry rantings of his brother, Ted. In fact, just a few months earlier, while helping his mother move out of her house in Chicago, he had discovered hundreds of angry letters written by his brother. The similarity was convincing enough for him to contact the FBI.

What the feds found behind Ted Kaczynski's cabin door on April 3, 1996, amounted to piles of incriminating evidence: ten binders full of data, meticulous notes

and diagrams of bombs; logs of experiments and test results, books on how to make bombs, chemicals used to make bombs, junkyard spare parts similar to the kind used in previous bombings, and a typewriter whose font matched that of the manifesto sent to the *New York Times* and *Washington Post.*

Why had it taken federal agents so long to make an arrest in this case? The answer points to the traits of the criminal himself. They had not been dealing with a typical suspect. This man was far less likely than most criminals to make a mistake. As a child, Ted Kaczynski was a math and science whiz. By skipping one grade in elementary school and his junior year in high school, he was able to enter Harvard at the age of 16. He went on to the University of Michigan to receive both his M.A. and Ph.D. degrees in mathematics, being remembered not only for meticulous and original work but also for his ability to solve math problems that had stumped his own professors. He even won a prize for his doctoral dissertation. These achievements landed him a faculty position at Berkeley, in the most prestigious mathematics department in the nation.

Kaczynski's ability to elude authorities can be attributed to his genius. There was nothing predictable about the pattern of traits he possessed, and that threw the feds off. For example, although he was a loner, a shy recluse, Kaczynski craved attention and recognition. Neighbors in Montana claimed that he never talked much about himself. They remembered him as a hermit, aloof and private, an eccentric fellow dressed in black or sometimes fatigues, who pedaled into town on a one-speed bicycle concocted out of spare parts. Yet on the day of his arrest, journalists saw another man. Unlike most criminals, who cover their faces as they take the "perp walk," Kaczynski looked straight into the cameras. In fact, he displayed an unapologetic arrogance, which led one journalist to remark that he had "the smile of the smartest kid in the class" (Thomas et al., *Newsweek*, 1996, 36).

He was also, despite his early academic achievements, a dropout of sorts, an underachiever for his talents, whose bombings appeared to be triggered by a strange need to compete with other terrorists. That is why, in the aftermath of the 1993 bombing of the World Trade Center in New York City by Islamic fundamentalists, the Unabomber struck again, targeting a geneticist in California and a scientist at Yale. And within five days of the bombing of a federal building in Oklahoma City, the president of the California Forestry Association received a deadly package.

One of the most curious ironies to be revealed about Kaczynski was his inability to fix anything mechanical. One neighbor reported that after his old pickup truck broke down, Kaczynski just let it sit until someone bought it from him. The new owner fixed the truck with a part that cost only $25.

What ultimately led to his capture was not something found in the FBI's vast computer system but something found in Ted Kaczynski's personality traits—his pride, his need to compete and to be recognized. It was the need to have his 35,000-word diatribe against industrial society published in the nation's two most prestigious newspapers that ultimately revealed his identity.

Many portraits have been painted of Ted Kaczynski. The people in Lincoln, Montana, saw a "harmless hermit on the hill." To his professors, he was a brilliant mathematician who had given up a promising career. His mother and his teachers saw him as a gifted child. But to federal authorities, he was the most wanted serial killer in American history.

FIGURE 5.1

Old Hag or Young Woman?

Source: Archives of the History of American Psychology—The University of Akron.

I n our everyday lives, we make judgments about the people around us. We seek to know and understand them. Are they kind, cruel, funny, or smart? Are they pretending to be other than they really are? We do not know. Since we are not privy to their thoughts, motivations, and feelings, we must rely on what we see—their behaviors—to infer what they are really like. As the case of the Unabomber shows, our perception of someone may differ dramatically from that of others. Try this test on yourself and a friend: Who do you see in Figure 5.1?

THE PROCESS OF ATTRIBUTION

The process by which we come to understand someone else is known as **attribution**. It involves a judgment about the factors that have caused a particular outcome. As we shall see, these causes may be either within a person (internal) or in the environment (external).

Theories attempting to explain the process of attribution can be traced back to the early work of Fritz Heider (1958). With an interest in interpersonal relations, he recognized that people make attributions about the causes of others' behavior for a number of interrelated reasons. First, such attributions help us make sense of the world by explaining the causes and effects associated with various relationships between people and the environment. This in turn helps us predict how people will behave in the future. Without this ability, our interactions with others would be filled with conflict, frustration, and surprise. But by making attributions, we gain an understanding of the world and feel at ease and in control of our environment.

Involving what Heider called "commonsense psychology," people make sense of what they observe by linking transient and changing behavior to dispositional properties. These relatively unchanging structures and processes, which underlie phenomena, make the world seem more stable, predictable, and controllable.

Consider a dispositional property such as ability. If a student memorizes spelling words quickly, solves math problems with ease, and reads above her grade level, her teacher might infer that she is intelligent. Learning and solving problems—behaviors that vary—are understood better when we link them to the more permanent property that we call intelligence. Based on this, we might feel confident in predicting that the bright student will succeed in college one day.

Heider used the term *commonsense psychology* to refer to the way we form ideas about other people and social situations in everyday life. He did not believe that it could replace scientific methods but suggested that it did provide insight into human behavior. Consider the following quotation, which Heider used to illustrate the commonsense psychology embodied in fables, novels, and other literary forms:

> Things are seldom what they seem.
> Skim milk masquerades as cream.
> (W. S. Gilbert, *H.M.S. Pinafore*)

Though Heider would not replace scientific methods with rhymes and stories, he did believe that they often contained truths that could be used to develop hunches and concepts (see Box 5.1).

We will examine three views of the attribution process in this chapter: Jones and Davis's theory of correspondent inferences, Kelley's model of causal attribution, and Weiner and colleagues' model of attributions of success and failure. Each of these models approaches the process of attribution in a distinct way, yet they all seek to address one question: How do we judge what someone is really like on the basis of the person's behavior?

BOX 5.1   COMMONSENSE PSYCHOLOGY EMBODIED IN LITERATURE

Appearances to the mind are of four kinds:
Things either are what they appear to be;
Or they neither are, nor appear to be; or
They are, and do not appear to be; or they
Are not, and yet appear to be. Rightly to aim
In all these cases is the wise man's task.
Epictetus, *Discourses*, 1.27.1

O what a goodly outside falsehood hath!
William Shakespeare, *The Merchant of Venice*, 1.3.103

Was ever book containing such vile matter
So fairly bound? O, that deceit should dwell
In such a gorgeous palace!
William Shakespeare, *Romeo and Juliet*, 3.2.183

There is no trusting to appearances.
Richard Sheridan, *The School for Scandal*, 5.2

Don't rely too much on labels,
For too often they are fables.
Charles Spurgeon, *Salt-Cellars*

I have often found persons of handsome appearance to be
The worst, and those of evil appearance to be the best.
Phaedrus, *Fables*, 3.46.

 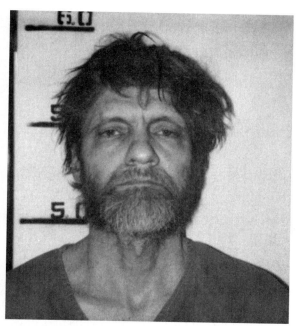

People can fool us. As a young man, Ted Kaczynski appeared to be a gifted student incapable of posing a threat to society. Ultimately, Kaczynski was recognized as the Unabomber—public enemy number one.

JONES AND DAVIS'S THEORY OF CORRESPONDENT INFERENCES

Jones and Davis's theory of **correspondent inferences** (1965) focuses on the way observers use different kinds of information to draw conclusions about the specific traits or dispositions of an actor. In attributing traits to an actor, observers begin by considering the effects that a particular action produces. Their analysis of these effects also takes into account alternative courses of action that an actor might take, as well as an assessment of their behavioral expectations for this particular actor.

Let us return to the case of the Unabomber to illustrate how observers might consider different pieces of information in making attributions about the disposition of an actor. For the feds, as well as the publishers of the *New York Times* and the *Washington Post*, the Unabomber's threat to blow up an American airliner created a life-or-death dilemma. Was this just a threat? Was this someone who delighted in manipulating the press—someone who liked to see others sweat? Or was this threat serious? To what extent did it correspond to an underlying violent disposition?

What would they consider as they attempted to answer these questions? According to Jones and Davis, they would begin by noting the effects produced by sending a threatening letter to the press (see Figure 5.2). The newspapers certainly noted a number of effects. One was to produce high anxiety and terror over the possibility that hundreds of innocent lives could be lost. Another was to draw attention to the Unabomber's concerns about the environment. A third was that the Unabomber himself would receive a lot of attention.

In assessing these effects, observers would also consider the alternative actions that the

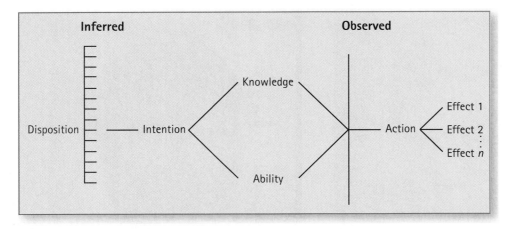

FIGURE 5.2

How Correspondent Inferences Are Made

Source: Jones and Davis 1965, 222.

Unabomber could have taken to express his grievances and concerns. For example, he could have worked through the political system or an environmental group to bring about the changes he sought. That action would have produced some effects common to the first course of action. For example, this would have drawn public attention to environmental problems associated with industrialization. Another common effect would have been that he could have received personal recognition for his efforts to solve a social problem.

In comparing the alternative actions open to the Unabomber, one noncommon effect stands out—the creation of fear and terror in the public. This unique effect provides us with a clue to the Unabomber's motivation for acting in a certain way. This, in turn, allows us to draw an inference about his underlying disposition. In this case, we could conclude that the Unabomber was a terrorist.

Assessing the Reliability of Correspondent Inferences

When we draw an inference about a person's disposition, based on the person's behavior, two factors can help us determine how confident we

should be in our assessment: the number of **noncommon effects** produced by an actor's behavior and the **social desirability** of the behavior itself. To illustrate how noncommon effects influence confidence, let us consider how a high school senior made her final decision about which college she would attend. Carla, a talented violinist who lives on the West Coast, was accepted by two prestigious universities to study music. One school was located in rural Pennsylvania, the other in New York City. She considered both schools seriously, noting that her decision to attend each would produce several effects (see Figure 5.3). In the end, she decided to attend the university located in New York.

The effects produced by Carla's decision to pursue her studies in New York included having her entire college education paid in full by a scholarship, earning a degree from one of the most prestigious music departments in the nation, and living in a major metropolitan area that offers unlimited cultural activities. Accepting the invitation to attend the college in Pennsylvania would have produced the effects of having her entire college education paid in full by a scholarship, earning a degree from one of the most prestigious music

FIGURE 5.3

Effects of Carla's Decision on Where to Study Music

departments in the nation, and living on a beautiful campus located in a rural area.

Based on a comparison of these effects, what can we confidently conclude about Carla? First, notice that earning a degree in music from a prestigious department and having a scholarship to cover all of her expenses are common to both universities. These facts, therefore, do not help us infer anything about her. But the third effect of her decision is noncommon. Living in a big city would give her the opportunity to experience rich cultural diversity. We can therefore conclude with confidence that Carla is a person who enjoys an urban lifestyle.

However, what if we learn that Carla's boyfriend, Mike, will also be attending the university in New York? This constitutes an additional noncommon effect, making it more difficult to know whether her decision was motivated by her preference for an urban lifestyle or her affection for Mike. As this example shows, the fewer noncommon effects of an action, the more confidence we have in our correspondent inferences.

Expectations about an actor's behavior also influence our perceptions. According to Jones and McGillis (1976), observers tend to pay little attention to behaviors that conform to their expectations and tend to focus instead on behaviors that deviate from usual patterns. Observers' expectations are shaped in two ways—either by cultural norms (social desirability) or by the categories to which people are assigned (**category-based expectations**).

Let us assume that all we knew about Ted Kaczynski was that he lived in Montana, checked books out of the library periodically, and rode a bicycle. What would we infer about him based on this information? As his neighbors might say, not much. Reading books is good for your mind; exercising is good for your health. Both are socially desirable.

Now imagine instead that we were privy to the information federal investigators had compiled and that we had access to his cabin immediately after his arrest. Surrounded by books on how to make bombs, the kind of "junkyard" spare parts that became the fingerprint of the Unabomber, and a typewriter whose font matched that of the Unabomber's manifesto, we might feel fully confident that Ted Kaczynski was a terrorist. Not only was this evidence of socially undesirable behavior, but he did not fit our category-based expectations of a Harvard graduate or former college professor.

These examples show how we can use both noncommon effects and social desirability to assess our confidence in a correspondent inference. These two factors illustrate what Harold H. Kelley (1967) has called the **discounting principle**, which he explains as follows: "The role of a given cause in producing a given effect is discounted if other plausible causes are also present" (8). As this suggests, noncommon effects and social desirability provide other plausible causes that can discount another particular cause.

KELLEY'S MODEL OF CAUSAL ATTRIBUTION

The Unabomber case shows that drawing inferences about someone's underlying disposition based on observations of his behavior might be more difficult than we think. Kaczynski was able to elude the feds for eighteen years. Whether he intended to mislead or deceive people is debatable. But one thing is clear—it played a role in making it tough to infer who he really was.

Another factor complicates the task of person perception. We may be led to draw false conclusions about someone because external factors can also cause people to behave in certain ways. Suppose that you were chosen as a juror for an armed bank robbery case. Witnesses testify that on the day of the robbery, four young women and a man filed through the front door of the bank, pulled out carbines from underneath their coats, and demanded that everyone get on the floor.

The 66-year-old guard on duty that day swears under oath that the young woman on trial knew what she was doing. According to his testimony, she had a gun, was not scared, and looked like she was ready to use it. Videotape from the bank's surveillance camera, which shows a hostile young woman shouting obscenity-laced threats, confirms the guard's observations. So does the testimony of the bank manager, who could see the lobby from his upstairs office. As it turns out, three people were shot in this robbery and left bleeding on the sidewalk outside the bank.

What would you conclude about the woman whose fate now lies in your hands? Based on what you had observed, you might conclude that she was a hardened criminal, greedy for money, and willing to commit an illegal act as a means to acquiring it. But later in the trial, her attorney reveals that she is Patty Hearst, the daughter of a millionaire and heiress to a fortune, who was kidnapped from her apartment in Berkeley, California, by the terrorist group who had robbed this bank. Now how would you interpret her behavior? Had the terrorists forced her to commit armed robbery? Or did her motivation lie within her?

This controversial case illustrates an important principle. If a person's behavior is caused by external factors, that behavior cannot be used to determine underlying traits or motivations. As it turned out, deciding whether Patty Hearst's behavior was the result of internal or external factors was not so simple.

How exactly do we decide whether an action was caused by internal or external factors?

According to Harold Kelley (1967, 1971), we must consider three things. First, we consider the **distinctiveness** of an entity. For example, does a person react to all entities or stimuli in a particular way, or is his reaction distinctive to one particular entity? Second, we consider **consensus**. How do other people respond to this entity? Do they all respond like the actor? Or is he the only one responding in a certain way? Third, we consider **consistency**. To what extent does a person respond to an entity in the same way over time and on different occasions? Is his behavior consistent?

To illustrate Kelley's model, consider the following example. Suppose that you and your college roommates decided to hire a band to play at a party to celebrate your graduation. You all agreed to split the cost equally. After the party, you rounded up your roommates for the money. Everyone paid up except Bob. He said he was disappointed in the band's performance and refused to pay. What are you likely to conclude? Was his behavior due to internal or external causes? Is Bob cheap or perhaps just simply hard to please? Or was the music really bad?

Let us consider Kelley's rules. Suppose that everyone else loved the music (consensus is low); from past experience with Bob, you know that he has refused to pay for this band before (consistency is high); and you have seen Bob refuse to pay for other forms of group activities (distinctiveness is low). Weighing these factors together, Kelley's theory suggests that you would attribute Bob's behavior to an internal cause—he is cheap or hard to please (see Figure 5.4).

But what if the outcome had been different? What if most of your roommates agreed that the band was lousy (consensus is high), Bob has refused to pay for this band before (consistency is high), and you have not seen Bob refuse to pay for other group activities before. Under these circumstances, Kelley would expect you to attribute Bob's behavior to external causes. In this case, the band really was bad.

ATTRIBUTIONS OF SUCCESS AND FAILURE

Minutes after Orel Hershiser won the fifth and final game of the 1988 World Series, Tony La Russa was asked to explain the defeat of his Athletics. In five games the Dodgers' pitchers had held the Athletics to 2 home runs, 5 extra-base hits, 11 runs and a team batting average of .177. La Russa answered: "It's been going on in baseball for 100 years. When pitchers make quality pitches, batters do not make good contact." Not far from where La Russa spoke an Oakland fan spotted Hershiser walking through the bowels of the stadium. The fan shouted: "You were lucky, Hershiser." Hershiser, without breaking stride, replied: "Oh yeah? Grab a bat, kid." Then, after a pause, he smiled. (Will 1990, 77)

As this sports anecdote shows, people may differ in their perceptions about the causes of success or failure. One sports fan attributed the Dodgers' success to Oral Hershiser's ability, while another claimed he was just lucky. These are just two of the four possible attributions that Bernard Weiner and his colleagues (1971) have proposed people make to explain success and failure. Effort and task difficulty are the other two possibilities.

According to Weiner and his colleagues, observers make attributions of success or failure in two steps. First, they determine whether the cause was internal or external (locus of control). Then they decide whether the behavior was stable or unstable (stability). Using this two-step process, observers classify the cause of a success or failure as ability, effort, task difficulty, or luck (see Figure 5.5).

Using this model, let us see how a professor might view the performance of a student who received an A on a multiple-choice exam. She could conclude that the student received an A because he is intelligent (a stable, internal attribution). Or she could decide that the exam was easy (a stable, external attribution). Not only could this student get A's on another exam similar to this one, but anyone could get an A. It is an easy task.

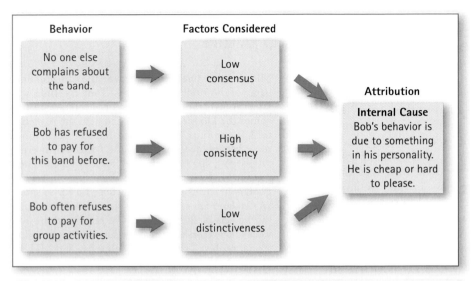

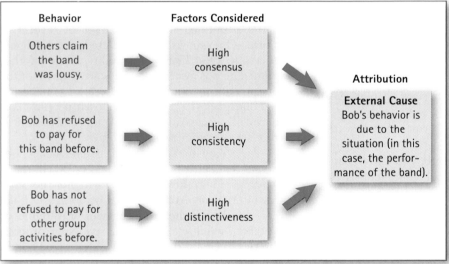

FIGURE 5.4

Making Attributions according to Kelley's Model of Causal Attribution

It is possible, however, that the student did well on this exam because he put forth a lot of effort (an unstable, internal attribution). In this case, the professor would not expect the student to score that well repeatedly. It was just his extraordinary effort this time.

Finally, the professor might believe that the student was just lucky (an unstable, external

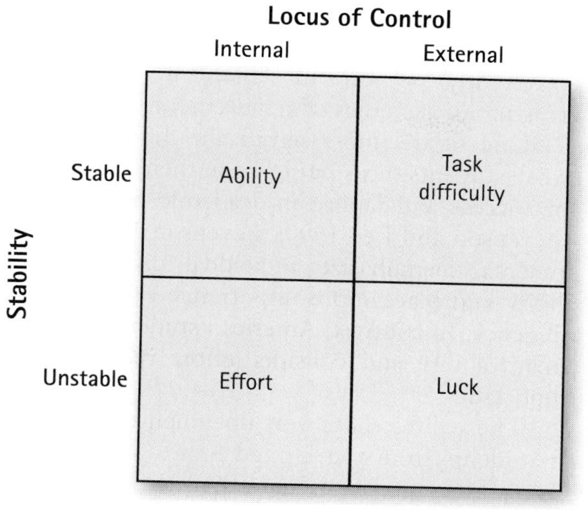

Locus of Control

FIGURE 5.5

Classification Scheme for Attributions of Success and Failure

Source: Weiner 1986, 46.

attribution). Although it is possible to guess well enough to get an A on a multiple-choice exam, it is unlikely that he will do it again.

As depicted in Figure 5.5, this model consists of two dimensions—locus of control (internal-external) and stability (stable-unstable). Weiner (1986) extended this model to contain yet a third dimension, which he called *controllability*. In contrast to the conept of stability, which refers to whether a cause is a relatively permanent feature of the external environment or of the internal dispositions of a person, controllability refers to the extent to which a cause is under a person's control.

Consider effort, for example. According to Weiner, this is an internal, unstable cause of a particular outcome. It is also controllable. So in the case of academic achievement, a student can decide to exert a great deal of effort or none at all. In contrast, ability—an internal, stable cause—is recognized as uncontrollable. We are born with certain abilities or talents and cannot change that.

Learned Helplessness

Although some critics question the validity of Weiner's three dimensional model, it does help us

understand everyday behavior and can even be useful in helping people overcome negative attitudes, which have been shaped by the experience of failure. Dweck (1975), for example, used the logic of this model to help children whose experience with failure led them to give up completely and adopt a defeatist attitude—a phenomenon called **learned helplessness** (Seligman 1975). She argued that a child's expectation for failure was rooted in his belief that it was due to his own lack of ability—something that was permanent, not under his control, and not going to change. By training children to attribute their failures to an unstable but controllable factor, such as effort, Dweck believed she could change their pessimistic attitudes.

In an experiment designed to test her hypothesis, Dweck proved to be correct. Children in this study were divided into two groups. In one condition, children were trained to reattribute the causes of their failure to effort, while children in another condition experienced only success. In the reattribution condition, children were given math problems to solve. After they completed the task, they were told that some of their answers were wrong but that it was due to their lack of effort. In the other condition, children were asked to solve the same math problems, but they were never led to believe that they had failed. After five weeks of training, the results showed that only children in the reattribution condition were prepared to deal with later failures without giving up.

Dweck's research raises a question about the degree to which children's perceptions of success and failure can affect their academic performance. In fact, international studies of academic performance suggest that these perceptions can exert a significant effect on children's attitudes toward school and learning (Stevenson and Lee 1990; Stevenson 1992; Stevenson and Stigler 1992).

Cultural Differences in Attributions of Success and Failure

Achievement consists of never giving up. . . . If there is no dark and dogged will, there will be no shining accomplishment; if there is no dull and determined effort, there will be no brilliant achievement.
Hsun Tzu, Chinese philosopher

In 1983, a blue-ribbon commission that had studied the American educational system declared us "a nation at risk." In response to this serious concern, and with a particular focus on the poor performance of American students on tests of mathematics

and science, researchers directed their attention to Asia, asking why Chinese and Japanese students consistently outperform American students on cross-national studies of achievement.

One of the most significant differences between students turns out to lie in their attributions for success and failure in academic performance (Stevenson and Lee 1990; Stevenson 1992). Asian students deemphasize individual differences in ability and place more importance on effort and diligence. In contrast, American students focus on innate ability and consider effort relatively less important.

These differences were documented in a study of students from the United States, Taiwan, and Japan (Stevenson and Lee 1990). In one part of this study, researchers asked fifth graders to rate their agreement with a number of statements, which assessed the influence of effort and ability in their academic performance (see Box 5.2). The results showed that students in all three cultures believed that children could do something about poor performance in reading and mathematics. However, American students showed the least agreement with the statement that children have the same ability in reading and mathematics and that the best student always works harder. In addition, American students also showed the strongest agreement with the statement that tests can show the child's natural ability.

BOX 5.2   ATTRIBUTIONS TO ACADEMIC ACHIEVEMENT

American and Asian students were asked, "To what extent do you agree with the following statements?" and told to respond to each using a 7-point scale.

1. If a person your age doesn't do well in math, there is probably nothing that person can do about it.
2. If a person your age doesn't do well in language arts, there is probably nothing that person can do about it.
3. Do you agree that everybody in your class has about the same ability in math?

4. Do you agree that everybody in your class has about the same amount of ability in language arts?
5. The best student in the class always works harder than the other students.
6. The tests you take can show how much or how little natural ability you have.
7. The best student in the class is always brighter than the other students.

Source: Stevenson and Lee 1990, 65.

Stevenson and Lee also examined mothers' beliefs about these factors. In one method, they asked mothers to rank four factors—effort, natural ability, difficulty of schoolwork, and luck or chance—in terms of their importance to academic performance. Then they were asked to assign points to the ranked factors to show the relative importance of each. The results showed that the emphasis given to effort relative to ability was much higher among Japanese and Chinese mothers than among American mothers.

In another assessment, mothers were asked to rate their agreement to a number of statements related to effort and ability. These findings indicated that Japanese mothers were most apt to agree that children have the same amount of ability in reading and mathematics. American mothers, in contrast, were most likely to agree that children were born with these abilities.

Finally, mothers were asked to rate a number of factors that could influence a child's school performance: studying hard, intelligence, study habits, a good teacher, home environment, parental assistance, the curriculum, and luck. The results showed that American mothers gave significantly lower ratings to effort than to study habits, a good teacher, home environment, and curriculum (see Figure 5.6, page 136). In contrast, for both Japanese and Chinese mothers, the only factor considered to be more important than effort was having a good teacher.

Interpreting their results from a cultural perspective, Stevenson and Lee argue that the attitudes of American and Asian students are shaped by the pervasive notions of their respective societies. Confucian beliefs, which stress the importance of effort and diligence and minimize the role of ability, encourage Asian students to persist in the face of failure or discouragement. The Western emphasis on individuality produces a different effect in American students. Shaped by a society that rewards people for their talents, they are far more likely to emphasize the innate ability responsible for people's achievements.

The implications of these conclusions are clear and point to solutions for improving the achievements of American students. If parents and teachers believe that effort can make a difference in a child's progress, they themselves will exert more effort to help the child. In addition, these expectations will transfer to the child, who will become more diligent in his work.

In the foregoing, we have examined how causal attributions influence our attitudes and behaviors. Consider, finally, the way they influence our feelings. Imagine that all of a sudden, the car next to you veers into your lane. The side of your car is smashed, and you will miss your plane to New York. According to Weiner (1986), the way you feel about this will depend on your causal attribution. If you learn that the driver of the car was talking on his cell phone and not paying attention to what he was doing, you will probably get angry. If you learn, however, that the driver veered to avoid hitting a child on a bicycle, you will probably be happy to learn that the child is safe.

BIASES IN THE ATTRIBUTION PROCESS

How closely do your perceptions reflect reality? Would you say that you process information objectively? The drawings in Figure 5.7 might reveal something that you don't know about the way you see things. For example, how many arms do you see in drawing (a)? Which portion of the vertical line is longer in (b)? Can you tell which lines are parallel in (c)? (*Answers:* When you focus on the center of drawing (a), it looks like the letter "E," but when you focus on the right side of the drawing, you see four arms. Surprisingly, the two lines in (b) are the same length. The arrows in the figure cause us to see the lower portion as longer than the top portion. All of the lines in (c) are parallel. The short lines crossing the longer ones cause the distortion in perception.)

As this exercise demonstrates, our perceptions are susceptible to errors. Although attribution theorists do lead us to believe that people are "naive scientists" rationally weighing information in an objective fashion, in fact, we are all susceptible to a

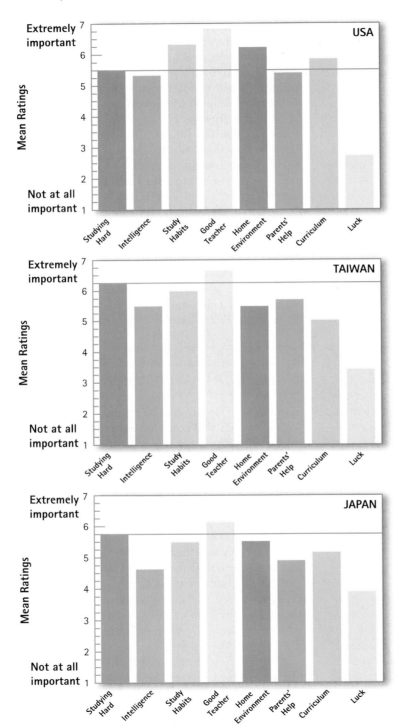

FIGURE 5.6

American and Asian Mothers' Ratings of Factors Related to School Achievement

Horizontal line represents rating for effort (studying hard).

Source: Stevenson and Lee 1990, 63.

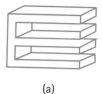

(a)

(b)

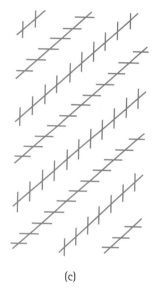

(c)

FIGURE 5.7

Optical Illusions

Source: Huffman 1971, 295–323.

number of attributional biases. All people do not have the ability to consider information in a logical manner, nor do all people take the time to do so. What is more, personal motivations often prevent us from being totally objective in judging the behavior of others. We turn now to some of the most common biases in the attribution process.

The Fundamental Attribution Error

Imagine the following situation. A few months after Dan landed a great job as an associate producer for a major network, he was assigned to cover the results of the presidential election. During that

broadcast, he saw his boss fly into a rage and throw a punch at another producer. He concluded that she had no respect for her colleague, had a violent temper, and was out of control.

This example illustrates a phenomenon that Heider (1944, 1958) called "behavior engulfs the field." Dan's perception of his boss was based too heavily on her behavior and not enough on the environment in which it occurred. He ignored the enormous pressure under which his boss was working to produce the best election night coverage. Perhaps her own boss's demand to receive the highest ratings, rather than her personality, made her act so aggressively. The tendency to overattribute others' behaviors to dispositions, and underattribute them to situations is so pervasive that Ross (1977) called it the **fundamental attribution error** (see Box 5.3).

Jones and Harris (1967) demonstrated how the fundamental attribution error operates in an experiment involving student essays about Fidel Castro, a controversial and unpopular dictator at the time of this study. The subjects in the experiment, college students, were asked to determine the attitudes of members of a debate team who had written speeches about Castro. The four conditions of this experiment were created as follows. First, subjects were divided into two main groups; one group was asked to read speeches of debaters who supported Castro, and the other was asked to read ones attacking him. These groups were then subdivided on the basis of what subjects were led to believe about the writer's freedom in choosing a position: half were told that the writer had made the choice, and the other half were told that the position had been assigned to the writer.

The results of this experiment are shown in Table 5.1. Subjects who believed that the writers freely chose their positions, pro or con, concluded that these choices reflected their true underlying attitudes. Thus subjects attributed more favorable attitudes toward Castro to writers who had freely written pro-Castro essays (56.92) and less favorable attitudes toward Castro to those who had freely written anti-Castro essays (17.38). These results suggest that the subjects were rational in the

---

BOX 5.3	CAUSES OF OTHERS' BEHAVIOR

Dear Ann Landers: You've often said that truth is stranger than fiction. Here's a lulu from your own backyard—the Chicago Tribune.

A man in California saw an ad in the paper for an "almost new" Porsche, in excellent condition—price $50. He was certain the printer had made a typographical error, but even at $5,000 it would have been a bargain, so he hurried to the address to look at the car.

A nice-looking woman appeared at the front door. Yes, she had placed the ad. The price was indeed $50. "The car," she said, "is in the garage. Come and look at it."

The fellow was overwhelmed. It was a beautiful Porsche and, as the ad promised, "nearly new." He asked if he could drive the car around the block. The woman said, "Of course," and went with him.

The Porsche drove like a dream. The young man peeled off $50 and handed it over, somewhat sheepishly. The woman gave him the necessary papers, and the car was his.

Finally, the new owner couldn't stand it any longer. He had to know why the woman was selling the Porsche at such a ridiculously low price. Her reply was simple: With a half-smile on her face, she said "My husband ran off with his secretary a few days ago and left a note instructing me to sell the car and the house, and send him the money."—Still Laughing in Wilmette

Landers 1996, 366

This letter shows how human beings seek to understand the causes of other people's behavior. Why? Because it helps them guide their own behavior. In this case, the man who wanted to buy the car was apparently so baffled by the woman's $50 price tag that he was not content to attribute her behavior simply to some quirky personality trait. That is, even though the woman's offer was crazy, he was not satisfied to apply the same description to her (a correspondent inference). Something did not add up. Her bizarre offer did not seem to fit her appearance or her demeanor. As he describes her, she was a "nice-looking woman" and behaved in a reasonable manner. In fact, as we learn, the cause of her behavior was her unfaithful husband, an external factor.

In most cases, we are more likely to attribute the causes of other people's behavior to their dispositions rather than to situational factors, a phenomenon called the *fundamental attribution error*. Research also shows that actors and observers differ in the way they make attributions.

Researchers demonstrated these kinds of differences in studies of letters written to Dear Abby and Ann Landers (Schoeneman and Rubanowitz 1985; Fischer, Schoeneman, and Rubanowitz 1987). Their results show that writers of letters to advice columnists tended to identify the cause of their problem in factors external to themselves (the situation or other people). For example, the researchers cite a letter written by a woman who identified her husband as the source of her problematic vacations: "Sidney is a drag on a trip" because "he has no interest in seeing new places or meeting new people" (Fischer, Schoeneman, and Rubanowitz 1987, 461). By contrast, readers of these letters were more likely to attribute the cause of the stated problem to the letter writer. In this case, they would fault the wife, not the husband, for failing to enjoy her vacations.

| TABLE 5.1 | ATTRIBUTION OF DEBATERS' ATTITUDES TOWARD CASTRO |

	Essay Position	
Choice Condition	Pro-Castro	Anti-Castro
Choice	59.62	17.38
No choice	44.10	22.87

NOTE: Higher numbers indicate more favorable attitudes toward Castro. The possible range of scores was from 10 (extremely anti-Castro) to 70 (extremely pro-Castro).

Source: Jones and Harris 1967, 6.

way they made attributions. With an external factor (no-choice condition) eliminated as a cause for writing either for or against Castro, subjects logically concluded that an internal factor (true opinions) influenced the debaters' choices.

The no-choice condition, however, suggests that some type of bias was operating. Despite the possible influence of an external factor (no-choice condition), subjects nevertheless attributed more favorable attitudes to debaters who had written pro-Castro essays (44.10) and less favorable attitudes to those who had written anti-Castro ones (22.87). Indeed, it appears that the behavior of the speechwriters, the most salient explanation for their attitudes, engulfed the field. As a result, it exerted the heaviest influence on the subjects' attributions.

Cultural Differences in the Operation of the Fundamental Attribution Error

If you have ever studied a foreign language, you are perhaps wondering whether the fundamental attribution error operates the same way across cultures. Consider the way the English expression "I am late" would be expressed in Spanish. Translated literally, the Spanish idiomatic expression means "The clock caused me to be late." As this shows, language itself may reflect the kinds of attributions we make. In cultures that stress individualism, people tend to focus on personal dispositions and therefore make internal attributions (Zebrowitz-McArthur 1988). This is less likely to be the case in cultures that place greater emphasis on contextual factors.

Miller (1984) demonstrated this kind of cultural influence in a study that compared how Americans differ from Hindus in India in their explanations of prosocial and deviant behaviors. Subjects in this study were asked to describe something a person they knew well had done recently. Two of the descriptions were supposed to involve some kind of prosocial behavior ("Describe something a person you know well did recently that you consider good for someone else"). Another two were supposed to involve some kind of deviant behavior ("Describe something a person you know well did recently that you considered a wrong thing to have done").

Miller's results showed little difference in the kinds of attributions made by school-aged children. However, as the age of the subject increased, so did the cultural differences. Thus American adults were more likely to make dispositional attributions than the Indians, whose explanations typically involved the situation. For example, an American adult narrated the following story about her neighbor:

> A neighbor of mine—she and her husband, they talk to us about a great number of things. She recently told me with a certain amount of even pride how she itemized her taxes to get back even more from the government—really outright cheating. On giving to charity she declared the maximum. And she knows and we know—'cause she tells us—that they didn't give anything to charity at all. (Miller 1984, 967)

According to Miller, this subject attributed the neighbor's behavior to personal characteristics—"That's just the type of person she is. She's very competitive."

In contrast, an emphasis on situational explanations for deviant behavior was seen in the stories of Hindu adults, as illustrated in the following story:

> I had to construct a house, and for that I had given advance money for Agent A to do that construction work. Agent A had promised—he had given in writing—that he would do that particular work. I gave him an advance of 1,500 rupees. He utilized it for his personal purposes, and then he never did that work or returned the money. That man, he deceived me up to the extent of 1,500 rupees. That's a great injustice. But I can go to the court of law. I have the documents, everything. (Miller 1984, 968)

In this case, the Hindu subject explained the man's behavior in terms of the agent's socioeconomic position—"The man is unemployed. He is not in a position to give that money." The results of

Miller's study clearly suggest that cultural differences influence the kinds of attributions people make.

In discussing the fundamental attribution error, we have only examined the way that observers' perceptions of actors may be distorted. As it turns out, the fundamental attribution error is unique to the way observers view the world. To understand why the attributional biases of actors and observers differ, let us turn now to a consideration of their different perspectives.

Actor–Observer Differences

Have you ever ended up in a dispute with someone yelling, "I just don't see it that way"? Chances are that you and the other person may never see it the same way. The simple explanation for this lies in the fact that actors and observers view things from different perspectives.

Imagine, for instance, the different viewpoints of a coach and a gymnast. As the gymnast looks outward, he directs his attention to what he sees—the equipment, his fans, and perhaps another competitor (external factors within the environment). As the coach looks outward, she sees these things as well. But her attention is drawn to the gymnast—to factors within him. These different perspectives lead actors and observers to make different kinds of attributions.

Let us say the gymnast falls off the balance beam. The coach is apt to attribute the mishap to an internal factor, perhaps lack of practice. The gymnast, by contrast, is more likely to claim that an external factor caused him to lose his concentration—for example, the noise of another competitor's music.

Jones and Nisbett (1971) claim that these kinds of differences in the way actors and observers make attributions are common. They say, "There is a pervasive tendency for actors to attribute their actions to situational requirements whereas observers tend to attribute the actions to stable disposition" (80). And they offer a number of explanations for this phenomenon, which is known as **actor-observer bias**.

What caused this gymnast to fall off this apparatus? Was it his fault, or did an equipment failure cause the accident?

First, as suggested by the example, the unique perspectives from which actors and observers view behavior make certain types of information more salient to each of them. From the actor's point of view, the most noticeable information exists in the environment. As she looks outward, she therefore tends to make attributions to external factors. Although the environment is also part of an observer's field of vision, it contains something the actor does not see—herself. In this case, the most prominent aspect of the environment is the actor, and an observer is more likely to make an attribution to her dispositions.

Second, actors and observers are privy to different information. Actors know how they have behaved over time and in different situations. They alone possess the history of their conduct. As a result, actors look to factors outside themselves for explanations of their behavior. In contrast, observers must rely on a minimal amount of information available to them. Based often on a single observation, they tend to assume that this act is representative of the actor's behavior over time and across situations. Consequently, they attribute the cause of a behavior to the disposition of the actor.

Actors possess two other kinds of information that observers do not—knowledge of their intentions and their feelings. Suppose a friend of yours overhears a conversation about the party you are planning for next Saturday. She is likely to conclude that you intentionally left her out. She is very hurt and concludes that you are just a fair-weather friend. In fact, you have kept this a guarded secret, but for another reason—it is a surprise party to celebrate her recent engagement.

The actor's knowledge of his own feelings can produce a similar effect. Suppose that while Paula is standing in the cafeteria line, a guy she would like to meet returns for more coffee. As she turns to say hello, he abruptly looks in the other direction and ignores her completely. Paula is devastated. Unfortunately, she does not realize that he has a crush on her but is simply too shy to speak to her.

Based on the assumption that the focus of our attention influences the kind of attribution we make, a number of researchers have designed studies using mirrors and cameras to manipulate the self-awareness of an actor (Duval and Wicklund 1973; Storms 1973). In a study involving mirrors, Duval and Wicklund (1973) hypothesized that an increase in objective self-awareness would increase the tendency for subjects to attribute causality to themselves. The researchers asked subjects to read a number of vignettes about a hypothetical situation involving two people as well as an outcome. Subjects were instructed to imagine themselves in the situation. A typical vignette read as follows:

> Imagine that you have selected and purchased a race horse. You enter the horse in a major race and hire a good jockey to ride him. The horse wins first place. To what degree did your actions cause the victory and to what degree did the actions of the jockey cause the victory? (26)

Before subjects entered the room to participate in this experiment, a large mirror was placed against the wall directly in front of their chair. For half of the subjects, the mirror was turned so they would face it directly (mirror condition). For the other half, it was turned so they only saw the wooden back (no-mirror condition). The results of the study confirmed the researchers' hypothesis. Subjects whose self-awareness was increased by the mirror did indeed make more self-attributions than subjects in the no-mirror condition.

The Self-Serving Attributional Bias

A curious thing happens during political campaigns in America. Perhaps you have noticed. Presidents take credit for booming economies, members of Congress will claim responsibility for passing legislation beneficial to the public, and mayors will boast about how they have lowered crime rates.

But have you ever heard a politician take responsibility for any problems? That is highly unlikely. During a recession, you are more likely to hear the president blame Congress for failing to cut taxes. Members of Congress, in turn, will attack the president for his lack of cooperation. And if the crime rate is on the rise, the media are at fault.

Actually, the tendency to take credit for success and to blame failure on someone or something else is not unique to politicians. We all do it. When we ace an exam, we brag about our intelligence. But if we fail, we complain about how unfair the exam was. Social psychologists call this tendency the **self-serving bias**.

Although this kind of attributional bias distorts reality, it can actually serve a number of positive functions. First, it protects our self-esteem. No doubt, we feel better about ourselves when we are responsible for only good things. Second, as noted earlier with regard to student achievement, when we attribute our success to our own effort, we create expectations that increase the likelihood that we will attempt similar kinds of tasks in the future.

Blaming the Victim: Belief in a Just World

During the opening statements to the jury in the civil trial of O. J. Simpson, Simpson's lawyer, Robert Baker, spared no mercy for Nicole Brown, one of the two victims in this tragedy. According to an

---

BOX 5.4	THE JUST WORLD SCALE

Rubin and Peplau (1975) designed the just world scale to measure the extent to which people believe others deserve their fates. What do you believe? Consider each item below and indicate whether you agree or disagree.

	Agree	Disagree
1. I've found that a person rarely deserves the reputation he has.	☐	☐
2. Basically, the world is a just place.	☐	☐
3. People who get "lucky breaks" have usually earned their good fortune.	☐	☐
4. Careful drivers are just as likely to get hurt in traffic accidents as careless ones.	☐	☐
5. It is a common occurrence for a guilty person to get off free in American courts.	☐	☐
6. Students almost always deserve the grades they receive in school.	☐	☐
7. Men who keep in shape have little chance of suffering a heart attack.	☐	☐
8. The political candidate who sticks up for his principles rarely gets elected.	☐	☐
9. It is rare for an innocent man to be wrongly sent to jail.	☐	☐
10. In professional sports, many fouls and infractions never get called by the referee.	☐	☐
11. By and large, people deserve what they get.	☐	☐
12. When parents punish their children, it is almost always for good reasons.	☐	☐
13. Good deeds often go unnoticed and unrewarded.	☐	☐
14. Although evil men may hold political power for a while, in the general course of history good wins out.	☐	☐

article in *Time* magazine, "Baker attacked her in his opening statement as a promiscuous woman who abused alcohol and drugs, had an abortion to get rid of a baby fathered by one of her boyfriends and ran with an unsavory crowd" (Zoglin 1996, 48). As shocking as this may sound, Baker's strategy was carefully designed to appeal to an attributional bias that leads people to perceive the causes of another's misfortunes as due to their own shortcomings rather than to situational factors. This perceptual distortion may result from a belief held by many people—that we get what we deserve in life, good or bad.

Known as **belief in a just world**, Rubin and Peplau (1973, 1975) trace this notion back to the biblical story of Job, whose friends try to persuade him to repent, arguing that suffering is the result of sin (Job 8:20). Although Job does not view the world as a just place, where people deserve the rewards and punishments that life bestows, many people have adopted this logic since ancient times (Selznick and Steinberg 1969; Hallie 1971). Thus, for example, Hallie (1971) demonstrated that many Germans living under the Nazi regime concluded that Holocaust victims must have deserved their fate. Do you tend to believe that people deserve their fates? Consider the items that Rubin and Peplau included in their just world scale (Box 5.4).

15. In almost any business or profession, people who do their job well rise to the top. ☐ ☐

16. American parents tend to overlook the things most to be admired in their children. ☐ ☐

17. It is often impossible for a person to receive a fair trial in the USA. ☐ ☐

18. People who meet with misfortune have often brought it on themselves. ☐ ☐

19. Crime doesn't pay. ☐ ☐

20. Many people suffer through absolutely no fault of their own. ☐ ☐

SCORING

Items that indicate the tendency to believe in a just world include: 2, 3, 6, 7, 9, 11, 12, 14, 15, 18, 19

How many of these items did you agree with? _____

Items that indicate the tendency to reject belief in a just world include: 1, 4, 5, 8, 10, 13, 16, 17, 20

How many of these items did you disagree with? _____

Add your answers to the questions above together for a total score. _____

The higher your total score, the stronger is your belief in a just world.

Note: The highest possible score is 20; the lowest possible score is 0.

Source: Adapted from Rubin and Peplau 1975, 69–70.

Lerner (1980) suggests that people cling to their belief in a just world out of a need to control what happens to them. Threatened by the idea that misfortune might occur haphazardly, people gain comfort in the belief that bad things happen only to those who deserve it. This kind of distortion, which is called **defensive attributional bias**, explains why Baker tried to convince jurors that Nicole Brown was a bad person. Presumably, this belief would appeal to jurors who did not want to believe that they, too, could be victims of such a heinous crime.

Although we would expect people who believe in a just world to admire successful people and support those in power, the unfortunate consequence of this belief is that they may also use it to justify the neglect or abuse of society's victims (Goffman 1963; Ryan 1971; Rubin and Peplau 1973, 1975). Thus Goffman (1963) has pointed out that even a person's physical disability might be viewed as proof of some kind of moral defect—"as just retribution for something he or his parents or his tribe did, and hence a justification of the way we treat him" (6).

IMPRESSIONS: HOW THEY INFLUENCE THE WAY OTHERS RESPOND TO US

> Keep up appearances; there lies the test;
> The world will give thee credit for the rest.
> Outward be fair, however foul within;
> Sin, if thou will, but then in secret sin.
> Charles Churchill, *Night*, 1.311

Perhaps it was this kind of commonsense psychology that motivated John Molloy to write a bestselling book titled *Dress for Success* (1988). Based on more than twenty-six years of research, including the opinions and subconscious reactions of over sixty thousand executives, Molloy (1988, 16) argues that "successful dress cannot put a boob in the boardroom, but incorrect dress can definitely keep an intelligent, able man out." How smart are you when it comes to dressing for success? Box 5.5 will help you determine your image IQ.

Whether you accept or reject the notion that "clothes make the man," research clearly indicates

---

BOX 5.5	TEST YOUR IMAGE IQ

According to John Molloy (1988) people who look successful are treated better than those who do not look successful. What do you know about looking successful? To give men a quick sense of their image IQ, Molloy designed the following quiz. It may also be useful for women who select clothing for the men in their lives.

1. What is the most effective raincoat color?
2. For which professionals are bow ties acceptable—and often preferred—attire?
3. What tie color makes men look sexy?
4. Should today's executive wear pants with cuffs or without them?
5. Are shirts with contrasting collars acceptable in conservative companies?
6. "Old money" Americans are most likely to distrust a man who (a) has disheveled hair, (b) is wearing a wrinkled suit, (c) is wearing shoes that are unshined or worn at the heels, (d) drives an old car.
7. Should suspenders always have button fasteners?
8. Should you wear stripes or solids if you are going to appear on television?
9. If you are a small man, will a dark, pinstripe suit make you look smaller and ineffective?

What should women consider when they are choosing clothes for themselves? Design a quiz for women who want to determine their image IQ.

Answers 1. beige; 2. waiter, clowns, college professors, and commentators; 3. bright red; 4. with cuffs; 5. yes, Lee Iacocca made them acceptable; 6. (c); 7. yes; 8. solids; 9. no, with the right accessories it will do the opposite.

Source: Molloy 1988, frontispiece.

that our appearance does influence the way others treat us. Let's consider how this happens.

Order Effects in Forming Impressions

Looking back over your dating experiences, what conclusions might you draw about the way your relationships developed? Did your best experiences with dates begin with good first impressions? Did anyone ever overcome a bad first impression to win your heart? Does it matter whether we learn about someone's good traits first or last?

A study conducted by Solomon Asch (1946) suggests that the order of personal traits is important in impression formation. Imagine yourself as a participant in his experiment. Subjects were divided into two groups. One group received a list describing a hypothetical person as *intelligent, industrious, impulsive, critical, stubborn,* and *envious.* The list for the other group contained the same adjectives but in reverse order: *envious, stubborn, critical, impulsive, industrious,* and *intelligent.* Try this yourself. Read the lists again. What kind of an impression do these two lists of adjectives give? Are they different?

The results of Asch's experiment suggest that they do give different kinds of impressions. Indeed, subjects exposed to the list that ran from positive to negative traits formed more positive impressions of the hypothetical person than subjects who read the traits in reverse order. The greater weight given to early information in impression formation is called the **primacy effect** (Luchins 1957).

Asch explained the results of his experiment by saying that the meaning of later adjectives was influenced by earlier ones. For example, once we regard someone as intelligent, our impression has already begun to form. As we add other traits, they tend to conform to our initial impression. So adjectives such as *impulsive* and *critical* are viewed more positively when they follow *intelligent.* Thus we are likely to think he has a creative spirit or the ability to think critically. In contrast, if our first impression leads us to believe the person is

envious, intelligence takes on a completely different meaning. Another explanation for the primacy effect suggests that we begin to pay less attention to incoming information once we have enough to form an impression (Dreben, Fiske, and Hastie 1979).

The primacy effect operates in a number of different ways and can have a significant influence in our lives. Suppose that you need a strong recommendation from your chemistry professor for medical school. In what way will her impression of you be influenced by patterns in your grades? Do students whose grades improve create a better impression than those who start out well and decline?

The evidence suggests that your best strategy is to start out well. In a study designed to determine how the primacy effect influenced impressions of others' intelligence, subjects were asked to observe someone taking a test that contained thirty multiple-choice items and resembled a standard college admissions test (Jones et al. 1968).

In one condition, subjects watched a person start out well but end up poorly. In another condition, the person got off to a bad start but eventually improved. In fact, the order of correct answers for these two conditions was simply flipped. And in both conditions the person taking the test answered fifteen questions correctly. After observing the person taking the test, subjects were then asked to rate the person's intelligence. The results of this study showed that people whose performance started out well but declined were judged more intelligent than people whose performance improved.

In some cases, the information received later may receive more weight than earlier information (Luchins 1957). This tendency, which is called the **recency effect,** can occur when people pay close attention to incoming information. The time which elapses between early and later information can also influence what kind of effect will be produced. Thus, as the time between early and later information increases, recency effects are more likely to occur.

The Self-Fulfilling Prophecy Effect of First Impressions

In George Bernard Shaw's play *Pygmalion* (which was later filmed as *My Fair Lady*), Eliza Doolittle captures the essence of what has been called the *self-fulfilling prophecy*, saying:

> You see, really and truly, . . . the difference between a lady and a flower girl is not how she behaves, but how she's treated. I shall always be a flower girl to Professor Higgins, because he . . . treats me as a flower girl, . . . but I know I can be a lady to you, because you always treat me as a lady, and always will. (Shaw 1916, Act 5)

As this suggests, Professor Higgins's first impression of Eliza as a flower girl had a tremendous influence on the way he treated her. She responded to his expectations and behaved accordingly. In a classic experiment on the self-fulfilling effects of first impressions, Rosenthal and Jacobson (1968) used Eliza's words to summarize their hypothesis that a teacher's expectations for her pupil's performance serve as an educational self-fulfilling prophecy. Teachers who expect pupils to excel get more out of them than teachers who expect less.

In this study, called the Oak School Experiment, researchers administered the "Harvard Test of Inflected Acquisition" to students in grades 1 through 6. Teachers were led to believe that this test predicted intellectual growth for the next year. From each of the eighteen classrooms at Oak School, researchers chose about 20 percent of the children to be labeled academic "spurters." Teachers were led to believe that the test indicated their potential when in fact the children had been chosen by means of a table of random numbers. The difference between these children and others in their class, then, existed solely in the mind of the teacher.

At the end of the school year, the children were tested again. The results showed that children in the experimental condition, the academic "spurters," gained more points in total IQ and especially in reasoning IQ than children in the control condition. What is more, when compared to children in the control condition, their teachers described them as more interesting, curious, and happy, with a significantly better chance of becoming successful in the future.

Rosenthal and Jacobson (1968) explained these results by saying that the teacher may have communicated her expectations for improved intellectual performance in a number of ways: through what she said and how she said it, by facial expressions, and even by the way she touched the child. While these results suggest the benefit of effects associated with positive expectations, they also suggest that children who are labeled as underachievers or troublemakers are also susceptible to the negative effects of a self-fulfilling prophecy.

The effect that an actor's first impression can produce via the expectations they create in an observer was also demonstrated in a study conducted by Snyder (1978). Male and female undergraduates at the University of Minnesota were led to believe that they were participating in a study of the "processes by which people become acquainted with each other." They were told that they would interact with a member of the opposite sex through telephone conversations. Prior to their initial contact, the male member of each pair received a Polaroid snapshot of the female. These photos served to create the impression that the woman was either attractive or unattractive. Based on Berscheid and Walster's (1974) research on stereotypes, Snyder expected a male subject to attribute certain personality traits to his partner depending on her physical attractiveness. He believed that men would attribute traits such as warmth, humor, and extroversion to physically attractive females while assuming that physically unattractive women would be serious, withdrawn, awkward, and socially inept.

The results confirmed Snyder's expectations. Women who were perceived by their male partners as physically attractive acted in a more

What kind of impression does the woman in the left photo give? How did she create the image she is trying to project? What kind of an impression does the man in the right photo give? Would you offer him a job based on his appearance?

friendly, likable, and sociable manner than the "unattractive" women. What is more, an analysis of the ratings made by judges who listened to the taped conversations between the men and women showed that the contributions made by men differed significantly, depending on the impression they had formed about the woman at the other end of the phone. Snyder concluded that the false impression created by the photos did in fact influence the interaction style between men and women.

According to Robert Merton (1948, 477), "The self-fulfilling prophecy is, in the beginning, a *false* definition of the situation evoking a new behavior, which makes the originally false conception come true." With evidence to support Merton's understanding of this phenomenon, Snyder cautioned that other widespread stereotypes—especially those involving gender, race, social class, and ethnicity—could influence social interaction in ways that produce their own reality.

SUMMARY

1. Attribution refers to the process by which we come to understand other people. In making judgments about others, we try to locate the causes of a particular outcome in either the person or in the environment.
2. Jones and Davis's theory of correspondent inferences explains how people consider information to draw conclusions about the specific traits of other people. Our confidence in inferences that we make about a person's disposition is influenced by the noncommon effects produced by a person's behavior and the social desirability of the behavior itself. These factors constitute the discounting principle.

3. Kelley's attribution model of causal attribution focuses on whether an action was caused by internal or external factors. Observers consider the distinctiveness of an entity, how many other people responded to the entity in the same way (consensus), and consistency over time and place.

4. Weiner's model of attributions focuses on the factors responsible for a person's success or failure. Observers decide whether the cause was internal or external and then whether the behavior was stable or unstable. Using this process, people ultimately conclude that success or failure was caused by one of four factors—ability, effort, task difficulty, or luck.

5. The fundamental attribution error refers to the tendency to exaggerate the role of a person's disposition as a cause of his behavior and to understate the role of situational factors. Cultural differences influence the kinds of attributions people make. In cultures that stress individualism, people tend to make internal attributions for behaviors they observe. In cultures that emphasize contextual factors, people tend to make external attributions.

6. The process of person perception differs for actors and observers, for several reasons. First, actors and observers are subject to actor-observer bias because they view behaviors from different perspectives. Second, actors and observers have access to different kinds and amounts of information. Third, actors know their intentions and feelings, while observers do not.

7. The idea that people get what they deserve in life is known as belief in a just world. This kind of attribution bias can give people the feeling that they can control what happens to them. Unfortunately, it also justifies the mistreatment of society's victims.

8. The impressions that people create can contribute to positive or negative outcomes. The primacy effect occurs when early information receives the most weight in forming an impression. The recency effect occurs when more weight is given to later information. In some cases, impressions contribute to a self-fulfilling prophecy. This occurs when a false definition of a situation evokes new behaviors that make the initial false impression come true.

KEY TERMS

CRITICAL REVIEW QUESTIONS

1. Politicians attempt to manipulate voters' perceptions of them in many ways. Consider the candidates currently running for office. Use each of the theories presented in this chapter to create a profile of these candidates.

2. Use the theories presented in this chapter to analyze the pattern of grades that your college transcript currently shows. What would an admissions committee for graduate school conclude about you?

3. How might the process of attribution operate in a murder case? What should jurors consider when they judge the defendant? What must they know about themselves in considering the murder victim?

SIX

Attitudes and Attitude Change

When I was a boy growing up in the South Bronx, my father was the dominant figure in my life. A Jamaican immigrant like my mother, who worked his way up to a foreman's job in Manhattan's garment district, Luther Powell never let his race or station affect his sense of self. West Indians like him had come to this country with nothing.

Every morning they got on the subway, worked like dogs all day, got home at 8 at night, supported their families and educated their children. If they could do that, how dare anyone think they were less than anybody's equal? That was Pop's attitude, and it became mine, too.

At home, my father was the neighborhood Solomon—the village wise man people came to for advice, for domestic arbitration or for help in getting a job. He would bring home clothes, seconds and irregulars, and end bolts of fabric from the company where he worked, and sell them at wholesale or give them to anybody in need.

He was totally unimpressed by rank, place or ceremony. Once, when I was a colonel stationed at Fort Campbell, Ky., I invited my parents to join us for Thanksgiving dinner. My father talked with generals as if he had known generals all his life, and then table-hopped through the mess hall, like Omar Bradley mixing with the troops before an invasion.

I was struck by his total aplomb: Luther Powell belonged wherever Luther Powell happened to be. He was a short man, just 5 feet 2 inches tall; but, like Napoleon, he was masterful.

Remembering him fondly on Father's Day, I realize how much of my own success I owe to his example. And when I think of that, I worry about the great many young people who will not be spending today with their own fathers.

—General Colin L. Powell (1999)

I n this touching Father's Day salute, General Colin Powell, one of America's most admired leaders, describes his father's attitudes toward work, family, education, the community, himself, and his place in society. By choosing this focus, General Powell recognizes the enormous impact that attitudes have on our thoughts, feelings, and behaviors. And he expresses concern for young people who do not have strong role models to shape their attitudes.

Today, attitude research is popular across the social sciences. But it is particularly central to social psychology, which seeks to understand the factors that influence the thoughts, feelings, and behaviors of human beings. The scope of attitude research is broad. It seeks to answer many questions: How do our attitudes shape our sense of who we are? How do attitudes guide our behavior? To what extent do other people, especially our parents, shape our attitudes? Are attitudes relatively stable, or do they change over time? And exactly how do attitudes form? We will attempt to answer these and many more questions in this chapter. To begin, we will attempt to define what we mean by *attitude*.

WHAT IS AN ATTITUDE?

Attitude is one of those words that is difficult to define but quickly used to capture the essence of what we mean (see Box 6.1). To have an attitude, get an attitude, or cop an attitude suggests hostility, aloofness, or a lack of cooperation (Parshall 1994). Lawrence Muhammad (1996), a journalist for the *Louisville Courier-Journal*, observed that bumper stickers "give attitude" and offered the following examples: "My Kid Beat Up Your Honor Student," "This Vehicle Insured by Smith & Wesson," and "The Best Man for the Job Is a Woman." Another journalist, Gerald Parshall (1994), used the word artfully when he referred to American slang as "words with attitude."

Most people grasp the meaning attached to the word *attitude*. Yet social scientists have

struggled to agree on a definition (Oskamp 1991). The word first appeared in the English language around 1710 (Fleming 1967). It originally referred to the posture, stance, or *physical* disposition of a figure, but social psychologists generally use the more modern meaning of a *mental* position or belief.

L. L. Thurstone (1946), a pioneer in attitude theory and research, defined *attitude* as "the intensity of positive or negative affect for or against an object" (39). Other definitions have come and gone since then as social psychologists have judged their importance and considered whether attitudes are learned or innate and whether they are lasting or temporary. One of the most widely accepted definitions of **attitude** today states that it "is a psychological tendency that is expressed by evaluating a particular entity with some degree of favor or disfavor" (Eagly and Chaiken 1993, 1). When we state our approval or disapproval, liking or disliking, attraction or aversion, we are expressing an attitude. The object of our everyday evaluations can be anything—a person, an idea, a group, a policy, even ourself (see Table 6.1.). Research on attitudes, however, has focused on specific kinds of attitudes: social and political attitudes, attitudes toward behavior, and attitudes selected for experimental purposes (Eagly 1992).

Social psychologists use attitude as a *hypothetical construct* to define a tendency or internal state of an individual (Eagly 1992). This tendency predisposes an individual toward evaluative responses that range in terms of favorability or unfavorability. These responses may or may not be expressed openly and can take one of three forms: cognitive, affective, or behavioral. The classification of evaluative responses into these three categories can be traced back to classical Greek and Hindu philosophers (McGuire 1985), and many social psychologists refer to them as the *basic components* of attitudes. Although research has revealed that all three components need not be expressed to show that an attitude exists, the tripartite division nevertheless serves as a useful conceptual model (Eagly and Chaiken 1993).

The **cognitive component** of attitudes refers to the thoughts that people have about an attitude

BOX 6.1   ON LANGUAGE: THE MOOD OF 'TUDE

To most of us, an attitude is something a person has: a cheerful frame of mind or negative outlook. The word is neutral, requiring some modifier to tell us what kind of attitude we're talking about.

To some, however, attitude—not preceded by the article *an*—has lost its neutrality and gained a new sense: pugnacity, sullen defiance, self-confidence tipping over into arrogance. This attitude has a hostile modifier built in.

The first inkling of a new sense in the Barnhart Dictionary files comes from *The New Yorker* in 1978, about a car-rental agency: "We have a very good atmosphere here. We enjoy our work. We don't have an *attitude.*"

Lewis Beale in *The Detroit Free Press* reports that *attitude* "is a uniquely post-modern way to look at the world. It's cynical, cool, a bit detached. . . . In the male of the species, it can include macho posturing; in the female, it's called bitchiness."

He provides a table for the age of attitude: Mickey Mouse needs it, Bugs Bunny has it, Bart Simpson has too much; John Le Carre needs it, Elmore Leonard has it, Norman Mailer has too much; in the animal world, gerbils need it, cats have it, ferrets have too much.

The same linguistic phenomenon was noted concurrently by Tony Gabriele in *The Newport News* (Va.) *Daily Press*, who had a character explain: "You don't have to be rich or famous to attitudinize; the lowliest street-corner lout can give you attitude just as well." The politeness and lack of affectation of the residents of Newport News made it an "attitude-impaired region."

To cop an attitude was prison slang for "to adopt a complaining demeanor" or "to whine," similar to the Yiddish "to kvetch"; it later changed to a more assertive "to project haughtiness" or "to stand up to the Man." Clipped to *'tude*, it is black English (which may have been its original source) for "confident posture."

Language is playing one of its cyclical tricks. The Latin *aptitudo*, "fitness," root of "aptitude," is also the source of *attitude*: the meaning has to do with the fitness of the arrangement of a body or figure. In the fine arts, this is expressed by sculptors or painters as "the disposition of a figure; the posture given to it to show a mood, humor or spirit."

From this physical positioning, *attitude* came to mean the mental or emotional state that the posture represented. Rodin's "Thinker" was in the physical position, with chin in hand, of being ultra-pensive; the artist's intention was to show that as his mental attitude.

By figurative extension, the word took on the sense of "opinion": in 1837, Thomas Carlyle wrote (prophetically) "the attitude of the Right Side is that of calm unbelief."

The slang sense in such vogue today reaches back for that original sense of fitness: what's suitable these days, according to those who seek just the right *'tude*, is a mixture of sassiness, brassiness, cockiness, self-assurance and defiance—in terms of posture, standing tall. Too much of this, of course, leads to the hostility and sullenness that is now called *an attitude problem.*

Source: Safire 1990.

TABLE 6.1   OBJECTS OF OUR ATTITUDES

Anything that can become an object of thought and evaluation can serve as an attitude object (Eagly and Chaiken 1993). The entity may be concrete (one's favorite sweater) or abstract (a particular political philosophy). Social psychologists view some attitude objects as key concepts or subjects worthy of special study. Examples include the following.

Attitude Object	Definition
Prejudice	Negative attitudes toward members of a group
Self-esteem	Attitudes toward the self
Values	Abstract goals, such as equality or freedom
Public opinion	Shared opinions and attitudes of large groups of people

object. Facts, knowledge, beliefs, information, opinions, and inferences are considered part of this component (Eagly and Chaiken 1993). For example, some people think that the primary cause of gun violence in America is the availability of guns. Others think the primary cause is the way parents raise their children, and still others think it is due to the influences of popular culture.

The **affective component** of attitudes refers to a person's emotions and feelings toward a particular attitude object. Consider the responses of children who have been asked, "When you are in school, do you ever fear for your physical safety?" Public opinion polls have also tried to measure the feelings of the public after the untimely deaths of people in the public eye, such as John F. Kennedy Jr. or Princess Diana. In these cases, pollsters wanted to know how people were responding to these tragedies—if they were upset or sad. In some cases, people might be given a full range of emotions from which to choose. In 1997, for example, Gallup asked the public, "Which of the following words best describes your reaction to these decisions by Janet Reno concerning independent counsels—are you *outraged, unhappy, indifferent, happy,* or *delighted?*"

Finally, the **behavioral component** refers to a person's actions with respect to an attitude object. In seeking the public's attitudes toward AIDS, Gallup sought to determine what kinds of steps people were actually taking to avoid contracting the disease. Their list of behaviors included avoiding elective surgery that would require blood transfusions, not associating with people they suspected might have AIDS, and avoiding the use of restrooms in public facilities (Moore 1997). The behavioral component also refers to intentions to act, which are not necessarily expressed in outward behavior (Eagly and Chaiken 1993). Studies of attitudes toward social and political issues often ask people to indicate how their position on an issue might affect the way they vote. For example, a 2000 Gallup poll asked, "Thinking about how the gun issue might affect your vote for major offices, would you only vote for a candidate who shares your views on gun control, would you consider a candidate's position on gun control as just one of many important factors when voting, or would you not consider gun control a major issue?" (2000b; see Figure 6.1).

MEASURING ATTITUDES

Today, public opinion polls track the attitudes of Americans from week to week and even from moment to moment when events stir debates on issues of national importance. In the weeks following the initially inconclusive November 7, 2000, presidential election, pollsters bombarded the public with questions: "Who do you consider to be the real winner of the election in Florida—Al Gore or George W. Bush, or are you unsure?" (Gallup 2000c). "How confident are you that the votes in Florida have been counted accurately?" (*Washington Post*/ABC News 2000). " Do you think dimpled or indented chads should or should not be counted as votes?" (*Washington Post*/ABC News 2000). While the two candidates disputed the methods used to measure the actual votes cast on election day, no one seemed concerned about the accuracy of ongoing public opinion polls. Pundits kept a close watch on these polls, believing that American attitudes could end the political future of either candidate in an instant.

It seems that measuring votes would be more accurate than measuring attitudes—unless you have to measure the intent of the voter. In that case, there might not be much difference between measuring votes and measuring attitudes. In fact, the main difficulty in measuring attitudes lies in the fact that we cannot observe them directly. Instead, we must infer them from observable responses or *indicators*. Evaluations that reveal a person's thoughts, feelings, or behaviors serve as indicators that researchers use to infer attitude. Next, we will review a number of methods that social psychologists have developed to measure attitudes.

Thoughts (Cognitive Component)
• The Second Amendment protects my right to own a gun.
• Too many children are accidentally killed with guns each year.

Attitude toward Gun Control

Feelings (Affective Component)
• I fear more school shootings.
• I am afraid to go out at night without some kind of weapon.

Behaviors (Behavioral Component)
• I voted for a candidate who supports gun control.
• I bought a gun and belong to the National Rifle Association.

FIGURE 6.1

Cognitive, Affective, and Behavioral Components of Attitude Formation

Bogardus's Social Distance Scale

In 1925, Emory Bogardus created the **social distance scale** to measure attitudes toward various racial or nationality groups. The instructions to respondents read as follows:

> According to my first feeling reactions, I would willingly admit members of each race (as a class, and not the best I have known, nor the worst members) to one or more of the classifications under which I have placed a cross.
>
> 1. To close kinship by marriage
> 2. To my club as personal chums
> 3. To my street as neighbors
> 4. To employment in my occupation in my country
> 5. To citizenship in my country
> 6. As visitors only to my country
> 7. Would exclude from my country

By ranking items systematically in order from acceptance into one's family to the exclusion from one's country, Bogardus created a way to assign scores to respondents that would indicate their attitudes toward members of various groups—Bulgarians, Canadians, the Dutch, and so on.

Thurstone's Method of Measuring Attitudes

In 1928, L. L. Thurstone published a paper titled "Attitudes Can Be Measured" that described a more precise measurement. The **Thurstone scale** would attempt to show the exact difference between one respondent's attitude and another's (Oskamp 1991). The method required to do this was far more complicated than Bogardus's approach. To begin, Thurstone assembled a large number of statements (about one hundred) that expressed varying degrees of favorability and unfavorablity about a particular subject of interest. A group of judges then placed the statements into eleven equally spaced categories on the basis of how favorable or unfavorable the statement was toward the attitude object, without considering their own attitude toward the subject. Items that showed wide disagreement among the judges were considered ambiguous and were excluded from the scale. Scale values were assigned to the statements chosen, based on the median favorability rating of the judges. The final scale consisted of about twenty statements that were chosen on the basis of two criteria. First, items were chosen that had scale values of approximately equal intervals along an 11-point scale of favorability. Second, items were chosen that showed high agreement among the judges' ratings.

These statements were randomly arranged on a questionnaire without any indication of their scale values. Respondents were then asked to identify only the items with which they agreed. Each person's attitude was then measured by calculating the average (mean or median) of the scale values associated with the chosen items.

Likert Scaling

One of the most popular methods for measuring attitudes today was developed a few years after Thurstone had proposed his scale. Seeking a simpler method for measuring attitudes, Rensis Likert (1932) proposed a method of summated ratings. Like Thurstone, he began by selecting a large pool of statements about the object of an attitude. However, unlike Thurstone's items, which included a variety of statements along an evaluative continuum, Likert's items were written so that agreement with an item expressed either a favorable or unfavorable attitude toward the object in a multiple-choice format. Consider a statement regarding attitudes toward the role of women in society: "Swearing and obscenity are more repulsive in the speech of a woman than of a man" (see Table 6.2). The responses on a Likert scale might be (A) I agree strongly, (B) I agree mildly, (C) I am neutral, (D) I disagree mildly, or (E) I disagree strongly. A respondent's total score for an attitude like this would be calculated by summing the scores on each item.

The range of responses on a **Likert scale** is not limited to five categories. A researcher might choose a 7-point scale or even a 100-point scale. Although a larger number of categories provides more information, Likert scales do not indicate the degree to which different respondents vary with respect to favorability or unfavorability—the distinguishing feature of Thurstone's scale.

Guttman Scaling

The scores obtained by using either the Thurstone or Likert scaling method have one serious drawback—respondents' scores do not have a unique meaning (Oskamp 1991). In other words, any given score can be produced in a variety of ways. Consider the total scores of subjects who responded to the questions on attitudes toward women in Table 6.2. The total score for a respondent who gave mostly neutral responses would be no different from a respondent who gave many "agree strongly" responses balanced by many "disagree strongly" ones.

To avoid this problem, Louis Guttman (1944) proposed a scaling method that would produce scores with unique meanings. A **Guttman scale** represents a hierarchy of attitudes, ranging from the least extreme to the most extreme (see Table 6.3). Consider a person's attitude toward handgun control. A respondent who holds a moderately favorable attitude on this issue should support items 1–5 in Table 6.3. A score of 5 indicates that he would "require a mandatory jail term for all persons carrying a handgun outside their homes or places of business without a license." This score is cumulative in the sense that we would assume that

TABLE 6.2	LIKERT SCALE

Attitudes toward Women

The statements listed below describe attitudes toward the role of women in society that different people have. There are no right or wrong answers, only opinions. You are asked to express your feeling about each statement by indicating whether you (A) agree strongly, (B) agree mildly, (C) are neutral, (D) disagree mildly, or (E) disagree strongly. Please indicate your opinion by blackening either A, B, C, D, or E on the answer sheet for each item.

1. Swearing and obscenity are more repulsive in the speech of a woman than of a man.
2. Women should take increasing responsibility for leadership in solving the intellectual and social problems of the day.
3. Both husband and wife should be allowed the same grounds for divorce.
4. Intoxication among women is worse than intoxication among men.
5. Under modern economic conditions with women being active outside the home, men should share in household tasks such as washing dishes and doing the laundry.
6. There should be a strict merit system in job appointment and promotion without regard to sex.
7. Women should worry less about their rights and more about becoming good wives and mothers.
8. Women earning as much as their dates should bear equally the expense when they go out together.
9. It is ridiculous for a woman to run a locomotive and for a man to darn socks.
10. Women should be encouraged not to become sexually intimate with anyone before marriage, even their fiancés.
11. The husband should not be favored by law over the wife in the disposal of family property or income.
12. The modern girl is entitled to the same freedom from regulation and control that is given to the modern boy.

Source: Spence, Helmreich, and Stapp 1973, 219–220.

TABLE 6.3	GUTTMAN SCALE

Attitudes toward Handgun Control

1. Institute a waiting period before a handgun can be purchased, to allow for a criminal records check.
2. Require all persons to obtain a police permit before being allowed to purchase a handgun.
3. Require a license for all persons carrying a handgun outside their homes or places of business (except for law enforcement agents).
4. Require a mandatory fine for all persons carrying a handgun outside their homes or places of business without a license.
5. Require a mandatory jail term for all persons carrying a handgun outside their homes or places of business without a license.
6. Ban the future manufacturing and sale of non-sporting-type handguns.
7. Ban the future manufacture and sale of all handguns.
8. Use public funds to buy back and destroy existing handguns on a voluntary basis.
9. Use public funds to buy back and destroy existing handguns on a mandatory basis.

Source: Teske and Hazlett 1985, 375.

he would agree with the less extreme positions that appear prior to this statement. We would also assume that he would not agree with more extreme positions on this issue (items 6–9).

Bogardus's social distance scale was based on the same reasoning. That is, respondents who express a very favorable attitude toward members of a particular ethnic group by indicating their willingness to accept them in their own family would presumably also indicate a willingness to accept them into a club or into their neighborhood. Conversely, respondents who express a very unfavorable attitude by indicating they would exclude them from their country would not presumably accept them into their neighborhood. Guttman argued that a scale that fits this cumulative pattern measures only one underlying attitude—that it is unidimensional (Oskamp 1991). Thurstone and Likert scales, on the other hand, may measure two or more underlying dimensions.

Although researchers have constructed a number of Guttman scales over the years, doing so is not an easy task (Eagly and Chaiken 1993). Selecting items that fit the Guttman scaling criteria remains intuitive, and many items are often tossed out or revised.

Semantic Differential Scaling

Another popular way of measuring attitudes today involves a method called the **semantic differential scale** (Osgood, Suci, and Tannenbaum 1957).

This scale measures the connotative meaning of the attitude object, that is, its implied meaning (Oskamp 1991). In contrast to the other methods, the semantic differential scale does not consist of specific statements about the attitude object. Instead, a respondent is asked to evaluate an attitude object by checking a point along a seven category continuum that stretches between a pair of adjectives that are opposite in meaning (see Table 6.4).

This method has several advantages (Eagly and Chaiken 1993). First, it is a simple method for measuring a person's evaluative response to an attitude object. Second, it allows researchers to study many different topics without having to construct new scales every time. And third, it allows researchers to compare attitudes across different attitude objects (such as social policies or social groups).

THE DEVELOPMENT OF ATTITUDES

John Rocker, star pitcher for the Atlanta Braves, earned the dubious distinction of being America's most prejudiced sportsman when his controversial comments about New York appeared in the December 1999 issue of *Sports Illustrated*. The interview with Jeff Pearlman took place in Rocker's minivan as they drove along Atlanta's Route 400. It was not long before Rocker spoke the words that would receive national attention for days to come: "Imagine having to take the [Number] 7 train to

TABLE 6.4	SEMANTIC DIFFERENTIAL SCALE	
	Americans	
Beautiful	–:–:–:–:–:–	Ugly
Bad	–:–:–:–:–:–	Good
Pleasant	–:–:–:–:–:–	Unpleasant
Dirty	–:–:–:–:–:–	Clean
Wise	–:–:–:–:–:–	Foolish

Source: Eagly and Chaiken 1993, 55.

the ballpark, looking like you're [riding through] Beirut next to some kid with purple hair next to some queer with AIDS right next to some dude who got out of jail for the fourth time right next to some 20-year-old mom with four kids. It's depressing." He continued to say: "The biggest thing I don't like about New York are the foreigners. I'm not a very big fan of foreigners. You can walk an entire block in Times Square and not hear anybody speaking English. Asians and Koreans and Vietnamese and Indians and Russians and Spanish people and everything up there. How the hell did they get in this country?" (Pearlman 1999, 2).

Rocker's shocking remarks caused a sensation. New Yorkers were outraged by his contempt. Nationwide, Americans condemned his hateful attitudes and expected the league to impose harsh sanctions on him. It did. He was suspended and fined $20,000.

It is hard to say how many people share Rocker's views. Many people would not express their prejudices so openly. Some of them might agree with matters he raises, such as wondering how foreigners get into this country. The reaction of most Americans, however, seemed to show that they were most concerned with a different question: How are hateful attitudes like that formed? And could a high-profile sports figure like Rocker shape similar attitudes in young fans?

We do have some answers to these questions. First, we know that people are not born with the kinds of attitudes Rocker expressed; they are learned predispositions (Allport, 1935; Doob, 1947; Campbell, 1963; Eagly and Chaiken 1993). Second, attitude formation occurs in a number of ways. And third, role models do have an impact on shaping attitudes in others. Learning theories can help us understand more about these processes. We will now consider the most important of these—classical conditioning, operant or instrumental conditioning, and social learning theory.

Classical Conditioning

Learning theories propose that we develop attitudes in the same way that we acquire habits. We learn to associate a particular stimulus with a particular response. In his famous experiments with dogs, discussed in Chapter 2, Ivan Pavlov showed how an unconditioned stimulus like meat would elicit an unconditioned response—salivation. He then created an association between meat and a bell, a neutral stimulus, by repeatedly pairing them. He discovered that eventually, the bell alone caused the dog to salivate. The dog had learned to associate the bell with salivating.

Animals are trained in this way to perform certain kinds of behaviors. But can classical conditioning explain the formation of attitudes in human beings? Research indicates that it can (Weiss 1968; Zanna, Kiesler, and Pilkonis 1970; Parish and

Whether sports figures like it or not, they do serve as role models. Young fans are likely to adopt the attitudes of athletes they admire, even the undesirable kinds of attitudes expressed by John Rocker.

Fleetwood 1975). To illustrate how this happens, consider how children develop positive or negative attitudes toward Halloween. The very notion of "trick or treat" suggests how the process operates. When a pleasant experience such as eating candy is paired with a tradition such as Halloween, children are likely to develop a positive attitude toward this holiday. By experiencing this pleasant association year after year, children begin to look forward to Halloween with keen delight. It is also possible, however, that some children might associate an unpleasant experience with Halloween and develop a negative attitude toward it. For example, strangers in unfamiliar costumes who jump out of bushes making loud, frightening noises often cause young children to cry. When Halloween is associated with this kind of unpleasant experience, children are more likely to develop a negative attitude toward it. Although few people seem to have negative attitudes toward Halloween, many approach other holidays with dread. According to classical conditioning theory, the experiences they associate with these holidays may well explain these kinds of attitudes.

Operant Conditioning

Operant or instrumental conditioning also explains how attitudes form. This process occurs when an individual's behavior is followed by something that either increases or decreases the likelihood that the behavior will be repeated. In his research with rats, B. F. Skinner observed that if an animal were rewarded for a particular behavior (for example, a rat receives a food pellet for pushing a lever), it would repeat that behavior. Skinner claimed that attitude formation in human beings occurs in a similar fashion. He even advocated the use of operant conditioning to teach children socially desirable attitudes. The idea is simple. Suppose parents want to teach their children that reading is good. According to Skinner (1948), children are likely to develop this attitude if their parents reinforce this behavior. When they notice their child reading, parents might compliment or praise him. Reinforcement can also come in a

nonverbal form—a parent might cast an approving smile when a child picks up a book.

Many studies in the late 1950s and 1960s sought to understand how operant conditioning shaped attitudes in human beings (Eagly and Chaiken 1993). In a typical experiment, the researcher would engage a subject in a conversation. He might ask the subject to answer questions or to construct sentences. As the interaction proceeded, the researcher would respond to certain verbal responses that the subject made with either approval or disapproval. For example, he might say "good," "uh-hmm," or "bad," "humph." Nonverbal communication, such as an approving or disapproving nod, also served as a form of reinforcement. These studies showed that subjects' verbal behavior could be operantly conditioned (Greenspoon 1955; Verplanck 1955; Insko 1965; Oakes 1967).

While Skinner advocated this method for shaping desirable attitudes in children, he also recognized that prejudiced attitudes are formed in the same way. Children learn racist, sexist, ethnocentric, and homophobic attitudes when parents or other important others express approval and reinforce them.

Social Learning Theory

Social learning theory also explains how attitudes are formed. It suggests that children can learn attitudes by simply observing and imitating other people. Albert Bandura (1977, 1986, 1992) agreed that learning can occur through operant conditioning as Skinner described, but he also claimed that it was unreasonable to believe that all learning occurred in this way. In his experimental research, he studied how nursery school children learned from adult models (Bandura 1965a). One of his best-known experiments involved the behavior of children who observed an adult attack a large, inflated Bobo doll. In one condition, the adult received soft drinks and candy after he hit the doll. In a second condition, another adult spanked the model with a magazine after he hit the doll. In a third condition, no consequences resulted when the adult hit the doll. Later the children were left alone to play with the Bobo doll.

The results showed that children who had observed the adult who was punished for hitting the Bobo doll were less likely to imitate this behavior. But did they learn anything from this model? To determine this, Bandura offered the children a reward for imitating what they had seen. In every condition, children were able to reproduce the behavior they had observed.

Parents serve as the first models for children. Eventually, however, children will imitate other models. Sports figures like John Rocker pose a threat to parents who do not want their children to develop prejudiced attitudes. So do other popular celebrities such as rap musicians whose lyrics promote intolerance, violence, vulgarity, and depravity.

THE FUNCTIONS OF ATTITUDES

Most of us spend a considerable amount of time trying to figure other people out. It is not easy. People's attitudes often do not seem to make sense. In the aftermath of President Clinton's impeachment, William Safire (1999) tried to understand Americans' attitudes toward this flawed man. He wrote:

> I love a mystery: what inspires the phenomenal loyalty to Bill Clinton?
>
> There he stands in the dock, impeached as a perjurer, certain of more censure, roundly denounced by even political allies for weaknesses that dishonored his office. . . .
>
> Through all the revelations of deceit, his wife steadfastly grasps his hand. His political party marches lockstep down the line to protect him. And the public, in opinion polls and at the polling booth, stand by him more staunchly with each step toward historic shame.
>
> That's loyalty across the board, the likes of which this nation has never seen before. What's behind it?

Safire suggested that it might be due to economic prosperity, respect for the presidency, shared political goals, and even blind love.

Human beings are not born with attitudes. Children learn attitudes by observing and imitating others.

The idea that people's needs and motives influence their attitudes is not new. In seeking to understand the reasons that people hold on to certain attitudes, Daniel Katz (1960) argued that attitudes serve a number of functions. Let us consider the four main functions that he described (see Table 6.5).

1. The **adjustment function**. Attitudes that help us satisfy our needs, help us reach a goal, or avoid an undesirable outcome serve an adjustment function. These kinds of attitudes are viewed as utilitarian or instrumental. This

function reflects the view that people seek to maximize their rewards and minimize their costs (punishments). Workers who express favorable attitudes toward a political party that promises to improve their financial situation illustrate the kind of utilitarian functions that some attitudes perform. Likewise, politicians whose attitudes simply mirror public opinion appear to have a goal—victory on election day.

2. The **ego-defensive function**. Attitudes can also protect our egos or self-images. We all use defense mechanisms for this purpose. However, people with internal conflicts, insecurities, and feelings of inferiority are more likely to form ego-defensive attitudes. Defensive attitudes take various forms, including rationalization, projection, and displacement. A student who blames her teacher for poor grades may have formed an ego-defensive attitude to deny her own failures. Prejudiced attitudes may also serve a defensive function. A popular explanation of prejudice, known as the scapegoat theory of prejudice, suggests that people gain a sense of superiority over a disadvantaged group by displacing their own feelings of inferiority onto members of this group.

3. The **value-expressive function**. In contrast to attitudes that serve to protect images of ourselves, value-expressive attitudes reveal who we are. They reflect cherished beliefs and values that are central to our self-image. A political candidate who claims he is a compassionate conservative, a new Democrat, or a liberal will seek to express attitudes that are consistent with these self-images.

4. The **knowledge function**. Attitudes also help us interpret the events that affect our lives. They provide a way for us to organize information and provide standards or frames of reference for understanding other people. As such, they serve a knowledge function. For example, we are more likely to support a political candidate who shares our views on important issues. That does not mean, however, that attitudes serving a knowledge function portray an accurate or truthful picture of the world. Walter Lippmann (1922/1991) made this point about stereotypes, claiming that they "are an ordered, more or less consistent picture of the world, to which our habits, our tastes, our capacities, our comforts and our hopes have adjusted themselves. They may not be a complete picture of the world, but they are a picture of a possible world to which we are adapted" (95).

The functions that Katz described reflect the primary focus of several popular twentieth century theories (Eagly and Chaiken 1993). For example, the adjustment function is based on principles of learning theory, while the ego-defensive function reflects psychoanalytic theory. The

TABLE 6.5 THE FUNCTIONS OF ATTITUDES

Function	Description	Theoretical Influence
Adjustment	Utility of attitudinal object in need satisfaction; maximizing external rewards and minimizing punishments	Behaviorism
Ego-defensive	Protecting against internal conflicts and external dangers	Freudian and Neo-Freudian
Value-expressive	Maintaining self identity; enhancing favorable self-image; self-expression and self-determination	Ego psychology
Knowledge	Need for understanding, for meaningful cognitive organization, for consistency and clarity	Gestalt psychology

Source: Katz 1960, 192.

BOX 6.2   FAMOUS PEOPLE EXPRESSING THEIR ATTITUDES

Our approach to life and the decisions we make can be influenced by the attitudes of others, especially famous people whose words have been immortalized. You might not even know who made the following statements. As you read them, ask yourself what function these attitudes served for the people who expressed them. Did they help these individuals interpret the events that affected their lives? Or did they reflect cherished beliefs and values that were central to their self-image?

"The basis of our government being the opinion of the people, the very first object should be to keep that right; and were it left to me to decide whether we should have a government without newspapers, or newspapers without a government, I should not hesitate a moment to prefer the latter."
—Thomas Jefferson, letter to Colonel Edward Carrington (January 16, 1787)

"Society in every state is a blessing, but government, even in its best state, is but a necessary evil; in its worst state, an intolerable one."
—Thomas Paine, *Common Sense* (1776)

"Is life so dear or peace so sweet as to be punished at the price of chains and slavery? Forbid it, Almighty God, I know not what course others may take, but as for me, give me liberty or give me death!"
—Patrick Henry, speech at the Virginia Convention (March 23, 1775)

"No one can make you feel inferior without your consent."
—Eleanor Roosevelt, *This Is My Story* (1937)

"Remember that time is money."
—Benjamin Franklin, "Advice to a Young Tradesman" (1748)

"To be prepared for war is one of the most effectual means of preparing for peace."
—George Washington, address to both houses of Congress (January 8, 1790)

---

value-expressive function is particularly well suited to theories that focus on the development of the self and self-presentation. And the knowledge function is compatible with cognitive theories that stress the idea that people seek to simplify, organize, and reduce inconsistencies in their cognitions (see Box 6.2).

CONSISTENCY THEORIES

For thousands of years, people have predicted that the world was about to end. Even though the Bible says that no one will know the exact date, this prediction has given rise to a number of millennial and messianic movements (Festinger 1957). One of the best-known cases involved the nineteenth-century Millerite movement. The leaders of this movement convinced a large number of people that the world would end in 1843. When it did not, they were initially bewildered. But they soon

found a reason. Arguing that William Miller had simply miscalculated the date, they renewed their efforts to recruit more members to the movement. It took three more disappointments before this movement finally died out.

As this case illustrates, it is difficult for people to abandon a strongly held belief. Instead they often seek to justify or rationalize the inconsistencies that threaten it. Two of the most influential theories of attitudes help us understand how people do this. They argue that people seek consistent relationships among their attitudes. That is, we like our beliefs, ideas, and behaviors to fit together. When inconsistencies disturb this pattern, people feel uncomfortable and seek to restore consistency.

Heider's Balance Theory

The earliest theory of **cognitive consistency** was developed by Fritz Heider (1958), who was interested in understanding the role that attitudes played in interpersonal relationships. Known as **balance theory**, the basic elements of his triangular model consist of a perceiver (P), another person (O), and an impersonal entity or attitude object (X). The relationships between pairs of elements in this model can be of two types: a sentiment relationship (attitudinal) or a unit relationship (nonattitudinal). *Sentiment relationships* refer to those that involve attitudes and therefore some kind of evaluation. For example, Jane (P) opposes stricter gun control laws (X). *Unit relationships*, by contrast, do not involve attitudes. Rather than evaluations, they characterize a relationship in terms of similarity, proximity, ownership, causality, or membership in a group (Oskamp 1991; Eagly and Chaiken 1993). For example, Steven's membership in Sigma Chi fraternity represents a unit relationship. The nature of both sentiment and unit relationships is designated by either a positive sign (+) or a negative sign (−).

Heider proposed that the relationships among the three basic elements created either a balanced or an imbalanced state within an individual. As Figure 6.2 shows, the relationships among P, O, and X can produce eight possible patterns. A balanced state exists when the relationships among elements are consistent. The model is stable and unlikely to change. However, if the relationships among the elements are inconsistent, an imbalanced state exists. According to Heider, individuals experience tension when the elements in this model do not fit together. In this case, the structure is unstable and likely to change.

To determine whether the elements in this model are balanced, you can perform a simple mathematical calculation. When all three relationships are positive, or when one is positive and two are negative, the model is balanced: $(+)(+)(+) = (+)$ and $(+)(−)(−) = (+)$. The model is unbalanced when two relationships are positive and one is negative, or when all three relationships are negative: $(+)(+)(−) = (−)$ and $(−)(−)(−) = (−)$.

Heider's balance theory suggests that we feel comfortable when people we like agree with us on issues and when people we dislike disagree with us. His theory also helps us understand our feelings when someone we like disagrees with us on an issue or when someone we dislike happens to agree with us on an issue.

Most of us can quickly grasp Heider's theory. It is intuitively appealing and provides an explanation for the distress we experience when we recognize inconsistencies in our attitudes. It also provides a model to explain how cognitive inconsistencies motivate people to change their attitudes. A number of consistency theories reflect the impact of Heider's original ideas, and research has supported his claim that people prefer balanced systems (von Hecker, 1993). At the same time, Heider's theory fails to adequately explain why some imbalanced states resist change. For example, why do people remain members of organizations (churches, political parties) when they disagree on serious issues?

Critics claim that Heider's theory is just too simple—that a triangle composed of three elements fails to accurately depict the complex structure of our attitudes. They also argue that Heider's model ignores the varying degrees of importance that we assign to the relationships between certain elements. For example, when we love someone, it is easy to overlook minor disagreements. That is, the strength of love is not comparable to the strength of agreement or disagreement on an issue. In fact, research shows that we often disagree with our friends, may like our opponents, and even be happy when someone we dislike agrees with us (Zajonc 1968; Sears and Whitney 1973; Oskamp 1991).

Festinger's Theory of Cognitive Dissonance

In 1957, Leon Festinger proposed another consistency theory, which he called **cognitive dissonance**. Like Heider, he believed that people seek consistency in their attitudes and opinions. He claimed that consistency is the usual state and was intrigued by the exceptions. He noted, for example, that an individual might believe in racial equality but object to integrated neighborhoods or that someone who knows that smoking cigarettes is dangerous to his health may nonetheless

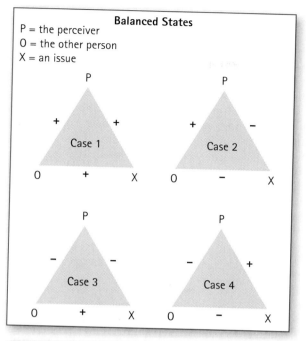

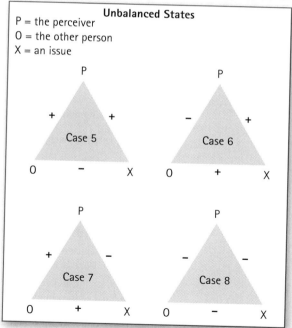

FIGURE 6.2

Eight Possible Patterns in Heider's Balance Theory of Cognitive Consistency

Do you like people who agree with you on an issue and dislike those who disagree with you? That is what we generally expect (cases 1–4). But what happens when someone you like disagrees with you on an issue or when someone you dislike happens to agree with you on an issue (cases 5–8)?

continue to smoke. Convinced that people could not psychologically accept these kinds of inconsistencies, Festinger argued that they would be motivated to restore consistency. And he undertook research to understand how they would respond to their own inconsistent attitudes in various situations.

Focusing on the cognitive component of attitudes, Festinger (1957, 3) defined the term **cognition** as "any knowledge, opinion, or belief about the environment, about oneself, or about one's behavior." He then considered cognitions in the form of sentences, such as "I smoke cigarettes," "I said the experimental task was fun," and "I voted for Ross Perot." According to him, the relationships between cognitions like these may be *consonant, dissonant,* or *irrelevant.*

Consonant relationships fit together; they are consistent in the sense that element *Y* follows from element *X*. The cognitions "I am a Democrat" and "I voted for John Kerry" are consonant. When elements do not follow this pattern but instead suggest the opposite—that element *Y* follows from the opposite of element *X*—a dissonant relationship

exists. For example, "I voted for George Bush" does not follow from "I am a Democrat." In some cases, cognitive elements are simply irrelevant, which means that one element has no bearing on the other one. The cognitions "I voted for Arnold Schwarzenegger" and "I chose to buy the Toyota over the Honda" are irrelevant. Table 6.6 illustrates some consonant and dissonant cognitions a person might hold simultaneously.

Like earlier consistency theorists, Festinger argued that dissonant cognitions caused people to feel tense or anxious. And he believed that this kind of psychological discomfort would motivate them to make their cognitions consonant. But he also recognized that the nature and structure of attitudes were more complex than Heider had assumed. Taking that into account, he proposed two key hypotheses:

1. When cognitive dissonance exists, individuals will feel pressure to reduce that dissonance.

2. The strength of that pressure will vary with the magnitude of the dissonance, which depends on the importance of the cognitions.

TABLE 6.6	DISSONANT AND CONSONANT COGNITIVE ELEMENTS	
Cognition	Dissonant Element	Consonant Element
I smoke cigarettes.	Smoking is a health hazard.	Smoking keeps my weight down.
I said the experimental task was fun.	I found the task dull.	I got $20 for saying the task was fun.
I do not practice safe sex.	AIDS is a deadly virus.	I am in a monogamous relationship and trust my partner completely.
I chose to buy the Toyota over the Honda.	Hondas get better mileage than Toyotas.	Toyota has a better repair record than Honda.
My friend Marie is pro-life.	I am pro-choice.	Marie is Catholic and believes in the teaching of the church.
I voted for George Bush.	I'm a registered Democrat.	The ballot was confusing.
I voted for John Kerry.	I'm a registered Republican.	Kerry will keep the economy in good shape.

Source: Adapted from Eagly and Chaiken 1993, 470.

To illustrate how people respond when they recognize inconsistencies in their cognitions, Festinger offered the example of a person who smokes cigarettes. He argued that the cognition "I know I smoke" was dissonant with the cognition "I believe smoking is bad for my health." A person's decision to stop smoking would depend on the pressure he feels, which depends on the importance attached to his cognitions. Some smokers might decide to give up cigarettes. But Festinger (1957) recognized that many smokers do not stop smoking. And he argued that they usually rationalized that decision. For example, smokers may say that even though smoking is unhealthy, (1) they enjoy it so much that it is worth the risk, (2) the health risks are not that serious, (3) they cannot avoid all things that are potentially dangerous, or (4) they would put on weight, which is also unhealthy, if they stopped. According to Festinger, people will try to reduce the dissonance they feel when they behave in ways that are inconsistent with their attitudes in one of three ways: by changing a cognition, by adding a cognition, or by reducing the importance of a cognition.

Festinger's approach to studying attitudes focused on cognitive processes, but it did not ignore human behavior. In fact, much of his work examined the relationship between attitudes and behavior. But his approach differed from previous attitude-behavior research. Departing from a widely held belief that attitudes determine behavior, he proposed just the opposite—that behavior determines attitudes. To think of it in another way, Festinger suggested that we are more likely to find reasons for the way we behave than to practice what we preach (Abelson 1972). This seemingly counterintuitive approach proved to be quite appealing.

According to Festinger, his theory could explain many everyday experiences and observations. Consider questions that most of us have pondered at one time or another: Why do we feel torn when we make tough decisions? Why do people listen to or even seek out some information voluntarily but totally ignore other messages? And why do we come to value experiences that involve great effort, sacrifice, or heartbreak? In the next section, we will consider these questions and other ways to apply cognitive dissonance theory.

The Consequences of Decision Making

Making decisions is often difficult, especially when the choices before us are equally attractive. Consider a talented gymnast who must decide whether to enter medical school or postpone that and train for the Olympics for the next four years. Festinger claimed that making decisions like this often arouses dissonance. When we make choices between two or more attractive alternatives, the undesirable aspects of our final decision are inconsistent with the desirable aspects of the unchosen alternative.

As Festinger's theory would suggest, the amount of cognitive dissonance produced by making a decision depends on the importance attached to it. As the importance or difficulty increases, so does the dissonance. It is also greater when the choice involves equally attractive alternatives and when the similarity between alternatives is low (Oskamp 1991). People often reduce the dissonance by subjectively altering their evaluations of the possibilities after they make their final decision. That is, we tend to like the chosen alternative more and the unchosen one less.

A number of studies have demonstrated **postdecision cognitive dissonance** (Brehm 1956; Aronson 1997; Murphy and Miller, 1997). In one study, researchers showed how the confidence of gamblers at a racetrack increased after they had placed their bet (Knox and Inkster 1968). Many studies have shown how consumers alter their perceptions of products after they buy them (Gilovich, Medvec, and Chen 1995; Murphy and Miller 1997). And other studies have shown how voters alter their perceptions of candidates on election day (Regan and Kilduff 1988).

Selective Exposure

Another result of making decisions is the tendency to seek out or pay attention to information that suggests that our attitudes are correct. Festinger originally referred to this phenomenon as voluntary and involuntary exposure to information. Today, social psychologists call it **selective exposure** (Frey and Wicklund 1978; Sweeney and Gruber 1984; Frey 1986). To illustrate how selective exposure operates, consider how different people respond to certain media messages. Whereas an atheist is likely to change the channel when a Billy Graham television special airs, a born-again Christian is likely to watch it with enthusiasm. A feminist is more likely to read *Ms.* magazine than *Playboy*. And a lifelong Democrat is more likely to listen to a speech given by Senator Hillary Clinton than one given by President George W. Bush. As these examples suggest, people seek information that supports their own worldview—ideas and views with which they already agree.

The idea that our preexisting attitudes influence what we tune in or tune out explains why political ads or political controversies seem to cause little change in people's opinions. We simply ignore the other side's point of view. A study of people's attitudes toward the Watergate scandal during the Nixon administration provided evidence to support the selective exposure hypothesis (Sweeney and Gruber 1984). At the time of the Watergate hearings in 1973, researchers interviewed people about the affair. The results showed that President Nixon's supporters avoided information about the scandal and paid less attention to the hearings than people who had supported Nixon's opponent, George McGovern, for president in 1972.

The Role of Social Support

Social groups play an important role in both creating and reducing cognitive dissonance (Festinger 1957). When other people express opinions or provide information that does not conform to our own attitudes, we may experience dissonance. On the other hand, when other people agree with us, they can provide substantial social support. The idea that social groups influence how people respond to cognitive dissonance was rooted in Festinger's theory of social comparison (1954). According to this theory, people compare themselves to others out of their need to evaluate their own behavior, abilities, expertise, and opinions. It is common for us to wonder if we hold the right attitudes. Should we do away with the electoral college? Is capital punishment right? Should the United States send peacekeeping troops abroad? When we find social support for our views, we are content. But when we discover that others do not share our opinions, we experience dissonance.

As Festinger suggested, we can try to reduce the dissonance we feel in a number of ways. We can change our attitude, discredit the group's position, or persuade the others to change their

Would you participate in or even listen to an anti-gun protest? The idea that we tune in to messages that reinforce our preexisting attitudes is called *selective exposure*.

opinions (Oskamp 1991). He also claimed that we might look for social support. We might actively seek out others who share our views or even recruit people who have not yet formed an opinion.

Festinger offered a number of examples to show how people seek social support to maintain consistency in their attitudes. One of these involved a field study of a doomsday group that Festinger had read about in a local newspaper (Festinger, Riecken, and Schacter 1956). Marion Keech, the leader of this group, claimed that she had received written messages from a number of "guardians" from outer space. One of these messages predicted that a cataclysmic flood would engulf most of the North American continent on a certain day just before dawn. Members of this group, however, would be rescued by a flying saucer, which would land in Keech's backyard. Convinced that the end of the world was near, many of Keech's followers quit their jobs and gave their belongings away.

Festinger and his colleagues believed that members of this group would experience a great deal of dissonance when their expectations were not met. And they were right. For hours after their expectations failed to materialize, the group sought to understand what had happened. Unable to deny their commitment to this prophecy, members of Keech's group provided social support to one another. Just hours after Keech's prophecy failed to come true, she received another message from God that allowed them to maintain consistency in their cognitions. It revealed that "he had saved the world and stayed the flood because of this group and the light and strength they had spread throughout the world that night" (Festinger 1957, 258).

The Induced Compliance Paradigm

What happens when people are persuaded to behave in a way that is inconsistent with their attitudes? Consider a vice-president who publicly supports the president's position on an issue even though he privately disagrees. What about a woman who marries a man even though she does not really love him? In some cases, people are able to deny that they acted in a way that is inconsistent with their attitudes. But most people are not able to do this.

Festinger and Carlsmith (1959) sought to understand how people reduced the dissonance produced by attitude-behavior discrepancies in an experiment that is now regarded as a classic. Their idea was to create a situation that would allow them to persuade subjects to behave in ways that were inconsistent with their attitudes. To get a sense of what these subjects experienced, imagine yourself in their experiment.

A researcher meets you at the door and explains that his study involves "measures of performance." He then shows you a large board with rows of square pegs. Your task is to move from row to row turning each of these pegs back and forth as you go. As you proceed, you begin to think what a waste of time this is. But you continue. After some time, the experimenter gives you a different task. Now he directs you to take spools of thread off of a pegboard and then put them back on.

You are anxious to leave when it looks like the experiment is over. But then the researcher asks you for some unexpected assistance. He now explains that you were a subject in the control condition. In the experimental condition, a confederate prepares subjects for these tasks by telling them the experiment is fun, fascinating, and exciting. Unfortunately, the person who usually plays the confederate role couldn't make it to the lab and another subject is now waiting outside. Can you help? The researcher says that he will pay you $1 if you would be willing to be the confederate today.

Suppose you do agree to help the researcher. In this case, he has created a situation that should produce cognitive dissonance. You have already formed an attitude toward the boring tasks you just performed ("It was a complete waste of time"). Now you will go into the waiting room and tell another subject how interesting the experiment is. In reality, you are not the confederate in this experiment. In fact, the subject you speak to is actually the confederate. And this experiment does not involve "measures of performance." It is designed to understand how people reduce the cognitive dissonance they experience when their privately formed attitudes clash with their public actions.

In Festinger and Carlsmith's experiment, only three of the fifty-one subjects refused to participate in this part of the experiment—to lie. The rest agreed to play the role of a confederate. In addition to the $1 incentive condition, Festinger and Carlsmith created a $20 incentive to play the confederate role. This variation was designed to see how a larger incentive would affect the subjects. Would it serve to justify lying? (Keep in mind that $20 was a lot of money for a student in the 1950s. Today, researchers would have to offer about $100 to create a comparable condition.)

Once the subjects told the person in the waiting room that the experiment was fun, they presumably believed that their participation in this experiment was over. But again, it was not. They were now asked to see the secretary in the psychology department to fill out a questionnaire required by subjects in all experiments. This questionnaire

asked them to evaluate the tasks they had performed.

Consider each of the conditions that Festinger and Carlsmith had created. Would subjects who were paid just $1 to lie now say that the experiment was interesting? Or would subjects who received $20 to lie be more likely to say this? The results for each of the conditions are shown in Figure 6.3. Students who received $1 for lying rated the tasks as more enjoyable than those who received $20. As Festinger and Carlsmith expected, the larger incentive ($20) served as a justification for behaving in a way that was inconsistent with one's attitude. The smaller incentive ($1), however, was not sufficient to justify a lie. In this case, Festinger and Carlsmith argued that subjects reduced the dissonance by actually changing their attitudes about the tasks.

Overjustification

Festinger and Carlsmith's classic experiment on counterattitudinal behavior demonstrates the effects of both **induced compliance** and **insufficient justification**. It also suggests that **overjustification** may produce some unintended effects. Forcing or bribing children to participate in activities that are intrinsically rewarding, such as sports, music, or other kinds of learning, can produce an unwanted effect. For example, consider children who attribute their effort in school to a monetary incentive ($25 for every A). Believing that their pleasure is due to the money, these children may never recognize that learning can be rewarding in and of itself. This analysis fits Harold Kelley's discounting principle, which suggests that the financial reward causes them to discount other possible causes for feeling good when they do well in school (Oskamp 1991).

Criticisms of Cognitive Dissonance Theory

For years, social psychologists accepted Festinger and Carlsmith's explanation for the results of their classic experiment. But it did not go unchallenged. Daryl Bem (1967) offered the first alternative

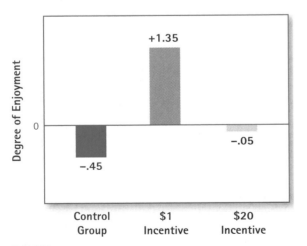

FIGURE 6.3

Subjects' Mean Ratings of Experimental Tasks in Festinger and Carlsmith's Induced Compliance Experiment

Source: Based on data in Festinger and Carlsmith 1959, 207.

explanation. Disputing the assumption that dissonance motivates people to change their attitudes, he explained the results in terms of **self-perception theory** (Bem 1972). He believed that we are likely to draw inferences about our own attitudes in the same way that we would draw inferences about other people's attitudes—on the basis of what we observe. In his original version of self-perception theory, Bem argued that people do not know their own attitudes until after they act (Bem and McConnell 1970). Eventually, he modified this extreme position, but he still claimed that we often do not know our internal states. And he claimed that when internal cues are weak, ambiguous, or uninterpretable, we are functionally in the same position as an outsider who is trying to determine our attitudes.

According to Bem, the subjects in Festinger and Carlsmith's experiment did not experience cognitive dissonance but rather drew inferences about their attitudes by acting as observers of their own behaviors. To fully understand what Bem meant, consider how people would make attributions about the subjects in this experiment based on what they see. In the $1 condition, an observer would see a subject tell a confederate that a task is enjoyable (even though that is unbelievable). Moments later, the observer sees the subject saying the same thing to a secretary. An observer, who considers all of the plausible causes for these statements, is likely to decide that a $1 incentive is not large enough to convince a subject to tell a lie. Therefore, he ignores it and concludes that the subject did enjoy the task. In this case, the observer makes an attribution to an internal disposition of the actor based on his most recent statement—"I enjoyed the task."

Now consider what an observer sees in the $20 condition. This time a subject tells a confederate that the task is enjoyable (again unbelievable). Soon after that, however, the subject tells the secretary the task was boring. What would the observer conclude about this subject's attitude? These contradictory statements pose a problem. However, in this case, there is a plausible cause for the subject's contradictory statements. The

observer can attribute the subject's first statement to the $20 incentive. As an external cause for this behavior, an observer is likely to conclude that this does not tell him anything about this subject's real attitude. Based on the subject's most recent behavior (his statement to the secretary), an observer is likely to conclude that the subject did not enjoy the task.

If people do make attributions about themselves in the same way that they make attributions about other people—on the basis of what they observe—self-perception theory would predict the same thing that cognitive dissonance does: that people in the $20 condition are less likely to believe that they really enjoyed the task than people in the $1 condition.

Thus self-perception theory and cognitive dissonance theory predict the same thing, but they are based on substantially different assumptions about attitudes and attitude formation (Fazio, Zanna, and Cooper 1977; Eagly and Chaiken 1993). Social psychologists conducted many studies, seeking to determine which theory provided the better explanation. Overall, the results proved to be largely inconclusive. Today, social psychologists believe that self-perception theory provides the better explanation in instances where attitudes are weak, ambiguous, or difficult to interpret. Cognitive dissonance theory is better in cases that involve long-standing, well-defined attitudes.

Attitudes and Behaviors

"We can measure attitudes, chart their trends over time, discover their relations to age, education, response latency, and a host of other social and psychological variables, but do attitudes as assessed by questionnaires and interviews relate to behavior outside the assessment situation?" (Schuman 1995, 72)

Richard La Piere (1934), an early symbolic interactionist, addressed this question in a classic study. Over a two-year period of time that began in 1930, he traveled across the United States with a young, foreign-born Chinese couple. Prejudice toward minorities and foreigners, as measured by social distance scales, was particularly high at this time in America. Seeking to determine how attitudes toward the Chinese were related to the way that people actually treated them, La Piere kept detailed records of the hotels, auto camps, and restaurants they visited. His notes indicated whether they were admitted to these places and, if so, how well they were treated. These records showed a surprising result. In a journey that covered about 10,000 miles, the group was accepted and served at 251 establishments. Only one auto camp refused to accept them.

La Piere sent a letter to each of the establishments they had visited six months later. He enclosed a survey, which included the question "Will you accept members of the Chinese race as guests in your establishment?" Of the 128 returned questionnaires, 92 percent said no.

What can we learn from La Piere's study? Is it fair to conclude that attitudes are not related to behavior outside of an assessment situation? For years after this classic study, empirical research supported this conclusion. But it was not taken seriously until 1955 when Herbert Blumer, another symbolic interactionist, questioned the definition attached to "attitude" and the assumption that attitudes influence behavior (Eagly and Chaiken 1993). At the same time, psychologists pointed out that the correlations between attitudes and behaviors were often weak (Green 1954; Campbell 1963; Festinger 1964). In a review of forty-two studies, Alan Wicker (1969) concluded that in most cases, verbal measures of attitudes were weakly related to behaviors. And he argued, "There was little evidence that people possess stable underlying attitudes that influence their overt behaviors" (Eagly and Chaiken 1993, 156). Festinger's research on cognitive dissonance, which suggested that behavior influenced attitudes, also raised questions about the causal direction between these two variables.

The debate took a new turn when critics pointed out that Wicker's review of the research focused on laboratory studies and excluded survey research (Eagly and Chaiken 1993). As a result, he failed to recognize that many studies of voting

behavior showed that voters' attitudes toward a candidate were fairly accurate predictors of their actual vote (Campbell et al. 1960). In fact, most of these studies showed a significant relationship between attitudes and behaviors (Schuman and Johnson 1976).

Seeking to explain why voting studies failed to support the weak-link conclusion of other studies, social psychologists recognized important differences in research designs. Some studies failed to account for differing levels of specificity between measures of attitudes and behaviors. To illustrate, consider voting studies. The typical question posed to respondents is "Whom do you intend to vote for?" The responses offered are specific—the name of a particular candidate such as John Kerry or George W. Bush. The voting behavior that is measured later is also specific—John Kerry or George W. Bush. In contrast, studies that showed a weak link between attitudes and behaviors failed to match the levels of specificity for attitudes and behaviors. So, for example, they might ask respondents a question about African Americans in general but measure their behavior toward a specific African American.

Although La Piere expressed this concern in the opening paragraphs of his 1934 essay, researchers failed to understand the significance of his point. In fact, La Piere's classic study was prompted by his belief that "social attitudes are seldom more than a verbal response to a symbolic situation" (230). To illustrate his argument, he offered the following example:

> Because it is easy, cheap, and mechanical, the attitudinal questionnaire is rapidly becoming a major method of sociological and socio-psychological investigation. The technique is simple. Thus from a hundred or a thousand responses to the question "Would you get up to give an Armenian woman your seat in a street car?" the investigator derives the "attitude" of non-Armenian males towards Armenian females . . . yet all that has been obtained is a symbolic response to a symbolic situation. The words "Armenian woman" do not constitute an Armenian woman of flesh and blood, who might be tall or squat, fat or thin, old or young, well or

poorly dressed—who might, in fact, be a goddess or just another old and dirty hag. And the questionnaire response, whether it be "yes" or "no," is but a verbal reaction and this does not involve rising from the seat or stolidly avoiding the hurt eyes of the hypothetical woman and the derogatory states of other street-car occupants. (230)

In his study, La Piere sent a letter to the establishments visited that asked about Chinese guests in general. But the behaviors he had measured were in response to a specific well-dressed, well-spoken, gracious Chinese couple accompanied by a middle-class white male companion. In his conclusions, La Piere (1934) claimed that the results of his study cast doubt on data obtained through survey research and argued that social psychologists should study attitudes through naturalistic observation. At the same time, he did not indicate that verbal responses never predict behavior (Schuman 1995). And he claimed that the behavior of southern whites toward blacks would have shown a stronger relationship toward their attitudes. His primary point was that verbal symbols are too abstract to give us any reliable idea about how someone might act in a real-life situation.

THREE STAGES OF ATTITUDE–BEHAVIOR RESEARCH

For years, research failed to provide a conclusive explanation for the puzzling relationship between attitudes and behavior. But it did move forward. Mark Zanna and Russell Fazio (1982) characterized this progress in terms of three stages, each identified by a unique research question. During the first stage, researchers asked, "Do attitudes predict behavior?" When years of research failed to provide a conclusive answer to this question, social psychologists moved to the second stage, asking, "Under what conditions can relatively good predictions be made about the relationship between attitudes and behaviors?" These studies pointed to situational, personality, and attitudinal factors (Oskamp 1991). The third stage finally

turned to a question of "how": "How do psychological processes operate in establishing connections between attitudes and behaviors?"

Research that sought to answer these questions showed that methodological refinements improve the correspondence between attitudes and behaviors (Oskamp 1991; Eagly and Chaiken 1993). For example, the use of multiple items to measure both attitudes and behaviors yields stronger correlations between these variables (Fishbein and Ajzen 1974, 1975; Weigel and Newman 1976; Jaccard 1979; Snyder and Kendzierski 1982). Keeping the measurements of attitudes and behaviors on the same level of specificity, as La Piere had argued, also strengthens this relationship. And the conditions under which measurements are made should be as similar as possible. For example, research shows that measuring an attitude anonymously while measuring a behavior through public observation introduces methodological problems (Green 1972).

Studies also indicated that researchers should consider the strength, stability, and complexity of attitudes. Attitude strength can be measured in several ways (Schuman 1995). Researchers may decide to measure the *extremity*, *intensity*, or *importance* of an attitude. Measured in any of these ways, social psychologists recognize that stronger attitudes are more likely to influence behavior than weaker ones. Polls that seek to predict the winner of an election are designed with this in mind. Consider the questions that the Gallup poll posed to Americans in the months preceding the 2000 presidential election. In March 2000, Gallup asked respondents, "What is the most important problem facing the country today?" About a month later, it took another approach. In that poll, it provided people with a list of twelve issues and asked them to rate how important each of these issues would be in influencing their vote for president in November (see Figure 6.4). As this suggests, if researchers hope to increase the correspondence between an attitude and a behavior, they must do more than measure the direction of an attitude. They must also assess the strength of that attitude.

Gallup Poll, March 10–12, 2000
What is the most important problem facing the country today?

Education	16%
Ethics/morals	15
Crime/violence	13
Taxes	11
Dissatisfied with government	11
Medicare/Social Security	9
Health care	8
Poverty	5
Drugs	5
Federal budget deficit/debt	4
International problems/foreign affairs	4
Race relations	4
Availability of guns	4
Welfare	3
Military/defense	3

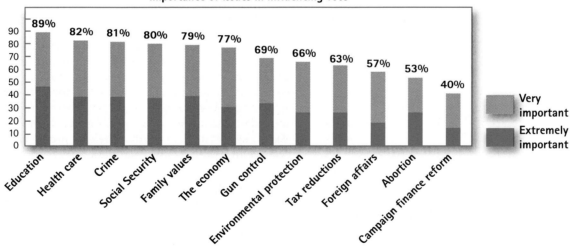

Gallup Poll, April 3–9, 2000
Importance of issues in influencing vote

FIGURE 6.4

Measuring the Strength of Attitudes: Two Approaches

Source: Gallup Organization, http://www.gallup.com

Pollsters use tracking polls like Gallup's to monitor the public's enthusiasm for presidential candidates. But reputable pollsters know that it is extremely risky to predict the winner of a race months in advance. The time that elapses between measuring an attitude and a behavior is another methodological concern. Research clearly shows that the shorter the time between measuring the intended vote and election day, the better the prediction.

What else should pollsters consider in trying to predict an election? Research suggests that they must also consider the stability of a person's attitude. Many studies show that stable attitudes are more likely to influence our behavior than more recently acquired ones (Doll and Ajzen 1992; Kraus 1995). This suggests that long-term members of the Democratic or Republican parties will vote along party lines. In close elections, the focus is likely to shift to the unknown factor—swing voters, whose attitudes are less stable and therefore less predictable.

Finally, let us consider how the correspondence between an attitude and behavior is affected by the complexity of our attitudes. Consider someone who has been a lifelong member of both the Democratic party and the Catholic church. How will this person vote? Will it be the Democratic candidate, even if he supports an abortion position that conflicts with that of the Catholic church? Or will this person cast a vote for the Republican candidate, who takes a position closer to the church's? As this suggests, our attitudes are complex. They must compete with other attitudes, values, and motives (Oskamp 1991). The issue of complexity is particularly important in assessing the relationship between prejudice and discrimination (Schuman 1972).

The second stage of attitude-behavior research identified a number of ways that methodological improvements could strengthen the link between attitudes and behavior. But it did not explain how psychological processes operate in establishing this connection. We will consider two theories that attempt to do just that.

The Reasoned Action Model

Fishbein and Azjen's theory of reasoned action (1975) proposes that the best predictions about an individual's behavior are based on his or her intentions (see Figure 6.5). If you plan to exercise three times a week, you are more likely to do so than

someone who does not intend to do so. How do **behavioral intentions** develop? According to Fishbein and Ajzen, they are shaped by two factors: an individual's attitude toward a behavior ("Exercising is good for my health") and a subjective norm (an individual's perception of what others think he or she ought to do: "My doctor recommended more exercise, my boyfriend will be pleased, and my friends value physical fitness").

An individual's attitude toward a specific behavior results from beliefs that this behavior will lead to certain outcomes and an evaluation of that outcome. A person's attitude toward exercising three times a week may be shaped by the belief that exercising will help her lose weight and that this is good for her health. Subjective norms are shaped by perceptions of what other important people expect us to do, as well as an individual's motivation to meet those expectations. Her doctor strongly urges her to exercise three times a week and she wants to follow his advice.

Fishbein and Ajzen's **reasoned action model** was widely accepted as a breakthrough in explaining the relationship between attitudes and behaviors. Though it specified just a few key variables, it could explain a variety of behaviors. It also addressed the problem La Piere recognized in trying to make predictions about an individual's behavior from an abstract verbal response (Schuman 1995). As the reasoned action model suggests, researchers should not measure attitudes toward an attitude object but rather attitudes toward a particular behavior. Thus it explains why research has failed to support the assumption that a negative attitude toward members of a particular minority group can predict a particular kind of behavior.

The Planned Behavior Model

The reasoned action model not only provided an explanation for years of mixed research findings but also suggested how researchers should design future studies. But questions remained. Critics argued that attitudes toward a behavior and subjective norms do not sufficiently account for behavioral intentions. In response to this criticism,

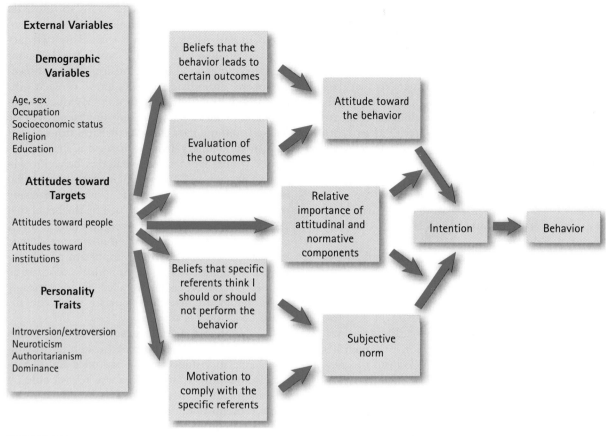

FIGURE 6.5

The Reasoned Action Model

Sources: Adapted from Ajzen and Fishbein 1980, 79–91.

Azjen (1985) recognized that while people may intend to behave in a certain way, they have varying amounts of control when it comes to accomplishing that. Suppose that you fully intended to vote on election day—you were registered and knew where you were supposed to go. But then something happened that was beyond your control. The night before the election, your flight home from an out-of-state business trip was cancelled due to bad weather. As it turns out, you got home an hour after the polls had closed.

Taking this problem into consideration, Ajzen modified the original theory to include a new variable—**perceived behavioral control**, which refers to someone's perception of how easy or difficult it is to perform a behavior (1985, 1988). This concept resembles Bandura's concept of self-efficacy—"the conviction that one can successfully execute (a given) behavior" (Bandura, 1977; Eagly & Chaiken, 1993). Suppose, for example, that you plan to get a law degree. Accomplishing this goal is not as easy as exercising three times a day. In this

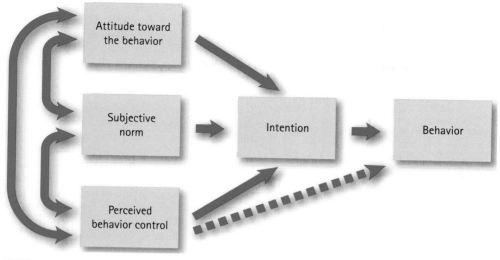

FIGURE 6.6

The Planned Behavior Model

Source: Ajzen 1987, 46.

case, the extent to which your intentions match your actual behavior depends on the amount of control you believe you have. Your perceived behavioral control will be influenced by whether you believe you have the ability and resources to achieve this educational goal.

Ajzen's **planned behavior model** is diagrammed in Figure 6.6. As this shows, perceived behavioral control influences one's intention to perform a behavior as well as the behavior itself. Recognizing that actual control was different from perceived behavioral control, Ajzen (1991) argued that an individual's perceptions do not necessarily reflect reality. According to Ajzen, actual control is more relevant than a person's perceptions in determining the link between control and behavior.

A number of studies have tested Ajzen's theory of planned behavior. Based on a review of these studies, Ajzen (1991) concluded that the inclusion of perceived behavioral control did improve the model's ability to predict behavior.

SUMMARY

1. When we evaluate a particular entity with some degree of favor or disfavor, we are expressing an attitude. Attitudes include cognitive, affective, and behavioral components.

2. Measuring attitudes is difficult because we cannot observe them directly. Researchers infer attitudes from evaluations that reveal a person's thoughts, feelings, or behaviors. Social psychologists have devised various methods for measuring attitudes. They include Bogardus's social distance scale, Thurstone's scale, Likert scaling, Guttman scaling, and semantic differential scaling.

3. People are not born with attitudes; they are learned. Learning theories that explain how

attitudes are formed include classical conditioning, operant or instrumental conditioning, and social learning theory.

4. Attitudes serve a number of functions. The most important are the adjustment, ego-defensive, value-expressive, and knowledge functions. Each is related to specific twentieth-century theoretical perspectives.

5. People prefer consistent patterns in their attitudes, beliefs, ideas, and behaviors. When they recognize that something does not fit, they feel uncomfortable and try to restore consistency. Two theories attempt to explain why people feel compelled to do this. Fritz Heider developed balance theory; Leon Festinger proposed a more complicated explanation in his theory of cognitive dissonance.

6. Making important decisions that involve equally attractive alternatives can cause postdecision cognitive dissonance. To reduce this kind of dissonance, people may alter their evaluation of the available choices after they make a decision. The tendency is to prefer what they have chosen. Selective exposure is the tendency to seek out information that suggests that our attitudes are correct. People also seek out social support for their attitudes.

7. Festinger and Carlsmith conducted a classic cognitive dissonance experiment to see what people do when they are persuaded to act in a way that contradicts an attitude. The results showed that they either justify the inconsistency or find another way to restore consistency.

8. Daryl Bem's self-perception theory provides an alternative explanation for the findings of Festinger and Carlsmith's cognitive dissonance experiment. According to this theory, subjects did not experience cognitive dissonance at all but instead drew inferences about their attitudes based on observations of their own behavior.

9. Richard La Pierre conducted a classic study of the relationship between attitudes and behaviors, which led him to conclude that attitudes are not related to behavior outside an assessment situation. Understanding the puzzling relationship between attitudes and behavior gradually proceeded from there in three stages that are characterized by specific questions. First, do attitudes predict behavior? Second, under what conditions can relatively good predictions be made about the relationship between attitudes and behaviors? And third, how do psychological processes operate in establishing connections between attitudes and behaviors? Research has shown that methodological refinements improve the correspondence between attitudes and behaviors.

10. Fishbein and Ajzen developed the reasoned action model to explain how psychological processes influence the link between attitudes and behavior. Ajzen modified the original model by adding the concept of perceived behavioral control. This new planned behavior model further improved the ability to predict behavior.

KEY TERMS

Attitude   152
Cognitive component   152
Affective component   154
Behavioral component   154
Social distance scale   155
Thurstone scale   155
Likert scale   156
Guttman scale   156
Semantic differential scale   158
Social learning theory   160

Adjustment function   161
Ego-defensive function   162
Value-expressive function   162
Knowledge function   162
Cognitive consistency   163
Balance theory   164
Cognitive dissonance   164
Cognition   166
Postdecision cognitive
   dissonance   167

Selective exposure   168
Induced compliance   170
Insufficient justification   170
Overjustification   170
Self-perception theory   171
Behavioral intentions   175
Reasoned action model   175
Perceived behavioral control   176
Planned behavior model   177

CRITICAL REVIEW QUESTIONS

1. Create different kinds of scales to show how you can measure an attitude on a specific issue.
2. How could you design an advertisement that would motivate an audience to change a particular attitude or behavior by creating cognitive dissonance?
3. Use the planned action model to show how the psychological process operates in linking attitudes toward a particular presidential candidate to voting for that candidate on election day.

SEVEN

The ABCs of Interpersonal Relationships

The enduring image of Britain's Queen Victoria is as a staid and stately dowager in black. But Victoria was a passionate young woman when she came to power in 1838 at the age of 18, unashamed at expressing her love for the man she would marry, Albert of Saxe-Coburg-Gotha.

Their relationship is today viewed as an epic love story. But it was not love at first sight. When they first met at the age of 16, neither Victoria nor Albert expressed much interest in the other (Hibbert 2000). In fact, she remarked that although he was handsome, he was also fat, unhealthy, and lacking in energy. Albert saw her even less favorably, believing they shared an interest in music but not much else.

On October 10, 1839, things suddenly changed between them. As Albert approached Victoria at a social gathering, she felt a powerful physical attraction to him.

> His blue eyes were "beautiful" [she wrote]; his figure, too, was "beautiful," no longer rather too fat as she had thought when they first met but broad in the shoulders with a "fine waist." All in all, he was so "excessively handsome," his moustache was so "delicate," his mouth so "pretty," his nose "exquisite." He really was "very fascinating." He set her heart "quite *going*." (Hibbert 2000, 107)

Victoria did not hesitate to share her feelings about Albert, especially her desire to marry him, with her close advisers. They recommended that she take a week to consider the idea; she did not. Just five days later, she decided to propose. Although it was not the prerogative of a nineteenth-century woman to do this, she knew that Albert would not take the liberty of proposing to a sitting queen. So she arranged a meeting. Both of them knew what would be said but were nervous. She finally spoke in a rush, saying that "it would make her 'too happy' if he would consent to what she wished" (Hibbert 2000, 109). He did. Later she wrote, "'Oh! To feel I was, and am, loved by such an Angel. . . . He is perfection; perfection in every way—in beauty—in everything. . . . Oh! How I adore and love him. . . . We embraced each other over and over again'" (109).

In his account of the courtship that followed, the historian Christopher Hibbert (2000, 109) described what would appear to be a fairy tale romance:

> It was clear to all at Court that she was blissfully happy. Her passion was plain to see: her eyes followed Prince Albert round the room. . . . Victoria and Albert sang duets together; they walked and rode together; they gave each other rings and locks of hair; he sat beside her while she signed papers, blotting the ink; he accompanied her when she reviewed a parade of soldiers in Hyde Park, wearing, she noted with admiration, a pair of white cashmere breeches with "nothing under them." They gazed at each other longingly, obviously dying for the moment when they could be alone together, to hold each other and to kiss; and, when they were alone, tears of happiness and pleasure poured down her cheeks as he took her face in his hands, whispering endearments, kissing her mouth "repeatedly."

Queen Victoria and Prince Albert were married on February 10, 1840. She wore a white satin dress and a sapphire brooch set with diamonds—Prince Albert's wedding gift to her. She would have preferred a simple ceremony in Buckingham Palace, but under pressure from her family, they were married in the Chapel Royal at Saint James's. Albert expressed the hope that there must never be a secret that they did not share. If anything could predict the success of this relationship, it was Albert's insight about the importance of intimacy.

Victoria and Albert had married for love. Although they did quarrel over the course of their marriage, they did not allow that to interfere with their relationship. Conflict never overshadowed the good times they enjoyed together. They developed numerous common interests. Evenings were particularly fun times. The prince still lacked his wife's energy, but he played games, danced, and spent time with their children. Physical attraction had first drawn them together, but their love grew from sharing pleasant times like these.

Alas, the royal couple did not live happily ever after. Prince Albert died at the age of 42. Stricken by grief, Queen Victoria hoped that she would die within a year. She even contemplated suicide. Her inability to cope with this loss was reflected in many ways. One of her daughters revealed that: "she cries a lot; then there is always the empty room, the empty bed, she always sleeps with Papa's coat over her and his dear red dressing-gown beside her and some of his clothes in the bed!" (Hibbert 2000, 290). The queen's feeling of loneliness and helplessness increased as time went on. She wrote:

> "Truly *the Prince was my entire self,* . . . my very life and soul. . . . I only lived through him My heavenly Angel! Surely there can never have been such a union *such trust and understanding* between two people. . . . I try to feel and think I am living on with him, and that his pure and perfect spirit is leading and inspiring me. . . . There is no one left to hold me in their arms and press me to their heart. . . . Oh! How I admired Papa! How in love I was with him! How everything about him was beautiful and precious in my eyes. Oh! How I miss all, all! Oh! Oh! The bitterness of this." (Hibbert 2000, 290)

From infancy to old age, our lives revolve around the intimate attachments we form with other human beings (Bowlby 1980). Social psychologists provide a simple explanation for this: we are driven by our instinct to survive. Not so simple, however, is understanding the complicated nature of human relationships. Prior to the nineteenth century, this task was left to writers, poets, and philosophers. In *The Two Gentlemen of Verona*, Shakespeare asks us to consider whether the love of a man for his friend is nobler than romantic love. In his opera *Tristan and Isolde*, Wagner teaches us about the overwhelming impact of love and desire. And Puccini dramatizes the fears of all lovers in *La Boheme*—"that passionate love cannot last and that we may suffer the agony of watching the beloved die before our eyes" (Tressider 1997, 76).

Queen Victoria's belief that true love involved the merging of two selves reflects a prevalent nineteenth-century attitude toward intimate relationships. And it shows how important self-disclosure had been in the development of her relationship with Prince Albert.

Certain Victorian views on romantic love still influence twenty-first century interpersonal relationships. For that reason, the story of Queen Victoria and Prince Albert provides some valuable insights. At the same time, it is not fair to suggest that our relationships offer the same experience. In this chapter, we will see traces of Victorian culture in theories about interpersonal relationships. But we will also consider how things have changed and try to gain some understanding of interpersonal relationships in the twenty-first century.

Over the course of our lives, we will form many relationships. Some will bring joy, happiness, and comfort. Others may cause sadness, depression, and despair. Some will be fleeting, others enduring. Some might constitute what we call love, others simply liking. These relationships will differ in fundamental ways, and each will serve a particular function.

Georg Simmel (1905/1964) identified a number of unique social relationships, including acquaintances, friends, lovers, and spouses. According to Simmel, these kinds of social relationships vary by the degree to which participants exchange knowledge about themselves. Referring to this process as **intimacy**, Simmel claimed that some kinds of relationships connect us with another person in terms of affection, another in terms of common intellectual interests, a third perhaps in terms of common experiences, and so on. In all cases, intimacy—reciprocal revelation and concealment—is involved.

In this chapter, we will examine how interpersonal relationships influence our thoughts, feelings, and behaviors. We will seek to answer a number of questions, including the following:

- Why are we attracted to some people and not to others?
- What is love? How does it differ from liking or infatuation?
- How do interpersonal relationships develop and become more serious?
- Why is ending a relationship so difficult?

ATTRACTION

Why are people attracted to one another? Why do certain people seem to exert an irresistible or compelling influence on us? As your own memories might suggest, there are many reasons that we are drawn to other people. We will begin first with an examination of the kinds of personal traits that attract us to certain people.

Personal Traits

Why do we like some people more than others? Social psychologists have attempted to answer this question in a variety of ways. In the late 1960s, Norman Anderson (1968) published a list of personality traits that subjects in one of his experiments associated with varying degrees of liking for other people. The experiment, which involved the rating of 555 adjectives that one might choose to describe other people, showed that subjects generally agreed about the personality traits that made people more or less likable. An analysis of the top ten likable traits indicated that six of them involved some form of trust: *sincere, honest, loyal, truthful, trustworthy,* and *dependable.* Traits that showed a lack of trust appeared at the bottom of subjects' lists: *untrustworthy, deceitful, untruthful, dishonest, phony,* and *cruel.*

Anderson believed that this list would be useful to other researchers. Since its publication, however, little research on this subject has been conducted. In 1979, *Psychology Today* conducted one of the few studies to examine why we like other people (Parlee 1979). In a comprehensive survey of friendship, magazine readers were asked to rate the importance of various qualities found in friends. Other questions sought to determine how friends spent time together, whether friendships involved reciprocal give-and-take, how similar friends were, the degree to which they shared their innermost thoughts and vulnerabilities, and why friendships cooled off or ended.

Although the sample for this survey did not fairly represent the attitudes of the American population, it did provide some insight into the personal traits that people value in friends. Consistent with Anderson's list of likable traits, respondents indicated that trust was a very important quality in a friend (see Table 7.1). Thus "keeping confidences" and "loyalty" topped the list of friendship qualities. The value placed on trust was also reflected in the list of activities shared by friends. Nine out of ten women indicated that they had an intimate talk with a friend in the last month. So did nearly eight in ten men. Other activities ranking at the top of the list included things that showed how friends depended on one another. For example, friends asked or were asked to do something for one another. The importance of trust also showed up in reasons given for ending a relationship. Among the top reasons for cooling or ending a relationship was the feeling of having been betrayed by a friend.

Familiarity

Familiarity is another factor that influences our attraction to certain people. In fact, research shows that our liking for political candidates and other packaged goods is affected by the degree to which we are exposed to their images. Greater exposure leads to higher levels of attraction and liking.

Mere Exposure

Robert Zajonc (1968) demonstrated the effect of **mere exposure** in a series of experiments. In one experiment, he studied how the frequency of exposure to nonsense syllables affected the extent to which subjects assigned favorable versus unfavorable ratings to them. In this particular study, subjects were told that the experiment involved "pronouncing foreign words." In fact, twelve seven-letter Turkish words served as the nonsense syllables. The procedure was fairly simple. First, the subjects would view the words on 3-by-5-inch cards for two seconds. As they did so, the experimenter would pronounce each word, after which the subjects would pronounce the word. The subjects were then told that the words were Turkish adjectives and that their next task would require

---

TABLE 7.1 **QUALITIES OF FRIENDSHIP**

Readers of *Psychology Today* were asked to respond to the question "How important to you is each of these qualities in a friend?" The table shows the percentage of respondents who said the quality was "important" or "very important."

Quality	Response (%)	Quality	Response (%)
Keeps confidences	89	Shares leisure (noncultural) interests	48
Loyalty	88	Shares cultural interests	30
Warmth, affection	82	Similar educational background	17
Supportiveness	76	About my age	10
Frankness	75	Physical attractiveness	9
Sense of humor	74	Similar political views	8
Willingness to make time for me	62	Professional accomplishment	8
Independence	61	Abilities and background different from mine	8
Good conversationalist	59	Ability to help me professionally	7
Intelligence	57	Similar income	4
Social conscience	49	Similar occupation	3

Source: Parlee 1979, 49. Reprinted with permission from *Psychology Today* magazine, Copyright © 1979 Sussex Publishers.

them to guess the meaning of each word. Since this was nearly impossible, they would only need to indicate on a 7-point scale whether the word meant something good or something bad.

In a second experiment, Zajonc substituted Chinese ideographs for the nonsense syllables. The results of both experiments showed that subjects were more likely to assign a positive rating to a nonsense syllable or a Chinese ideograph as the frequency of exposure increased. In a third experiment, Zajonc asked subjects to evaluate how much they liked a series of faces based on their photographs in a college yearbook. Again the results showed that liking increased with the number of times the subjects viewed the pictures.

The mere exposure effect also suggests that we should prefer images of ourselves that are more familiar. To demonstrate this preference, Theodore Mita, Marshall Dermer, and Jeffrey Knight (1977) designed an ingenious experiment. They believed that people would like a mirror image of themselves better than the true image that others saw since they saw their mirror image more often. To test their hypothesis, these researchers asked subjects to bring a close friend to the experiment. At the beginning of the experiment, the subjects posed for two frontal photographs. One of these photographs was processed so it appeared as the subjects' mirror image. The other one, which showed how they appeared to others, was designated as their true image. Later, both the subject and a friend were asked to indicate which photograph they liked better. The results of this experiment also lent support to the idea that mere exposure leads to liking—subjects preferred their mirror images, while their friends liked the true ones better.

Since the publication of Zajonc's original research, more than two hundred experiments have investigated the relationship between exposure and liking (Bornstein 1989). Researchers have studied how it operates in advertising (Sawyer 1981), social perceptions (Saegert, Swap, and Zajonc 1973), food preferences (Pliner 1982), verbal learning (Grush 1976), and subliminal influences on behavior (Bornstein, Leone, and Galley 1987). The results of these studies show over and over again that familiarity leads to liking.

Proximity

Have you ever stopped to consider the role that location plays in the relationships you have formed over the years? Did your best childhood friends live in your neighborhood? Did you share the same homeroom with your high school friends? What about the friendships you have made in college? Would you say that most of your closest friends are people who lived close by? If you fit the typical pattern, you answered yes to most of these questions.

Proximity—geographical location and distance—influences our relationships. In fact, we are more likely to marry someone who lives in our neighborhood, sits next to us in class, or works with us (Bossard 1932; Clarke 1952; Katz and Hill 1958; Burr 1973). In an analysis of five thousand marriage license applications issued in Philadelphia, James Bossard (1932) discovered that one-third of the couples lived within five blocks of each other; half of them lived only twenty blocks apart.

A number of other studies have demonstrated the importance of location in the formation of friendships. In one well-known study, Leon Festinger, Stanley Schacter, and Kurt Back (1950) studied how the physical layout of an apartment complex called Westgate West affected the development of friendships among residents. This complex, which was specifically designed for married students, provided an ideal setting for a field experiment. For one thing, it allowed researchers to make observations in an unobtrusive way. It also guaranteed the random assignment of subjects to different conditions. Couples were not allowed to choose their own apartments but were randomly assigned to one when it became available.

Westgate West consisted of seventeen separate two-story buildings, each containing ten nearly identical apartments, five on each floor. Residents who lived on the second floor reached their apartments by stairs located at either end of

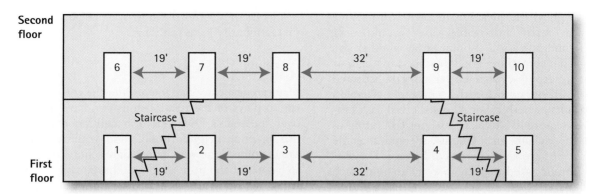

FIGURE 7.1

Configuration of a Standard Ten-Unit Building in the Westgate West Apartment Complex

Source: Adapted from Festinger, Schacter, and Back 1950.

the building. Figure 7.1 shows the configuration of the apartments and the stairwells. The distance between the two middle apartments (3 and 4, 8 and 9) was 32 feet. The distance separating other adjacent doors was 19 feet. And the maximum distance between two doors on the same floor was 89 feet.

The results of this study showed that residents of Westgate West were more likely to develop friendships with their next-door neighbors than with neighbors who lived two doors away. They were even less likely to make friends with neighbors who lived three doors away and so on. People who lived on different floors were also less likely to become friends than people living on the same floor. These findings suggest that the distance between apartments explained these particular patterns. However, the physical distance between apartment doors on the same floors was relatively short. An additional finding offered another explanation. As it turns out, couples who lived near the stairs or mailboxes developed more friendships with people in their building than residents who did not live near these gathering places. According to the researchers, the actual physical distance between doors was less important in determining friendships than the *functional distance* between residents. The chance of meeting and socializing with other residents was in fact affected by the design of the building.

William Whyte (1956) also demonstrated the importance of proximity in his classic study *The Organization Man.* Most of this study focused on the organizational activities of men at work. But Whyte also examined how relationships developed among these men after working hours—how they and their families formed friendships in Park Forest, a community that was built specifically for them. The architects who designed the layout for the 105 courts in this community introduced variety into the neighborhood by varying the lengths of the streets and by staggering the arrangement of apartments around parking bays. As a result, no two courts or blocks were alike. As in Festinger's study, residents of this community could not choose where they lived but were assigned to a specific location. Whyte was therefore able to focus on location as an important variable in the development of friendships.

Using a map of Park Forest, Whyte kept track of social activities, the location of civic leaders, and patterns of friendships (see Figure 7.2). As it turned out, the physical design of Park Forest had a remarkable effect on the web of friendships that formed. He discovered that parties as well as the

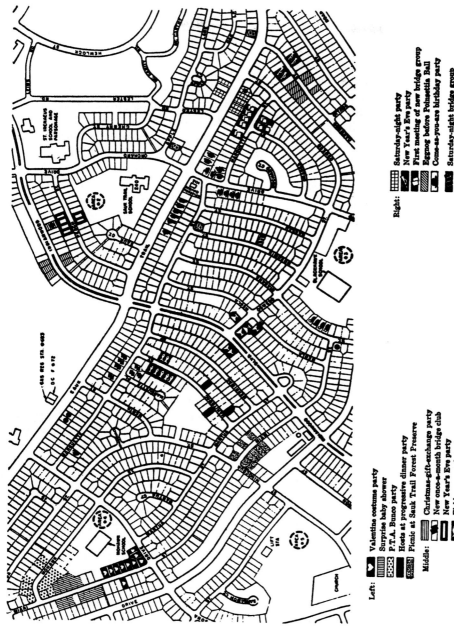

Left:
- Valentine costume party
- Surprise baby shower
- P.T.A. Bunco party
- Hosts at progressive dinner party
- Picnic at Sauk Trail Forest Preserve

Middle:
- Christmas-gift-exchange party
- New once-a-month bridge club
- New Year's Eve party
- Fishhouse punch party
- Meeting of "the Homemakers"
- Pre-dance cocktails
- Breakfast after Homesteaders dance

Right:
- Saturday-night party
- New Year's Eve party
- First meeting of new bridge group
- Eggnog before Poinsettia Ball
- Come-as-you-are birthday party
- Saturday-night bridge group
- Gourmet Society

FIGURE 7.2

Social Groupings in Park Forest

Source: Whyte 1956, 338–339.

geographical concentrations of civic leaders could not be attributed to chance. Friendship groups usually formed along and across streets but rarely included people who lived on the side of the back-yard. Residents who had adjacent driveways were more likely than others to be friends, exchange gossip, and baby-sit for one another. Whyte also noticed that courts within this community developed certain traits. One resident recognized the same thing, saying, "I can't put my finger on it . . . but as long as I've been here this court has had an inferiority complex. We never seem to get together and have the weenie roasts and anniversary parties that they have in B18 across the way" (Whyte 1956, 332). Residents in other courts observed the same thing. In some cases, they even expressed relief at having been assigned to a "good court."

Physical Attractiveness

Although we might preach that "beauty is only skin deep" or that "you should not judge a book by its cover," research shows that most people do, in fact, place a great deal of importance on physical attractiveness (Walster et al. 1966; Berscheid, Dion, Walster, and Walster 1971; Krebs and Adinolfi 1975; Reis, Nezlek, and Wheeler 1980; Reis et al. 1982). Charles Darwin would not be surprised. In his 1871 book *The Descent of Man and Selection in Relation to Sex*, he wrote, "Both sexes, if the females as well as the males were permitted to exert any choice, would choose their partners not for mental charms, or property, or social position, but almost solely from external appearance."

Blind Dates

We might not like to admit it, but most of us have had a dating experience that suggests just how important physical appearance is. In an article about dating at a small college in the 1930s, Willard Waller (1937, 731) recounted the story of a 30-year-old alumnus who was the unfortunate victim of the importance placed on physical appearance:

"While I was at X college . . . I had just one date. That was a blind date, arranged for me by a friend. We went to the dorm, and after a while my girl came down and we were introduced. She said, 'Oh, I'm so sorry. I forgot my coat. I'll have to go get it.' She never came down again. Naturally I thought, 'Well, what a hit I made!' "

Is physical attraction that important? Elaine Walster and a team of colleagues (1966) conducted one of the first field studies to answer that question. Their subjects included 376 men and 376 women who were students at the University of Minnesota. These students had purchased tickets to a dance that was held on the last day of "Welcome Week"—an event designed to orient incoming first-year students to the university. This dance was advertised with many other events in the handbook for freshmen, but it was not a regular event. The researchers planned the dance to test their hypotheses about the factors that influenced dating behavior. The ad read as follows: "Here's your chance to meet someone who has the same expressed interests as yourself." It went on to say that a computer would match students with a date based on information they would provide about their interests and personality. The tickets cost only $1. Many students responded to the ad, but only the first 376 males and 376 females were allowed to purchase tickets.

When they bought their tickets, the subjects passed four confederates who quickly rated their physical attractiveness. They were then led to another room to fill out a questionnaire. In addition to a few demographic questions, students were asked to rate their own popularity with the opposite sex and to describe their nervousness about blind dates. Another set of questions measured the students' self-esteem. And a few questions asked subjects about their expectations about their computer date. For example, to what degree did they expect their date to be physically attractive, personally attractive, and considerate? Two days later, students were assigned a date. The matches were random with one exception: a man was never matched to a taller woman. The dance began at

8:00 P.M. At 10:30 P.M., during the intermission, the subjects filled out another questionnaire to evaluate the dance and to rate their dates.

What did the results reveal? Did more attractive subjects have higher expectations for their dates than less attractive ones? What did nervousness about the blind date or self-esteem predict about the subjects' evaluations of their dates? And just how important was physical attraction? As it turns out, more attractive subjects did have higher expectations for their dates. But the most important finding of this study showed that physical attractiveness was the most important factor in determining whether subjects liked their dates. And to the researchers' surprise, women were just as likely as men to indicate this. In fact, the only important determinant of whether subjects subsequently asked their computer match out on another date was how attractive they were. In this study, intelligence and personality were not better predictors of liking than physical attractiveness. However, the researchers did acknowledge that these factors might be more important when people have more time to get acquainted.

The Matching Hypothesis

Do the results of Walster's study surprise you? If so, you are not alone. In fact, Walster and her colleagues had actually predicted that the students in their computer dating study would choose dates similar to themselves in terms of physical attractiveness. In discussing their unexpected results, these researchers realized that their study failed to consider many factors that normally operate in dating behavior. For one thing, they had eliminated the fear of rejection that people often feel when they decide to ask someone out on a date. Recall that subjects in their study were guaranteed a date; they thought that a computer would pair them with someone who had similar interests.

The researchers also realized that the short duration of the dance caused subjects to focus on physical attractiveness since they did not have enough time to consider other important factors

such as personality. Finally, the researchers suggested that a study with older subjects would be more likely to support their matching hypothesis than one that involved 18-year-old freshmen. They argued that after the most desirable dates remove themselves from the "dating market," people realize that time is running out and settle for someone who is less attractive. Based on these considerations, the researchers modified their hypothesis. They proposed that the matching hypothesis would be supported under more realistic dating conditions, which allowed for the possibility of rejection (Berscheid, Dion, Walster, and Walster 1971).

Many experiments were designed to test the modified matching hypothesis (Berscheid, Walster, and Walster 1971; Stroebe et al. 1971; Huston 1973). In one study, Walster and Walster (1969) redesigned the original "computer matching dance" to allow for the possibility of being rejected by a date. In another study, Ellen Berscheid and colleagues (1971) used photographs of the opposite sex to examine how subjects' realistic choices of dates differed from their idealistic ones. To create these two conditions, the researchers asked the subjects to select a person they would like to date from six photographs. Some of the subjects were told that the person they chose could refuse to go out with them, while others were told that their date was guaranteed. Both of these studies supported the matching hypothesis.

Evolutionary Studies

Study after study shows that physical attractiveness is the most important factor in determining whom we like, whom we want to date, and whom we eventually marry (see Box 7.1). But what kinds of physical attributes make men and women more attractive to someone of the opposite sex? Are there universal standards for beauty, or is beauty culturally defined? Consider some of the people who have made *People* magazine's annual list of the "most beautiful people": Julia Roberts, Tom Cruise, Catherine Zeta-Jones, Harrison Ford, Queen Raina of Jordan, Denzel Washington,

BOX 7.1	LOVE AND BEAUTY

The swiftest cue for love has always been human beauty, striking with the speed and force of an arrow and bringing the strongest of us to our knees. The relationship between love and perceived beauty has been celebrated in widely different cultures for centuries. Islamic love poetry is devoted almost exclusively to the praise of ideal beauty, whilst the art of Hindu temples is peopled with divinely beautiful figures symbolizing love. In the ancient Greek pantheon, Aphrodite is the goddess of beauty as well as love. . . .

The obvious and sensible argument that other qualities are more lasting has little effect on anyone who has ever fallen in love. Beauty creates a hunger; our recognition that it is ephemeral makes it all the more heartbreaking and desirable.

Source: From *The Secret Language of Love* by Megan Tressider. © 1997 by Megan Tressider. Used with permission of Chronicle Books LLC, San Francisco. Visit ChronicleBooks.com.

Michelle Kwan, Ben Affleck, and Tina Turner. What do these "beautiful" people share in common?

For centuries, artists, philosophers, and scientists have viewed beauty in terms of universal standards (Hatfield and Rapson 1996). Aristotle claimed that a perfect balance—the Golden Mean—embodied a universal ideal. However, ideas about beauty seem to change over time and from one culture to another. In her book *American Beauty*, Lois Banner (1983) described four radically different definitions of American beauty for the period between 1800 and 1921. Before the Civil War, female attractiveness was defined as a "frail, pale, willowy woman." In the years following that war, beautiful women were defined as "buxom, hearty, and heavy." By the end of the nineteenth century, the "tall, athletic, patrician Gibson girl" became the model of beauty. Within twenty years, the "skinny, waifish flapper" became popular.

Many studies have investigated the influence of physical attractiveness on human behavior, but relatively little research has attempted to determine the origins of what constitutes physical attractiveness (Langlois et al. 1987). The reason appears to rest in the assumption that definitions of beauty are learned and therefore vary from time to time and culture to culture. So what can social psychologists tell us about universal versus culturally defined beauty? Even though historical differences seem to support the belief that "beauty is in the eye

of the beholder," a number of recent studies suggest that universal standards do in fact exist.

In one of the first studies designed to determine the basis of human beings' judgments about physical attractiveness, Judith Langlois and her associates (1987) examined infants' liking for attractive faces. In two separate experiments, these researchers measured infants' preferences for the faces of adult females by timing how long the babies looked at them. Both studies showed that babies spent more time looking at attractive faces than at unattractive ones. These results challenged the assumption that beauty is in the eye of the beholder, since infants could not yet feel the impact of cultural definitions of beauty. But it did not provide all of the answers. Even though it suggested that universal standards do exist for physical attractiveness, it did not specifically identify what is physically attractive. Like most studies on physical attractiveness, the researchers had a panel of judges determine which photographs of female faces were attractive and which were not. The judges did agree, but on what?

A number of studies have provided some answers to that question. In one experiment, seventy-five undergraduate males rated the attractiveness of fifty black-and-white photographs of females (Cunningham 1986). Twenty-three of these pictures were taken from a yearbook of a women's college. The other twenty-seven were selected

Definitions of beauty vary over time. At the end of the nineteenth century in the United States, the Gibson girl (left) represented the model of beauty. Twenty years later, the flapper (right) set the new beauty standard.

from a yearbook of a Miss Universe international pageant program. In addition to the subjects' ratings, each of these photographs was evaluated in an objective way—precise measurements were made for various facial features using a micrometer (see Figure 7.3). The results showed that the subjects did rate the photographs of the beauty pageant contestants as more attractive than the photographs taken from the college yearbook. And the correlations between the subjects' attractiveness ratings and the measurements of facial features provided an explanation.

The kinds of eyes that drew more positive attractiveness ratings were higher and wider and spaced at a somewhat greater distance than less attractive eyes. Dilated pupils and the expressive quality of higher eyebrows were also seen as more attractive. Subjects also preferred smaller noses and chins. Prominent cheekbones and narrower cheeks, which suggest maturity, were associated with greater attractiveness. According to Cunningham (1986), the babylike features of attractive eyes and small chins and noses might produce caretaking or affectionate responses in others. The

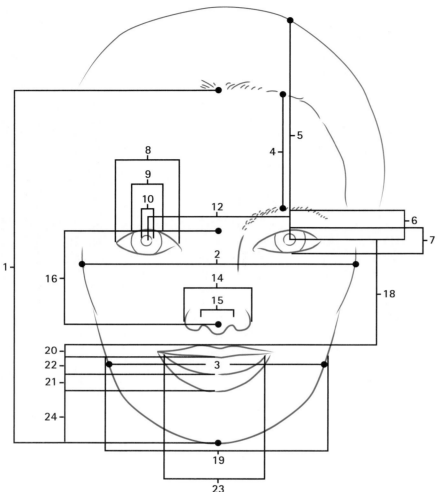

FIGURE 7.3

Measuring Beauty

Precise measurements of twenty-four aspects of photographs of women were made in preparation for an experiment intended to identify the exact determinants of facial features that make women attractive to men. The results showed a preference for wider-spaced eyes, dilated pupils, higher eyebrows, prominent cheekbones, and smaller noses and chins.

Source: Cunningham 1986, fig. 1.

mature features, in contrast, bestowed a certain status that elicited respect.

Research on male attractiveness also shows preferences for certain facial features (Keating 1985; Cunningham, Barbee, and Pike 1990). Attractive men possess prominent cheekbones and a large chin—features that signify maturity and dominance. But several other features fit the baby-like ones that judges prefer in females—higher and wider eyes and a small nose. Overall, this combination suggests that physically attractive men are

rugged but cute. According to Cunningham, these features may produce feelings of respect and nurturance in observers.

If physical attractiveness is defined by the size and relative distance of facial features, then does a Golden Mean really exist? Judith Langlois and Lori Roggman (1990) found evidence to support that argument. But they were not the first to devise a method to test this idea. Sir Francis Galton (1879) constructed one more than a century earlier. By superimposing many individual photographs on a photographic plate, he was able to create a composite photograph that was more attractive than any individual one. He described the resulting photo as "one that represents no man in particular, but portrays an imaginary figure possessing the average features of any given group of man" (341).

Langlois and Roggman (1990; Langlois, Roggman, and Musselman 1994) used a modern computer to create the same kind of image. After digitalizing the photographs of college students, the computer averaged them together to create one composite face. This process eliminated the irregularities of all the individual faces to create a "perfect" face. Ratings by student judges showed that these imaginary composite faces were preferred over individual faces in most cases.

A number of other studies show that symmetry is characteristic of physical attractiveness (Grammer and Thornhill 1994; Gangestad and Thornhill 1997; Shackelford and Larsen 1997). But is an average face the most attractive one? To answer this question, David Perett, K. A. May, and S. Yoshikawa (1994) had subjects compare an "average" composite face shape to an exaggerated version of it. To create an "average" face shape, the researchers averaged the faces from a sample of

sixty female Caucasians between the ages of 20 and 30. Another composite face was made using the photographs of the fifteen most attractive females. That composite was altered once more to exaggerate the shape differences from the "average" composite by 50 percent. The results showed that attractiveness is not averageness. The subjects who rated these three images preferred the second composite more than the first one. And they rated the third composite as the most attractive. To assess the generality of these effects, the researchers replicated the study using composite images of 342 Japanese high school girls. The results showed the same pattern of preferences. What is more, it made no difference whether the subjects who rated the images were Asian or Caucasian.

Measuring facial features to determine standards of beauty is a relatively new idea, but measuring other parts of the body is not. In fact, most people know that 36-24-36 (referring to inches) describes an hourglass figure—the "perfect" proportions for a woman's bust, waist, and hips. Charles Atlas, the "97-pound weakling" whose transformed body turned him into the world's most famous bodybuilder, became the model that boys and men sought to emulate. But do women really find muscular men attractive? And do men

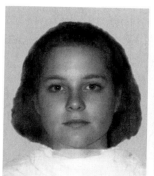  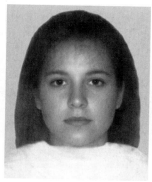 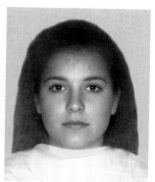

Which of these females do you find most attractive? Research conducted by Langlois and Roggman (1990) suggests that you will prefer the photo on the far right. This image is the final composite face created by mathematically averaging the digitized faces of 32 individual female faces. From left to right, the images are composites of four faces, eight faces, sixteen faces, and thirty-two faces.

find women with an hourglass figure or a Barbie doll shape (originally the unrealistic equivalent of 39-18-33) more attractive than women with more natural shapes? Are these the standard measurements that define physical attractiveness in men and women?

Scientific studies, which have examined desirable male and female body proportions, provide some answers (Wiggins, Wiggins, and Conger 1968; Beck, Ward-Hull, and McLear 1976; Singh 1993, 1995b; Singh and Young 1995). In her examination of the preferred proportions for female figures, Devendra Singh (1993, 1995a) showed that subjects found females whose waists were 30 percent smaller than their hips (a low waist-to-hip ratio) as more attractive than females with a high waist-to-hip ratio. In another study, Singh (1995b) showed that subjects found men whose waist-to-hip ratio was high (0.9 and 1.0) as more attractive than men whose figures were more curvaceous (with a low waist-to-hip ratio). And like other studies, her study did not show that women view "muscle men" as having the ideal body (see also Beck, Ward-Hull, and McLear 1976). How can we explain these findings?

Many studies suggest that Darwin was correct—that if men and women had their choice, they would not select partners on the basis of intelligence, property, or social position. They would simply base it on physical appearance. Evolutionary psychologists would agree. Based on their belief that natural selection operates to ensure the survival of the fittest, they argue that the physical features associated with beauty reflect good health, strength, and fertility. In fact, research shows that attractive men and women are more resistant to parasites and other diseases (Gangestad, Thornhill, and Yeo 1994).

THEORIES OF INTERPERSONAL RELATIONSHIPS

Our initial attraction to someone can lead to friendship, romance, even marriage. In this section, we will consider a number of theories that seek to explain how interpersonal relationships develop. In the process, we will address a number of questions:

"It isn't that I don't love you. It's just that I've evolved and you haven't."

- How do our attitudes influence our interpersonal relationships? Do birds of a feather flock together, or do opposites attract?
- How do our relationships with our parents influence our ability to form healthy adult relationships?
- Do some people give too much or too little in their relationships? What effect does this have on the people who are involved?
- When do relationships become too costly to maintain?
- How do people form close relationships that last?

Balance Theory: Attitudes and Interpersonal Relationships

I never considered a difference of opinion in politics, in religion, in philosophy, as cause for withdrawing from a friend.

—Thomas Jefferson

Some people believe that opposites attract. Others argue that "birds of a feather flock together." What do you think (see Box 7.2)? Most social psychologists believe that people are more likely to be attracted to someone who holds similar attitudes and that similarity contributes to lasting relationships. As discussed in Chapter 6, Fritz Heider (1958) was one of the first to study how attitudes influence interpersonal relationships. According to his *balance theory*, we feel comfortable when someone we like agrees with us on issues and when people we dislike disagree with our position. His theory also helps us understand our feelings when someone we like does not share our attitudes or when someone we dislike happens to hold the same ones.

How can we apply Heider's model to interpersonal relationships? Consider the following example. Matt and Kelley just started dating. Just for fun, they decide to complete a survey that measures attitudes toward the roles played by American men and women today. They both agree that women should stay home to raise children for the first five years. Matt is particularly happy that they agreed. A couple of months ago, he broke up with Amy, who strongly believed that women should not have to give up their careers to stay at home with children. Disagreement over this issue caused a lot of tension in their relationship, and the conflict ultimately ended their relationship.

In this case, the relationships among the basic elements in Heider's model—two people (P and O) and an attitude object (X)—created imbalance. We can represent the imbalance in the situation

---

BOX 7.2 | **THE ODD COUPLE**

Would a faithful, conservative Republican ever consider dating a staunch, liberal Democrat? It seems highly unlikely. But it does happen. Consider the case of Mary Matalin and James Carville—two outspoken political strategists whose allegiance to the party faithful put them in warring camps during the 1992 presidential campaign. As the political director for George H. W. Bush's reelection campaign, Matalin frequently lambasted Clinton, criticizing him for everything from his budget plan to his alleged affairs. James Carville, Clinton's chief defender, not only responded to these attacks but, similarly, took aim at Bush. In fact, he launched aggressive assaults on Bush, calling him "Chicken George" for refusing to debate Clinton and reminding the public about his "Read My Lips" pledge of no new taxes. While these political enemies duked it out on the campaign trail, grabbing every chance to publicly whip their opponent, they fell in love and married in 1993. As frequent guests on *Meet the Press*, Tim Russert introduces them as they are widely regarded: Washington, D.C.'s "odd couple."

with Matt and Amy mathematically as $(+)\,(+)\,(-) = (-)$. Even though they liked each other initially, their disagreement over child care caused tension and eventually ended the relationship.

Research shows that people do like others who share similar attitudes. What is more, as the number of similar attitudes increases, so does the attraction between two people (Gonzales et al. 1983). Attitude similarity also bodes well for the length of friendships (Griffin and Sparks 1990). Dating and marriage patterns clearly reflect the effect that similarity has on relationships (Benokraitis 2005). In this respect, social background is even more important than attitudes in determining whom we marry. Study after study shows a predominant pattern of **homogamy**—the tendency to marry someone about the same age, in the same social class, with the same level of education, raised in the same religion, and so on.

Attachment Theory: Building the Foundation for Healthy Adult Relationships

What do you remember about the first person you ever loved? Did spending time with this person make you feel safe, secure, and happy? How important was this person's attention and approval? What happened when you were separated from this loved one? For most people, first loves often involve strong emotional bonds or attachments. Some people describe this experience as falling in love or as maintaining a special bond—loving someone. Others remember the pain and sorrow associated with the ultimate loss of love (Bowlby 1969).

John Bowlby, a British psychiatrist, was one of the first to study the role of emotional attachments in interpersonal relationships. Arguing that human beings are driven by their need to connect with other people, he wrote:

> Intimate attachments to other human beings are the hub around which a person's life revolves, not only when he is an infant or a toddler or a schoolchild but throughout his adolescence and his years of maturity as well, and on into old age. From these intimate attachments a person draws his strength and enjoyment of life and, through what he contributes, he gives strength and enjoyment to others. (Bowlby 1980, 442)

Focusing on the kinds of emotional responses that infants and children displayed when they were separated from their mothers, Bowlby sought to understand how the loss of a mother figure affected the development of an individual's personality. He wanted to know how the connection that is established between an infant and its primary caregiver influenced the development of other relationships. Could interference with an attachment process explain why some people become anxious and angry when their needs are not met? Could it block a person's capacity to form deep relationships later in life? Based on his observations of the interaction between infants and mothers, Bowlby (1969) concluded that early attachments to primary caretakers have a powerful and long-lasting impact. According to his **attachment theory**, early attachments form the basis of an individual's happiness, security, and self-confidence (Shaver, Hazen, and Bradshaw 1988).

Mary Ainsworth (1979), an American psychologist who set out to test Bowlby's attachment theory, identified three distinct styles of attachment: secure, anxious/ambivalent, and avoidant. **Secure attachment** results when a primary caretaker is accessible to a child and responds to his needs. Trust, a critical factor in the development of this style of attachment, develops through a number of different infant-caretaker interactions (feeding, body contact, and responses to crying). **Anxious/ambivalent attachment** results when a primary caretaker is not available or fails to respond to a child's needs. Children with this kind of attachment style cry more than secure children. They also show great distress when separated from their caretakers but express anger when they return. **Avoidant attachment** results when a primary caretaker avoids or rejects a child. Comparing these kinds of caretakers to those who create secure or anxious/ambivalent attachment styles, Ainsworth characterized them as more rigid and compulsive. They also tended to express more anger and irritation. Children with this attachment style may appear indifferent to their caretakers and ultimately become "detached."

So how might the particular kind of bond formed between an infant and its caregiver serve as a model for later intimate relationships? A number of studies provide some answers (Shaver, Hazan, and Bradshaw 1988; Hazan and Shaver 1994; Mikulincer and Florian 1996; Koski and Shaver 1997; Fraley and Shaver 1998) In an account of their groundbreaking studies on romantic love, Philip Shaver, Cindy Hazan, and Donna Bradshaw (1988) proposed that many adult responses to romantic love parallel those that infants experience when they form attachments to their primary caretakers. They note, for example, behavior and emotional similarities in eye contact, smiling, efforts to maintain close proximity, desire for physical contact, and distress over separation. They also point out that both kinds of relationships involve a desire to share discoveries with one another as well as a powerful empathy (Feeney and Noller 1996). At the same time, they recognized important differences. For example, they characterized infant-caregiver relationships as asymmetrical caregiving, whereas adult relationships involved reciprocal caregiving. And they noted that romantic love involves a component of sexuality that is absent from infant-caregiver relationships.

Hazan and Shaver (1987) designed two studies to examine the effect that early attachment styles had on the relationships that adults form. In both studies, they asked subjects to describe their feelings about an important romantic love relationship. They were given the following choices:

Secure: "I find it relatively easy to get close to others and am comfortable depending on them and having them depend on me. I don't often worry about being abandoned or about someone getting too close to me."

Avoidant: "I am somewhat uncomfortable being close to others; I find it difficult to trust them completely, difficult to allow myself to depend on them. I am nervous when anyone gets too close, and often love partners want me to be more intimate than I feel comfortable being."

Anxious/ambivalent: "I find that others are reluctant to get as close as I would like. I often worry that my partner doesn't really love me or won't want to stay with me. I want to merge completely with another person, and this desire sometimes scares people away."

Subjects in these studies were also asked to respond to a "love quiz," which sought to measure how they had experienced an important love relationship. For example, had they ever experienced love at first sight, did they fear close relationships, were they prone to jealousy, and did they experience emotional extremes? Finally, they were asked to answer some questions about themselves and to describe their relationships with their parents.

The results of these studies showed that slightly more than half of the subjects classified themselves as having a secure attachment style. About a quarter indicated an avoidant style, and about 20 percent described themselves as anxious/ambivalent. These attachment styles were linked to a number of interesting differences in how these subjects experienced love. Secure lovers tended to have longer relationships (on average, 10.02 years, compared with 4.86 years for anxious/ambivalent and 5.97 for avoidant). They also had more positive experiences with love, describing them as especially happy, friendly, and trusting. And they indicated that they accepted and supported their lover despite the other's faults. Anxious/ambivalent subjects portrayed their important love relationships as ones that involved obsession, the desire for reciprocation and union, emotional highs and lows, extreme sexual attraction, and jealousy. Finally, avoidant subjects showed a greater tendency to fear intimacy, to experience emotional extremes, and to feel jealousy in their important love relationships.

Differences related to attachment styles also appeared in subjects' attitudes toward romantic love, themselves, and others (see Table 7.2). Secure

TABLE 7.2	ATTACHMENT THEORY: ATTITUDES TOWARD ROMANTIC LOVE

In two studies that sought to understand "love as attachment," Shaver, Hazan, and Bradshaw (1988) used a number of items to measure what Bowlby called "working models of relationships." The subjects were asked to describe how they saw themselves, how they saw others, and how they saw the course of romantic love over time by checking or not checking each of the items below.

	Avoidant	Anxious/ Ambivalent	Secure
1. The kind of head-over-heels romantic love depicted in novels and movies doesn't exist in real life.	.25	.28	**.13**
2. Intense romantic love is common at the beginning of a relationship, but it rarely lasts forever.	**.41**	.34	.28
3. Romantic feelings wax and wane over the course of a relationship, but at times they can be as intense as they were at the start.	**.60**	.75	.79
4. In some relationships, romantic love really lasts; it doesn't fade with time.	.41	.46	**.59**
5. It's easy to fall in love. I feel myself beginning to fall in love often.	.04	**.20**	.09
6. It's rare to find someone you can really fall in love with.	.66	.56	**.43**
7. I am easier to get to know than most people.	.32	.32	**.60**
8. I have more self-doubts than most people.	.48	.64	**.18**
9. People almost always like me.	.36	.41	**.68**
10. People often misunderstand me or fail to appreciate me.	.36	.50	**.18**
11. Few people are as willing and able as I am to commit themselves to a long-term relationship.	.24	**.59**	.23
12. People are generally well intentioned and good-hearted.	.44	.32	**.72**

NOTES: Results for items 1–6 are from the newspaper sample and were replicated in the university sample; results for items 7–12 are from the university sample only. Statistically significant differences between means within a row are indicated by boldface type.

Source: Shaver, Hazan, and Bradshaw 1988, 82.

subjects were more likely to say that romantic feelings wax and wane but could at times be as intense as in the beginning. And they indicated that in some relationships, romantic love never fades. Avoidant subjects did not believe in the kind of head-over-heels romantic love depicted in novels and movies. They thought it was rare to find someone to fall in love with and did not believe that romantic love lasts forever. Finally, anxious/ambivalent subjects said that it is easy to fall in love and that they often felt themselves beginning to fall in love. However, like avoidant subjects, they also indicated that "real" love is hard to find.

Self-attitudes and attitudes toward others also showed differences among attachment styles. Secure subjects felt they were easier to get to know than most people, believed that other people almost always liked them, and thought that other people were generally well intentioned and good-hearted. Anxious/ambivalent subjects had more self-doubts, felt that they were misunderstood and underappreciated, and believed that few people were as willing as they were to commit themselves to a long-term relationship. The attitudes of avoidant subjects tended to fall between the extremes of secure and anxious/ambivalent subjects and somewhat closer to the anxious subjects.

Studies that support the findings of Hazan and Shaver's groundbreaking research continue to mount (Brennan and Shaver 1995; Baldwin et al. 1996; Jones and Cunningham 1996; Mickelson, Kessler, and Shaver 1997). These studies show that nearly seven in ten adults form secure attachments. These individuals form close relationships easily and do not worry about being abandoned. Secure lovers enjoy sexuality within an ongoing relationship and feel comfortable sharing their ideas and feelings with their partners (Feeney and Noller 1990; Simpson, Rholes, and Nelligan 1992; Feeney 1996). They view their parents' marriages as good and portray their parents positively—as affectionate, fair, and caring.

About two in ten adults display traits associated with avoidant attachment styles. These individuals express fears about getting close to others or say that being independent and self-sufficient is very important to them (Bartholomew and Horowitz 1991). They find it difficult to trust their partners, tend to invest less in their relationships, are more likely to engage in brief sexual encounters, experience emotional highs and lows, and are more likely to end relationships. Finally, they tend to describe their parents as more demanding, critical, and uncaring.

About 10 percent of adults fit the anxious/ ambivalent attachment style. These individuals commonly report falling in love at first sight. These relationships often involve obsession, the desire for reciprocation and union, and extreme sexual attraction. Individuals with an anxious/ ambivalent attachment style are also less trusting and tend to be more possessive and jealous. Conflicts often become highly emotional and angry (Simpson, Rholes, and Phillips 1996). And it is not uncommon for these individuals to break up with the same person over and over again. In contrast to secure adults, anxious/ambivalent individuals view their parents' marriage as unhappy, and they describe the parents as more intrusive and demanding.

Bowlby's ideas, which inspired others to conduct research on the attachment process, contributed to radical changes in the care of children

Hospitals that encourage parents to interact with their newborn babies recognize the developmental benefits described by studies on attachment theory.

(Feeney and Noller 1996). Hospitals have changed their policies, which at one time limited the amount of time that parents could spend with their sick children. Now mothers are encouraged to spend a lot of time with their children and to get involved in basic care such as feeding. Some of the most dramatic changes involve the birth of a child. Fathers no longer wait in another room while women give birth. Instead they take an active role in the childbirth process. And they are encouraged to spend time interacting with their new infants for the duration of the hospital time.

Social Exchange Theory

On April 22, 2001, the *New York Times* ran the first personal ads from readers looking for love. In a period of declining advertising sales for the newspaper, an industry analyst applauded the move, saying that it made sense to expand its definition of classified advertising to include personal ads (Kilgannon 2001). Seeking companionship and marriage in a newspaper ad is not as new as the *New York Times*'s decision might suggest. In the 1880s, newspaper ads for "mail-order brides" appeared across the United States (Bolig, Stein, and McHenry 1984), and many newspapers and magazines have carried ads placed by both men and women since the 1960s. Finding love in a personal ad might not sound very romantic (see Box 7.3). But just how different is it from the way that most Americans make decisions about whom they should date and marry?

Social exchange theory, probably the most influential theory of interpersonal relationships today (also see Chapter 9), suggests that it is not that different. This theory assumes that human beings are rational and that social interaction resembles a business transaction. It views people as bookkeepers who keep a mental record of the rewards, costs, and profits (rewards minus costs) of their interpersonal relationships. Acting like wise businessmen, the parties in an exchange process look for the best deals. Therefore, they also consider the alternatives when they assess the costs and benefits of a particular relationship. Seen from the bottom line, this theory proposes that parties in an exchange process are concerned with their own interests and seek in their negotiations to maximize their own rewards. It also suggests that most people will decide to end a relationship when its costs outweigh its rewards.

BOX 7.3	PERSONAL ADS

Many people place personal ads in newspapers in search of love, adventure, and friendship. Within a space of about one square inch, advertisers must describe the qualities they offer and the ones they seek. Do these ads work? What kinds of traits draw the most responses? Before you answer, consider a sample of typical ads.

TRUE BLUE
Single black male, 30, 6 feet, 170 lbs., financially secure, athletic, sincere. In search of attractive black female, 25–30, who enjoys outdoor activities, children, and dogs.

BOOK WORM
Athletic single white male, 58, enjoys reading, bicycling, and hiking. Seeking intelligent single white female, 50–58, with similar interests.

GOLD DIGGER
Single white female, 25, slim blonde beauty. Enjoys shopping, travel, and great food. Seeking financially independent single white male, 30–40.

ROMANCE AND MORE
Divorced black male, 63, professional. Enjoys candlelit dinners, poetry, and classical music. In search of black female, 55–65, who enjoys travel and the arts.

SEEKING ADVENTURE
Outgoing divorced white female, 42, dark hair/brown eyes, 5'7", 130 lbs. Seeks wild adventure with successful athletic male, 37–55.

SOULMATE
Intelligent single white female, 25, 5'4", 120 lbs., seeking liberal, romantic, professional, single male, 28–35.

Research provides a somewhat surprising answer for the questions posed above. As it turns out, the age of the advertiser was the most important factor in successful ads (Rajecki, Bledsoe, and Rasmussen 1991). The advertisers who received more responses were relatively younger women (an average of 35 years) and older men (an average age of 43.9 years).

These ideas can be traced to certain nineteenth-century thinkers, especially economists and philosophers who stressed individual activity and choice (Wallace and Wolf 1999). Georg Simmel, who also favored this view of human behavior, believed that social interaction always involves some form of reciprocity and should therefore be considered a form of exchange. According to Simmel (1905/1964, . . . 387), "All contacts among men rest on the schema of giving and returning the equivalence." People who sign prenuptial agreements are particularly aware of how this *norm of reciprocity* operates. With the hope of guaranteeing an equitable exchange, they formalize the conditions of their relationship by designating how they will divide money, property, and other assets should their marriage end in divorce. This kind of exchange bears a close resemblance to economic models of exchange. However, social exchange theorists also consider the kinds of intangible commodities that are typically exchanged in interpersonal relationships—love, companionship, status, security, recognition, help, time, and effort. They view these kinds of intangible commodities as investments in a relationship.

Simmel's ideas influenced the thinking of many social exchange theorists, including George Homans (1961), who is widely recognized for his contributions in the 1960s. Rooted in both elementary economics and behaviorist psychology, Homans's version of exchange theory is based on five propositions (see Table 7.3). The first three portray humans as rational beings who act in their own self-interest. Thus he argues that people will repeat behaviors that are rewarded by another person, people will repeat past behaviors when a current situation resembles one that was rewarded in the past, and the frequency of a person's behavior will depend on the value the person attaches to the other person's behavior.

To illustrate how we can apply these first three propositions to interpersonal relationships, consider the case of Jane and Bill, two college students who have been dating for about a year. At the end of the school year, Jane decides to move from her sorority house to an apartment. She asks Bill if he could help her move the weekend after final exams. This was not the first time that Jane had asked Bill to help her. Just a few months earlier, he helped her move an antique chest that her grandmother had given her for her birthday. Jane was not strong enough to move heavy furniture by herself, and she really valued Bill's help. Bill, in turn, was particularly pleased by the way Jane had shown her

---

| TABLE 7.3 | HOMANS'S FIVE PROPOSITIONS OF SOCIAL EXCHANGE THEORY |

1. *Stimuli proposition:* If in the past the occurrence of a particular stimulus-situation has been the occasion on which a man's activity has been rewarded, then the more similar the present stimulus-situation is to the past one, the more likely he is to emit the activity, or some similar activity, now.

2. *Frequency proposition:* The more often within a given period of time a man's activity rewards the activity of another, the more often the other will emit the activity.

3. *Value proposition:* The more valuable to a man a unit of the activity another gives him, the more often he will emit activity rewarded by the activity of the other.

4. *Satiation proposition:* The more often a man has in the recent past received a rewarding activity from another, the less valuable any further unit of that activity becomes to him.

5. *Expectations and emotions proposition:* The more to a man's disadvantage the rule of distributive justice fails of realization, the more likely he is to display the emotional behavior we call anger.

Source: Homans 1961, 53–55, 75.

appreciation. He was more than happy to help Jane move again.

According to Homans, Jane and Bill engage in activities that involve rewards and costs. While it might seem that Jane is getting the most out of this relationship, the exchange is bound to involve far more than Bill's physical strength. If Bill finds Jane attractive, this relationship might involve an exchange of beauty for brawn. Of course, there are probably many intangible rewards in this exchange, not to mention the appreciation that Jane shows for Bill's consideration and efforts.

You might wonder how long a relationship like this might last. According to Homans, people are likely to stay in relationships as long as both parties are profiting from the exchange. This might sound simple, but determining the net outcome of an exchange process involves considerations above and beyond attaching values to the absolute rewards and costs of a relationship. Homans recognized this in his fourth proposition by pointing out a unique aspect of rewards: they lose value when people receive them too frequently and gain value when people are deprived of them. Homans then argued that when one party's needs or desires are satiated, the costs might then exceed the rewards. And at this point, the relationship may end.

Understanding the concept of profit requires a clear explanation of what Homans meant by costs. He did not view them as punishments but instead defined them as a value forgone. According to Homans (1961, 59), "For an activity to incur a cost, an alternative and rewarding activity must be forgone." In our example, Bill's cost for helping Jane might be the pleasure he forgoes by not going to a ballgame with his buddies. Choosing to participate in one type of activity precludes the possibility of participating in another one (which might offer more or fewer rewards) (Shaw and Costanzo 1970). According to Homans, both parties take this into consideration in the exchange process.

In his fifth proposition, Homans proposed that rewards are also influenced by our expectations. People become angry when they do not receive an expected reward. In contrast, they will be pleased if they receive an unexpected one. For example, a woman who expects but does not receive flowers on Valentine's Day is likely to be very upset with the man who failed to remember her. On the other hand, a woman who is surprised by a simple Valentine's card is likely to be thrilled.

In his last proposition, Homans suggested that people consider not only the costs and rewards of their interpersonal relationships but also whether the social exchange is fair and equitable. He suggests that an individual is likely to wonder, "Did he get as much reward from the other, less the cost to himself in getting that reward, as he had the right to expect? And did the other get from him, at a certain cost to the other, no more reward then *he* had the right to expect?" (Homans 1961, 74). Homans referred to the "justice in the distribution of rewards and costs between persons" (74) as the problem of **distributive justice**. As a general rule, he believed that "a man in an exchange relation with another will expect that the rewards of each man be proportional to his costs—the greater the rewards, the greater the costs—and that the net rewards, or profits, of each man be proportional to his investments—the greater the investments, the greater the profit" (75).

Equity Theory

Homans's concept of distributive justice was modified by other social exchange theorists and reformulated in terms of the following equation:

$$\frac{\text{Outcomes of person A}}{\text{Contributions of person A}} = \frac{\text{Outcomes of person B}}{\text{Contributions of person B}}$$

This equation represents the fundamental principle of **equity theory**—that equity exists when the ratio of one person's outcomes and contributions in a relationship equals the ratio of the other person's outcomes and contributions. Equity theory, an offshoot of social exchange theory, seeks to explain how people will react when they believe they are involved in an unfair relationship (Walster, Berscheid, and Walster 1973). This theory is based on three basic propositions:

1. People seek to maximize their outcomes, which are defined by rewards minus costs.

2. When people perceive a relationship as inequitable, they will feel distressed. The greater the inequity, the greater the distress.

3. People who perceive inequity in a relationship will attempt to restore equity.

To illustrate how the equity formula works, recall our example of Bill (person A) and Jane (person B). Suppose we could assign numbers to the contributions and outcomes that these two people make and receive in their relationship. Let's say that Bill's outcomes amount to 154 units and that his contributions are 132 units. If Jane's outcomes are 126 units and her contributions are 108, does equity exist? According to this equation, it does. Although Bill's outcomes are greater than Jane's, this relationship is balanced or equitable because Bill also contributes more than Jane. Mathematically, the ratio of outcomes to contributions on both sides of the equation sign equals 7/6. That is, 154/132 and 126/108 both equal 7/6.

It is actually difficult to put a number on the outcomes and contributions of a relationship. Some couples might keep track of the chores they do, or they might know exactly how much of their paycheck goes toward the maintenance of their household. But social psychologists argue that even then a "rewards-minus-costs" formula cannot provide a good picture of the true outcomes of their relationships (Thibaut and Kelley 1959a; Wallace and Wolf 1999). Recognizing the problem with evaluating the outcomes of a relationship, John Thibaut and Harold Kelley (1959a) proposed that people make two types of comparisons when they evaluate the outcomes of their relationships.

The first kind, the **comparison level**, refers to the outcome an individual believes he deserves from a particular relationship. This standard is based on direct personal experience. Thus, for example, your current relationship might be better than the one you had last year but not as good as the one you had three years ago. The comparison level indicates the acceptable outcome for a relationship. If the outcome of a particular relationship exceeds the comparison level, we should be satisfied. If it falls short of the comparison level, we are likely to seek a different relationship.

When we evaluate our relationships, we also compare them with other relationships that we might pursue. Thibaut and Kelley (1959a) called this standard the **comparison level for alternatives**. Consider a dilemma that many attractive coeds might face. Sherri is currently dating Fred. She feels he is the best boyfriend she has ever had. However, she just learned that Dan, a longtime interest, just broke up with his girlfriend. Even though she is satisfied with Fred, she may well break up with him to seek a relationship with Dan. In this case, her relationship with Fred is above her comparison level, but it is below her comparison level for alternatives. You might know someone who illustrates the opposite problem—someone who has remained in an unhappy relationship for a long time because they can find no one better. This describes a relationship that falls below one's comparison level but above the comparison level for alternatives.

When people feel that they are involved in an inequitable relationship, they will try to restore balance. According to equity theory, people try to do this in two ways. One way is to change the actual rewards and costs in a relationship. This involves a change in behavior. For example, if a wife believes that her husband does less housework than she does, she can try to convince him to split up the chores more equally. If that does not work, she can alter the division of labor herself by doing less work. Individuals can also try to restore equity psychologically. In this case, the wife might convince herself that she really does not work that hard or that her husband contributes more to the household by putting in long hours at the office.

Common sense suggests that when the disadvantaged person in a relationship recognizes inequity, she will seek to restore actual balance. But what about the advantaged person who has nothing to gain and something to lose? Equity theory still maintains that this person will feel uneasy. In fact, she might even feel guilty for taking advantage of the other person. In this case, the advantaged person is likely to take the psychological approach to restoring equity. By doing so, she does not have to alter the actual balance, just the perception of it. She might even view the disadvantaged person as deserving the inequitable ratio of outcomes to contributions. People who subscribe to the idea that the world is a fair place—the "belief in a just world" (see Chapter 5)—are particularly likely to use this kind of reasoning. For them, people simply get what they deserve.

Power and Control: The Principle of Least Interest

Have you ever had a friend who waits by the phone for a call from her boyfriend? Maybe you know a guy who showers attention and gifts on his girlfriend. Maybe that person is you. If you have ever felt dependent on another person for the receipt of rewards, you understand the role that **power** plays in a relationship. In his analysis of the courtship process, Willard Waller (1937) found relationships that involved some degree of exploitation. In these cases, he observed that the person who showed the least interest in continuing the relationship gained control. Referring to this as the **principle of least interest**, Waller argued that people who care too much relinquish their power. Dependent on the other person for a reward, they willingly defer to the other person's wishes. Equity theory predicts that relationships like this—where one person derives more benefits than the other—will not last. When the costs for the disadvantaged person become too great, he or she will end the relationship.

Self-Disclosure

Honest men esteem and value nothing so much in this world as a real friend. Such a one is as it were another self, to whom we impart our most secret thoughts, who partakes of our joy, and comforts us in our affliction; add to this, that his company is an everlasting pleasure to us.

—Pilpay

Most of us would agree with Pilpay, including Georg Simmel, who argued that secrets tie people together in a special way. Simmel, you may recall, claimed that social relationships vary by the degree to which participants exchange knowledge about themselves. In an essay on friendship and love, he wrote that the ideal of friendship aims at "an absolute psychological intimacy" (1905/1964, 325). According to Simmel, close relationships connect us with another through reciprocal revelations about ourselves, mutual understanding and receptivity, and affection.

Today, social psychologists share Simmel's belief that intimacy is one of the most important factors differentiating various types of relationships. Achieving intimacy involves **self-disclosure**, a special kind of conversation in which we reveal personal information about ourselves to another person—our family background, attitudes, values, concerns, needs, dreams, and feelings (see Box 7.4). We give that person a glimpse of who we are—our self. Social psychologists differentiate two types of self-disclosure. In **descriptive self-disclosure**, people talk about the facts of their lives, such as their place of birth or their parents' occupations. When they talk about their feelings or personal opinions—shame for violating a law, love for a pet, or attitude toward abortion—it is called **evaluative self-disclosure**.

Irving Altman and Dalmas Taylor (1973) described the process of self-disclosure in their **social penetration theory**. According to them, close relationships progress through the development of increasing intimacy. When people first meet, they

BOX 7.4	A SELF-DISCLOSURE QUESTIONNAIRE

Instructions: The answer sheet you have been given has columns with the headings "Mother," "Father," "Male Friend," "Female Friend," and "Spouse." You are to read each item on the questionnaires and then indicate on the answer sheet the extent that you have talked about that item to each person, that is, the extent that you have made yourself known to that person. Use the rating scale that you see on the answer sheet to describe the extent that you have talked about each item.

1. My personal views on sexual morality—how I feel that I and others ought to behave in sexual matters
2. What I would appreciate most for a present
3. What I enjoy most and get the most satisfaction from in my present work

4. How I really feel about the people that I work for or work with
5. All of my present sources of income—wages, fees, allowance, dividends, etc.
6. The facts of my present sex life—including knowledge of how I get sexual gratification; any problems that I might have; with whom I have relations, if anybody
7. Things in the past or present that I feel guilty or ashamed and guilty about
8. My present physical measurements, for example, height, weight, waist, etc.

Source: Jourard and Lasakow 1958, 91–92.

reveal little about themselves, sticking instead to superficial subjects like sports or the weather. As relationships develop into more intimate ones, people begin to reveal more private things about themselves. The knowledge that partners divulge to one another penetrates to deeper levels. It also expands to cover the wider aspects of who they are.

Intimacy connects people like nothing else. Part of its bonding strength lies in the way that it develops: it is never immediate but builds gradually over time. As described by social penetration theory, it involves the norm of reciprocity. That is, in the early stages of a relationship, people tend to match the level of information they reveal. For example, if one person talks about high school experiences, the other person is likely to share the same kinds of stories. As relationships develop further, reciprocity levels off and diminishes. In established relationships, reciprocity is less likely, and one partner might respond instead with support and understanding (Archer 1979; Laurenceau, Barrett, and Pietromonaco 1998).

Revealing information about oneself is important in the development of a relationship. But it is not risk-free. Lifting the mask to uncover hidden aspects of the self exposes our vulnerabilities. Revealing the self in a slow reciprocal manner provides some protection. It allows us to gradually determine how much we can trust the other person.

As you might recall, research shows that trust is the central trait of liking and friendship (Anderson 1968; Parlee 1979). The reason seems obvious: trust involves the process of self-disclosure. Social psychologists who study trust note that in the beginning of a relationship, people carefully reveal aspects of themselves that are both precious and vulnerable (Parlee 1979). If this self-disclosure is respected and accepted by the other party, trust begins to develop. This process must continue in a reciprocal fashion in order for the relationship to deepen. The development of trust is slow. It might takes months or even years. Destroying it, however, can happen in an instant—in a single betrayal.

Whereas self-disclosure generally fosters the positive development of a relationship, revealing too much too fast can actually threaten it. People who disclose things about themselves too quickly risk creating a negative impression; they can also cause the other person to feel threatened (Kaplan et al. 1974).

Unique Aspects of the Self-Disclosure Process

Self-disclosure occurs in all kinds of close relationships, and research has focused on many aspects of this process. One of the most studied questions involves the role that gender plays in self-disclosure. Theories of gender role socialization suggest that males learn to inhibit their emotions, while society encourages females to express them (Lindsey 1997). Based on her analysis of conversational styles, Deborah Tannen (1990) concluded that differences in gender role socialization influence the way that men and women communicate as adults. Women, who place particular value on intimacy, use conversations to achieve closeness—to seek and give support. Men, who place more value on independence, use conversations to achieve and maintain status. Using jokes and stories to jockey for a superior position, men develop conversational styles that make them good public speakers. Women, in contrast, develop conversational styles that minimize status differences and encourage intimacy. This gives them an advantage when it comes to communicating on an interpersonal level—what Tannen calls private speech. With these kinds of theories in mind, social psychologists have asked, Who is more likely to initiate self-disclosure—men or women? Does one gender disclose more than the other? And do men and women differ in the kinds of things that they disclose about themselves?

Most studies show that gender differences do exist. For one thing, women are more likely to initiate self-disclosure than men are (Arliss 1991). They will not, however, disclose information if they expect a negative or uncaring response. Men are more likely to disclose private information to women than to other men. But they are likely to hold back if they anticipate an emotional response. Research also shows that women are particularly good at eliciting intimate self-disclosures (Miller, Berg, and Archer 1983; Pegalis et al. 1994; Shaffer,

Pegalis, and Bazzini 1996). The reason appears to lie in gender-specific conversational traits that encourage others to "open up." For example, women tend to be good listeners. They also encourage further communication by showing interest and concern. Thus they might say, "I understand how you feel," and reinforce it nonverbally with attentive facial expressions. Women also use questions to gain greater insight into other people's feelings and perceptions. So, for example, they might ask, "Do you think that was intentional?" (Benokraitis 2005).

When it comes to revealing information about themselves, women are somewhat more likely than men to do so (Rotenberg and Chase 1992; Clark and Ayers 1993; Derlega et al. 1993; Stein and Brodsky 1995). Gender differences also involve the kinds of things that men and women reveal about themselves (Rubin et al. 1980). Men are less willing to express their fears and more hesitant to reveal their weaknesses than women are (Cunningham 1981). They are more likely than women to disclose factual information and to express positive emotions (Rubin et al. 1980). Women tend to express their feelings and are more likely than men to express negative emotions. In terms of the specific kind of information they reveal, women are more likely than men to express their feelings toward their parents and closest friends as well as their fears and accomplishments. Men, in contrast, are more likely to talk about the things they are most proud of, things they like most about their partners, and their views on politics.

Gender is not the only factor that influences levels of self-disclosure. Research shows that self-disclosure is more likely to occur when people feel distressed, anxious, depressed, frightened, or angry (Stiles, Shuster, and Harrigan 1992). We are also more likely to reveal personal things about ourselves when we anticipate future interaction with others or want to cultivate a relationship with them (Shaffer, Pegalis, and Bazzini 1996). And research shows that people with secure attachment styles tend to disclose more about themselves than people with other attachment styles (Keelan, Dion, and Dion 1998).

As Pilpay suggested, imparting secret thoughts to another person can bring us everlasting pleasure. Sharing our happiness and receiving comfort for our pain and suffering are just two of the benefits associated with self-disclosure. Being singled out as the recipient of confidential information flatters most of us. Social psychologists have suggested that we are pleased because we attribute the self-disclosure to the fact that this person likes us, trusts us, and would like to develop a closer relationship (Wortman et al. 1976). In fact, studies show that people feel rewarded when someone shares personal information with them. Our attraction to this person increases, and we are more likely to disclose something to them (Collins and Miller 1994). Viewed from the perspective of social exchange theory, reciprocal self-disclosure increases partners' liking and trust for one another, eases communication problems, and helps balance the costs and rewards of a relationship (Benokraitis 2005).

ESTABLISHING RELATIONSHIPS

As we learned early in this chapter, many factors account for our attraction to other people. In some cases, we are motivated to pursue a friendship or a platonic relationship. Similar values and activities draw us together and act as strong bonds. In speaking of our affection for friends, we say that we like them. When sexual attraction becomes one of the reasons for pursuing a relationship, it becomes more complicated. To understand this special kind of social interaction, let us consider what happens during courtship and dating.

Courtship and Dating

Courtship practices date back to the twelfth century (Tressider 1997). Inspired by Arabic and Moorish ideals, the nobility of southern France introduced the arts of courtly love. This new concept of love combined two ideas prevalent at the time: male chivalry and the idealization of women (Schwartz and Scott 2000). Emerging in the guise

of theater, this romantic playfulness was designed to amuse bored wives. It provided ladies of the court with an acceptable way to practice their skills of flirtation without the risks of an illicit affair.

Over time, the rules of courtship changed. In the nineteenth century, when courtship was considered a prelude to marriage, the process served to test a man's economic and social suitability for a woman. In many ways, the dating practices of the twentieth century (see Box 7.5) differed little from the courtship practices of the nineteenth. High school dances provided a way for boys and girls to assess the other person's qualities and potential. Even though dating practices today do not seem to resemble those of the past, they still serve the same purpose as the process by which people select mates.

Flirting

Courtship and dating involve a special kind of social interaction called flirting. Some people are masters when it comes to flirting. Others seem to have no clue. How would you rate yourself? Your answer probably reflects your understanding of this unique kind of social interaction. The subject of flirtation caught the interest of Georg Simmel, who referred to this kind of behavior as *coquetry* (see Box 7.6). Appearing as a special subject in an essay written on the broader topic of sociability, he portrayed flirtation as a playful game of offers and refusals between men and women. This characterization suggests that the outcome of this particular kind of social exchange will not produce any serious consequences. We might conclude, therefore, that the players' attitudes and behaviors reflect that. But in fact, as Simmel describes it, players are quite cautious. They engage in behaviors apparently designed to protect their egos. According to him, flirtation involves a gray area between acceptance and refusal, which he describes as a vacillation between a half "yes" and a half "no." Masters of this game protect their own vulnerabilities while they skillfully assess the desires of the other player.

BOX 7.5	RULES OF THE DATING GAME

If dating is a game, what are the rules? Is this a game whose rules are always changing? Or is this a game like Simmel described where rules have no place?

In 1995, Ellen Fein and Sherrie Schneider wrote a book claiming that there were some "time-tested" rules. According to them, these rules emerged sometime around the second decade of the twentieth century—when their grandmothers were dating. Fein and Schneider recognize that these rules seem crazy, but they claim that they are neither immoral nor outlandish—"just a simple working set of behaviors and reactions that, when followed, invariably serve to make most women irresistible to desirable men" (2). Their critics disagree, arguing that the rules are a form of manipulation and an unhealthy approach to relationships. What do you think? Consider a sample of their rules:

- Be a "creature unlike any other."
- Don't talk to a man first (and don't ask him to dance).
- Don't stare at men or talk too much.
- Don't meet him halfway or go Dutch on a date.
- Don't call him and rarely return his calls.
- Always end phone calls first.
- Don't accept a Saturday night date after Wednesday.
- Fill up your time before the date.
- Always end the date first.
- Don't see him more than once or twice a week.
- Don't tell him what to do.
- Don't open up too fast.

Whether you approve of these rules, or not, you might realize why they might work. "Playing hard to get," which was the term their grandmothers used to describe these rules, involves one of the basic principles of social exchange theory. Women who are not readily available for dates may appear more valuable or desirable than women who might appear to drop everything on a moment's notice to go on a date. In fact, Willard Waller described the same strategy in his study of college coeds in 1937. Referring to courtship as the "rating and dating complex," he claimed that a coed's prestige depended on dating more than anything else. And "here as nowhere else, nothing succeeds like success. Therefore, the clever coed contrives to give the impression of being much sought after even if she is not" (730). Several of Fein and Schneider's rules also put women in the position of having power as a condition of a date. Consider where the power lies when women date men who (1) are willing to pay for the entire date, (2) relentlessly call a woman who rarely returns phone calls, and (3) must make every move in the flirtation process. These are men who are dependent on the woman for the receipt of rewards. These rules might work, but women should recognize that by following them, they have considerably narrowed their pool of eligible dating partners and have probably eliminated many desirable mates.

The unique character of this special kind of social behavior led Simmel to claim that observers had a certain right to speak of "its 'art,' not only of its 'artifices.'"

Margaret Mitchell, the author of *Gone with the Wind*, would agree with Simmel. In fact, Scarlett O'Hara, the main character of her novel, was a master of this "art." Showing how Scarlett could pull men on with one hand and push them off with another, Mitchell described the playful interaction that ensued between Scarlett and every man she met. Today, novels, television programs, and films depict the flirtation process in rich detail. And many books on this subject fill the self-help section

of bookstores. It is therefore surprising that few scientific studies have examined this unique form of social interaction.

Studies of the Flirtation Process

Irenäus Eibl-Eibesfeldt (1989), an ethologist at the Max Planck Institute in Germany, is credited with conducting the first serious study of flirting. When he undertook this research in the 1960s, he was well aware of the role that instinct played in the unique patterns of behaviors that many animals display when they want to attract a mate. Traveling to cultures around the world—from Samoa to

BOX 7.6	GEORG SIMMEL ON COQUETRY

In the sociology of sex, we find a play-form: the play-form of eroticism is coquetry. In sociability, it finds its most facile, playful, and widely diffused realization. Generally speaking, the erotic question between the sexes is that of offer and refusal. Its objects are, of course, infinitely varied and graduated, and by no means mere either-ors, much less exclusively physiological. The nature of feminine coquetry is to play up, alternately, allusive promises and allusive withdrawals—to attract the male but always to stop short of a decision, and to reject him but never to deprive him of all hope. The coquettish woman enormously enhances her attractiveness if she shows her consent as an almost immediate possibility but is ultimately not serious about it. Her behavior swings back and forth between "yes" and "no" without stopping at either. She playfully exhibits the pure and simple form of erotic decisions and manages to embody their polar opposites in a perfectly consistent behavior: its decisive, well-understood content, that would commit her to one of the two opposites, does not even enter.

This freedom from all gravity of immutable contents and permanent realities gives coquetry the character of suspension, distance, ideality, that has led one to speak, with a certain right, of its "art," not only of its "artifices." Yet in order for coquetry to grow on the soil of sociability, as we know from experience it does, it must meet with a specific behavior on the part of the male. As long as he rejects its attractions or, inversely, is its mere victim that without any will of his own is dragged along by its vacillations between a half "yes" and a half "no," coquetry has not yet assumed for him the form that is commensurate with sociability. For it lacks the free interaction and equivalence of elements that are the fundamental traits of sociability. It does not attain these until he asks for no more than this freely suspended play which only dimly reflects the erotically definitive as a remote symbol; until he is no longer attracted by the lust for the erotic element or by the fear of it which is all he can see in the coquettish allusions and preliminaries. Coquetry that unfolds its charms precisely at the height of sociable civilization has left far behind the reality of erotic desire, consent, or refusal; it is embodied in the interaction of the mere silhouettes, as it were, of their serious imports. Where they themselves enter or are constantly present in the background, the whole process becomes a private affair between two individuals: it takes place on the plane of reality. But under the sociological sign of sociability from which the center of the personality's concrete and complete life is barred, coquetry is the flirtatious, perhaps ironical play, in which eroticism has freed the bare outline of its interactions from their materials and contents and personal features. As sociability plays with the forms of society, so coquetry plays with those of eroticism, and this affinity of their natures predestines coquetry as an element of sociability.

Source: Simmel 1905/1964, 50–51.

South America, western Europe, the United States, Africa, and the Far East—he discovered that the flirting and courtship behaviors of men and women were fairly universal. Equipped with a specially designed camera that allowed him to shoot pictures from the side when the lens pointed in another direction, he captured a number of nonverbal gestures that signaled interest in a member of the opposite sex. What is more, these behaviors followed a similar sequence. For females, it began by smiling at a male. Soon thereafter, her eyes would widen as her eyebrows arched. Then she would quickly lower her eyelids, tuck her chin down slightly and coyly to one side, avert her gaze, and cover her mouth as she giggled (Rodgers 1999).

Other gestures commonly displayed during flirtation show submissiveness or safety. For example, flirting couples may place their palms up on a table or knee to reassure the other person of their harmlessness (Goleman 1995; Rodgers 1999). Shrugging the shoulders, another submissive gesture, signals helplessness. Females may combine a shrug with a tilted head, a posture that elongates the neck and signals vulnerability, submissiveness, and physical attraction.

One of the best studies on this subject was conducted by Timothy Perper and Susan Fox (1980a, 1980b), who spent more than three hundred hours observing the social interactions between men and women in bars located in New Jersey and New York City (see also McCormick and Jesser 1983). They reported that flirtation is "a sequence of behavior, mostly nonverbal, which brings two people into increasing sociosexual intimacy" (Perper and Fox 1980b, 23). This perspective led them to conclude that American women usually take the first steps in this process by making a subtle move, such as standing close to men

who interest them. They also claimed that women appear to know more than men about the process of flirting. Based on hours of observation, they noted:

> Typically, women are exquisitely familiar with what occurs during flirtations while men are generally quite ignorant. Women can describe in great detail how they and other women flirt and pick up men, and what men do (and just as frequently, what men do *not* do). In contrast, . . . [most] men were unfamiliar with all or most of the events of flirtations. Even quite successful men had no idea how they attracted women and what

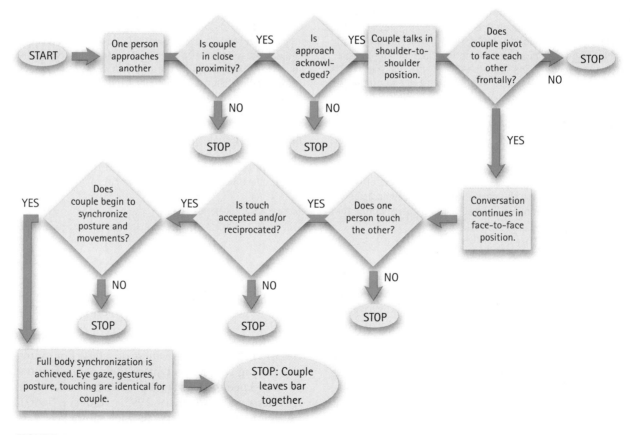

FIGURE 7.4

Flirtation in Bars

Source: McCormick and Jesser 1983, 77, based on Perper and Fox 1980a, 1980b.

happened during a flirtation. Often men create vast and complex theories . . . but they seem to possess little or no information. (Perper and Fox 1980a, 4)

This conclusion might suggest that women have more power than men during a flirtatious interaction, but Naomi McCormick and Clinton Jesser (1983) argue that flirtations are not under the control of one person. In fact, they claim that both parties in a successful flirtation influence each other at each step in a sequence of behaviors. Based on the model proposed by Perper and Fox, they describe the reciprocal influence of men and women in the stages of a flirtation as shown in Figure 7.4.

Functions of Courtship and Dating

Today, as in the past, courtship and dating help people select a mate. It provides a way to assess the qualities they consider most important for an intimate relationship. It also serves two other purposes in the development of interpersonal relationships: confirmation of a social self and anticipatory socialization.

Confirmation of a Social Self. The interaction that takes place in dating provides us with valuable information about who we are (Knox and Schacht 2000). When two people interact on a date, they constantly assess themselves from the other's perspective. How does he view me? Does she find me attractive, charming, or intelligent? Will he want to go out on another date? As our discussion of flirting suggested, this kind of interaction provides us with important clues about how we are mutually affecting one another. If the other person responds to us positively through speech and gestures, we feel good about ourselves. Dating, therefore, gives us a way to confirm our self-concept (Knox and Schacht 2000).

Anticipatory Socialization. For many people, dating teaches them how to interact with someone of the opposite sex. Males and females learn how to negotiate differences, such as the timing and degree of sexual expression (Knox and Schacht 2000). Throughout the process, individuals acquire skills that are necessary for the maintenance of long-term relationships (communication skills, empathy, and companionship).

SUMMARY

1. Personality traits play an important role in determining whom we like. The traits that we associate with likable people reflect the importance of trust.

2. Familiarity also influences our attraction to certain people. Repeated exposure to people or objects increases our liking for them. Promixity also influences the development of friendships.

3. Physical attractiveness is an important factor in determining whom we like, whom we want to date, and whom we eventually marry. Universal standards of beauty do exist. Scientific studies of male and female bodies also show a preference for certain proportions in figures. Evolutionary psychologists argue that natural selection explains these findings, in that the physical features associated

with beauty reflect good health, strength, and fertility.

4. Heider's balance theory proposes that we like people who share attitudes similar to our own, and research bears this out. In fact, as the number of similar attitudes increases, so does the attraction between two people. Research also shows a predominant pattern of homogamy—the tendency to marry someone about the same age, in the same social class, with the same level of education, raised in the same religion, and so on.

5. According to attachment theory, adult relationships are influenced by the kinds of bonds that develop between infants and their caregivers during early childhood development. Researchers have

identified three distinct types of attachment styles—secure, anxious/ambivalent, and avoidant —linked to differences in adults' attitudes toward romantic love, toward themselves, and toward others.

6. According to social exchange theory, human beings enter into relationships that offer the best balance between rewards and costs. The parties in these relationships engage in a type of social exchange that involves a variety of intangible commodities such as love, companionship, time, and effort. As long as both parties feel they profit from the exchange in a relationship, they will stay together. When people believe that the exchange in a relationship is unfair, however, they will try to restore balance.

7. Achieving intimacy in a relationship involves self-disclosure, the revealing of personal information. Talk about factual matters is called descriptive self-disclosure; talk about feelings or personal opinions is known as evaluative self-disclosure. According to the theory of social penetration, close relationships progress through increasing levels of intimacy. This involves the norm of reciprocity. Revealing personal information is not risk-free; doing so in a slow reciprocal manner provides some protection and allows us to gradually determine how much we can trust the other person.

8. Courtship and dating can be traced back to the twelfth century. Although the rules have changed, this interaction still serves as the process by which people select mates. Flirtation plays an important role in courtship and dating. Simmel described this as a playful game of offers and refusals. Eibl-Eibesfeldt described the process as a sequence of rituals and gestures. Men and women hold equal power during the flirtation process. In addition to selecting a mate, courtship and dating serve two other important functions: confirmation of a social self and anticipatory socialization.

KEY TERMS

Intimacy   183

Mere exposure   184

Homogamy   196

Attachment theory   196

Secure attachment   196

Anxious/ambivalent attachment   196

Avoidant attachment   196

Social exchange theory   200

Distributive justice   202

Equity theory   202

Comparison level   203

Comparison level for alternatives   203

Power   204

Principle of least interest   204

Self-disclosure   204

Descriptive self-disclosure   204

Evaluative self-disclosure   204

Social penetration theory   204

CRITICAL REVIEW QUESTIONS

1. Consider a relationship that has caused problems for you. Which of the theories presented in this chapter provides the best explanation for the trouble you experienced? Provide an analysis of that relationship based on that theory.

2. Consider how e-mail operates in developing relationships today. Do you think it facilitates or hinders the process of self-disclosure?

3. Describe how the process of flirtation occurs on a college campus (in a class, at a party, or at the library). How can signals be misunderstood? What kinds of "lines" do college students use to initiate contact with someone who interests them? Is the process of flirtation a game that mature adults should avoid?

EIGHT

Dimensions of Love and Marital Relationships

How Do I Love Thee?

How do I love thee? Let me count the ways.
I love thee to the depth and breadth and height
My soul can reach, when feeling out of sight
For the ends of being and ideal grace.
I love thee to the level of every day's
Most quiet need, by sun and candlelight.
I love thee freely, as men strive for Right;
I love thee purely, as they turn from Praise.
I love thee with the passion put to use
In my old griefs, and with my childhood's faith.
I love thee with a love I seemed to lose
With my lost saints—I love thee with the breath,
Smiles, tears, of all my life!—and, if God choose,
I shall but love thee better after death.

—Elizabeth Barrett Browning

Part of the marvel of this poem is recognizing just how difficult it is to put the emotion it expresses into words. "How do I love thee?" the poet asks. The question itself gives us pause. It is a tough question. And yet it captures the essence of an experience that most of us can relate to. What we feel may seem irrational, if only because it seems to defy any succinct definition. And of course, the poet recognizes that when she writes, "Let me count the ways." Love is not a simple emotion. At times it seems to tug at the heart for no reason. It seems to control us—we do not control it. Yet if we stop to think for a moment, we can identify specific reasons for the love that we feel for someone.

Part of the appeal of this poem may also lie in curiosity about the man who inspired the poet to write so eloquently about love. Who was the object of such great affection? How did they meet? What was the attraction? How did they keep their love alive? And what kind of relationship would cause the poet to wish it to last for eternity?

We know the answers to some of these questions. Elizabeth Barrett Browning was born in 1806. She was the oldest child in a family of twelve children—four girls and eight boys. Her parents' marriage, which lasted twenty-seven years, ended when her mother died in 1832. Elizabeth was her father's favorite for many years. This did not, however, make Elizabeth's life easy. Edward Barrett was a tyrant who never wanted any of his children to marry. And this was not the biggest obstacle in Elizabeth's life: a horse-riding injury to her spine at the age of 15 left her a semi-invalid. She thereafter suffered damage to her lungs from lying on her back for long periods of time.

By the time Elizabeth was 36 years old, she had become a popular English poet. Much of her day was spent lying on her couch reading and writing. One day a poem written by a certain Robert Browning called "Pippa Passes" caught her interest. That particular poem is remembered best for the line "God's in his heaven—all's right with the world." She sought out more of his poetry. Two years later, she mentioned him in a poem of her own, comparing him to William Wordsworth and Alfred, Lord Tennyson (Engel 2002). Browning, long an admirer of Barrett's, was flattered and took the opportunity to write to her. Although he was six years her junior and not nearly as famous, he did not hesitate to show an interest in her. In his letter, he asked if they could meet. And he ended his note boldly, writing, "I love your verses with all my heart, dear Miss Barrett. I do, as I say, love these books with all my heart—and I love you too."

Elizabeth put him off until spring. Part of the reason was her father, who constantly reminded her that he would never allow her to marry. But the couple did meet on May 20, 1845, and spoke for over an hour.

Even though Elizabeth's dog, Flush, bit Robert when he entered the room, the suitor remained undeterred. For him, it was love at first sight, and he knew immediately that he wanted to marry her. Their courtship continued for a year through daily correspondence and weekly visits. But it was a highly guarded secret. Elizabeth knew that if her father ever learned of their meetings, she would never see Robert again.

On September 12, 1846, Elizabeth Barrett married Robert Browning in a secret ceremony. Nine days later, Elizabeth left her father's home forever. The couple, along with Flush and Elizabeth's maid, sailed to Italy. It was only after they were married that Elizabeth showed Robert the collection of love sonnets she had written during their courtship. When he read them, he knew they were the finest poems she had ever written. To maintain their privacy, they were published under the title *Sonnets from the Portuguese*. No one was fooled; the public readily recognized that Elizabeth Barrett Browning was the poet.

Robert and Elizabeth Barrett Browning lived happily in Florence, Italy, until her death in 1861. They had one child, a son, born in 1849. Nothing expresses Elizabeth's deep love for her husband more than the final lines of Sonnet 43—"How Do I Love Thee?"—in which she expresses the hope that God will allow her to love Robert even better after death.

Elizabeth Barrett Browning's poem gives us much insight into the meaning of love. Because we bring our own experiences to it, our interpretations are bound to vary. Nonetheless, we are sure to agree on some things. Wayne Dyer (2002), a psychologist who is known for explaining how we can apply the "wisdom of the ages" to our modern lives, offers this interpretation:

> In this sonnet, a woman pours out her deep love for the man she loves and says to us all that being in love is not the result of a thunderbolt crashing down on you, rendering you speechless and wilting you by the magnitude of the love energy. It is not purely physical attraction that makes one feel so in

love. No, it is a multitude of little things that constitute the feeling of romantic love. As the sonnet says, "I love thee to the level of every day's most quiet need." (108)

LOVE

Like Queen Victoria and Prince Albert, whose love was documented at the start of Chapter 7, Robert and Elizabeth Browning were influenced by the culture of nineteenth-century England. These two historical examples illustrate how individuals meet, fall in love, and develop long-lasting relationships. They also show that good interpersonal relationships have many dimensions. We will now examine how close interpersonal relationships grow, develop, and sometimes end. Let us begin with ideas about the multidimensional nature of love.

Historical Ideas about Love

What is love? For centuries, lovers, poets, and writers have tried to capture its meaning (see Box 8.1). Love is an elusive concept, not easily defined. However, you may recognize the feelings and have perhaps experienced some of its

symptoms. If you attempt to define *love*, you will realize that this one word has multiple meanings. What is more, the meanings we attach to it refer to a wide range of feelings and designate various types of relationships. Consider, for example, the differences between romantic love, parental love, and brotherly love.

Confusion over the word *love* has a long history (Short 1990). In his book *Sex and Love in the Bible*, William Cole (1959) traces it to the Old Testament. As he points out, the Aramaic word *aheb* in the Old Testament refers to both the love of God and the love of man. It also referred to several other kinds of human love, including love for one's neighbor and sensual love for the opposite sex.

The New Testament contributed to the confusion in a different way. Whereas the original Greek texts recognized the multiple meanings of love, these distinctions were sometimes lost when the Bible was translated into English. To see how translation altered the meaning of specific passages, consider the five Greek words that were all translated as *love*:

1. *Epithymia:* sensual love or sexual desire.
2. *Eros:* yearning for unity. In English, *eros* implies only passion and sex, but for Greeks it had a broader meaning, including yearning for unity with God.

| BOX 8.1 | LOVE: PUTTING IT INTO WORDS |

Love is patient, love is kind. It does not envy, it does not boast, it is not proud. It is not rude, it is not self-seeking, it is not easily angered, it keeps no record of wrongs. Love does not delight in evil but rejoices with the truth. It always protects, always trusts, always hopes, always perseveres.

—1 Corinthians 13:4–7

Let me not to the marriage of true minds
Admit impediments. Love is not love
Which alters when it alteration finds,
Or bends with the remover to remove:

O, no! it is an ever-fixed mark.
That looks on tempests and is never shaken;
It is the star to every wand'ring bark,
Whose worth's unknown, although his height be taken.
Love's not Time's fool, though rosy lips and cheeks
Within his bending sickle's compass come;
Love alters not with his brief hours and weeks,
But bears it out even to the edge of doom:—
　　If this be error and upon me proved,
　　I never writ, nor no man ever loved.

—William Shakespeare, Sonnet 116

3. *Philia:* brotherly love, the kind of love between close friends and companions who have many things in common.

4. *Storge:* family affection, the love shared by parents and children.

5. *Agape:* self-giving love. This kind of love, which is associated with Jesus, refers to the "self-giving devotion" to others regardless of their merits.

Social Psychological Definitions of Love

How do social psychologists view love? Zick Rubin (1970) emphasized love as a social psychological variable by defining it as "an attitude held by a person, involving predispositions to think, feel, and behave in certain ways toward that other person" (265). And he argued that love differed significantly from liking. To demonstrate the difference, Rubin created a questionnaire that contained thirteen measures for each (see Table 8.1). His love scale consisted of items commonly associated with romantic love: the desire to be with or depend on a partner, the desire to help the partner, absorption with the partner, trust, and tolerance. In contrast, the liking scale included items that showed respect, admiration, and similarity to oneself.

Other social psychologists recognize the cognitive, emotional, and behavioral responses that Rubin suggests (Berscheid and Walster 1978; Lee 1988; Sternberg 1988b). And they have proposed models of love based on the nature of these responses. Ellen Berscheid and Elaine Walster (1978) were among the first social psychologists to recognize the multiple meanings attached to love. They proposed that two kinds of love exist: passionate and companionate. Passionate love involves intense emotions that are linked to sexual feelings. The physiological responses that accompany passionate love are often described as the "chemistry" between two people. When people experience this kind of love, they feel an acute longing to be with the loved one. They become totally absorbed with that person and frequently find it difficult to study, work, or concentrate on anything

else. When they see their loved one, they may feel butterflies in their stomach or even lose their appetite. Others feel like they are floating on air. Social psychologists have described this experience as a state of wildly fluctuating moods. In fact, the highs and lows of passionate love can swing from blissful ecstasy to utter despair. It is therefore not surprising that passionate love produces fragile attachments.

Companionate love, which does not produce the same kind of emotional intensity as passionate love, is characterized by more durable attachments. People who experience this kind of love are more likely to describe it as a steadier, calmer state. Although people who experience companionate love feel less intense affection for the other person, they do feel a certain closeness. The attachments they form are based on qualities that produce stable, enduring relationships: trust, respect, and admiration.

THEORIES OF LOVE

For years social psychologists avoided studies of love, arguing that it was not a topic worthy of respect (Livermore 1993). This attitude resulted in part from Senator William Proxmire's 1974 campaign against wasting government research funds on frivolous subjects such as love. But in the 1980s, the importance of this subject was recognized. In the next section we will explore two major theories that attempt to explain love.

John Lee's Styles of Loving

John Lee (1988) proposed one of the best-known theories of love. His research on this subject began with an exhaustive study of the writings of great novelists. After that he examined nonfictional accounts of love, including observations made by Plato, Ovid, Andreas Cappellanus, and Castiglione. Finally, he considered the thoughts of recent psychologists. All in all, he recorded over four thousand descriptions of some aspect of love. He discovered that love could not be described in a

TABLE 8.1	RUBIN'S MEASUREMENTS OF "LOVING" VERSUS "LIKING"

Love Scale Items

1. If _____ were feeling badly, my first duty would be to cheer him/her up.
2. I feel that I can confide in _____ about virtually everything.
3. I find it easy to ignore _____'s faults.
4. I would do almost anything for _____.
5. I feel very possessive toward _____.
6. If I could never be with _____, I would feel miserable.
7. If I were lonely, my first thought would be to seek _____ out.
8. One of my primary concerns is _____'s welfare.
9. I would forgive _____ for practically anything.
10. I feel responsible for _____'s well-being.
11. When I am with _____, I spend a good deal of time just looking at him/her.
12. I would greatly enjoy being confided in by _____.
13. It could be hard for me to get along without _____.

Like Scale Items

1. When I am with _____, we are almost always in the same mood.
2. I think that _____ is unusually well-adjusted.
3. I would highly recommend _____ for a responsible job.
4. In my opinion, _____ is an exceptionally mature person.
5. I have great confidence in _____'s good judgment.
6. Most people would react very favorably to _____ after a brief acquaintance.
7. I think that _____ and I are quite similar to each other.
8. I would vote for _____ in a class or group election.
9. I think that _____ is one of those people who quickly wins respect.
10. I think that _____ is an extremely intelligent person.
11. _____ is one of the most likable people I know.
12. _____ is the sort of person whom I myself would like to be.
13. It seems to me that it is very easy for _____ to gain admiration.

Source: Rubin 1970, 267.

single statement. And he concluded that there were different kinds of love that could be described by a clustering of symptoms. Capturing the wide range of experiences associated with love, Lee's list of symptoms included jealousy, fidelity, unselfishness, intense preoccupation with the loved one, and insomnia. His analysis identified a number of unique clusters of symptoms, to each of which he attached a label. For example, he described *mania* as "a cluster of physical distress (like loss of sleep), intense preoccupation, jealousy, possessiveness, ambivalence (love-hate), and belief in the power of love to overcome all odds" (56).

Based on what he had learned from this first step, he then conducted 112 personal interviews with white, heterosexual couples under the age of 35. Lee asked subjects to tell him about their stories of love, using a method called the "Love Story Card Sort." Choosing from among fifteen hundred cards, subjects told a variety of stories. The results of these interviews led Lee to conclude that people experience many different kinds of love. Using color as an analogy for love, he argued that love comes in many different shades. Like the hues on an artist's color wheel, he proposed that the different kinds of love we experience result from blending three primary styles of loving—*eros* (red), *ludus* (yellow), and *storge* (blue). The beauty of this model lies in the idea that there is not just one "true" kind of love. There are many different kinds to experience. According to Lee, most of us will find that our preference for a certain style of loving will vary over time just as our color preferences do. To understand how this works, let us first consider the three primary styles of loving.

Primary Styles of Loving. Eros refers to passionate love. According to Lee (1988), this kind of love provides evidence that love is *not* blind. In fact, people who experience eros are likely to describe it as "love at first sight." The experience involves an immediate, powerful physical attraction. Erotic lovers are attracted to certain physical types. For example, a man might prefer a tall, slim, blond woman with blue eyes. Or he might have several versions of his "ideal" type. Erotic lovers seek exclusive relationships, but they are not possessive and do not fear rivals. The desire for sexual intimacy is the focus of this kind of love.

Ludus takes the form of a game. It is playful, casual, and carefree. Neither commitment nor serious emotional involvement characterizes this style of loving. In fact, the pleasure of ludus lies in playing the game rather than winning it. People who prefer the ludic style often date several people at the same time and discourage partners from becoming attached. They view sex as fun and do not fall in love. Jealousy and possessiveness play no role in this kind of love.

Storge (pronounced "stor-gay") is an affectionate form of love that typically develops between siblings and friends. This kind of love, which focuses on companionship, is peaceful and steady. Storgic lovers may be embarrassed to say, "I love you." They may be surprised by the question "Do you love me?" and are likely to respond, "Of

According to John Lee, people experience many kinds of love. Eros, a passionate style of love, involves physical attraction (left). Ludus refers to a playful style of love (center). And storge is the kind of love that usually develops between friends (right).

course, I do. Why would you ask?" Unlike other styles of love, storgic love grows slowly and is long-lasting.

Secondary Styles of Loving. **Mania** refers to the kind of love "that strikes the lover like a bolt from the blue—or from the gods" (Lee 1988, 45). This secondary style of love is derived from a combination of eros and ludus. It describes lovers who are intensely jealous, possessive, and obsessively preoccupied with their lover. Though they need repeated reassurances that they are loved, these kinds of lovers often hold themselves back, fearing that they will love too much without an equal return. This style of love may give rise to a "hate-love" relationship. According to Lee, manic lovers may not even like their lovers and would not choose them as friends. He discovered that this style of love is common among the young, who are anxious to experience the excitement of love. For them, it is an experience with valuable lessons about how deeply they may love someone else. In other cases, they may fall into a cycle of manic love. In this case, this style reflects a desperate need to be in love. Manic lovers do not really love the other person but are "in love with love itself."

Pragma combines ludus and storge. Pragmatic lovers take a practical approach to love. While they do not necessarily focus on the physical traits they might desire in a partner, they do have a "shopping list" of practical qualities they want. In considering who might be a *compatible* partner, pragmatic lovers look for people who have similar interests, and they are likely to take similar attitudes and backgrounds into account (religious affiliation, social class, education, political attitudes). In the past, parents who arranged marriages for their children relied on this style of love. Today, computer dating and matching services reflect this preference for finding the right mate.

Agape (pronounced "ah-gah-pay"), the kind of love promoted by Christianity, is derived from eros and storge. It is selfless and giving, an altruistic kind of love that expects nothing in return. This kind of love is guided by the head rather than the heart. People who subscribe to this style of love feel a duty to love and care for the beloved. This kind of gentle, patient love is rare. According to Lee, people who prefer this style of love probably practice celibacy and do not have a lover or a mate.

In considering the kind of love that people may experience, Lee recognized that we are not limited to just one of the styles he described. He viewed his descriptions as portraits that are typical of each style. Although people may prefer one style over another, we often experience many styles over a lifetime. For example, erotic love probably characterizes the beginning of many relationships. Over time, however, the style of love might change, taking on characteristics that are more typical of the storgic style (friendship or companionship). Lee also argued that long-lasting relationships relied on compatibility between love styles. It is unlikely that someone who prefers an erotic style would remain in a relationship with someone who prefers the pragmatic or storgic styles.

Robert Sternberg's Triangular Model of Love

Robert Sternberg (1988b) proposed another popular theory of love to explain the different forms that love takes over time. According to his triangular theory of love, eight kinds of love are produced by a combination of three key components: intimacy, passion, and commitment. Each of these components has a unique course of development—some develop quickly, and others take time (see Table 8.2). At some points in a relationship, both people might experience the same degree of a particular component. For example, passion tends to be intense for both people at the beginning of a relationship. As relationships develop, however, the importance of these elements tends to change. As it does, so does the relationship. To understand how Sternberg's three basic elements can produce many different kinds of love, let us begin by examining each one separately.

The Intimacy Component. Intimacy, the emotional component of love, describes the closeness and affectionate feelings of connection that people

TABLE 8.2	DISTINGUISHING INFATUATION AND LOVE	
Questions to Ask	**If It's Romantic Infatuation**	**If It's Real Love**
The Nature of the Attraction		
1. What is your main interest? What attracts you most?	Person's "physical equipment"; the body; what responds to the senses.	The total personality; whole person; what's *in* the body.
2. How many things attract you?	Few—though some may be very strong.	Many or most.
The Course of the Romance		
3. How did the romance start?	Fast (hours or days).	Slowly (months or years).
4. How consistent is your level of interest?	Interest varies, comes and goes; many peaks and valleys; not consistent or predictable.	Evens out; gets to be dependable, consistent, can predict it.
5. What effect does the romance have on your personality?	Disorganizing, destructive, you act strangely, are not "yourself."	Organizing, constructive; you're a better person.
6. How does it end?	Fast—*unless* there's been mutually satisfying sex.	Slowly; takes long time; you may never be quite the same.
Two Views of You Two		
7. How do you view each other?	You live in a one-person world. You see the other as faultless, idealizing him or her.	You add the new relationship to former ones. You are more realistic, admitting other's faults but loving anyway.
8. How do others view you two? What's the attitude of friends and parents?	Few or none approve of the relationship.	Most or all approve. You get along well with other's friends and parents.
Dealing with Double Trouble		
9. What does distance (long separation) do to the relationship?	Withers away, dies; can't stand this added stress.	Survives; may even grow.
10. How do quarrels affect the romance?	They get more frequent, more severe, and will kill relationship.	They grow less frequent, less severe.
The Inner World of Love		
11. How do you feel about and refer to your relationship?	Much use of *I/me/my; he/him/his; she/her/hers;* little feeling of oneness.	Speak of *we/us/our;* feel and think as a unit, a pair; togetherness.
12. What's your ego response to the other?	Mainly selfish, restrictive; "What does this do for *me?*"	Mainly unselfish, releasing; concerned equally for other.
13. What's your overall attitude toward the other?	Attitude of taking; exploit and use the other.	Attitude of giving, sharing; want to serve other's needs, wants.
14. What is the effect of jealousy?	More frequent, more severe.	Less frequent, less severe.
Total Pattern of the Clues	Kid stuff; romantic infatuation	The real thing; true love.

SUMMARY CLUE: In real love, you love the other person so much that you want him or her to be happy—even if you may not be allowed to share that happiness.

Source: Short 1990, 186.

experience in loving relationships. The bond people feel results from reciprocal self-disclosure. Mutual understanding, support, and concern for the welfare of a loved one characterize this component of love (Sternberg and Grajek 1984).

Drawing on Berscheid's theory of emotions (1983), Sternberg proposed that intimacy develops over time. Readily apparent at the beginning of a relationship, it increases steadily. After that, it continues to grow but at a slower rate. Eventually it levels off and then disappears beneath the surface of the relationship. Berscheid observed that when a disruption occurs in a close relationship, it causes emotions to increase. This is particularly common in the early stage of a new relationship, when two people do not know each other well and cannot predict what the other will do. A disruption at this point causes uncertainty and, consequently, intensified emotions. Although uncertainty wreaks havoc on our emotional states, it actually aids the development of intimacy.

Once a relationship is established, intimacy may seem to disappear. That could suggest that a relationship is dying out. But it could also mean that a relationship is thriving—that the couple are growing together with such ease that they are not even aware of their interdependence. In this case, only some kind of disruption—a separation, death, or divorce—might show how they feel about one another. That led Sternberg to ask, "Is it any wonder that some couples realize only after a divorce that they were very close to and dependent on each other?" (Trotter 1992, 147).

The Passion Component. Passion, the motivational aspect of love, refers to the "chemistry" between two people. It describes the romantic feelings and desires that are produced by physical attraction—the intense desire to be united with the loved one. In contrast to intimacy, passion develops rapidly. Although people initially feel a powerful sexual attraction, they get used to it—get habituated—and the intense attraction begins to diminish. Sternberg compared this pattern to the kind of addiction people experience with certain substances—coffee, cigarettes, or alcohol. That is,

once habituation takes hold, even increased amounts of these drugs no longer produce the same effect. At the same time, it is difficult to break these habits. And people experience withdrawal symptoms. When someone loses a lover, the withdrawal symptoms can cause great pain. Common reactions include depression, irritability, and loss of appetite.

The Commitment Component. Commitment, the cognitive component of love, involves the short-term decision to love someone and the long-term commitment to maintain that love. Remaining faithful to one's partner for a lifetime is viewed as a rational choice. The course of commitment is fairly simple. It starts at zero, when people first meet. As they get to know one another, it begins to increase. If the relationship is going to be long-term, the level of commitment tends to increase gradually in the beginning and then speed up. Commitment eventually levels off for long-term relationships. However, if a relationship begins to fail, commitment will decline. And if the relationship ends, commitment returns to zero.

Combining the Key Components of Love. As Figure 8.1 shows, Sternberg positioned intimacy, passion, and commitment at the vertices of a triangle. He then described eight subsets of love that resulted when they were combined:

- *Nonlove* lacks all three components. It characterizes most interpersonal relationships, which are casual and do not involve any meaningful kind of love. Acquaintanceships fit this kind of love.
- *Liking* involves a high degree of intimacy but absent or low levels of passion and commitment. It is the type of love characteristic of friendships.
- *Infatuation* involves a high degree of passion but low levels of intimacy and commitment. It is the kind of love most often described as "love at first sight."
- *Empty love* involves a high degree of commitment but low or absent levels of intimacy and passion. People who stay together for the sake

Marriages that last fifty years show the strength of a couple's commitment—the cognitive component in Sternberg's model of love.

of children or for religious reasons may experience this kind of love.

- *Romantic love* involves both passion and intimacy but no commitment. High school romances that end when people leave for college represent this kind of love.
- *Companionate love* involves both intimacy and commitment but no passion. Married couples who no longer have passionate sex but still share interests and enjoy one another's company belong in this category.
- *Fatuous love* involves commitment and passion but no intimacy. People who meet and marry within a few weeks often experience fatuous love. Hollywood marriages or whirlwind courtships are examples.
- *Consummate love* involves all three components—intimacy, passion, and commitment. This kind of complete love is difficult to achieve and to maintain.

LOVE AND MARRIAGE

In his historical account of the relationship of Queen Victoria and Prince Albert, Christopher Hibbert (2000) described a fairy tale romance and a marriage based on love (see Chapter 7). He did not neglect to point out, however, that the public and one newspaper in particular believed that Albert was marrying for money, and they strongly disapproved of this reason. Although marrying for romantic love had become the ideal motive by the middle of the nineteenth century, practical marriages were not unusual. In fact, one advice book on marriage written by a Boston physician named Pomeroy in the late 1880s spelled out a number of unromantic considerations: "convenience, policy, friendship, position, influence, money" (Gay 1984, 102).

Today, most Americans are unlikely to admit that their reason for marrying might involve practical considerations like these. However, a number of social psychologists do view marriage in terms of an exchange. Erving Goffman (1952) claimed that people recognize this even before they marry.

A proposal of marriage in our society tends to be a way in which a man sums up his social attributes and suggests to a woman that hers are not so much better as to preclude a merger or a partnership in these matters. (456)

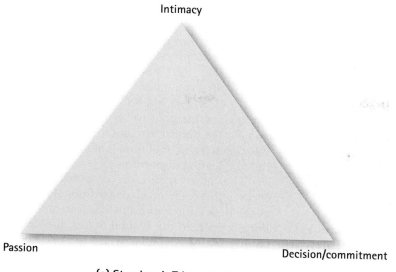

(a) Sternberg's Triangular Model

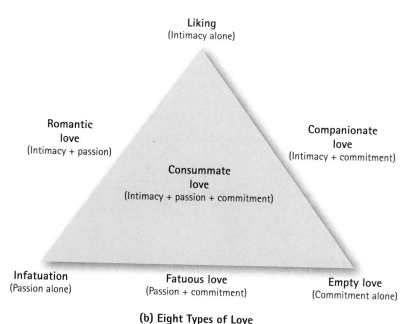

(b) Eight Types of Love

FIGURE 8.1

Sternberg's Triangular Model
and Eight Types of Love

Source: Sternberg and Barnes 1988, 121–122.

What are these social attributes? Is love one of them? A number of surveys have tried to get some answers. In one international study of attitudes toward love and marriage (Levine et al. 1995), respondents were asked, "If a man (woman) had all the other qualities you desired, would you marry this person if you were not in love with him (her)?" The results showed significant cross-cultural variations. The majority of Americans (85 percent) said they would not get married if they were not in love (see Table 8.3). But marrying for love is not a universal expectation. Young people in a number of other countries do not consider love a prerequisite for marriage and willingly enter into arranged marriages. As Table 8.3 shows, about half of those in Pakistan and India indicated that they would marry someone they did not love if the person had the other qualities they desired in a marital partner. What are those qualities?

Qualities Sought in Marital Partners

As it turns out, men and women in most societies look for the same kinds of qualities in a mate (Buss et al. 1990). Seeking to identify the personality characteristics that men and women in different societies value, David Buss designed an impressive cross-cultural study. His sample included over ten thousand men and women from thirty-seven countries, located on six continents and five islands. Buss and his research team asked their subjects to consider eighteen traits and to rate the desirability of each one in selecting a mate. The results showed that men and women throughout the world appreciate many of the same traits (see Table 8.4). In fact, the overall pattern for the top four traits turned out to be identical for men and women: (1) mutual attraction—love, (2) dependable character, (3) emotional stability and maturity, and (4) pleasing disposition.

The most significant cross-cultural differences in this study involved traditional values such as the desire for home and children and chastity. For example, in the United States, the desire for home and children ranked seventh for women and ninth for men. In China, it ranked second for both men and women. The Chinese also gave chastity a higher ranking. Men ranked it third, and women ranked it sixth. For men and women in the United States, this quality ranked near the bottom of the list. Cultural differences also appeared among preferences for certain personality traits. For

---

TABLE 8.3	LOVE AND MARRIAGE: CROSS-CULTURAL COMPARISONS

"If a man (woman) had all the other qualities you desired, would you marry this person if you were not in love with him (her)?"

	Respondents' Answers (%)		
Country	No	Yes	Undecided
United States	85.9	3.5	10.6
Brazil	85.7	4.3	10.0
England	83.6	7.3	9.1
Mexico	80.5	10.2	9.3
Australia	80.0	4.8	15.2
Hong Kong	77.6	5.8	16.7
Philippines	63.6	11.4	25.0
Japan	62.0	2.3	35.7
Pakistan	39.1	50.4	10.4
Thailand	33.5	18.8	47.5
India	24.0	49.0	26.9

Source: Levine et al. 1995, 561.

TABLE 8.4	TRAITS CONSIDERED IN MATE SELECTION
By Men	**By Women**
1. Mutual attraction—love	1. Mutual attraction—love
2. Dependable character	2. Dependable character
3. Emotional stability and maturity	3. Emotional stability and maturity
4. Pleasing disposition	4. Pleasing disposition
5. Good health	5. Education and intelligence
6. Education and intelligence	6. Sociability
7. Sociability	7. Good health
8. Desire for home and children	8. Desire for home and children
9. Refinement, neatness	9. Ambition and industriousness
10. Good looks	10. Refinement, neatness
11. Ambition and industriousness	11. Similar education
12. Good cook and housekeeper	12. Good financial prospect
13. Good financial prospect	13. Good looks
14. Similar education	14. Favorable social status or rating
15. Favorable social status or rating	15. Good cook and housekeeper
16. Chastity (no previous experience in sexual intercourse)	16. Similar religious background
17. Similar religious background	17. Similar political background
18. Similar political background	18. Chastity (no previous experience in sexual intercourse)

NOTE: Traits are ranked in descending order of importance.

Source: Buss et al. 1990, 19.

example, subjects from France, Japan, Brazil, the United States, Spain, and Ireland found traits such as a pleasing disposition, an exciting personality, and an easygoing demeanor highly desirable. People from South Africa (Zulu), China, India, and Iran placed far less emphasis on these traits.

Buss also found cross-cultural gender similarities. For example, men across cultures tended to rank physical attractiveness higher than women did. In contrast, women were more likely than men to give a higher ranking to qualities such as ambition and industriousness. Buss explained these particular findings in terms of evolution. Males seek physically attractive, younger women because of their greater reproductive potential. Females

desire qualities that will ensure the survival of off-spring—men who show the potential for making money.

The Process of Mate Selection

On June 13, 1998, David Weinlick married Elizabeth Runze before two thousand people who had gathered to witness the nuptials at the Mall of America. Weinlick and Runze were complete strangers. This arranged marriage became a national news story when the media learned about the unusual manner by which the bride was going to be selected. Tired of being asked when he was going to get married, Weinlick set the June 13 wedding date arbitrarily with no one special in mind. A close friend then suggested that friends and family should help him choose the bride. They began the screening process with a pool of candidates who had been nominated as the "woman of his dreams" on a Web site. The final candidates arrived at the mall at 10:00 A.M. on June 13. The interview process included questions such as "Why should I let you marry our Dave?" Family members also considered whether they would like the potential bride. Weinlick's sister remarked, "I'm picking a sister-in-law, someone who is going to be there at Christmas" (*Washington Post*, February 12, 2001). So far, the marriage is working. Although husband and wife had no relationship on the day of their wedding, they did share a strong commitment to make the marriage work. Passion and intimacy followed.

Would you trust your friends or family to make such an important decision? Even though you might not hand the process over to them like Weinlick did, they might have more influence than you think. Although it is not entirely clear how the process works, the process used by Weinlick may not be all that different from what actually happens. As it turns out, this couple had several important things in common. They both lived in Minnesota and were well matched in terms of age, race, education, and social class.

How important is similarity? As noted in Chapter 7, most people marry someone with a similar background, a pattern that sociologists call homogamy (Qian and Preston 1993; Blackwell 1998; Kalmijn 1998). Although you might believe that you are choosing a spouse from a large pool of eligible partners, our culture actually limits whom we consider. According to **filter theory**, people seeking spouses sift eligible candidates through successive levels of criteria (Kerckhoff and Davis 1962; Klimek 1979). As Figure 8.2 shows, the most important filters are geographical proximity; social class; race, ethnicity, and religion; physical attraction; and age. Pressure from family and friends also plays an important role in the filtering process.

Geographical proximity. The population of potential mates is first limited by geographical proximity. Although you may know people who have met their spouses over the Internet, most people have met them in high school, college, at work, or in community activities (Benokraitis 2005). In a nationwide survey, Ed Laumann and his colleagues (1994) found that 66 percent of married couples were introduced by someone they knew (family, friends, coworkers, and so on). One-third of the couples said that they met at a party given by a friend or at a social club or organization.

Social class. Most people marry someone from the same social class. In fact, it is uncommon for us to meet people outside our own social class. Social networks operate against this. Neighborhoods, schools, and other organizations make it more likely to meet someone in the same social class. Membership in the same social class suggests that people are fairly equal in terms of wealth. But it also suggests that they share similar attitudes, values, and lifestyles (Benokraitis 2005). Social class is such an important filter that even when people from different ethnic groups intermarry, they are likely to be of the same social class (Benokraitis 2005).

Race, ethnicity, and religion. At the next level, potential mates are sifted according to racial, ethnic, and religious similarities. These groups may vary significantly in terms of attitudes, beliefs, and values. Most religions oppose interfaith marriages. And interracial dating is still relatively rare. As a result, most people marry within their own groups.

Physical attractiveness. As research has repeatedly shown, people prefer to date the most attractive person possible. However, when it comes to marriage, we tend to marry someone who is similar to us in terms of physical attractiveness.

Age. We are most likely to marry someone close to our own age. In the United States, the

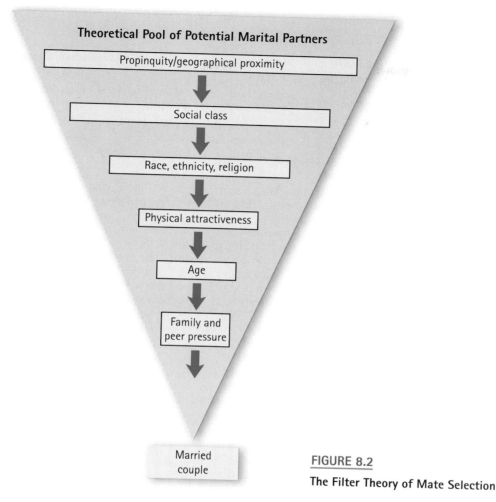

Theoretical Pool of Potential Marital Partners

Propinquity/geographical proximity

Social class

Race, ethnicity, religion

Physical attractiveness

Age

Family and peer pressure

Married couple

FIGURE 8.2

The Filter Theory of Mate Selection

man is typically two to three years older than the woman.

Family and peer pressure. Stories like *Romeo and Juliet* and *West Side Story* suggest that families and friends exert a powerful influence on mate selection. Do these stories distort reality? Research on teenage dating shows that parents exert little influence on their children's dating choices (Leslie et al. 1986; Longmore et al. 2001). But what does this really show? When parents decide to live in a

certain neighborhood, they influence the pool of eligible partners for their children: who the children meet at school, church, and other places in that community (Benokraitis 2005).

Before couples decide to marry, they should compare their social backgrounds. They should also discuss a number of subjects. In his book *Sex, Love, or Infatuation*, Ray Short (1990) suggests that the list should include roots, values, children, money, sex roles, places to live, main interests,

---

BOX 8.2   SHOULD YOU MARRY?

The sociologist Ray Short (1990) suggests that before people get married, they make sure they are on the same social wavelength. He advises people to discuss a wide range of subjects and to ask a lot of questions. His list includes the following:

Roots. How similar are you as to: Social class? Racial, national, and ethnic roots? City vs. country backgrounds? Religions?

Values. What is very important to you: Religion? Money? Social position and acceptance? Prestige? Sex before/after marriage? Who decides?

Children. Do you like them? Want them? How many? What about birth control? If so, what kind? Who's responsible for it?

Money. How much is enough? Who will make it? Save it? For what? Spend it? On what? Who'll budget, pay bills, do the shopping? (More married couples fight about money than any other thing.)

Sex roles. Who'll make decisions? Will both work? Will you share home chores? If babies come, will the wife work outside the home?

Where and how to live. Region? Rural or urban? Fancy or modest?

Main interests. Hobbies? Vocation plans? Education? Recreation likes and dislikes?

Investment in your future. What do you plan to do about war, pollution, poverty, and so on?

Concepts of marriage. For keeps? Trust and fidelity? Companionship?

Major goals and hopes for the future. What do you want out of life? How will you get there from here? Who can help? (70)

According to Short, the more that people agree on key issues like these, the better their chances for a successful marriage. From his perspective, married couples should be friends as well as lovers. And that means that two people should resemble one another in many ways—ideas, activities, sentiments, and goals.

---

concepts of marriage, and major goals and hopes for the future (see Box 8.2).

Marital Expectations: Myth versus Reality

> "They dream in courtship but wake in marriage."
>
> Geoffrey Chaucer, *Canterbury Tales*, "Wife of Bath's Prologue"

In a study of young adults' attitudes toward love and marriage, researchers with the National Marriage Project concluded that people today have very high expectations for marriage (Whitehead and Popenoe 2001). "The centuries-old ideal of friendship in marriage, or what sociologists call companionate marriage, may be evolving into a more exalted and demanding standard of a spiritualized union of souls" (6). In fact, 94 percent of never-married single people said they wanted to marry their soul mate. At the same time, these young adults also appeared realistic about marriage. A substantial majority (86 percent) recognized that marriage is hard work and a full-time job. And more than eight in ten say that one of the reasons for divorce is "too much focus on expectations for happiness and not enough hard work needed for a successful marriage" (6).

Social psychologists recognize that unrealistic expectations about love and marriage can set couples up for serious disappointments (see Box 8.3). David Knox and Caroline Schacht (2000) identify a number of myths that give young couples unrealistic ideas of what to expect in marriage.

Myth 1: Our Marriage Will Not Be like the Unhappy Ones We See. Even though we all know people who have unhappy marriages, we commonly assume that ours will be different. This assumption is rooted in the deceptive nature of

BOX 8.3	LOVE: ILLUSION AND REALITY

The initial stages of a love affair may be sustained largely through illusion, although few would relinquish its early euphoria on that account. Love is far more than "falling in love," however. It . . . [is] also a stripping away of illusion to acknowledge and love the fallible human within. It is this kind of clear-sighted, honest love that provides, for many people, the most "real" and enduring experience in life.

Source: From *The Secret Language of Love* by Megan Tressider. © 1997 by Megan Tressider. Used with permission of Chronicle Books LLC, San Francisco. Visit ChronicleBooks.com.

courtship. Many couples assume that their undying love for one another is special—that it alone will carry them through rough times. Influenced by this expectation, many couples fail to realize that good marriages take effort. Each partner must monitor the relationship and tend to its needs when necessary.

Myth 2: Married People Make Each Other Happy. Most Americans expect the person they marry to make them happy. After all, isn't that why we marry for love? Even attachment theory argues that the object of our love produces feelings of comfort, joy, and happiness. In fact, spouses do have a great impact on one another's happiness. That does not mean, however, that marriage ensures happiness. To expect another person to make us happy is unrealistic. Many circumstances outside of marriage still affect us. For example, a spouse might be able to comfort us after the death of a parent, but he or she can only do so much. Likewise, it may be difficult, if not impossible, for a spouse to relieve the anxiety that our boss, work, or something else produces.

Myth 3: We Will Not Have Serious Disagreements. Most couples know they will have disagreements over the course of their marriage. However, they might not believe that their arguments could threaten the stability of their relationship. Arguing itself is not a good predictor of a doomed relationship; according to John Gottman (1999), it is the *way* couples argue. In his research on marriages, he discovered that four kinds of negativity are lethal to a relationship: criticism, contempt, defensiveness, and stonewalling.

Myth 4: My Spouse Will Satisfy All of My Needs. Some people believe that the person they marry will or should satisfy all of their needs. This might mean that we want our partner to be intellectually stimulating or to provide emotional support for personal problems, warmth and affection, or sexual intimacy. While soap operas may lead us to believe that loving partners meet each other's every need, this expectation is unrealistic. We should not rely on one person but should seek support from other friends and family members as well.

Myth 5: More Love Means Less Conflict. Contrary to what you might think, more love does not mean less conflict (Sprecher and Felmlee 1993). In fact, research shows that deeper love can lead to increasing levels of conflict over time. Intense love can turn to frustration when partners fail to meet unrealistic expectations. Ironically, their desire for a better relationship than the one they have may cause conflict to escalate.

Marital Relationships

Knowing what to expect in a marriage could reduce disappointments, yet little research on good marriages exists (Benokraitis 2005). However, three studies do provide some insight into the kinds of marriages that people have: Cuber and Haroff's classic identification of marital types, Lavee and Olson's study of married couples in therapy, and Wallerstein and Blakeslee's typology of good marriages.

Cuber and Haroff's Marital Types. In the 1960s, John Cuber and Peggy Haroff undertook a study of the relationships of 437 upper-middle-class men and women aged 35 to 55. Although this study did not provide a representative sample of married couples, it does give us some insight into the kinds of marriages that men and women experience. Based on personal interviews conducted with these men and women, Cuber and Haroff (1965) identified five distinctive marriage styles: the conflict-habituated, the devitalized, the passive-congenial, the vital, and the total.

The **conflict-habituated marriage** is characterized by tension and conflict that are largely controlled. Arguments do not settle issues, nor are they intended to do so. In fact, the reason for the conflict is often unimportant. Some psychiatrists have even suggested that couples in these kinds of marriages have a need to fight and that their spats actually keep their marriages from falling apart.

Couples in **devitalized marriages** describe themselves as having been deeply in love at the beginning of the relationship. They recall spending time together, enjoying sex, and closely identifying with one another. Over time, however, they drift apart, spend little time together, share fewer interests and activities, and report less sexual satisfaction. When they do spend time together, it is out of a sense of obligation. And it usually involves joint entertaining, activities with children, and participating in community responsibilities. Although these relationships endure, some couples are resentful and disillusioned. Others accept the result but are ambivalent. One spouse in such a marriage said, "I wish life would be more exciting, but I should have known it couldn't last. In a way, it's calm and quiet and reassuring this way, but there are times when I get very ill at ease—sometimes downright mad. Does it *have* to be like this?" (Cuber and Haroff 1965, 54–55).

Passive-congenial marriages resemble devitalized ones, except that passivity exists from the start. Couples in these kinds of marriages begin with low expectations and therefore experience little disillusionment. These are marriages based on practical considerations. One wife expressed it this way:

> We have both always tried to be calm and sensible about major life decisions, to think things out thoroughly and in perspective. When he asked me to marry him, I took a long time to decide whether he was the right man for me and I went into his family background, because I wasn't just marrying him; I was choosing a father for my children. (Cuber and Haroff 1965, 51)

In **vital marriages**, partners are intensely bound together psychologically. They value sharing and togetherness, and they put their relationship above everything else. For them, sexual fulfillment is a very important part of marriage. One man described his marriage as follows:

> The things we do together aren't fun intrinsically— the ecstasy comes from being *together in the doing.* Take her out of the picture and I wouldn't give a damn for the boat, the lake, or any of the fun that goes on out there. (Cuber and Haroff 1965, 55)

Couples in vital marriages do experience conflict. However, the way partners handle it differs significantly from the way that men and women in conflict-habituated marriages do. In vital marriages, couples disagree over specific issues. And they seek to resolve the conflict quickly through compromise.

The last kind of relationship, the **total marriage**, resembles the vital marriage in most respects. There are simply more facets to it. Partners' lives are more fully enmeshed. They spend more time together—whether that involves work or play. Although couples in total marriages can have serious differences of opinion, they do not allow conflict to affect their relationships. This type of relationship is rare, but it does exist.

Lavee and Olson's Study of Couples in Therapy. Yoav Lavee and David Olson (1993) found similar kinds of marital relationships in their study of more than eight thousand couples who had taken part in either marital therapy or marital enrichment

TABLE 8.5 LAVEE AND OLSON'S TYPOLOGY OF MARITAL RELATIONSHIPS

Dimensions	Type of Marriage						
	Vitalized (9%)	Balanced (8%)	Harmonious (8%)	Traditional (10%)	Conflicted (14%)	Financially Focused (11%)	Devitalized (40%)
Personality issues	✓	✓	✓	✓	×	×	×
Communication	✓	✓	✓	×	×	×	×
Conflict resolution	✓	✓	✓	×	×	×	×
Financial management	✓	×	✓	✓	×	✓	×
Leisure activities	✓	✓	✓	✓	✓	×	×
Sexual relationship	✓	✓	✓	×	✓	×	×
Children and parenting	✓	✓	×	×	×	×	×
Family and friends	✓	✓	×	✓	✓	×	×
Religious beliefs	✓	✓	×	✓	✓	×	×

✓ = generally satisfied on this dimension; × = problems on this dimension.

Source: Adapted from Benokraitis, Nijole V., *Marriages and Families: Changes, Choices, and Constraints*, 4th Edition, © 2005. Reprinted by permission of Pearson Education, Inc., Upper Saddle River, NJ., page 271. Based on data in Lavee and Olson 1993.

programs. As Table 8.5 shows, they identified seven types of marriages that varied along a number of dimensions. Because the couples in this study sought marriage counseling, we cannot generalize these findings to the general population. Nevertheless, this study does reveal the kinds of problems that couples experience in different kinds of relationships. For example, couples in devitalized marriages report problems across the board: personality issues, communication, sexual relationships, parenting, religious beliefs, and so on. The problems in harmonious marriages revolve around family and friends, religious beliefs, and parenting. In vitalized marriages, couples reported general satisfaction on all of the dimensions considered.

Wallerstein and Blakeslee's "Good Marriage."
The married couples in Lavee and Olson's study provide some insight into different kinds of marital relationships. But this sample was composed of people who had volunteered for marriage counseling and therefore focused on troubled relationships. Few studies have examined "good marriages," in which both spouses agree that the relationship is satisfying (Wallerstein and Blakeslee 1995). Seeking to learn more about these kinds of relationships, Judith Wallerstein designed a qualitative study of fifty couples whose marriages were considered lasting and happy. These couples had faced the same problems, crises, and temptations as other married couples, but they had overcome them to build lasting and happy marriages. Like other studies, the couples in this study did not constitute a representative sample. All of them lived in Northern California; were well educated, middle-class, and predominantly white; and had been married at least nine years. The final sample did, however, represent marriages over different periods of time. In nearly equal numbers, these marriages had begun in the 1950s, 1960s, 1970s, and early 1980s.

One of the most important goals of Wallerstein's study was to discover what people in good marriages meant by "happy." Personal interviews thus began with the question "Tell me what's good about this marriage." Later, the couples were asked to describe what was disappointing about it. These personal interviews provided a rich source of information about good marriages. Couples talked about their love for and friendship with their partners. They discussed sex and passion, commitment, and common values. The interviews also revealed that these couples did not agree all of the time. In fact, men and women described longstanding differences and angry conflicts.

Describing love, on the other hand, was more difficult for couples in this study. In fact, every one of the participants hesitated to define it. They did, however, talk about how much they valued, respected, and enjoyed their spouses. And they expressed appreciation for their partner's responsiveness to their needs. These were not just marriages that had lasted a long time. The men and women in these relationships found them satisfying and considered their marriages personal triumphs.

After the study was done, Wallerstein recognized that there were four distinct types of good marriages: the romantic marriage, the rescue marriage, the companionate marriage, and the traditional marriage. Although relationships rarely fit one category perfectly, most fit one better than the others. Each of the four types could also be characterized by a potentially dangerous hidden aspect, which Wallerstein called the "antimarriage." According to her, every marriage has a negative

aspect that could at some point begin to dominate the relationship. Although she did not believe that this spelled the end for a relationship, it could lead to a lifeless one.

The key characteristic of the **romantic marriage** is a passionate sexual relationship. Couples who experience this kind of relationship feel that they were destined to be together, and memories of their first meeting and courtship maintain the special bond between them. The antimarriage in romantic marriage rests in its potential for husbands and wives to develop a self-absorbed, childlike preoccupation with one another to the exclusion of everyone else, including children.

Couples in a **rescue marriage** provide each other with comfort for past unhappiness. Healing is the central theme of their lives together. The potential danger in this kind of relationship involves the reenactment of past traumas. When this happens, one spouse may tolerate the abuse, mistakenly believing that this is just the way life is. Ironically, the initial foundation of this type of relationship—the hope for healing and comfort—can end up forgotten.

The **companionate marriage** is probably the most common type of relationship among younger

In traditional marriages, raising children can cause problems if it diverts too much attention from the couple's own relationship.

BOX 8.4	NINE TASKS CENTRAL TO THE SUCCESS OF A MARRIAGE

1. To separate emotionally from the family of one's childhood so as to invest fully in the marriage and, at the same time, to redefine the lines of connection with both families of origin.
2. To build togetherness by creating the intimacy that supports it while carving out each partner's autonomy. These issues are central throughout the marriage but loom especially large at the outset, at midlife, and at retirement.
3. To embrace the daunting roles of parents and to absorb the impact of Her Majesty the Baby's dramatic entrance. At the same time the couple must work to protect their own privacy.
4. To confront and master the inevitable crises of life, maintaining the strength of the bond in the face of adversity.
5. To create a safe haven for the expression of differences, anger, and conflict.
6. To establish a rich and pleasurable sexual relationship and protect it from the incursions of the workplace and family obligations.
7. To use laughter and humor to keep things in perspective and to avoid boredom by sharing fun, interests, and friends.
8. To provide nurturance and comfort to each other, satisfying each partner's needs for dependency and offering continuing encouragement and support.
9. To keep alive the early romantic, idealized images of falling in love while facing the sober realities of the changes wrought by time.

Source: Wallerstein and Blakeslee 1995, 27–28.

couples. Reflecting the social changes since the 1970s, partners in this kind of relationship value friendship and equality. They also seek to balance their emotional investment at work with their emotional investment in family relationships. The antimarriage in this kind of relationship involves the possibility that it could degenerate into a brother-and-sister relationship—one that lacks both sexual passion and emotional intimacy.

The defining trait of the **traditional marriage** is its clear-cut division of roles and responsibilities. The woman takes primary responsibility for the home, while the man assumes the role as the primary wage earner. If partners in this kind of relationship focus too narrowly on raising children and begin to view each other only as parents, they risk the danger of developing a relationship in which they have little in common.

Wallerstein's study of happy marriages led her to conclude that a good marriage is built on the successful achievement of a series of psychological tasks that partners address together (see Box 8.4). The inspiration for this idea came from Erik Erikson's theory of psychosocial development (see Chapter 3), which focuses on human potential and,

particularly, on what can go right in each of the eight major stages of life. Wallerstein noticed that when marriages were on track, couples were engaged in these tasks. In contrast, work on these tasks had hardly begun in many divorced families. What is more, resolving the crisis for a particular task often broke the relationship apart.

ENDING RELATIONSHIPS

Neil Sedaka got it right: "Breaking up is hard to do." However, it is easier to do before marriage. In fact, breaking up is a natural part of the dating process, and it accounts for most of the intimate male-female breakups among American couples (Hill, Rubin, and Peplau 1976). If the mate selection system were perfect, more couples would discover through dating that they are ill-suited for one another, end their relationships, and move on to someone else.

While many dating couples do actually recognize problems in their relationships, they are unable or unwilling to end the relationship. For them, the costs of terminating the relationship may seem too high. Unfortunately, many couples ultimately discover that the psychological costs of ending a marriage are far greater than ending a dating relationship. Most of this chapter has focused on how interpersonal relationships are established and maintained. However, it is also important to understand why some relationships end. In this section, we address three main questions: Why do people end their relationships? What is the process? And what are the costs?

Reasons for Breaking Up

Social psychologists offer a number of reasons for why intimate relationships end. Social exchange theorists suggest that the costs of the relationship simply outweigh the rewards—that inequity exists. Little or no intimacy, which might result from a lack of self-disclosure, or weak attachment might also explain why some relationships fail. And poor communications skills, especially destructive ways of expressing grievances, contribute to unsuccessful relationships (Gottman 1999).

In a study of why college students ended their relationships, David Knox and his colleagues (1997) found that the majority of men and women said that another person was involved in some way for the breakup. As Table 8.6 shows, the most frequently mentioned single reason for breaking up was too many differences or different values (43 percent of respondents). However, a number of specific reasons point to another person: 18 percent mentioned "cheating," 15 percent said, "I met someone new," 13 percent indicated that their partner met someone new, 6 percent said they went back to a previous lover, and 5 percent said the partner went back to a previous lover. Altogether, 57 percent indicated that another person was the reason for a breakup. These results suggest that the principles of social exchange theory are operating. In assessing their current relationships, it appears that couples not only consider the balance of rewards and costs but also compare their relationships to alternative ones. If they perceive the alternatives as more desirable, the current one is likely to end.

TABLE 8.6	REASONS COLLEGE STUDENTS GIVE FOR ENDING RELATIONSHIPS
Reason	**Percentage**
Too many differences or different values	43
Got tired of each other	27
Cheating	18
Dishonesty	18
Separation	15
I met someone new	15
Partner met someone new	13
Parental disapproval	13
Violence or abuse	9
Alcohol or drug use	7
I went back to a previous lover	6
Partner went back to a previous lover	5

NOTE: Respondents could give more than one reason.

Source: Data from Knox et al. 1997, 451.

In an earlier study of engagement and marriage, Burgess and Wallin (1953) argued that couples who are less attached to one another or who are less intimate are most likely to end their relationships. Research over the years has supported their hypothesis. Hill, Rubin, and Peplau (1976) found that "love" versus "liking," as measured by Rubin's loving-versus-liking scale (see Table 8.1), was a good predictor for the survival or breakup of a relationship. Subjects who indicated that they "loved" their partner were more likely to stay together than those who indicated that they "liked" their partner. This study's measures of intimacy included attachment, as measured by Rubin's "love" items; dating exclusively; and seeing one's partner daily. This study also showed that two measures of intimacy were totally unrelated to ending relationships: having had sexual intercourse and having lived together.

In their study of engagement and marriage, Burgess and Wallin (1953) indicated that "slight emotional attachment" was an important reason for breaking up. However, they also cited "unequal attachment" as another important reason. The idea that "unequal attachment" will precipitate the end of a relationship is consistent with social exchange theory. Peter Blau (1964) formulated this hypothesis when he said:

> Commitments must stay abreast for a love relationship to develop into a lasting mutual attachment. . . . Only when two lovers' affection for and commitment to one another expand at roughly the same pace do they tend mutually to reinforce their love. (84)

The results of the study conducted by Hill and his associates (1976) show support for Blau's expectation. In their study, only 23 percent of the couples who reported equal attachment ended their relationship. Alternatively, 54 percent of couples in which at least one partner indicated unequal attachment broke up. Hill's study also supported the idea that "birds of a feather flock together"—that people who share similar attitudes and social, physical, and intellectual characteristics are more attracted to one another. In his study, couples who stayed together were better matched in terms of age, educational aspirations, intelligence, and physical attractiveness.

The Process and Costs of Breaking Up

"Few experiences in life are capable of producing more emotional distress, anguish, and suffering than the dissolution of an important relationship" (Simpson 1987, 683). Unfortunately, most of us will experience this pain at some point in our lives. When couples dissolve relationships, partners often grieve the loss of their loved one (Kaczmarek, Backlund, and Biemer 1990). The emotional highs that accompany the attachment process at the beginning of a romantic relationship (feelings of security, acceptance, and happiness) are now replaced by emotional lows (anxiety, self-doubt, and sadness). For many people, the loss of one's partner is the most traumatic experience of their lives (Holmes and Rahe 1967; Bowlby 1980; Simpson 1987).

In addition to deep sadness, people often experience other emotions, including anger and guilt. Curiously, people who initiate the break up may experience more emotional turmoil, especially guilt, than their spurned partners (Baumeister and Wotman 1992). For some people, feelings of anxiety and insecurity are devastating. Overcome by self-doubts, their self-esteem and self-confidence may suffer from painful questions such as "What is wrong with me?" "Will I ever fall in love again?" "Will I spend the rest of my life alone?" and "Will I ever get married?"

One interesting aspect is the role that power plays in determining who initiates the end of a relationship. Peter Blau (1964) suggested that when a partner recognizes an imbalance in the rewards and costs of a relationship, it is not always the less involved person (the more powerful one) who decides to end it:

> Whereas rewards experienced in the relationship may lead to its continuation for a while, the weak interest of the less committed or the frustrations of the more committed probably will sooner or later prompt one or the other to terminate it. (84)

People can feel emotionally devastated when relationships end. Healing a broken heart is not easy, but developing new romantic interests can help.

much to bear. The end is often precipitated by something that is regarded as "the last straw."

Men and women differ when intimate relationships fall apart (Hill, Rubin, and Peplau 1976; Choo, Levine, and Hatfield 1996). Women are more likely than men to feel joy or relief immediately following a breakup. They are also more likely to blame their partners for the split. Men tend to feel the greater impact of breaking up. Studies show that following the breakup, they are less likely to feel guilty but more likely to feel depressed, lonely, and less free (Hill, Rubin, and Peplau 1976). To distract themselves from the painful separation, men are also more likely than women to immerse themselves in work or sports.

Why can't men and women avoid all of this pain and decide to remain friends after breaking up? In some cases, they do. But again, there are significant gender differences. Hill, Rubin, and Peplau (1976) found that when couples remain friends, either the man had precipitated the breakup, or it had been a mutual decision. If the woman initiated the breakup, she was more inclined to walk away.

The reluctance of partners to disengage themselves from an intimate relationship in which they have become heavily invested is understandable (Hill, Rubin, and Peplau 1976). As Howard Becker (1960) pointed out, when people invest their time and energy in a relationship and even forgo alternative relationships to remain in it, ending it can be very costly in terms of emotional pain. However, it is often the right thing to do. Having the courage to terminate a dating relationship that is plagued by problems and frustrations can save people from the far more painful process of divorce. It is also important to initiate new relationships after breaking up. Research shows that finding a new romantic interest helps heal a broken heart.

The study by Hill and his associates (1976) supports Blau's expectation. In the majority of cases, the partner who was less involved in the relationship had a greater desire to end it. However, in a significant minority of breakups, the more involved partner wanted the relationship to end. For these people, the costs of remaining in the relationship—the frustration and pain—became too

SUMMARY

1. Love is not easy to define, and the word itself has many meanings.

2. Early social psychological definitions of love involved the distinction between liking and loving.

John Lee concluded that there are different kinds of love and that people may experience several types of love over a lifetime.

3. Robert Sternberg proposed that there are eight kinds of love, produced by a combination of three basic components: intimacy, passion, and commitment. Each of these components runs a unique course of development and may differ in degree for the parties in a relationship at any particular point.

4. Most Americans marry for love, but people in other countries do not consider love a prerequisite. Nevertheless, men and women in most societies do look for the same kinds of qualities in a mate. The top four traits are mutual attraction, dependable character, emotional stability and maturity, and a pleasing disposition.

5. Although people might believe that the pool of eligible marital partners is large, cultural factors limit whom we consider. Filter theory proposes that we sift eligible candidates through successive levels of criteria that include geographical proximity; social class; race, ethnicity, and religion; physical attraction; and age. In fact, most people marry someone with a similar background.

6. Many young people today hope to marry their soul mate. Unfortunately, unrealistic expectations for love may set them up for serious disappointments.

7. Cuber and Haroff's description of five marital types shows a clear contrast between marriages that are characterized by vital relationships and those that lack vitality for various reasons. Lavee and Olson's study of marital relationships casts a similar portrait of the characteristics of happy marriages. In her study of good marriages, Judith Wallerstein identified four distinct types of good marriages: the romantic marriage, the rescue marriage, the companionate marriage, and the traditional marriage. A good marriage is built on the successful accomplishment of a series of psychological tasks that partners address together.

8. Ending an intimate relationship is difficult, but it is a natural part of the dating process. The reasons for breaking up vary. In some cases, relationships end because the costs of a relationship outweigh the rewards. In other relationships, problems with intimacy appear to be the most important factor. While people experience a number of common reactions when their relationships end, few people react in exactly the same way.

KEY TERMS

Eros   220
Ludus   220
Storge   220
Mania   221
Pragma   221
Agape   221

Passion   223
Commitment   223
Filter theory   228
Conflict-habituated marriage   232
Devitalized marriage   232
Passive-congenial marriage   232

Vital marriage   232
Total marriage   232
Romantic marriage   234
Rescue marriage   234
Companionate marriage   234
Traditional marriage   235

CRITICAL REVIEW QUESTIONS

1. Which of the definitions of love given in this chapter do you prefer? How does that definition provide insight into your preferred style of love, as described by John Lee?

2. Compare the theories of love presented in this chapter. What does the research on attachment theory (Chapter 7) suggest about these theories?

3. Consider Table 8.2, "Distinguishing Infatuation and Love." Use this checklist to write some guidelines for dating and courtship in the twenty-first century.

NINE

Altruism
and Moral Development

On September 1, 1939, Germany invaded Poland. Hundreds of thousands of refugees fled eastward ahead of the Nazi horde. Many knew they were primary targets for persecution. They were prominent Jewish leaders—members of political parties, lawyers, teachers, writers, journalists, physicians, and rabbis. They thought they would be safe in eastern Poland. But that belief soon faded. The Soviet Union invaded eastern Poland on September 17. Polish forces were quickly overpowered. By October, the German and Soviet invaders had divided Poland between them.

Escaping the Nazis brought some relief to Jews who would now live under Soviet rule. But they did not fool themselves. It would be a hard life. They expected material deprivation and knew that their chances for emigration were slight. Viewing their lives from this perspective, many a refugee lamented, "Our death sentence has been commuted to life imprisonment" (Bachrach and Kassof 2001, 8). But they had not yet given up. Their next hope lay in neighboring Lithuania—at the time an independent nation. Crossing the border into Lithuania was not easy, but that did not stop the most determined. Unfortunately, Lithuania did not provide a safe haven for long. On June 15, 1940, Soviet tanks rolled through the streets of Vilna, the capital. This time the refugees felt trapped. In the words of one of them, Samuel Soltz, "their way to the free world was now closed" (51).

As it turned out, the refugees did have one last hope to escape. If they could obtain the necessary documents to travel through foreign countries, they could eventually be free. But they did not have much time. After the Soviet Union annexed Lithuania, it announced that all foreign consulates in the Baltic States would close by late summer, when diplomatic services would be centralized in Moscow. By this time, the refugees had anticipated all possible escape routes. As one refugee later recounted:

"We had memorized atlases and the globe and had become experts in outlining to ambassadors and consuls the most intricate travel routes. . . . By the time the Soviets seized Lithuania, only two routes remained possible: south through Turkey toward Palestine or east through the Soviet Union." (Bachrach and Kassof 2001, 55)

It was at this point in their long journey that the refugees would meet the first good Samaritans—the Dutch. Pessla and Isaac Lewin remembered their experience. Pessla, who had grown up in the Netherlands, renounced her Dutch citizenship when she married Isaac, a Polish Jew. Hoping that this would not stand in her way, she wrote to the Dutch ambassador asking for entry to the Dutch West Indies. He responded by asking her to mail him her passport. On the passport, he wrote, "For the admission of aliens to Surinam, Curaçao, and other Dutch possessions in the Americas, an entry visa is not required" (Bachrach and Kassof 2001, 60). What Ambassador de Decker failed to note was that they also needed permission from the local colonial governor—something that was rarely granted. In fact, the deceit was intentional. And it worked. When Isaac Lewin presented his wife's passport to Jan Zwartendijk, the acting Dutch consul in Lithuania, the official did not hesitate to copy de Decker's notation into Lewin's safe-conduct document.

Other refugees learned about the Curaçao visas and were soon making their way to Zwartendijk's office. Although Zwartendijk had little confidence that the documents would guarantee the refugees' freedom, he worked nonstop to grant all requests. But this was only one of the documents they would need. The route to Curaçao required them to travel across the vast Soviet Union to Vladivostok, from there to Japan, and then by boat to Curaçao by way of the Panama Canal. They now needed help from the Japanese. Chiune Sugihara, Japan's acting consul, would become the next good Samaritan. In an urgent message to his superiors, Sugihara sought advice, indicating that every day almost one hundred people came to his office requesting visas. The bureaucrats' slow response forced him to make his own decision. Later he wrote:

"I finally decided that it was completely useless to continue the discussions with Tokyo; I was merely losing time. . . . I gave visas to all who came to me, regardless of whether or not they could produce some kind of document proving they were going to another country." (Bachrach and Kassof 2001, 66)

Zwartendijk and Sugihara never met. But the freedom of these refugees hung on their willingness to cooperate. And it was remarkable! For a few weeks in the summer of 1940, they "became an unofficial team" (Bachrach and Kassof 2001, 68).

Years later, Zwartendijk recalled with wry amusement that during the eight-day period when they were both issuing visas, he received telephone calls from Sugihara imploring him to slow down: "He could not keep up, the street was full of waiting people." Sugihara issued visas at a furious pace, stamping as many as 260 in a single day, the bulk while Zwartendijk was still issuing Curaçao notations." He continued to approve visas for more than three weeks after Zwartendijk closed his office on August 2. (68)

With the visas that Zwartendijk and Sugihara had issued in hand, the refugees left Lithuania and made their way across the Soviet Union on the Trans-Siberian Railroad. From Vladivostok they took a boat to Japan. Many of the refugees who were stranded in Kobe were eventually sent to Shanghai, China, where they remained until 1947. It had been a long, harrowing journey.

Commenting on the moral depth of Zwartendijk and Sugihara, Rabbi Irving Greenberg, chair of the United States Holocaust Memorial Council, wrote:

"The Talmud says *yesh koneh olamo b'sha'ah achat*—there are some people who earn immortality/ eternity in an hour's work. In this case, it was two weeks of work, issuing papers and stamps and visas, etc., until they were forced to shut down." (Bachrach and Kassof 2001, xiv)

World War II was perhaps history's most brutal example of man's inhumanity against man. The barbaric persecution and extermination of six million Jews in a period of about five years will forever stand as evidence of the dark side of human nature. And yet as many as half a million non-Jews put their own lives at risk to help Jews escape and survive (Oliner and Oliner 1988).

Does it take special greatness to become a good Samaritan? The story of Zwartendijk and Sugihara shows that it does not. So do the stories of the ordinary people who risked their lives and even died on September 11, 2001, helping complete strangers. In the case of these fallen heroes, many did earn immortality in an hour's work. The pure, selfless altruism of good Samaritans raises a number of questions that we will address in this chapter:

- What motivates people to help others?
- Are differences in the tendency to help others learned? How do cultures differ in terms of the social norms that prescribe helping behavior?

- What kind of prosocial moral reasoning is involved in the kind of altruism shown by Zwartendijk and Sugihara?

DEFINING ALTRUISM

Stories of human compassion and selfless acts taken out of concern for the well-being of another human being date back to ancient times. In the New Testament parable about the Good Samaritan (Luke 10:29–37), Jesus taught that we should love our neighbor as we do ourselves (see Box 9.1). It was not, however, until the middle of the nineteenth century that this kind of behavior became known as **altruism**. Social psychologists give Auguste Comte (1851–1854/1973) credit for coining this term, pointing out that it is rooted in the Latin word *alter*, which means "other" (Oliner and Oliner 1988). Viewing altruism as the primary virtue in his religion of humanity, Comte summarized this religion's moral code as "living for others."

By the end of the nineteenth century, altruism had received some attention from other prominent social scientists. Herbert Spencer, who used the

BOX 9.1	THE GOOD SAMARITAN (LUKE: 10:29–37)

"A certain man was going down the lone road from Jerusalem to Jericho and he fell among robbers, who stripped him of all that he had, and beat him, and then went away, leaving him almost dead. It happened that a certain priest was going down that road, and when he saw the man lying there, he passed by on the other side. And a Levite also, when he came to the place, and saw the man, he, too, went by on the other side. But a certain Samaritan, as he was going down, came where this man was, and as soon as he saw him, he felt a pity for him. He came to the man and dressed his wounds, pouring oil and wine into them. Then he lifted him up and set him on his own beast of burden, and walked beside him to an inn. There he took care of him all night. And the next morning he took out from his purse two shillings, and gave them to the keeper of the inn, and said, 'Take care of him, and if you need to spend more than this, do so. When I come again I will pay it to you.'

"Which one of these three do you think showed himself a neighbor to the man who fell among the robbers?"

The scribe said, "The one who showed mercy on him."

Then Jesus said to him, "Go and do thou likewise."

By this parable Jesus showed that "our neighbor" is the one who needs the help that we can give him, whoever he may be.

Source: Bennett 1993, 141.

Mother Teresa (left), Martin Luther King, Jr. (top right), and Oprah Winfrey (lower right) are known for helping others. Which provides an example of altruism?

word throughout his writings, pointed out how sharply it contrasted with another popular concept, **egoism**, the idea that human behavior is motivated by self-interest (Budd 1956). This led him to suggest that as a private motive, altruism would influence the equilibrium between the self and society. Émile Durkheim also recognized the value of altruism, arguing that all societies depended on it—that they could not survive unless individuals made sacrifices for the sake of society (Oliner and Oliner 1988). But most social scientists ignored altruism until the middle of the twentieth century, when Pitirim Sorokin (1948, 1950a, 1950b, 1954) began to study it as a social psychological phenomenon.

For Comte, the defining trait of altruism was **selflessness**—an unselfish regard for the welfare of others (Oliner and Oliner 1988). Most social psychologists today would agree. They would, however, also point out that altruism does not refer to all kinds of helping behavior. For example, even though Peace Corps volunteers and firemen dedicate their lives to helping other people, many social psychologists do not regard their behavior as a form of altruism. Instead, they refer to it as **prosocial behavior**.

To distinguish altruism from prosocial behavior, social psychologists consider the specific meaning attached to selflessness as well as the motivation associated with a certain behavior. For example, they would want to know if the actor derived any benefit from the act—whether it be monetary or simply a feeling of satisfaction or gratification. And they would consider a number of motives, including the simple intention of helping, adherence to social norms, personal values (love or compassion), personal principles, or internal states (such as empathy) (Oliner and Oliner 1988). Most definitions of altruism today specify that it refers to acts that are carried out voluntarily by individuals who have no concern for themselves and who have no expectation of any kind of reward (Simmons 1991; Schroeder et al. 1995). Prosocial behavior is a broader category of helping behavior that does not stress personal motives, whereas altruism must involve some kind of clear self-sacrifice.

THEORETICAL EXPLANATIONS OF HELPING BEHAVIOR

Why do we help others? The answer is not simple. When he was asked why he had helped World War II refugees, Chiune Sugihara said that he "acted according to a sense of human justice and of love for mankind" (Bachrach and Kassof 2001, xiv). Zwartendijk never answered this question directly. But one of his colleagues, A. M. de Jong, the Dutch consul-general in Sweden, implied that they sympathized with the refugees and felt an obligation: "We . . . , who enjoyed the privilege of living in freedom, felt obliged to find possibilities to help everyone who was trying to escape from the area of the tyrants" (64).

Social Exchange Theory

These answers suggest that what these good Samaritans did was altruistic—that they did have an unselfish regard for the welfare of others. But many explanations for why we help others suggest that our motivations are actually egoistic (Batson et al. 1981). In fact, they suggest that the decision to help involves a cost-benefit analysis. Consider, for example, social exchange theory. As explained in Chapter 7, this theory contends that we enter into relationships because we derive some personal benefit from doing so (Homans 1961). It suggests that no act is truly altruistic—that when we step forward to offer assistance, we expect to get something out of it. Even the most altruistic among us might admit that we benefit from good acts (see Box 9.2).

Some people consider this a cynical way to view good deeds. And they might point out that helping others involves far more costs than rewards. Social exchange theorists would agree that

---

BOX 9.2   ABRAHAM LINCOLN ON ALTRUISM

Even the most altruistic among us might admit that we get something out of helping others. F. C. Sharp illustrated this point with the following incident from the life of Abraham Lincoln.

Mr. Lincoln once remarked to a fellow-passenger on an old-time mud-coach that all men were prompted by selfishness in doing good. His fellow-passenger was antagonizing this position when they were passing over a corduroy bridge that spanned a slough. As they crossed this bridge they espied an old razor-backed sow on the bank making a terrible noise because her pigs had got into the slough and were in danger of drowning. As the old coach began to climb the hill, Mr. Lincoln called out, "Driver, can't you stop just a moment?" Then Mr. Lincoln jumped out, ran back, and lifted the little pigs out of the mud and water and placed them on the bank. When he returned, his companion remarked: "Now, Abe, where does selfishness come in on this little episode?" "Why, bless your soul, Ed, that was the very essence of selfishness. I should have had no peace of mind all day had I gone on and left that suffering old sow worrying over those pigs. I did it to get peace of mind, don't you see?"

Source: Sharp 1928, 75.

costs are incurred. But they would also identify the variety of rewards that accompany behaviors that benefit individuals. For example, people who return lost wallets or lost pets often receive a financial reward in exchange for their thoughtfulness. What is more, good deeds often bring a number of intangible rewards: respect, admiration, and recognition from others. Social exchange theorists would even say that feeling good because we helped someone else is a reward that we derive from this interaction. From this perspective, helping is done to serve one's own self-interest—its motivation is egoistic.

Batson's Model: The Empathy–Altruism Hypothesis

Must we be pessimists and conclude that true altruism does not exist? Are we always motivated by selfish interests? Was Auguste Comte wrong to believe that people can act in selfless ways? Daniel Batson and his colleagues provide some answers to these questions (Batson 2001; Batson et al. 1981, 1983). According to them, helping behavior can involve egoistic motivations. People may weigh the costs and benefits of offering help to others. But not always. Batson argues that true altruism

does exist and that the telltale sign is **empathy**—"an other-oriented emotional response (e.g., sympathy, compassion) congruent with the . . . welfare of another person" (Batson and Oleson 1991, 63). For example, when we hear that a child has died in a car accident, we might feel empathy—the sort of sadness that her parents are feeling. The public's reaction to the deaths of beloved personages such as Princess Diana or John F. Kennedy Jr. shows that complete strangers can experience empathy. And nothing illustrates this concept better than the reactions of millions of people worldwide to the tragic deaths of thousands of Americans in the attacks that occurred on September 11, 2001.

In Batson's empathy-altruism model of helping behavior, a person's motivation for helping may involve urges that are either egoistic or altruistic (Batson et al. 1981) (see Figure 9.1). *Egoistic motivation* operates when someone helps because he expects a reward (e.g., money, admiration, self-esteem) or when someone is trying to avoid personal pain (e.g., guilt or shame). If, however, a person helps because he wants to increase the benefits of another or decrease that person's distress, Batson labels it *altruistic motivation*.

According to Batson and Coke (1981), two distinct emotional states are produced when we

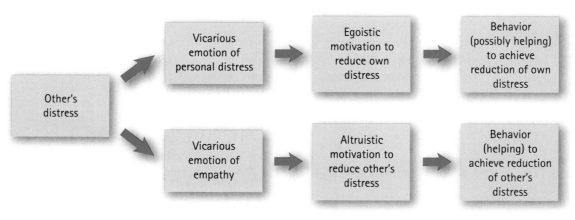

FIGURE 9.1

Batson's Empathy–Altruism Model of Helping Behavior

Source: Batson, Fultz, and Schoenrade 1987, 25.

watch another person experiencing distress. One state, *empathic concern*, involves emotions like compassion, softheartedness, and warmth, and it generates an altruistic motivation for helping. The other state, *personal distress*, includes feelings such as fear, worry, and shame and produces an egoistic motivation to reduce an individual's *own* distress. Batson's model shows two separate paths for altruistic and egoistic motivations, but he does believe

that we can take both paths simultaneously (Batson 1991). That is, we might feel empathy for the person needing help but also reduce our own level of distress (see Box 9.3).

To test the empathy-altruism hypothesis, Batson and his colleagues (1981, 1983) designed experiments to show how personal distress differs from empathy. In one experiment, the researchers told the subjects that they were studying how

---

BOX 9.3   MEASURING EMPATHY: THE INTERPERSONAL REACTIVITY INDEX

Respondents are asked to indicate the degree to which each item describes them by choosing the appropriate point on a scale running from 0 ("does not describe me well") to 4 ("describes me very well").

Scoring: Items indicated by an (R) are first reversed (0 = 4, 1 = 3, 3 = 1, 4 = 0), and then responses to the items making up each subscale are summed separately. Each subscale consists of seven items; thus scores on each subscale can range from 0 to 28. Subscales are the Fantasy (FS) scale, the Perspective Taking (PT) scale, the Empathic Concern (EC) scale, and the Personal Distress (PD) scale.

1. I daydream and fantasize, with some regularity, about things that might happen to me. (FS)
2. I often have tender, concerned feelings for people less fortunate than me. (EC)
3. I sometimes find it difficult to see things from the "other guy's" point of view. (PT) (R)
4. Sometimes I don't feel very sorry for other people when they are having problems. (EC) (R)
5. I really get involved with the feelings of the characters in a novel. (FS)
6. In emergency situations, I feel apprehensive and ill-at-ease. (PD)
7. I am usually objective when I watch a movie or play, and I don't often get completely caught up in it. (FS) (R)
8. I try to look at everybody's side of a disagreement before I make a decision. (PT)
9. When I see someone being taken advantage of, I feel kind of protective toward them. (EC)
10. I sometimes feel helpless when I am in the middle of a very emotional situation. (PD)
11. I sometimes try to understand my friends better by imagining how things look from their perspective. (PT)
12. Becoming extremely involved in a good book or movie is somewhat rare for me. (FS) (R)
13. When I see someone get hurt, I tend to remain calm. (PD) (R)
14. Other people's misfortunes do not usually disturb me a great deal. (EC) (R)
15. If I'm sure I'm right about something, I don't waste much time listening to other people's arguments. (PT) (R)
16. After seeing a play or movie, I have felt as though I were one of the characters. (FS)
17. Being in a tense emotional situation scares me. (PD)
18. When I see someone being treated unfairly, I sometimes don't feel very much pity for them. (EC) (R)
19. I am usually pretty effective in dealing with emergencies. (PD) (R)
20. I am often quite touched by things that I see happen. (EC)
21. I believe that there are two sides to every question and try to look at them both. (PT)
22. I would describe myself as a pretty softhearted person. (EC)
23. When I watch a good movie, I can very easily put myself in the place of a leading character. (FS)
24. I tend to lose control during emergencies. (PD)
25. When I'm upset at someone, I usually try to "put myself in his shoes" for a while. (PT)
26. When I am reading an interesting story or novel, I imagine how *I* would feel if the events in the story were happening to me. (FS)
27. When I see someone who badly needs help in an emergency, I go to pieces. (PD)
28. Before criticizing somebody, I try to imagine how *I* would feel if I were in their place. (PT)

Source: Davis 1994, 56–57.

people worked under aversive conditions. The subject then watched a confederate named Elaine receive a series of shocks. Elaine's discomfort was plain to see. During a break following the first trial, she told the subject that she was particularly sensitive to the electric shock because of a childhood accident—she had fallen against an electric fence. The researcher then suggested that the subject might switch places with the confederate for the second trial. What would the subject do? How would people who felt personal distress differ from people who felt empathy?

Showing that these two kinds of motivations were qualitatively distinct posed a challenge. Batson and his colleagues assumed that all subjects would feel both personal distress and empathy when they saw the victim receive electric shocks. But how would the subject interpret the arousal of these feelings? To manipulate subjects' interpretations, their experiment included a misattribution technique. At the beginning of the experiment, subjects were told that they would actually participate in two studies simultaneously. One study supposedly involved the effect of a drug called Milletana on short-term memory. The other one, which involved the electric shock, was designed to study how people worked under aversive conditions.

All subjects received the Milletana at the beginning and were told that they would participate in the second experiment while the drug took effect. In fact, Milletana was just a placebo. And the researchers were using it to manipulate the subjects' interpretations of the arousal of their feelings. To create the necessary conditions for the misattribution of feelings, the researchers further explained that the drug had a side effect. In the empathy condition, subjects were told that the drug "produces a clear feeling of uneasiness and discomfort, a feeling similar to what you might experience while reading a particularly distressing novel" (Batson et al. 1981, 298–299). This explanation was designed to reduce the subject's feeling of personal distress. The researchers reasoned that instead of attributing the arousal they felt to their own personal distress,

they would interpret it as empathy for the victim. In the personal distress condition, the subjects were led to believe that the drug "produces a clear feeling of warmth and sensitivity, a feeling similar to what you might experience while reading a particularly distressing novel" (298). This explanation was designed to reduce the subject's feeling of empathy. In this case, the researchers believed that the subjects would attribute their empathy to the drug and believe that their emotional arousal was due to their own personal distress. Did the misattribution technique work? Interviews with subjects following the experiment showed that it did.

In addition to the misattribution technique, the researchers also manipulated the ease of escaping from the situation. This part of the design was based on the researchers' expectations about theoretical differences between egoistic and altruistic motivations for helping others. If the motivation for helping was egoistic, the subject could alleviate his own personal distress in one of two ways: by helping or by leaving the situation. However, if the motivation for helping were altruistic, the subject would not leave the situation but would help (offer to switch places with the victim). As the researchers pointed out, the specific kind of motivation for helping could not be inferred from a single behavior but rather only from a pattern of helping responses. Table 9.1 shows the patterns associated with each type of motivation.

The results of this experiment provided support for the empathy-altruism hypothesis. In the empathy condition, the subjects were more likely to help the victim by offering to switch places with her regardless of whether or not they could leave after the first trial. In contrast, subjects in the personal distress condition were more likely to leave if they had the opportunity. They switched places with the victim only when that was the only way to relieve their own personal distress.

Although some social psychologists still argue that true altruism does not exist, evidence continues to mount in support of the empathy-altruism hypothesis (Sibicky, Schroeder, and Dovidio 1995; Batson et al. 1997; Batson 2001).

TABLE 9.1 MOTIVATION TO HELP IN BATSON'S MODEL

Difficulty of Escape	Type of Motivation (Level of Empathic Emotion)	
	Egoistic (Low Empathy)	Altruistic (High Empathy)
Easy	Low	High
Difficult	High	High

Source: Batson et al. 1981, 292.

Evolutionary Theories: A Genetic Explanation for Altruism

Certain small birds—robins, thrushes, and titmice, for example—warn others of the approach of a hawk. They crouch low and emit a distinctive thin, reedy whistle. Although the warning call has acoustic properties that make it difficult to locate in space, to whistle at all seems at the very least unselfish; the caller would be wiser not to betray its presence but rather to remain silent and let someone else fall victim. (Wilson 1996, 77)

This kind of unselfish behavior, which might be described as altruism in human beings, is not uncommon in nature. Other animals risk their own lives by sounding warning calls. When a circling hawk sets its sights on a group of ground squirrels, one squirrel will sound a shrieking alarm call even though that makes the individual squirrel a prime target for the predator (Dugatkin 2000). Other forms of cooperative behavior are common among other animals. When a dolphin is injured, other dolphins may lift it to the surface so it can continue to breathe (Sienbenaler and Caldwell 1956; Schroeder et al. 1995; Wilson 1996). Bees will attack an intruder who threatens their beehive, even though bees die shortly after they sting a victim (Schroeder et al. 1995; Wilson 1996). And some varieties of ants, bees, rodents, and birds spend their entire lives working for the sake of the group, even raising the offspring of others instead of having their own (Dugatkin 2000).

Why do animals act in these unselfish ways, especially when doing so may put their lives at risk? Ironically, the explanation may lie in Charles Darwin's theory of natural selection (1859, 1871). For years, the altruistic behavior of animals posed a problem for evolutionary theorists who supported Darwin's belief in the "survival of the fittest." According to Darwin, altruistic animals risk the survival of their genes by engaging in self-sacrificing behaviors that threaten their long-term reproductive potential. So how would evolution explain the kind of self-sacrifice that scientists have observed in animals?

The answer lies in the level at which natural selection takes place. Darwin believed that it occurred at the level of the individual. But evolutionary theorists now believe it takes place at the level of genes (Wilson 1992; Settle 1993). Once an individual's genes have been transferred to a gene pool, natural selection can take place at this level. Scientists describe three ways by which altruistic genes are passed on: kin selection, reciprocity, and group selection.

KIN SELECTION

Some of the most dramatic examples of altruism among other animals involve self-sacrifice by parents to benefit their offspring. Many ground-nesting birds, such as the killdeer, attempt to distract predators who threaten their young. As the predator approaches, the parent leaves the nest to attract attention to itself, limping as if its wing were injured. The predator, spying easy prey, is lured away from the nest to stalk the "injured" parent. At the last possible moment, the bird abandons all pretense and takes to the air, leaving the predator confused and hungry. The animal that threatened the nest is now distracted and some distance away; it is unlikely that it will be able to find the nest and the helpless young birds in it. In this way, the young are saved, but only at great risk to the parent. (Schroeder et al. 1995, 102–103)

As it turns out, cooperative behavior may actually increase the likelihood that one's genes are passed on to the next generation (Hamilton 1964). Instead of emphasizing the survival of an individual's genes, a theory known as **kin selection** focuses on the survival of the individual's gene pool. It proposes that we are more likely to act altruistically when it comes to saving our relatives. Consider, for example, a mother who sounds an alarm call to protect her children even though she puts her own life at risk. As long as she saves the lives of at least two children, she has succeeded in passing her genes on to the next generation. This kind of genetic benefit extends to other relatives as well (see Table 9.2). For example, if the warning call of a squirrel saves the lives of two siblings, who on average share 50 percent of its genes, it was worth the risk. If the squirrel saves more than two siblings, the benefit far outweighs the risk (Dugatkin 2000).

Whether or not kin selection operates in the human population remains an open issue, but this theory does have its supporters (Rushton 1989; Caporael and Brewer 1991). It might well explain why we tend to help people similar to ourselves. It is less clear how it would explain altruism within larger, unrelated groups of people.

Reciprocal Altruism

Kin selection theory is the most popular evolutionary explanation for helping behavior among animals. It does not, however, explain why animals help nonrelatives. In this case, evolutionary theorists suggest that "doing unto others as you would have them do unto you" involves a cost-benefit analysis (Dugatkin 2000). According to Lee Dugatkin, one of the reasons that people abide by the Golden Rule is that human beings are "remarkable scorekeepers." When it comes to altruistic behavior, he suggests that we are more likely to cooperate with people who have helped us in the past and less likely to cooperate when future interaction is uncertain.

Known as **reciprocal altruism**, this theory suggests that helping in the short run increases the probability that our genes will be protected in the future (Trivers 1971). Robert Trivers coined the term *reciprocal altruism* to describe the genetic tendency for mutual helping. As an explanation for why nonkin help one another, he argued that

---

TABLE 9.2	KIN SELECTION CHART: WHEN IS A RELATIVE WORTH SAVING?	
Relative	Degree of Relatedness	Number of Relatives Who Must Hear Your Screams
Sibling	1/2	≥ 2
Parent	1/2	≥ 2
Grandparent	1/4	≥ 4
Grandchild	1/4	≥ 4
Uncle or aunt	1/4	≥ 4
Cousin	1/8	≥ 8
Spouse	0	—

Source: Dugatkin 2000, 44.

"natural selection favors . . . altruistic behaviors because in the long run they benefit the organism performing them" (35).

Why? Consider Trivers's "drowning man model." A drowning man has a 50-50 chance of surviving if no one tries to save him. The man will definitely drown if the person attempting the rescue does so. However, if a rescuer is successful, the drowning man will live. What would most people do? If this were an isolated situation, a simple cost-benefit analysis suggests that no one would attempt to save the drowning man. But Trivers takes a different angle and considers the long-term benefit of saving the drowning man. If one good turn deserves another, the drowning man could reciprocate this act of kindness at a future point in time (Trivers 1971; Dugatkin 2000). From this perspective, the relatively low cost of saving the drowning man is well worth the risk. In other words, the long-term benefit amounts to an increased chance of propagating one's genes.

Reciprocal altruism cannot operate if "cheaters" take help but fail to give it when it is their turn. Yet it seems that natural selection would favor cheating (Trivers 1971; Dugatkin 2000). Why should someone who has already received a benefit ever reciprocate in kind? The simple answer is that cooperating yields more benefits than cheating. According to Trivers, natural selection ultimately punishes cheaters.

Group Selection

The third mechanism by which altruistic genes might evolve is through **group selection**. According to this perspective, groups consisting of cooperative members are more likely to survive and pass on their genes than groups composed of selfish members (Schroeder et al. 1995; Dugatkin 2000). Although common sense might suggest that this mechanism could work, critics cite serious problems. Consider just one—how long it would take for an entire group to perish. In fact, it would take so long that selfish group members would enjoy a considerable advantage over cooperative members (Krebs and Miller 1985; Schroeder

et al. 1995). Altruism could not evolve in a system like this, where selfish members outlive cooperative ones.

Evolutionary theories provide interesting explanations for cooperative behavior in animals and human beings. But they are still controversial. To argue that soldiers who die in the line of duty are programmed like bees who sacrifice their lives to protect a beehive is a stretch.

THE PROCESS OF HELPING

Imagine the following. One evening around dusk, you hear a loud disturbance outside your window. A young woman is struggling with a man. You do not recognize either one of them and cannot make out their conversation. But it looks like the woman needs help. What do you do?

The reactions of other people who have found themselves in similar situations do not necessarily suggest what you are likely to do. But they have served as lessons and inspired research that seeks to understand why some people would help and others would not. One incident that occurred more than forty years ago still causes experts to wonder if anyone would come to our aid if we were the victims of a crime. The case involved the attack on Kitty Genovese, a 28-year-old bar manager who was returning home from work at 3 A.M. As she walked from her car toward her apartment building in the borough of Queens, New York City, a man grabbed her and stabbed her with a hunting knife. Crying out, she screamed, "Oh my God, he stabbed me. Please help me! Please help me!" (Dorman 2002). Her plea brought people to their apartment windows. One witness warned the assailant that he was being watched, shouting out, "Let that girl alone." Although that caused the assailant to retreat, he waited across the street to see what would happen next. When no one came to his victim's aid, he returned to stab her again. Her repeated cries brought thirty-eight witnesses to their windows to view the attack. But again, no help followed. For more than half an hour, Kitty Genovese was raped and stabbed. Someone finally called the police after the attack had ended. By that time, she was dead. In interviews with the police, the witnesses offered many explanations for failing to help her. Some believed it was a lovers' quarrel; others claimed that they were too frightened to help. Tragically, some said they simply did not want to get involved.

Many articles, books, and studies have sought to explain the reactions of the thirty-eight witnesses to Kitty Genovese's murder. Of these, one stands out as providing the best explanation: Bibb Latané and John Darley's book *The Unresponsive Bystander: Why Doesn't He Help?* (1970). Although they acknowledged that the witnesses to this attack did nothing to help the victim, these authors did not believe that "apathy," "indifference," or "unconcern" were accurate explanations of why witnesses had failed to act. Instead, they argued that "people often help others, even at great personal risk to themselves." And they claimed that "for every 'apathy' story, one of outright heroism could be cited" (4) (see Box 9.4).

The Decision-Making Perspective

Arguing that sometimes people help and that sometimes they do not, Latané and Darley (1970) set out to understand "what determines when help will be given" (4). In their model of the intervention process, they proposed that we make a series of decisions, not just one, when we decide to help someone. Figure 9.2 illustrates the five decisions involved in this process.

Noticing that Something Has Happened. The act of helping begins when we notice that something is wrong. Our senses usually make us aware of things that are unusual. A crying child expresses distress, an automobile horn warns of a potential fender bender, and smoke usually means fire. Unfortunately, our environment can cause us to ignore or block out signs that tell us something is wrong. In a crowded shopping mall, we might easily ignore the cries of a lost child. Inside our air-conditioned cars with the music blasting, we are unlikely to hear a honking horn or even the siren of a police car or fire engine. And we might not detect smoke if we live in a polluted city.

Interpreting the Event as an Emergency. Noticing that something is wrong or out of the ordinary does not automatically lead us to intervene and help. We must next decide whether the situation is an emergency. In many cases, the situation is ambiguous. Seeing a man forcing a "jimmy stick" inside the window of a car might mean that he is stealing it. But he might also be the owner who has locked his keys inside. A coed crying outside a dormitory might need help, but she might also be feeling the effects of too much alcohol.

BOX 9.4	REGINALD DENNY'S GOOD SAMARITANS

Thirty years after the Kitty Genovese incident, another highly publicized incident showed us that good Samaritans do live among us. On April 29, 1992, Reginald Denny found himself in the middle of one of the worst riots ever to break out in the United States. As he sat in his truck at an intersection in South Central Los Angeles, four African American teenagers pulled him out and began to kick, punch, and beat him. As Bobby Green, a 29-year-old African American trucker, viewed this scene on TV, he saw the assailants smash Denny in the head repeatedly with a brick. Recognizing that he was only about half a mile away, Green jumped off his couch and headed out to provide the victim with some assistance. Three other witnesses left nearby homes to come to Denny's aid: Titus Murphy, Lei Yuille, and Terri Barnett. Fighting off the four assailants, these four African Americans pushed Denny back into his truck and drove him to the hospital. According to the doctors, these four good Samaritans saved Denny's life. When he was interviewed later, Green explained his reaction, saying, "I saved another man's life because to me, he was another human being who needed my help" (Chavez 2002).

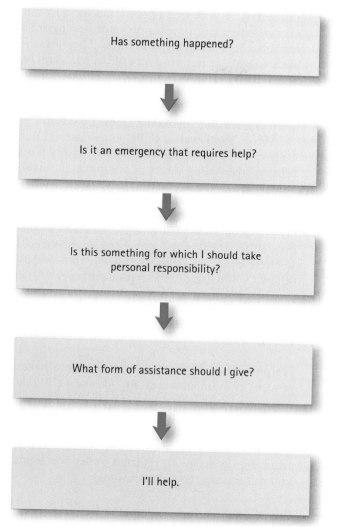

FIGURE 9.2

Deciding to Help: Latané and Darley's Model

Source: Adapted from Latané and Darley 1970.

Assuming Personal Responsibility. Once we have noticed that something is wrong and have interpreted the situation as an emergency, we must next determine whether we should assume personal responsibility. In making this decision, we are likely to consider a number of questions. First, does the victim "deserve" help? Second, do we have the expertise or competence necessary to help? Third, do other bystanders share responsibility for helping?

Whether we decide to take personal responsibility for helping someone else depends on whether we think the victim deserves our help. Consider the difference between a student who slips and falls because he is drunk and an elderly professor who loses his balance through no fault of his own. We may well decide that people who drink too much liquor deserve neither sympathy nor help. Most people, however, would not hesitate to offer assistance to an elderly person.

To illustrate how competence influences our decisions to help others, consider the following situation. You are driving home along a busy street through an unfamiliar neighborhood. You notice a man jump from his car holding a baby. He is upset and calls for help, crying that his child has stopped breathing. What are you likely to do? If you are a doctor or have some medical expertise, you might rush over and offer assistance immediately. Assuming personal responsibility in this case is clearly linked to your competence and expertise. Your reason for not helping in this situation is probably not because you do not care but rather because you don't know how to help. In the past, even some doctors have been unwilling to help in these kinds of emergencies out of their concern for being sued for malpractice. Fortunately, many states have now passed good Samaritan laws that prevent doctors from being sued for actions taken under emergency conditions (Northrop 1990; Taylor 1990; Rosenberg 1992).

Finally, the degree to which we feel personally responsible for helping is also influenced by the number of other people who might assume responsibility. Latané and Darley (1970) referred to this phenomenon as the **diffusion of responsibility**—the tendency for bystanders to diffuse the responsibility for helping among themselves. When only one person is present in an emergency, responsibility for helping falls squarely on her shoulders. But when many people are present, each person feels less responsibility for helping.

Determining the Appropriate Form of Assistance. At this point in making decisions about helping, we must decide what form of assistance is appropriate. Should I jump into a lake to save a drowning child, or should I call the lifeguard? Should I break up a fight between my fraternity brothers, or should I call the police? When we make these kinds of decisions, we are choosing either direct or indirect assistance. Jumping into the water to save a drowning child provides direct assistance, whereas calling for the lifeguard is a form of indirect assistance. Likewise, stepping in to stop a fight is direct assistance, whereas calling

authorities is indirect. These kinds of decisions may be based on an assessment of our personal strength, expertise, or competence. They are also likely to involve an assessment of the costs and rewards. If you cannot swim, you are unlikely to risk your own life to save a child if a lifeguard is nearby. Fraternity brothers may resent your calling the police if you are able to end the conflict yourself.

When the benefits of helping someone outweigh the costs, we are more likely to offer our help. In some cases, the costs are minimal. Giving directions to a lost motorist involves little cost and is likely to make us feel good. Responding to other simple requests, such as giving the time of day or holding a door open for someone, similarly involve little effort or risk and are likely to be appreciated. In these cases, we derive a reward from helping others. Not helping can also produce costs. Others may perceive us as self-centered and uncaring. We might also experience guilt or come to view ourselves negatively—as cowardly, lacking compassion, or selfish.

Helping. The final step in the decision-making process is implementing the decision. At this point, we usually have little trouble. If you have decided to put out a fire yourself, you will reach for the fire extinguisher. If you decide that you are not qualified to administer CPR, you will call 911 instead. If you decide to return a wallet you found, you will contact the wallet's owner.

Situational Factors Influencing Helping Behavior

The Kitty Genovese case raised many questions about why people fail to help someone in an emergency situation. As you considered the details of that case, you probably thought of many reasons why witnesses did not help. And it might have caused you to think about situations in which you failed to help. Most of us have driven past a stranded motorist without stopping to offer assistance. Many people ignore homeless people who beg for assistance from the doorway of a building. And how often have we told others that we cannot answer a question for them right now? Social psychologists have identified a number of situational factors that influence our decisions to help. They include time, the presence of others, size of place, and moods and emotions.

Time

Have you ever hurried past someone who needed help and thought, "I can't stop now. I'll be late for class"? If so, then you realize that time is an important situational factor that people consider in deciding whether they will help. When they thought about the reasons why people fail to help in an emergency situation, John Darley and Daniel Batson (1973) were reminded of the Good Samaritan parable (see Box 9.1), in which a Samaritan stops to help a man who has been beaten by robbers after two other men have passed and offered no assistance. Inspired by this story, Darley and Batson designed an experiment to determine how situational factors influence a person's tendency to help a stranger in need. In this study, they focused on two variables that might affect the inclination to stop and help: time demands (feeling hurried)

and the specific thoughts that preoccupy a person's mind.

The subjects in this experiment were students from the Princeton Theological Seminary, who believed they were participating in a study on religious education and vocations. When they arrived for the study, an assistant gave some of them the parable of the Good Samaritan and told them that the researchers would like them to record a short talk on that topic. Subjects in another condition were asked to speak about jobs or professions that were well suited for seminary students—ones they would enjoy or be effective in. Both groups were given a few minutes to consider what they would say. They were then given directions to another building, where the equipment for recording the talk was located.

In one of the experimental conditions, the researchers told the subjects, "It'll be a few minutes before they're ready for you, but you might as well head on over. If you have to wait over there, it shouldn't be long" (Darley and Batson 1973, 104). In another condition, the researcher checked his watch and said, "Oh, you're late. They were expecting you a few minutes ago. We'd better get

Opportunities to help others are often right in front of us. Why don't people stop to help?

moving. The assistant should be waiting for you so you'd better hurry" (103–104). As the seminary students made their way over to the other building, they passed a man who "was sitting slumped in a doorway, head down, eyes closed, not moving" (104). When they walked past him, he coughed and groaned but did not raise his head. What would they do?

The results of this experiment showed that subjects who were pressured to rush to the next building were less likely to offer help than subjects who thought they had plenty of time. Amazingly, the topic of their speech made no difference in whether they stopped to help. In fact, the researchers noted that "on several occasions, a seminary student going to give his talk on the parable of the Good Samaritan literally stepped over the victim as he hurried on his way!" (107).

The Presence of Others: The Bystander Effect

One of the most baffling aspects of the Kitty Genovese case was the number of people who saw the attack—thirty-eight. Why didn't one of them call the police? As Latané and Darley (1970) would later propose, the answer might ironically point to the large number of witnesses. In situations where many bystanders are present, people tend to assume that someone else will take responsibility—that someone else has already called the police. As the number of bystanders increases, our own sense of personal responsibility decreases. Latané and Darley referred to this diffusion of responsibility as the **bystander effect**.

Darley and Latané (1968) conducted a number of experiments to test the bystander effect. One of the best-known studies was designed to simulate the situation present in the Kitty Genovese case. Students at New York University were led to believe that they were participating in an experiment about the problems that undergraduates face at a large urban university. To ensure their anonymity, these subjects would sit in separate booths and would participate in a discussion through an intercom system. Only one person could speak at a time over this system, but everyone in the experiment could hear what was said. The researcher also assured the subjects that even he would not eavesdrop on the conversation.

The subjects were assigned to different conditions, which differed in terms of the number of subjects who were supposedly participating in the discussion. The discussion was actually taped and involved no other participants. At the beginning of the discussion, one of the participants mentioned the kinds of problems he had as an epileptic. When it was his turn to speak again, it sounded like he was falling into a seizure. The subject heard the following:

> I-er-um-I-I need-er-if-if could-er-er-somebody er-er-er-er-er-er-er give me a little-er-give me a little help here because-er-I-er-I'm-er-er-h-h-having a-a a real problem-er-right now and I-er-if somebody could help me out it would-it would-er-er s-s-sure be-sure be good . . . because-er-there-er-er-a cause I-er-I-uh I've got a-a one of the-er-sei-er er-things coming on and-and-and I could really-er-use some help so if somebody would-er-give me a little h-help-uh-er-er-er-er-er c-could somebody-er-er-help-eruh-uh-uh (choking sounds). . . . I'm gonna die-er-er-I'm . . . gonna die-er-help-er-er-seizure-er-[chokes, then quiet]. (Darley and Latané 1968, 379)

The results of this experiment provided strong support for the bystander effect. In the condition where subjects thought they were the only ones witnessing an epileptic seizure, 85 percent left their booths to help. As the number of bystanders increased, the percentage of subjects attempting to help decreased. When subjects thought the discussion involved one other bystander, 62 percent went to help. But when subjects thought five bystanders were present, only 31 percent went to the victim's aid.

Researchers have also observed the effect of group size on helping in studies of organ donations (Simmons, Klein, and Simmons 1977). Simmons and her colleagues reported that the willingness of individuals to donate a kidney to a sibling dropped from 51 percent when one sibling was qualified to be the donor to 0 percent when ten or eleven siblings could do so.

Study after study provides solid support for the bystander effect (Latané and Nida 1981). Curiously, many of these studies show that people do not believe that the presence of others influences their decisions about helping.

Size of Place

Among the reasons offered to explain why so many people failed to help Kitty Genovese was New York City itself. What if this had happened in a small town? Would people have responded differently? We are likely to think so. So would sociologists, who have long considered the differences between small towns and cities (Tönnies, 1887/1988; Durkheim 1893/1964; Simmel 1905/1964; Wirth 1938; Bellah et al. 1985). In his analysis of the transition from agricultural to industrial societies, Émile Durkheim (1893/1964) compared the close bonds created by small traditional communities to the more impersonal ties of big cities. Focusing on the intense stimulation of cities, Georg Simmel (1905/1964) proposed that factors such as the rhythm of life and the ever-changing onrush of impressions caused individuals to react with their heads instead of their hearts. This tendency was reinforced by the nature of the city, which he viewed as the seat of economic activity. Thus, he wrote, "punctuality, calculability, exactness are forced upon life by the complexity and extension of metropolitan existence" (413). In contrast to the warm, personal relationships that develop in small towns, he described the anonymity of metropolitan relationships, which contributed to a matter-of-fact attitude in everyday social encounters. Attributing the cause of this blasé attitude to the intense stimulation of the city, Simmel described the "reserve" that city dwellers develop. In the eyes of small-town people, he thought city dwellers must appear cold and heartless. According to him, however, city dwellers were rational in their distrust of strangers, something that people from small towns, where everyone knew everyone else, would not understand.

Many twentieth-century urban theorists recognized the traits that Simmel associated with the city dweller—alienated, unresponsive, and unhelpful (Wirth 1938; Milgram 1970; Levine et al. 1994). In making the distinction between the attitudes of people from small communities versus modern metropolises, Robert Bellah and his colleagues (1985) wrote:

> The classical idea of friendship made sense more readily in the small face-to-face communities that characterized early American society than it does to us. In such small communities, it was obvious that people not only helped one another and enjoyed one another's company but also participated mutually in enterprises that further the common good. (116)

Research on the effects of city size confirms stereotypical expectations that people in large cities are less likely to help strangers in need (Holahan 1977; Steblay 1987). In one of the best studies designed to determine the relationship between community size and helping behavior, Paul Amato (1983) examined various types of helping behavior in fifty-five Australian communities with population sizes ranging from under one thousand to over three million. The kind of help required in a particular situation varied from a simple request like writing down your favorite color for a class project to a serious situation where a man with a bandaged leg collapsed on a sidewalk. As expected, the general trend showed that people in small towns were more likely to offer assistance than people in larger cities.

Where do you think your hometown might rank in terms of helping behavior? A study conducted by Levine and his colleagues (1994) might tell you (see Table 9.3). Based on an examination of six types of helping behavior in thirty-six U.S. cities, they found that population density was the strongest predictor of whether a stranger would offer assistance.

Moods and Emotions

Consider the following hypothetical situations. How would your mood in each case influence what you do?

- When you check the scores for your last chemistry exam, you are thrilled to learn that

TABLE 9.3	COMMUNITY SIZE AND HELPING			
City	Region	Population[a]	Score[b]	Rank
Rochester, NY	Northeast	Medium	10.81	1
Houston, TX	South	Large	10.74	2
Nashville, TN	South	Medium	10.69	3
Memphis, TN	South	Medium	10.66	4
Knoxville, TN	South	Small	10.62	5
Louisville, KY	South	Small	10.58	6
Saint Louis, MO	North Central	Large	10.58	7
Detroit, MI	North Central	Large	10.55	8
East Lansing, MI	North Central	Small	10.54	9
Chattanooga, TN	South	Small	10.54	10
Indianapolis, IN	North Central	Medium	10.46	11
Columbus, OH	North Central	Medium	10.42	12
Canton, OH	North Central	Small	10.35	13
Kansas City, MO	North Central	Medium	10.33	14
Worcester, MA	Northeast	Small	10.24	15
Santa Barbara, CA	West	Small	10.17	16
Dallas, TX	South	Large	10.13	17
San Jose, CA	West	Medium	10.11	18
San Diego, CA	West	Large	10.05	19
Springfield, MA	Northeast	Small	9.92	20

[a]Based on estimates for metropolitan or primary statistical area for 1989. Small = 350,000–650,000; medium = 950,000–1,450,000; large = 2,000,000 or more.

[b]Average of standardized score ($M = 10$, $SD = 1.0$) for the six measures.

Source: Data from Levine et al. 1994, 72.

you received an A. An hour later, a friend asks if you would donate blood to the local Red Cross. Do you agree or beg off?

- You were just fired from your job. On your way home, you pass a homeless person who asks for change. What do you do?
- You just cheated on an exam. After you turn it in, the professor asks a favor—would you tutor another student who is having problems in the class? What do you say?

Research shows that our moods do affect how helpful we are. In some cases, the research shows

what we might expect. In other cases, the research suggests that the decision to help is more complicated. The results of this research should help you understand the answers you gave to the three hypothetical situations.

Good Moods. Research consistently shows that good moods increase people's willingness to do good deeds (Berkowitz 1987). And that tends to be true regardless of the reason for the good mood. Whether it is due to feeling successful (Isen 1970), an unexpected reward (Isen and Levin 1972), remembering pleasant experiences (Rosenhan,

Underwood, and Moore 1974), or simply beautiful weather (Cunningham 1979), a good mood has a positive effect when it comes to helping others.

Alice Isen conducted a number of studies to determine how a momentary emotional state might influence a person's tendency to donate money to a good cause or to help a stranger. Two of these studies focused on moods produced by feelings of either success or failure (Isen 1970). In one study, teachers in a suburban school system were told that they were participating in an experiment designed to assess the relationship between perceptual and motor skills and creativity. They were also told that if they scored either very high or very low, they would be asked to participate in a second session. They were then given a battery of tasks to measure their abilities. After the experimenter added up their scores, they were led to believe that they had either succeeded or failed on the battery of tasks. While they waited to participate in the second session, a confederate entered the room carrying a can labeled "Junior High Air-Conditioning Fund." She mentioned that this room had just recently been air-conditioned and that they were raising funds to air-condition the junior high school library. She continued to say that she thought this was a good place to put a can to collect donations and placed it on the table next to the subject. How did the mood created by either their success or failure affect their generosity? The results showed that subjects who believed they had been successful donated significantly more money than subjects who believed they had failed.

In a similar study, Isen (1970) used an identical procedure to create conditions of success or failure. For this study, however, she measured how likely subjects were to help a confederate who entered the room carrying an armload of books and notebooks. As the confederate approached the subject, she stepped over some wires and dropped a book. Again the results showed that subjects in the success condition were more likely than those in the failure condition to help a stranger. The results of these studies led Isen to conclude that the "warm glow of success" has a positive effect on

helping behavior. People who feel good due to success are more generous and helpful than people who feel bad.

Good moods that result from other kinds of positive experiences also lead us to treat others with kindness and generosity. In another study, Isen and Paula Levin (1972) created a positive mood by secretly putting change in the return slot of a public telephone. As they expected, shoppers who found the coins were more likely than shoppers who were not rewarded to later help a confederate who dropped a folder of papers when they crossed paths. In another variation, Isen and her colleagues compared the helpfulness of subjects who had received a free sample of stationery with those who had not (Isen, Clark, and Schwartz 1976). In this particular study, the researchers first delivered a free packet of stationery to subjects in the good mood condition in their homes. After they had received the free stationery, a confederate called them on the phone. Some were contacted immediately, others at intervals of five, ten, or twenty minutes. When the subject answered, the confederate indicated that she had dialed the wrong number and had just run out of change. She then asked if the subject would look up the correct number, make the call, and leave a message. The results of this study showed that the good mood produced by the free gift did lead people to be helpful. In contrast to people who had not received free stationery (the control condition), they were more willing to help a stranger. This study also showed that as time passed, the effect of the good mood diminished.

Why are people in a good mood so likely to help others? A number of factors account for this difference. One overriding reason is that good moods produce a number of effects that promote positive behavior. One simple effect is that good moods make people more optimistic (Forgas and Moylan 1987). They lead people to expect the best possible outcome for an event or action undertaken (Erber 1991; Mayer et al. 1992; Wegener, Petty, and Klein 1994). Good moods also increase the tendency to recall positive memories, which may themselves involve helping behaviors (Bower, Monteiro, and Gilligan 1978; Isen et al. 1978).

Finally, the tendency for someone in a good mood to help others may also result from that person's desire to stay in a good mood and helping is a way to do that (Isen and Simonds 1978; Wegener and Petty 1994).

Bad Moods. Although Isen's studies on the effects of feeling success or failure suggested that bad moods are likely to hamper our willingness to help someone else, many other studies show the opposite result. In fact, research on the effects of negative moods does not provide a simple answer (Carlson and Miller 1987). If a bad mood is severe enough, people may focus entirely on themselves to the exclusion of everyone else's needs. A man who is grieving the loss of his young wife may be so absorbed with his own needs that he might easily ignore those of his children. Of course, this is an extreme case. And sometimes helping when we are in a bad mood can make us feel better (Cialdini et al. 1987). In some cases, bad moods increase helpfulness (Cialdini, Darby, and Vincent 1973; Kidd and Marshall 1982), but in other cases it has a negative effect (Aderman 1972; Isen, Horn, and Rosenhan 1973).

Can anything explain these mixed findings? One model provides an explanation. Robert Cialdini and his associates proposed the **negative state relief model** to explain the decisions that people in bad moods make about helping others (Cialdini, Kenrick, and Baumann 1982; Cialdini et al. 1987). They argue that people will help someone else if they believe that doing so will alleviate their own suffering. According to this model, improving our own mood becomes the deciding factor in whether or not we help. So, for example, we might volunteer to speak to a group of parents who are grieving the death of a child if we believe it will relieve our own sadness. If, however, we expect the cost of helping to be greater than the reward—if we fear that our mood could deteriorate even further—we are unlikely to offer assistance. As this suggests, the motivation for helping is egoistic (Schroeder et al. 1995).

This model also provides an explanation for another pattern of inconsistent research findings.

A number of studies show that bad moods reduce the tendency for children to help but make it more likely for adults to help (Isen, Horn, and Rosenhan 1973; Kenrick, Baumann, and Cialdini 1979). According to Cialdini, Kenrick, and Baumann (1982), altruism does not provide the same kind of reward for children and adults. Tangible rewards for altruism like candy or toys are effective motivators for children, who have not developed the ability to view the world from the perspective of others. The intangible reward that adults feel from helping another person is a product of the socialization process. Unlike children, their ability to view the world from the perspective of others is likely to elicit sympathy and the desire to offer help when possible.

Guilt. Research shows that feeling guilty also makes us more inclined to help others (Carlsmith and Gross 1969; McMillen and Austin 1971; Regan, Williams, and Sparling 1972; Salovey, Mayer, and Rosenhan 1991). One explanation for this tendency suggests that when people feel responsible for hurting someone else, they will take an opportunity to "balance the scales" (Regan, Williams, and Sparling 1972). Acts of altruism—even when they are not directed at the harmed person—reduce a person's guilt.

Researchers have conducted a number of field experiments to test this hypothesis. In one study, a college-age male confederate approached women who were walking alone at a shopping center with a simple request. He told them that he needed a photograph of himself for a project he was working on and asked her if she would help. He then showed her an expensive-looking camera and said that even though it was somewhat sensitive, she would only need to focus it and snap a shot. After showing her how to operate the camera, he stepped back to have the picture taken. But when she pushed the button, the shutter would not work. At that point, the confederate gave one of two explanations. In the control condition, he said that the camera was old and "acts up a lot." After telling her that it was not her fault, he thanked her and walked away. In the guilt condition, he suggested that the woman had jammed the camera by turning some of the dials. He then said that the camera would have to be fixed, thanked her perfunctorily, and walked away. A few stores down from where this interaction occurred, a college-age female confederate was posted. After she saw the first experimenter contact the subject, she turned away from them and waited until the woman came her way. In this part of the experiment, the confederate held a bag of groceries with a corner torn so that candy would fall out of it when her path crossed the subjects. Would the subject bother to tell this stranger that candy was falling out or help pick it up? The results showed that feeling guilty about breaking the camera did influence whether someone offered help to a stranger later. Fifty-five percent of the subjects who thought they broke the camera (guilty condition) offered the stranger help, compared to only 15 percent of the women in the control condition.

Researchers have also manipulated guilty feelings by inducing subjects to lie (McMillen and Austin 1971). In one experiment, the procedure involved a confederate who engaged subjects in a conversation about the experiment they were about to take part in. The confederate, who supposedly entered the waiting room looking for a lost book, told these subjects that the experiment involved a multiple-choice test for which most of the correct answers were "B." After the confederate left, the experimenter came in and asked the subjects if they knew anything about the current experiment. None of them admitted that they did. They then took the multiple-choice test. When they finished, the experimenter told them they could leave. But he also asked if they had time to help him score some of the questionnaires. The results showed that subjects in the guilt condition, who presumably felt guilty for lying, were more likely to comply with this request. According to the researchers, agreeing to help served to restore the damage that lying had done to their self-esteem.

Guilt provides a powerful motivation for helping others. In some cases, people may do good deeds to compensate others for the harm they have caused. Social psychologists also suggest that when

people hurt others, they damage their own self-esteem. Balancing the scales would allow them to restore the positive image they once had of themselves. By helping others, they come to view themselves as "decent" people, worthy even of their own self-respect (Schroeder et al. 1995). Roberta Simmons (1991) found evidence of this kind of thinking in her research on kidney donors. In one interview, a successful donor said:

> "It's a tangible, quantifiable evidence of something I've done that I'm proud of. Sometimes if you've done a series of things wrong, or for any reason you start to develop doubts about your own worth, you say, 'Wait a minute, I'm not all bad. [I donated a kidney.]'" (9)

CULTURAL AND SOCIAL INFLUENCES ON HELPING BEHAVIOR: SOCIAL NORMS

Another explanation for why people help lies in **social norms**—socially constructed expectations for how we ought to act. In contrast to empathy, which occurs on an individual level, social norms operate at the level of society (Simmons 1991). In many cultures, helping others is so highly valued that it is regarded as a virtue. It is the biblical Golden Rule: "Do unto others as you would have others do unto you" (Matthew 7:12). Different versions of this social norm have been expressed over time (see Box 9.5). As a primary principle in the teachings of Confucius, it appeared in the *Analects*, a collection of his most famous teachings:

> Tzu-kung asked, saying, "Is there one word which may serve as a rule of practice for all one's life?" The Master said, "Is not *reciprocity* such a word? What you do not want done to yourself, do not do to others." (*Analects* 15:23)

Social norms that prescribe how we ought to help vary somewhat from culture to culture, but social psychologists recognize two main classes (Schroeder et al. 1995). The first class consists of

BOX 9.5	THE GOLDEN RULE

Leviticus 19:18 (c. 1000 B.C.E.): "Thou shalt not avenge, nor bear any grudge against the children of thy people, but thou shalt love thy neighbor as thyself."

The Hahabharata (c. 150 B.C.E.): "This is the sum of all true righteousness: deal with others as thou wouldst thyself be dealt by. Do nothing to thy neighbor which thou wouldst not have him do to thee hereafter."

John Wycliffe, translation of Luke 6:31 (1389): "As ye will that men do to you, and do ye to them in like manner."

Thomas Hobbes, *Leviathan* (1651): "Whatsoever you require that others should do to you, that do ye to them."

John Stuart Mill, *Utilitarianism* (1863): "To do, as one would be done by, and to love one's neighbor as one's self, constitute the ideal perfection of utilitarian morality."

Source: Shermer 2004, 25–26.

norms that invoke rules of fairness, including the norm of reciprocity (Gouldner 1960), the principle of equity (Walster, Walster, and Berscheid 1978), and beliefs about justice (Lerner 1980). The second class of social norms contains rules that address questions of social responsibility, such as the degree to which we are obligated to help less fortunate members of society.

Norm of Reciprocity

"If you don't go to somebody's funeral, they won't come to yours."

—Yogi Berra

According to the **norm of reciprocity,** we should help those who help us—"tit for tat" (Gouldner 1960). The idea is not new. The earliest

Adhering to the norm of responsibility, volunteers in soup kitchens serve people who depend on others for help.

collection of English colloquial sayings, which was printed in 1546, includes another familiar proverb "One good turn asketh another." Alvin Gouldner, who regarded reciprocity as a moral norm, traced the idea back to Cicero (106–43 B.C.E.), who said, "There is no duty more indispensable than that of returning a kindness. . . . All men distrust one forgetful of a benefit" (161).

Individuals learn the norm of reciprocity through the socialization process. As a moral principle, children may learn about the Golden Rule or the good Samaritan as part of their religious training. Stories like Aesop's tale "The Lion and the Mouse" teach children that if they help someone, the favor is likely to be returned at some point in the future. Taking turns, which is learned by playing games, also teaches children that reciprocation is an important social skill (Schroeder et al. 1995).

As noted in Chapter 7, the norm of reciprocity plays an important role in relationships. Acts of mutual helpfulness indicate the desire to establish and maintain stable relationships (Schroeder et al. 1995). Accepting help creates a state of indebtedness, which motivates the recipient to reciprocate. The failure to return a favor or repay a kindness usually signifies the end of a relationship. Two studies illustrate how people recognize and respond to the norm of reciprocity. In the first one, researchers mailed Christmas cards to complete strangers (Kunz and Woolcott 1976). Confirming the idea that we feel pressure to reciprocate a thoughtful gesture, about 20 percent of these strangers returned a holiday greeting card. Another study of gift giving at Christmas showed that reciprocation between family members follows a set of unwritten rules that specify obligations to various kin based on the closeness of the relationship (Caplow 1984). Overall, if we give a Christmas gift to a family member, we expect one in return. The exception to this rule applies to children, who are not expected to reciprocate with adults. Theodore Caplow summarized the importance of the norm of reciprocity in exchanging Christmas gifts as follows:

Middletown people find themselves compelled to give Christmas gifts to their close relatives, lest they inadvertently send them messages of hostility. In this community, where most people depend on their relatives for emotional and social support, the consequences of accidentally sending them a hostile message are too serious to contemplate, and few are willing to run the risk." (1320)

Research on the norm of reciprocity lends support to the principle that "one good turn deserves another." Although reciprocity is more likely to occur when we expect future interaction with the person who has done us a favor, it also occurs when we do not expect to see the person again (Goranson and Berkowitz 1966; Carnevale, Pruitt, and Carrington 1982). Studies also show that even though the particular person giving assistance may not benefit from her kindness, someone else probably will (Berkowitz and Daniels 1964).

Principle of Equity

The norm of reciprocity motivates us to repay a kindness or return a favor. If you help a friend move, you will expect a favor in return. But it cannot be any favor. It must be fair. What is fair? The principle of equity, discussed in Chapter 7, provides an answer. It says that equity or fairness exists when the contributions that people in a social interaction make balance out the benefits they receive. In other words, people expect to get as much out of a relationship as they put into it (Walster, Walster, and Berscheid 1978). When the exchange is equitable, the relationship is considered stable. If, however, one person perceives an uneven exchange, inequity exists. In this case, the relationship is unstable, and the disadvantaged person will seek to restore equity.

Equity theory is often used to explain why people become upset when they believe they got less than they deserved in a relationship. However, it also explains people's reactions when they feel that they have received too much (Greenberg and Shapiro 1971; Staub 1978). In an effort to restore equity, people might try to reciprocate a favor as soon as they can (Walster, Walster, and Berscheid 1978). In cases where recipients of aid are not able to reciprocate, equity theory predicts they might come to dislike the person who helped (Schroeder et al. 1995). In fact, one cross-cultural study showed that subjects in the United States, Japan, and Sweden did develop negative attitudes toward others when they could not reciprocate help (Gergen, Morse, and Bode 1974). Social psychologists suggest that this could explain the anti-American attitudes of people living in nations that receive foreign aid from the United States (Schroeder et al. 1995).

Beliefs about Justice

Melvin Lerner (1980) proposed that ideas about fairness are also based on beliefs about what people deserve. People get what they deserve because the world is just and fair. Thus whether someone deserves a particular outcome is a reflection of specific behaviors or personal attributes. For example, Lerner points out, "If one fails to prepare [or] take normal precautions [or] does not produce sufficient quantity or quality, then one is entitled to a certain amount of failure, suffering, deprivation—negative consequences" (11). People who subscribe to this belief in a just world might deny help to a homeless man, arguing that his fate was his own fault (he was fully responsible for it). The same people might act generously to a homeless child, who is seen as undeserving of deprivation. In this case, helping would be motivated by an interest in making the world a just place once more (Schroeder et al. 1995).

Social psychologists recognize that society has much to gain from relationships that are based on reciprocity and fairness (Simmel 1905/1964; Hobhouse 1906; Putnam 2000). By fostering stable relationships, these norms contribute to a stable society (Schroeder et al. 1995). Georg Simmel (1905/1964) suggested that reciprocity contributed to the equilibrium and cohesion of society, writing that "all contacts among men rest on the schema of giving and returning the equivalence" (387). In his examination of prosocial behavior in America today, Robert Putnam also recognized the value of reciprocity, but he did not believe the exchange was necessarily equivalent. Noting how networks within a community foster reciprocity, he cited the T-shirt slogan used by the Volunteer Fire Department of Gold Beach, Oregon: "Come to our breakfast, we'll come to your fire" (21).

Norm of Responsibility

Our society must make it right and possible for old people not to fear the young or be deserted by them, for the test of a civilization is the way that it cares for its helpless members.

—Pearl Buck, *My Several Worlds*

The **norm of responsibility** tells us that we should help people who are dependent on us (Berkowitz 1972; Schwartz 1975). Adherence to this norm is particularly strong when it comes to children. Parents are expected to care for their children until they reach maturity. Teachers should help their students, especially those with the greatest needs. And to harm a child is considered a despicable crime. As Pearl Buck recognized, this norm extends to all helpless members of our society. Children should care for their elderly parents. Pedestrians at a busy intersection should help a blind person cross the street. And people who witness an accident should seek to help an injured person. While the norm of responsibility usually remains an unwritten rule, laws have been passed to ensure that people help in emergencies or in situations where failing to act could harm someone in need. Thus, for example, some states have enacted "good Samaritan" laws.

In some instances, we may not feel any sense of responsibility to someone who needs help. Consider an individual who has lost his job because of an alcohol or drug addiction. In this case, people may justify their unwillingness to help on the basis of other important social norms—self-reliance, hard work, and individualism. These kinds of justifications became particularly obvious in Americans' attitudes toward the homeless in the 1990s.

Compassion fatigue—a term coined to describe Americans' apparent lack of concern for the homeless—may actually suggest that Americans came to blame the homeless for their own plight. Blaming the victims in this case is linked to social norms that have a particularly strong influence in the United States. Would people in other cultures have more sympathy for the homeless? A number of studies suggest they would.

Research shows that attitudes toward dependent members of society vary cross-culturally (Bontempo, Lobel, and Triandis 1990; Miller, Bersoff, and Harwood 1990; Miller 1994; Baron and Miller 2000). In their studies of cross-cultural differences in perceptions of social responsibility, Joan Miller and her colleagues chose subjects from the United States and India. The selection of these particular groups was based on an obvious difference: American culture tends to value individuality and self-reliance, whereas Hindu Indian culture tends to stress interdependence and mutual aid—obligations to the welfare of the group (Dumont 1970; Lukes 1973; Kakar 1978; O'Flaherty and Derrett 1978).

Seeking to understand how the attitudes of these subjects would differ, Miller and her colleagues designed a study that would show how obligations to help varied by the magnitude of a recipient's need and by the relationship between the donor and recipient of help. Subjects from each culture consisted of 180 individuals taken equally from three age levels: college, sixth grade, and second grade. The procedure required subjects to evaluate hypothetical situations that involved varying levels of need. Consider an example:

Amy is a 30-year-old woman who likes to draw. One day, she found out that an art store, which was going out of business, was having a big sale. Amy wanted to go to the sale to see if she could get any good bargains there. The art store was on Banyon Street—a street on the other side of town. Amy did not know where Banyon Street was.

So Amy asked her best friend Lisa for directions to Banyon Street. Amy told Lisa that she wanted to get to the sale early, while there were still lots of art supplies left to buy. But Lisa was busy reading an exciting book and did not want to be interrupted. So Lisa refused to give her friend directions to Banyon Street. Because of this, by the time Amy was finally able to get to the art store, there were few art supplies left. (Miller, Bersoff, and Harwood 1990, 35–36)

In this case Amy's need was relatively minor. In some cases, the need was extreme: not driving someone who was bleeding to the hospital, not donating blood to someone who needed it, or not administering mouth-to-mouth resuscitation to someone who had stopped breathing. In other cases, the need was moderate: giving aspirin to someone suffering from a migraine headache, providing comfort to someone about to undergo knee surgery, giving a ride to someone who is the main speaker at a ceremony. For each of these situations, the relationship between the provider and recipient of help also varied (parent or child, friend or stranger). For each of these hypothetical situations, subjects were asked a series of questions, including one that showed whether they felt a moral obligation to help the person.

The results of this study lent support to the researchers' cross-cultural expectations (see Table 9.4). In cases of extreme need—where a person's life was endangered—both Americans and Hindu Indians felt a moral obligation to help. But cultural differences appeared when the level of need and the relationship between the donor and recipient of help varied. Overall, Hindu Indians felt a social responsibility to help regardless of the particular role relationship or magnitude of need. But the pattern for Americans differed along both of these dimensions. Except in the case of a parent-child relationship where the incident involved moderate need, the percentage of Americans feeling a moral obligation to help friends or strangers dropped significantly under conditions of moderate and low need.

These findings suggest that Hindu Indians hold a broader and stricter view of social responsibilities than Americans do. According to Miller and her colleagues, the more sociocentric perspective of their culture led Hindu Indians to regard

| TABLE 9.4 | DIFFERENCES IN PERCEPTIONS OF SOCIAL RESPONSIBILITY |

Numbers show the percentage of subjects indicating that people have an obligation to help.

Incident Type	Parent			Friend			Stranger		
	Second Grade	Sixth Grade	College	Second Grade	Sixth Grade	College	Second Grade	Sixth Grade	College
India									
Extreme need	98	100	98	98	98	100	100	100	100
Moderate need	100	98	97	100	100	100	100	97	100
Minor need	97	98	92	98	100	93	95	97	73
United States									
Extreme need	100	100	100	98	100	97	97	95	97
Moderate need	95	94	95	78	92	65	65	53	47
Minor need	75	63	44	58	85	33	53	47	23

Source: Adapted from Miller, Bersoff, and Harwood 1990, 38.

the needs of others as a moral obligation (Dumont 1970; Kakar 1978; O'Flaherty and Derrett 1978; Baron and Miller 2000). In contrast, the more individualistic perspective of Americans influenced their tendency to consider the obligation to help against the competing values of individuality and personal freedom (Dumont 1965; Lukes 1973; Baron and Miller 2000).

Unwelcome Help

Most people appreciate acts of kindness and welcome help when it is needed. But this is not always true. In some cases, offers of assistance may be rebuffed. Imagine how a successful executive might react if he lost his job. It would not be surprising if he responded in anger to a close friend who might offer advice about job hunting. His wife might react in the same way to neighbors offering assistance, claiming that they do not need any free handouts. What explains reactions that clearly indicate that help is unwelcome?

One theory, the **threat-to-self-esteem model**, suggests that the answer lies in the complex web of internalized norms that influence a person's feelings of self-worth. According to this theory, offers of assistance may conflict with other important social norms (Fisher, Nadler, and Witcher-Alagna 1982; Fisher, Nadler, and De Paulo 1983). For example, while the Golden Rule teaches us the virtue of helping others, it represents only one of many rules that teach us how we ought to live. Americans raised according to the Protestant work ethic learn the value of self-reliance and independence (Weber 1930; Fisher, Nadler, and Witcher-Alagna 1982). Norms of fairness and equity, which stress the importance of reciprocity, also guide our everyday behavior. When an offer of assistance collides with these internalized norms, it can threaten a person's self-esteem (Fisher, Nadler, and Witcher-Alagna 1982).

The threat-to-self-esteem model proposes that a person's reaction to assistance depends on how help is offered. Giving help in a loving and concerned way sends a positive message—that the individual is worthy of assistance. It provides self-support. If, on the other hand, the giver somehow suggests the relative inferiority or dependence of the recipient, it sends a negative message that threatens his self-esteem. Providing help in a way that allows for some kind of fair exchange also produces a positive effect that contains elements of self-support. However, if help is given so that it prevents the recipient from feeling that she can reciprocate, it creates an inequitable relationship. When people find themselves in this situation—receiving more than they give—they feel the uneasiness of violating the ethical principle of fairness in dealing with others (Walster, Berscheid, and Walster 1973). This model also proposes that recipient characteristics influence their reactions to offers of assistance. High-achieving individuals who place great value on their autonomy are particularly susceptible to threats to their self-esteem. They will react more negatively to offers of assistance and aid.

LEARNING TO HELP

Social norms cannot tell us who will act like a good Samaritan when we face a decision to help a stranger in need. But this explanation does suggest that the shared expectations of the culture into which we are born shape our altruistic and prosocial tendencies. While specific ideas about helping vary from culture to culture, the process by which people come to know the norms of their group is similar. We learn the norms of our group through the process of socialization.

In this section, we will begin with theories that explain how we learn the helping norms of our society. We will then consider how these theories are related to a special kind of cognitive development—moral reasoning. As we will see, the reasons we help others change over the course of the socialization process (Schroeder et al. 1995).

Rewarding Altruism and Prosocial Behavior

A number of studies show how rewards influence helping behavior in children (Fischer 1963; Mills and Grusec 1989). In one early study, researchers showed that rewarding 4-year-old children with bubble gum increased their tendency to share marbles with other children (Fischer 1963). Adults are also more likely to act in helpful ways when they are rewarded rather than punished for doing so (Moss and Page 1972). Consider the results of a field study conducted on a street corner in Dayton, Ohio (Moss and Page 1972). The procedure involved a confederate who asked subjects for directions as they passed by. In the reward condition, she treated the subjects with courtesy. Communicating her appreciation both verbally and nonverbally, she smiled and said, "Thank you very much, I really appreciate this." But in the punishment condition, she spoke rudely, saying, "I can't understand what you're saying; never mind, I'll ask someone else." Not far from where this happened, the subject passed another confederate, who dropped a small bag but continued to walk on without noticing. Would the behavior of subjects who had been rewarded differ from that of subjects who had been punished? The results showed that it did. As Table 9.5 shows, subjects who received a polite thank-you for giving directions were more likely

TABLE 9.5	FREQUENCY OF OFFERING HELP		
	Reinforcement		
Help Offered	Positive	Negative	Control
Physical	27	12	14
Verbal	10	5	4
No help	3	23	2

Source: Adapted from Moss and Page 1972, 366.

than subjects who were treated rudely to later offer help to a confederate.

Do tangible rewards such as bubble gum differ from intangible rewards such as praise or gratitude? The answer is yes (Schroeder et al. 1995; Shaffer 2000). For one thing, tangible rewards are more effective in children than in adults. Compared to children, adults are more likely to respond to intangible rewards such as those that involve feelings of compassion, personal values, or a sense of obligation. The reasons we help others change over the course of the socialization process. Young children may attribute their helpful behavior to the tangible reward itself rather than to a concern for another person (Shaffer 2000). Instead of seeing an altruistic motive behind their actions, children only recognize the tangible reward for helpful behavior. They have not yet internalized the value of helping. An intangible reward such as verbal praise promises to have a longer-lasting impact, especially if it comes from a warm and kind person (Shaffer 2000; Mills and Grusec 1989).

Modeling Altruism and Prosocial Behavior

Another way people learn social norms that promote altruistic or prosocial behavior is by watching others model this kind of behavior. According to Albert Bandura (1977, 1986), children learn a great deal from simply observing models. Parents who practice what they preach provide children with an effective model. When they stop to help a stranded motorist, agree to do a favor for a neighbor, or call the police when someone needs special help, they model behaviors that tell children how they ought to behave. In contrast, parents who admonish their children to "do as I say, not as I do," provide poor models for expected kinds of behavior. In this case, children are again likely to imitate the behavior they observe and ignore what they consider hypocritical advice (Rushton 1975).

One study that showed the effectiveness of modeling prosocial behavior involved sixth-grade girls who played a pinball game to win chips that could be traded for candy and toys (Midlarsky, Bryan, and Brickman 1973). Before the girls took their turn, an adult showed them how to play, modeling either charitable or selfish behaviors. In the charitable condition, the adult put the chips she had won into a canister labeled "Money for Poor Children." In the selfish condition, the adult dropped all of her chips into a canister labeled "My Money." Regardless of whether the adult modeled charitable or selfish behavior, she encouraged the girls to be charitable. In reminding them about the poor children, she emphasized how happy they would be to receive the prizes that the chips could buy. The results showed that children do learn prosocial behaviors through modeling. Girls who watched a model give money to the poor children donated an average of nineteen chips, while those who had observed the selfish model gave only an average of ten chips.

Adults are also more likely to help if they see someone model prosocial behavior. James Bryan and Mary Ann Test (1967) designed a field study to see how models influence people who see them helping someone in distress. This experiment involved two scenes staged on a busy Los Angeles highway. In both cases, a traveler appeared to have gotten a flat tire. As drivers along the highway passed the first motorist with car trouble, they could see that she was getting help from another passerby. Shortly thereafter, about one-fourth of a mile down the road, another woman appeared to have a flat tire. Do helpful models set a good example for other motorists? The results of this study suggest they do. In a control condition, where motorists did not see someone helping the first stranded woman, only thirty-five stopped to help the second woman. In contrast, fifty-eight people stopped to help the second woman after they had seen the first woman being helped.

Further support for the hypothesis that modeling behavior increases helpfulness came from a second study involving charitable donations from Christmas shoppers (Bryan and Test 1967). In this case, the researchers wanted to know if shoppers who observed a model dropping money into a

Salvation Army kettle would be more likely to make a donation themselves. The results showed that in fact they were. When a confederate modeled charitable behavior, sixty-nine shoppers followed suit. In the no-model condition, only forty-three shoppers made a donation.

Parents may provide the best models for promoting prosocial behavior. But that depends on the kind of relationship they have developed with their child. Warm and nurturing relationships, in which the child views the parent as powerful, produce the strongest modeling effects (Schroeder et al. 1995). Evidence for the particularly strong influence of these kinds of parents appears in a number of studies. For example, many accounts of the Christians who risked their own lives to help Jews escape the Nazis during World War II include interviews with rescuers who describe their parents in this way (London 1970; Oliner and Oliner 1988). London (1970) claimed that these individuals had "an intense identification with a parental model of moral conduct" (245). Many white social activists who participated in the civil rights movement in the 1960s saw the same qualities in their parents (Rosenhan 1970).

Learning from models does not have to involve real people (Bandura 1977, 1986). Children also learn how to behave by watching fictional or animated characters in television programs and movies. Since American children watch an average of four hours of television per day, viewing these models could have a significant impact. The potential influence of aggressive and violent models has generated a great deal of concern and many studies. Less attention has been focused on the positive impact that helpful models might have. Yet research shows that watching media characters model prosocial behavior can increase helpful behavior in children (Sprafkin, Liebert, and Poulos 1975; Ahammer and Murray 1979).

In her review of the impact of television shows with prosocial themes, Susan Hearold (1986) concluded that the positive impact of helpful themes was far greater than the negative impact of antisocial themes. Citing *Mister Rogers' Neighborhood* as an example of a program with prosocial messages and drawing on the work of Stein and Friedrich (1975), she identified a number of common themes:

> cooperation, sympathy, sharing, affection, friendship, understanding the feelings of others, verbalizing one's own feelings, delay of gratification, persistence and competence at tasks, learning to accept rules, control of aggression, adaptive coping with frustration, fear reduction, self-esteem, and valuing the unique qualities of each individual. (Hearold 1986, 67)

A number of studies show that combining television programs that have these kinds of themes with training in prosocial behavior exerts a strong positive influence on levels of children's helping behaviors (Schroeder et al. 1995; Friedrich-Cofer et al. 1979; Friedrich and Stein 1975).

Mr. Rogers found a variety of ways to teach children prosocial messages such as friendship, cooperation, and sharing.

THE DEVELOPMENT OF PROSOCIAL ATTITUDES AND ACTIONS

The tendency to help others increases as children mature (Staub 1979). Some of the factors that may explain this change include children's understanding and acceptance of social norms, the ability to take the perspective of others, the capacity to empathize, and feelings of greater social responsibility and competence (Piliavin and Charng 1990). The reasons that children give for helping others—their moral reasoning abilities—also change with age (Piliavin and Charng 1990; Schroeder et al. 1995). Social psychologists have described the changes in children's motivations for helping and have proposed several models to explain the developmental process that accompanies these changes. We will consider two popular theories: Cialdini's socialization model (Cialdini and Kenrick 1976; Cialdini, Kenrick, and Baumann 1982) and Bar-Tal and Raviv's cognitive-learning model (Bar-Tal, Sharabany, and Raviv 1982).

Cialdini's Socialization Model of Charitable Behavior

In their socialization model of charitable behavior, Cialdini, Kenrick, and Baumann (1982) describe three steps to show how children's motivations for helping change over time. At the first step in this model, children view altruistic behavior either in a neutral manner or even as punishing, since they could see it as a loss of rewards. When they move to the second step in this model, children become aware of the social norms that prescribe prosocial and altruistic behavior. They do not, however, internalize them. Their motivations for helping at this point are linked to external rewards. The internalization of norms that promote helping occurs in the third step of this model. At this point, charitable behavior is intrinsically rewarding—it alone can make us feel good (Schroeder et al. 1995).

Bar-Tal and Raviv's Cognitive-Learning Model

Daniel Bar-Tal and Amiram Raviv (1982) propose a cognitive-learning model of helping behavior that suggests that both the amount and the quality of help that children offer improve as they mature. Changes in the quality of children's helping are reflected in their motives for helping. For example, young children are motivated to help for hedonistic reasons, to comply with adult requests, or from primitive empathy. Older children, however, are more likely to help because of high levels of empathy, sympathetic distress, or internalized norms. Based on an analysis of different kinds of motivations, Bar-Tal and Raviv identified six phases in the development of helping behavior. Table 9.6 shows these phases next to the three steps that Cialdini had proposed. As a comparison of these models shows, development progresses from the egocentric motivations of young children to a final stage where individuals help because they really want to and because it makes them feel good. In both models, the norms for prosocial behavior are internalized by the final stage of development.

Moral Reasoning about Prosocial Behavior

The two models of helping behavior we have just discussed suggest that children and adults make decisions about prosocial behavior in different ways. According to these particular theories, individuals progress through a series of stages that reflect the increasingly more sophisticated reasons and motivations for helping others. At the lowest levels in these stage theories, the reasons for helping would not lead us to define the behavior as altruistic (Eisenberg 1982). For example, if a child shares his toys with a playmate because his mother promises to buy him ice-cream later, the child's motivation for a reward disqualifies the behavior as altruistic. Recognizing the child's motivation in this case seems easy enough. But other cases are bound to be more difficult. And that poses a problem for social psychologists who need to make these kinds of distinctions. One solution for this

TABLE 9.6 THE SOCIALIZATION AND COGNITIVE-LEARNING MODELS

Cialdini's Socialization Model	Bar-Tal and Raviv's Cognitive-Learning Model
Stage 1: Presocialization	**Phase 1: Compliance—concrete**
Individuals are unsocialized about helping and rarely act altruistically because it involves a loss of resources.	Individuals help because they have been ordered to do so, with explicit threat of punishment.
	Phase 2: Compliance
	Individuals help if an authority requests them to do so. The threat of actual punishment is no longer needed.
Stage 2: Awareness of norms	**Phase 3: Internal initiative—concrete**
Individuals help because they have learned that people expect them to help and may punish them if they do not. They are concerned about social approval.	Individuals help because they expect a tangible reward.
	Phase 4. Normative behavior
	Individuals help because they know social norms about helping and are concerned about social approval.
	Phase 5. Generalized reciprocity
	Individuals help because they believe that the recipient would and should reciprocate.
Stage 3: Internalization	**Phase 6. Altruistic behavior**
Individuals help because it makes them feel better.	Individuals help because they want to benefit the other person. Helping increases their self-esteem and satisfaction.

Source: Schroeder et al. 1995, 132; based on Cialdini, Kenrick, and Baumann 1982; Bar-Tal and Raviv 1982.

problem involves an analysis of a person's moral reasoning about prosocial behaviors (Eisenberg 1982).

Kohlberg's Theory of Moral Development

Theories of moral reasoning focus on the principles that individuals use to judge right from wrong (Schroeder et al. 1995). Ideas about the way individuals reason about prosocial behavior have been strongly influenced by Lawrence Kohlberg (1963, 1984), who proposed that children pass through a series of stages of moral reasoning as they mature. According to Kohlberg, the principles on which they base their moral decisions differ qualitatively from one level to the next.

Kohlberg based his theory of moral development on the work of Jean Piaget, who believed that moral development depends upon a child's level of cognitive development. Like Piaget, Kohlberg believed that children pass through a series of sequential stages, which differ significantly in terms of the criteria that children use to think about a particular problem. As children progress from one stage to the next, the way they think about something becomes more sophisticated.

Kohlberg identified six stages of moral development, which he divided into three major levels. As Table 9.7 shows, an individual's level of moral development is not determined by whether he decides an action is right or wrong but rather by the specific reasoning he uses. To discover how

TABLE 9.7	KOHLBERG'S STAGES OF MORAL DEVELOPMENT	

Stage of Development	Typical Comments on the Morality of Heinz's Stealing a Drug (see text)
Level 1: Premoral	
Stage 1: Obedience and punishment orientation. The child obeys rules to avoid punishment; "conscience" is the irrational fear of punishment.	**Pro**—He should steal the drug. It isn't really bad to take it. It isn't like he didn't ask to pay for it first. The drug he'd take is only worth $200; he's not really taking a $2,000 drug.
	Con—He shouldn't steal the drug; it's a big crime. He didn't get permission, he used force and broke and entered. He did a lot of damage, stealing a very expensive drug and breaking up the store too.
Stage 2: Naive hedonistic and instrumental orientation. The child's action is motivated by a desire for reward or benefit. The rightness of the conduct is judged in terms of the extent to which a given action satisfies oneself.	**Pro**—It's all right to steal the drug because she needs it and he wants her to live. It isn't that he wants to steal, but it's what he must do to get the drug to save her. **Con**—He shouldn't steal it. The druggist isn't wrong or bad; he just wants to make a profit. That's what you're in business for, to make money.
Level 2: Morality of Conventional Role Conformity	
Stage 3: "Good boy" morality. The child is oriented toward seeking approval of others; consideration is given to needs and intentions of others.	**Pro**—He should steal the drug. He was only doing something that was natural for a good husband to do. You can't blame him for doing something out of love for his wife; you'd blame him if he didn't love his wife enough to save her.
	Con—He shouldn't steal. If his wife dies, he can't be blamed. It isn't because he's heartless or that he doesn't love her enough to do everything that he legally can. The druggist is the selfish or heartless one.

Sources: Kohlberg 1963; comments from Kohlberg 1984, 49.

people reason about different moral issues, Kohlberg presented subjects with a series of stories that involved a particular dilemma. The best-known of these vignettes involves a conflict that requires the main character to decide whether to steal if it would save his wife's life. As you consider this story, keep in mind that Kohlberg was interested in how subjects reasoned about the moral decision, not the specific answer they gave.

In Europe, a woman was near death from a special kind of cancer. There was one drug that doctors thought might save her. It was a form of radium that a druggist in the same town had recently discovered. The drug was expensive to make, but the druggist was charging $2,000, or 10 times the cost of the drug, for a small (possibly life-saving) dose. Heinz, the sick woman's husband, borrowed all the money he could, about $1,000, or half of what he needed. He told the druggist that his wife was dying and asked him to sell the drug cheaper or to let him pay later. The druggist replied, "No, I discovered the drug, and I'm going to make money from it." Heinz then became desperate and broke into the

Stage of Development	Typical Comments on the Morality of Heinz's Stealing a Drug (see text)
Stage 4: Law and authority maintain morality. The child is oriented toward "doing one's duty," respect for authority, and maintaining the social order.	**Pro**—You should steal it. If you did nothing, you'd be letting your wife die; it's your responsibility if she dies. You have to take it with the idea of paying the druggist. **Con**—It is a natural thing for Heinz to want to save his wife but it's still always wrong to steal. He still knows he's stealing and taking a valuable drug from the man who made it.
Level 3: Self-Accepted Moral Principles **Stage 5: Morality of contract, individual rights, and democratically accepted law.** The child is concerned with balancing the rights of the individual and the protection of society.	**Pro**—The law wasn't set up for these circumstances. Taking the drug in this situation isn't really right, but it's justified to do it. **Con**—You can't completely blame someone for stealing, but extreme circumstances don't really justify taking the law in your own hands. You can't have everyone stealing whenever they get desperate. The end may be good, but the ends don't justify the means.
Stage 6: Morality of individual principles of conscience. The child is concerned about self-condemnation for violating his or her own principles. The child's own conscience is the guide, and that guide is based on abstract, universal moral principles.	**Pro**—This is a situation which forces him to choose between stealing and letting his wife die. In a situation where the choice must be made, it is morally right to steal. He has to act in terms of the principle of preserving and respecting life. **Con**—Heinz is faced with the decision of whether to consider the other people who need the drug just as badly as his wife. Heinz ought to act, not according to his particular feelings toward his wife, but considering the value of all the lives involved.

store to steal the drug for his wife. Should Heinz have done that? (Kohlberg 1969, 379)

Based on subjects' moral reasoning about dilemmas like this, Kohlberg proposed that moral development involves three main levels, which contain stages that are sequential and universal. The three main levels in Kohlberg's model reflect fundamental differences in the way people reason about moral issues. At the first level, preconventional morality, children make moral decisions

based on their own needs and expectations about the rewards and punishments of a particular decision. When children progress to the second level, conventional morality, they no longer think in hedonistic terms but consider the shared expectations of the social group. Conformity and maintenance of the social order serve as the primary criteria for moral reasoning at this level. At the third level, postconventional morality, individuals make decisions based on their own internalized moral values and principles. In making decisions at this level, individuals do not consider their identification with particular groups.

Table 9.7 shows each of the stages that fall within these broader levels. For each of these stages, Kohlberg described the kind of reasoning that subjects used to judge the decision that Heinz made. As this table shows, the actual decision that Heinz made does not determine the subject's level of moral development. It is rather the reasoning that the subject used.

Eisenberg's Model of Prosocial Reasoning

Kohlberg's model of moral development shows how children's reasoning about moral questions changes and develops as they mature. But does it adequately explain the way children think about prosocial behavior? Nancy Eisenberg (1982, 1986) pointed out that Kohlberg's model was based on subjects' responses to hypothetical dilemmas that involved violations of rules or laws, punishments, social obligations, and authority. According to her, these kinds of dilemmas do not tap into prosocial moral reasoning. After all, how often do prosocial actions involve or even require breaking the law or disobeying authority? To understand prosocial moral reasoning, the dilemmas should involve conflicts between a person's own wants and needs and those of others. Helping should bear some kind of personal cost.

Based on this argument, Eisenberg (1982) designed and presented her own prosocial moral dilemmas to children and then asked them what they should do. A typical example read as follows:

> One day a girl (boy) named Mary (Eric) was going to a friend's birthday party. On her (his) way she (he) saw a girl (boy) who had fallen down and hurt her (his) leg. The girl asked Mary to go to her house and get her parents so the parents could come and take her to the doctor. But if Mary did run and get the child's parents, she would be late

for the birthday party and miss the ice cream, cake, and all the games. What should Mary do? Why? (231)

Based on children's responses to these kinds of dilemmas, Eisenberg proposed the model of prosocial moral reasoning shown in Table 9.8. At the lowest level of development, children's decisions to help are based on hedonistic concerns—how helping will satisfy their own needs or wants. As they mature, children begin to consider other people's needs, which may be expressed simply as "He's hungry." At mid-levels, their responses indicate the ability to empathize with others: "I'd feel bad if I didn't help because he'd be in pain." And at the most advanced level, reasoning is based on the internalization of values and norms that show a concern for the welfare of others. At this stage, children also reveal how they would feel about themselves if they did not help: "I would feel bad if I didn't help because I'd know that I didn't live up to my values."

The link between Eisenberg's model of prosocial moral reasoning and Cialdini's and Bar-Tal and Raviv's models is easy to recognize. All of these models emphasize the motivations children have for helping (Schroeder et al. 1995). Eisenberg's model of prosocial moral reasoning also resembles Kohlberg's model of moral development, but it is not identical. For example, the responses of her subjects were often coded into categories of moral judgment that resembled those in Kohlberg's stages. The pattern of development also appears similar—from the egocentrism of infants to the interpersonal orientation of adults, which in both models is tied to the ability to take the perspective of another. But there are also significant differences between these two models. Eisenberg does not assume that the stages in her model are fixed in sequence or universal. Instead, she offers her model as one that describes an age-related sequence of prosocial moral development in middle-class American children.

TABLE 9.8	**EISENBERG'S STAGES OF PROSOCIAL MORAL REASONING**

Stage 1: Hedonistic, pragmatic orientation

The individual is concerned with selfish, pragmatic consequences rather than moral considerations. "Right" behavior is that which is instrumental in satisfying the actor's own needs or wants. Reasons for assisting or not assisting another include consideration of direct gain to the self, future reciprocity, and concern for others whom the individual needs and/or likes.

Stage 2: Needs of others orientation

The individual expresses concern for the physical, material, and psychological needs of others even though the other's needs conflict with one's own needs. This concern is expressed in the simplest terms, without clear evidence of role taking, verbal expressions of sympathy, or reference to internalized affect such as guilt ("He's hungry" or "She needs it").

Stage 3: Approval and interpersonal orientation and/or stereotyped orientation

Stereotyped images of good and bad persons and behavior and/or considerations of others' approval and acceptance are used in justifying prosocial or nonhelping behaviors. For example, one helps another because "It's nice to help" or "He'd like him more if he helped."

Stage 4a: Empathic orientation

The individual's judgments include evidence of sympathetic responding, role taking, concern with the other's humanness, and/or guilt or positive affect related to the consequences of one's actions. Examples include "He knows how he feels," "She cares about people," and "I'd feel bad if I didn't help because he'd be in pain."

Stage 4b: Transitional stage

Justifications for helping or not helping involve internalized values, norms, duties, or responsibilities or refer to the necessity of protecting the rights and dignity of other persons; these ideas, however, are not clearly and strongly stated. References to internalized affect, self-respect, and living up to one's own values are considered indicative of this stage if they are weakly stated. Examples include "It's just something I've learned and feel."

Stage 5: Strongly internalized stage

Justifications for helping or not helping are based on internalized values, norms, or responsibilities, the desire to maintain individual and societal contractual obligations, and the belief in the dignity, rights, and equality of all individuals. Positive or negative affects related to the maintenance of self-respect and living up to one's own values and accepted norms also characterize this stage. Examples of stage 5 reasoning include "She'd feel a responsibility to help other people in need" and "I would feel bad if I didn't help because I'd know that I didn't live up to my values."

Source: Eisenberg 1982, 234.

SUMMARY

1. August Comte, who coined the term *altruism*, considered its defining trait to be an unselfish regard for the welfare of others. Most social psychologists today would agree, but they would also distinguish altruism from another kind of helping behavior called prosocial behavior.

2. Social exchange theory offers one explanation for why we help others. This theory suggests that helping others is actually done to serve one's own self-interest—that the decision to help involves a cost-benefit analysis.

3. Daniel Batson argued that true altruism does exist and that empathy is the true sign. Batson's empathy-altruism model proposes that a person's motivation for helping may involve motivations that are either egoistic or altruistic.

4. Evolutionary theories of altruism propose that animals that risk their own lives by acting in unselfish ways to help other animals do so because of natural selection. According to this theory, natural selection operates at the level of genes, not at the level of the individual. Altruistic animals may risk their own lives to save their gene pool. Altruistic genes are passed on via kin selection, reciprocity, and group selection.

5. The 1964 murder of Kitty Genovese prompted Latané and Darley to investigate the factors that determine when people will help others in need. Their model includes a series of decisions that people make when they decide to intervene to help someone.

6. Social psychologists have identified a number of situational factors that influence a person's decision to help others. They include time, the presence of others, size of place, and moods and emotions.

7. The bystander effect offers one explanation for why people fail to help in an emergency. This effect involves the diffusion of responsibility, which means that as the number of bystanders watching an emergency increases, an individual's own sense of responsibility decreases. Research provides solid support for the bystander effect.

8. The idea that the size of a community affects the likelihood of people helping others has been around for a long time. Both Durkheim and Simmel explained why helping behavior is more likely to occur in smaller, traditional communities than in cities. And research confirms the expectation that people in large cities are less likely to help strangers.

9. Studies show that our moods can influence whether we decide to help others. Overall, good moods have a positive effect on helping behavior. The effect of bad moods is not as predictable. In some cases, they increase the tendency to help others. But bad moods can also have negative effects. Cialdini's negative state relief model provides a good explanation for the pattern of inconsistent findings for the effects of bad moods. Feeling guilty also makes people more inclined to help others. One explanation suggests that people do good deeds to compensate others for the harm they have caused. Hurting others can also damage a person's self-esteem. Helping others can restore the positive image these people once had of themselves.

10. Social norms also explain why people help others. The norm of reciprocity, the principle of equity, and beliefs about justice belong to a class of social norms that invoke rules of fairness. A second class of norms address questions of social responsibility—when or under what circumstances we are obligated to help others.

11. Although people usually appreciate help, it is sometimes rejected. The threat-to-self-esteem model provides one explanation. If assistance from someone conflicts with other important social norms, it can threaten a person's self-esteem. High achievers who value their autonomy are particularly susceptible to threats to their self-esteem.

12. People learn social norms that promote altruistic or prosocial behavior in various ways. Rewarding helpful behavior is successful in both children and adults. Tangible rewards are more effective with children than with adults, but intangible rewards are likely to have a longer-lasting impact. Modeling is another effective way to teach altruistic or prosocial behavior. And learning from models does not have to involve real people. Hearold's review of television programs with prosocial themes also showed that the positive impact of helpful themes was far greater than the negative impact of antisocial themes.

13. The tendency to help others increases as children mature. Social psychologists have proposed several models to explain the developmental process associated with the acquisition of prosocial attitudes and actions. These models include Cialdini's socialization model of charitable behavior and Bar-Tal and Raviv's cognitive-learning model.

14. Ideas about the way individuals reason about prosocial behavior have been strongly influenced by Lawrence Kohlberg, whose theory of moral development focuses on the principle that individuals use to judge right from wrong. Nancy Eisenberg developed a model of prosocial moral reasoning that resembles Kohlberg's model of moral development. Her model's hypothetical dilemmas, however, focused on conflicts between a person's own wants and needs and those of others. And helping in these cases involved some kind of personal cost.

The pattern that Eisenberg observed in the development of prosocial reasoning is similar to that observed by Kohlberg—from the egocentrism of infants to the interpersonal orientation of adults. But Eisenberg does not assume that the stages in her model are fixed in sequence or universal.

KEY TERMS

Altruism   243
Egoism   244
Selflessness   244
Prosocial behavior   244
Empathy   246

Kin selection   250
Reciprocal altruism   250
Group selection   251
Diffusion of responsibility   254
Bystander effect   256

Negative state relief model   260
Social norms   261
Norm of reciprocity   262
Norm of responsibility   264
Threat-to-self-esteem model   266

CRITICAL REVIEW QUESTIONS

1. Émile Durkheim argued that all societies depend on altruism. Do you agree or disagree? What would an evolutionary theorist say about this claim?
2. Research shows that the size of a community influences altruistic and prosocial behavior. How, then, would you explain the responses of people in New York City after the terrorist attack on September 11, 2001?
3. What role should schools play in teaching children altruistic and prosocial behavior?

TEN

Aggression

On October 24, 2002, after a three-week reign of terror, it all came to an end. A police team armed with submachine guns closed in and captured John Allen (Williams) Muhammad and Lee Malvo as they slept in their 1990 blue Chevrolet Caprice. They were parked in a lot just off a highway outside Washington, D.C. When the police opened the trunk of the car and discovered a built-in sniper perch, little doubt existed that these two men were the snipers who had terrorized the Washington, D.C., area for twenty-two days. By the time these snipers had been apprehended, ten innocent people were dead—murdered in cold blood. Four others had been shot, and police were looking into unsolved murders across the country.

The shooting spree started on October 2. The first shot, fired into the window of a Michael's craft store, claimed no victim. But less than an hour later, James Martin, 55, was dead, struck as he walked across a parking lot. On October 3, one innocent victim after another was gunned down. The first victim of the day was a 39-year-old landscaper; the second, a 54-year-old cabdriver; then a 34-year-old woman sitting on a bench, a 25-year-old mother vacuuming her minivan, and later that evening, a 72-year-old man standing on a corner. The victims were all anonymous targets, executed at random. The sniper's marksmanship was exceptional. The victims died from a single bullet. Although witnesses heard the shots, the sniper was able to make a fast getaway, leaving little evidence for the police.

As the bloody rampage continued day after day, panic set in. As reported by *Newsweek* magazine:

> Nothing seemed to ease the dread that shadowed anyone who stepped outside. Sidewalk cafés were empty. Gas-station owners parked trucks between the pumps and the street, attempting to lure back customers, who warily crouched behind their cars while their tanks filled. Schools went into "code blue" lockdown, keeping students inside, curtains drawn. Playing fields were off-limits. All around the region, the sniper had succeeded in making the irrational seem rational. (Smalley and Miller 2002, 27–28).

On October 7, the first clues to the identity of the sniper were found in the grass outside Benjamin Tasker Middle School, where a 13-year-old student was critically wounded as he got out of his aunt's car. A tarot card depicting Death was left with a simple message: "Mister Policeman, I am God." Next to the card was a spent shell casing. On October 19, the sniper left a letter for police demanding $10 million along with a threat: "Your children are not safe anywhere at anytime." The clues provided little insight into the mind of this sniper. It seemed that he was simply playing a cat-and-mouse game with law enforcement and the media.

The bewildering nature of this crime left experts with little to say. But everyone else seemed to have a theory.

> Computer geeks swore the killer was modeling himself after One Shot, One Kill, a popular videogame. No, said highbrow-cop-show fans, he was re-enacting a script from *Homicide,* the defunct television drama. Amateur serial-killer historians speculated that the sniper might be paying homage to Son of Sam on the 25th anniversary of his New York killing spree. (Smalley and Miller 2002, 28)

Within days of the snipers' arrest, information about them provided some explanation for their cold-blooded acts of aggression. According to two ex-wives, Muhammad was a violent man who turned particularly threatening when disputes involved custody of his children. In 1999, his second wife filed for divorce and was granted a restraining order against him. She claimed that Muhammad had physically intimidated her and threatened her. In a court document, she wrote, "I have had my phone number changed three times in five days. I am afraid of John. He is behaving very, very irrational" (Ripley 2002, 37). He vanished ten days after these court papers were filed, taking his three children with him. Did his frustration over child custody battles play a role in his murderous rampage?

Perhaps it was frustration that had grown during his career in the army. Although he had received many

medals for his military service, an army officer claimed that "all but one of them are basically awarded for just showing up" (Ripley 2002, 37). He had nonetheless one remarkable military achievement to his credit: He had risen through three levels of army marksmanship and had become an expert with the M-16 rifle. He had learned how to aim, fire, and kill human targets.

The second sniper, 17-year-old Lee Malvo, called Muhammad his "play" father. Was he simply being an obedient son—a child eager to please his father? Or was he acting out a military role—just obeying orders? At the time of his arrest, it was hard to determine the cause of his aggression.

Muhammad and Malvo are not the first serial killers to paralyze American communities with fear. Nor do they represent the only kind of aggression that threatens the public. Today, Americans identify terrorism as the most important problem facing the country. The war in Iraq comes in second. School shootings have now slipped from our memories. And the most common kind of aggression—interpersonal violence—rarely appears on the list of the country's most important problems. What causes human aggression? Do normal people engage in acts of aggression? Is aggressive behavior learned? Or are human beings born with instincts that lead them to fight and kill? Does frustration explain explosive forms of aggression like road rage? What explains the aggressive behavior of spectators and players at competitive sports events? And is it fair to blame the media for the escalating violence in America? Finally, what can we do to reduce aggression? These are some of the questions we will address in this chapter.

DEFINING AGGRESSION

Aggression is so common in American life that few of us stop to consider how to define it (see Box 10.1). It is easy to recognize. The front page of the newspaper provides story after story of human aggression: war, terrorism, sniper shootings,

When 17-year-old Lee Malvo was arrested for playing a role in the Washington, D.C. sniper shootings, the cause of his aggression was unclear.

domestic violence, road rage, sports violence, and child abuse. It seems obvious. But social psychologists struggle to define it. Why the confusion? Consider a few examples.

> A football player tackles an opponent and breaks his leg.
>
> A fireman grabs a child who is choking on a piece of hard candy and forcefully squeezes her chest to dislodge it.
>
> A mother spanks her 7-year-old for lighting matches in a closet.
>
> A soldier murders a young woman; he considered her an enemy.
>
> A police officer fatally wounds a teenager who is aiming an automatic rifle at his classmates.
>
> A teenager knocks a young woman down in a New York subway and runs off with her purse.

In each of these examples, the injury of another human being is the consequence of an action. Does that make all of these examples of aggression? Let us complicate matters further. Some terms portray aggressive behavior as a positive quality. In the competitive business world, the "aggressive salesman" or the "go-getter" is viewed as a rising star. *Aggressive* in this context reflects an energetic or enterprising attitude. People who are aggressive in this way do not sit around waiting for something to happen; they initiate things and follow through.

Storr (1968) argued that a single drive explains aggressive behavior, whether it is constructive or destructive. This drive motivates an eager beaver to earn an M.B.A. from Harvard with the dream of great wealth. That same drive would also explain the behavior of someone who takes the shortcut—the mugger who attacks a Wall Street banker as he is stepping away from the ATM. Is it that simple? Can aggression be explained by one drive?

Most social psychologists reject such a broad definition of aggression. Some have even rejected the idea of motivation altogether. Arnold Buss (1961), who offered one of the earliest definitions of aggression, ignored subjective explanations that involved intention. He chose instead to favor the approach of behaviorists: Aggression was simply "the delivery of noxious stimuli to another [person]." This early definition failed, for obvious reasons. For one thing, accidentally injuring another person is different from intentionally doing so (Berkowitz

---

BOX 10.1   AGGRESSIVE LANGUAGE

Language suggests a great deal about our everyday understandings of aggression. Judging by common American expressions, we seem to approach just about everything in an aggressive manner. We refer to the "aggressive salesman"—one who takes the hard sell approach in trying to persuade us to buy a product. This guy might be "under the gun," that is, "under pressure from above to produce desirable performance results" (Harragan 1977, 103). The business world has adopted aggressive language like this directly from the military. Other common expressions include:

- *Under fire:* Under intense pressure to perform or vindicate oneself in a clash of opinions. (103)
- *Shoot:* Let's hear what you think. (102)
- *Bite the bullet:* Face an extremely painful but unavoidable fact. (100)
- *Blitzed* or *bombarded:* "Saturated a market region with a sudden explosion of advertising, promotion, and sales incentives. A concentrated, short-term activity, as when introducing a new or improved product or 'attacking' a competitor's dominance in a market" (Harragan 1977, 100).

Military terms are also common in sports. For example, a *gunner* refers to a basketball player who shoots a lot. The same term may be used to describe a fiercely competitive student. If the thought of aggression seems foreign to intellectual pursuits, think again. Storr (1968) argues that language says it all: "The words we use to describe intellectual effort are aggressive words. We *attack* problems, or *get our teeth into* them. We *master* a subject when we have *struggled with* and *overcome* its difficulties" (4).

In *The Argument Culture*, Deborah Tannen (1998) describes life in America as a pervasive warlike atmosphere. She writes:

The war on drugs, the war on cancer, the battle of the sexes, politicians' turf battles—in the argument culture, war metaphors pervade our talk and shape our thinking. Nearly everything is framed as a battle or game in which winning or losing is the main concern. (4)

She is in favor of "stopping America's war of words," claiming that living in this kind of contentious atmosphere corrodes our spirit.

1993). A motorist who causes an accident due to hazardous road conditions is clearly different from someone who intentionally rams his vehicle into another one because he is angry for getting stuck in a traffic jam. Even people with good intentions act in ways that hurt us. Consider a surgeon who performs a liver transplant to save a patient's life. Today, most social psychologists view **aggression** as "any form of behavior that is intended to injure someone physically or psychologically" (Berkowitz 1993, 3).

Social psychologists have refined this definition of aggression by recognizing one additional distinction: the difference between *hostile* and *instrumental* aggression (Feshbach 1964; Berkowitz 1993). **Hostile aggression** involves an impulsive emotional response that aims to injure a victim. An example of this type of aggression would be an adolescent who becomes angry and then attacks a classmate because she made insulting remarks about his mother. In contrast, **instrumental**

aggression aims to achieve a particular goal. This kind of aggression is not impulsive but requires thought and planning. A teenager who knocks a woman down in a New York subway and runs off with her purse illustrates this kind of aggression. His aggression is not triggered by anger but rather by his intent to steal her money. This aggression is instrumental in achieving that goal.

Arnold Buss and his colleagues designed an aggression questionnaire that taps into different kinds of aggression (see Table 10.1, pages 284–285). What do your responses to this questionnaire tell you about aggression in your personal life?

Aggression: Human Nature or Learned Behavior?

To what extent can human nature explain aggression? Are human beings born with instincts that program them to fight and kill? Or are these behaviors learned? Philosophers and other great thinkers have considered these questions for centuries (Berkowitz 1993; Baron and Richardson 1994; Geen and Donnerstein 1998). As noted in Chapter 2, Thomas Hobbes (1651/1904) believed that human beings are basically selfish, seeking to maximize their own self-interest at the expense of others. From this perspective, the inevitable outcome for social life looks bleak. It suggests that human beings will live in a state of war—an existence that Hobbes described as "solitary, poor, nasty, brutish, and short." These beliefs led him to argue that society would have to impose external controls over the egoistic nature of human beings. In contrast, Jean-Jacques Rousseau (1762/1968) viewed human beings as "noble savages." Born as gentle creatures, society's restrictive controls cultivated the hostile and aggressive behavior of human beings. Adam Smith (1759/1999) offered another view. He did not believe that society needed to impose controls on individuals at all. Instead, he argued that human beings do it themselves through sympathy. Today, the term *empathy* is used to describe what he meant—"the shared feeling that results when we observe other people in emotional states, the compassion we feel for their sorrow, the resentment when they are slighted, the joy when they triumph" (Davis 1994, 2).

Social psychologists consider both nature and nurture in their theories of aggression. In the next section, we will consider theories that explain the role that nature might play.

Instinct Theories

The earliest theories of aggression proposed that human beings are programmed for aggressive behavior—that it is deeply rooted in human instincts (Baron and Richardson 1994). For these early theorists, human instincts provided the best explanation for why wars have forever plagued the human race (Berkowitz 1962). Albert Einstein, one of the most prominent thinkers of the twentieth century to address this problem, wondered why propaganda could so easily incite human beings to war (Berkowitz 1962). In a letter to Sigmund Freud, Einstein (1933) suggested that the explanation lay within human beings themselves—that it was relatively easy to activate human beings' "lust for hatred and destruction" and elevate it to "the power of a collective psychosis" (18). Freud agreed.

Freud did not identify a specific instinct for aggression in his early thinking. Instead, he proposed that the life instinct, *eros*, guided human behavior toward the preservation and reproduction of life and that aggression resulted when the path for this instinct was blocked. After witnessing the brutality and destruction of World War I, however, he argued that a separate instinct for aggression did exist. Referring to it as *thanatos*, the death instinct, he claimed that its energy drives human beings toward destruction and the termination of life. Like Hobbes, he saw the outcome of social life as bleak. Summing up his revised theory, he wrote:

> The fateful question for the human species seems to me to be whether and to what extent their cultural development will succeed in mastering the disturbance of their communal life by the human instinct of aggression and self-destruction. . . . Men have gained control over the forces of nature to such an extent that with their help they would have no difficulty in exterminating one another to the last man. (Freud 1930/1962, 92)

Konrad Lorenz (1966, 1974), a Nobel Prize–winning ethologist, proposed another instinct-based explanation of human aggression. Like Freud, he believed that the cause of war was rooted in a human instinct for aggression. Unlike Freud, however, he viewed aggression as an evolutionary adaptation. According to Lorenz, human beings, like other animals, are born with an instinct to fight. This instinct for aggression serves a number of important functions. First, fighting among animals of the same species distributes them over the land in a way that protects their food supply. Second, aggression operates in sexual selection. By dominating weaker members of the species, the strongest animals guarantee that their genes will be passed on—the ones best suited for the long-term survival of the species.

But why do human beings, unlike other animals, kill members of their own species? Lorenz offered an interesting evolutionary explanation. In

TABLE 10.1 THE AGGRESSION QUESTIONNAIRE

Aggression takes several forms. Arnold Buss and his colleagues identified five of them: physical aggression, verbal aggression, anger, hostility, and indirect aggression. Most people experience some form of aggression off and on. Although aggression is generally viewed in a negative way, some components suggest a normal reaction. Others indicate that people think for themselves and feel free to express an opinion. What are you like?

To assess your own level of aggression, indicate "yes" or "no" for the following sample items from Buss's questionnaire.

Component	Yes	No
Physical Aggression		
1. I may hit someone if he or she provokes me.	☐	☐
2. I have become so mad that I have broken things.	☐	☐
Verbal Aggression		
1. I often find myself disagreeing with people.	☐	☐
2. I tell my friends openly when I disagree with them.	☐	☐
Anger		
1. I flare up quickly but get over it quickly.	☐	☐
2. I have trouble controlling my temper.	☐	☐

addition to a fighting instinct, he argued that non-human animals also possess instincts that restrain them from delivering fatal blows to their victims. To illustrate how these instincts operate, he described how fighting between dogs usually ends when one innately signals his submissiveness:

> I have repeatedly seen that when the loser of a fight suddenly adopted the submissive attitude, and presented his unprotected neck, the winner performed the movement of shaking to death, in the air, close to the neck of the morally vanquished dog, but with closed mouth, that is, without biting. (Lorenz 1963, 133)

Lorenz argued that strong inhibitions that prevent animals from killing members of their own species evolved in dangerous carnivores whose sharp teeth and claws easily kill prey. These instinctive mechanisms did not, however, evolve in weaker animals like human beings who are not physically equipped to kill with their bare hands

Component	Yes	No
Hostility		
1. I wonder why sometimes I feel so bitter about things.	☐	☐
2. At times I am so jealous I can't think of anything else.	☐	☐
Indirect Aggression		
1. I have been mad enough to slam a door when leaving someone behind in the room.	☐	☐
2. I sometimes spread gossip about people I don't like.	☐	☐

When you can honestly describe yourself by responding "YES" to a lot of statements like these examples, it may be a sign that you have a higher level of aggression than others your age. If you compare the number of "YES" responses you give to these statements with the average number of "YES" answers given by your friends or classmates, you can get an idea of how real test scores are sometimes evaluated. For a well-developed test like the AQ, actual scores are evaluated by comparing a single person's scores to scores for hundreds or even thousands of people of different ages and in different settings.

and teeth. In contrast to dangerous carnivores, human beings instinctively flee danger rather than confront it. This reaction to danger changed, however, when human beings developed lethal weapons—knives, bows and arrows, guns, and nuclear arms.

Instinct theories of human aggression are not widely supported today. Critics cite many specific problems with these theories, including the argument that human beings are fundamentally different from lower animals. Instincts also fail to explain significant cross-cultural differences in aggressive behavior such as homicide rates. Most social psychologists cite the lack of empirical evidence as the most important reason for rejecting the idea that instincts explain human aggression.

Biological Theories

In the September 1997 issue of *Esquire* magazine, Mike McAlary recounted the story of Vincent La Marca, a former homicide detective for the Long

Beach, Long Island, police department. According to McAlary, he is "the hero cop whose life is poised between two murders" (92). His father, Angelo, was executed in Sing Sing prison for kidnapping and murdering a one-month-old baby in 1956. Forty years later, La Marca's son Joey was arrested for brutally murdering a 24-year-old homeless man. The detective who discovered Joey's victim speculated that drugs or liquor played a role in the murder: "The killer or killers were in a raw, bloody rage. The . . . murder was not a thinking crime" (90).

This real-life case raises questions about the genetic nature of aggression. Is it inherited? The idea that criminal tendencies are inherited was popularized by a nineteenth-century Italian physician named Cesare Lombroso. Influenced by Darwin's theory of evolution, Lombroso argued that criminals were *atavists*, evolutionary throwbacks who were biologically disposed toward antisocial behavior (Berkowitz 1993; Barkan 1997). As evidence for this theory, he offered the body measurements of Italian prisoners, which he argued resembled primitive men more than contemporary ones. The distinctive features that he associated with criminal atavists included sloping foreheads, abnormally long arms, large skulls and jaws, and hairy bodies. The methodological flaws in Lombroso's research eventually discredited his theory. Nonetheless, his belief that biological factors contribute to criminal behavior still influences research today (Vold and Bernard 1986; Rafter 1992).

Genetics: Do We Inherit Aggression?

Research that seeks to reveal the biological basis of aggression attempts to show a link between biological similarities and behavioral similarities (Livingston 1996). Many of these studies have tried to establish this link by showing a genetic basis for criminal behavior. The logic behind their approach suggests that if heredity does influence aggressive behavior, then people with similar genes will commit the same kinds of crimes. An easy way to establish this relationship is to examine the criminal records of family members. If one brother is sitting on death row for murder, does he have a brother with a similar record for violent offenses? The problem with this comparison is that it fails to separate hereditary influences from the influences of being raised in a similar environment. Researchers have taken two approaches to solve this problem.

Twin Studies. One approach involves the comparison of fraternal and identical twins (Berkowitz 1993; Baron and Richardson 1994). Identical twins develop from a single fertilized egg and therefore share identical genes. Geneticists call them *monozygotic twins*. In contrast, fraternal twins result when two separate eggs are fertilized at the same time. These *dyzygotic twins* do not share identical genes and are no more similar than ordinary brothers and sisters. Researchers assume that both types of twins experience similar environmental influences (Berkowitz 1993). So if identical twins show more similarity in aggressive behavior than fraternal twins, logic suggests that it is due to their unique biological trait (identical genes).

A number of studies dating back to the early twentieth century show that the degree of similarity, or **concordance**, between different types of twins indicates a genetic influence (Hollin 1989). Overall, the pattern shows more similarity in the crimes committed by identical twins than by fraternal twins. A number of other studies that compared identical twins to other siblings also provide evidence for a genetic influence on aggressive behavior (Ellis 1982; Rowe and Osgood 1984; Taylor 1984; Rowe 1985, 1986; Carey 1994).

Karl Christiansen (1977) provided strong evidence for the hereditary influence on criminal behavior in a study based on data gathered in Denmark. His analysis involved close to eight hundred pairs of twins from a sample of approximately 3,900 sets of twins. For each of the pairs he selected, one of the twins had been convicted of a crime. He then checked to see if the other twin had a criminal record. His results showed that the concordance rate for identical twins was more than twice that for fraternal twins. The concordance rate was,

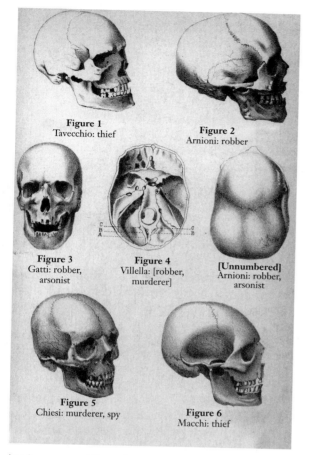

Figure 1
Tavecchio: thief

Figure 2
Arnioni: robber

Figure 3
Gatti: robber,
arsonist

Figure 4
Villella: [robber,
murderer]

[Unnumbered]
Arnioni: robber,
arsonist

Figure 5
Chiesi: murderer, spy

Figure 6
Macchi: thief

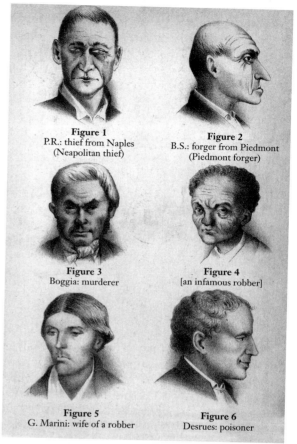

Figure 1
P.R.: thief from Naples
(Neapolitan thief)

Figure 2
B.S.: forger from Piedmont
(Piedmont forger)

Figure 3
Boggia: murderer

Figure 4
[an infamous robber]

Figure 5
G. Marini: wife of a robber

Figure 6
Desrues: poisoner

Lombroso argued that criminals were evolutionary throwbacks with distinctive physical features such as large skulls and jaws and sloping foreheads.

moreover, greatest when the crime involved another person rather than a property crime.

Some critics argue that the high concordance rate for identical twins can be explained by greater similarity in their experiences (environmental influences). They claim that identical twins spend more time together, share more friends, are treated more alike by their parents and teachers, and are more attached to one another (Livingston 1996). They simply have more similar experiences than fraternal twins. And these things, critics argue, produce the greater degree of similarity in attitudes and behavior (Dalgard and Kringlen 1978; Walters and White 1989; Walters 1992).

Parent-Child Studies: Biological versus Adoptive Parents. A second approach that researchers take in studying the genetic component of aggressive behavior involves a comparison of the criminal behavior of parents and children. One way to separate the effects of nature and nurture is to study children who were adopted soon after birth. Using this approach, Sarnoff Mednick and his colleagues analyzed the criminal records of all Danish children adopted between 1924 and 1947 (Mednick, Gabrielli, and Hutchings 1983, 1987; Van Dusen et al. 1983). To determine whether criminal behavior had a biological basis, they then examined the criminal records of the child's biological

TABLE 10.2   CRIMINAL CONVICTIONS OF ADOPTED SONS AND THEIR FATHERS

Sons are more likely to be convicted of a crime if their biological fathers have a criminal record than if their adoptive fathers do.

Adoptive Father Convicted?	Biological Father Convicted?	
	No	**Yes**
No	14%	20%
Yes	15	25

Source: Baron and Richardson 1994, 247; data from Mednick, Gabrielli, and Hutchings 1987.

and adoptive parents. Their analysis provided support for an hereditary basis for criminal behavior. As Table 10.2 shows, adopted sons were more likely to have a criminal conviction if their biological parent had one.

Although this study suggests a genetic basis for aggressive behavior, the researchers point out that the type of crime committed by an adopted child was not necessarily the same as that committed by the biological parent. In fact, the results of this study showed more support for a genetic basis for property crimes than for violent crimes. This suggests that it is not aggression that is inherited but rather another trait, such as impulsivity or dominance, that might in turn influence aggression (Barratt and Pattan 1983; Mednick, Gabrielli, and Hutchings 1987). This study lends support for a biological basis for criminal behavior, but it does not suggest that environmental influences play no role. In fact, Table 10.2 shows that the adopted children most likely to have a criminal conviction were influenced in some way by both biological and adoptive parents.

The Brain's "Aggression Center"

Another biological explanation for aggression focuses on the brain and the sympathetic nervous system. Theoretically, this influence is significant, since different parts of the brain influence basic drives, emotions, learning, judgment, and decision making (Baron and Richardson 1994). But scientists who study the brain as a biological explanation

for aggression focus on a specific part of the brain—the amygdala. Located within the limbic system, this almond-shaped structure is often called the "aggression center." Scientists recognized the connection between the amygdala and aggressive behavior by the early twentieth century. Heinrich Kluver, a psychologist, and Paul Bucy, a neurosurgeon, discovered that lesions of the amygdala produced a mellowing effect on rhesus monkeys (Kassin 1998). Later experiments showed that stimulating the amygdala causes violent outbursts in otherwise gentle animals (Moyer 1976).

Researchers have also discovered that lesions on the amygdala of epileptic patients reduce violent outbursts (Mark and Ervin 1970; Baron and Richardson 1994). The case of a patient named Julia shows a direct link between the amygdala and aggressive behavior (Kassin 1998). She had suffered from epilepsy since childhood and would periodically have seizures that brought violent outbursts including temper tantrums and fits of rage. By the time she reached the age of 21, she had attempted suicide four times and had stabbed a woman in the chest with a knife for simply bumping into her. The neurosurgeon who evaluated Julia discovered abnormal discharges from the amygdala and was able to cause violent outbursts by stimulating this part of her brain. To treat her condition, part of her amygdala was surgically destroyed.

While understanding how the amygdala might play a role in aggression, operating on the brain to change a person's behavior raises serious ethical questions and limits this kind of research (Valenstein 1986; Baron and Richardson 1994).

Hormones and Aggression

Are men more aggressive than women? It seems so. The evidence clearly shows a pattern of sex differences in aggression, which exists across cultures (Baron and Richardson 1994). The dramatic difference in violent crime rates for men and women explains why one of the most popular explanations of crime has focused on the "male hormone," testosterone (Barkan 1997). Hormones offer a plausible explanation, since the level of testosterone is more than ten times higher in males than in females (Baron and Richardson 1994).

Many studies show a correlation between testosterone levels and aggression or criminality. They have not, however, demonstrated a causal relationship. What is more, they also suggest that mediating factors influence the specific way that hormones influence behavior. A few studies show the complicated relationship between hormones and aggression. James Dabbs and his colleagues conducted a series of studies involving prison inmates (Dabbs et al. 1988, 1995; Dabbs, Hargrove, and Heusel 1996; Dabbs 2000). In one study that lasted over six years, they collected data for more than seven hundred male inmates (Dabbs et al.

1995; Dabbs 2000). To measure inmates' testosterone levels, they collected saliva samples by having the subjects spit a teaspoonful of saliva into a plastic vial. They then examined the prison records to evaluate whether the crimes they had committed were violent or nonviolent. They also measured aggressive behavior on the basis of how often they had violated prison rules. Their results showed that testosterone levels were associated with both the type of crime committed and with prison rule violations. As Figure 10.1 shows, men convicted of violent crimes showed higher levels of testosterone than men who were convicted of nonviolent crimes. Similarly, men who had violated prison rules had higher testosterone levels than men who had not violated them.

Dabbs and colleagues' research on women inmates (1988) revealed a more complicated picture. In this case, the researchers had to further differentiate violent crimes on the basis of whether the woman had been provoked to commit the offense. For example, was a woman provoked by an abusive husband to murder him? Was she acting in self-defense? Using this finer distinction, this study showed that levels of testosterone were lower for women who had been provoked to commit a violent crime than for women who had not been provoked.

In another study, Dabbs and Morris (1990; Dabbs 2000) analyzed the relationship between

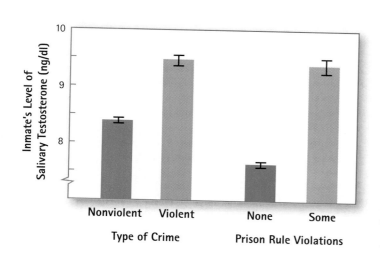

FIGURE 10.1

Relation of Inmate Testosterone Level to Original Crime Committed and Rule Violations in Prison

Source: Dabbs 2000, 78.

testosterone levels and antisocial behavior for 4,462 male military veterans. After undergoing medical examinations, which included measuring testosterone levels, the veterans provided information about their military experience, family, work, and background. To analyze the data, Dabbs and Morris divided their subjects into a high-testosterone group (the 10 percent with the highest levels) and a low-testosterone group (everyone else). These two groups differed significantly in terms of specific kinds of misbehaviors (see Table 10.3). Men in the high-testosterone group were "more likely to misbehave in school as children, get into trouble with the law as adults, use drugs and alcohol, go AWOL in the Army, and report having ten or more sex partners in one year" (Dabbs 2000, 82).

Researchers have examined the relationship between hormones and aggression in a variety of ways. So far, however, their studies are inconclusive and provide no clear picture of how hormones influence aggressive behavior (Baron and Richardson 1994). But we have learned some things. First, although studies do show a correlation between testosterone and aggression, they have not established a causal direction. In fact, several studies show that aggression increases testosterone. Second, although testosterone does not bear directly on aggression, it might affect certain personality traits that do (e.g., impulsiveness, risk taking, or dominance). These particular traits may also interfere with the formation of relationships that would reduce aggressive behaviors (Barkan 1997). Third, the evidence suggests that social factors somehow mediate the influence of hormones.

Biology appears to play some role in aggression. But exactly how it operates is unclear, and the evidence suggests that something outside human beings "triggers" the aggressive response. We will now consider explanations of aggression that focus on these triggers.

SITUATIONAL AND SOCIAL EXPLANATIONS OF AGGRESSION

Situational and social factors offer another explanation for aggression. One of these explanations focuses on the relationship between high temperatures and aggressive behavior. The other examines the effect that one situation can have on a later incident.

Temperature and Aggression

I pray thee, good Mercutio, let's retire;
The day is hot, the Capulets abroad,

TABLE 10.3 **DELINQUENCY AMONG MALE MILITARY VETERANS**

Numbers show the percentage of normal- and high-testosterone men engaging in the different behaviors.

| | Testosterone Level | | |
Behavior	Normal	High	Risk Ratio
Childhood delinquency	12%	18%	1.5
Adult delinquency	10	23	2.3
Hard drug use	10	25	2.5
Marijuana use	22	48	2.2
Alcohol abuse	12	16	1.3
Military AWOL	6	13	2.2
Many sex partners	23	32	1.8

Source: Dabbs 2000, 82.

And, if we meet, we shall not 'scape a brawl,
For now, these hot days, is the mad blood
stirring

—William Shakespeare, *Romeo and Juliet*

William Shakespeare linked weather conditions with hot tempers and aggression in a number of his plays, including *King Lear* and *The Merchant of Venice*. He was not the only one to believe that hot temperatures could lead to violent outbursts. Cicero wrote, "The minds of men do in the weather share, dark or serene as the day's foul or fair" (cited in Geen and Donnerstein 1998, 248). Do tempers flare when temperatures rise? The first attempt to scientifically test this commonly held belief involved the analysis of various types of crimes by weather conditions in the late nineteenth century (Anderson 1989). As other explanations of aggression began to attract attention, research on the effect of weather conditions declined. Interest in weather effects returned when riots erupted in a number of U.S. cities in 1967.

Seemingly recognizing the wisdom of ancient philosophers and medieval writers, the media soon associated the violence that spread from city to city with "the long hot summer" (Berkowitz 1993).

Does scientific evidence support the temperature hypothesis? A number of studies indicate that an association does exist between temperature and aggression (Baron and Ransberger 1978). In an extensive analysis of seventy-nine riots that occurred in U.S. cities between 1967 and 1971, Merrill Carlsmith and Craig Anderson (1979) found a clear relationship between temperature and aggressive acts: Riots were more likely to break out on hot days than on cool ones (see Figure 10.2). Researchers have also shown a pattern between violent crimes and hot temperatures in a number of American cities, including Minneapolis (Cohn 1993), Dallas (Harries and Stadler 1988), Indianapolis (Cotton 1986), Dayton (Rotton and Frey 1985), and Houston (Anderson and Anderson 1984). It has also been shown that violent crimes occur more frequently in hotter cities and regions

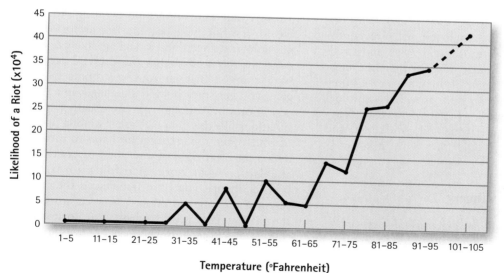

FIGURE 10.2

Temperature and Aggression

The likelihood of urban violence increases as temperatures rise.
Source: Adapted from Carlsmith and Anderson 1979.

(Anderson and Anderson 1998; Anderson et al. 2000). Hot temperatures are also linked to aggressive behaviors in sports (Reifman, Larrick, and Fein 1991). One study showed that the number of batters hit by balls during major league baseball games rose steadily with the temperature.

Do these natural studies prove that hot temperatures cause people to lose their tempers, to riot, and to commit violent crimes? This interpretation fails to recognize that correlation does not prove causation. In fact, we could make a different argument—that hot weather produces a number of effects: It not only makes people more irritable, but it also draws them out of their hot homes into the streets, where they gather with other angry people. Natural studies can only suggest that heat increases aggression in people. But laboratory experiments, which allow researchers to tightly control other influences, provide additional evidence to support the temperature-aggression hypothesis. In one laboratory experiment, William Griffitt and Roberta Veitch (1971) compared students who completed a questionnaire in a room at normal room temperature to students who did so in a room heated to 90 degrees. Students in the high-temperature condition reported feeling more aggressive and tired. They also expressed more hostility (harsher judgments) toward a stranger of the same sex. A number of other experiments have provided additional support for these findings (Bell 1980; Rule, Taylor, and Dobbs 1987; Anderson, Anderson, and Deuser 1996).

Excitation Transfer Theory

It is all too common in today's sport world for physical aggressiveness to escalate into violence, psychological aggressiveness into hostility toward opponents, and competitiveness into a callous preoccupation with outcome, or "winning at all costs." On our lust for success and our covetousness of physical prowess that we associate with it, we Americans often tolerate brutality and idolize savage bullies.

—William Dudley, *Sports in America*

Why is it that sports events often turn into mayhem on the field, court, or ice? **Excitation transfer theory** offers one explanation. Dolph Zillmann (1983) was the first to propose that arousal that is produced in a particular situation can be transferred later to another incident. Zillmann grounded his theory in Stanley Schacter and Jerome Singer's theory of emotions (1962), which proposed that people search for clues in the environment to understand what they are feeling (see Chapter 4). Their research showed that when someone in close proximity is acting silly, people who do not understand their feelings tend to attribute their own arousal to euphoria. If, on the other hand, someone close by is angry, people are likely to assume that they are also angry.

Zillmann extended this idea to explain how arousal at one point in time can influence an aggressive response at a later time. Exercise can cause the kind of arousal that Zillmann describes. Consider how you feel after participating in an aerobics class. If you have pushed yourself to have a good workout, you may feel and observe the physiological effects: increased heart rate, elevated blood pressure, rapid breathing, and sweating. After resting for a while, you become less aware of these physiological effects and in fact are likely to be unaware of the arousal that the exercise produced. Now suppose that on your way home from the gym, you get stuck behind a teenager in a driver's education car. Although you are usually patient in situations like this, you feel anger welling up inside of you. When the teenager hesitates to turn when he has the clear right of way, you lose your temper and lay on your horn. According to excitation transfer theory, you have transferred the residual physical excitation produced by your workout to the driver's education student. You do not make that connection, however, because you are most aware of the current situation, not the aerobics class that ended thirty minutes ago.

A number of studies have shown that people do transfer arousal created in one situation to a later incident. The sources of arousal included physical exercise (Zillmann, Katcher, and Milavsky 1972), violent movies (Zillmann 1971), erotica

(Donnerstein and Hallam 1978), and noise (Donnerstein and Wilson 1976).

Frustration–Aggression Theory

Have you ever lost your last quarter in a vending machine? If you were really hungry, you probably kicked the machine. Every so often, we find ourselves so frustrated that we lose our temper. It is a common experience. Social psychologists have been examining the link between frustration and aggression for more than six decades (Dollard et al. 1939).

John Dollard and his colleagues at the Yale University Institute of Human Relations formulated the first theory of aggression to focus on frustration. In their 1939 monograph, *Frustration and Aggression*, they argued that a few basic ideas could explain nearly all kinds of human aggression (Berkowitz 1989). The basic postulate of **frustration-aggression theory** stated that "Aggression is always a consequence of frustration" (Dollard et al. 1939, 1). **Frustration** was "an interference with the occurrence of an instigated goal-response at its proper time in the behavior sequence" (7). In other words, frustration occurs when something prevents us from enjoying an expected reward (see Box 10.2).

Frustration was the key to understanding aggression, according to these researchers. To stress this point, they clarified their statement further, saying that "the occurrence of aggressive behavior always presupposes the existence of frustration and, contrariwise, that the existence of frustration always leads to some form of aggression" (Dollard et al. 1939, 1). What is more, if an individual does not relieve his frustration through an act of aggression, it lingers within the person, disposing him to future aggression.

Frustration-aggression theory claims that people tend to direct their aggression toward the primary source of their frustration. In some cases, however, we direct it toward another target, a process called **displacement**. This is likely to occur if we fear retaliation from the person who is the actual source of frustration. In some cases, this

The excitation transfer model of aggression suggests that the arousal that people experience at sporting events can be linked to an aggressive incident later.

might be a person in a position of authority. Consider a student who claims that her professor gives unfair exams and blames him for her poor grades. Although the professor is the primary source of her frustration, confronting him directly might cause him to lower her grade even further. Frustration-aggression theorists argue that her frustration will continue to build and that eventually she will relieve it by displacing her aggression on a safe target. It might be her roommate, a close friend, or even a pet. This innocent victim becomes a **scapegoat**.

Can the explanation for acts of aggression be as simple as frustration-aggression theory suggests? Is frustration the key? A number of studies provide evidence to support the basic frustration-aggression hypothesis. In a classic experiment, researchers compared how children behaved when their desire to play with attractive toys was blocked (Barker, Dembo, and Lewin 1941). Children were shown a room full of attractive toys. The researchers let children in one group play with the

BOX 10.2	FRUSTRATION: THE EFFECT OF THWARTED EXPECTATIONS

Evils which are patiently endured when they seem inevitable become intolerable when once the idea of escape from them is suggested.

— Alexis de Tocqueville,
The Old Regime and the French Revolution

The concept of frustration can be understood in many ways. In their original definition of frustration, Dollard and his colleagues (1939) emphasized the importance of people's expectations. Leonard Berkowitz (1993) clarified what they meant, saying that "they basically defined frustration as an external condition that prevents a person from obtaining the pleasures he or she had expected to enjoy" (31). He further pointed out that the absence of a reward does not amount to frustration.

According to Berkowitz (1993), hopelessness does not create frustration; it is rather the expectation of improved conditions that causes it. This explains why deprivation alone is not likely to cause social unrest or even a revolution. Alexis de Tocqueville, a respected observer of nineteenth-century American society, pointed out that citizens will "patiently endure" hardship when they expect nothing more. They become angry when the promise of something better—a desired goal—is thwarted. Applying de Tocqueville's argument to the conflict that took place in Tiananmen Square in Beijing, China, in 1989, Berkowitz (1993, 32) wrote:

> The student protests in China in May and June of 1989 can certainly be understood this way. The government's economic liberalization and the introduction of western technology had awakened the young people's hope for political liberalization. The political repression which they had previously suffered in silence became an evil which they could no longer accept.

toys immediately. They allowed children in the other group to look at the toys but made them wait twenty minutes before they could play with them. The results of this experiment showed that the children who had to wait to play with the toys were more destructive with them than the children who were allowed to play with the toys immediately.

Naturalistic studies also support the link between frustration and aggression (Hovland and Sears 1940; Hepworth and West 1988). In an examination of real-world data, Hovland and Sears (1940) analyzed the relationship between cotton prices and the number of black lynchings in the southern United States between 1882 and 1930. They found that lower cotton prices were correlated with more lynchings. Viewing this as evidence supporting the frustration-aggression hypothesis, they argued that a drop in cotton prices produced frustration in white southerners. The subsequent lynching of black southerners was a consequence of that frustration. They became the scapegoats.

Criticisms of Frustration–Aggression Theory

Although research provides support for frustration-aggression theory, critics fault the absolute nature of its propositions. Does aggression *always* result from frustration? Does frustration *always* lead to aggression? Critics also question the proposition that acts of aggression function like a valve to reduce built-up frustration and further aggression. Do these criticisms have any merit? Let us consider each one in turn.

Does Aggression Always Result from Frustration? Critics point out that many factors other than frustration may account for human aggression (Berkowitz 1993; Baron and Richardson 1994). For example, the aggression of the terrorists who attacked the United States on September 11, 2001, presumably resulted from their commitment to a holy war. Likewise, soldiers who carry out the orders of their superiors to bomb enemy targets are not necessarily engaging in acts of aggression that result from frustration. They may result from a sense of duty, patriotism, or even the prospect of attaining the status of a war hero (Baron and Richardson 1994). Similarly, teenage boys may engage in acts of violence as part of an initiation rite for gang membership, not from some kind of frustration. As these cases illustrate, aggression does not necessarily result from the blocking of goal-directed behavior. Instead, it can result from other desires and needs: money, status, acceptance, even sadistic tendencies (Baron and Richardson 1994).

Does Frustration Always Lead to Aggression?

Social psychologists also point out that frustrated people do not always respond by physically attacking or verbally abusing others (Baron and Richardson 1994). Consider students who start college with the dream of becoming a doctor. Reaching this goal is difficult. It may be blocked by poor grades, personal problems, or a lack of financial resources. When students recognize that their goal is blocked, they react in different ways. Some may feel defeated, discouraged, or disheartened; they may lose interest in school altogether. Others may feel relieved. Some students may show resilience and change their majors or focus on other goals.

Although frustration may lead to aggression, studies show that aggression is only one of many kinds of responses people have (Berkowitz 1969). Studies also show that when people interpret the cause of frustration as justified or unintentional, they are less likely to respond with aggression. People who do respond to frustration with aggression have often learned to respond that way and are prompted to do so by cues that trigger aggressive behavior (Carlson, Marcus-Newhall, and Miller 1990).

Do Acts of Aggression Function like a Valve to Reduce Built-Up Frustration and Further Aggression?

According to frustration-aggression theory, "Any act of aggression is a catharsis that reduces the instigation to all other acts of aggression" (Dollard et al. 1939, 53). We have all experienced **catharsis** when we have given in to the need to "blow off some steam" or to "get something off

our chest." Catharsis alleviates pressure building within us, providing a satisfying feeling of relief.

The idea that we can alleviate bottled-up emotions is not new (Baron and Richardson 1994). Aristotle claimed that "exposure to emotion-provoking stage drama could produce a vicarious 'purging' of the emotions" (321). Freud also referred to the process of catharsis, suggesting that it released pent-up psychic tension. The popularity of this concept, however, appears to come from the explanation that Dollard and his colleagues attached to it in the original version of frustration-aggression theory (Baron and Richardson 1994).

The notion that venting anger could reduce future acts of aggression led many psychotherapists to encourage their patients to express their hostile feelings (Baron and Richardson 1994). Support for the idea was so strong in the 1960s that one popular book claimed that "couples who fight together are couples who stay together—provided they know how to fight properly" (Bach and Wyden 1970, 1). This approach to relationships reflected the philosophy of the encounter group movement, which encouraged people to throw off their inhibitions and just let it all out. Some therapists believed that punching pillows, smashing objects, or hitting the target of their frustration with a foam bat would reduce the urge to act aggressively (Howard 1970; Berkowitz 1973). Others encouraged verbal aggression. In his audiotaped course on dating, Bach told his female audience, "Don't be afraid to be a real shrew, a real bitch! Get rid of your pent-up hostilities! Tell them where you're really at! Let it be total vicious, exaggerated hyperbole!" (quoted in Straus 1974, 13).

Critics were quick to point out that no scientific evidence supported this approach (Straus 1974). In fact, several reviews of the evidence for catharsis concluded that it was simply a myth (Hokanson 1970; Berkowitz 1973; Steinmetz and Straus 1974). Israel Charney (1974, 52) claims that "fighting fairly" may be only a modern psychological version of blood-letting—harmless but useless in some cases and injurious in others.

Counter to the catharsis proposition, research suggests that expressing anger and hostility actually increases conflict (Straus 1974; Geen, Stonner, and Shope 1975). In a study of 2,143 couples, Straus and his colleagues found clear evidence that verbal aggression produces an escalation in aggression. Couples who engaged in little or no verbal aggression reported little or no violence. In contrast, over 80 percent of the most verbally aggressive couples had engaged in at least one physical fight during the year of this study (Straus, Gelles, and Steinmetz 1980, 169).

Cues for Aggression

People who do respond to frustration with aggression have often learned to respond that way (Carlson, Marcus-Newhall, and Miller 1990). Leonard Berkowitz (1965) argued that cues in the environment play a role in determining the kind of response that follows frustration. Weapons such as guns, knives, or baseball bats may signal the kind of response that should follow. According to Berkowitz (1981, 11), "The finger pulls the trigger, but the trigger may also be pulling the finger." The anger that accompanies frustration may dispose an individual toward an aggressive response. But the actual response that results is influenced by the presence or absence of aggression cues.

Berkowitz demonstrated the effect of weapons as cues for aggression in an experiment conducted at the University of Wisconsin (Berkowitz and Le Page 1967). Each subject was paired with a confederate and told that the study concerned physiological reactions to stress. The partners would observe how the other one performed on an assigned task and then evaluate it by delivering from one to ten electric shocks. The subject was then led to a separate room to work on the problems. After they finished, subjects received either one shock or seven shocks from the confederate as an indication of how well they had solved the problem. The researchers reported that subjects who received seven shocks were angered by the confederate's evaluation as well as by the mildly painful shock that it brought.

In the next part of the experiment, the subject evaluated the confederate's performance on a task. At this point, he was taken to a "control room," where he would deliver the shocks to indicate his evaluation of the confederate's performance on the task. The researchers created three conditions to determine how weapons might influence an aggressive response. In one condition, they placed a 12-gauge shotgun and a .38-caliber revolver on the table next to the shock key. In another condition, two badminton racquets and some shuttlecocks were placed on the table. To explain why these objects were lying on the table, the experimenter pushed them aside and said that someone else must have left them there after another experiment. This explanation was not given to subjects in a third condition, who saw no objects on the table next to the shock key.

The results support Berkowitz's aggression cue hypothesis (see Figure 10.3). The effect of weapon cues on subjects who had been angered by a confederate was clear. These subjects responded with the most aggressive behavior, delivering on average 5.8 shocks to the confederates who had provoked their anger. In contrast, subjects in the nonangry conditions delivered the least number of shocks.

Berkowitz's Reformulated Theory: The Cognitive Neoassociation Model

Fifty years after the formulation of the original aggression-frustration hypothesis, Berkowitz (1989) argued that it had largely withstood the test of time. The bulk of the research provided strong evidence consistent with the hypothesis first proposed by Dollard and his colleagues (1939). He viewed the core proposition of this theory as valid but offered a major modification. As he explained, "Frustrations are aversive events and generate aggressive inclinations only to the extent that they produce negative affect" (Berkowitz 1989, 71). From his perspective, frustrations were but one kind of unpleasant event that could ultimately result in aggression. Other kinds of unpleasant events that might lead to unpleasant feelings (negative affect) include personal insults, stress, or physical pain. According to this reformulation, frustration did

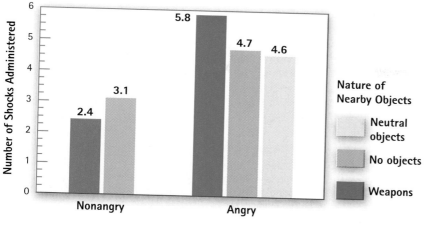

FIGURE 10.3

Berkowitz's Aggression Cue Theory

Mean number of shocks given as a function of the presence of weapons.

Source: Berkowitz 1993, 72.

not lead to aggression. Instead, the negative affect that was created by an unpleasant experience did so (see Figure 10.4).

According to Berkowitz's **cognitive neo-association model**, when people feel bad, they tend to be angry and aggressive. This idea seems simple, but the relationship between negative affect and open aggression is actually complex (Berkowitz 1993). In Berkowitz's model, a person passes through several stages after experiencing an unpleasant event. The negative feelings that are produced by an unpleasant event initially evoke feelings, thoughts, and memories that activate an impulse to either flee the situation or to stay and fight—the "flight or fight response." Several factors influence a person's impulse to escape or remain in a situation, including one's genetic makeup, past learning, and perceptions about the safety or danger of the situation.

This *primitive associational reaction* determines the specific path that individuals will take from here. People who proceed down the path of aggression-related tendencies will experience primitive or rudimentary feelings of anger; those who proceed down the path of escape-related tendencies will experience rudimentary fear. These primitive feelings are transformed in the next stage by "higher-order" thinking. At this point, a

number of factors begin to play a role in "constructing" a person's emotional experience. For example, to determine the appropriate emotional response for a situation, people may consider past experiences or social rules. Their thoughts are also likely to involve attributions for the causes of their feelings, ideas about the nature of an emotional response, and anticipation of the consequences of an event. The higher-order thinking at this stage differentiates the rudimentary feelings of the previous stage. Some of them become more intense; others are suppressed.

Berkowitz's reformulation of aggression-frustration theory offers new ways of explaining aggression. For one thing, it provides an alternative explanation for aggression that appears to result from frustration. Other researchers have used it to revise the explanation of temperature effects on aggression (Anderson, Anderson, and Deuser 1996). And it promises to explain the connection between media violence and aggression (Berkowitz 1984; Geen and Donnerstein 1998)

Learning Theories of Aggression

Albert Bandura proposed one of the most popular explanations of how people learn aggression (1973,

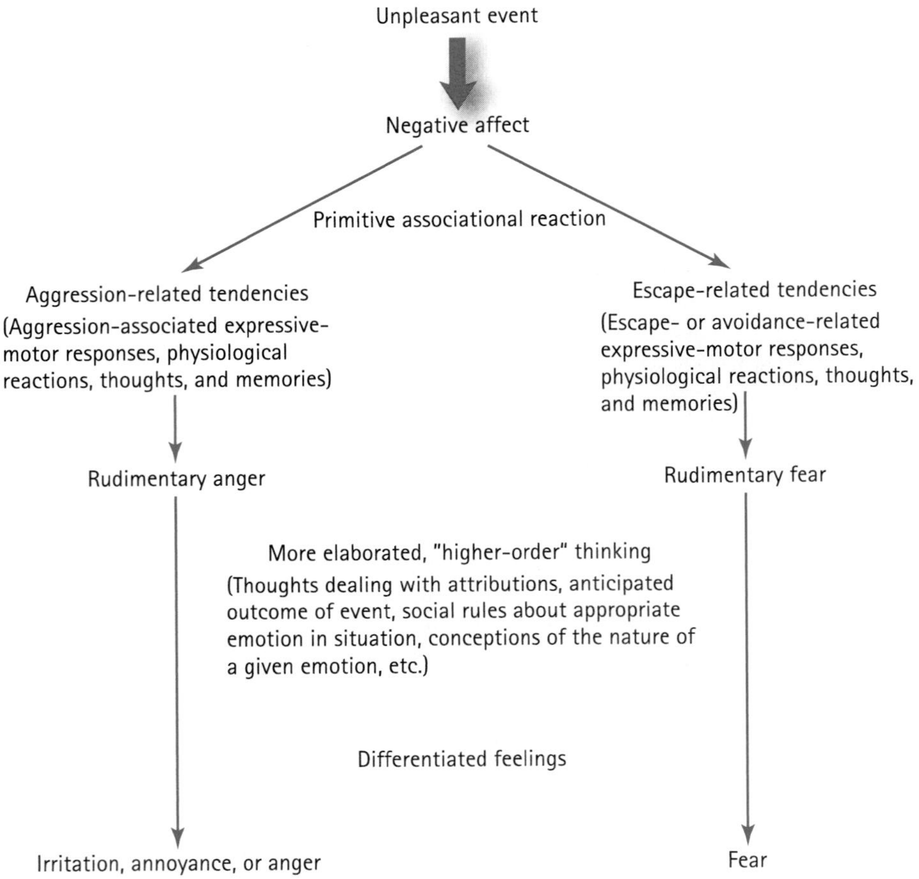

Unpleasant event

Negative affect

Primitive associational reaction

Aggression-related tendencies
(Aggression-associated expressive-
motor responses, physiological
reactions, thoughts, and memories)

Escape-related tendencies
(Escape- or avoidance-related
expressive-motor responses,
physiological reactions, thoughts,
and memories)

Rudimentary anger

Rudimentary fear

More elaborated, "higher-order" thinking
(Thoughts dealing with attributions, anticipated
outcome of event, social rules about appropriate
emotion in situation, conceptions of the nature of
a given emotion, etc.)

Differentiated feelings

Irritation, annoyance, or anger

Fear

FIGURE 10.4

Berkowitz's Cognitive Neoassociation Theory

Source: Berkowitz 1993, 57.

1983). According to his social learning theory (see Chapter 6), children learn to behave in aggressive ways in the same way that they learn other social behaviors—both through direct experience and by observing models. Bandura claimed that a complete explanation of aggressive behavior involves three questions: How is aggression acquired? How is aggression instigated? And how is aggression regulated? Table 10.4 shows each of these components in detail.

Acquiring Aggressive Behavior

Like any other social behavior, aggression involves the acquisition of "intricate skills that require extensive learning" (Bandura 1983, 4). Consider prize fighters. Recognizing the skills that he had acquired and developed through rigorous training, Mohammed Ali promoted himself, proclaiming, "I float like a butterfly, sting like a bee." No one would deny that Ali was born with athletic gifts

TABLE 10.4	BANDURA'S SOCIAL LEARNING THEORY

Aggression is *acquired* through:

    Biological factors (e.g., hormones, neural systems)

    Learning (e.g., direct experience, observation)

Aggression is *instigated* by:

    Influence of models (e.g., arousal, attention)

    Aversive treatment (e.g., attack, frustration)

    Incentives (e.g., money, admiration)

    Instructions (e.g., orders)

    Bizarre beliefs (e.g., delusions of paranoia)

Aggression is *regulated* by:

    External rewards and punishments (e.g., tangible rewards, negative consequences)

    Vicarious reinforcement (e.g., observing others' rewards and punishments)

    Self-regulatory mechanisms (e.g., pride, guilt)

Source: Baron and Richardson 1994, 32.

and the physical ability to become a world champ, but he had to learn the fancy footwork that would make him an elusive target as well as the punches that would knock out his opponent. Learning aggression is part of the training required for many other occupations. As part of their basic training, soldiers learn how to fight, fire weapons, and drop bombs. Policemen are trained to physically apprehend and, if necessary, shoot an armed and dangerous suspect. Human beings learn these kinds of

Law enforcement officials learn aggressive behavior as part of their occupational training.

BOX 10.3   LESSON FROM A SOUTH BRONX CHILDHOOD

Down the block from us was a playground. It was nearby and we didn't have to cross a street to get there. We were close in age. My oldest brother, Daniel, was six, next came John, who was five, I was four, and my brother Reuben was two. Reuben and I were unable to go to the playground by ourselves because we were too young. But from time to time my two oldest brothers would go there together and play.

I remember them coming inside one afternoon having just come back from the playground. There was great excitement in the air. My mother noticed right away and asked, "Where's John's jacket?"

My brother John responded, "This boy . . . this boy he took my jacket."

Well, we all figured that was the end of that. My mother would have to go and get the jacket back. But the questioning continued. "What do you mean, he took your jacket?"

"I was playing on the sliding board and I took my jacket off and left it on the bench, and this boy he tried to take it. And I said it was my jacket, and he said he was gonna take it. And he took it. And I tried to take it back, and he pushed me and said he was gonna beat me up."

To my mind John's explanation was clear and convincing, this case was closed. I was stunned when my mother turned to my oldest brother, Daniel, and said, "And what did you do when this boy was taking your brother's jacket?"

Daniel looked shocked. What did he have to do with this? And we all recognized the edge in my mother's voice. Daniel was being accused of something and none of us knew what it was.

Daniel answered, "I didn't do nuthin'. I told Johnny not to take his jacket off. I told him."

My mother exploded. "You let somebody take your brother's jacket and you did nothing? That's your younger brother. You can't let people just take your things. You know I don't have money for another jacket. You better not ever do this again. Now you go back there and get your brother's jacket."

My mouth was hanging open. I couldn't believe it. What was my mother talking about, go back and get it? Dan and Johnny were the same size. If the boy was gonna beat up John, well, he certainly could beat up Dan. We wrestled all the time and occasionally hit one another in anger, but none of us knew how to fight. We were all equally incompetent when it came to fighting. So it made no sense to me. If my mother hadn't had that look in her eye I would have protested. Even at four years old I knew this wasn't fair. But I also knew that look in my mother's eye. A look that signified a line not to be crossed.

My brother Dan was in shock. He felt the same way I did. He tried to protest. "Ma, I can't beat that boy. It's not my jacket. I can't get it. I can't."

My mother gave him her ultimatum. "You go out there and get your brother's jacket or when you get back I'm going to give you a beating that will be ten times as bad as what that little thief could do to you. And John, you go with him. Both of you better bring that jacket back here."

Source: Canada 1995, 4–5.

aggressive behaviors; they acquire the knowledge and skills to act in these ways. It is not something they are born with.

Rewarding Aggression. One of the ways that aggression is acquired is by reinforcement. When aggressive behavior is rewarded, the tendency to repeat similar behavior is increased. Bullies are often directly reinforced for aggressive behavior. Toys, candy, and money are often the rewards they seek by pushing and punching other children. Parents

of the bully's victims often teach their children how to retaliate (see Box 10.3). To reinforce the lesson, parents are likely to admire and praise their son for sticking up for himself when a bully tries to push him around. A number of studies show that material rewards such as toys, candy, and money reinforce and increase aggressive behavior (Borden, Bowen, and Taylor 1971; Buss 1971; Borden and Taylor 1976). Intangible rewards like social approval or status also serve as effective incentives for aggression (Gentry 1970; Geen and Stonner 1971).

Children not only learn how to aggress against other people, but also learn when to aggress and against whom they can aggress. Parents serve as the primary models for aggressive behavior. Other models include teachers, siblings, peers, and even characters that appear in mass media.

Modeling Aggression. Albert Bandura and his colleagues demonstrated how children learn aggression through observation in a series of classic experiments that involved an inflatable Bobo doll (Bandura, Ross, and Ross 1961, 1963; Bandura 1965a). In one experiment, a child was brought to a room where he could observe an adult assembling Tinkertoys. In the experimental condition, the adult stood up after one minute and walked over to the Bobo doll. He then began to attack the doll— he punched it, sat on it, and hit it with a mallet. As he engaged in this kind of aggressive behavior, the adult also yelled at the doll: "Sock him in the nose!" "Kick him!" "Pow!" The adult modeled this kind of behavior for nine minutes while the child watched. In the control condition, the adult played quietly with the Tinkertoys, totally ignoring the Bobo doll. Not long after the children had observed the adult model, they were taken to another room where they saw a variety of interesting toys. At this point, the researcher attempted to frustrate the children by telling them that these were her best toys and that she had to "save them for the other children." The children were then taken to another room where they were left to play with another assortment of toys, including the Bobo doll.

During this part of the experiment, the researchers rated the amount of aggressive behavior displayed by children in the two conditions. The results showed that children who had observed an aggressive adult attack and shout at the Bobo doll tended to imitate what they had observed. They kicked, punched, and hit the doll. And they shouted verbal assaults.

Families provide the primary models for aggressive behavior (Baron and Richardson 1994). Children who witness physical violence between their parents reenact what they learn in other relationships, especially their own marriages. In his book *The Violent Home*, Richard Gelles (1987) presents evidence showing that children who see parents engage in physical violence are more likely than those who do not to get involved in physical fights with their own spouses later.

Researchers who study family violence call the transmission of aggressive behavior from one generation to the next the "cycle of violence" (Steinmetz 1977; Emery 1982; Kruttschnitt, Heath, and Ward 1986; Widom 1989). Suzanne Steinmetz (1977) describes the cycle of violence as follows:

> The conflict-resolution methods used by husbands and wives to resolve marital conflict . . . are imitated by their children much in the "monkey see, monkey do" manner when these children interact with their siblings. Furthermore, when these children mature and marry, they appear to use these methods, which are a firmly entrenched part of their behavior repertory, to resolve marital conflict, and, continuing the cycle, transfer this method to their children in the form of the disciplinary techniques they utilize. (118)

Did your parents model aggressive behavior that predisposes you to domestic violence? The Conflict Tactics Scale developed by Murray Straus and Suzanne Steinmetz might give you some idea (see Table 10.5).

FACTORS MEDIATING AGGRESSION

What factors influence decisions about aggressive behavior? We will consider two: social norms and the process of dehumanization.

Social Norms and Aggression

Thou shalt not kill.

An eye for an eye, a tooth for a tooth, a hand for a hand, a foot for a foot.

Spare the rod, spoil the child.

All societies have rules to maintain social order. Certain acts of aggression are regarded so

TABLE 10.5	STRAUS AND STEINMETZ'S CONFLICT TACTICS SCALE

Here is a list of things which your mother and father might have done when they were trying to solve a problem. Taking all disagreements into account, not just the most serious ones, indicate how frequently each of them did the following during a conflict. Using the following code to rate how your mother and father solved the problem: 0 = Never, 1 = Almost Never, 2 = Sometimes, 3 = Almost Always, 4 = Always.

	Mother	Father
Tried to discuss the issue calmly	☐	☐
Did discuss the issue calmly	☐	☐
Got information to support the issue	☐	☐
Brought in someone else to try and help settle things	☐	☐
Argued a lot but did not yell or scream	☐	☐
Yelled, screamed, or insulted each other	☐	☐
Sulked and refused to talk about it	☐	☐
Threw something (but not at the other) or smashed something	☐	☐
Threw something at the other	☐	☐
Stomped out of room	☐	☐
Pushed, grabbed, or shoved the other	☐	☐
Hit (or tried to hit) the other person with something hard	☐	☐
Threatened to hit or throw something at the other	☐	☐
Hit (or tried to hit) the other person but not with anything	☐	☐
Threatened to break up the marriage by separation or divorce	☐	☐

Source: Adapted from Steinmetz 1977, 155.

seriously that they are the subjects of commandments or laws. The biblical commandment says flatly, "Thou shalt not kill." Laws, however, which are backed up by the power of the state, are not always so straightforward. In some cases, murder is a capital crime. But not always. Under some conditions, it is defined as self-defense.

Social norms that are designed to maintain the social order recognize that aggression works two ways. Though aggression may threaten the social order, some forms of aggression are necessary to maintain it. As a result, social norms specify a number of things: who has the right to act aggressively, under what circumstances, and in what form. To illustrate how these norms operate, consider the following examples. The police have the authority to use force in arresting criminal suspects. But they

must follow the rules. If they use unnecessary aggression, they may be accused of brutality. Parents have the right to discipline their children. But social norms specify the difference between acceptable discipline and child abuse. Soldiers are expected to defend their country and are trained to kill the enemy. The rewards for serving their country in this way include promotions, glory, and medals. But murdering innocent civilians is not regarded as legitimate. Soldiers who do so can be court-martialed.

Dehumanizing the Enemy

Look carefully at the face of the enemy. The lips are curled downward. The eyes are fanatical and far away. The flesh is contorted and molded into the shape of monster or beast. Nothing suggests this man ever laughs, is torn by doubts, or shaken by tears. He feels no tenderness or pain. Clearly he is unlike us. We need have no sympathy, no guilt, when we destroy him.

In all propaganda, the face of the enemy is designed to provide a focus for our hatred. He is the other. The outsider. The alien. He is not human. If we can only kill him, we will be rid of all within and without ourselves that is evil. (Keen 1986, 16)

Soldiers justify killing an enemy on the basis of patriotism or the need to defend freedom (Berkowitz 1993). Terrorists may do it in the name of God. But most people—even trained soldiers—find it difficult to do. Yet horrific stories of violence fill the history books. The brutal extermination of millions of Jews during World War II led social psychologists to investigate how ordinary human beings could bring themselves to participate in such extreme forms of brutal aggression. How could ordinary human beings treat other human beings with such ruthless, callous disregard?

One explanation is that inflicting harm is easier when people convince themselves that their victims are subhuman—monsters that deserve to be hurt, even exterminated (Berkowitz 1993). Adolf Hitler's calculated effort to arouse hatred toward the Jewish population of Europe provides a particularly disturbing example of how this can be accomplished. Under the authority of Joseph Goebbels, the Nazi propaganda minister, Fritz Hipler produced a film titled *The Eternal Jew*. As images of swarming rats filled the screen, the film compared them to German Jews, saying that they were carriers of disease and destruction (Williams and Cooper 2002). In analyzing the intended message of this film, one commentator remarked, "When other human beings are compared to rats and vermin that spread disease, it takes no great leap of imagination to know what you're expected to do with the creatures" (326).

Depicting the enemy as vermin is a common propaganda play. In *Faces of the Enemy*, Sam Keen (1986) describes the **dehumanization** effects of

Thinking of the enemy as subhuman creatures who deserve a fate worse than death is encouraged by propaganda that portrays them in "devil terms."

propaganda. The intent is to convince the masses—our side—that unlike us, these others are faceless creatures who are not hurt when struck. They do not fear death or love their children. The enemy is subhuman, lacks individuality, and deserves to be exterminated. Racist stereotypes are particularly effective in portraying the enemy in ways that prevent us from recognizing our own humanity in them. During the Vietnam War, soldiers referred to the enemy in degrading terms: They were "gooks," "dinks," and "slopes."

Dehumanizing the enemy makes it easier to destroy him. Making him human again reverses the effect. Thus, Keen (1986, 26) observed, "front-line soldiers frequently report that when they come on an enemy dead and examine his personal effects—letters from home, pictures of loved ones—the propaganda image fades and it becomes difficult or impossible to kill again."

MEDIA EFFECTS ON AGGRESSION

> In 1995 two men entered a New York City subway, poured a flammable liquid on the clerk sitting inside the toll booth, set him on fire, and then left him trapped inside to burn to death. Was life imitating art? A few weeks earlier, a character named Torch enacted a similar scene in the movie *Money Train.* (Hiebert and Gibbons 2000, 124).

Is media violence harmful to children? Many respected scholars and organizations contend that it is. But what does the research show? In fact, research conducted since the early 1960s provides no clear answer. Feshback and Singer (1971), who conducted the first field study on television and aggression, recognized the difficulty in designing any study of media effects. They wrote:

> The verdict of research on these issues is ambiguous. Clear-cut answers are difficult to provide because the issue is not simply whether violence in television stimulates, reduces, or has no effect upon children's aggression. Many variables may have a

critical bearing upon the effects of exposure to aggression on television. These variables include the type and degree of violence depicted; the overall dramatic context; the outcome of the violence; the personal attractiveness of the aggressor; the justifiability of the aggressive acts depicted; the degree of prior exposure; the age, intelligence, aggressive predisposition, emotional state, and stability of the audience; and the nature of the viewer's aggressive reaction. And this list is by no means exhaustive. (xii)

Social psychologists do recognize one thing. To understand the results of the many studies conducted on media violence, we must carefully consider the particular research method used.

Experimental Studies of Media Violence

Bandura's classic Bobo doll studies in the early 1960s mark the beginning of researchers' investigations into the effects of media violence on children (Bandura, Ross, and Ross 1963; Bandura 1965a). As described earlier in this chapter, some of the Bobo doll experiments involved the direct observation of live models. But Bandura also designed some of the experiments to determine whether children would imitate the aggressive behavior of television models. Instead of viewing actual models, he had children watch filmed scenes of the adult model attacking the Bobo doll.

After they viewed the film, the children were taken to another room where they saw an assortment of toys, including a Bobo doll like the one in the film. The researchers viewed the behavior of the children through a two-way mirror for ten minutes. The results of this experiment showed that children did imitate the aggressive behavior of the televised model when the model was rewarded and when he suffered no consequences. Children who saw the televised model punished for aggressive behavior did not spontaneously imitate him. Bandura did show, however, that they had learned the modeled behavior. When these children were offered rewards to reproduce the modeled behavior, they were able to do so without difficulty.

Leonard Berkowitz (1974) also examined the impact of media violence on aggressive behavior in a number of experiments. In one experiment, he showed how cues in the environment can prompt an aggressive response in individuals who have experienced some kind of frustration (Berkowitz and Geen 1966). At the beginning of the experiment, adult subjects met a confederate who posed as a fellow subject. The researchers intentionally varied his name. One group of subjects was introduced to Bob *Kelly*, another group met Bob *Dunne*, and a third group greeted Bob *Riley*. Shortly after this introduction, the confederate insulted the subject by criticizing his performance on a task. The subjects then viewed a six-minute film clip. Some of them viewed a scene from the movie *Champion*, which showed a boxer named Midge Kelly receive a brutal beating from another boxer named Bob Dunne. Other subjects watched a nonaggressive film clip of a track race. After they watched these films, subjects were then put in a position to administer shocks to the confederate. The researchers were obviously interested in determining whether the name of the confederate would influence the amount of punishment he received from the subjects. They assumed that subjects would associate Bob Kelly with the victim in *Champion*, Midge Kelly. Likewise, they thought subjects would make a connection between Bob Dunne and the boxer Dunne, who had given Kelly the beating. No connection was expected for the name Bob Riley, since no character by the name of Riley appeared in this film.

The results indicated that the name of the confederate did influence the aggressive response of the subjects. As Figure 10.5 shows, the confederate named Bob Kelly received the most shocks. According to Berkowitz and Geen (1966), subjects in this experiment took the opportunity to lash out at the confederate who had insulted them. The association established by a common name strengthened the aggressive response in subjects.

Can the results of laboratory studies be generalized to real life? Some social psychologists cite this as a serious weakness with experimental studies (Freedman 1984). And they identify a number of specific concerns. First, they argue that punching a Bobo doll or pushing "shock" buttons in a laboratory are poor measures of aggression. Subjects may view these behaviors as acceptable, even encouraged by the researchers. In addition, these particular forms of aggression would not lead a subject to fear retaliation or punishment. Subjects might also assume that the researcher approves of the media violence chosen for the experiment. Second, experiments have used films or programs

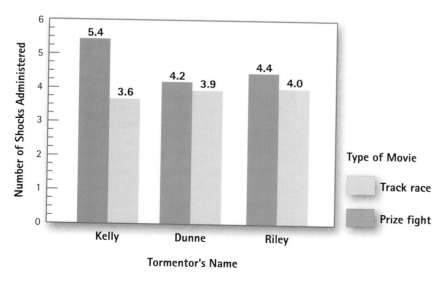

FIGURE 10.5

Media Violence and Aggression

Mean number of shocks given as a function of tormentor's name and type of movie seen.

Source: Berkowitz 1993, 221; data from Geen and Berkowitz 1966.

that were edited to test a specific hypothesis. The specific scenes chosen were viewed out of context and were probably selected to maximize the effect of violent media. What is more, people usually view a mixture of violent and nonviolent programs. Critics argue that one isolated clip does not produce the same effect that a film or program viewed under more typical circumstances does. Finally, critics say that measuring aggression immediately after viewing media violence is not comparable to what happens in the real world.

Field Studies

Concerns about the artificial conditions of laboratory experiments led researchers to design field studies to better approximate real-world experiences. Instead of short media clips, the researchers showed real movies and television programs in their entirety. In some cases, they mixed violent and nonviolent media. And they extended the length of these studies so they could make multiple observations of subjects' behavior after repeated exposure to many different media depictions of violence.

Feshback and Singer (1971) conducted the first field study on the effects of television violence on human aggression. While the typical child in a typical home was the ideal subject for their study, practical considerations led them to draw subjects (all boys) from seven residential schools and institutions located in Southern California and the New York City area. The subjects were assigned to one of two conditions. In the aggressive condition, the boys watched television programs that contained violence such as *Gunsmoke*, *The Untouchables*, and *Have Gun, Will Travel*. Boys in the nonaggressive condition watched programs such as *Leave It to Beaver*, *Bewitched*, and *The Flintstones*. The boys had to select programs from a designated list and were required to watch at least six hours of television a week for six weeks. The researchers evaluated the boys using personality tests and attitude scales at the beginning and end of the six-week period. They also rated the boys' behavior daily during the experimental period.

The results of this study showed that the boys' exposure to aggressive television programs did not increase aggressive behavior. In fact, fighting occurred twice as often in boys who had watched nonaggressive programs as in boys who had watched the aggressive ones. According to Feshback and Singer, watching aggressive television programs actually reduced the aggressive tendencies in certain kinds of boys—those who came from relatively low socioeconomic backgrounds. These results suggest that viewing media violence can have positive effects—that it allows viewers to blow off steam. But critics point out that the violent programs were actually more popular than the nonviolent ones (Freedman 1984). As a result, the higher levels of aggression displayed by subjects who viewed the nonviolent programs may have resulted from greater frustration and disinterest.

In a field experiment conducted by Friedrich and Stein (1973), nursery school children were assigned to three groups to watch specific kinds of television programs. In one group, the children watched violent cartoons (*Superman*), in another they watched neutral television programs, and in a third group they saw prosocial programs (*Mr. Rogers*). The children viewed the programs on twelve days over the course of four weeks. The researchers observed the children during free play time and recorded several measures of aggressive behavior (physical, verbal, object, and fantasy aggression). The results of this experiment showed no significant differences for most measures of aggression for most groups.

Other field studies show that viewing violent media increases aggression. In one three-week field study that was conducted in Belgium, researchers compared the behavior of adolescent boys in a private institution before and after they viewed either aggressive or neutral films (Leyens et al. 1975). During the first week, the researchers observed the boys to establish a baseline for their behavior. The subjects were then divided into two groups. Every night over the course of the next week, one group viewed an aggressive film while the other group viewed a neutral one. Researchers continued to monitor the boys' behavior during this week. Observation of the boys' behavior continued during the third movie-free week, to determine if the exposure to the films during the treatment week had any long-term effects. The results of this study showed that physical aggression increased significantly in subjects who had viewed the aggressive films; subjects who watched the neutral films did not show an increase in aggressive behavior. Two comparable studies conducted later in the United States showed similar results (Parke et al. 1977).

Finally, a study conducted by Wendy Josephson (1987) provides evidence to support not only the claim that violent media increase aggressive behavior but also Berkowitz's theory that cues can trigger aggressive responses. Canadian schoolboys in the second and third grades viewed a fourteen-minute excerpt of a television program that was either violent or nonviolent. The violent program began with a group of snipers killing a police officer in cold blood. The dead officer's partner was then shown joining a SWAT team so he could avenge the slain officer's murder. Right before the SWAT team descended on the snipers, the snipers were shown communicating back and forth with walkie-talkies. At the end of the excerpt, the SWAT team knocked the snipers unconscious or killed them. The nonviolent program showed state highway patrol officers coaching a boys' motocross team. The race was exciting but involved no violence. Prior to viewing these programs, the boys had been frustrated during a short cartoon, when the television picture became distorted and then turned to snow.

After viewing the television programs, the boys were taken to the school gym to play a game of hockey. Before the game started, the boys were interviewed by a referee who explained that this pregame interview would give the observers information about the players so they could do a "play-by-play" of the game "like they do on the radio" (Josephson 1987, 884). Some of the boys were interviewed with a tape recorder; others were interviewed with walkie-talkies. The boys then played a nine-minute hockey game during which four observers evaluated the degree of aggression displayed by each of the boys. Measures of aggression included pushing other players, tripping them, elbowing them, hitting them with a hockey stick, and using abusive language.

The results of Josephson's experiment showed that the boys who showed the greatest degree of aggression were those who had viewed the violent program and had been interviewed with walkie-talkies. Boys who had viewed the violent program and had been interviewed with a tape recorder showed less aggression, and those who watched the motocross race showed the least. These results support Berkowitz's aggression cue theory. The walkie-talkies, which served as the aggression cues, apparently triggered aggressive thoughts that were primed by scenes in the violent television program. What is more, the influence of the violent program and the aggression cue was greater for highly aggressive boys (as judged by their teachers). Boys who were already predisposed to aggressive behavior were most susceptible to these influences.

Correlational Studies

Many correlational studies have also sought to determine how viewing media violence affects human behavior (Stein and Friedrich 1975; Freedman 1984; Friedrich-Cofer & Huston 1986). These studies have involved thousands of subjects from diverse ethnic backgrounds, socioeconomic statuses, and ages (Eron et al. 1972; Singer and Singer 1981; Huesmann 1982; Milavsky et al. 1982; Huesmann, Lagerspetz, and Eron 1984; Singer, Singer, and Rapaczynski 1984). Most of these studies show a positive correlation between viewing media violence and aggressive behavior (Freedman 1984; Friedrich-Cofer and Huston 1986). The meaning of these results, however, depends on two questions. First, what is the causal direction between viewing media violence and aggressive behavior? And second, how might a third variable influence the observed correlation between these two variables of interest?

Longitudinal studies provide one way for researchers to establish causality. These kinds of studies seek to determine whether early childhood

Does viewing violent television programs harm children? The question remains open after more than forty years of research.

socioeconomic status and IQ. This analysis did not reveal the influence of additional variables.

In one notable longitudinal study, Rowell Huesmann and his colleagues (1984) gathered data over a twenty-two-year period of time. Starting in 1960 with 8-year-old subjects who resided in Columbia County, New York, they collected data on subjects' television viewing habits and aggressive behavior at three ages: 8, 18, and 30. The results of this study showed a correlation between early viewing of violent television programs and self-reported measures of aggressive behavior at age 30. The correlation remained even after the researchers controlled for the effects of intelligence, social class, and parenting behavior.

A number of correlational studies have also been conducted outside the United States (Eron 1980, 1982; Huesmann 1982). In collaboration with colleagues in Finland, Poland, Australia, and the United States, Leonard Eron compiled data for a large number of subjects in grades 1 through 5. Although the correlations in countries outside the United States were less consistent, the results still showed a positive correlation between viewing violent television programs and aggressive behavior.

Summary of Research on Media Effects on Aggression

Summarizing the results of the extensive body of research on media violence and aggression is difficult. Some social psychologists are inclined to argue that media violence does harm children. Most argue that there is a relationship between viewing violent media and aggressive behavior (Hearold 1986; Wood, Wong, and Chachere 1991; Comstock and Scharrer 1999). But supporting the argument that viewing media violence harms children on the basis of existing research is difficult. Experiments show that viewing violence in a laboratory increases aggression. Unfortunately, this methodology is subject to many weaknesses. The mixed results of field studies provide little support for either side of the argument. Correlational studies show an association between television violence

viewing of violent media increases the aggressive behavior of an adult. The basic procedure for these kinds of studies involves obtaining measures of television viewing and measures of aggressive behavior. A study of nursery school children by Singer and Singer (1981) illustrates this approach. The parents of 3- and 4-year-old children kept a diary of their children's television viewing along with a record of their behavior. The data were collected over a one-year period in four waves. The results showed that children who watched a lot of television, especially action programs, were more likely to engage in aggressive behavior. Recognizing that a third variable might have influenced this association, the researchers analyzed the influence of

and aggression, but they cannot establish a causal relationship. In summarizing his comprehensive review of the literature, Jonathan Freedman (1986) came to the same conclusion that Feshback and Singer did (1971): The effect of media violence on individuals depends on many variables. Other researchers agree. In their review of the literature, Haejung Paik and George Comstock (1994, 546) concluded, "The findings obtained in the last decade and a half strengthen the evidence that television violence increases aggressive and antisocial behavior, this to a varying degree, depending on the choice of the variables considered."

METHODS FOR REDUCING AGGRESSION

> In the 5,600 years of recorded human history, there have been some 14,600 wars—a rate of more than 2.6 per year. Moreover, it has been estimated that only 10 of the 185 generations of human beings that have lived during this period have known the blessings of uninterrupted peace. (Baron and Richardson 1994, 309)

The record of human aggression does not offer much hope for global peace in the near future. Weapons of mass destruction threaten everything from biological and chemical warfare to all-out nuclear annihilation. Can anything reduce the mounting aggression and violence that we witness every day? Most of the research on aggression to date has focused on its causes rather than on ways that we might reduce it (Baron and Richardson 1994). Though much still needs to be explored in terms of the ways that we might reduce aggression, we can comment on four possibilities: punishment, nonaggressive models, cognitive factors, and incompatible responses.

Punishment

Most criminal justice systems around the world assume that the threat of punishment deters crimes (Baron and Richardson 1994). Although threatened punishment can deter aggression, most

systems of justice fail to achieve this goal and often promote rather than reduce aggression. Why? In order for punishment to work, several conditions must exist. First, the aggressors must believe that punishment for aggressive behavior is a certainty, not just a threat. Second, they must believe that they have little to gain from aggressive behavior. And third, the anticipated punishment must be severe. For actual punishment to work, it must follow aggression immediately and be delivered in a predictable way. In addition, the aggressors must consider it legitimate.

Nonaggressive Models

If aggressive role models increase aggression, can nonaggressive role models, who respond with restraint and calm behavior even when they are provoked, decrease aggression? A number of experiments suggest that nonaggressive models can in fact produce this effect (Baron and Kepner 1970; Baron 1971; Donnerstein and Donnerstein 1976). Research has also shown that prosocial models are effective in encouraging children to act in altruistic ways (Hearold 1986).

Cognitive Factors

Our reactions to other people rely heavily on our perceptions of them. When we respond to people who have provoked our anger, we consider the cause of their behavior—did they intend to hurt us? If we believe that they acted with malice, we are likely to respond in kind. However, if we recognize that they did not intend to hurt us and they provide a reasonable explanation for their behavior, we are not likely to respond with aggression. For this reason, apologies are particularly effective in reducing aggression.

Incompatible Responses

Reactions that are incompatible with aggression can also decrease it (Baron 1983a; Baron 1983b; Baron 1993). When an aggressor identifies with the pain and suffering of his victims, he is likely to experience an empathic response that will reduce his aggression. This kind of reaction is unlikely to occur if the aggressor is very angry or when he believes the attack is justified. Under these circumstances, he may even enjoy watching his victim suffer. Humorous or mildly erotic materials are also responses that are incompatible with aggression and are effective in reducing it.

SUMMARY

1. Aggression refers to behavior that aims to injure someone. Hostile aggression involves an impulsive emotional response that injures a victim. In contrast, instrumental aggression seeks to achieve a particular goal.

2. Early theories of aggression focused on the role that instincts play in programming human beings for aggression. Critics cite many weaknesses with instinct theories of aggression, including the fact that they fail to explain significant cross-cultural differences.

3. Researchers have conducted a variety of studies seeking to determine whether there is a genetic basis for aggression. Studies that compare the criminal records of fraternal versus identical twins provide some evidence for a genetic influence on aggressive behavior. So do studies that examine the criminal records of children and their biological and adoptive parents. They do not, however, identify the specific genetic trait responsible for aggression. It is possible that another trait such as impulsivity or dominance influences aggression.

4. Another biological explanation for aggression focuses on the brain and sympathetic nervous system. Scientists have recognized a link between the amygdala and aggression since the early twentieth century. Research on this connection is limited by ethical guidelines, however.

5. Researchers have also considered how hormones influence aggression. Biology appears to play some role in aggression, but exactly how it operates is unclear. And the evidence suggests that something outside human beings triggers the aggressive response.

6. A number of studies indicate that ambient temperature has an effect on aggression. Riots are more likely to break out on hot days than on cool ones.

7. Excitation transfer theory explains how nonobvious factors can trigger aggression. According to this theory, physiological arousal produced in one situation can be transferred later to another. Studies show that a variety of sources can produce this effect, including physical exercise, violent movies, erotica, and noise.

8. Frustration-aggression theory provides a good explanation for a common experience. When something prevents us from enjoying an expected reward, we feel frustrated and respond with aggression.

9. People who respond to frustration with aggression have often learned to respond that way. And weapons such as guns, knives, or baseball bats may serve as cues in determining their response.

10. Leonard Berkowitz's cognitive neoassociation model takes frustration-aggression theory a step further by stipulating that frustrations are adverse events that generate aggressive inclinations only to the extent that they produce negative affect. Other unpleasant events, such as insults, stress, or physical pain, could also produce negative affect that could lead to aggression. According to Berkowitz, the relationship between negative affect and open aggression is quite complex. His more complicated model offers new ways of explaining aggression.

11. According to Albert Bandura's social learning theory, children learn to behave in aggressive ways in the same way that they learn other social behaviors—through direct experience and by observing role models.

12. Some forms of aggression are necessary to maintain the social order. Social norms specify who has the right to act aggressively, under what circumstances, and in what form.

13. Even when wars are justified, soldiers can find it difficult to kill another human being. One strategy that makes it easier to destroy an enemy is to dehumanize him. Various propaganda techniques are used to accomplish this, including portrayals of the enemy as subhuman beings who lack individuality and who deserve to be exterminated.

14. Although many scholars argue that media violence is harmful to children, research still provides no clear answer. The effect of media violence on individuals depends on many variables.

15. Most of the research on aggression has focused on its causes rather than on ways that we might reduce it. But social psychologists have considered four key strategies: punishment, nonaggressive models, cognitive factors, and incompatible responses.

KEY TERMS

Aggression   282
Hostile aggression   282
Instrumental aggression   282
Concordance   286
Excitation transfer theory   292

Frustration-aggression theory   293
Frustration   293
Displacement   293
Scapegoat   293
Catharsis   295

Cognitive neoassociation
  model   297
Dehumanization   303

CRITICAL REVIEW QUESTIONS

1. Complete the Aggression Questionnaire presented in Table 10.1. Use the theories presented in this chapter to explain your aggression score. For example, describe how you have learned to respond to frustration.

2. Which of the theories presented in this chapter provides the best explanation for school shootings?

3. Is propaganda used today to make it easier to destroy an enemy? Provide some evidence to support your position.

ELEVEN

Prejudice

On June 7, 1998, one of the most vicious hate crimes in recent times occurred in the early morning hours along the dark backroads of Jasper, Texas. Its victim was James Byrd Jr., a 49-year-old black man. Journalists described what happened as a "modern-day lynching" (King 2002).

The warm summer evening started out on a pleasant note for Byrd, who was one of about forty guests attending an anniversary party held by Jimmie Mays and his wife. By all accounts, everyone had fun. Guests ate, drank, danced, and played cards until early morning. Like many of the partygoers, Byrd had a lot to drink and left the party drunk. Friends watched him zigzag across the road as he headed home on foot, but they did not think it necessary to offer him a ride. It was not the first time he had left a party in this state, and he always made it home safely.

At about the same time, another party was ending on the other side of town. But three of the men at that party were just getting started. Anxious to find some excitement elsewhere, they piled into a 1982 Ford pickup truck and took off. With several beers already under their belts, the trio continued to drink beer that was stored in a red-and-white cooler in the back of the truck. At one point, one of them thought it would be fun to wind a chain around a mailbox and drag it down the street. This prank entertained them for a short time.

Then they spotted Byrd stumbling home. Shawn Berry, the owner and driver of the truck, called out to him, asking if he would like a ride. Byrd recognized Berry and decided to take him up on the offer. He jumped into the back of the truck. Up front, one of Berry's passengers, John William King, flew into a rage. Using violent racist language, he ranted and raved about picking up a black man. Berry did not take him seriously and just laughed it off. Moments later, the group stopped at a small convenience store and switched places. Byrd got up front with Berry, while King and Russell Brewer, the other passenger, jumped into the rear of the truck. As they continued their early-morning joy ride, Berry turned off the main road onto an unmarked logging road. After a while, King banged on the roof of the truck and told Berry to stop.

Before he had time to turn off the truck, King and Brewer jumped from the rear and violently pulled Byrd from the cab. They then began to beat him mercilessly. Berry watched in horror but did nothing to stop the attack. As it continued, Brewer grabbed a can of black paint and sprayed it directly into Byrd's face. Finally, a blow to his head knocked Byrd unconscious. He fell to the ground and did not move again. Then King and Brewer grabbed the chain from the back of the truck and attached it to the hitch of the pickup. They fastened the other end around Byrd's ankles. Then all three white men climbed back into the cab of the truck and took off, dragging James Byrd behind them. At one point, Byrd's body came loose. With the intention of recovering it, the driver slammed on the brakes and then backed up—right over Byrd. Someone jumped out and reattached Byrd's mangled body to the chain. Then they took off again, continuing to drag him along. Hurtling from one side of the road to the other, Byrd's body finally hit a culvert, which decapitated him.

Describing what happened, Joyce King (2002, 27) wrote, "What was left of his body was released from the chain near a small black cemetery, holy ground where speechless ancestors witnessed the deed. His dismembered body sent a message to all: You could be next!"

From the beginning, the sheriff investigating this crime knew that it was not just a hit-and-run case. In fact, the evidence showed that it was a violent hate crime. One of the most incriminating pieces of evidence was a lighter inscribed with three interlocking K's. It was also engraved with the word "Possum," which turned out to be the nickname given to King while serving time in prison for burglary. The depth of King's racist hatred was written all over his body. Tattoos he had gotten in prison included a burning cross, a Confederate flag, Nazi swastikas, a baby Jesus with horns, and a black man hanged.

Russell Brewer had befriended King in prison. The initiation rites of prison life had given Brewer a reputation for being a "tough little man" (King 2002, 89). Members of the Confederate Knights of America respected Brewer for his toughness and invited him to join. Brewer accepted the invitation and sealed his allegiance with a bloody thumb print pressed onto an agreement that pledged allegiance to the "sacred principles of Aryan racial supremacy" (King 2002, 89). Brewer realized that membership in the CKA gave him the kind of protection he needed to survive prison life. He was a loyal follower and recruited others for the group. King was his twelfth recruit.

Shawn Berry did not have a reputation for being a racist. In fact, he had grown up with blacks and considered them friends. But Berry did have a rough childhood and got into mischief. He quit school before he made it into the ninth grade and went to work. William Sparks, who would become Berry's probation officer, described him this way: "He was something of an enigma; he had a good work ethic and likable personality, but couldn't stay out of trouble" (King 2002, 85). In fact, his first serious run-in with the law occurred shortly after he had made friends with King. At King's suggestion, they broke into a machine shop and stole cigarettes. They were both sentenced to ninety days in boot camp for the crime. Berry earned the reputation for being unable to say no, of just going along with the bad ideas suggested by others. He did, however, avoid a more serious run-in with King, which had landed King in prison. Although King wrote to Berry while he was serving his sentence, their relationship cooled. Berry was put off by King's racist attitudes and language. Unfortunately, their paths did cross again. And Berry's predilection for getting into trouble and his inability to say no resulted in the tragic death of James Byrd Jr. Berry's involvement in this particular hate crime raised a moral question seldom addressed: How guilty are people who do not actually participate in a violent crime but at the same time fail to stop it?

Hate crimes pose puzzling and disturbing questions. For example, what motivates someone to hate and hurt a complete stranger? And why are particular groups the target of hate crimes? In the case of James Byrd Jr., he knew Shawn Berry, a friendly neighbor. He did not know the other two assailants, who were nevertheless filled with hatred for him simply because he was black. To answer such questions, we must begin by examining the distinguishing feature of all hate crimes—prejudice.

PREJUDICE

What is **prejudice**? Gordon Allport (1979, 6) defined it as "thinking ill of others without sufficient warrant." Its origin can be traced to the Latin word *praejudicium*, which meant to prejudge without knowledge or experience (Feagin and Feagin 2003, 11). Today, the term *prejudice* is commonly used to refer to negative attitudes held about members of certain racial or ethnic groups. Social psychologists emphasize that prejudice exists in people's minds (Schuman et al. 1997; Farley 2000). Thus the concept refers to people's thoughts and feelings rather than their behaviors.

Viewing prejudice in this way provides an explanation for the inconsistencies that we often observe in people's responses to members of different groups (see Box 11.1). Consider an individual who believes that members of a particular group are intellectually inferior to his own group but neither dislikes them nor wants to hurt them. These inconsistencies have led social psychologists to propose that prejudice has three distinct dimensions: beliefs about a group (*cognitive prejudice*), feelings about a group (*affective prejudice*), and behavioral tendencies toward a group (*conative prejudice*) (Kramer 1949; Triandis 1971; Farley 2000). This multidimensional conceptualization of prejudice suggests that one kind of prejudice might be reduced without influencing other kinds (Farley 2000). For example, educational campaigns might change a person's faulty beliefs about members of a

---

BOX 11.1	AN AMERICAN DILEMMA

In 1963, Oscar Handlin wrote a review of Gunnar Myrdal's classic study of race relations in the United States, *An American Dilemma* (1944). He began:

> Few serious studies of American society have been more widely read than Gunnar Myrdal's social-science classic, *An American Dilemma*. Its analysis of the Negro problem in the United States has been a magnet to scholars and a catalyst to political groups. Its recommendations have helped shape the strategy of every organization interested in legislation and in judicial interpretations.

By the end of the twentieth century, Myrdal's classic was still regarded as "one of the most significant pieces of scholarship to come out of this era" (Schuman et al. 1997, 11). The study framed the treatment of blacks in America as a moral issue that focused on cherished American beliefs and values. Pointing out the inconsistency between prejudice and values such as equality, justice, and liberty, Myrdal (1944) wrote:

> The American Negro problem is a problem in the heart of the American. It is there that the interracial tension has its focus. It is there that the decisive struggle goes on. . . . The "American Dilemma," referred to in the title of this book, is the ever raging conflict between, on the one hand, the valuations preserved on the general plane, which we shall call the "American Creed," where the American thinks, talks, and acts under the influence of high national and Christian precepts, and, on the other hand, the valuations on specific planes of individual and group living, where personal and local interests; economic, social, and sexual jealousies; considerations of community prestige and conformity; group prejudice against particular persons or types of people; and all sorts of miscellaneous wants, impulses, and habits dominate his outlook. (xlii)

Educational campaigns attempt to teach tolerance by promoting positive beliefs about members of different races and creeds.

particular group but have no effect on how much the prejudiced person likes them.

STEREOTYPES

The tendency to ignore the distinct traits of individual members of a group is characteristic of each dimension of prejudice (Allport 1979). When this kind of incorrect overcategorization involves beliefs, it is called a **stereotype**. Allport defined *stereotype* as "an exaggerated belief associated with a category" and added that "its function is to justify (rationalize) our conduct in relation to that category" (191). Negative stereotypes typecast members of many groups: The Irish are "lazy drunkards," Jews are "crafty," Italian Americans belong to the Mafia, and blacks are oversexed. These kinds of stereotypes are rooted in social precedents and cultivated in popular culture. But they fail to portray reality and are often gross distortions of it.

Walter Lippmann, a well-respected twentieth-century journalist, offered a widely accepted explanation of why human beings use stereotypes. Describing them as "pictures in our heads," he claimed that "the attempt to see all things freshly and in detail, rather than as types and generalities, is exhausting, and among busy affairs practically out of the question" (1991, 88). He went on to say that "there is neither time nor opportunity for intimate acquaintance. Instead we notice a trait which marks a well known type, and fill in the rest of the picture by means of the stereotypes we carry about in our heads" (89). Lippman viewed stereotypes as the "fortress of our tradition" and argued that culture creates and develops them. He described the process by which this occurred as follows:

> For the most part, we do not first see and then define; we define and then see. In the great blooming, buzzing confusion of the outer world, we pick out what our culture has already defined for us, and we tend to perceive that which we have picked out in the form stereotyped for us by our culture. (81)

Anthropologists have noted that our culture defines the world in a way that favors our own beliefs, values, attitudes, and ways of doing things. William Graham Sumner (1906/1960), a sociologist, referred to this tendency as *ethnocentrism*, describing it as "the view of things in which one's own group is the center of everything, and all others are scaled and rated with reference to it" (27–28). In other words, we tend to view our own group, the **in-group**, in positive terms but to see members of any other group, an **out-group**, in negative terms, as falling short of our own standards. The result is stereotyping and prejudice.

Three studies of Princeton University students illustrate in-group and out-group biases and how they can change over time (Katz and Braly 1933; Gilbert 1951; Karlins, Coffman, and Walters 1969). The procedure in each study required subjects to identify traits that applied to a variety of ethnic groups. The list of traits included adjectives such as *sly, superstitious, ignorant, industrious, reserved, intelligent, talkative,* and *loyal to family ties.* These studies showed several notable trends. For example, the tendency to attach negative stereotypes to blacks declined steadily from 1933 to 1967. By 1967, the percentage of students who picked traits such as *superstitious, lazy, happy-go-lucky,* and *ignorant* to describe blacks had dramatically declined. A similar pattern emerged for several other groups. The frequency of six traits ascribed to Italians declined substantially from 1933 to 1950: *artistic, impulsive, passionate, quick-tempered, musical,* and *imaginative.* The only trait to show an increase was *very religious.* The stereotypes of Chinese as *superstitious* and *sly,* perceptions held by about one-third of the subjects in 1933, had nearly disappeared by 1967. Finally, whereas nearly half of subjects identified Turks as *cruel* in 1933, only 9 percent did so in 1967.

The tendency to view one's own group more positively than an out-group is also reflected in the connotation attached to a particular trait. The perception of an identical trait—whether it implies something positive or negative—depends on membership in either the in-group or an out-group (Merton 1949; Allport 1979; Farley 2000). For example, if you ask people what traits they admire in Abraham Lincoln, they are likely to say *thrift, hard work, ambition, eagerness for knowledge,* and *devotion to human rights.* Yet if you ask people to identify the traits that cause people to dislike Jews, they might give the same list. In this case, however, these same traits come to imply negatives: *Thrift* implies tight-fistedness, *hard work* becomes pushiness, and so on. Robert Merton (1949) made this comparison to argue that stereotypes alone do not explain prejudice (see Box 11.2). As this shows, classification as a member of an in-group or out-group influences an individual's perception of someone as either positive or negative.

HOW PREJUDICE IS LEARNED

One of the simplest explanations of prejudice is that people learn negative attitudes toward members of other groups in the same way they learn other attitudes—through the socialization process. Children are not born with prejudiced attitudes. From birth through childhood, they may be trained to think, feel, and act with hostility toward members of certain groups. The process of acquiring a particular set of attitudes may involve direct reinforcement, punishment, or simply observing a model.

The Socialization Process

Parents who laugh at racist jokes or sexist stereotypes set examples that children are likely to imitate. When children reenact the modeled behavior, their parents may then reinforce prejudice by smiling, laughing, or rewarding it in some other way. Parents may likewise express disapproval if their child expresses positive attitudes toward members of other groups, makes friends with a child of another race, or shows an interest in dating a person outside her own group.

Selective exposure and modeling are two of the most effective ways by which attitudes are acquired (Farley 2000). Parents can deliberately choose to expose their children to a particular set of influences by enrolling them in certain schools, joining exclusive clubs, or putting them in particular after-school programs. This can result in limited experiences within homogeneous groups. The

| BOX 11.2 | MERTON ON "IN-GROUP VIRTUES AND OUT-GROUP VICES" |

So much for out-groups being damned if they don't (apparently) manifest in-group virtues. It is a tasteless bit of ethnocentrism, seasoned with self-interest. But what of the second phase of this process? Can one seriously mean that out-groups are also damned if they do possess these virtues? One can.

Through a faultlessly bisymmetrical prejudice, ethnic and racial out-groups get it coming and going. The systematic condemnation of the out-grouper continues largely *irrespective of what he does*. More: through a freakish exercise of capricious judicial logic, the victim is punished for the crime. Superficial appearances notwithstanding, prejudice and discrimination aimed at the out-group are not a result of what the out-group does, but are rooted deep in the structure of our society and the social psychology of its members.

To understand how this happens, we must examine the moral alchemy through which the in-group readily transmutes virtue into vice and vice into virtue, as the occasion may demand. Our studies will proceed by the case-method.

We begin with the engagingly simple formula of moral alchemy: the same behavior must be differently evaluated according to the person who exhibits it. For example, the proficient alchemist will at once know that the word "firm" is properly declined as follows:

I am firm,

Thou art obstinate,

He is pigheaded.

There are some, unversed in the skills of this science, who will tell you that one and the same term should be applied to all three instances of identical behavior. Such unalchemical nonsense should simply be ignored.

With this experiment in mind, we are prepared to observe how the very same behavior undergoes a complete change of evaluation in its transition from the in-group Abe Lincoln to the out-group Abe Cohen or Abe Kurokawa. We proceed systematically. Did Lincoln work far into the night? This testifies that he was industrious, resolute, perseverant, and eager to realize his capacities to the full. Do the out-group Jews or Japanese keep these same hours? This only bears witness to their sweatshop mentality, their ruthless undercutting of American standards, their unfair competitive practices. Is the in-group hero frugal, thrifty, and sparing? Then the out-group villain is stingy, miserly, and penny-pinching. All honor is due the in-group Abe for his having been smart, shrewd, and intelligent and, by the same token, all contempt is owing the out-group Abes for their being sharp, cunning, crafty, and too clever by far. Did the indomitable Lincoln refuse to remain content with a life of work with the hands? Did he prefer to make use of his brain? Then, all praise for his plucky climb up the shaky ladder of opportunity. But, of course, the eschewing of manual work for brain work among the merchants and lawyers of the out-group deserves nothing but censure for a parasitic way of life. Was Abe Lincoln eager to learn the accumulated wisdom of the ages by unending study? The trouble with the Jew is that he's a greasy grind, with his head always in a book, while decent people are going to a show or a ball game. Was the resolute Lincoln unwilling to limit his standards to those of his provincial community? That is what we should expect of a man of vision. And if the out-groupers criticize the vulnerable areas in our society, then send 'em back where they came from. Did Lincoln, rising high above his origins, never forget the rights of the common man and applaud the right of workers to strike? This testifies only that, like all real Americans, this greatest of Americans was deathlessly devoted to the cause of freedom. But, as you examine the statistics on strikes, remember that these un-American practices are the result of out-groupers pursuing their evil agitation among otherwise contented workers.

Source: Merton 1949, 482–483.

prejudices of models are often acquired without question, and this tends to be particularly effective when children view these models as all-knowing and all-powerful (Allport 1979).

Children who grow up in a prejudiced environment do not question the attitudes they hold; they consider them appropriate (Farley 2000.) And they will not hesitate to express their prejudices (see Blake and Dennis 1943; Richert 1974; Allport 1979; Mielenz 1979; Garcia-Coll and Vazquez-Garcia 1995). Once children have internalized the prejudiced attitudes and beliefs of significant agents of socialization, they become highly resistant to change and are likely to persist through adulthood (Ehrlich 1973). In a study of ethnocentrism and antiblack attitudes in the Deep South in the 1950s, E. T. Prothro (1952) argued that situational, historical, and cultural factors play a more important role in the formation of prejudice than personality factors alone. To test his hypothesis, he designed a study that measured ethnocentric personalities as well as specific antiblack attitudes. His findings showed that while a large proportion of the subjects were low on general ethnocentrism, they still held antiblack attitudes. According to him, these results do not support a personality theory of prejudice but instead suggest that southerners internalized the social norms of their community, which included strong prejudices against African Americans.

Parents are not the only ones to teach children racial attitudes. Other agents of socialization include peers, schools, and mass media. The sociologist John Farley (2000) claims that "society itself can be a powerful teacher of bias" and argues that "the racial attitudes most people learn are the dominant attitudes of their society" (31). Nothing illustrates this process better than the role that popular culture and the media play in creating and perpetuating stereotypes.

The Media as Agents of Socialization

Parents are the most powerful agents of socialization, but the media play a significant role in teaching people about a society's norms, values, and social structure (statuses, roles, groups, and institutions). Newton Minow, former chairman of the Federal Communications Commission, claimed that television ranked alongside home, church, and school as one of the great influences on a child. And he wrote that by the time American children reach the first grade, most of them have spent what amounts to three school years in front of the television set (Minow and Le May 1995, 18). What exactly do children learn from the media? How do the media shape perceptions about particular groups in society? Do the media teach racial attitudes?

To answer these questions, let us first consider how the media influence perceptions of the real world. Walter Lippmann (1922/1991) claimed that the function of news was to "make a picture of reality upon which the citizen can act" (358). Most people today assume that the news, documentary films, and history books accurately portray the "real" world. But critics argue that the media, even the evening news, distort reality. And a growing body of research suggests that the media do not reflect the reality of the social world (Croteau and Hoynes 2003). Some critics say, So what? They argue that most media are not trying to reflect reality. In fact, they are trying to do the opposite—to create a media product that allows audiences to escape reality. Science fiction, for example, is pure fantasy.

The problem is that all media products, even "make-believe fantasies," are vehicles for commenting on the social world (Croteau and Hoynes 2003). In some cases, writers and creators intentionally send messages about racial attitudes in society. Norman Lear's *All in the Family* is perhaps the best example of a program that was designed to raise awareness about racist attitudes in America. But even science fiction programs like *Star Trek* have incorporated messages about race relations into scripts. In one episode, Captain Kirk and Lieutenant Uhuru kissed. It was the first interracial kiss on an American television program (Croteau and Hoynes 2003). Programs like these appear to teach positive lessons about race relations, but they do not always succeed. In fact, research shows that in the case of *All in the Family*, the program was less effective in changing racial attitudes than in reinforcing already existing prejudice (Vidmar and Rokeach 1974). Whereas Norman Lear's intention was to portray Archie as an

The media comment on the social world in ways that produce both positive and negative results. The program *Will and Grace* (top) has been successful in promoting positive messages about diversity. Although this was the intent of the producers of *All in the Family*, many viewers saw Archie Bunker (bottom) as a "lovable bigot."

ignorant bigot, audiences viewed him as a "lovable bigot" (Wilson, Guttierez, and Chao 2003).

If programs that are designed to reduce prejudice actually reinforce it, then how damaging are programs that recklessly cast characters in stereotypical roles? Wilson and Gutierrez (1995) answered this question by first pointing out that stereotyping has been used as a tool in entertainment from the inception of the dramatic arts. They note, for example, that stereotypes are used to telegraph the differences between heroes and villains. Stereotypes are "shortcuts to character development and form a basis for mass entertainment and literary fare" (61). But they argue that when stereotypes are coupled with prejudice, they cause great damage to race relations and human development. Elaborating on this main point, they wrote:

> In the absence of alternative portrayals and broadened news coverage, one-sided portrayals and news articles could easily become the reality in the minds of the audience. Whites might be seen in a wide range of roles in a movie, ranging from villains to heroes. In contrast, Blacks were most often seen as comical mammys, wide-eyed coons, or lazy, shuffling no-goods. There were no alternative portrayals to counter the stereotypes. (44)

MOTIVATIONAL EXPLANATIONS FOR PREJUDICE

World War I inspired scholars to consider the factors that cause human aggression, but it did not lead them to ask why hate was directed toward members of certain groups. This turned out to be a question the world would ask after it learned about the systematic extermination of over six million Jews during World War II. The most influential postwar study to examine this kind of prejudice was conducted by a group of Berkeley researchers that included Theodor Adorno and Else Frenkel-Brunswick, two social scientists who had fled Nazi Germany (Adorno et al. 1950). Adopting the psychoanalytic perspective, they designed a study that attempted to answer two questions (Farley 2000): First, is prejudice associated with a particular personality type? And second, if it is, then how is that kind of personality created?

The Authoritarian Personality

The results of this study of prejudice were published in Adorno and colleagues' 1950 book *The Authoritarian Personality*. As the researchers expected, a set of personality traits was linked to bias against members of out-groups. Overall, they concluded that people with an **authoritarian personality** tended to rigidly adhere to conventional values, to uncritically accept authority figures, to regard weak or different people negatively, and to

think in stereotypical ways. People with an authoritarian personality also tended to view morality in black-and-white ways, as absolutely right or wrong (see Table 11.1).

The psychoanalytical approach taken by Adorno and his colleagues is compatible with two explanations for how prejudice operates: scapegoating and projection. *Scapegoating*, another term for *displacement*, refers to the tendency for people to direct their aggression toward a safe target rather than the real source of their frustration. For example, people who feel frustrated at work are unlikely to verbally or physically abuse their bosses. Instead, they may displace it toward members of a minority group who may seem powerless or unable to retaliate. *Projection* refers to a process that allows individuals to eliminate their own undesirable traits by criticizing others for possessing them. According to this explanation, people who attack members of an out-group for being lazy or stupid are either unable or unwilling to correct these flaws in themselves. By projecting these characteristics onto someone else, they can safely reject their own deficiencies without rejecting themselves. By putting others down, these people elevate themselves. According to Adorno and colleagues, people with authoritarian personalities are particularly likely to engage in scapegoating and projection.

Adorno's research revealed two other patterns linked to authoritarian personalities. First, prejudiced people were sensitive to status. They showed a need to rank other people and to defend their own position. Second, almost all prejudiced people were raised in very strict homes. As children, they were taught to obey their parents without questioning authority and were subject to severe discipline.

Taking all of their findings together, Adorno and his colleagues (1950) described the process by which an authoritarian personality acquires the tendencies for scapegoating and projection:

- Strict, rigid, and demanding parents produce feelings of frustration and aggression in children. This results in part from a child's realization that affection is conditional, that it

TABLE 11.1	THE AUTHORITARIAN PERSONALITY: F-SCALE ITEMS

Adorno and his colleagues (1950) designed a scale to measure the characteristics of people who have an authoritarian personality. They identified nine basic characteristics and developed items to measure each one. Examples for each characteristic are shown here.

1. **Conventionalism: Rigid adherence to conventional values**
   - Obedience and respect for authority are the most important virtues children should learn.
   - A person who has bad manners, habits, and breeding can hardly expect to get along with decent people.
   - The businessman and the manufacturer are much more important to society than the artist and the professor.

2. **Authoritarian submission: Uncritical acceptance of authority**
   - Every person should have complete faith in some supernatural power whose decisions he obeys without question.
   - Young people sometimes get rebellious ideas, but as they grow up, they ought to get over them and settle down.

3. **Authoritarian aggression: Aggressiveness toward people who do not conform to authority or conventional norms**
   - An insult to our honor should always be punished.
   - There is hardly anything lower than a person who does not feel a great love, gratitude, and respect for his parents.

4. **Anti-intraception: Opposition to the subjective or imaginative; rejection of self-analysis**
   - When a person has a problem or worry, it is best for him not to think about it but to keep busy with more cheerful things.
   - Nowadays more and more people are prying into matters that should remain personal and private.

5. **Superstition and stereotypical thinking**
   - Some people are born with an urge to jump from high places.
   - Someday it will probably be shown that astrology can explain a lot of things.

6. **Concern with power and toughness**
   - An insult to our honor should always be punished.
   - People can be divided into two distinct classes: the weak and the strong.

7. **Destructiveness and cynicism**
   - Human nature being what it is, there will always be war and conflict.
   - Familiarity breeds contempt.

8. **Projectivity: Projection outward of unconscious emotions; belief that the world is a wild and dangerous place**
   - Nowadays when so many different kinds of people move around and mix together so much, a person has to protect himself especially carefully against catching an infection or disease from them.
   - Most people don't realize how much our lives are controlled by plots hatched in secret places.

9. **Exaggerated concern with sexual "goings-on"**
   - Sex crimes, such as rape and attacks on children, deserve more than imprisonment; such criminals ought to be publicly whipped or worse.
   - The wild sex life of the old Greeks and Romans was tame compared with some of the goings-on in this country, even in places where people might least expect it.

Source: Farley, John E., *Majority-Minority Relations,* 4th Edition, ©2000. Reprinted by permission of Pearson Education, Inc., Upper Saddle River, NJ.

depends on behavior that is approved by the parent. Children are expected to obey the rules and face severe punishment for their failure to do so. This causes and reinforces a child's fear of parents.

- In these kinds of families, parent-child relationships are defined by dominant and submissive roles. Children are taught to obey and respect authority and to accept society's hierarchical (ranking) system for members of different groups.
- This kind of training produces frustration and aggression, which cannot be directed against the authority figures, who have produced these feelings. As a result, individuals displace their aggression toward safe targets that will not retaliate—members of low-ranking out-groups. This reflects "uncritical acceptance of the in-group and violent rejection of the out-group" (482).
- The emphasis placed on rigid adherence to cultural norms and concern for one's social status cause authoritarian personalities to minimize or deny their own imperfections and faults. Individuals are likely to rid themselves of undesirable traits by projecting them onto members of out-groups.

Critics fault Adorno's research on the authoritarian personality on both methodological and theoretical grounds (Oskamp 1991; Farley 2000). An obvious methodological problem involves three of the four scales that measure the authoritarian personality. The wording of items in these scales is biased toward an "agree" response. Because some respondents, known as yea-sayers, tend to agree with nearly all of the statements they consider, the failure to provide them with an opportunity to "disagree" raises questions about the fairness of these measures (Cohn 1953; but compare Ray 1980). Critics also point out that this theory considers only right-wing or fascist authoritarianism, whereas liberals and radicals may also have authoritarian attitudes (Kirscht and Dillehay 1967; Simpson and Yinger 1985).

Nevertheless, social psychologists recognize that prejudice does meet the needs of certain personality types (Farley 2000). And most of them view scapegoating and projection as processes associated with prejudice. Additional support for Adorno's theory comes from research that continues to show that prejudice is linked to certain personality traits (Altemeyer 1988; Doty, Peterson, and Winter 1991).

Intergroup Competition

Another motivational explanation of prejudice focuses on groups' competition for society's scarce resources. These kinds of theories recognize that only the wealthiest people can afford to live in a penthouse in New York City, that admission to the best schools is limited, and that access to the president of the United States is reserved for powerful people. According to these theories, intergroup competition develops as members of society's dominant group seek to maintain their advantaged position while members of the subordinate group seek greater equality.

Realistic Conflict Theory

According to **realistic conflict theory**, prejudice is a consequence of these groups' competition for scarce resources and power (Le Vine and Campbell 1972). For example, competition between blacks and whites for high-paying jobs causes prejudice when one group perceives the other group as a threat to its own members' chances of achieving that goal. Hostility between groups is likely to grow during periods of high unemployment when competition for a handful of jobs intensifies. However, it can also occur when the economy starts to improve. In this case, even though conditions are getting better for everyone, members of one group may experience greater fortune than members of another group. Although members of the group making slower gains may not consider themselves deprived, they may experience **relative deprivation**. Their perception that the other group is making faster gains than they are contributes to hostility and conflict. For example, social psychologists argue that the "long hot summers" from 1964 to 1968, when riots erupted in cities across the United States, resulted at least in part from perceptions of relative deprivation. From their perspective, black Americans did not see their standard of living improving as quickly as that of whites. Relative deprivation resulted when blacks' high aspirations mixed with their feelings of dissatisfaction (Sears and McConahay 1973).

The Group Position Model

Lawrence Bobo (1999) has proposed an explanation of intergroup competition that emphasizes the relative status positions of groups in a "racialized social order." Bobo's **group position model** is built on Herbert Blumer's (1958) theory of prejudice, which combined ideas from classical prejudice models with a sociological explanation of group relations. Blumer did not reject social learning theories of prejudice, but he claimed that the best explanation of racial prejudice must involve normative ideas about the position of one's own group in society vis-à-vis an out-group. This model's emphasis on group position indicates that prejudice involves the classification of people into racial categories. That, in turn, determines the relationships between members of different groups. One of the unique features of this theory is its focus on the historical development of group relations and the group interests that characterize a racially or ethnically stratified social order.

According to Blumer (1958), the in-group's sense of position in society involves four elements: (1) *group identity*, a belief in the superiority of the in-group (ethnocentrism); (2) *out-group stereotyping*, a view of out-group members as "alien and different"; (3) *preferred group status*, a sense of entitlement to certain rights, resources, statuses, and privileges; and (4) *perceived threat*, a perception that out-group members want a share of the in-group's rights, resources, statuses, and privileges. Leaders play an important role in the development of these beliefs through public debates and political struggles with other groups. Perceptions of group position are not, therefore, fully explained by social learning models of prejudice. Bobo and Hutchings (1996) emphasize that "feelings of competition and hostility emerge from historically and collectively developed judgments about the positions in the social order that in-group members should rightfully occupy relative to members of an out-group" (955).

Bobo's version of the group position model extends Blumer's original model in two ways. First, it broadens the scope of attitudes beyond those of the in-group (dominant group) to include those of the out-group (subordinate group). Second, it focuses on the individual level of perceptions of threat. These modifications stretch the model beyond the assessment of prejudice as simply negative stereotypes or negative feelings.

To test this new model, Bobo and Hutchings (1996) analyzed data from the 1992 Los Angeles County Social Survey (LACSS). Respondents in this study included 625 whites, 483 blacks, 477 Latinos, and 284 Asians. Four measures evaluated respondents' perceptions of threat for scarce social resources. Using a scale ranging from "strongly agree" to "strongly disagree," subjects were asked to respond to the following items:

Job competition: More good jobs for (Asians/Blacks/Hispanics) means fewer good jobs for members of other groups.

Political competition: The more influence (Asians/Blacks/Hispanics) have in local politics the less influence members of other groups will have in local politics.

Housing competition: As more good housing and neighborhoods go to (Asians/Blacks/Hispanics), the fewer good houses and neighborhoods there will be for members of other groups.

Economic competition: Many (Asians/Blacks/Hispanics) have been trying to get ahead economically at the expense of other groups. (958)

This study provided some support for classical theories of prejudice, including social learning theory.

Overall, however, these theories failed to explain the complexity of the results. In summarizing their findings, Bobo and Hutchings argued that Blumer's group position model provided the best explanation.

The results of another study provide additional support for the group position model (Bobo and Garcia 1992; Bobo 1999). In this case, researchers analyzed data from a survey that concerned a heated controversy over the rights of the Chippewa Indians to fish and hunt in Wisconsin. To show how people expressed their own sense of perceived threat, Bobo used several examples from open-ended comments made by three respondents:

> A 40-year-old White male who worked as a machinist said: "Well, I don't know. It seems that the government is just backing them up and we pay for the license and the stocking programs and they seem to be getting ahead of us and away with everything." Or as a 57-year-old White male truck driver saw it: "If they are getting food stamps and welfare coming out of our taxes, I'm paying for them living without working. I'm working for them." Or in the words of a 40-year-old White female who worked as a bookkeeper: "It goes back to the same thing. They get quite a bit handed to them that they're doing [nothing] for. But the middle-class people who work, [they] don't get anything handed to them." (Bobo 1999, 459)

As Bobo pointed out, these perceptions do not necessarily reflect reality. They do, however, illustrate how people react to the feeling that they are losing ground to members of another group.

Social Dominance Theory

Social dominance theory also focuses on the relative status positions of different groups in society. According to this theory, the structures of all human societies tend to resemble systems of group-based social hierarchies (Sidanius and Pratto 1999). A **group-based social hierarchy** is the "social power, prestige, and privilege that an individual possesses by virtue of his or her ascribed membership in a particular socially constructed group such as race, religion, clan, tribe, lineage, linguistic/ethnic group, or social class" (32). The dominant group, which sits at the top of the hierarchy, enjoys a disproportionately large share of valuable social resources such as power, wealth, high social status, the most expensive homes, and the best health care. Subordinate groups at lower levels of the hierarchy have limited access to these valuable resources. In contrast to the dominant group, these groups are relatively powerless, have low social status, and live in modest or miserable housing. Their educational and occupational opportunities are limited, and they have access to relatively poor health care.

A number of social processes maintain this social hierarchy (see Figure 11.1). The most direct influences are aggregated individual discrimination, institutional discrimination, and behavioral asymmetry. *Aggregated individual discrimination* refers to the kind of discrimination that occurs between individuals every day. Discrimination in hiring is an obvious example. Subtle acts, like failing to consider voting for a political candidate because of the individual's race or gender, also fit into this category. *Institutional discrimination* involves rules and procedures that operate in places like courtrooms, banks, hospitals, schools, and retail shops. Four kinds of *behavioral asymmetry* also operate to maintain the social hierarchy. The first kind involves **in-group bias** or ethnocentrism, which is stronger for the dominant group. The second kind refers to **out-group favoritism** or deference, where subordinate group members favor members of the dominant group over their own. The third kind, **self-debilitation**, refers to the self-destructive behavior of subordinate group members, whose response to negative stereotypes results in a self-fulfilling prophecy. And the fourth kind, **ideological asymmetry**, refers to a more subtle kind of influence that operates through legitimizing ideologies that serve to either reinforce or weaken the social hierarchy.

Legitimizing myths also influence the maintenance of a group-based social hierarchy. These myths involve attitudes, values, beliefs, stereotypes, and ideologies that justify the social practices of a

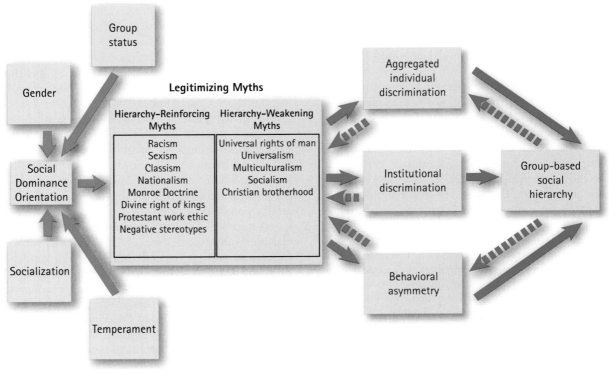

FIGURE 11.1

Social Dominance Theory

Source: Sidanius and Pratto 1999, 40.

particular social system. Some myths reinforce the group-based social hierarchy. Obvious examples include racism, sexism, and classism. The Protestant work ethic, a set of beliefs that operates to stress American values such as individualism, responsibility, and hard work, represent a more subtle yet powerful influence that reinforces the group-based social hierarchy. Other myths weaken the group-based social hierarchy. Examples of these kinds of myths include the universal rights of man, socialism, and the Christian brotherhood.

Finally, an individual's **social dominance orientation** also exerts an influence on maintaining a group-based social hierarchy. This variable, which is the most psychological component in social dominance theory, is affected by group status, gender, socialization, and temperament. Table 11.2 shows items that are used to measure a person's social dominance orientation. Differences in the extent to which individuals reinforce a group-based social hierarchy tap into whether they approve or disapprove of inequality and dominance. Research shows that dominant group members tend to score higher on measures of social dominance orientation than subordinate group members (Pratto et al. 1994, 2000; Sidanius, Pratto, and Bobo 1996; Phillips and Ziller 1997; Whitley 1999). Men also score higher than women (Pratto et al. 1994; Sidanius, Pratto, and Bobo 1994).

TABLE 11.2	SOCIAL DOMINANCE ORIENTATION

The following statements represent a sample of items from a social dominance orientation scale. The response scale ranged from 1 = very negative to 7 = very positive. Items 5–8 were reverse-coded.

1. Some groups of people are simply inferior to other groups.
2. It's OK if some groups have more of a chance in life than others.
3. To get ahead in life, it is sometimes necessary to step on other groups.
4. Inferior groups should stay in their place.
5. All groups should be given an equal chance in life.
6. We would have fewer problems if we treated people more equally.
7. We should strive to make incomes as equal as possible.
8. No one group should dominate in society.

Source: Sidanius and Pratto 1999, 67.

COGNITIVE THEORIES OF PREJUDICE

Cognitive explanations of prejudice maintain that bias is simply a result of the way individuals organize their thoughts about the world (see Chapter 2). From this perspective, stereotyping is not a result of hostility, scapegoating, competition, or an authoritarian personality but results instead from the sorting of people into groups.

Social Categorization

To understand how this cognitive process works, consider how people sort things in the environment into categories. Animals, plants, and objects are placed into categories on the basis of similarities and differences (Wilder 1986). For example, at a certain age, children recognize that birds and dogs belong in the animal category. Within that category, specific differences suggest even more well-defined categories (collies versus German shepherds, blue jays versus hawks). This same cognitive process helps us simplify our social world. We sort people into categories on the basis of gender, race, religion, ethnicity, nationality, and other traits. Classifying people into groups reduces the amount of information we have to process and makes social interaction easier.

The process of social categorization is natural and necessary in a complex social world. But this simple way of sorting the world into categories also results in prejudice. By assigning people to groups on the basis of obvious physical or social characteristics, we lose important information about these individuals. Instead of recognizing their unique traits, we interact with them on the basis of expectations associated with their membership in a particular group. In other words, we interact with them on the basis of stereotypes. Social psychologists recognize three kinds of biases that result from faulty cognitive processes: the illusory correlation, the self-fulfilling prophecy, and the ultimate attribute error.

The Illusory Correlation. One of the most common errors that human beings make in processing information is to perceive a link between two variables when in fact little or no relationship exists. This flaw, called an **illusory correlation**, explains how stereotypes arise and persist (Mullen and Johnson 1995; Haslam, McGarty, and Brown 1996; McConnell, Leibold, and Sherman 1997; Shavitt et al. 1999; Fiedler 2000). To understand how this happens, consider a common stereotype: "Gypsies are thieves and con artists." Meeting a gypsy would be an unusual experience for most Americans, a memorable experience. Suppose our interaction with a gypsy is negative—we discover that our wallet is missing right after we bumped into this person. The two unusual events are linked. Even though the relationship between these two variables may be small or nonexistent, we are likely to overestimate the strength of the correlation (Johnson and Mullen 1994).

Illusory correlations tend to involve distinctive people and events (Hamilton 1981; Hamilton, Stroessner, and Mackie 1993). Members of minority groups are therefore particularly susceptible to this kind of faulty cognitive link, which manifests itself as a stereotype. David Hamilton and Robert Gifford (1976) conducted a classic experiment that demonstrated exactly how people create illusory correlations. The subjects in this experiment viewed a series of thirty-nine slides that described a behavior performed by a particular individual. To keep the experiment simple, these individuals were described as a member of Group A or Group B. Twenty-seven of the behavioral descriptions were moderately desirable; twelve of them were moderately undesirable. An example describing a desirable behavior read, "John, a member of Group A, visited a sick friend in the hospital."

After they viewed the slides, the subjects evaluated members of these two groups in three ways. First, they rated the individuals on a series of characteristics. Items measuring an interpersonal dimension included *popular, sociable, irritable,* and *unhappy.* An intellectual measure included adjectives such as *industrious, intelligent, lazy,* and *foolish.* Six of the words for each of these measures were positive and four were negative. Second, subjects identified the group of the person who had performed the behavior in each of the thirty-nine slides. Descriptions for the behaviors were listed from 1 to 39, beginning with the phrase "A member of Group _____ ." Subjects merely wrote A or B to identify the individual's group. Third, subjects were then told how many of the thirty-nine statements had described members of Group A and Group B. Then they were asked to indicate how many of these statements described undesirable behaviors.

Since the goal of this experiment was to examine "paired distinctiveness," the researchers manipulated the frequency of two variables: (1) the number of members in each group, and (2) desirable versus undesirable behaviors. To avoid any bias that might be associated with a real minority group, the researchers manufactured their own minority group by simply varying the number of members in each group: Group A contained twenty-six members, while Group B had only thirteen. The researchers also made the behaviors distinctive in terms of statistical frequency: Desirable behaviors occurred more frequently than undesirable ones. The ratio of desirable to undesirable behaviors was 9:4 for both groups (for Group A, eighteen desirable ones versus eight undesirable ones; for Group B, nine desirable ones versus four undesirable ones). Note, however, that two-thirds of the behaviors described members of Group A. That is, of the thirty-nine statements, twenty-six described Group A members and thirteen described Group B members. So statistical frequency defined both Group B and an undesirable behavior as distinctive.

The results of this experiment showed that even though the proportion of undesirable behaviors was the same for both groups, subjects overestimated how often members of Group B engaged in these acts. These findings provide support for the notion that an illusory correlation results from the co-occurrence of unusual events.

In the real world, the media are particularly guilty of creating perceptions that perpetuate beliefs about these kinds of spurious relationships (Wilson, Gutierrez, and Chao 2003; Allan 1999). Consider how young black teenagers appear on the evening news—as drug dealers or victims of a drug deal gone bad. The failure to balance the coverage of black teenagers with positive stories feeds the negative stereotype of black teenagers as dangerous juvenile delinquents and creates an illusory correlation (see Box 11.3).

The Self-Fulfilling Prophecy. One of the dangers of faulty cognitive processes is the possibility

| BOX 11.3 | STEREOTYPICAL SELECTION |

Although conflicts between Whites and other racial groups have been numerous throughout American history, none of the conflict resolutions have resulted in the disappearance of non-Whites from the American social landscape. News media reportage, therefore, moves into another phase designed to neutralize White apprehension of people of color while accommodating their presence. Information items that conform to existing White attitudes toward other groups are then selected for inclusion in news media and given repeated emphasis until they reach thematic proportions.

Examples include news stories that ostensibly appear to be favorable to non-Whites, as in the cases of "success stories," where a person has risen from the despair of (choose one) the reservation, the ghetto, the barrio, Chinatown, or Little Tokyo. These stories accomplish the two objectives of stereotypical selective reporting: (a) The general audience is reassured that non-Whites are still "in their place" (i.e., the reservation, ghetto, etc.) and (b) those who escape their designated place are not a threat to society because they manifest the same values and ambitions as the dominant culture and overcome the deficits of their home communities. In the early 1980s, one of the nation's largest metropolitan newspapers headlined a story concerning a Black woman's appointment to the presidency of a major university with reference to her being the "granddaughter of [a] former slave." The headline fulfilled the objectives of stereotypical selection by invoking the image of Black slavery even though the issue had no relevance to the instant "news" event. Similarly, the same newspaper headlined a story on the election of its city's first Asian American councilman with a reference to his being the "grandson of a Chinese laundryman." At a moment of signal personal achievement, the newspaper came

forth to put the persons of color "in their place" and thereby legitimize their accomplishments in the eyes of the Anglo audience. At the same time, such stories tangentially give credit to the social system that tolerates or praises upward mobility of non-Whites without facilitating it.

Other types of thematic stories also appear during the stereotypical selection phase of news coverage and, unfortunately, they are far more numerous. In the years since the 1968 issuance of the Kerner Commission report, the news media have responded to the call for better reporting of non-White groups with imbalanced coverage. People of color are more likely to pass the gatekeeper if they are involved in "hard news" events, such as those involving police action, or in the "colorful" soft news of holiday coverage, such as Chinese New Year, Cinco de Mayo, and Native American festivals. Other reporting in recent years has emphasized non-Whites on "welfare" who live in crime-infested neighborhoods; lack educational opportunity, job skills, and basic language skills; and, in the circumstance of Latinos and Southeast Asians, are probably not documented U.S. citizens.

The news media have served to reinforce existing stereotypes. The old stereotypes of non-Whites as violent people who are too lazy to work and who indulge in drugs and sexual promiscuity are prominent. In fact, the preponderance of such reporting has led some observers to say the news media have offered an image of non-Whites as "problem people," which means they are projected as people who either have problems or cause problems for society. The legacy of news exclusion thus leads to the general audience seeing people of color as a social burden—the "us versus them" syndrome carried to another dimension.

Source: Wilson and Gutierrez 1995, 156–158.

that our biases might actually contribute to the fulfillment of our expectations. Robert Merton (1948) called it the self-fulfilling prophecy (see Chapter 5). He wrote:

> The self-fulfilling prophecy is, in the beginning, a *false* definition of the situation evoking a new behavior which makes the originally false conception

come *true*. The specious validity of the self-fulfilling prophecy perpetuates a reign of error. For the prophet will cite the actual course of events as proof that he was right from the very beginning. (195)

A number of studies suggest how this might operate in the real world (Rosenthal and Jacobson 1968; Word, Zanna, and Cooper 1974). In a classic experiment discussed in Chapter 5, Rosenthal and Jacobson showed how teachers' expectations influenced students' performances. Researchers have also shown that experimenters' expectations influence the responses of their subjects (Roethlisberger 1949; Rosenthal 1971). These studies led Carl Word and his associates (1974) to propose that the racial attitudes of a white interviewer might operate in the same way to influence the performance of black job applicants. Based on Merton's self-fulfilling prophecy, they argued that the racial attitudes of a white interviewer were linked to nonverbal behaviors that influenced the interaction that occurred with black job applicants. For example, the prejudice of a white interviewer might be communicated nonverbally by the degree of eye contact established during the interview, the physical distance separating her from the applicant, or the degree to which she leaned toward the applicant during the interview. The researchers believed that the response of the job applicant would be tailored to these nonverbal signals to create a self-fulfilling prophecy.

To test their hypothesis, the researchers set up two experiments. In the first one, white college students were asked to interview applicants for a job. Some of the applicants were white; others were black. The results of this first study showed that when a white interviewer met with black job applicants, he sat farther away, made more errors in speaking, and ended the interview sooner than when he met with white applicants. To determine how these nonverbal behaviors influenced the applicants, the researchers then conducted a second experiment in which they intentionally controlled and varied the behavior of the interviewers to replicate how the interviewers in the first experiment had interacted with black or white applicants. The results of this study showed that the nonverbal behavior did in fact influence the performance of job applicants. The results of this study provided support for the argument that self-fulfilling prophecies do operate in interracial interactions. In summarizing their findings, the researchers emphasized that

analyses of black-white interactions, particularly in the area of job-seeking blacks in white society, might profit if it were assumed that the "problem" of black performance resides not entirely within the blacks, but rather within the interaction setting itself. (Word, Zanna, and Cooper 1974, 120)

The Ultimate Attribution Error. We spend a lot of time trying to figure out other people. Who are they? What makes that person tick? How is she likely to respond to me? Although attribution theories assume that people weigh information logically, our perceptions of others involve a number of biases. For example, as noted in Chapter 5, the fundamental attribution error leads us to make internal attributions for the causes of other people's behavior. Instead of taking situational factors into account, we tend to focus on a person's disposition. When we consider why a person has been unemployed for two months, we tend to blame the person—he is not looking hard enough for a job, he doesn't have enough education, he has poor interpersonal skills. In fact, a poor economy—too few jobs—may fully explain why that person is unable to find a job.

This kind of attribution error also operates beyond the level of the individual. Consider how people make judgments about members of outgroups: "*They* are not intelligent enough to get into college," "*They* are too lazy to run a successful small business," and so on. Stereotypes like these ignore situational explanations for the behavior of individuals and focus on dispositional traits that characterize all members of a particular group. Thomas Pettigrew (1979) called this bias the **ultimate attribution error**.

Social Identity

Cognitive theories of prejudice also explain how social identities contribute to in-group and out-group biases (Tajfel 1982b). Henri Tajfel (1981, 255) defined **social identity** as "that part of the individuals' self-concept which derives from their knowledge of their membership of a social group (or groups) together with the value and emotional significance of that membership." This definition resembles a concept derived from the theory of symbolic interaction (Stryker 1987, 2002; Stryker and Serpe 1982; Capozza and Brown 2000; see Chapter 4). Both of them assume multiple definitions of the self that rely on the social context.

To understand the importance of social identity, consider the groups and organizations to which you belong (political parties, religious groups, nationality, college, or place of work). Membership in these kinds of social categories defines us in terms of a category's specific characteristics. It provides us with a self-definition that becomes part of our self-concept (Hogg and Terry 2001). This social identity tells us how we ought to think, feel, and behave in certain situations. And it influences our perceptions of in-group and out-group members. Let us now consider how these perceptions contribute to several other kinds of biases.

In-Group Bias. The process of sorting people into social categories creates two basic distinctions: the in-group and the out-group. As discussed earlier, the in-group refers to the category to which we assign ourselves. The out-group includes everyone else. We are the insiders; they are the outsiders. This basic "us versus them" distinction is susceptible to a number of biases or prejudices.

The first bias is the tendency to view members of our own group more positively than members of out-groups. Sumner (1906/1960) described this in-group bias in terms of the positive characteristics that described the relationships among members of the in-group—loyalty, peace, and order. In fact, studies show that in-group members have more favorable perceptions of their own members, view their own behavior more positively than members of out-groups, and expect to be treated better by members of their own group (Allen and Wilder 1975; Brewer 1979; Mackie, Worth, and Asuncion 1990).

Assumed Similarity Effect. Categorizing people into in-groups and out-groups also distorts perceptions of similarities and differences between members of different groups. People tend to see greater similarities among members of their own group and greater differences with members of other groups. One study that showed this effect found that university commuter students believed they held more similar attitudes than students who lived in the same fraternity on campus (Holtz and Miller 1985).

Out-Group Homogeneity Bias. Finally, members of in-groups tend to view members of other groups as different from themselves but nearly indistinguishable from one another. The columnist Art Buchwald provided one of the best examples to illustrate this kind of bias (Park and Rothbart 1982). He recounted a conversation that he had with a black friend about a headline that read "Blacks Seriously Split on Middle East." Buchwald's friend asked him why whites expected blacks to agree on this complicated issue. And then he pointed out that we do not see headlines like "White People Send Stock Market Prices Tumbling on Wall Street." Buchwald responded, "We expect blacks in this country to be in agreement on everything . . . but it isn't news if the whites are divided" (Buchwald 1979, 23).

The tendency to minimize the differences among members of other groups is called the **out-group homogeneity bias**. It is reflected in comments such as "They all look alike" or "They all do that." A number of studies illustrate how this particular bias operates. One study showed that sorority sisters saw members of their own group as having more distinct traits than members of other sororities (Park and Rothbart 1982). Another study showed that engineering and business students recognized more variability among members of their own majors than among students in other disciplines (Judd, Ryan, and Park 1991; Park, Ryan, and Judd 1992).

The failure to recognize unique traits among members of other groups may be due to a lack of interaction with them (see Box 11.4). For example, how difficult would it be to identify the physical

| BOX 11.4 | CORRECTING DISTORTED PERCEPTIONS THROUGH INTERACTION |

Tom Wicker, raised in the South, had limited interactions with blacks until he embarked on a ten-day journey on a military troop train from Seattle to Norfolk with twenty-seven black soldiers and two white soldiers.

[Those] 10 days had been the time of [Wicker's] discovery that black people were just that—people, individuals, human as he was, hurting, laughing, loving, worrying in much the same fashion about much the same things, whatever the inexcusable and ineradicable differences in their experience.
    The blacks still were preoccupied, as he was, with families, jobs, schooling, girls. No two of them were much alike in temperament or personality. Some he liked; some he did not. One was better read than he; another was mentally deficient, or so it seemed; another had a flashing wit; still another organized a profitable black market for food and tobacco, out of whatever obscure sources of supply. Some [created] disciplinary problems, as both the white boys did. Others shared plans and memories as equals with young Tom Wicker. Since in 10 days all the men on the car got only one shower—at the St. Louis YMCA, to which they were marched from the city's magnificent old railroad station one blessed evening—it turned out that whites when dirty smelled as bad as blacks when dirty. In such close quarters, it became apparent that black penises were no bigger than white and no more thought about by their possessors, which was constantly. The only major difference, other than skin color, was that, with one or two exceptions, the blacks were not as well educated as the whites, although all had gone to school. (1975, 162–163)

Source: Park and Rothbart 1982, 1067.

traits of a stranger who sat next to you for ten minutes on a bus? Now consider how easy it would be to describe the traits of your best friend. Differences in the frequency of social interaction may likewise account for perceptions that members of out-groups hold similar opinions, values, and beliefs while members of our own group have unique ones (Linville and Fischer 1993).

Social Identity Theory

The process of sorting people into social categories produces a number of negative effects and biases. Of those discussed so far, social psychologists have paid particular attention to in-group biases. Much of the research on this kind of bias has sought to explain the positive feelings among members of the in-group and the negative feelings between members of in-groups and out-groups. Group conflict theories suggest that in-group bias results from group members' desires to maximize their own reward. But that does not appear to be the only explanation.

    To gain a better understanding of in-group favoritism, Henri Tajfel conducted a number of experiments that involved "minimal group" situations (Tajfel and Billig 1974; Tajfel and Turner 1979; Tajfel 1982a). Subjects in these experiments were first assigned to groups created solely for the purpose of these experiments. Members of these groups had no prior interaction, held no stereotypical beliefs about these newly formed groups, and were not involved in any kind of intergroup competition. In one experiment, subjects were randomly assigned to groups on the basis of a coin toss. In another study, assignment to a group was based on subjects' opinions of artists that they knew nothing about. The results of these experiments showed that the favoritism that subjects showed toward members of their own group was simply related to their arbitrary assignment to the same group. In fact, studies show that the simple act of classification into a group produces favoritism toward one's own group (Tajfel et al. 1971; Turner 1978; Brewer 1979; Brewer and Brown 1998).

    Why does categorization in a group, by itself, produce in-group favoritism? Tajfel (1982a) and Turner (1987) argue that the answer lies in a powerful benefit derived from membership in a group:

Self-esteem can be boosted through identification with an in-group. This explanation, which is known as **social identity theory**, is based on three main assumptions:

1. People sort the social world into categories: in-groups and out-groups.
2. Membership in a particular group provides people with a social identity, which provides a sense of self-esteem.
3. A person's self-esteem, which is tied to membership in a particular group, can be boosted by identification with the in-group.

As mentioned earlier, our membership in a group or an organization defines us in terms of the specific characteristics of that social category. It provides us with a social identity that tells us how we ought to think, feel, and behave. But social identities are also evaluative, and they provide an assessment of our group and its members compared to other relevant groups (Hogg and Terry 2001). Groups and their members try to maximize favorable in-group comparisons, which ultimately serve to boost the self-esteem of individual members. Whether an individual's self-esteem is reinforced by identification depends on the belief that the in-group is superior to other out-groups. Nowhere, perhaps, is this more evident than among sports fans, who enjoy "basking in the reflected glory" of their team (Cialdini et al. 1976). Robert Cialdini and his associates described it well:

> Fans of championship teams gloat over their team's accomplishments and proclaim their affiliation with buttons on their clothes, bumper stickers on their cars, and banners on their public buildings. Despite the fact that they have never caught a ball or thrown a block in support of their team's success, the tendency of such fans is to claim for themselves part of the team's glory; it is perhaps informative that the chant is always "We're number one," never "They're number one." (p. 367)

This observation led Cialdini and his colleagues to design an experiment to examine the "basking in glory" phenomenon. Using subjects from seven universities with victorious intercollegiate football teams, they found support for the idea that people like to publicly announce their identification with a winning team. In this study, university students were more likely to wear apparel that indicated their academic affiliation after their football team had won a game (Cialdini et al. 1976; Cialdini 1993).

Reducing Prejudice

Reducing prejudice and discrimination was the ultimate goal of the civil rights movement. In his famous 1963 speech, Martin Luther King Jr. echoed this hope when he said, "I have a dream that my four little children will one day live in a nation where they will not be judged by the color of their skin but by the content of their character." The civil rights movement did lead to the enactment of laws designed to prevent discrimination. These laws protected the voting rights of minorities, made it illegal for employers to discriminate in hiring practices, and outlawed discrimination in the sale or rental of housing. In general, they made it illegal to discriminate on the basis of race, religion, color, or national origin. They did not, however, eliminate hatred toward members of certain groups. Hate crimes today, as in the case of James Byrd Jr., reflect deeply held prejudices and hatred. So does this mean that laws promise little hope for better race relations? What kinds of solutions do work?

As it turns out, we have learned some valuable lessons from the historic decisions that have shaped civil rights laws in the United States. Consider the case of *Brown* v. *Board of Education of Topeka*, the unanimous 1954 U.S. Supreme Court decision that overturned the eighteenth-century doctrine of "separate but equal" educational facilities for blacks and whites and outlawed segregated schools. Recognizing the significance that this decision had for understanding race relations, Elliot Aronson (1999, 227) wrote, "This decision launched our nation into one of the most exciting, large-scale social experiments ever conducted." In fact, social psychologists did learn how contact between children of different races affected racial attitudes.

The Contact Hypothesis

A number of studies had already suggested that contact between members of different races did reduce prejudice. In one study, Morton Deutsch and Mary Ellen Collins (1951) examined the attitudes of black and white Americans who lived in public housing developments that were desegregated after World War II. In one condition, black and white families were randomly assigned to buildings that were segregated by race. In a second condition, black and white families were assigned to integrated buildings. Over a period of months, white residents living in integrated buildings reported more favorable attitudes toward black neighbors than whites living in segregated housing. Studies of American soldiers also showed that increased contact between the races reduced prejudice. In a comprehensive study of World War II soldiers, Samuel Stouffer and his colleagues (1949)

showed that after the military changed its policy toward racially segregated troops, levels of prejudice declined significantly among white soldiers.

Encouraged by the findings of these studies, social psychologists hoped that desegregated schools would reduce prejudice among children of different races. And in some cases it did—but not always. Contact alone was not enough to reduce prejudice (Allport 1979; Amir 1969). In fact, as Gordon Allport (1979) had pointed out in his **contact theory**, several conditions must exist before contact between members of different groups can effectively reduce prejudice, including cooperative interdependence, equal status, intimate contact, and institutional support. Why are these specific conditions so necessary? And how do they operate?

A well-known study conducted by Muzafer Sherif and his colleagues (1961) provides some answers (see also Sherif 1966). This study, which was designed to examine group behavior, took place in a boys' summer camp. After their arrival, the boys were randomly divided into two groups. Loyalty to their own group developed over the course of a week as the boys worked, played, and lived

The contact hypothesis suggests that interaction among children in racially mixed groups can reduce prejudice under certain conditions.

together. The two groups then met to compete in various games such as football, baseball, and tug-of-war. These and other kinds of contests created intense conflict and hostility between the groups. Initial efforts to reduce in-group bias and out-group hostility failed. Eliminating the competition did not work. Neither did lectures about friendship. Uniting the two groups to compete against another rival group proved somewhat successful, but the researchers noticed that this solution also widened the conflict.

Eventually, the researchers discovered a solution. They created situations that required the cooperative interdependence of both groups. In one case, a serious emergency arose when the water supply system broke down. The joint efforts of all boys were required to repair it. Another problem arose when a truck that was supposed to pick up their food stalled. Using a rope that had ironically created conflict in an earlier tug-of-war battle, the boys pulled the truck and got it running. Working together toward goals that were important to both groups eventually reduced the intergroup conflict and hostility. This experiment clearly showed the necessity of cooperative interdependence and an important common goal in reducing intergroup hostilities. A number of other favorable conditions were also present. The boys at the summer camp all held equal status. The informal camp setting allowed intimate contact between members of different groups over a fairly long period of time. And the adults in this situation supported social norms that promoted friendship between boys of different groups.

The Jigsaw Classroom

Sherif's study played an important role in developing strategies to reduce conflict between racially mixed groups of students in newly desegregated schools in the United States. Elliott Aronson and his colleagues developed one of the most well-known techniques, called the **jigsaw classroom** (Aronson et al. 1978; Aronson and Bridgeman 1979; Aronson and Gonzalez 1988; Brown and Campione 1994; Wolfe and Spencer 1996; Aronson

and Patnoe 1997; Walker and Crogan 1998). The method involves the cooperative learning of small groups of racially mixed students. To promote cooperation among members of the group, a lesson is divided into separate tasks. Each student is then expected to take responsibility for one of these tasks. Although each one in turn will assume the role of teacher, no one in the group assumes the role of leader. So every member is viewed as having equal status. In a jigsaw classroom, learning the material requires the cooperative interdependence of all group members. It involves a great deal of face-to-face interaction, which fosters the development of friendships. Finally, because teachers supervise these activities, students recognize that they have institutional support.

Aronson believed that when students work together to accomplish an important common goal, friendships are more likely to develop than bitter animosities between rivals. In fact, research shows that this technique is effective in reducing prejudice in racially mixed classrooms (Aronson and Gonzalez 1988; Brewer and Brown 1998).

THE MEDIA'S ROLE IN REDUCING PREJUDICE

From the beginning of American history, the media have shaped and maintained prejudice. Some people believe that the long history of damaging media stereotyping has come to an end. But some critics argue that Americans have just been bamboozled into believing that. The filmmaker Spike Lee argued that the public does not recognize how American popular culture perpetuates stereotypical racist images. In an effort to drive this point home, Lee produced the satirical film *Bamboozled*, which sparked intense controversy because of its depiction of blackface. Movie critic Roger Ebert claimed that Lee went too far, saying, "I think his fundamental miscalculation was to use blackface itself. He overshoots the mark. Blackface is so blatant, so wounding, so highly charged, that it obscures any point being made by the person

TABLE 11.3	FIGHTING MEDIA STEREOTYPES	
Stereotype	**Stereotype-Buster**
1. Asian Americans as foreigners who cannot be assimilated	1. Portraying Asians as an integral part of the United States; more portrayals of acculturated Asian Americans speaking without foreign accents
2. Asian Americans restricted to clichéd occupations (e.g., grocers, martial artists, prostitutes)	2. Asian Americans in diverse, mainstream occupations
3. Asian racial features, names, accents, or mannerisms as inherently comic or sinister	3. Asian names or racial features as no more unusual than those of whites
4. Asians relegated to supporting roles in projects with Asian or Asian American content	4. More Asian and Asian American lead roles
5. Asian male sexuality as negative or nonexistent	5. More Asian men as positive romantic leads
6. Asian women as "China dolls" (i.e., exotic, subservient, compliant, industrious, eager to please)	6. Asian women as self-confident and self-respecting, pleasing themselves as well as their loved ones
7. Asian women as "dragon ladies" (i.e., inherently scheming, untrustworthy, and back-stabbing)	7. Whenever villains are Asian, it's important their villainy not be attributed to their ethnicity
8. Asians who prove how good they are by sacrificing their lives	8. Positive Asian characters who are still alive at the end of the story
9. Asian Americans as the "model minority" (i.e., over-achievers with little emotional life)	9. The audience empathizing with an Asian character's flaws and foibles
10. Asianness as an "explanation" for the magical or supernatural	10. Asian cultures are no more or less magical than other cultures

Sources: Croteau and Hoynes 2003, 205, adapted from janet.org/~manaa/a_stereotypes.html.

wearing it." But Lee countered his argument, saying, "One could make the argument that certain parts of rap, you might say gangster rap, those videos could be construed as a contemporary minstrel act. You could possibly say some shows on television are borderline minstrel shows. This film does a great thing; it poses questions" (quoted in Patterson and Wilkins 2002, 273). In fact, it does.

Lee is not the only one to challenge stereotypical imagery (Croteau and Hoynes 2003). A number of organizations offer suggestions for alternative portrayals. For example, the Media Action Network for Asian Americans (MANAA) assembled a list of common Asian stereotypes with alternative portrayals (see Table 11.3). Instead of casting actors into clichéd occupations such as grocers, this group suggests more diverse mainstream ones. Like other groups, the MANAA also suggests that more Asians be cast in lead roles.

SUMMARY

1. Prejudice refers to negative attitudes held about members of certain racial or ethnic groups. It has three distinct dimensions: beliefs about a group (cognitive prejudice), feelings about a group (affective prejudice), and behavioral tendencies toward a group (conative prejudice). This suggests that one kind of prejudice might be reduced without influencing the other kinds.

2. Stereotypes ignore the distinct traits of individual members of a group and exaggerate beliefs associated with the group. Stereotyping and prejudice can result from the tendency to view our own group (the in-group) in positive terms but to see members of other groups (the out-groups) in negative terms.

3. Prejudice is not inborn; it is learned through direct reinforcement, punishment, or observing a model. Children acquire racial attitudes from parents, peers, schools, and the mass media.

4. The authoritarian personality theory holds that a set of personality traits is linked to prejudice. People with an authoritarian personality tend to adhere rigidly to conventional values, accept authority figures uncritically, regard weak or different people negatively, and to think in stereotypical ways. This theory is compatible with two explanations for how prejudice operates: scapegoating and projection.

5. Other theories—realistic conflict theory, the group position model, and social dominance theory—explain prejudice in terms of competition for scarce resources. Intergroup competition develops as members of society's dominant group seek to maintain their advantaged position while members of the subordinate group seek equality.

6. Cognitive explanations of prejudice maintain that bias is simply a result of the way individuals organize their thoughts about the world. From this perspective, stereotyping is not the result of hostility, scapegoating, competition, or an authoritarian personality but from the sorting of people into groups. Three kinds of bias result from faulty cognitive processes: the illusory correlation, the self-fulfilling prophecy, and the ultimate attribution error.

7. Cognitive theories of prejudice also explain how social identities contribute to in-group and out-group biases. Social identity theory holds that self-esteem can be boosted through identification with an in-group.

8. Efforts to reduce prejudice in the United States have been challenging. One of the best-known techniques is the jigsaw classroom.

KEY TERMS

Prejudice 315
Stereotype 316
In-group 317
Out-group 317
Authoritarian personality 321
Realistic conflict theory 323
Relative deprivation 323
Group position model 324

Social dominance theory 325
Group-based social hierarchy 325
In-group bias 325
Out-group favoritism 325
Self-debilitation 325
Ideological asymmetry 325
Legitimizing myths 325
Social dominance orientation 326

Illusory correlation 327
Ultimate attribution error 330
Social identity 330
Out-group homogeneity bias 331
Social identity theory 333
Contact theory 334
Jigsaw classroom 335

CRITICAL REVIEW QUESTIONS

1. Should the media be allowed to broadcast racist messages? What position has the U.S. Supreme Court taken on the argument that certain hate crimes fall under the protection of the First Amendment's right to free speech?

2. Do American values contribute to prejudice? If so, which ones? Use one of the theories presented in this chapter to support your position.

3. Provide specific examples to show how faulty cognitive processes such as the illusory correlation contribute to prejudice.

TWELVE

Conformity, Compliance, and Obedience

In 1969, a high school history teacher in Palo Alto, California, decided to teach his students a lesson they would never forget (Strasser 1981). It all began during a lecture on World War II, when Ron Jones's students asked him why the Germans blindly followed Adolf Hitler and the Nazis. Why didn't they question the slaughter of friends and neighbors, millions of Jews? How could they deny what had happened? Jones could not answer their questions. After doing some research, he decided that the best way to teach this lesson was through an experiment. It lasted only a week but would have a lifelong impact.

The experiment began on a Monday in the form of a lesson about discipline. Praising the self-discipline of athletes, dancers, and artists who exert great effort to perfect their skills, Jones proceeded to show his class the power of discipline. He began by demonstrating how a certain seating posture made them more alert. Then they practiced a number of drills that required students to obey orders. He also established new rules for his classroom, which resembled the basic training that soldiers receive when they enter military service. These new rules were designed to increase punctuality and respect for authority. To his surprise, the students accepted these new rules with enthusiasm.

Jones seriously considered ending the experiment the next day. But the intensity and degree of student compliance intrigued him. So on Tuesday, he proceeded with a lesson on the value of community. Referring to his own personal experiences, he told the class, "Community is the bond between people who work and struggle together for a common goal. It's like building a barn with your neighbors." He went on to say, "It's the feeling that you're part of something that's more important than yourself. . . . You're a movement, a team, a cause" (Strasser 1981, 42).

The students' unhesitating acceptance of this experiment puzzled Jones. He could not understand why they didn't question his authority or this Gestapo-style behavior.

But he continued. To demonstrate the power of community, he created simple rituals. One of these involved the chanting of the basic lessons: "Strength through discipline. Strength through community." These rituals gave students a sense of belonging. Regardless of their academic talents, all of them came to feel competent and equal.

When class ended on Tuesday, Jones provided students with another sign of their group membership—a special hand gesture that symbolized membership in "The Wave." He called it the Wave salute. To his amazement, his entire class returned the salute without any prompting.

On Wednesday, the experiment continued with the institution of sanctions for deviating from group norms. At the beginning of class, Jones distributed membership cards to all of the students. Some cards were marked with a red X. Students who received these cards were given a special role. They were expected to report any students who violated the rules. Once more, Jones was surprised by the students' response. This time, many stood up in class and openly expressed how much they valued this experience. And they asked why he did not teach like this before. In fact, this teaching style was effective. Jones could see significant improvements in his students' performance. But would they do anything he asked?

To find out, he asked students to recruit new members to the Wave. Acceptance to the group required the recommendation of an active member and a demonstration that the recruit knew the rules and pledged to obey them. When recruits met these requirements, Jones would then give them a membership card. This recruitment request was accepted enthusiastically by all but three students who had begun to question the experiment. They had expressed their concerns to their parents, who called Jones to learn more about that week's lessons. Jones was again surprised and disappointed when these thoughtful and intelligent parents accepted his explanation so easily.

The degree to which students embraced the Wave was reflected in their behavior. Many of them expected strict adherence to the rules and punished students who violated them. Others did not question the group and simply accepted their new roles.

By Thursday, even Jones recognized changes in his own behavior. He had become a dictator. He came to understand how ordinary people accept an ascribed role and then fit their self-concept to it. He knew the experiment had to end. It was a mistake, and it had gone too far. But he was also gravely concerned about the psychological damage that it would do when students realized what had happened.

Planning to end it on Friday, he told his students that the Wave was not just a classroom exercise. It was a nationwide program that was recruiting students across the country to work for political change. He emphasized that they were selected to participate because they were special. And he added that they could make society a better place by spreading the lessons they had learned over the past week. He ended by inviting them to a rally that would take place in the auditorium on Friday at noon. At that time a national presidential candidate would address members of the Wave. The excitement was contagious. Students expressed their support, shouting, "We can do it!" Other students encouraged Wave members to wear white shirts and to bring their friends.

By noon on Friday, the school auditorium was packed. Jones turned down the lights and plugged in a television set. For minutes, the audience stared at a test pattern. Finally, a student yelled, "There is no leader, is there?" At that point, Jones turned off the television set and began to explain:

> "You thought you were so special! Better than everyone outside of this room. You traded your freedom for what you said was equality. But you turned your equality into superiority over non-Wave members. You accepted the group's will over your own convictions, no matter who you had to hurt to do it. . . . Yes, you all would have

made good Nazis. . . . You would have put on the uniforms, turned your heads and allowed your friends and neighbors to be persecuted and destroyed. You say it could never happen again, but look at how close you came." (Strasser 1981, 134)

R on Jones taught his students a painful lesson. In fact, the potential pain caused by an experiment like this makes it highly unlikely that it would happen in any classroom today. Colleges and universities have strict guidelines to protect human subjects from the kind of harm that experiments like this cause. Nevertheless, many college students face situations that involve the kind of social influence involved in Jones's experiment. Consider the hazing rituals and traditions of fraternities and sororities that serve as the rites of passage for new members. Members and pledges enthusiastically accept the rules of these groups and comply with leaders' requests. In some cases, this involves silly antics that pose no serious threat to pledges, such as wearing a costume to class. Or it might involve harmless rituals, gestures, or dress codes. Often, however, the activity involves the excessive consumption of alcohol, which has resulted in many tragic accidents and deaths (Nuwer 1999).

How do these kinds of pressures resemble what Jones created? Much of this chapter is devoted to answering that question. We will also consider some questions that Jones's experiment did not answer. For example, a few students at Cubberly High School resisted and challenged the influence of Jones and members of the Wave. But this minority failed to exert any influence of its own. Instead, they were punished and ostracized from the group. Are minorities powerless to exert influence? If not, in what does their power lie?

Jones's experiment also suggested that social influence could be reduced to strategies or techniques. What kinds of strategies and techniques are we susceptible to in our everyday lives? How can we defend ourselves against tactics that are designed to get us to comply with others' requests? And finally, we are socialized from childhood to obey authority. But there are situations that require us to disobey authority. When is disobedience justified? Let us now begin to answer these questions.

SOCIAL INFLUENCE

Ron Jones's classroom experiment was designed to teach students a lesson about **social influence**. This refers to the exercise of power by a person or group to produce changes in an individual's thoughts, feelings, or behaviors. The question that prompted Jones to teach this particular lesson was not new. In fact, it appeared in a well-known essay by Max Weber (1977, 78), asking, "When and why do men obey?"

Responses to Social Influence

This question focuses on **obedience**, one of three specific behaviors that reflect social influence. The others are **conformity** and **compliance**. In each case, someone is trying to change another person's behavior. Obedience refers to a behavioral response to a command or direct order. In this case, we may feel a duty to obey authority or pressure to follow an order. We might even feel threatened. Social influence also operates in more subtle ways to produce conformity and compliance. Consider the last time you conformed to the actions of a crowd. Few people remain seated at sporting events when the national anthem begins. Most of us stand and sing without thinking about it because everyone is doing it. Social influence also operates when someone asks us to do a favor. Have you ever bought a box of Girl Scout cookies that you did not want? Would you refuse to donate a dollar to a good cause? In these cases, we are likely to comply with a person's request.

The reactions of crowds gathered at sporting events show how social influence operates in subtle ways to produce conformity.

Processes of Social Influence

These three kinds of behaviors do not necessarily provide an accurate reflection of our thoughts or feelings. When we go along with someone's request just to please him or to avoid an unfavorable reaction, we are not necessarily doing so because we agree with him. So when we comply, that does not mean that our privately held attitudes or beliefs have changed. For example, if the president of our sorority pledges support for greater diversity in the Greek system, we might publicly express agreement with her position. We might even sign a petition in front of her to support changes that would bring about greater diversity. If we do not really agree with her but are simply attempting to gain her favor, our behavior illustrates the process of compliance (Kelman 1961).

Herbert Kelman (1961) describes two other processes of social influence. In contrast to compliance, **identification** involves the acceptance of the influencing agent's role. This occurs when an individual admires or likes someone and adopts that person's attitudes, values, and beliefs as his own. Kelman and Hamilton (1989) offer the bizarre case of Patricia Hearst as a classic example of this kind of response to social influence. After she was kidnapped by members of the radical Symbionese Liberation Army (SLA), she came to adopt the group's attitudes and beliefs. As a member of this group, she participated in an armed bank robbery that led to her capture. She was tried for this crime as Tanya, the new name that she had taken as a member of the SLA, and was convicted. Even though her kidnapping indicated that she was originally forced to join this group, prosecutors argued that she eventually became a convert. Following her capture, Hearst fluctuated between her two identities but eventually reverted to her original identity as Patricia Hearst.

The third process of social influence, **internalization**, occurs when people adopt new attitudes or beliefs that are congruent with their existing value system. A medical student who participates in a marathon that raises money for breast cancer demonstrates acceptance of this event's purpose, which is consistent with the value he places on saving lives.

Recognizing the difference between compliance and internalization provides important information about individuals. If they are simply complying, we should see them express their privately accepted attitudes when the agent of social influence is absent.

CLASSIC STUDIES OF CONFORMITY

The two most famous researchers into the phenomenon of conformity are Muzafer Sherif and Solomon Asch.

Muzafer Sherif's Study: The Autokinetic Effect

Muzafer Sherif (1935) conducted one of the first experiments to provide insight into the process of conformity. Recognizing a key contribution that Émile Durkheim (1965) made to the process of norm formation, Sherif credited him with the idea that "norms take shape in out-of-the ordinary situations, when the usual rules and routines of daily living are not applicable" (Sherif and Sherif 1969, 201).

To create an "out-of-the-ordinary situation" in the laboratory, Sherif decided to use an optical illusion called the *autokinetic effect*. It is the visual perception that a single small light will appear to move erratically in many directions when shined in a completely darkened room. This illusion is well known by astronomers who study heavenly bodies in the dark evening skies. Because the autokinetic effect is an optical illusion, no one can measure exactly how far the spot of light moves—perceptions vary from individual to individual. So the subjectivity of this experience provided an ideal way to study how a group influenced the judgments of individual members.

The subjects in Sherif's experiment were first taken separately into a completely dark room and told that when they were ready, they would see a point of light that would soon appear to move.

Their task was to estimate how far it moved. Later the subjects were brought into the darkened room with one or two other subjects and again asked to estimate out loud how far the light moved. In the last part of the experiment, the subjects were again taken separately into the room and asked to estimate how far the light moved. The results of this experiment showed that the estimates that subjects made independently changed when they estimated the distance in the presence of other subjects. Over the course of several group sessions, the estimates made by group members converged (see Figure 12.1). In the last part of the experiment, when subjects were asked to again make individual estimates of the distance moved, they tended to stick close to the estimate established by the group.

These findings provide support for the idea that conformity is likely to occur in situations where individuals cannot rely on objective measures or standard rules. But what about situations that do rely on objective measures? Will people still tend to conform to an emerging group norm? Let us turn to another classic experiment that attempted to answer that question.

Solomon Asch's Conformity Study

Most people can understand why subjects conformed in Sherif's experiment. Situations that involve subjective perceptions are more fluid than those where the right answer can be measured in some objective way. Recognizing this fundamental difference, Solomon Asch (1955) designed an experiment to see how other people influenced a subject's response when the right answer was made perfectly clear. Imagine yourself in the situation that Asch created for the subjects in this classic study. You are seated with a group of seven other college students. The experimenter tells you that he will show you a series of cards that show a standard line on the left with three comparison lines to the right, marked A, B, and C. When it is your turn, you are to choose the comparison line that matches the standard line.

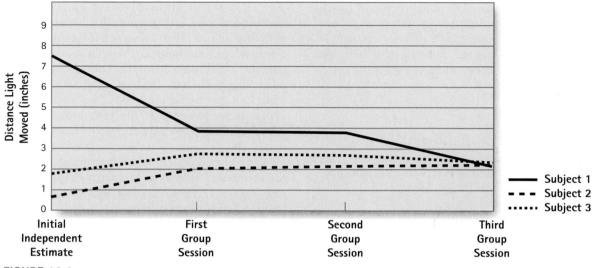

FIGURE 12.1

Sherif's Experiment on Conformity in Groups

Individuals were asked separately to estimate how far a light seemed to move in a darkened room. They were then paired with two other subjects, and all were asked to repeat their estimates. After several such sessions, the estimates made by all group members tended to converge. (Each line in the graph represents one individual.)

Source: Data from Sherif 1936, 103.

Figure 12.2 shows one of the cards that Asch used in the experiment. On this particular card, the length of the standard line was 10 inches. The lengths of the comparison lines were as follows: A = 8.75 inches; B = 10 inches; C = 8 inches. The experimenter begins with the first subject, who indicates that line B matches the standard line. The next five subjects agree that line B is correct. You had also chosen line B and say so when your turn comes. The last subject also agrees. Nothing seems unusual for the next couple of trials. The answer you have chosen is the same as the other subjects. But then the situation changes. It seems clear that the correct comparison line on the card in front of you is A. But no one else agrees. As each subject takes his turn, they each indicate that line B is the correct match. You are sure that line A is the correct line, but how could five other people be wrong? What do you do?

Over the course of several more trials, you discover that no one else agrees with your answer. You sit there in disbelief, wondering how the others could see the card so differently. What you do not know is that all of the other subjects in the experiment are confederates who have been instructed to give the wrong answer. Asch designed it this way to find out what would happen when "social consensus contradicted clear-cut perceptual evidence" (Sherif and Sherif 1969, 120).

The results of this study showed just how much influence the majority can exert on an individual. One-third of the subjects conformed to the group's answer even though they had privately identified the correct comparison line. Only thirteen of the fifty subjects stuck with the answer they had decided was the correct one over the course of these trials. Most of the subjects conformed at least once during the experiment.

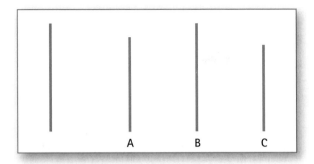

FIGURE 12.2

Asch's Experiment on Conformity in Groups

Which comparison line, A, B, or C, is the same length as the standard line at left?

Source: Adapted from Asch 1955, 32.

WHY PEOPLE CONFORM

In seeking an explanation for why people conform, social psychologists have focused on two distinct types of group influence: **informational social influence** and **normative social influence**. The first kind is based on people's need to be right, while the second kind involves the desire to be liked. We are all susceptible to these powerful influences.

Informational Social Influence: The Need to Be Right

Every so often, we find ourselves in situations that cause us to seek information about what is happening. Consider the reaction of people in the World Trade Center on September 11, 2001, when they heard a loud explosion. Most people did not know what had happened. Even people on the streets below looked at one another in disbelief, speculating about the smoke that began to pour from the upper floors of the building. In living rooms across the nation, television viewers watched intently as news reporters tried to gather and provide information as quickly as possible.

Not knowing how to respond to this out-of-the-ordinary situation led people to avidly seek information about what had happened. Through various forms of social interaction, but particularly that which took place between eye-witnesses and news media, the public eventually arrived at a definition of the situation. Nothing indicates how important this kind of informational social influence is more than the public's reaction, which was to remain tuned to news stations for hours on end. In later accounts of how people on the upper floors of the World Trade Center responded to definitions of the situation, we learned that many people were able to escape safely. Others, however, returned to their offices based on the faulty information that everything was OK. They died when the buildings collapsed. As this example illustrates, people conform when they believe that someone else's interpretation of an ambiguous situation is better than their own. Acting on one definition of the situation, many people followed the crowd and ran for the stairways to reach safety. The people who returned to their desks also conformed. But in that case, they responded to the instructions of someone, who did not interpret the situation accurately. Sherif's experiment also illustrates how informational social influence operates. In that ambiguous situation, subjects sought information from one another to determine how far the pinpoint of light had moved.

Normative Social Influence: The Desire to Be Liked

In 1993, before even reaching the legal drinking age, Chad Saucier died from consuming too much alcohol during a pledge Christmas party held at the Phi Delta Theta fraternity house at Auburn University (Nuwer 1999). Following a fraternity tradition, he and fellow pledges swapped bottles of liquor with their big brothers and gulped down the contents. Although bottle exchanges violated the rules of both the university and the Phi Delta Theta's national organization, it was a custom highly resistant to change. Pledges view traditions

---

BOX 12.1	HAZING

Hazing occurs when a group perceived to have power over a newcomer requires someone to do any of the following:

- Engage in servitude, run errands, and perform so-called favors
- Participate in intimidation; use derogatory terms to refer to pledges; terrorize; use verbal abuse or create a hostile environment
- Engage in acts of degradation such as required nudity, partial stripping, rules forbidding bathing, and games played while someone is in a state of undress
- Engage in rough rituals involving physical force, paddling, electric shocks, beatings, calisthenics, and sexually demeaning behavior
- Sing explicit songs and perform sexist, racist, or anti-Semitic acts, including denying someone membership in an organization on the basis of religion, skin color, or ancestry
- Employ deception and deceptive psychological "mind games"
- Suffer from sleep deprivation (six or fewer hours of sleep a night)
- Coerce or be coerced by others to consume any substance, concoction, drug, or alcoholic beverage, regardless of whether the person being coerced is of legal drinking age or appears to be participating willingly
- Keep vile, sexist pledge books, or require alumni or members to sign such books
- Participate in road trips and in the so-called "kidnapping" of pledges or in their abandonment
- Require or use peer pressure to get someone to agree to undergo branding, tattooing, chemical burning, burns with cigarettes or cigars, and any mutilation of the skin whatsoever
- Participate in dousing of initiates involving dangerous or objectionable substances such as chemicals, animal scents used by hunters or anglers, urine, human or animal feces, cleaning fluids, objects to be retrieved from toilets, and spoiled foods capable of causing or transmitting diseases or bacterial infections
- Make someone eat or drink objectionable, unusual, or spicy concoctions, substances, liquids, and foods
- Participate in boxing and wrestling matches, unauthorized swimming across lakes, ponds, and rivers, or hold competitions that are demeaning to those who participate
- Ask pledges to perform daily duties such as phoning members to awaken them
- Demand that pledges learn trivia about members and about the chapter, perform foolish pranks, and attend all-night pledging-related sessions; ask prospective members to learn chapter history if such a request interferes with academic study
- Require initiates to wear silly or unusual clothing or objects; require initiates to ask members or alumni to sign articles of clothing or flesh; force initiates to carry objects such as spears, paddles, oars, bricks, concrete blocks, stuffed animals, live animals, and so forth
- Require initiates to perform calisthenics, jogging, and exercise sessions or to engage in athletic contests such as football games in which members have protective gear and pledges do not
- Require raids on rival schools, groups, or organizations
- Require the performance of dangerous stunts or throw out dares that a prospective member feels obligated to take
- Demand that pledges keep silent or refrain from visiting their parents or nongroup members
- Hold activities during ordinary class times and study sessions, or that interfere with legitimate extracurricular, school-sponsored activities
- Extort money or demand fees not approved by the school or by the fraternal organization's headquarters and board of directors
- Participate in pledge lineups or anything leading to sleep deprivation
- Engage in harassment or shunning to coerce new individuals into quitting or to punish an initiate who has reported hazing to superiors
- Participate in illicit scavenger hunts requiring thievery or property destruction
- Engage in any activity that treats an initiate as a nonperson, an object to make sport of, or a being to be held in low regard because he or she has not yet been accepted as a member
- Require pledges to sleep in a closet, bathroom, or other unsatisfactory quarters

Source: Nuwer 1999, 35–37.

like this one as rites of passage that give their lives meaning and a sense of belonging. Saucier is only one of a large and growing number of college students who have died from hazing incidents in fraternities and sororities (see Box 12.1).

Why do college students engage in activities that are known to end in tragedy? Why do they blindly follow the leader even when it could end their young lives? The answer, it seems, is rather simple. In his book *Wrongs of Passage* (1999), Hank Nuwer argues that they are "dying to belong" (129). In other words, they conform to the expectations of the group because they want to be accepted and liked. All human groups have rules that define what is expected in order to belong, "what is done and what should be done; what is expected, good, desired, and even ideal, as well as what is bad or forbidden" (Sherif and Sherif 1969, 184). These rules are called *social norms*. Other terms that refer to social norms include *traditions*, *customs*, *laws*, *mores*, *taboos*, and *folkways*. Social norms regulate social life and ensure a certain degree of orderliness. So conforming to the group's expectations usually brings acceptance and other rewards. People who refuse to conform or deviate in ways that make them appear different from other group members will not win the acceptance of other group members. Instead, they are likely to be ridiculed and punished in various ways (see Box 12.2).

When people conform because they want to be accepted by the group, they are feeling the effect of normative social influence. The need to belong is rooted in the social nature of human beings. And that explains why conformity is more common than deviance. Even people who regard themselves as nonconformists and reject the normative regulation of behavior have been shown to adapt their own rules and standards over time (Sherif and Sherif 1969). To illustrate this tendency, Sherif and Sherif (1969) noted that "anarchists opposed to marriage in New York's bohemian circles . . . established informal liaisons as socially acceptable, while consigning marriage to the latitude of objectionable behavior. To remain 'good' bohemians, the couple that married kept the fact a secret from their bohemian friends" (188; see also Ware 1935).

Members of fraternities and sororities conform to the expectations of these groups because they want to be accepted and liked.

WHEN PEOPLE CONFORM

Our need to be right and our desire to be liked help us understand why we conform. Social psychologists also recognize that we are more likely to conform in certain kinds of situations than in others. Let us now consider two of the most important situational factors affecting conformity: group size and group cohesiveness.

Group Size

How does group size affect the tendency to conform? Research shows that conformity increases with group size up to a certain point (Asch 1955; Rosenberg 1961; Gerard, Wilhelmy, and Conolley 1968; McGuire 1968; Campbell and Fairey 1989). In an early study of group size, Asch (1955) manipulated the size of the majority from two to fifteen. His results showed that conformity does not increase significantly after the group reaches four or

BOX 12.2   A TEST FOR NONCONFORMITY

*If a man does not keep pace with his companions, perhaps
It is because he hears a different drummer. Let him step to the
music which he hears, however measured and far away.*
—Henry David Thoreau, *Walden*

What traits do noncomformists possess? Social psychologists have used the following scales to measure this concept.

PERSONAL VALUES SCALES

Please read over the following statements and for each one indicate (by a check in the appropriate space) whether it is something you *always admire* in other people, something you *always dislike*, or something that *depends on the situation* whether you admire it or not.

Creativity (Originality)	Always Admire	Depends on Situation	Always Dislike
Being able to create beautiful and artistic objects	☐	☐	☐
Developing new and different ways of doing things	☐	☐	☐
Constantly developing new ways of approaching life	☐	☐	☐
Inventing gadgets for the fun of it	☐	☐	☐
Trying out new ideas	☐	☐	☐
Being original in one's thoughts and ways of looking at things	☐	☐	☐
Always looking for new roads to travel	☐	☐	☐
Doing unusual things	☐	☐	☐
Creating unusual works of art	☐	☐	☐
Being an innovator	☐	☐	☐
Creating beautiful things for the enjoyment of other people	☐	☐	☐
Devoting one's entire energy to the development of new theories	☐	☐	☐
*Doing routine things all the time	☐	☐	☐
*Not having any new ideas	☐	☐	☐
*Enjoying a routine, patterned life	☐	☐	☐
*Doing things the same way that other people do them	☐	☐	☐
*Abiding by traditional ways of doing things	☐	☐	☐
*Repeating the ideas of others, without any innovation	☐	☐	☐
*Working according to a set schedule that doesn't vary from day to day	☐	☐	☐
*Painting or composing or writing in a traditional style	☐	☐	☐
*Keeping one's life from changing very much	☐	☐	☐

	Always Admire	Depends on Situation	Always Dislike
Independence			
Being a freethinking person who doesn't care what others think of his opinions	☐	☐	☐
Being outspoken and frank in expressing one's likes and dislikes	☐	☐	☐
Being independent	☐	☐	☐
Standing up for what one thinks is right, regardless of what others think	☐	☐	☐
Going one's own way as one pleases	☐	☐	☐
Being a nonconformist	☐	☐	☐
Being different from other people	☐	☐	☐
Encouraging other people to act as they please	☐	☐	☐
Thinking and acting freely, without social restraints	☐	☐	☐
Living one's own life, independent of others	☐	☐	☐
Being independent, original, nonconformist, different from other people	☐	☐	☐
*Conforming to the requirements of any situation and doing what is expected of one	☐	☐	☐
*Going along with the crowd	☐	☐	☐
*Acting in such a way as to gain the approval of others	☐	☐	☐
*Keeping one's opinions to oneself when they differ from the group's	☐	☐	☐
*Being careful not to express an idea that might be contrary to what other people believe	☐	☐	☐
*Always basing one's behavior on the recognition that one is dependent on other people	☐	☐	☐
*Acting so as to fit in with other people's way of doing things	☐	☐	☐
*Always checking on whether or not one's intended actions would be acceptable to other people	☐	☐	☐
*Never acting so as to violate social conventions	☐	☐	☐
*Suppressing one's desire to be unique and different	☐	☐	☐
*Working and living in harmony with other people.	☐	☐	☐

*Reverse-scored.

Sources: Robinson, Shaver, and Wrightsman 1991, 729, based on Scott 1965, 245–260.

five people. Milgram, Bickman, and Berkowitz (1969) studied this question with a field experiment that was conducted on a sidewalk in New York City. They sought to determine how the number of people who stopped and looked up would affect other people who passed by. They used groups of one, two, three, five, ten, and fifteen people. The results of this study showed that conformity increased from one to five persons and then leveled off (see Figure 12.3).

Cohesiveness: Collectivist versus Individualistic Group Cultures

Is conformity universal, or does it vary from culture to culture? A number of studies indicate that culture does influence the degree to which people conform (Bond 1988; Triandis et al. 1988). Using a modified design of Asch's classic group pressure experiment, Milgram (1961) compared the degree to which French and Norwegian students conformed. His results showed that conformity was higher among Norwegians. Milgram offered a cultural explanation for the observed differences, claiming that Norwegian society was "highly cohesive." "Norwegians have a deep feeling of group identification," he wrote, "and they are strongly attuned to the needs and interests of those around them" (51). In contrast, he saw French society as one that had a "tradition of dissent and critical argument," which would explain the low level of conformity found in French students (51).

The results of a meta-analysis by Rod Bond and Peter Smith (1996) provide further support for the idea that cultural values influence conformity. Based on studies conducted in seventeen countries, Bond and Smith found that subjects in collectivist cultures like China are more susceptible to normative social influence than subjects in individualistic cultures like the United States.

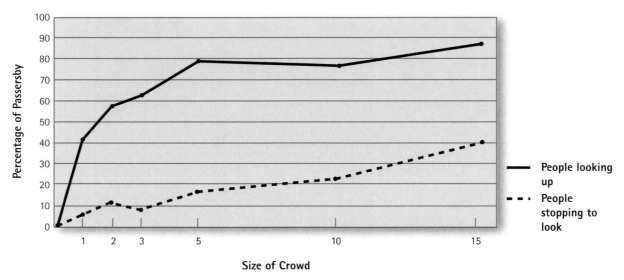

FIGURE 12.3

The Impact of Group Size on Conformity

Mean percentage of passersby who looked up and who stopped to look as a function of the size of the stimulus crowd assembled by the researchers.

Source: Milgram, Bickman, and Berkowitz 1969, 80.

Minority Influence: Moscovici's Consistency Theory

Research clearly shows the powerful influence of the majority. But history provides many examples of the extraordinary influence that minorities can have. Notable individuals whose minority influence changed the worlds in which they lived include Galileo, Darwin, Christ, Freud, Marx, and Einstein (Crano 1994). Martin Luther King Jr. influenced the attitudes of a nation toward racial injustices that had become deeply embedded in cultural norms. So did Nelson Mandela. How do minority individuals like these change the worlds in which they lived? Why do they stand as exceptions to the classical models of conformity?

Serge Moscovici (1994) provides some answers. He begins by arguing that throughout our lives, we repeatedly confront a dilemma, "the familiar dualism between the wish to rebel against shared conventions and the wish to strictly comply with them" (234). As he points out, this idea is not new but rather a presumption of social theories. Max Weber made the distinction "between the hierarchical bureaucratic institutions which ensure order in everyday life as well as the stability of collective relationships and the charismatic communities that are gathered together by the revelation of a creed, an ideal, bringing about social mutations, social big bangs" (Moscovici 1994, 234). Émile Durkheim made the distinction "between the routine states of life in common and the states of collective effervescence during which a society is renewed and sometimes changes its foundations after some political or religious revolution" (234–235). American sociologists recognize the distinction "between social structures and collective movements" (235). And social psychologists recognize this distinction as the difference between the need to conform and "the desire to change and innovate" (235).

Moscovici points out that social influence operates in two ways. Both majorities and minorities can serve as sources of social influence. Both are also targets of it. He refers to the influence of majorities as **social control** and argues that this kind of influence can be understood as the reproduction and stability of existing beliefs. In contrast, minority influence refers to **social change** and can be understood as innovation or change in existing

Nelson Mandela showed the world that minority influence can bring about dramatic social change.

beliefs. For Moscovici, the appeal of social change lies in his assumption that conformity of opinion can be damaging to the well-being of a group. Minority dissent offers a solution for this problem. But how can minorities exert their influence? Moscovici offers a theory based on three central concepts: the minority, conflict, and the semantics of influence.

The Concept of the Minority

Moscovici attaches a specific meaning to the concept of minority. To help us understand this concept, he begins with a reference to John Stuart Mill's essay *On Liberty* (1859), in which he discusses the value of two opposing opinions. Mill wrote:

> If either of the two opinions has a better claim than the other, not merely to be tolerated, but to be encouraged, it is the one which happens at the particular time and place to be in minority. That is the opinion which, for the time being, represents the neglected interests, the side of human well-being that is in danger of obtaining less than its share. (186)

According to Moscovici (1994), we immediately grasp what Mill means by minority. Claiming that we have all experienced this idea and emotion, he draws on George Herbert Mead's description of the self. In describing the interaction between the "I" and the "me" (see Chapter 4), Moscovici writes, "The 'I' designates in each of us not only an inner force facing the 'me' that tends to comply with the outer norms of the group, but chiefly a force tending to react in a vigorous, reflexive manner—especially in situations where a change is necessary" (237). The qualities of the "I" are clearly reflected in the artist, inventor, and scientist. But we all experience the reflexive influence of the "I" and the "me." The "I" acts to reconstruct society as well as the "me." The interaction between the "I" and the "me" produces new ways of seeing things and dramatic social change. According to Moscovici, this experience motivates certain individuals to change the world. It reflects

the "dualism between the tendency to conform and the tendency to innovate" (237). And it captures what Moscovici means by a minority that disagrees with a majority.

Conflict: Dissensus versus Consensus

The second concept in Moscovici's theory is a specific kind of conflict, which involves two opposing desires that minority groups and individuals arouse: the desire to approach new ideas versus the wish to avoid the conflict they produce. A number of prominent social thinkers have recognized the value of this kind of conflict, including Charles Horton Cooley (1909), who wrote, "Conflict, of some sort, is the life of society, and progress emerges from a struggle in which individual, class, or institution seeks to realize its own idea of good" (199). According to Moscovici (1994), minority influence depends on the ability of a group or individual to create this kind of conflict and to manage it effectively. Arguing that revolutionary change is possible, he claims that minority dissent is the key catalyst. But he does not imply that minorities alone are capable of innovation. In addition, he points out that minorities are viewed as irrational, eccentric nonconformists who should be avoided.

Research supports Moscovici's suggestion that people dislike minorities (Bassili and Provencal 1988). In a factor analysis of the traits attributed to minorities, John Bassili and Allison Provencal found that people regarded minorities as more assertive, less agreeable, more honest, more competent, and more consistent than majorities. This suggests a positive image of "strength, conviction, integrity, and consistency" (12). Yet the study clearly showed that minorities are disliked.

These findings offer some insight into Moscovici's claim that majorities tend to draw away from minorities, even though they are attracted to them. What is the attraction? Moscovici (1994) argues that they are

> seen as figures of awesome power whose action can exemplify the difference between progress and stagnation, knowledge and ignorance, freedom and

bondage. Therefore, they stand at the head of a lineage of people who have fought, vanquished, discovered, or created, so that ordinary people look upon them with admiration or envy or both. They are the heroes of mankind—artists, rulers, saints, scientists, and philosophers who inspire and lead, search and enlighten, and whose lives stand out as examples to the unrecognized potentials within each of us. (241)

Even though people may dislike minorities and the conflict they produce, research shows that minority dissent does provide benefits to the group (Nemeth and Wachtler 1983; Volpato et al. 1990; Mucchi-Faina, Maass, and Volpato 1991). Studies show that minority dissent leads people to take in more information, to think in more creative ways, and to find more solutions to problems (Nemeth 1994). At the same time, pressures to conform stifle the creativity of group members.

The Semantics of Influence

The third concept in Moscovici's theory led him to ask, "What is 'the power of the powerless'"? (a reference to a phrase coined by Czech President Vaclav Havel). Recognizing that minorities lack status, expertise, and credibility, Moscovici (1980) concluded that the power lies in a particular behavioral style—consistency (see also Maass, West, and Cialdini 1987). Describing the value of this trait, Moscovici (1994, 247) wrote, "Whether expressed by the repetition of arguments, a firm position, or coherence between what one says and what one does, it is felt to be an index of deep conviction, courage, or certainty."

Moscovici and his colleagues demonstrated the power of consistency in an early experiment, which resembled Asch's conformity study (Moscovici, Lage, and Naffrechoux 1969). The study involved the rating of color slides by a group of six subjects. In contrast to Asch's experiment, the majority of subjects in the experimental condition were not confederates but naive participants. The minority consisted of two stooges. Subjects were asked to judge whether the slides were blue or green. In reality, all of the slides were blue. In one experimental condition, the stooges consistently rated the slides as green. In this case, the results showed that about one-third of the naive subjects identified at least one slide as green and 8 percent of all ratings were described as green. When the stooges' responses were inconsistent, their influence on the majority was minimal. And in the control condition, which involved twenty-two naive subjects, only one subject identified two of the slides as green. Wendy Wood and her colleagues (1994) confirmed the power of consistency in a meta-analysis of ninety-seven studies.

COMPLIANCE

Have you ever come under the influence of a salesperson who quickly convinced you to buy something you did not need? Most of us have a few things in our closet to attest to that. Persuading others to yield to our wishes and commands might develop naturally. But social psychologists also recognize that people learn and master the art of gaining compliance from others. These people are called *compliance professionals* (Cialdini and Trost 1998).

How do these masters of persuasion get us to comply with their requests? The answers are found in studies that have accumulated for more than half a century. Beginning with research instituted during World War II to learn about programs of persuasion and public information (e.g., Lewin 1947; Hovland, Lumsdaine, and Sheffield 1949; Stouffer et al. 1949), social psychologists proceeded to investigate how the compliance process operates in a multitude of everyday situations. Whether the request is as small as buying a candy bar from a Boy Scout or as large as making a risky investment with one's lifetime savings, it probably involves one of six basic principles: reciprocation, consistency, social proof, liking, authority, and scarcity (Cialdini and Trost 1998).

In the book *Influence: Science and Practice*, Robert Cialdini (1993) shows how compliance professionals skillfully integrate these principles into tried-and-true strategies for getting us to agree to their requests. He begins by openly admitting that he has been a sucker for sales pitches, fund-raisers, and other tactics of compliance professionals his entire life. In fact, recognizing that he was an easy mark for their pitches, Cialdini spent years researching the process of compliance. At first, his research involved laboratory experiments. He eventually realized that he needed to work directly with the compliance professionals— salespeople, fund-raisers, advertisers—people who are in the business of getting us to say yes. Assuming the role of a participant observer, he answered newspaper ads for sales trainees and allowed the professionals to teach him their methods. After three years as a participant observer, Cialdini concluded that there are thousands of compliance strategies.

These strategies, he notes, produce automatic, unthinking compliance from people. And he argues that the fast pace of modern living will increase this kind of mindless compliance in the future. To help us understand how these strategies operate, he identifies and then explains the basic principles on which they rest. Warning us that we are sitting ducks for these skilled compliance professionals, he provides useful tips to help us recognize and avoid their traps.

Basic Principles of Compliance

Several of the basic principles of compliance operate exactly as we would expect. For example, we are more likely to agree to a request or to do a favor for someone we like. We are also likely to comply with people who are regarded as having legitimate authority, even if we do not like them. In this case, we do it because we are trained through the socialization process to respect and obey authority figures. The principle of social proof is also straightforward. As a form of informational social influence, it operates in the compliance process by providing clues to how we ought to behave. In this case, people determine how they ought to behave by observing what other people

do. Complying with the "cleanup rules" of a fast-food restaurant involves nothing more than seeing what other patrons do with their trays.

The principles of reciprocity, consistency, and scarcity also operate in ways that we would expect. But compliance professionals often devise strategies based on these principles that are not so obvious. For that reason, let us take a closer look at each of them.

Reciprocity

If someone gave you a birthday gift, would you feel obligated to buy her one? Most people do. The reason lies in a social norm found in most human societies—the **principle of reciprocity**—that teaches people that if someone does you a favor, you should repay it in kind (Gouldner 1960). In fact, in most societies this feeling of indebtedness is so strong that the expression "much obliged" often replaces the phrase "thank you" (Cialdini 1993).

This principle operates in all settings. In fact, many careers depend on it. Consider the political system. Politicians who violate the rule of reciprocity are unlikely to survive long. Many have used it skillfully to their advantage. Cialdini (1993) offered the successful record of President Lyndon Johnson as an example:

> Political analysts were amazed at Lyndon Johnson's success in getting so many of his programs through Congress during his early administration. Even Congress-members who were thought to be strongly opposed to the proposals were voting for them. Close examination by political scientists has found the cause to be not so much Johnson's political savvy as the large score of favors he had been able to provide to other legislators during his many years of power in the House and Senate. As President, he was able to produce a truly remarkable amount of legislation in a short time by calling in those favors. (28–29)

Providing further support for his reasoning, Cialdini argues that President Carter failed to recognize the value of reciprocity. In contrast to

Johnson, Carter came into office boasting that he was indebted to no one. Unfortunately, no one felt indebted to him either.

The norm of reciprocity is powerful because it offers benefits to society. By producing a sense of obligation to repay a favor, this norm contributes to the development of stable relationships. Through the process of socialization, we are taught that if we violate the norm of reciprocity, we will pay the consequences. We are therefore particularly susceptible to the tactics of compliance professionals who use this strategy. A common tactic is to do a favor before making a request. When the U.S. government offers financial aid to a Third World country, it creates a sense of future obligation. Charities that send us return address labels expect something in return. And perfume samples are never really free. Cialdini claims that the best defense against this strategy is to accept a favor but be prepared to recognize it as a trick.

Consistency

> If, as it appears, automatic consistency functions as a shield against thought, it should not be surprising that such consistency can also be exploited by those who would prefer that we respond to their requests without thinking. (Cialdini 1993, 65)

A number of social psychologists argue that people feel a need for consistency in their thoughts and actions (Heider 1946; Newcomb 1953; Festinger 1957). In fact, the **principle of consistency** forms the basis of a number of popular theories, including balance theory and cognitive dissonance. According to these theories, the need for consistency is a primary motivator of human behavior (Cialdini 1993). In his research on compliance, Cialdini wondered if this need could compel people to do things they would ordinarily not do. He concluded that there was "no question about it. The drive to be (and look) consistent constitutes a highly potent weapon of social influence, often causing us to act in ways that are clearly contrary to our own best interests" (61).

One reason that people prefer consistency is because it is efficient. In our complicated modern lives, it is easier to respond automatically—in a way that appears to be consistent with our fundamental values and beliefs. We do not have time to think about the issues or to consider all of the information (Cialdini 1993). Instead, we choose this easy way out.

The consistency principle operates particularly well after people make an initial commitment. For example, if a school principal convinces parents to volunteer thirty minutes a week to school activities, this commitment bodes well for future requests that involve the school. In addition, the desire for consistency often causes people to actively seek reasons to support their commitment decisions. Cialdini argues that this explains why hazing rituals for fraternities and sororities are so effective (see Box 12.3). The more pledges suffer, the stronger their commitment. Once they pass the test, they rationalize their suffering on the basis of how much they sacrificed to belong. From their perspective, it was all worthwhile.

Cialdini recognizes the value of consistency, but he also sees the danger in it. Consistency is usually a sign of honesty, stability, and sound reasoning. People who act consistently appear trustworthy. In contrast, those who act inconsistently seem two-faced, wishy-washy, or mentally ill. Consistency is not, however, always a good sign. In fact, it may reflect an unthinking, automatic approach to a complicated world. Ralph Waldo Emerson captured this idea in his essay *Self-Reliance* when he wrote, "A foolish consistency is the hobgoblin of little minds" (see Box 12.4, page 358).

Warning us against the danger of consistency pressures, Cialdini says that we should be sensitive to two internal signals. First, our stomach will tell us when we are feeling resistance to commitment and consistency pressures. In this case, we should simply explain that we recognize the foolishness in the consistency tactic. Second, our heart will give us a signal. In this case, Cialdini (1993) recommends that we ask a crucial question: "Knowing what I know, if I could go back in time, would I make the same commitment?" (106).

BOX 12.3	INITIATION RITES

In *Influence: Science and Practice* (1993), Robert Cialdini argues that primitive initiation rites are not just a relic of the past. After describing the rituals of an African tribe, the Thonga, he describes six incidents of hazing that occurred in the United States in college fraternities. Why are human beings so willing to suffer for acceptance into a group? Does greater suffering lead to higher levels of commitment? If so, why?

Before you answer, consider the tests that adolescent Thonga boys must pass to be accepted as men. Then consider what male college students are willing to do to become members of a college fraternity.

When a boy is somewhere between 10 and 16 years of age, he is sent by his parents to "circumcision school," which is held every 4 or 5 years. Here in company with his age-mates he undergoes severe hazing by the adult males of the society. The initiation begins when each boy runs the gauntlet between two rows of men who beat him with clubs. At the end of this experience he is stripped of his clothes and his hair is cut. He is next met by a man covered with lion manes and is seated upon a stone facing this "lion man." Someone then strikes him from behind and when he turns his head to see who has struck him, his foreskin is seized and in two movements cut off by the "lion man." Afterward he is secluded for

three months in the "yard of mysteries," where he can be seen only by the initiated. . . .

During the course of his initiation, the boy undergoes six major trials: beatings, exposure to cold, thirst, eating of unsavory foods, punishment, and the threat of death. On the slightest pretext, he may be beaten by one of the newly initiated men, who is assigned to the task by the older men of the tribe. He sleeps without covering and suffers bitterly from the winter cold. He is forbidden to drink a drop of water during the whole three months. Meals are often made nauseating by the half-digested grass from the stomach of an antelope, which is poured over his food. If he is caught breaking any important rule governing the ceremony, he is severely punished. For example, in one of these punishments, sticks are placed between the fingers of the offender, then a strong man closes his hand around that of the novice, practically crushing his fingers. He is frightened into submission by being told that in former times boys who had tried to escape or who had revealed the secrets to women or to the uninitiated were hanged and their bodies burned to ashes. (Whiting, Kluckhohn, and Anthony 1958, 359–360)

Do the rites of passage described here sound familiar? Cialdini argues that college fraternities expect pledges to pass similar kinds of tests in order to become members. Enduring suffering and hardship during the traditional

Scarcity

Anyone who has ever searched for an apartment in Manhattan understands the **principle of scarcity**. You hear about a studio apartment on the Upper East Side for rent, $1,200 a month. You call immediately. You meet with the superintendent, who tells you that it will not last long. If you are interested, you must make a decision on the spot. You hesitate—it has no window. But the price is right and the location is great. You tell him that you will think about it and get back to him. You call an hour later and it is already rented. You learned your lesson and rent the next apartment you see.

Nice apartments in New York City are rare, so this was not necessarily the best example to illustrate the scarcity principle. But it does show how

people react when they believe something will not last (see Box 12.5, page 359). Consider a few more examples. A real estate agent is likely to claim that it is a hot market and that lake homes sell quickly. A furniture salesperson will warn you that the sale ends tomorrow. And an auctioneer will stress that an item is one-of-a-kind.

In each of these cases, the scarcity principle is operating. We are likely to assign a greater value to an item simply because it is rare or will not be available for long. This strategy, which is often used in business, may involve a pitch that specifies a time deadline or a limited number of goods (Cialdini 1993). One reason that the scarcity principle works so well is that it threatens our freedom. According to psychological reactance theory, when people feel that their freedom will be restricted in

fraternity "Hell Week" is the cost associated with acceptance into one's fraternity of choice. In some cases, the cost is very high. Consider the following examples drawn from newspaper reports of hazing rituals (Cialdini 1993, 82–84).

- *Beatings.* Fourteen-year-old Michael Kalogris spent three weeks in a Long Island hospital recovering from internal injuries suffered during a Hell Night initiation ceremony of his high school fraternity, Omega Gamma Delta. He had been administered the "atomic bomb" by his prospective brothers, who told him to hold his hands over his head and keep them there while they gathered around to slam fists into his stomach and back simultaneously and repeatedly.
- *Exposure to cold.* On a winter night, Frederick Bronner, a California junior college student, was taken 3,000 feet up and 10 miles into the hills of a national forest by his prospective fraternity brothers. Left to find his way home wearing only a thin sweatshirt and slacks, Fat Freddy, as he was called, shivered in a frigid wind until he tumbled down a steep ravine, fracturing bones and hurting his head. Prevented by his injuries from going on, he huddled there against the cold until he died of exposure.
- *Thirst.* Two Ohio State University freshmen found themselves in the "dungeon" of their prospective fraternity house after breaking the rule requiring all pledges to crawl into the dining area prior to Hell Week meals. Once

locked in the house storage closet, they were given only salty foods to eat for nearly two days. Nothing was provided for drinking purposes except a pair of plastic cups in which they could catch their own urine.
- *Eating of unsavory food.* At Kappa Sigma house on the campus of the University of Southern California, the eyes of eleven pledges bulged when they saw the sickening task before them. Eleven quarter-pound slabs of raw liver lay on a tray. Thick cut and soaked in oil, each was to be swallowed whole, one to a boy. Gagging and choking repeatedly, young Richard Swanson failed three times to down his piece. Determined to succeed, he finally got the oil soaked meat into his throat where it lodged and, despite all efforts to remove it, killed him.
- *Punishment.* In Wisconsin, a pledge who forgot one section of a ritual incantation to be memorized by all initiates was punished for his error. He was required to keep his feet under the rear legs of a folding chair while the heaviest of his fraternity brothers sat down and drank a beer. Although the pledge did not cry out during the punishment, a bone in each of his feet was broken.
- *Threats of death.* A pledge of Zeta Beta Tau fraternity was taken to a beach area of New Jersey and told to dig his "own grave." Seconds after he complied with orders to lie flat in the finished hole, the sides collapsed, suffocating him before his prospective fraternity brothers could dig him out.

some way, they are likely to respond by wanting something even more than before (Brehm 1966; Brehm and Brehm 1981). One of the places where this principle operates particularly well is with censored or banned information (Cialdini 1993). Consider a typical teenager's reaction to knowing that his school has banned a certain book from its reading list. Research suggests that even students who hate to read will rush out and buy the book (Zellinger et al. 1974).

Specific Techniques for Gaining Compliance

Now that we have considered the basic principles underlying the compliance process, let us examine some specific techniques used by salespeople, fund-raisers, and other compliance professionals.

We will consider three of the most common ones: the foot in the door, the door in the face, and lowballing.

The Foot-in-the-Door Technique. One way to persuade people to comply with a request is called the **foot-in-the-door technique**. Compliance professionals know that if you can convince someone to do a small favor for you, he is more likely to agree to a larger favor later. Jonathan Freedman and Scott Fraser (1966) demonstrated how this technique works in a classic experiment. Identifying themselves as working for the Committee for Safe Driving, they asked a group of homeowners if they would sign a petition to support safe driving. Nearly all of the homeowners agreed to this small request. Two weeks later, the experimenters

BOX 12.4	RALPH WALDO EMERSON ON SELF-RELIANCE

Emerson had a reputation as an individualist. These excerpts from his essay *Self-Reliance* show two things: first, the importance he placed on individualism and non-conformity, and second, the idea that consistency can be harmful. Emerson warns us about thoughtless consistency and conformity. And he points out that great thinkers relied on themselves, not on society's rules, laws, or customs.

These are the voices which we hear in solitude, but they grow faint and inaudible as we enter into the world. Society everywhere is in conspiracy against the manhood of every one of its members. Society is a joint-stock company, in which the members agree, for the better securing of his bread to each shareholder, to surrender the liberty and culture of the eater. The virtue in most request is conformity. Self-reliance is its aversion. It loves not realities and creators, but names and customs.

Whoso would be a man, must be a nonconformist. He who would gather immortal palms must not be hindered by the name of goodness, but must explore if it be goodness. Nothing is at last sacred but the integrity of your own mind.

A foolish consistency is the hobgoblin of little minds, adored by little statesmen and philosophers and divines. With consistency a great soul has simply nothing to do. He may as well concern himself with his shadow on the wall. . . . If you would be a man speak what you think to-day in words as hard as cannon balls, and to-morrow speak what to-morrow thinks in hard words again, though it contradict everything you said to-day. Ah, then, exclaim the aged ladies, you shall be sure to be misunderstood! Misunderstood! It is a right fool's word. Is it so bad then to be misunderstood? Pythagoras was misunderstood, and Socrates, and Jesus, and Luther, and Copernicus and Galileo, and Newton, and every pure and wise spirit that ever took flesh. To be great is to be misunderstood.

---

approached the same people and another group of homeowners who had not been asked to sign the petition. This time they asked if they could put a large, unattractive sign in their front yards that read "Drive Carefully." The results confirmed the researchers' expectation. More than half of the people who had signed the petition allowed the researchers to put the sign out front. Only 17 percent of the homeowners who had not been asked to do the smaller favor agreed to the larger request.

Why does this strategy work? According to social psychologists, the foot-in-the-door technique is successful because it involves perceptions about who we are. When someone agrees to do a small favor, he comes to view himself as someone who is willing to help. This self-perception operates later when someone asks for a bigger favor. Research also shows that this technique works particularly well with people who prefer consistency (Guardagno et al. 2001).

The Door-in-the-Face Technique. Another strategy for gaining compliance, the **door-in-the-face technique**, involves just the opposite approach. In this case, someone begins with a large request followed by a smaller one. Cialdini and his colleagues (1975) demonstrated how this operates in an experiment. In one condition, they contacted students and asked them if they would chaperone adolescents from the county juvenile detention center for a two-hour trip to the zoo. When they were approached in this way, 17 percent of them agreed to do so. In the door-in-the-face condition, the researchers started with a much larger request. They told students that they were seeking volunteers to work as nonpaid counselors for the county juvenile detention center and that the position involved a commitment of two hours a week for two years. As the researchers expected, this long-term commitment was too much to ask. In fact, all of the students turned down the request. When they refused, the researchers then made a smaller request. Would they volunteer to chaperone adolescents from the county juvenile detention center on a two-hour trip to the zoo? This strategy worked. Fifty percent of the students agreed to the smaller

BOX 12.5	SWINDLED!

NEW YORK—Daniel Gulban doesn't remember how his life savings disappeared.

He remembers the smooth voice of a salesman on the telephone. He remembers dreaming of a fortune in oil and silver futures. But to this day, the 80-year-old retired utility worker does not understand how swindlers convinced him to part with $18,000.

"I just wanted to better my life in my waning days," said Gulban, a resident of Holder, Fla. "But when I found out the truth, I couldn't eat or sleep. I lost 30 pounds. I still can't believe I would do anything like that."

Gulban was the victim of what law enforcement officials call a "boiler-room operation," a ruse that often involves dozens of fast-talking telephone salesmen crammed into a small room where they call thousands of customers each day. The companies snare hundreds of millions of dollars each year from unsuspecting customers, according to a U.S. Senate subcommittee on investigations, which issued a report on the subject last year.

"They use an impressive Wall Street address, lies and deception to get individuals to sink their money into various glamorous-sounding schemes," said Robert Abrams, the New York State attorney general, who has pursued more than a dozen boiler-room cases in the past four years. "The victims are sometimes persuaded to invest the savings of a lifetime."

Orestes J. Mihaly, the New York assistant attorney general in charge of the bureau of investor protection and securities, said the companies often operate in three stages.

First, Mihaly said, comes the "opening call," in which a salesman identifies himself as representing a company with an impressive-sounding name and address. He will simply ask the potential customer to receive the company's literature.

A second call involves a sales pitch, Mihaly said. The salesman first describes the great profits to be made and then tells the customer that it is no longer possible to invest. The third call gives the customer a chance to get in on the deal, he said, and is offered with a great deal of urgency.

"The idea is to dangle a carrot in front of the buyer's face and then take it away," Mihaly said. "The aim is to get someone to want to buy quickly, without thinking too much about it." Sometimes, Mihaly said, the salesman will be out of breath on the third call and will tell the customer that he "just came off the trading floor."

Such tactics convinced Gulban to part with his life savings. In 1979, a stranger called him repeatedly and convinced Gulban to wire $1,756 to New York to purchase silver, Gulban said. After another series of telephone calls the salesman cajoled Gulban into wiring more than $6,000 for crude oil. He eventually wired an additional $9,740, but his profits never arrived.

"My heart sank, " Gulban recalled. "I was not greedy. I just hoped I would see better days." Gulban never recouped his losses.

Source: Kerr 1983.

request—three times the number who had agreed without an initial large request.

Robert Cialdini (1993) argues that this strategy involves the principle of reciprocation. Instead of calling it the door in the face, he prefers to call it the **rejection-then-retreat technique**. The rule of reciprocation operates because the parties view this as a process of compromise. When someone turns down a large request, she is likely to view the person who asked for the favor as making a concession. To reciprocate the concession, she is then likely to agree to the second request.

All kinds of negotiations illustrate how the rejection-then-retreat strategy works. It clearly operates on Capitol Hill, where legislators write bills packed full of items that will serve as compromises in the bargaining process. Labor unions often take extreme positions when they negotiate new contracts, recognizing that they will have to make a series of concessions before they accept a final deal. Even children approach their parents with extreme requests, fully understanding how the compromise process operates.

Talented negotiators realize just how far they can go and take positions that will allow for reciprocal concessions (Cialdini 1993). To show how this operates in natural settings, Cialdini describes how television writers and producers have used this strategy in negotiations with network censors. Recognizing Garry Marshall as one of the best negotiators for getting around the censors, he cites an article from *TV Guide:*

> But Marshall . . . not only admits his tricks . . . he seems to revel in them. On one episode of his [then] top-rated *Laverne and Shirley* series, for example, he says, "We had a situation where Squiggy's in a rush to get out of his apartment and meet some girls upstairs. He says, 'Will you hurry up before I lose my lust?' But in the script we put something even stronger, knowing the censors would cut it. They did; so we asked innocently, well, how about 'lose my lust'? That's good, they said. Sometimes you gotta go at 'em backward."
>
> On the *Happy Days* series, the biggest censorship fight was over the word *virgin*. That time, says Marshall, "I knew we'd have trouble, so we put the word in seven times, hoping they'd cut six and keep one. It worked. We used the same pattern again with the word *pregnant*." (Russell 1978, 40)

The Lowball Technique. Lowballing involves the principles of consistency and commitment (Cialdini 1993). Consider how this might operate in the purchase of a car. Suppose you are checking out the cars at a dealership when a salesperson approaches you and entices you with an offer that is $1,000 below the best price you've seen for the car you want. Of course, this offer is not designed to pan out. Its aim is rather to commit you to this dealership. The commitment process gets under way when you take the car out for a spin, begin to discuss the financing, and fill out the paperwork. As the consistency principle would suggest, you begin to justify this purchase with mounting reasons (Teger 1980; Brockner and Rubin 1985). Then the manager of the dealership enters the picture. He tells you that the salesperson made a mistake in the calculations and that he could not possibly sell the car for that price. But he also points out that the new price is fair and that his dealership offers the best service in town. Would

you buy the car? If you are like most people, you do (Cialdini 1993). Of course, that really depends on whether or not you view this as a trick.

Obedience to Authority

We have considered a number of examples in this chapter that illustrate how people unthinkingly conform or comply with the expectations of leaders or members of groups to which they seek admission. Ron Jones's students blindly committed themselves to the Wave. They strictly obeyed and enforced rules without questioning them. Fraternity and sorority members engage in activities that are called traditions but often harm and even kill pledges. And we are all susceptible to the strategies of compliance professionals. In the last section of this chapter, we will consider the third kind of behavior that reflects social influence: obedience to authority.

The My Lai Massacre. One of the best examples to illustrate how this operates occurred during the Vietnam War in a small village called My Lai. The incident, which came to be known as the My Lai massacre, was captured in images that later appeared in *Life* magazine:

> piles of bodies jumbled together in a ditch along a trail—the dead all apparently unarmed. All were oriental, and all appeared to be children, women, or old men. Clearly there had been a mass execution, one whose image would not quickly fade. (Kelman and Hamilton 1989, 2)

The details of exactly what happened here on March 16, 1968, became the focus of a long congressional investigation and the subject of numerous books. Lieutenant Colonel Frank Barker and his staff had planned the operation with the intent of disbanding the 48th Viet Cong Battalion. Exactly what he ordered, however, was unclear. No written orders existed, and witnesses gave conflicting accounts of what had been discussed during military briefings. But Lieutenant Colonel Barker did state that he expected only Viet Cong to remain in the village after 7 A.M. on the day of the

Law enforcement officers must obey the orders of superiors or face disciplinary action. If, however, an order is illegal, they have a duty to disobey it.

mission. He assumed that innocent villagers would be at the market. The plan, which was considered a search-and-destroy mission, would involve the destruction of the area. Despite conflicting testimony, the evidence suggested that Barker's orders were to destroy houses, dwellings, livestock, and food supplies.

Did Barker order the killing of civilians? Again, that was unclear. The only conclusion the investigators could draw was that he had given little or no instructions in that regard. According to the final report, this allowed for serious misunderstandings, and it left soldiers with a great deal of latitude for interpretation. That was further complicated by a particularly emotional funeral the day before for a sergeant who had been killed by a booby trap. Did that predispose these soldiers to revenge? Many of these questions remain unanswered because Barker was killed in action in June 1968.

What became known during the investigation was the extent of the atrocities committed. The report included clear evidence that this was a war crime. As the report indicated, innocent civilians were brutally murdered:

Nineteen-year-old Nguyen Thi Ngoc Tuyet watched a baby trying to open her slain mother's blouse to nurse. A soldier shot the infant while it was struggling with the blouse, and then slashed it with his bayonet. Tuyet also said he saw another baby hacked to death by GIs wielding their bayonets. Le Tong, a twenty-eight-year-old rice farmer, reported seeing one woman raped after GIs killed her children. Nguyen Khoa, a thirty-seven-year-old peasant, told of a thirteen-year-old girl who was raped before being killed. GIs then attacked Khoa's wife, tearing off her clothes. Before they could rape her, however, Khoa said, their six-year-old son, riddled with bullets, fell and saturated her with blood. The GIs left her alone. (Hersh 1970, 72)

The soldiers who participated in the My Lai incident were not crazy or insane. In fact, an army unit that investigated this incident described the men as "average" for the time, place, and war (Kelman and Hamilton 1989). In his report on the massacre, Seymour S. Hersh (1970) wrote that most of the men had volunteered for the draft and were between the ages of 18 and 22. Almost half of the soldiers were African Americans, and a few were Mexican Americans. Few had attended college, and their favorite source of reading material was comic books. Like soldiers who have committed similar kinds of crimes in wars since the beginning of time, these men were just like us—average people.

One of the most troubling aspects of this incident was that many of these murders were organized. The investigation identified Lieutenant William Calley as the authority primarily responsible for this organized crime. He was tried for 102 murders and convicted of 22 in 1971. Although other soldiers also stood trial, he was the only one convicted in the My Lai massacre.

Stanley Milgram's Experiment. What causes average people to act in ways that we regard as so abnormal? What if you found yourself in that situation? Would you question the orders of the person in command, or would you obey orders without hesitating? Stanley Milgram (1965, 1974) designed a classic experiment hoping to answer to these questions. It is now also remembered for the ethical questions it raised about research that involves human subjects.

As Milgram's experiment is described, try to imagine yourself as one of his subjects. You have been chosen to participate in a study on learning and memory that was advertised in the newspaper. When you arrive for the experiment, you meet another participant who is sitting in the waiting room. The experimenter comes in and explains that the study seeks to understand how punishment affects learning. He then asks you to draw straws to decide who will play the role of the teacher. The straws indicate that you will be the teacher. Your job appears simple enough. You must simply teach your student, the other subject, pairs of words. After you have gone through the list of word pairs, the student will then be tested to determine how many of the pairs he remembers correctly. At that point, your job will change. Now you must punish the student for making mistakes.

The punishment for incorrect answers involves an electrical shock that will be delivered through a machine that can deliver from 15 to 450 volts. You are seated in front of this machine, where you see levers that label the full range of shocks that you will deliver each time the learner makes a mistake. The lower levels of shock are labeled "Slight Shock." "Danger: Severe Shock" appears near the highest levels. And next to the 450 volts you simply see "XXX." To get an idea of how painful these shocks are, the experimenter attaches an electrode to your arm and flips the lever for 45 volts. As you can imagine, the shock is very painful. The electrodes are now attached to the learner who is strapped into a chair, and you are ready to begin. The experimenter indicates that when the learner makes his first mistake, you should administer 15 volts as the punishment. For each subsequent mistake, you should increase the shock by 15 volts.

To test how much the student has learned, you will read the first word of the pair and then give four possible answers. The student will respond by flipping a switch that will turn on a light that is located on the machine. At first, it seems that the student has mastered the list of word pairs. But then he starts to make mistakes. You proceed as instructed to administer the punishment in increasing levels of 15 volts. When you reach the 75-volt level, the learner responds in pain. At 120 volts, he lets out a painful yelp and tells you that it really hurts. And by 150 volts, he is begging you to stop and complains of heart problems. What do you do?

If you are like most subjects, you look to the experimenter for further instructions. But he does not tell you to stop; he says that you should continue. You obey reluctantly. As the voltage increases, the learner continues to complain about the pain. You continue to look for a sign from the experimenter that you should stop. But he never gives any indication to stop.

At what point would you stop? Would you go all the way and administer 450 volts? How many people in this experiment do you suppose gave the highest level of shock? These are the questions that Milgram sought to answer with this experiment. When he asked a small group of Yale psychology majors and psychiatrists this question, they thought that fewer than 2 percent of the subjects would deliver the maximum level of shock. Far from these expectations, however, the actual results showed that 65 percent of the subjects (twenty-six out of forty) delivered the highest level of shock, 450 volts. (In truth, the learner did not receive any actual shocks; he was a confederate who had been instructed to fake his suffering.)

Crimes of Obedience

When you think of the long and gloomy history of man, you will find more hideous crimes have been committed in the name of obedience than have ever been committed in the name of rebellion.
—C. P. Snow, *The Two Cultures and the Scientific Revolution*

Milgram's experiment demonstrated that most people obey the orders of an authority figure with little resistance. Like crimes committed in wars, his experiment fits what Kelman and Hamilton (1989) call a "crime of obedience." The distinguishing feature of this kind of crime involves two opposing social norms: the duty to obey versus the duty to disobey. The duty to obey finds its origin in the concept of authority, which is supported by widely accepted social norms. In Western society, these norms are found in religious and moral teachings. They assume a variety of forms in different social institutions and are backed up with serious consequences for individuals who violate them. For example, obedience to authority is the first lesson that soldiers learn. This norm is so important to the operation of the military that it is regarded as a law and is strictly enforced.

But social institutions also recognize that certain situations require us to disobey the orders of authority figures. Evidence of these countervailing norms exist in the Bible as well as military laws that specify the conditions under which disobedience is expected and where obedience would be met with punishment.

Max Weber's essay *Politics as a Vocation* (1918/1977) was one of the first to address the question of obedience to authority. Recognizing that the state can exist only if the dominated obey

authority, Weber asked, "When and why do men obey? Upon what inner justifications and upon what external means does this domination rest?" (78). Referring to the notion of legitimate domination (authority), or the right to command, Weber claimed that genuine domination involves voluntary compliance or an interest in obedience. He then described three pure types of legitimate authority: traditional, charismatic, and legal or rational authority. When legitimate authority rests on tradition, people obey because they believe in the sanctity of immemorial traditions. Charismatic authority lies in a devotion to the exceptional characteristics of a leader. And legal or rational authority rests on an acceptance of legally enacted rules.

Modern conceptions of authority view it as a relationship of roles (Kelman and Hamilton 1989). Each role is defined in terms of the other party in the relationship, reflecting the shared assumption that authorities have the right to command and citizens have a duty to obey them. The difference between authority and absolute power is made clear by this assumption, which emphasizes the right to command and the duty to obey. The language associated with the concept of authority also reflects this distinction. For example, words like *orders, obedience, obligation,* and *duty* suggest how the nature of an authority relationship differs from that defined by sheer power.

Justified Disobedience. One of the most remarkable findings of the My Lai investigation showed that more than one soldier refused to obey Lieutenant Calley's orders to murder innocent civilians. When he was asked if he had fired at the villagers, Private James Joseph Dursi said:

> "No. I just stood there. Meadlo turned to me after a couple of minutes and said, 'Shoot! Why don't you shoot! Why don't you fire!' He was crying and yelling. I said, 'I can't! I won't!' And the people were screaming and crying and yelling. They kept firing for a couple of minutes, mostly automatic and semi-automatic." (Hammer 1971, 143)

When do people resort to justified disobedience? As it turns out, this decision is difficult for most of us. In fact, our tendency is to presume that authorities have legitimacy (Kelman and Hamilton 1989). What is more, questioning authority usually requires the adoption of a new ideology that then justifies a new order. New ideologies are a collective product, which explains why justified disobedience usually occurs as a collective effort.

Strong social norms that teach us to follow the rules and that encourage obedience also contribute to our tendency to regard authority as legitimate. Obedience to the rules and laws is regarded as normal. Acts of disobedience thus require another set of norms that tells us when we have a duty to disobey authority. These norms specify the grounds for determining when authority is illegitimate.

Scholars offer a number of examples that specify the conditions under which we have a duty to disobey authority. The Code of Maimonides states it clearly: "If a king ordered violation of God's commandments, he is not to be obeyed" (Laws of Kings 3:9). Jewish law contains a similar version of this norm regarding the military (Kelman and Hamilton 1989). In his analysis of the law, Kirschenbaum (1974) points out that the duty to obey is not absolute. In fact, if the order is illegal, a soldier must disobey or else take personal responsibility for his actions.

Historical examples teach us important lessons about the circumstances that require us to disobey authority. One of the most important lessons came from the civil rights movement of the 1950s and 1960s. Drawing on ideas that can be traced back to Saint Augustine, the Reverend Martin Luther King Jr. (1963/2000) captured it eloquently in a letter to his colleagues:

My Dear Fellow Clergymen:

While confined here in the Birmingham city jail, I came across your recent statement calling my present activities "unwise and untimely." . . . You express a great deal of anxiety over our willingness to break laws. This is certainly a legitimate concern. Since we so diligently urge people to obey the Supreme Court's decision of 1954 outlawing segregation in the public schools, at first glance it may seem rather paradoxical for us consciously to break laws. One may well ask, "How can you advocate breaking some laws and obeying others?" The answer lies in the fact that there are two types of laws: just and unjust. I would be the first to advocate obeying just laws. One has not only a legal but a moral responsibility to obey just laws. Conversely, one has a moral responsibility to disobey unjust laws. I would agree with St. Augustine that "an unjust law is no law at all." . . .

Now, what is the difference between the two? How does one determine whether a law is just or unjust? A just law is a man-made code that squares with the moral law or the law of God. An unjust law is a code that is out of harmony with the moral law. To put it in the terms of St. Thomas Aquinas: An unjust law is a human law that is not rooted in eternal law and natural law. Any law that uplifts human personality is just. Any law that degrades human personality is unjust. All segregation statutes are unjust because segregation distorts the soul and damages the personality. (570–571)

SUMMARY

1. Social influence refers to the exercise of power by a person or group to produce changes in an individual's thoughts, feelings, or behaviors. Three kinds of behaviors reflect social influence: conformity, compliance, and obedience. Conformity refers to a change in a person's thoughts or behaviors that moves him or her toward those of a group. Compliance suggests that how we behave or the attitudes we express do not necessarily reflect that these have been internalized. We may comply to please someone or to avoid an unfavorable reaction. Obedience to authority is a form of voluntary compliance that rests on a person's belief that someone has the right to make a request or give an order.

2. Sherif and Asch conducted two classic experiments to understand why people conform. Sherif's study

illustrated how informational social influence operates. In ambiguous situations where people cannot rely on objective measures to determine the right answer, they will conform to the group norm because they want to be right. Asch's study showed that even when the right answer is clear, people still tend to conform. In this case, the reason lies in the desire to be liked.

3. Situational factors such as group size and group cohesiveness influence the tendency to conform. Cultural values like individualism and collectivism also influence conformity.

4. Although conformity is usually a result of the influence of the majority, the minority can also exercise its influence. Maintaining consistency is an effective way for minorities to do this.

5. Compliance professionals use many strategies to get people to agree to their requests. These strategies are based on six basic principles: reciprocation, consistency, social proof, liking, authority, and scarcity. Specific techniques for gaining compliance include the foot-in-the-door technique, the door-in-the-face technique, and lowballing.

6. The My Lai massacre is an example of the social influence called obedience to authority. Milgram's classic experiment on obedience suggested that most people will obey the orders of an authority figure.

7. Crimes of obedience involve opposing social norms: the duty to obey versus the duty to disobey. One of the most remarkable findings of the My Lai investigation showed that more than one soldier refused to obey the order to murder innocent civilians. In a letter to his fellow clergymen, Martin Luther King Jr. explained why people have a moral responsibility to disobey unjust laws.

KEY TERMS

Social influence   341
Obedience   341
Conformity   341
Compliance   341
Identification   342
Internalization   342

Informational social influence   345
Normative social influence   345
Social control   351
Social change   351
Principle of reciprocity   354
Principle of consistency   355

Principle of scarcity   356
Foot-in-the-door technique   357
Door-in-the-face technique   358
Rejection-then-retreat technique   359
Lowballing   360

CRITICAL REVIEW QUESTIONS

1. How do college students use fashion to express their individuality today? Is this really an expression of conformity? If so, what function do these "fashions" really serve?

2. Consider the last time you bought something you did not need. Who was the compliance professional who successfully convinced you to make the purchase? What strategy was used?

3. Under what conditions do people have the duty to disobey the requests or orders of authority figures?

THIRTEEN

Groups
and Organizations

On September 11, 2001, four small groups of men carried out terrorist missions that shocked the world. At 8:45 A.M., Mohammed Atta and his group crashed American Airlines flight 11 into the North Tower of the World Trade Center in New York City at a speed of more than 378 miles an hour. Hitting at about the ninety-sixth floor, floors 94 to 99 were completely destroyed upon impact. Less than twenty minutes later, at 9:03 A.M., Marwan Al-Shehhi and his group guided United Airlines flight 175 into the South Tower of the World Trade Center. As the world watched, an inferno engulfed the upper floors of these buildings; all 110 stories would collapse. Other events began to unfold outside of Washington, D.C. At 9:38 A.M., Hani Hanjour and his group of terrorists crashed American Airlines flight 77 into the southwest side of the Pentagon. Americans watched and listened as news of yet another hijacked flight trickled in. At 9:16 A.M., the FAA announced that United Airlines flight 93 had probably been hijacked. Passengers aboard the flight learned about the other hijackings through conversations on cell phones. Their attempts to stop their hijackers probably prevented an attack on another Washington, D.C., target. But tragically, all aboard flight 93 died when it crashed near Shanksville, Pennsylvania.

It did not take long for officials to realize that America was under attack by a terrorist group. In his efforts to calm the nation, President George W. Bush vowed to bring these terrorists to justice. But, he warned, it would take time. Rooting out the terrorists—Osama bin Laden and the members of Al Qaeda—would require a strategy far more complicated than the plan that led to their attacks on New York and Washington, D.C. And the cost of the American operation promised to be staggering—far more than the $500,000 that Al Qaeda spent on the 9/11 attacks.

The Al Qaeda attack on America showed just how serious underestimating the power of an enemy can be. It did not, however, provide any ideas for how we might manage and counter this threat. And that is what President Bush could not explain and what stumped the authorities responsible for national security. Where would the ideas come from? According to Rohan Gunaratna (2002), a leading expert on Al Qaeda, they would come from a full understanding of this terrorist group.

We now know that Al Qaeda is a sophisticated terrorist organization. Individual members are highly committed to Al Qaeda and loyal followers of Osama bin Laden, a wealthy Saudi expatriate. But understanding how it operates presents a daunting challenge: Al Qaeda is unlike any other terrorist group. United States intelligence agencies that had tracked and studied terrorist groups since 1968 failed to see the vast threat sprawl across four continents. In fact, they did not even know the name of Osama bin Laden's group until 1998 after it had attacked U.S. diplomatic targets in East Africa. Gunaratna has provided the most complete picture of Al Qaeda to date. His investigation, which took five years, involved an analysis of hundreds of telephone and e-mail communications. He interviewed more than two hundred rank-and-file terrorists in more than fifteen countries and, remarkably, managed to interview top leaders of Al Qaeda.

The picture he paints shows a complex organization that is goal-oriented, not rule-oriented. It is not locked into a fixed structure but is capable of changing as circumstances dictate. To get an understanding of what we face, consider the various descriptions offered by Gunaratna (2002):

> Al Qaeda is the first multinational terrorist group of the twenty-first century, and it confronts the world with a new kind of threat. (1)
> Al Qaeda is above all else a secret, almost virtual, organization, one that denies its own existence in order to remain in the shadows. (1)
> Although its ideology is puritanical, Al Qaeda is an essentially modern organization, one that exploits up-to-date technology for its own ends,

relying on satellite phones, laptop computers, encrypted communications websites for hiding messages, and the like. (15)
> Al Qaeda cuts across historical and sectarian barriers, drawing its membership from all strata of society. However, it remains an overwhelmingly Sunni group, doctrinally and otherwise. (16)

These descriptions lead us to ask a number of questions. First, in what way does Al Qaeda resemble a multinational corporation? Second, how does such a large organization carry out missions that require such high levels of secrecy and trustworthiness? Third, how does it reconcile its puritanical ideology with its use of modern technology? Fourth, how does the organization recruit such diverse members? And finally, what makes this group so cohesive? Let us take a quick look at some of the answers that Gunaratna suggests.

In some respects, Al Qaeda appears to resemble other multinational organizations. Its high command operates in the form of a vertical leadership structure that develops strategy and provides the tactical resources to its horizontal network of cells and associate organizations (Gunaratna 2002). This unusual organizational structure provides the best defense against enemy intelligence. The vertically structured part of Al Qaeda includes three top levels. Osama bin Laden, the *emir-general*, sits on top. Directly below him are the *shura majlis*, his consultative council. Below this council sit four operational committees: military; finance and business; *fatwa* (religious decrees) and Islamic study; and media and publicity.

To appreciate the complexity of each committee, consider just one, the finance and business committee. According to Gunaratna (2002), intelligence agents have never seen such a sophisticated financial group within a terrorist organization. This committee, which manages Al Qaeda's money across four continents, consists of professional bankers, accountants, and financiers. To protect the identities of parties involved in the transfer of money, this committee has created a number of legitimate organizations such as banks, companies, and charities. In many respects, it operates like any multinational corporation.

Gunaratna even notes that "some have likened it to the Ford Foundation, where researchers present projects and after careful consideration some are funded while most are discarded" (91).

The complexity of the financial and business committee requires the assistance of intelligent and highly educated personnel. They, like all Al Qaeda members, must meet the highly selective criteria that this organization uses to determine its membership. According to Gunaratna (2002), Al Qaeda screens out "only the most committed, most trustworthy and most capable operatives. Islamists from all over the world regard it as the very highest honor to be accepted as a full Al Qaeda member; in fact they almost fight to get in" (11).

This explains one of the most surprising features of Al Qaeda—its diversity: Members come from all strata of society—poor and rich, illiterate and highly educated, professional bankers and warriors. Though these social differences could divide them, members' commitment to achieving the goals of Al Qaeda makes this a highly cohesive group. They display a kind of passionate commitment that no amount of money could buy and no kind of military training could produce. No higher level of commitment exists: Al Qaeda members are willing to die for the organization. This extraordinary commitment is rooted in Al Qaeda's ideology and reflects the personal quality that determines who will be chosen. Gunaratna (2002) explains the power of ideological commitment:

Most of Al Qaeda's 9/11 pilots and their accomplices did not undergo extensive military training; rather, their psychological conditioning and willingness to die for Allah were considered the operational priorities. Al Qaeda also believes that commitment to the ideology of the organization frees its members from "conceptual problems." Although the media refer to 9/11 and the USS *Cole* attacks as "suicide" operations, Islamist military groups consider them to be "martyrdom" attacks, given that suicide per se is forbidden in Islam. Hence another qualification to join Al Qaeda is a willingness to "do the work and undergo martyrdom for the purpose of achieving the goal and establishing the religion of majestic Allah on earth. (97)

This kind of commitment produces a unique cohesiveness. It binds members together on an impersonal basis. They often do not know one another. And in fact, this organization is intentionally designed that way. Secrecy is crucial to the successful operation of this terrorist group. But how does it keep secrets so well? Its unique organizational structure helps. Gunaratna (2002) explains:

Al Qaeda's global terrorist network strictly adheres to the cellular (also known as the cluster) model, "composed of many cells whose members do not know one another, so that if a cell member is caught the other cells would not be affected and work would proceed normally." Cell members never meet in one place together; nor do they in fact know each other; nor are they familiar with the means of communication used between the cell leader and each of its members. (102)

Loyalty to Osama bin Laden also explains the strength of members' commitment to Al Qaeda. Viewed as a legitimate authority figure, he derives much of his power from his personal charisma. Gunaratna (2002) explains bin Laden's rise to power as follows:

In terms of leadership qualities, Osama is the model Islamist, the preeminent leader of the pioneering vanguard. He possesses "charismatic and authoritarian leadership, depends upon a disciplined inner core of adherents, and promotes a rigorous socio-moral code for all followers"—the ideal characteristics of an Islamist leader. (118)

Gunaratna's five-year study of Al Qaeda shows why this terrorist group poses such an awesome threat. Because Al Qaeda can reinvent itself as circumstances require, it poses a challenge even to experts who have spent their careers studying groups and organizations. At the same time, it conforms to much of what we know and understand about groups. Even though Al Qaeda lacks a fixed structure, its designers recognized that parts of it had to resemble the structure of a modern multinational organization to achieve its goals. They also saw how the need for secrecy could be controlled by group size. And Al Qaeda's leaders clearly understood the power of commitment that is rooted in ideology. As this shows, Al Qaeda has an extraordinary understanding of how groups and organizations influence individuals.

Did underestimating this enemy indicate that intelligence agencies lacked an adequate understanding of how groups operate? Or did it just show how difficult it is to recognize and control these kinds of terrorist groups? Research on groups and organizations suggests that the answers to both questions might be yes. To understand why, this chapter begins with a focus on why groups form and how their structures help them accomplish their goals. It ends by focusing on research that examines conflict and cooperation.

SOCIAL GROUP DEFINED

Groups influence individuals' thoughts, feelings, and behaviors. Yet one of the most important things to keep in mind is that a group cannot be reduced to its individual parts (Durkheim 1898; Simmel 1905/1964). Émile Durkheim (1898) emphasized this feature of a group when he wrote, "The group thinks, feels, and acts quite differently from the way in which its members would were they isolated. If we begin with the individual, we shall be able to understand nothing of what takes place in the group" (104).

Durkheim's insight into the unique nature of a social group leads us to ask, What exactly is a *group?* Sociologists exclude both the simple gathering of people and the social categorization of them from their definition of *group.* They would not refer to an assembly of people waiting for a bus as a group. Nor would they refer to middle-class, white women as a group. The feature lacking in both cases is something that Durkheim suggested when he referred to *members.*

Belonging to a group suggests that an individual has developed an identity as a group member (Popenoe 2000). This occurs through a process that involves the acceptance of a group's meanings and social norms. We might then define a **social group** "as two or more people who have a common identity and some feeling of unity, who interact, and who share certain goals and expectations" (84). This definition captures many of the characteristics sociologists associate with the nature of a group (Levine and Moreland 1998; McGrath, Arrow, and Berdahl 2000).

Primary versus Secondary Groups

Sociologists make another important distinction when they consider the concept of the group. They recognize the difference between primary and secondary groups. We often take this distinction for granted in our everyday lives as we move with ease between small, intimate groups and large, impersonal ones. But the difference is significant. Small groups (primary groups) operate differently than large organizations (secondary groups). Consider the difference between a college fraternity or sorority and the college's office of admissions. As a member of the fraternity or sorority, you will be treated like a close friend or family member. Other members greet you by your first name and make you feel at home. In contrast, you are likely to stand in line to speak with an official when you visit the college's office of admissions. Your name is not important—you are now viewed as just a number when you register for classes. This kind of impersonal treatment is characteristic of secondary groups.

Charles Horton Cooley (1909) was the first to apply the term *primary* to a social group. With the intention of suggesting the notion of first, he used this concept with reference to groups that played an important role as the first agents of socialization. He considered the family as the most important primary group but recognized children's play groups as well. Today, a **primary group** would refer to any group in which relationships resemble those of a family. Fraternities and sororities, certain sports teams, some church groups, and a variety of social groups qualify as primary groups. The key characteristics of these family-type relationships

Primary groups operate differently than secondary groups. Close friends (top), members of a primary group, interact face to face, communicate freely, and provide emotional support to one another. Employees of large companies (bottom), members of a secondary group, interact in an impersonal way on a temporary basis to achieve a particular goal.

are face-to-face interaction on a regular basis, free and open communication that involves reciprocal self-disclosure, and emotional support.

One of the most salient features of a **secondary group** is its impersonal nature. Communication is not casual and personal but formal. For example, the Internal Revenue Service is likely to contact taxpayers by mail, not visit them at home. Memos are a common form of communication at work. And most colleges do not personally inform students about their final semester grades but rather mail them to their homes.

Reasons for Forming or Joining Groups

People form groups or join existing ones because they fill several human needs (Baumeister and Leary 1995). The need to belong may be rooted in human survival. In fact, groups help individuals meet two specific kinds of needs that reflect basic differences between primary and secondary groups (Popenoe 2000). In some cases, groups help us satisfy *instrumental* needs—that is, they help us accomplish goals that require a group effort. Gathering and accumulating food supplies, building homes, and caring for children fall into the category of instrumental needs. Groups accomplish these goals better than individuals do.

The human need to belong is also related to our *expressive* needs. We all need emotional support—love and affection, security, encouragement, acceptance, and recognition. In addition to meeting these needs, groups also provide a way for people to express who they are. Families may be the best group to meet expressive needs, but other primary groups also contribute to our emotional well-being. Sports teams, fraternities and sororities, church groups, and schools provide emotional support for their members. Even groups that are usually regarded as harmful to society can meet these kinds of basic emotional needs. Gangs are a good example. In his book *Islands in the Street*, Martin Jankowski (1991) identifies a number of reasons that people join gangs. Some join with the hope of gaining financial security, some of them seek opportunities to socialize, others feel a need for physical protection, and some just want the protective group identity that a gang provides (see Box 13.1).

BOX 13.1	WHY ADOLESCENTS JOIN GANGS

For more than a decade, from 1978 to 1989, Martin Sanchez Jankowski studied gangs in Los Angeles, New York City, and Boston. Acting as a participant observer, he sought to gain insight into the behavior of individuals in a gang, the behavior of the gang as a collective, and the rise and decline of gangs. Unlike most studies of gangs, he chose not to focus on the delinquent activities of gangs. Studies like that, he felt, attempt to theorize about delinquency, not about gangs as groups or organizations. And that explains why the research has produced limited explanations of the behavior of gangs and why they persist.

In fact, studying gangs as groups and organizations oriented Jankowski to a completely different set of variables. It led him to ask a number of important questions: Why do people join gangs? How do gangs operate? What can we learn from the organizational structures of gangs? What kinds of roles do leaders play? And what function does ideology play in a member's commitment to a gang? In answering these questions, Jankowski discovered that most of the theories on gangs provided inadequate explanations for why they emerge and for why they persist.

He found part of the explanation in the answer to the first question: Why do people join? Jankowski identified many reasons why people join gangs—and they all fit the answer that group research supports: because membership in a gang fills several human needs. Interviews with gang members showed that these needs included money,

physical protection, a place of refuge, recreation, independence from parents, and a commitment to the community.

Consider the reasons that three different gang members gave for belonging to a gang. "Street Dog," a 15-year-old Puerto Rican who had belonged to a gang in New York City for two years, said:

> "Hey, the club [the gang] has been there when I needed help. There were times when there just wasn't enough food for me to get filled up with. My family was hard up and they couldn't manage all of their bills and such, so there was some lean meals! Well, I just needed some money to help for a while, till I got some money or my family was better off. They [the gang] was there to help. I could see that [they would help] before I joined, that's why I joined. They are there when you need them and they'll continue to be." (Jankowski 1991, 42)

Chico, a 17-year-old member of an Irish gang in New York City, said, "When I first started up with the Steel Flowers, I really didn't know much about them. But to be honest, in the beginning I just joined because there were some people who were taking my school [lunch] money, and after I joined the gang, these guys laid off" (Jankowski 1991, 45).

Junior J., a 17-year-old gang member living in New York, said:

Many social groups meet both instrumental and expressive needs. For example, even though students attend college to meet an instrumental goal—a diploma that will give them more job opportunities—most of them also expect to do a lot of partying. Working with classmates on group projects helps students acquire the knowledge and skills required in certain professions. It also provides a way to establish friendships that can provide a social life that will satisfy a number of emotional needs.

GROUP STRUCTURE

Think of the last time you joined a new group. Whether it was a new church group, a sports team, or an exercise group, you probably had an experience common to all new group members—you felt a little uncomfortable. Why did you feel this way? The answer is rather simple. In the beginning, new group members do not know how they fit in or what is expected of them. But over time, as people interact, a group structure evolves. This structure consists of norms, statuses, and roles.

Robert Bales (1950), an early leader in small group research, argued that social structures evolve in groups because people seek a predictable social environment. Until group members establish stable patterns of group interaction, they feel a certain degree of uneasiness. They do not know how to behave. The social structure of a group—

"I been thinking about joining the gang because the gang gives you a cover, you know what I mean? Like when me or anybody does a business deal and we're members of the gang, it's difficult to track us down 'cause people will say, oh, it was just one of those guys in the gang. You get my point? The gang is going to provide me with some cover." (Jankowski 1991, 44)

If these particular reasons seem unique for gangs, other do not. For example, Jankowski (1991) claims that "the gang provides individuals with entertainment, much as a fraternity does for college students or the Moose and Elk clubs do for their members" (42). And he cites a reason given by Fox, a 23-year-old from New York, to make the point:

"Like I been telling you, I joined originally because all the action was happening with the Bats [gang's name]. I mean, all the foxy ladies were going to their parties and hanging with them. Plus their parties were great. They had good music and the herb [marijuana] was so smooth. . . . Man, it was a great source of dope and women. Hell, they were the kings of the community so I wanted to get in on some of the action." (45)

Jankowski's study also revealed a surprising reason for gang membership: commitment to the community. Pepe, a 17-year-old member, expressed it well:

The Royal Dons [gang's name] have been here for a real long time. A lot of people from the community have been in it. I had lots of family in it so I guess I'll just have to carry on the tradition. A lot of people from outside this community wouldn't understand, but we have helped the community whenever they've asked us. We've been around to help. I felt it's kind of my duty to join 'cause everybody expects it. . . . No, the community doesn't mind that we do things to make some money and raise a little hell because they don't expect you to put in your time for nothing. Just like nobody expects guys in the military to put in their time for nothing." (47)

Jankowski's approach to studying gangs shows the value of research on groups and organizations. Although much of the research has involved groups that are involved in harmless activities, the findings also apply to groups that are viewed as dangerous or that threaten the stability of society. As the introduction to this chapter shows, understanding how groups and organizations operate can help us solve serious social problems.

norms, statuses, and roles—provides members with information about how they should behave and relate to others in the group.

Group Size

How does the size of a group affect human behavior? Many social psychologists have asked this question, including Georg Simmel (1905/1964), who provided some of the earliest insights into groups. He, like Durkheim, did not believe that a group was the sum of its individual parts. In addition, he recognized that the nature of a group varies depending on its size. Simmel found the **dyad**, the smallest group, particularly interesting. According to him, the relationship between two parties offered a degree of intimacy that was impossible with larger groups. To make his point, he argued that when a person shares a secret with someone else, it no longer remains his property. It is also most secure when it is shared with only one other person. The parties in a dyad interact only with one another, not with a collectivity. The social structure of this group therefore rests solely on them and ceases to exist if either party chooses to leave the group. If a dyad expands by one to form a **triad**, the nature of the group changes dramatically. This addition creates both direct and indirect relationships, which can unite or separate group members. From Simmel's perspective, this meant that a third party could serve as either a mediator or an intruder.

Most groups are small and consist of only two or three people (Desportes and Lemaine 1988; Mullen and Copper 1994). Social psychologists have offered a number of explanations for this tendency. First, people might avoid large groups because the possibility of so many different relationships may cause confusion (James 1951). Second, people may prefer small groups because they might feel that they can control what happens to them (Lawler 1992). And third, group members' satisfaction in larger groups may decline because they may not feel that they have input to decisions (Wagner 1995).

Group Social Status

Whether a group is large or small, a multinational corporation or a clique of friends, its structure includes a **status system**. This system reflects the distribution of power among group members (Robinson and Balkwell 1995; Levine and Moreland 1998). Status within a group indicates one's rank in terms of authority, prestige, and power. The status system in the U.S. Army illustrates the degree to which groups distribute power at different levels. At the top of this hierarchy, generals hold the most power and are given the most respect. Privates, who hold the lowest rank, must obey the orders of their superiors and salute them. Rankings in schools often take the form of classes: freshman, sophomore, junior, senior. Other groups use titles such as president, vice-president, secretary, and treasurer.

Recognizing where members fit in the status system contributes to positive social interaction. Individuals may convey their group status in either verbal or nonverbal ways. For example, members with higher status tend to speak more frequently, to interrupt others more often, to criticize, and to give orders. They are also spoken to more often (Kelley 1951; Skvoretz 1988). Nonverbal signs of higher status include an erect posture, strong eye contact, and physical intrusiveness (Leffler, Gillespie, and Conaty 1982).

Social psychologists have devoted much attention to how status systems develop in groups. Status systems like that of the U.S. Army support the view that status is a position that individuals earn by helping a group achieve a goal, by adhering to group norms, and by putting the group's interest above their own (Levine and Moreland 1998). But research also shows that status systems can develop within minutes of a group's formation (Barchas and Fisek 1984). This suggests that status systems are based on other factors as well. In fact, research shows that status is ascribed on the basis of sex, race, and even attractiveness (Ridgeway 1991).

Joseph Berger and his associates (Berger, Rosenholtz, and Zelditch 1980; Berger, Wagner, and Zelditch 1985) offer a theory to explain these mixed findings. According to Berger's **expectation states theory**, group members form expectations about the likely contributions of individuals to the group's goals from the first meeting. These expectations are based on a number of personal traits, which are either obvious or become known during group interaction. Although goal-directed characteristics such as relevant experience carry a lot of weight in forming these expectations, irrelevant traits such as sex and race are also considered. Higher status is assigned to members whose characteristics look more promising. Members' status evaluations can change as their actual contributions are recognized, but members who receive low status in the beginning may have difficulty in convincing members of their value (Ridgeway 1982).

Group Norms

How can you tell the difference between a group and a simple gathering of individuals? One key difference is a set of **group norms**. These shared expectations about how group members ought to behave are a key characteristic of social groups. George Homans (1950) described one of the earliest investigations of group norms in a classic field study conducted at the Western Electric Company's Hawthorne Works in Chicago. This particular study, called the Bank Wiring Observation Room, lasted from November 1931 to May 1932. Its primary aim was to reveal the factors that affected the output of workers, especially certain characteristics of group behavior.

The group selected for this study was taken from a department that assembled switches for office telephone equipment. It consisted of fourteen men: nine wiremen, three soldermen, and two inspectors. Although these men worked individually on a specific task, a finished bank of terminals required the cooperation of workers in each subgroup. The telephone equipment began with a wireman, who wired the terminals of the banks together. The equipment then moved to a solderman, who fixed the connections in place. Finally, the inspector tested and examined the work. Each of these jobs took a different amount of time. For

example, one solderman could handle the connections made by about three wiremen. The company had therefore organized the men into three soldering units. The nature of this work meant that wiremen generally set the pace for the other workers. It was also possible, however, for the others to limit the day's output by failing to keep up with the wiremen.

The daily output for workers was important because it partially determined their weekly salary. Although workers were paid an hourly wage rate, their salary also depended on the total number of terminal banks completed and shipped. This group piecework system was designed to increase productivity. But the results of this study showed that these workers had their own idea about what made for a "fair day's work": approximately two finished pieces of equipment, which amounted to 6,600 connections. Workers did not believe that they should work any harder and fashioned their behavior in ways that kept this output level fairly constant. Homans (1950) described what they did as follows:

> They tended to work hard in the morning, until the completion of a day's work was in sight, and then to take it easy in the afternoon as quitting time approached. As the pressure lessened, conversation, games, and the preparation of tools and equipment for the next day's work took more and more time. (60)

As this suggests, the productivity of these workers was not limited by fatigue. Instead, it was maintained by group norms that let workers know what the group expected. Describing how these group norms operated, Homans wrote:

> If a man did turn out more than was thought proper, or if he worked too fast, he was exposed to merciless ridicule. He was called a "rate-buster" or a "speed king," but at the same time a man who turned out too little was a "chiseler." He was cutting down the earnings of the group. The fact that the men had set an upper limit on output did not mean they believed in doing no work at all. And ridicule was not the only penalty a nonconformist

had to suffer. A game called "binging" was played in the Observation Room, especially by Hasulak (W7), Oberleitner (W8), Green (W9), and Cermak (S4). If, according to the rules of this game, a man walked up to another man and hit him as hard as he could on the upper arm—"binged" him—the other then had the right to retaliate with another such blow, the object being to see who could hit the harder. But binging was also used as a penalty. A man who was thought to be working either too fast or too slow might be binged. (60–61)

These shared expectations about how group members ought to behave are a key characteristic of social groups.

William Whyte provided another early example of how group norms operate in a classic study, *Street Corner Society* (1943). Taking the role of a participant observer, Whyte spent over a year studying street-corner gangs in an Italian neighborhood in the North End of Boston (February 1937 to May 1938). Prior to his investigation, sociologists had assumed that slum districts like this one were disorganized communities. He discovered that it was highly organized, though not reflective of middle-class values.

Whyte systematically studied the social structure of these gangs, identifying key characters, group norms, and group roles. Figure 13.1 shows the hierarchical structure of the Nortons, a gang whose name identified the street where its leader had been born. The Nortons included thirteen men between the ages of 20 and 29. Every member knew his relative position in the gang and recognized Doc as the leader. Mike and Danny, who ranked directly below Doc, were regarded as his lieutenants. Long John held an anomalous position. His special relationships with the top three members gave him a unique kind of influence. He had little authority over the followers in the group. But as Doc explained,

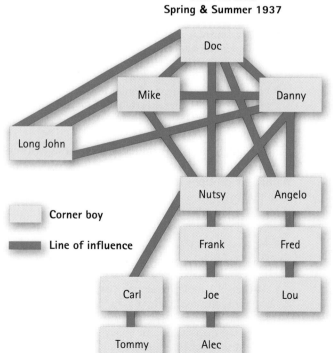

The Nortons
Spring & Summer 1937

Corner boy

Line of influence

FIGURE 13.1

Social Structure of a Boston Street–Corner Gang

Source: Whyte 1943, 13.

they had to respect him because the leaders gave him so much attention.

The members of the Nortons met almost every night at about the same time in the same restaurant or tavern. They had a regular table where seats were determined by custom. Even members of other local groups recognized the Nortons' right to sit in these claimed seats. The regular interaction of the Nortons produced a code of mutual obligations that was fundamental to the group's cohesiveness. "The code of the corner boy requires him to help his friends when he can and to refrain from doing anything to harm them" (Whyte 1943, 256). Living up to this code of obligations varied with a member's status. Members with lower status were free to violate their obligations without serious penalty. But the leader was expected to meet his obligations; if he failed, his position was threatened.

Group Roles

Whyte's analysis showed that group norms can take the form of role expectations. For example, as the leader of the Nortons, Doc was expected to spend more money on his followers than they would on him. Small groups involve all kinds of roles. If you work in the newsroom of a local television station, these roles coincide with job titles: producer, director, writer, reporter, weather person, anchor. This holds as well in hospitals that have highly specialized staffs of nurses, doctors, administrators, and so on. Schools, sports teams, the military, government bureaucracies—all groups and organizations have roles that tell us how the people are supposed to behave.

What kinds of roles typically emerge in groups? Robert Bales (1950) was one of the first researchers to study this question. He found that roles make a particular contribution to a group's function. For example, within small groups, he identified two types of leadership roles. **Instrumental leaders** are task-oriented and seek to help groups achieve their particular goals. In contrast, **expressive** or **socioemotional leaders**

try to keep groups together. These leaders are most concerned with group unity and harmony.

Phillip Zimbardo (1972) and his colleagues conducted a classic study that showed how roles operate in groups (Haney, Banks, and Zimbardo 1973). These researchers believed that the roles we play are influenced by our membership in certain groups. Seeking to understand this process more fully, they designed a study that focused on the roles that prisoners and guards take in a prison situation. To make this experiment seem real, Zimbardo transformed a basement at Stanford University into a mock prison. The subjects for this study were recruited through newspaper ads. Using psychological tests and physical exams to determine their suitability for this experiment, Zimbardo screened seventy men who had responded to his ad. He chose twenty-four male subjects who appeared to be stable, normal college students from middle-class families. These subjects were then randomly assigned to take the role of either prisoner or guard.

To make this experiment as real as possible, the local police arrested the prisoners at home. They were informed about their rights, searched, handcuffed, and then taken to the police station, where they were booked and fingerprinted. When they arrived at the mock prison, these subjects were again treated like real prisoners. They were stripped naked, searched, sprayed for lice, and issued a uniform and linens. At that point, they were taken to a 6-by-9-foot prison cell, where they remained with two other "prisoners."

Although this experiment was supposed to last two weeks, the researchers stopped it after six days out of concern for the subjects (Zimbardo 1972). The subjects came to play their roles too well. The "guards" began to treat the "prisoners" like animals and took pleasure in dehumanizing them. They ordered the prisoners to sing songs, laugh, or stop smiling at their command. One of the guards described his own experience as follows:

> I was surprised at myself. . . . I made them call each other names and clean the toilets out with their bare hands. I practically considered the prisoners

cattle, and I kept thinking: I have to watch out for them in case they try something. (Zimbardo et al. 1973, 42)

As the guards enacted this kind of aggressive behavior, the prisoners became increasingly passive and depressed. In some cases, they displayed psychosomatic illnesses or fits of crying. In both cases, these subjects took on the roles that were dictated by their membership in a particular group.

Group Cohesiveness

The cohesiveness of a group has drawn more attention than any other feature of group structure (Levine and Moreland 1998). A practical reason may explain the popularity of this focus. Researchers want to know what makes some groups more successful than others. Does cohesiveness explain why some sports teams win repeatedly? Does it explain why some military units have more victories than others?

One of the problems with this concept involves its nature. This problem is reflected in the variety of terms that researchers use to refer to this concept: *solidarity*, *morale*, and *climate* (Levine and Moreland 1998). Émile Durkheim (1897), who used the term *cohesiveness* to mean solidarity, is recognized for his pioneering work on the powerful influence of a group's cohesiveness in his study of suicide. He observed that suicide rates are lower in groups characterized by higher levels of cohesion: Catholics were less likely to commit suicide than Protestants. He also recognized how the increased cohesiveness of groups during wars was linked to lower suicide rates.

Today, social psychologists use the term **group cohesiveness** to refer to the property of a group that binds members together (Dion 2000). Using a variety of methods to measure group cohesiveness, researchers have identified a number of nonverbal behaviors associated with highly cohesive groups (Piper et al. 1983; Tickle-Degen and Rosenthal 1987; Levine and Moreland 1998). Members of these groups tend to "stand or sit close together, pay attention to one another, show signs of mutual affection, and coordinate their behavior" (Levine and Moreland 1998, 428). Researchers have also found certain verbal behaviors to be more prevalent in highly cohesive groups (Owen 1985; Eder 1988; Budman et al. 1993). For example, members of these groups tend to actively engage in conversations, to disclose things about themselves, and to invent a special jargon (Levine and Moreland 1998).

What makes some groups more cohesive than others? Researchers have identified a number of factors. First, assigning people to groups is enough to produce some cohesion (Hogg 1987). Second, time is an important factor. The more time group members spend together, the greater the cohesion (Terborg, Castore, and De Ninno 1976; Griffith and Greenlees 1993). Third, liking or affection among members contributes to higher levels of cohesion (Lott and Lott 1965). Fourth, groups that provide more rewards for its members are more cohesive (Ruder and Gill 1982; Stokes 1983). Finally, external threats, as Durkheim argued, can increase cohesion (Dion 1979; Harrison and Connors 1984).

BEHAVIOR IN GROUPS

Groups affect the behavior of individuals in a number of interesting ways. Musicians who perform in front of audiences, athletes who compete in packed stadiums, and even schoolchildren who must recite poems in front of classmates recognize the effect that groups have on their behavior. Sometimes groups enhance our performance; sometimes they impair it. Groups also affect our motivation. Who is not tempted to let the other members of a group do most of the work? And what about the pressure that groups exert on us to conform? Social psychologists have learned a great deal about how groups affect the behavior of individuals.

Social Facilitation

What effect does the mere presence of others have on our behavior? Norman Triplett (1898) posed this question over a century ago. As a bicycling enthusiast, Triplett had observed that cyclists performed better when they raced together instead of alone. Intrigued by his hunch that the presence of others produced this effect, he designed the first experiment in social psychology. He asked children to wind up the string on a fishing reel under two conditions—either alone or in the presence of other children. The results showed that subjects wound the string faster when other children were present.

The tendency to perform better in the presence of others was originally called **social facilitation**. In an early series of studies, Floyd Allport (1920, 1924) observed subjects as they worked on a variety of tasks such as solving easy multiplication problems, composing refutations for logical arguments, and just marking out the vowels in a newspaper column. His results showed that subjects performed better when other people were in the room. And the effect produced by the presence of others operated not only when people worked on the same task but even when they were merely present in the room.

Curiously, social facilitation is not just a human phenomenon. It operates in other species as well. Researchers have observed it in ants, cockroaches, and birds (Chen 1937; Zajonc and Sales 1966; Zajonc, Heingartner, and Herman 1969; Rajecki, Kidd, and Ivins 1976; Bond and Titus 1983; Guerin 1986). In an early demonstration of this effect, Chen (1937) showed that ants dug three times more sand when they were surrounded by other ants than when they were alone.

Social psychologists soon recognized a problem with the concept of social facilitation. It did not always work. In fact, in some cases, the presence of others inhibited the performance of an individual—a response called *social inhibition*. Allport (1920) observed this negative effect in his early study of subjects who were asked to write refutations to a logical argument. The quality of the subjects' writing was actually worse when they wrote in the presence of other people. Pessin (1933) also showed this effect in another early study that involved memory tasks.

These mixed findings stalled research on social facilitation until the 1960s, when Robert

Contestants of nationwide spelling bees who falter when they perform in front of an audience illustrate an effect called social inhibition.

Zajonc (1965) took another look. Gaining insight from experimental psychology, he began with a well-known principle—that arousal enhances dominant responses. With a focus on what constitutes the dominant response, the mixed findings began to make sense. Consider how this might operate in your own performance on tasks. If you are asked to perform an easy task, the dominant response is likely to be the correct answer. But what if you are asked to perform a new task that is difficult? In this case, the dominant response is most likely to be the incorrect answer.

Zajonc's insight into the effect of others on an individual's performance modified the original concept of social facilitation. Today it refers to the tendency for individuals to perform better on simple tasks but to do worse on difficult ones when others are present. A large body of research supports Zajonc's theory of social facilitation. In fact, two separate meta-analyses of over three hundred experiments provide ample evidence (Bond and Titus 1983; Guerin 1986). One of the most interesting studies conducted to show this effect involved observations of people playing billiards in a college student union (Michaels et al. 1982). Working unobtrusively, researchers first identified the players as either above or below average in their shooting ability. Then four confederates approached the players and served as an audience for several more rounds. As Zajonc's theory would predict, the performance of the good players improved—their accuracy rose from 71 to 80 percent. In contrast, the poor players' performance deteriorated—their accuracy dropped from 36 to 25 percent.

Research thus demonstrates that arousal precipitates a dominant response in subjects. But why did the presence of others produce arousal? Zajonc offered a simple explanation. He claimed that humans have an innate tendency to become aroused when other people are present. This explanation is appealing because it accounts for the results of both human and animal studies.

A second explanation called **evaluation apprehension** fails to explain why animals become aroused in the presence of others, but it does provide a convincing reason for why people do. According to Nickolas Cottrell (1972), arousal is a reaction that people experience when they realize that others are judging them. To determine the value of this explanation, Cottrell and his colleagues (1968) modified a study that Zajonc and Sales (1966) had conducted, which showed that the mere presence of others affected subjects. The original experiment showed how social facilitation operated on a memory task that involved nonsense syllables. In the modified experiment, Cottrell eliminated the effect that evaluation apprehension might have on subjects by blindfolding observers during the exercise. The results showed that subjects who saw an audience observe them did better on rehearsed tasks than subjects who performed for a blindfolded audience.

This explanation accounts for performances that either improve or worsen when we believe that others are evaluating us. When we perform easy tasks, our awareness of being judged motivates us to do our best. However, if the task is difficult, the pressure may cause us to do poorly. Studies provide support for evaluation apprehension (Gastorf, Suls, and Sanders 1980; Seta 1982; Worringham and Messick 1983; Seta and Seta 1995).

The third explanation offered for the arousal caused by the presence of others is called the **distraction-conflict theory** (Sanders, Baron, and Moore 1978; Baron 1986). According to this theory, an audience produces arousal in someone who is performing a task because it divides her attention between the audience and the task. She may overcome the distraction of an audience on an easy task by simply increasing her concentration. But if the task is difficult, the distraction is likely to impair her performance. Research shows that audiences are not the only distractions that produce this effect. Flashing lights do the same thing (Baron 1986).

Social Loafing

If you could work alone on a class project or in a group, which would you prefer? Your answer probably depends on the grade you expect and how the instructor plans to evaluate your contribution. Although there are many benefits to cooperative learning, teachers recognize a problem. When each group member's work cannot be evaluated individually, people tend to put in less effort than when they work alone. Social psychologists call this group effect **social loafing** (Latané, Williams, and Harkins 1979).

Max Ringelmann (1913), a French agricultural engineer, undertook the first study of social loafing in the 1880s (see Kravitz and Martin 1986). Aiming to learn more about work efficiency, Ringelmann measured the effort that individual men exerted to pull a rope compared to the amount they put forth when they worked in groups of seven or fourteen. Although social facilitation suggests that they would perform this simple task better in the presence of others, the results showed just the opposite. Working alone, the men pulled an average of 85 kilograms. When they worked in a group of seven, the average weight was 65 kilograms per man, and in groups of fourteen, the average was only 61 kilograms.

Nearly a century after Ringelmann first identified this particular group effect, Bibb Latané, Kipling Williams, and Stephen Harkins (1979) referred to it as social loafing. They and other researchers have shown how it operates in a variety of simple tasks including swimming, writing songs, cheering, clapping, and moving through a maze (Karau and Williams 2001). The reason that social loafing occurs gives us insight into what motivates group members to work together. According to Steven Karau and Kipling Williams (1993), the amount of effort that individuals put forth on a group task involves two things: first, an individual's belief about the importance of her contribution, and second, the value the individual places on the success of the group's goal. If an individual believes that her contribution will be "lost in the crowd"—that it will not be noticed or evaluated—she is likely to relax and put less effort into the task.

A number of studies have examined the role that accountability plays in social loafing (Karau and Williams 1993). The results of these studies

suggest an interesting insight into one of the explanations for social facilitation—evaluation apprehension. In studies of social loafing, subjects assume that they are evaluated only when they work on tasks alone. They must take full responsibility for their contribution. Working in a group reduces individual members' concern about evaluation, since it would be difficult to determine their individual contribution. In this case, responsibility is diffused across all group members, and it contributes to social loafing (Kerr and Bruun 1981; Harkins and Jackson 1985).

SOCIAL IMPACT THEORY

Social facilitation and social loafing focus on how groups influence individuals' performance on tasks. But this is not the only way that groups affect the behavior of human beings. Groups also pressure individuals to conform, to adopt the norms and values of the group, and in some cases to engage in destructive behaviors like riots or even pack suicides. Peer pressure from junior high school classmates may convince some teenagers to smoke, do drugs, or join gangs. College fraternities and sororities pressure members to participate in philanthropic activities such as dance marathons. But these Greek groups also make headlines for hazing rituals and traditions that are degrading, cruel, and sometimes life-threatening. A number of cults have also made headlines for convincing their members to participate in mass suicides.

As these examples suggest, groups vary in the amount of influence they exert on individual members. What factors determine the level of this influence? Bibb Latané (1981) argued that three features affect the amount of influence felt by individual members. According to his **social impact theory**, these are the group's size, strength, and immediacy.

Size refers to the number of people in the group. According to Latané, as the number of group members increases, so does the impact of the group on an individual. When it comes to conformity, research shows that the effect of size levels off at a point. Asch (1955) and others have shown that the impact of size does not change much once a group reaches four or five people.

Group strength refers to an individual's evaluation of the group's importance. This judgment is based on an assessment of the group's status, power, and credibility. College fraternities and sororities often have reputations as "better" or "worse" to belong to. Willard Waller (1937), one of the first to comment on this ranking system, argued that success in dating was largely determined by one's membership in one of the better Greek houses. As college students prepare to enter the job market, they are likely to recognize the status of a Fortune 500 company as a factor determining their career decisions. Later, they might make decisions about country clubs on the same basis. This group feature clearly influences how individuals behave, from conformity in the way individual members dress to the attitudes they openly express.

Immediacy, the second factor in Latané's model, refers to the proximity of the group to an individual member. Measured in terms of both space and time, this feature focuses on how close the group is to the individual. For example, a presidential candidate would have more impact on party members at personal gatherings than he would have through a thirty-second political ad that is broadcast on television.

Latané explained social impact theory by comparing it to light falling on a surface. The total illumination varies on the basis of the number of light bulbs, the bulbs' wattage, and the distance of the bulbs from the surface. Conceived in this way, Latané's model provides further insight into the way that social facilitation and social loafing operate. Consider the differences illustrated in Figure 13.2. Diagram (a) shows how social facilitation influences an individual's performance. In this case, the target of influence is a single individual, who feels the impact of many audience members. As the size of the group (source of influence) increases, so should the impact on the individual. Diagram (b) shows how social loafing occurs. Now the target includes many group members, not just one individual member. The source, represented

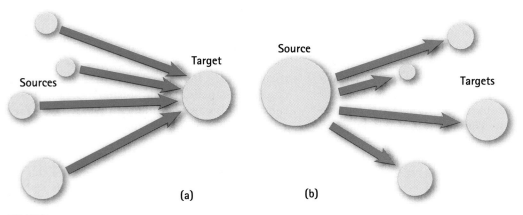

FIGURE 13.2

Latané's Social Impact Theory

Social facilitation occurs when many sources (the audience) focus on a single target performer (a). Social loafing occurs when a single source (an outsider) directs attention to a group of target performers (b). In this latter case, the extent of social loafing reflects the number of performers involved.

Source: Adapted from Latané 1981, 344, 349.

by a single circle, represents the influence of one outsider. As the size of the group grows, the responsibility felt by individual members is diffused across them. This results in social loafing.

GROUP PERFORMANCE: DECISION MAKING IN GROUPS

Groups play a critical role in the operation of all types of organizations (Levine and Moreland 1998). Whether a military mission succeeds or fails ultimately depends on the performance of smaller units within a much larger organization. Presidents and prime ministers confer with groups of advisers to make decisions about domestic and international issues. And teams of doctors make life-and-death decisions about their patients. In consultation, they might decide whether conjoined twins can survive an operation to separate them. In each of these cases, achieving a desired goal depends on the performance of the group. Why do some groups perform better than others? Some answers can be found in the process by which groups make decisions.

Recall Émile Durkheim's astute observation that "the group thinks, feels, and acts quite differently from the way in which its members would were they isolated" (1898, 104). Georg Simmel (1905/1964) made a similar observation. From his perspective, the individual possesses qualities superior to the ones that he contributes to the group. How superior? He quotes the German philosopher Fritz Schiller: "Seen singly, everybody is passably intelligent and reasonable; but united into a body, they are blockheads" (32). What do you think? Research provides some answers.

The Effect of Task Type

One of the first things that social psychologists consider in evaluating group performance is the type of task that groups work on. The question they seek to answer is this: Can a group perform the task better than an individual? The answer depends on the kind of task. The basic variations include additive tasks, conjunctive tasks, and disjunctive tasks.

If the task is an **additive task**, the group's performance is determined by the sum of individual efforts. Consider a small group of volunteers that attempts to push a lost whale back out into the ocean. In this case, the group's effort is the sum of all of the members' individual efforts. And one of the most important determinants of success will be whether the volunteers coordinate their efforts effectively. One person cannot save the whale. But together they have a chance. This is a key characteristic of additive tasks: The group effort is generally better than the effort of one person.

To complete a **conjunctive task** successfully, all group members must succeed. The Bank Wiring Observation Room study showed how conjunctive tasks depend on all group members. Completing a bank of terminals required the efforts of the wireman, the solderman, and the inspector. Any one of these group members could slow down the process of completing the task. As this demonstrates, the group's performance on conjunctive tasks depends ultimately on the weakest member of the team.

If a group is working on a **disjunctive task**, the effort of one member is enough for the group to achieve its goal. Consider a team of scientists who must find a computer glitch to prevent a spacecraft from going off course. One member can solve the problem. In this case, the group's performance depends on the strongest member of the team.

Brainstorming

Suppose you are the executive producer for a new television sitcom. Over the past few weeks, your ratings have begun to slip. You need fresh ideas. What is your best strategy? Should you ask your writers to work independently, or should you gather your staff together for a brainstorming session? Alex Osborn (1963), the 1950s advertising executive who invented the **brainstorming technique**, would advise you to have your writers work in a group, for his technique is an approach to problem solving in which all members of a group contribute ideas spontaneously and simultaneously.

The strategy is simply to encourage people to come up with as many ideas as they can without worrying about how they will be evaluated. According to Osborn (1963), productive brainstorming sessions require that participants follow four basic rules:

1. *Criticism is ruled out.* Adverse judgment of ideas must be withheld until later.

2. *"Free-wheeling" is welcomed.* The wilder the idea, the better; it is easier to tame down than to think up.

3. *Quantity is wanted.* The greater the number of ideas, the more the likelihood of useful ideas.

4. *Combination and improvement are sought.* In addition to contributing ideas of their own, participants should suggest how ideas of others can be turned into *better* ideas or how two or more ideas can be joined into still another idea. (156)

Brainstorming in groups remains a popular strategy today. Unfortunately, research shows that it is in fact not particularly effective in generating new ideas (Paulus, Larey, and Ortega 1995; Paulus, Brown, and Ortega 1997; Paulus, Larey, and Dzindolet 1998, 2000; see also Mullen, Johnson, and Salas 1991; Stroebe and Diehl 1994). Why not? Social psychologists offer a number of reasons (Paulus and Brown 2003). First, the group actually prevents individual members from generating multiple ideas. Since only one person can speak at a time, this distracts other members from the process of coming up with more ideas (Diehl and Stroebe 1991). What is more, they may forget their own ideas as they listen to another person present an idea. Second, if individuals believe that their ideas are not important or crucial to the group's success, they may participate less. And third, even though group members are encouraged to offer ideas without fear of criticism, they are still likely to feel the effect of evaluation apprehension (Camacho and

Paulus 1995). Despite the evidence that shows that brainstorming is not an effective group strategy, businesses and other organizations continue to use it (Levine and Moreland 1998). The reason, it appears, lies in the perception that it does work (Paulus et al. 1993). This may result from group members' difficulty in separating their own ideas from those of other members once the meeting is over (Stroebe, Diehl, and Abakoumkin 1992).

Groupthink

" 'How could we have been so stupid?' President John F. Kennedy asked after he and a close group of advisers had blundered into the Bay of Pigs invasion" (Janis 1971, 43). Irving Janis answered Kennedy's question after studying it for two years. According to him, this historic fiasco resulted from a faulty decision-making process that involved **groupthink**. Janis coined this term to refer to a mode of thinking that characterizes cohesive ingroups. Instead of critically examining alternative solutions to a problem, these groups seek concurrence. Members avoid harsh judgments of their leaders and other in-group members to prevent disunity.

Janis developed the concept of groupthink based on an analysis of a number of historic fiascoes that resulted from defective foreign policy decision making. These included British Prime Minister Neville Chamberlain's decision to support a policy of appeasing Adolf Hitler in 1937 and 1938, Admiral Kimmel's failure to heed warnings in the fall of 1941 that Pearl Harbor was in danger of being attacked by the Japanese, President Kennedy's Bay of Pigs debacle, and President Johnson's decision to escalate the war in Vietnam despite intelligence reports that such efforts would be futile (Janis 1982). Other social psychologists recognized the symptoms of groupthink in the way that President Nixon and his advisers made decisions about the Watergate coverup.

Janis's analysis of these events led him to identify the antecedent conditions and symptoms of groupthink. As Table 13.1 shows, antecedent

TABLE 13.1	GROUPTHINK	
Antecedents of Groupthink	**Symptoms of Groupthink**	**Flawed Decision Making**
High level of group cohesiveness	Illusion of invulnerability	Incomplete survey of alternatives
Group isolation	Belief in morality of group	Failure to examine risks of alternatives
Directive leadership	Stereotypes of out-groups	Poor information search
High stress	Self-censorship	Failure to create contingency plans
	Direct pressure on dissenters	
	Mindguards	

Source: Based on Janis 1982, 244.

conditions lead to concurrence seeking within the group. The symptoms of groupthink then become apparent and lead to symptoms of defective decision making.

One of the most important symptoms of groupthink is the feeling of invulnerability that leads the group to disregard clear signs of danger. Janis describes the case of Admiral H. E. Kimmel, who failed to prepare for an attack on Pearl Harbor, as the most poignant example of the illusion of invulnerability. When Kimmel's intelligence chief told him that they had lost radio contact with Japanese aircraft carriers, Kimmel made a joke about it: "What, you don't know where the carriers are? Do you mean to say that they could be rounding Diamond Head [at Honolulu] and you wouldn't know it?" (Janis 1971, 44). In fact, that's exactly what the Japanese were doing.

The absence of contrary views indicates another deadly symptom of groupthink—self-censorship. Group members may not express their opposition to a policy or their doubts about it for several reasons. Some might believe it could damage the group's morale. Others might fear criticism from other group members or rejection from the group. Arthur Schlesinger, one of Kennedy's advisers, admitted that he had serious doubts about the Bay of Pigs invasion. But he did not express his opinion because he was afraid that "others would regard it as presumptuous of him, a college professor, to take issue with august heads of major government institutions" (Janis 1982, 32).

Janis's analysis led him to describe a faulty decision-making process that resulted from groupthink. The symptoms included a failure to consider alternative options, assess the risks associated with the decision, or make contingency plans. Although these should serve as red flags to policymakers and other groups that make decisions with potentially serious consequences, tragic events repeatedly suggest that groupthink accounts for poor decisions. For example, critics claimed that the 1986 space shuttle *Challenger* disaster would have been avoided if the decision makers at NASA had heeded warnings about the problems with O-ring seals. NASA's failure to learn a lesson about the effect of groupthink contributed to a second disaster on February 1, 2003, when seven members of the shuttle *Columbia* died when their vehicle disintegrated upon reentering the atmosphere. In a broad indictment of NASA's decision-making process, an investigation board blamed NASA's culture for failing to heed clear signs of danger (see Box 13.2).

How can groups protect themselves against groupthink? Janis offered a number of suggestions. First, the leader should remain impartial during group discussions. Second, outside experts, who are not part of the in-group and have no interest in maintaining the cohesiveness of the group, should be invited to offer their opinions. Third, the leader should divide the group into subcommittees that first meet alone to discuss the issue and then later meet together to discuss their ideas. Fourth, at least one group member should take the role of the

| BOX 13.2 | NASA'S CULTURE: THE COLUMBIA DISASTER |

On February 1, 2003, NASA grieved over another tragedy when the shuttle *Columbia* broke apart upon reentering the atmosphere, killing all seven members of the crew. Analysts concluded that the physical cause of the accident occurred when a 1.7-pound chunk of foam insulation hit *Columbia*'s left wing at more than 500 miles per hour during the shuttle's ascent on January 16. The tragedy evoked memories of the 1986 *Challenger* tragedy that resulted from a failure in O-rings.

Although investigations into both tragedies discovered different technical reasons for the two disasters, the *Columbia* report identified a common problem—NASA culture. In its 248-page report, the *Columbia* Accident Investigation Board rated NASA's management problems as equal in importance to the technical ones (Wald 2003). "Members of the board said that by the time of the *Columbia* mission NASA managers had become complacent about safety, and lower-level engineers were reluctant to raise issues that might interfere with a mission" (15).

Sean O'Keefe, a NASA administrator, told reporters that the accident was primarily a result of poor data, not a failure of communication (Sawyer and Smith 2003). But in fact, a long record of e-mails suggests that NASA culture discouraged engineers and technicians from expressing their concerns about possible problems. Indications of trouble were spotted on the second day of the flight when analysts detected signs of the debris strike on a video of the shuttle launch. This prompted the director of the Mission Evaluation Room to ask for further technical evaluation. The task was assigned to engineers at Boeing, the primary subcontractor for the shuttle program. Although the company's familiarity with the *Columbia* mission made it well suited for the assignment, it posed a conflict since Boeing stood to be penalized for a mission failure. Boeing issued three reports about the debris within ten days of the mission launch. Playing down the safety risk, the engineers gave no indication that the debris strike posed a threat to the shuttle.

Others involved with the mission disagreed with these conclusions and expressed concerns that led nowhere. One group of safety experts at the Johnson Space Center recommended that the Defense Department take pictures of *Columbia* as it orbited. Decision makers rejected the request. The concerns of other engineers who spotted trouble were also disregarded. In fact, the record of e-mails between engineers and technicians indicated wide concern over the damage caused by the debris strike and the risk it posed to *Columbia* and its crew. But these concerns never reached senior NASA officials.

The report prepared by the *Columbia* Accident Investigation Board placed the blame on NASA culture, saying:

> Management decisions made during *Columbia*'s final flight reflect missed opportunities, blocked or ineffective communications channels, flawed analysis, and

devil's advocate to make sure that ideas do not go unchallenged and that alternatives are considered. Finally, to avoid self-censorship, the leader can ask for a secret vote or for members to write down their opinions without identifying themselves.

Group Polarization

One of the supposed dangers of groupthink is the tendency for groups to make risky decisions that are not justified by available information (Hart 1991; Levine and Moreland 1998). Tragedies such as the *Challenger* and *Columbia* disasters cause

investigators to raise this question over and over again. James Stoner (1961) was the first to raise this question. As the topic for his master's thesis in industrial management at MIT, Stoner created dilemmas that involved a decision that would have a significant impact on a person's life. His subjects considered the dilemmas and then offered their advice about how much risk the person should take. They then discussed the dilemma with other members of a group and came up with a group decision about the level of risk to take. Although most people assumed that groups would be more conservative than individuals in making decisions,

ineffective leadership. Perhaps the most striking is the fact that the management . . . displayed no interest in understanding a problem and its implications. (Sawyer and Pianin 2003)

NASA's culture problem is not new. The flaws in NASA's decision-making process resemble the kind that Irving Janis (1971) identified in a number of historical cases. According to one newspaper report:

Outside experts and sources close to the board NASA appointed to investigate the disaster say they suspect the engineering staff fell victim to a form of "groupthink," in which they avoided confronting head-on the imminent possibility of the agency's signal failure—the loss of a shuttle and its crew. (Sawyer and Smith 2003)

The *Columbia* Accident Investigation Board recommended that NASA make a number of fundamental changes in its culture to prevent another disaster, including a system of external policing. But it was not optimistic about NASA's compliance, saying, "The changes we recommend will be difficult to accomplish—and will be internally resisted." NASA administrator O'Keefe was more optimistic, expressing his intention to fully comply with the board's recommendations. With a space program and human lives at stake, we can only hope that NASA makes a genuine effort to avoid the pitfalls of groupthink.

An investigation of the Columbia *disaster placed part of the blame on groupthink, a flaw in the way that groups make decisions.*

his findings showed just the opposite. The phenomenon, which became known as the **risky shift**, has now been tested in many studies with an instrument called the Choice Dilemma Questionnaire (see Box 13.3).

The results of early studies confirmed Stoner's conclusion that groups tend to make riskier decisions than individuals. But later research showed that some groups make more conservative decisions. Researchers eventually realized that the shift is related to the initial opinions of group members. If group members express conservative opinions in the beginning, further discussion leads in that direction. Conversely, if group members start out with risky opinions, the shift moves that way. Serge Moscovici and Marisa Zavalloni (1969) called this tendency **group polarization**.

Explanations for group polarization involve both informational and normative influence (Levine and Moreland 1998; see also Kaplan 1987; Eagly and Chaiken 1993). The most popular informational influence explanation is called the **persuasive arguments perspective**. According to this explanation, individuals are influenced during discussions by ideas that support their own initial position as well as by new ideas that they have not

| BOX 13.3 | CHOICE DILEMMA QUESTIONNAIRE |

Subjects are asked to read a number of stories that involve a dilemma. They are then asked to choose the level of risk they would be willing to take if they were in that position. Consider the following story (Kogan and Wallach 1964, 256–257):

> Mr. B, a 45-year-old accountant, has recently been informed by his physician that he has developed a severe heart ailment. The disease would be sufficiently serious to force Mr. B to change many of his strongest life habits—reducing his workload, drastically changing his diet, giving up favorite leisure-time pursuits. The physician suggests that a delicate medical operation could be attempted, which, if successful, would completely relieve the heart condition. But its success could not be assured, and in fact, the operation might prove fatal.

Imagine that you are advising Mr. B. Listed below are several probabilities or odds that the risky play will work. Check the lowest probability that you would consider acceptable for the risky surgery to be attempted.

_____ Place a check here if you think Mr. B. should not have the operation no matter what the probabilities.

_____ The chances are 9 in 10 that the operation will be a success.

_____ The chances are 7 in 10 that the operation will be a success.

_____ The chances are 5 in 10 that the operation will be a success.

_____ The chances are 3 in 10 that the operation will be a success.

_____ The chances are 1 in 10 that the operation will be a success.

After subjects made their own decisions about this dilemma, they were asked to discuss the dilemma with a group and come to a unanimous decision about the risk they would be willing to take.

considered (Burnstein and Sentis 1981). Group members tend to offer more arguments and stronger ones for their initial position than for positions they oppose. And their position is strengthened when individuals repeat and restate their ideas during group discussions (Brauer, Judd, and Gliner 1995). The persuasive arguments perspective also explains the process of "depolarization"—a shift to the middle, which happens when group members are about evenly divided on an issue (Burnstein and Vinokur 1977; Burnstein 1982; Brauer, Judd, and Gliner 1995).

The second explanation for group polarization, the **social comparison perspective**, involves normative influence. As Leon Festinger (1954) argued, people are motivated to evaluate their own opinions by comparing them to those of others. This comparison occurs during group discussions where individuals discover how similar or dissimilar their attitudes are to those of other members. One particular explanation proposes that individuals view extreme positions as socially desirable. Their own desire to be liked may cause individuals to shift toward a more extreme position than that of other members of the group. This shifting is a form of one-upmanship, which ultimately causes the group polarization (Brown 1974; Myers 1978).

Research supports both the persuasive arguments explanation and the social comparison explanation of group polarization (Isenberg 1986; Zuber, Crott, and Werner 1992). Martin Kaplan (1987) argues that a number of variables affect the impact of informational and normative influence on group polarization. For one thing, it depends on whether the issue involves a judgmental task or an intellective one. The goal of the group also plays a role. That is, what does the group consider more important—maintaining harmony or arriving at the correct decision? The orientation of individual group members also has an effect. Are members oriented to the task or to relationships? And finally, the impact depends on the kind of response required in the group, whether it is public or private. Kaplan argues that the combination of a judgmental task, an emphasis on group harmony, relationship-oriented individual members, and a public response favors the normative influence explanation. Intellective tasks combined with a desire for arriving at the correct decision, task-oriented individual members, and private responses tends to support the informational explanation of group polarization.

Clark McCauley and Mary Segal (1987) recognized the process of group polarization in the decision making of terrorist groups. According to them, terrorist groups do not start out with extreme positions but develop them gradually over time. One explanation for a shift to extremist positions focuses on how the same membership develops more extreme opinions and behaviors over time. McCauley and Segal argue that this shift occurs as a result of normal group dynamics and resembles the process of group polarization that has been observed in studies of college students.

LEADERSHIP IN GROUPS

Be not afraid of greatness. Some are born great, some achieve greatness, and some have greatness thrust upon 'em.
—William Shakespeare, *Twelfth Night, 2.5*

It was a hard decision: Who should appear on the front cover of the December 31, 2001/January 7, 2002, issue of *Time* magazine as the "person of the year"? The question really boiled down to leadership. Did New York City Mayor Rudolph Giuliani deserve the honor for his leadership in the wake of 9/11, or did the honor belong to President George W. Bush, who had calmed and united the country after the terrorist attacks? As it turns out, Giuliani appeared on the cover. Both men were recognized for their abilities to lead the nation in a time of crisis. But the hardest question really remained unanswered: What makes a great leader?

Social psychologists are joined by historians, political scientists, and psychologists in searching for the answer to this question (Fiedler 1967; Burns 1978; Hollander 1985; Simonton 1987; Bass 1990, 1997; Klenke 1996; Chemers, Watson, and May 2000). Two well-known theories of leadership look for the answer, but in opposite directions—one inward toward certain characteristics of the individual, the other outward toward the situation.

The Great-Person Theory

The **great-person theory of leadership** proposes that individuals who possess certain personality traits are likely to emerge as leaders no matter what the situation is. In an attempt to identify specific personality traits, a number of studies have examined the differences between leaders and followers (Forsyth 2000). And it appears that leaders and followers do differ in certain traits. For example, leaders tend to surpass other group members in terms of the abilities and skills needed to help a group reach its particular goals. They tend to be somewhat more intelligent than followers, have stronger interpersonal skills, and have more confidence in their ability to lead (Chemers, Watson, and May 2000). They are also more flexible, empathic, and emotionally stable (Hogan, Curphy, and Hogan 1994). Finally, leaders tend to seek recognition and power. They are ambitious, geared toward achievement, and willing to take responsibility (Whitney, Sagrestano, and Maslach 1994).

The Situation

The terrorist attacks on September 11, 2001, tested the leadership abilities of both Rudolph Giuliani and George W. Bush. They both passed the test. But what if this situation had never occurred? Were they simply in the right position at the right time? If this had not happened, would they both be left out of the history books? Did the situation provide them with a challenge that many others could handle? Or were they born to lead?

Mayor Rudolph Giuliani and President George W. Bush were both considered for *Time* magazine's "person of the year" for leadership they demonstrated after 9/11.

According to the situational perspective on leadership, possessing certain leadership traits does not mean that an individual will become a leader. The situation plays a critical role. Fred Fiedler (1967) proposed one of the most popular theories of this kind. According to his **contingency theory of leadership**, a leader's style along with the particular situation determines his or her effectiveness. Fiedler claims that leaders exhibit one of two styles of leadership. **Task-oriented leaders** focus on the group's goal; their primary interest rests in getting the job done. In contrast, **relationship-oriented leaders** pay attention to the feelings of group members and how those affect relationships with other group members.

Which leadership style is more effective? Fiedler (1967) argues that the answer depends on the situation. Some situations give leaders a great deal of control and influence, and some do not. In a high-control situation, a leader is well liked, respected, and viewed as having legitimate authority; the task is structured and clearly defined. A situation that involves high control is the construction of a new home. An experienced building supervisor with clear plans can effectively guide skilled workers without much trouble. His crew is likely to respect and like him.

In a low-control situation, the leader has poor relationships with group members and is not viewed as having much legitimate authority; the task is poorly structured and might involve a complex problem. Consider a new teacher who is asked to take the role of a team leader at her school. If the team project involves a complicated task such as revising the curriculum for her department, she is likely to encounter many problems from more experienced teachers, who are unlikely to accept her authority.

Fiedler's research showed that task-oriented leaders were more effective in either very high or very low control situations. In contrast, relationship-oriented leaders were most effective in moderate-control situations. These results suggest why situational characteristics determine the effectiveness of leaders. In highly controlled situations, people are likely to follow the directions of a task-oriented leader without complaining or resentment. Clear-cut tasks reduce conflict that might arise between leaders and followers. These kinds of smoothly operating groups do not require a leader who must pay attention to members' feelings or relationships. In low-control situations, where the task is not clearly defined, group members are likely to welcome the direction of a task-oriented leader who can get the job done. Relationship-oriented leaders operate best in moderate-control situations, where relationships among members play a more important role in the group's productivity.

CONFLICT AND COOPERATION

People in groups often cooperate to achieve a common goal. The magic of championship basketball teams may in fact be due to that special kind of chemistry that fosters cooperative teamwork. Sometimes, however, an individual member wants to be the star. In this case, he might well put his own interests above the team's and compete with his teammates for all of the glory. Groups can also compete or cooperate with one another. The futile attempts to resolve the bitter conflict between Israelis and Arabs leave many doubts about long-lasting peace.

Social psychologists have long sought to understand conflict and how it might be resolved (Thibaut and Kelley 1959b; Deutsch 1973; Allison, Beggan, and Midgley 1996; Levine and Thompson 1996; Pruitt 1998). So have researchers in every field of the social sciences. Parties engaged in conflict include individuals, groups, organizations, and nations (Pruitt 1998). Conflict can therefore range from arguments and fistfights to all-out war. In the final section of this chapter, we will examine the creative approaches that social psychologists have taken to studying conflict and cooperation.

Social Dilemmas

Social psychologists have paid much attention to a special kind of conflict called a **social dilemma**. This term refers to a situation that involves a choice between self-interest and collective interest (Pruitt 1998). The dilemma amounts to this: If the parties involved in a situation decide to act in their own self-interest, all parties are worse off than if they had acted cooperatively. In other words, this is a situation in which the welfare of the group is sacrificed in the interest of one party. Many social problems involve social dilemmas, from "failing to help colleagues and loafing on the job to arms races and the collapse of ecosystems" (471).

Garret Hardin (1968) offered a classic example of a social dilemma in the article "The Tragedy of the Commons," which appeared in *Science* magazine. He asked readers to imagine a pasture that is available to everyone for grazing cattle. This arrangement might work for hundreds of years if wars and diseases maintain the population of human beings and animals below the sustenance level of the pasture. The tragedy of the commons starts when herdsmen act in their own self-interest and decide to increase the size of their herds. The overgrazing of the pasture eventually destroys it.

A number of environmental problems involve social dilemmas—choices between self-interest and collective interest (Yamagishi 1995). The issue may involve the interests of individuals over the community when it comes to the air, water, or forests. The use of public goods also illustrates the concept of social dilemma. Consider people who listen to public broadcasting but make no financial contribution to pay for it. Known as the *free rider problem*, this example illustrates how a decision made out of self-interest jeopardizes the welfare of the group. If everyone decides to free-ride, the lack of funding will end public broadcasting.

The Prisoner's Dilemma

One way that social psychologists study social dilemmas is through simulated games. The best-known game is the *prisoner's dilemma*. Imagine the following scenario. The police have arrested two suspects for a serious crime. The district attorney is convinced that both of them are guilty. Unfortunately, she does not have enough evidence to convict either one of them. She decides to question them separately and comes up with a deal to persuade them to confess. If neither suspect confesses, she will convict each of them of a lesser crime that would result in a two-year sentence. If both of them confess, she will recommend a sentence of ten years for each of them. If one of them confesses but the other does not, she will recommend a light sentence for the one who confesses (one year), but she will use that confession to convict the other suspect of the serious crime and will recommend the maximum sentence—twenty years. Figure 13.3 shows the choices available to the

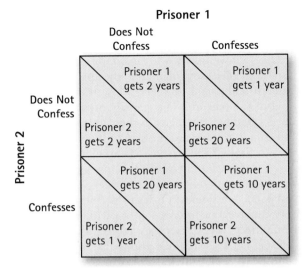

Prisoner 1

Does Not
Confess   Confesses

Prisoner 2

Does Not
Confess

Prisoner 1
gets 2 years

Prisoner 1
gets 1 year

Prisoner 2
gets 2 years

Prisoner 2
gets 20 years

Confesses

Prisoner 1
gets 20 years

Prisoner 1
gets 10 years

Prisoner 2
gets 1 year

Prisoner 2
gets 10 years

FIGURE 13.3

The Prisoner's Dilemma

Source: Adapted from Tucker 1955.

suspects. If you were in this situation, what would you do?

This example illustrates why conflict is difficult to resolve. If one suspect expects the other one to confess, then it is in his best interest to confess as well. Of course, the best mutual outcome occurs if neither of them confesses. In that case, they both get off with a minor sentence. This situation poses a difficult question: How much can they trust one another? And that creates the dilemma. If one of them is convinced that he can trust the other one, will he choose to put his own self-interest above that of the group?

At least two thousand studies have examined how people respond to games like the prisoner's dilemma (Dawes 1991). Instead of facing prison terms, however, subjects play for chips, money, or points. This research shows that people handle the conflict in these games much like real-life conflict. Although the best way to resolve conflict involves trust, people more often distrust the other party. As a result, this leads to an escalation of the conflict so that in the end no one wins (Kelley and

Thibaut 1978; Insko and Schopler 1998; Pruitt 1998; Budescu and Erev 1999).

The Trucking Game

When conflict arises between individuals or groups, one of the parties will probably try to reduce it by using a threat. Teachers might threaten students with more homework if they waste time in class. Parents may threaten to cut off their children's allowance if they ignore household chores. And attempts to reduce international conflict often involve threats such as sanctions and embargoes. But do threats work?

Morton Deutsch and Robert Krauss (1960) designed the *trucking game* to answer this question. This game simulated a conflict situation for two players. At the start, the researchers told the players to pretend that they were the heads of two trucking companies—one was called Acme, the other Bolt. Their task was to deliver merchandise to a given destination in the shortest amount of time. For each delivery, the players would make 60 cents minus their operating expenses, which would be based on the time it took—1 cent per second. For example, if the trip took 20 seconds, the player would make 40 cents.

The players were then shown a map of the routes to their destination (see Figure 13.4). Although both players started out in different locations and had separate destinations, the most direct route required both of them to travel across the same one-lane road. As the map shows, this was designed to create a conflict situation. If both players decided to take this quick route, one of them would have to wait for the other to cross before she could begin. Both players could take an alternate route, but this road was significantly longer and would cost them at least 10 cents more.

To study how the players might use threat to resolve the conflict, Deutsch and Krauss also told some players that they could control a gate that would block the path of the other truck. Gates were placed at the end of the one-lane road closest to each player's starting point. In all, the researchers created three conditions: (1) no threat (no gates),

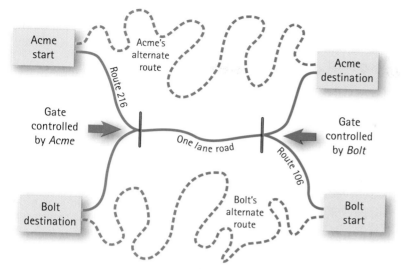

FIGURE 13.4

Road Map for the Trucking Game

Source: Deutsch and Krauss 1960, 183.

(2) one-sided threat (one player controlled a gate), and (3) two-sided threat (both players controlled a gate). During the game, neither player knew exactly where the other was except when they met on the one-lane road. At that point, one of them had to back up before the other could pass.

What did Deutsch and Krauss learn from this experiment? Overall, players made the most money in the no-threat condition and lost the most money in the two-sided threat condition (see Table 13.2). Does this simulation provide insight into the way conflict and threats operate in real life? After all, parties who become involved in conflict are rarely silent. What would happen if

the heads of Acme and Bolt had communicated? Deutsch and Krauss (1962) created two more conditions to find out. In one condition, communication was voluntary—the players were free to say as much or little as they wanted. In a second condition, the researchers made them communicate during each trial. Again, the results did not reveal a positive picture for ways to resolve conflict. Overall, the players' winnings did not increase significantly when they were forced to communicate in the no-threat or two-sided-threat condition. Their losses were cut a little in the one-sided-threat condition when the players were forced to communicate.

TABLE 13.2 **TRUCKING GAME RESULTS: MEAN PAYOFFS AFTER 20 TRIALS**

	Means		
Variable	(1) No Threat	(2) Unilateral Threat	(3) Bilateral Threat
Summed payoffs (Acme + Bolt)	203.31	−405.88	−875.12
Acme's payoff	122.44	−118.56	−406.56
Bolt's payoff	80.88	−287.31	−468.56

Source: Adapted from Deutsch and Krauss 1962, 58.

The explanation for these results might seem obvious: Threats do not foster trust. What is more, when players could use an intercom system to communicate, they did so in ways that undermined trust. Other studies have shown that communication can reduce conflict if people understand how to use it to build trust (Kerr and Kaufman-Gilliland 1994).

SUMMARY

1. For social psychologists, a group differs significantly from a simple gathering of individuals. A group consists of at least two interacting people who hold common expectations, seek common goals, share an identity, and feel a sense of unity or interdependence.

2. Social structures evolve in groups as people interact. The basic elements of a group's social structure are norms, statuses, and roles. These elements contribute to a predictable social environment by giving members information about how they should behave and how they should relate to others in the group. Also important is group cohesiveness.

3. Groups influence our thoughts, feelings, and behaviors in various ways. Social facilitation and social loafing focus on how groups influence individuals' performance on tasks. Groups also pressure individuals to conform by adopting the norms and values of the group. In some cases, this pressure leads group members to engage in destructive behaviors like riots.

4. Various factors and processes influence a group's performance. Groups are more efficient than individuals sometimes but not always. Group performance may vary with the specific tasks a group is given. Brainstorming, a popular strategy for generating ideas in a group, is not as effective as once thought. Groupthink can lead groups into serious judgment errors. Decision making in groups can be subject to group polarization, the tendency to shift opinions in an extreme direction.

5. According to the great-person theory of leadership, personality traits play the most important role in determining who emerges as a leader. Leaders do possess certain traits that distinguish them from followers. Situational theories of leadership reject the idea that personality explains leadership. They focus instead on characteristics of the situation. Fiedler's contingency theory of leadership illustrates how situations influence the effectiveness of a leader. According to this theory, some situations give leaders greater control and influence than others. And who emerges as an effective leader depends on the style of leadership chosen for a particular situation.

6. Although members of a group often cooperate to achieve a common goal, their own self-interests may conflict with the collective interest of the group, posing a social dilemma. Games such as the prisoner's dilemma and the trucking game have been designed to study this kind of conflict.

KEY TERMS

Social group   370
Primary group   370
Secondary group   371
Dyad   374
Triad   374
Status system   374

Expectation states theory   375
Group norms   375
Instrumental leaders   377
Expressive (socioemotional) leaders   377
Group cohesiveness   378

Social facilitation   379
Evaluation apprehension   380
Distraction-conflict theory   380
Social loafing   381
Social impact theory   381
Additive task   383

CRITICAL REVIEW QUESTIONS

1. What does a good leader know about the way groups operate? For example, what should the president of the United States know about groups before taking office?
2. Give specific examples to show how social facilitation and social loafing operate in college classes.
3. Suppose that you must decide whether to work alone or with a small group on a class project. If you want to get an A, what should you consider about the specific tasks that the project involves?

FOURTEEN

Collective Behavior and Social Movements

New Yorkers who were standing on the sidewalk in Lower Manhattan recalled how it all began. Marking the time as 8:45 A.M., David Blackford told a *New York Times* reporter that he heard a jet engine and looked up (Kleinfield 2001). "I saw this plane screaming overhead," he said. "I thought it was too low. I thought it wasn't going to clear the tower." He was right. Within moments, the plane crashed into the north face of One World Trade Center. Alerted to the crash, the media quickly focused cameras on the building as smoke and fire began to envelop it. As they watched on their monitors, morning news anchors remarked that it appeared that an accident had occurred. But in fact, it was no accident. That seemed evident to eyewitnesses on the ground. Another one, Robert Pachino, told a reporter, "There was no engine trouble. He didn't try to maneuver. This plane was on a mission" (A1). About fifteen minutes later, media broadcasters voiced Pachino's fears when they saw a second plane crash into Building Two. It was a terrorist attack. And now it seemed that these terrorists had even calculated the timing between these two crashes to manipulate the media. It had given broadcasters enough time to capture the image of an American symbol as it was defaced and then obliterated. In living rooms across the nation, Americans witnessed an attack on their cherished beliefs and values.

This terrorist act produced immediate effects. People in the streets of Lower Manhattan panicked. Running for their lives, some were stomped by the crowd. Others remembered being hysterical and dumbstruck. Some appeared paralyzed as they watched the inferno in disbelief. When police officers warned them that the buildings could collapse, some gravitated closer together. Grabbing the hand of a stranger, one woman began to recite the Lord's Prayer. But as smoke rising from the towers took the form of an atomic mushroom cloud, everyone began to run. Moments later, from their vantage point ten blocks north of the World Trade Center, they looked back in horror as first one building and then the other collapsed. "People cried at what they saw: a crystalline sky with nothing in it" (Kleinfield 2001, A7). Soon lines of people, five to eight deep, stretched out from pay phones.

The effects of these terrorist acts were not limited to the streets of New York City. From disbelief and horror to fear, sadness, anger, anxiety, and sleeplessness, people across the United States experienced a wide range of common reactions. The attack threatened to shatter the world as they knew it. The resulting uncertainty produced a powerful bond. Complete strangers gathered to share information, to express their feelings, to pray for victims, and to seek comfort at prayer vigils. Messages quickly swept the Internet urging people to show their unity by flying their American flags at half-mast. The response was overwhelming—stores across the country could not keep flags in stock.

The September 11 attacks on America showed how the acts of a small group of terrorists profoundly affected the thoughts, feelings, and behaviors of millions of people. It provided priceless information about a kind of behavior that is unpredictable and difficult to study. How do crowds act when they come under the attack of an enemy? What happens when people find themselves in a building that is on fire and on the verge of collapsing? How do people witnessing these events react? These questions address the main topic of this final chapter: collective behavior. Social psychologists would consider much of what happened on September 11 a particular kind of collective behavior called disaster behavior. We will see that collective behavior comes in many forms. The last section of this chapter is devoted to one of the most important kinds: social movements.

COLLECTIVE BEHAVIOR

Collective behavior refers to a wide variety of behaviors involving two or more individuals. It includes disaster behavior, panics, fashions, fads, crazes, riots, public opinion, propaganda, rumors, urban legends, and social movements. What do these different kinds of collective behavior have in common? That is a difficult question to answer (Marx and McAdam 1994), but social psychologists do agree that they have a number of common characteristics.

Collective behavior is unexpected and emerges as a response to a common stimulus. It is unpredictable in terms of when or where it will occur. In contrast to organizational behavior, which conforms to social norms, collective behavior is characterized by modified norms that may conflict with dominant norms. Collective behavior can spread quickly within the same environment, passing from one person to the next. It may also spread from one place to another. People recognize that something out of the ordinary is happening (Marx and McAdam 1994).

It is easy to recognize these characteristics in various kinds of collective behavior. Consider the following examples:

- A crowd that flocks to the scene of a disaster, fire, or accident
- Demonstrations or riots that spread from city to city across the United States
- A mysterious illness with no known medical cause that spreads among workers
- A social movement that turns into a violent revolution

Even though defining collective behavior is difficult, identifying the kinds of behaviors that occur in temporary gatherings is not. Clark McPhail (1991) provided a list of forty different forms (see Table 14.1). As he argued, people engage in these kinds of collective behaviors at all types of gatherings around the world.

Crowds and Crowd Behavior

The most widely recognized form of collective behavior is the crowd (Turner and Killian 1987). Whether it takes the form of a lynch mob, a rioting crowd, or curious spectators, this term refers to a temporary gathering of people in close proximity,

TABLE 14.1	ELEMENTARY FORMS OF COLLECTIVE BEHAVIOR IN COMMON	
Collective Orientation	**Collective Vocalization**	**Collective Verbalization**
1. Clustering	1. Ooh-, ahh-, ohhing	1. Chanting
2. Arc-ing, ringing	2. Yeaing	2. Singing
3. Gazing, facing	3. Booing	3. Praying
4. Vigiling	4. Whistling	4. Reciting
	5. Hissing	5. Pledging
	6. Laughing	
	7. Wailing	

Collective Gesticulation (Nonverbal Symbols)

1. Roman salute (arm extended forward, palm down, fingers together)
2. Solidarity salute (closed fist raised above the shoulder level)
3. *Digitus obscenus* (fist raised, middle finger extended)
4. #1 (fist raised shoulder level or above, index finger extended)
5. Peace (fist raised, index finger and middle fingers separated and extended)
6. Praise or victory (both arms fully extended overhead)

Collective Vertical Locomotion	**Collective Horizontal Locomotion**	**Collective Manipulation**
1. Sitting	1. Pedestrian clustering	1. Applauding
2. Standing	2. Queueing	2. Synchroclapping
3. Jumping	3. Surging	3. Finger-snapping
4. Bowing	4. Marching	4. Grasping, lifting, waving an object
5. Kneeling	5. Jogging	5. Grasping, lifting, throwing an object
6. Kowtowing	6. Running	6. Grasping, lifting, pushing an object

Source: McPhail 1994, 164.

who share a common focus of attention and who exert a mutual influence on one another. A crowd is not synonymous with a social grouping. In fact, a number of features clearly distinguish a crowd from other kinds of social groupings (Turner and Killian 1987). One distinguishing feature is the *uncertainty* of a crowd, the result of both an unstructured situation and the absence of preexisting expectations about how people ought to behave in that situation. Crowds also tend to be permissive and ignore normal social constraints. But these characteristics alone do not give rise to crowd behavior. It is a crowd's sense of urgency to act now, coupled with a heightened suggestibility that is shaped by a crowd's mood that do so.

Types of Crowds

Herbert Blumer (1939/1969) identified four types of crowds: a casual crowd, a conventional crowd, an expressive crowd, and an acting crowd. The individuals in a **casual crowd** interact with little emotional involvement. For example, they may be curious spectators who share attention in the noisy arrival of emergency vehicles. They are aware of other individuals in the crowd and may speak to them casually. But the interaction is brief and relatively insignificant.

A **conventional crowd** interacts in a more structured situation, and it recognizes a set of conventional norms. Audiences attending a play or students gathered for a prescheduled school assembly are conventional crowds. The interaction among individuals in these crowds is minimal and fairly predictable.

An **expressive crowd** assembles for an event that is designed to allow individuals to release their emotions. The festivals of preliterate cultures included a wide range of activities for this purpose, including singing, dancing, feasting, and competitions. Today, we see similar behaviors at sports events, New Year's Eve celebrations, and parades. These events create situations that allow individuals to release their emotions in spontaneous ways that are invigorating. The unique trait of an expressive crowd is "that excitement is expressed in physical movement merely as a form of release instead of being directed toward some objective" (Blumer 1951a, 179).

An **acting crowd** differs from an expressive crowd in one important respect: Its activity is directed toward a clear objective. For example, the goal of individuals in a crowd that panics when it discovers that the building is on fire is to escape to safety. The behavior of individuals in this kind of acting crowd is motivated by fear, is competitive, and is directed toward a specific goal. But acting crowds can be motivated by other emotions. In fact, many acting crowds are angry and hostile. And they direct these emotions toward a single target. Lynch mobs provide a good example.

Panic

Panic is a form of collective behavior that results when a group views a situation as threatening. The presence of a "hysterical belief" can produce panic by transforming a poorly defined situation into a generalized threat (Marx and McAdam 1994). When members of a crowd panic, they experience fear and alarm. But their behavior is not just an emotional release. It is competitive and directed toward a specific goal—escaping to a safe place.

Orson Welles's 1938 Halloween radio broadcast serves as one of the best examples of the effects that panic produces. At 8 P.M. Eastern time from a New York radio station, he and a group of actors broadcast Howard Koch's adapted version of H. G. Wells's novel *War of the Worlds*. To make this fantasy seem realistic, they interrupted the radio program with simulated news broadcasts, which reported that Martians had landed in New Jersey and had launched a devastating attack on the United States. Americans gathered around their radios, listening intently to the details of this invasion. Many believed that the end of the world was at hand. Newspapers the next day described the "tidal wave of terror that swept the nation" (Cantril 1941, 3).

The reactions of listeners in 1938 ranged from feelings of anxiety to hysterical crying. Many people felt an overwhelming impulse to escape, which led them to jump into their cars and rush to their loved ones. One college student reported his reaction later in an interview conducted by Hadley Cantril (1941), who undertook a comprehensive study of what had happened:

> "One of the first things I did was to try to phone my girl in Poughkeepsie, but the lines were all busy, so that just confirmed my impression that the thing was true. We started driving back to Poughkeepsie. We had heard that Princeton was wiped out and gas was spreading over New Jersey and fire, so I figured there wasn't anything to do—we figured our friends and families were all dead. I made the 45 miles in 35 minutes and didn't even realize it. I drove right through Newburgh and never even knew I went through it. I don't know why we weren't killed. My roommate was crying and praying. He was even more excited than I was—or more noisy about it anyway; I guess I took it out in pushing the accelerator to the floor." (51–52)

Another interview provided insight into some real fears that Americans had in 1938:

"Sylvia Holmes, a panic-stricken Negro housewife who lived in Newark, thinking the end of the world was near, in her excitement overstepped the bounds of her usual frugality. 'We listened getting more and more excited. We all felt the world was coming to an end. Then we heard "Get gas masks!" That was the part that got me. I thought I was going crazy. It's a wonder my heart didn't fail me because I'm nervous anyway. I felt if the gas was on, I wanted to be together with my husband and nephew so we could all die together. So I ran out of the house. I guess I didn't know what I was doing. I stood on the corner waiting for a bus and I thought every car that came along was a bus and I ran out to get it. People saw how excited I was and tried to quiet me, but I kept saying over and over again to everybody I met: "Don't you know New Jersey is destroyed by the Germans—it's on the radio." I was all excited and I knew that Hitler didn't appreciate President Roosevelt's telegram a couple of weeks ago. While the U.S. thought everything was settled, they came down unexpected. The Germans are so wise they were in something like a balloon and when the balloon landed—that's when they announced the explosion—the Germans landed. . . . It was eleven o'clock and we heard it announced that it was only a play. It sure felt good—just like a burden was lifted off me.' " (53–54)

This broadcast caused such a panic that the Federal Communications Commission called the program "regrettable" and later adopted regulations to prevent it from happening again.

People panic in response to all kinds of threats. It frequently occurs aboard ships, in congested buildings that are on fire, and in places where a catastrophe has occurred (Cantril 1941). Financial crises also cause panic. Consider what happens when there is a run on a bank or when the stock market crashes. Mysterious illnesses, property damage, and reports of alien invasions are also common triggers of panic (Marx and McAdam 1994) (see Box 14.1).

Fashion, Fads, and Crazes

"The gods and heroes wear beards," proclaimed Robert de Valcourt, a Victorian. And the late Victorian man, determined to look both god and hero, sprouted an infinite variety of facial adornment. This hairiness was a marked departure. No founding father sported a beard: Uncle Sam wore none until 1858. Then beards and mustaches suddenly bloomed everywhere. Gold prospectors and fast-shooting marshals made them a mark of virility. Distinguished thinkers like Carl Schurz gave them an air of intellectuality. Finally, Abe Lincoln, growing a beard after a little girl said it might help his looks, established facial hair as a male status symbol of the era.

—Bowen 1968, 193

Beards, mustaches, and hairstyles are **fashions**, much like clothing and other kinds of adornment. They are transitory and suggest that someone is

---

BOX 14.1	PANIC IN INDIA

On August 20, 2002, the *New York Times* printed the following account of an unusual series of events that occurred in India.

Reports of a flashing space creature, or maybe a mutant bug that glows at both ends, have created panic in the country's most populous state [Uttar Pradesh], setting off riots and lynchings that have killed more than a dozen people. Victims report being scratched by something flashing blue, red or green that strikes only at faces and only at night. Some police officers declared that the "face-clawing monster" is an extraterrestrial being. Terrified villagers have killed people suspected of being one, and one person died on Sunday when the police fired on a crowd storming their post 40 miles from the state capital, Lucknow. A scientist investigating the incidents said he believed that the most likely explanation in the drought-stricken state was lightning balls, common during prolonged dry spells.

Hairstyles, including beards and mustaches, illustrate one of the unique forms of collective behavior. Being fashionable during the nineteenth century required careful grooming. Some men preferred long, narrow beards with sideburns (left). Others combined a medium-length beard with a mustache (center). And some men added a little flare to a neat, short beard by curling the ends of their mustaches (right).

either up-to-date or outmoded (Vago 1999). Herbert Blumer (1939/1969, 341–342) described fashion as "a continuing pattern of change in which certain social forms enjoy temporary acceptance and respectability only to be replaced by others more abreast of the times." This pattern of fleeting popularity may be called a "fashion cycle" (Vago 1999), and indeed, some fashions in clothing and hairstyles do seem to come and go in a recurrent way. Dwight Robinson (1976) found a "most remarkable" relationship between the "width of skirt wave, which rose and fell between 1811 and 1926, and the beard wave, which rose and fell between 1842 (or very possibly 1840) and 1956" (136–137). He did not explain why these two fashions were linked in this way.

What can we learn from studying fashion? Both Georg Simmel and Thorstein Veblen recognized that fashion plays a role in assigning status in modern societies. Veblen (1911/1930) explained fashion in terms of "conspicuous consumption"—spending money for the explicit purpose of advertising one's wealth. Simmel (1904/1971) claimed that members of the upper classes engage in a constant effort to distinguish themselves from members of the lower classes by adopting new styles. In an attempt to raise their own status, members of the lower classes imitate those of the upper classes. As a fashion spreads across the population, it no longer distinguishes the social classes and is quickly replaced by a newer fashion.

Fads, like fashions, are cultural patterns, but the life spans of fads are even shorter than those of fashions. This kind of collective behavior is adopted by the masses with extraordinary enthusiasm for a brief time. It involves something particularly unusual or novel, spreads quickly, and then disappears. In some cases, people use fads to express their identity (Turner and Killian 1987). Think of teenagers who wear punk hairstyles and clothing or college students who wear baseball caps backward (Trinkhaus 1994; Vago 1999).

John Lofland (1985) identified four types of fads:

- Object fads: Kilroy pins, hula hoops, Rubik's Cube, baseball cards, bumper stickers, clothing, posters
- Activity fads: eating goldfish, streaking, bungee jumping, flagpole sitting, phone booth stuffing, the wave (sports audiences)
- Idea fads: astrology
- Personality fads or fad heroes: Elvis Presley, the Beatles, Michael Jordan, Madonna, Britney Spears

What is the difference between a fad and a **craze**? That is hard to say. Kingsley Davis (1949) claimed that they could sometimes be distinguished by "the quickness with which they alternate, the utter superficiality of their content, and the irrationality and intensity of the temporary fascination for them" (79). The tulip mania that occurred in Holland in the 1630s is one of the best examples of a craze (Mackay 1841; Menschel 2002). Robert Menschel described it as follows:

> By 1630 the Dutch people in particular were becoming obsessed with the growing and trading of tulips. Amateur growers began to bid up the price of certain species that were especially popular or that had the potential of winning prizes, and by 1634 an adjunct to the Amsterdam stock exchange had been set up for the trading of tulips. The rage to own tulips became such that "persons were known to invest a fortune of 100,000 florins in the purchase of forty roots." Soon, everyone who had a few square yards of back garden was growing bulbs, and at first all were winners as the price of bulbs kept rising. Stories of common people cultivating rare bulbs and suddenly becoming rich abounded, and working men began to quit their jobs in order to have more time to grow and trade tulips. . . .
>
> The height of tulipmania was between 1634 and 1637. The price of prime bulbs soared to the present equivalent of $110,000. As the mania expanded, the fabric of society began to unravel. . . .
>
> Visitors to Holland were astounded, and Charles Mackay recounts the story of an ignorant English sailor off a visiting ship in Rotterdam happening to eat a tulip bulb from a garden, thinking it was an onion. Its owner turned out a lynch mob, and the sailor was committed to debtors' prison for ten years. (12–13)

Both fads and crazes spread quickly among college and high school students. Marx and McAdam (1994) argue that friendship networks are part of the reason. Students who live in group quarters like dormitories, fraternities, or sororities are easy to organize for these kinds of collective behavior. In fact, one of the most memorable fads of the twentieth century—streaking—erupted on college campuses across the United States in 1974. During the mere four months it lasted, it spread to high schools, sports events, and even a national broadcast of the Emmy Awards.

COMMUNICATION AND COLLECTIVE BEHAVIOR

Communication plays a central role in collective behavior. In some cases, it can create panic or mass hysteria. As Orson Welles's radio broadcast of *The War of the Worlds* showed, the mass media can exert a powerful influence over a large part of the population. Although the effects of that broadcast were unexpected, other forms of media are intentionally designed to produce a given effect. Consider Hitler's use of propaganda to win support for his domestic and foreign policies (see Box 14.2). The film *Triumph of the Will*, produced by Leni Riefenstahl at Hitler's request, is "widely regarded as the most powerful, influential propaganda film in nonfiction cinema history" (Williams and Cooper 2002, 348; see also Everson 1971; Barsam 1992).

Today, the mass media play a central role in the transmission of other kinds of information that are also considered collective behavior: rumors, gossip, urban legends, and public opinion. At one time, people spread rumors and gossip informally through personal conversations. Today, telephone lines, faxes, and the Internet provide modern channels for this kind of collective behavior.

BOX 14.2	TRIUMPH OF PROPAGANDA

The most famous piece of propaganda produced during World War II was Leni Riefenstahl's film of the 1924 Nazi Party rally at Nuremberg, *Triumph of the Will*. When it premiered in 1935 it was hailed as a masterpiece. Frank Capra, a Hollywood filmmaker, was called in to produce American films to counteract what he called "the classic powerhouse propaganda film of our times." He recalls:

> Shortly after General Marshall ordered me to make the *Why We Fight* films for our servicemen, I saw Leni Riefenstahl's terrifying motion picture, *Triumph of the*

Will. The film was the ominous prelude of Hitler's holocaust of hate. Satan couldn't have devised a more blood-chilling super-spectacle.

. . . It was at once the glorification of war, the deification of Hitler, and the canonization of his apostles. Though panoplied with all the pomp and mystical trappings of a Wagnerian opera, its message was blunt and brutal as a lead pipe: We, the *Herrenvolk* [master race], are the new invincible gods! *Triumph of the Will* fired no gun, dropped no bombs. But as a psychological weapon aimed at destroying the will to resist, it was just as lethal. (Capra 1972, 362–363)

Rumors

A **rumor** is unsubstantiated information that spreads informally, most often by word of mouth. Rumors may contain some truth, but they are often inaccurate and difficult to stop. Consider rumors about the deaths of beloved celebrities. To this day, Elvis fans continue to question whether he really died in 1977. And rumors of Elvis sightings fill the tabloids. In 1969, Paul McCartney of the Beatles suffered the opposite fate: Rumor had it that he had died in an automobile accident and had been replaced by a double. Fans were encouraged to consider the evidence. For example, Paul was the only Beatle wearing a black flower in a picture that appeared on the sleeve of their album *Magical Mystery Tour*. Rumors of his death persisted despite his own denials.

Rumors like these may seem harmless, and they may simply provide entertainment for the people who generate and transmit them (Marx and McAdam 1994). But rumors have the potential to cause significant harm. In fact, this concern during World War II prompted the earliest research on this topic (Rosnow and Fine 1976; Marx and McAdam 1994). One feature that we should consider when it comes to the harm that rumors cause is the potential to actually precipitate certain kinds of collective behavior. For example, a rumor that the stock market is going to crash or that the banks

are about to fail can trigger a panic. People may rush to sell their stocks or to withdraw their money from the bank. Rumors have also been known to trigger riots. According to Marx and McAdam (1994, 27), "A rumor that police had beaten a pregnant black woman whose car they had stopped played an important role in triggering the Watts riot in Los Angeles in 1975. The incident actually involved a routine stop of a black male."

Research shows that a number of factors contribute to the generation and transmission of rumors: personal anxiety, uncertainty about a situation, the credibility of a rumor, and the rumor's relevance to an individual (Rosnow 1991; Marx and McAdam 1994). The social function of rumors also plays a role. For example, rumors may help people figure out what is happening in a situation or indicate what should be done about a particular problem. They can also help people reach agreement or recognize meaning in an unclear situation.

Urban Legends

Consider the following claims (Roeper 2001). Are they fact or fiction?

- As the result of a settlement in a class action lawsuit, Gerber, the baby food maker, is giving children born between 1985 and 1997 a $500 savings bond.

- A psychic who had predicted the Oklahoma City bombing later appeared on the Oprah Winfrey show and predicted that a mass murder would take place at a state college on Halloween.
- As part of a recycling program that will turn old shoes into playground surfaces and basketball courts, Nike is offering a brand-new pair of tennis shoes to anyone who sends in an old pair of tennis shoes.

Not one of these claims is true. They are all **urban legends**. This form of collective behavior refers to modern morality tales that happen to anonymous others—the friend of a friend of a friend (Segaloff 2001). These stories often involve a gruesome murder, sex, or just plain stupidity. For example, have you heard the one about the "vanishing hitchhiker" or the moviegoer who contracted AIDS when someone pricked her with a sticker in the theater that read "Welcome to the World of AIDS"? (see Roeper 2001; Segaloff 2001).

It is difficult to trace the origin of urban legends because most of them develop from rumors that spread quickly from person to person. And even though they are supposedly designed to teach a lesson, it is often difficult to figure out what that lesson is (see Box 14.3). However, if you are familiar with the story about the schoolgirl who discovers a nest of cockroaches in her hair because she neglected to wash it, maybe you have learned a lesson.

Public Opinion

Another form of collective behavior that involves communication is **public opinion**. The meaning of this term revolves around the concept of the **public**, which refers to a dispersed collection of people who share opinions on a variety of social issues: war, gun control, education, health care, social security, and so on. *Public* is not synonymous with *audience*, *mass*, or *crowd* (Turner and Killian 1987). In contrast to these kinds of collectivities, a public discusses an issue with the expectation that its members' collective opinion will influence the decisions of another group or individual. Taking this into account, public opinion, then, refers to "that which is communicated to decision makers as a consequence of the functioning of a public" (180).

The media play an important role in reporting public opinion. Newspapers and magazines publish public opinion in the form of letters to the editor. And they regularly report the results of public opinion polls. Today, many newspapers and broadcasters conduct joint public opinion polls to measure the public's attitudes toward controversial issues. These joint efforts include the *New York Times*/CBS News polls, the *Washington Post*/ABC News polls, and the *Wall Street Journal*/NBC News polls.

Does the public approve of the way the president is handling his job? Should the United States take military action to depose foreign dictators? Should same-sex marriages performed in one state

---

BOX 14.3   AN URBAN LEGEND

Urban legends are supposed to teach us lessons. But what is the lesson in the following urban legend about a state trooper?

A small town discovered that it could cut the money it was spending on traffic cops by parking an empty police car behind a highway billboard and propping a uniformed mannequin in the front seat. The appearance of a "hidden" policeman would scare speeders into slowing down. Before long the decoy was discovered and, like a road sign in rural areas, soon became a target for gun-toting joyriders. Intent on stopping his affront to the law, a young crusading state trooper stationed himself in the car to catch the shooter. Instead, he caught a bullet. (Segaloff 2001, 188)

be recognized by the other states? Such questions identify issues that citizens consider when they vote. And politicians, decision makers, and the public study the answers obtained in these kinds of opinion polls.

But what shapes public opinion? How much impact do the mass media have? Do they have the power to influence public opinion on issues as serious as war? These are difficult questions to answer. And they raise concerns about another kind of collective behavior—propaganda.

Propaganda

As you saw in Box 14.1, **propaganda** refers to intentional attempts to influence mass audiences through techniques that involve spoken, written, or visual representations (Ellul 1966; Nelson 1996; Williams and Cooper 2002). During the early phase of a propaganda campaign, appeals are aimed at the audience's emotions and prejudices. For example, Adolf Hitler fueled hatred for Jews by depicting them as the source of Germany's problems. And they were not his only

targets. When Jesse Owens, an African American, won the gold medal in the 1936 Olympics in Munich, Hitler expressed his disappointment that Owens's Aryan competitors had lost to a person of an "inferior" race (Williams and Cooper 2002).

Although propaganda is usually associated with governmental institutions, especially during times of war, other social institutions use propaganda extensively. Public relations firms, advertising agencies, and even churches use propaganda to persuade audiences to support their goals (see Box 14.4). In fact, the term *propaganda* was coined by the Roman Catholic Church in 1622 when Pope Gregory XV established the Congregation for the Propagation of the Faith (Williams and Cooper 2002). The propaganda of the church was designed for educational and missionary purposes, to further the goals of this institution.

During World War I, the United States government established the Committee for Public Information (CPI) to create propaganda campaigns to "sell the war" to the American public. The CPI used a variety of methods to stir up and maintain

---

BOX 14.4   "TORCHES OF LIBERTY": FEMINIST STAND OR PR STUNT?

On the surface it seemed like an ordinary publicity stunt for "female emancipation," the pre-Depression equivalent of women's liberation. A contingent of New York debutantes marched down Fifth Avenue in the 1929 Easter Parade, each openly lighting and smoking cigarettes. It was the first time in the memory of most Americans that any woman who wasn't a prostitute had been seen smoking in public.

It was dubbed the "torches of liberty contingent" by Edward Bernays, its brilliant behind-the-scenes organizer. Bernays, a nephew of Sigmund Freud, later admitted that he had been paid a tidy sum to orchestrate the march by George Washington Hill, president of the American Tobacco Company. But long before the public learned who had engineered the parade, it had achieved its goal of breaking the taboo against female smoking. Within months, in fact, the politest of American ladies

were puffing in public and sales of Hill's Lucky Strikes were soaring.

The event is still hailed in public relations lore as a "triumph." Some people consider it *the* coup that launched a whole new, distinctively American industry.

Most of us are aware of public relations. "That's just a lot of PR," we say, with smug confidence that we have pierced the veil of hype around us rather than be taken in by some anonymous huckster. But few outside the public relations industry know how well PR really works, and fewer still realize how often we are persuaded by it. Nor do many of us know how much of our "news" and other information originates from the desks of public relations practitioners. "The best PR is never noticed," says the proud unwritten slogan of the trade.

Source: Stauber and Rampton 1995, 1–2.

support for the war effort, including posters, pamphlets, speakers' bureaus, and films.

> A famous World War I poster in the United States defined the enemy in stark form: A German soldier was painted holding his bayoneted rifle menacingly before him. On the bayonet, stuck through and dripping blood, was an infant. The bottom of the poster held the words "The Hun." (Ryan and Wentworth 1999, 47)

Fascists and Communists developed their own propaganda techniques in the 1920s and 1930s to exert influence over the masses in Germany and the Soviet Union. Josef Goebbels, who was appointed by Hitler to serve as the minister of propaganda for the Nazi Party, believed he could make a science out of propaganda. One of Goebbels's projects shows just how successful propaganda techniques can be in producing certain effects. It was a film called *The Eternal Jew*, which was shot in the Warsaw ghettos of 1940. With the intention of provoking intense hatred toward Jews, this film compared Jews to swarming rats. Bill Moyers (1982) identified the unique purpose of this depiction:

> Looking at Fritz Hippler's film *The Eternal Jew*, we must keep reminding ourselves that the purpose of propaganda is action. The viewers were expected to do something about what they saw. When other human beings are compared to rats and vermin that spread disease, it takes no great leap of imagination to know what you're expected to do with the creatures.

The United States also engaged in propaganda campaigns during World War II. The government recruited scholars, journalists, filmmakers, cartoonists, and public relations firms to design media that would persuade the American public to support the war effort. One of the most memorable images of this effort was "Rosie the Riveter," who targeted the American woman. This particular campaign was designed to recruit women to work in the defense industry in jobs that were traditionally viewed as men's work—building tanks, bombs, aircraft, and so on. Recognizing the

need to alter perceptions of traditional gender roles, the creators of these messages promoted the strength and patriotism of working women. Slogans like "We Can Do It" and popular songs and images such as "Rosie the Riveter" convinced women to do their part for America.

Detecting Propaganda

How good are you at detecting propaganda? You might not find it difficult to recognize this kind of intentional persuasion in an editorial cartoon that portrays the enemy in a dehumanized form, often as a symbol of evil—a monster, a serpent, or vermin. But it is often difficult to spot propaganda, which is intentionally designed to mislead us. And it comes in many forms. Just consider a short list:

Rosie the Riveter, one of the most recognized poster girls of World War II, demonstrates how propaganda is designed to manipulate attitudes.

black propaganda, disinformation, doublethink, indoctrination, brainwashing, dogma, hidden agenda, ideology, dirty tricks campaign, double-speak, and psychological warfare (Nelson 1996).

Perhaps you think you could spot an outright lie. But many people are fooled. Consider one example from the 1991 Persian Gulf War (Operation Desert Storm). On October 10, 1990, the Congressional Human Rights Caucus heard testimony from people about Iraqi human rights violations. The emotional account of what a 15-year-old Kuwaiti girl had seen in a hospital in Kuwait City was later reported in the news and then repeated over and over again in the months preceding Desert Storm. To protect her family, who remained in Kuwait, she was simply identified as Nayirah. Crying throughout her testimony, she was quoted as saying:

> I saw the Iraqi soldiers come into the hospital with guns, and go into the room where . . . babies were in incubators. They took the babies out of the incubators, took the incubators, and left the babies on the cold floor to die. (Stauber and Rampton 1995, 173)

This story became part of an official congressional record, was reported on radio and television programs, was told to the UN Security Council, and was repeated by President Bush himself. According to John MacArthur (1992), who thoroughly investigated the story, "Of all the accusations made against the dictator, none had more impact on American public opinion than the one about Iraqi soldiers removing 312 babies from their incubators and leaving them to die on the cold hospital floors of Kuwait City" (58). What the American public did not know was that Nayirah's father was Kuwait's ambassador to the United States. Only after the war did we learn that her testimony was false. This was not the first time that a horrific story had won the sympathy of the American public. It is a common form of black propaganda—an outright lie. And similar tales had been used successfully in previous wars. "During World War I, for example, the Allies said (falsely) that the Germans were chopping off the hands of Belgian babies and turning corpses into soap" (Nelson 1996, 128). The American public believed that story as well.

The first serious study of propaganda in the United States was prompted by a concern about the nature of mass audiences (Williams and Cooper 2002). The ease with which fascists and Communists garnered support for their extreme political positions led many observers to view audiences as crowds or mobs. More specifically, they were seen as

> undifferentiated aggregates with no strong sense of shared communal interests, not as individuals acting and deciding for the common good. From this perspective, a member of the masses is not responsible for his or her actions, is easy to incite to action, feels enormous pressure to conform to the behavior of the crowd and, therefore, is easy to manipulate. (326)

This perception caused alarm over the potentially damaging influence of propaganda and led to the creation of the Institute for Propaganda Analysis (IPA) in 1937.

In its analysis of propaganda, the IPA identified seven common devices. Each of these appeals to human emotions such as fear, hatred, pride, selfishness, and love. These are the tools of propagandists. Let us consider how each of these propaganda devices works.

Name calling is a technique that encourages audiences to make judgments about others without considering the evidence. Name calling appeals to emotions such as hate and fear. The names that propagandists attach to the enemy are called "devil terms." They have included *fascist, dictator, Red, muckraker, alien, outside agitator,* and *Constitution wrecker.*

Glittering generalities refers to the propagandist's use of "virtue words" to identify his own cause. These terms appeal to emotions such as love, generosity, and brotherhood. The propagandist uses words that imply ideals such as "truth, freedom, honor, liberty, social justice, public service, the right to work, loyalty, progress, democracy, the American way, Constitution defender" (Jackall 1995, 219).

Transfer is a device used by propagandists to link something we respect and revere to a program or cause that they want us to accept. Consider the following example:

Cartoons such as Uncle Sam represent a consensus of public opinion. Those symbols stir emotions. At their very sight, with the speed of light, is aroused the whole complex of feelings we have with respect to church or nation. A cartoonist, by having Uncle Sam disapprove a budget for unemployment relief, would have us feel that the whole United States disapproves relief costs. By drawing an Uncle Sam who approves the same budget, the cartoonist would have us feel that the American people approve it. (Jackall 1995, 220)

Testimonials are personal stories designed to persuade us to support a certain position. The testimonial strategy was particularly successful for President Ronald Reagan, who included anecdotes from average Americans in his speeches to promote his policies (Williams and Cooper 2002).

Plain folks is a device that emphasizes the similarity between a persuader and her audience. Politicians rely on this strategy during election years to woo voters. They will appear in expensive suits to speak before Wall Street bankers, but they are likely to take off their jackets and roll up their sleeves to speak to an audience of factory workers. Williams and Cooper (2002) provide an excellent real-life example of plain folks: "During the months of troop buildup before the Persian Gulf War, Saddam Hussein frequently appeared on Iraqi television moving among his troops, enduring their conditions, wearing similar clothes and eating their food with them" (332).

Card-stacking refers to the practice of offering evidence that "stacks the deck" in favor of the propagandist's position. According to the IPA:

He uses under-emphasis and over-emphasis to dodge issues and evade facts. He resorts to lies, censorship, and distortion. He omits facts. He offers false testimony. He creates a smoke-screen of clamor by raising a new issue when he wants an embarrassing matter forgotten. He draws a red herring across the trail to confuse and divert those in quest of facts he does not want revealed. He makes the unreal appear real and the real appear unreal. He lets half-truth masquerade as truth. . . . By means of this device propagandists would convince us that a ruthless war of aggression is a crusade for righteousness. (Jackall 1995, 221)

The *band wagon* encourages people to follow the crowd. The propagandist encourages us to support a position or engage in a certain behavior because "everybody's doing it." He appeals to our identity as a member of a particular group—race, religion, gender, occupation, and so on. He then attempts to capture the prejudices, fears, and biases common to the group to get people to jump on the band wagon. Americans who wrap yellow ribbons around their trees to symbolize support for returning soldiers are demonstrating the concept of the band wagon.

EARLY THEORIES OF COLLECTIVE BEHAVIOR

The earliest theory of collective behavior is identified with the work of Gustave Le Bon (1895/1960)—and rightfully so. But Charles Mackay had already identified and described historical examples of collective behavior almost fifty years earlier in his *Extraordinary Popular Delusions and the Madness of Crowds*, which was published in 1841. Referring to them as "moral epidemics," he claimed that they showed how "easily the masses have been led astray." In the preface, Mackay wrote:

We see one nation suddenly seized, from its highest to its lowest members, with a fierce desire of military glory; another as suddenly becoming crazed upon a religious scruple; and neither of them recovering its senses until it has shed rivers of blood and sowed a harvest of groans and tears, to be reaped by its posterity. At an early age in the annals of Europe its population lost their wits about the sepulcher of Jesus, and crowded in frenzied multitudes to the Holy Land; another age went mad for fear of the devil, and offered up hundreds of thousands of victims to the delusion of witchcraft. At another time,

Tying yellow ribbons around trees, posts, and fences illustrates a propaganda strategy called the band wagon.

the many became crazed on the subject of the philosopher's stone and committed follies till then unheard of in the pursuit.

Mackay's purpose in writing the book was not to explain the madness of crowds; it was simply to trace the history of these "delusions." He did, however, make this observation: "Men, it has been well said, think in herds; it will be seen that they go mad in herds, while they only recover their senses slowly, and one by one."

Contagion Theory

Credit for the first scientific explanation of the "madness" of crowds does go to Le Bon, who outlined his theory of collective psychology in 1895 in *La Psychologie des Foules* (The Psychology of Crowds). Recognizing how crowds transform individuals, he proposed the idea of a collective mind:

> Whoever be the individuals that compose it, however like or unlike be their mode of life, their occupations, their character, or their intelligence, the fact that they have been transformed into a crowd puts them in possession of a sort of collective mind

which makes them feel, think, and act in a manner quite different from that in which each individual of them would feel think and act were he in a state of isolation. (1895/1960, 27)

Le Bon's exposure to the unruly behavior of crowds during the turbulent second half of the nineteenth century clearly contributed to his thinking about collective behavior. He had personally witnessed violent strikes and out-of-control crowds between 1869 and 1871 (McPhail 1991). These upsetting experiences left him with a fear of crowds. And they motivated him to develop scientific principles of crowd behavior that could be used to control crowds.

According to Le Bon, the transformation that affected individuals in a crowd developed under particular conditions. One of those conditions was the loss of personal responsibility that resulted from the anonymity of a crowd. Combined with a feeling of invincibility that comes from the crowd, individuals lose their "conscious personality." Arguing that this then led to the formation of a "collective mind," Le Bon claimed that this organized crowd "forms a single being, and is subjected to the *law of the mental unity of crowds*" (McPhail 1991, 4). Without fully explaining this law, he implied that it caused individuals to be suggestible in a manner similar to that experienced by people who were hypnotized. And he proposed that crowds follow the suggestions of a leader just like individuals who act according to the suggestions of a hypnotist.

Le Bon called the state created by the combination of these conditions *contagion*, and he considered it a form of collective hypnosis. Describing it, he wrote:

> We see, then, that the disappearance of the conscious personality, the predominance of the unconscious personality, the turning by means of suggestion and contagion of feelings and ideas in an identical direction, the tendency to immediately transform the suggested ideas into acts; these, we see, are the principal characteristics of the individual forming part of a crowd. He is no longer himself but has become an automaton who has ceased to be guided by his will. (1895/1960, 32)

Le Bon's **contagion theory** on the psychology of crowds was widely accepted in Europe and in the United States. And he is still viewed as the primary contributor to theories of crowd behavior (McPhail 1991). Building on his ideas, Robert Park and Ernest Burgess, two American sociologists, coined the term collective behavior in 1921 when they recognized it as an important field of study. Among the most significant additions they made in explaining collective behavior were the concepts of social unrest and the mechanism of "circular reaction" (McPhail 1991). Using these concepts to explain collective behavior, they wrote:

> The most elementary form of collective behavior seems to be what is ordinarily referred to as "social unrest," . . . [which] is transmitted from one individual to another . . . so that the manifestations of discontent in A communicated to B, and from B reflected back to A, produce the circular reaction. (Park and Burgess 1921, 382)

Herbert Blumer (1939/1969) wove these basic ideas together in his model of the *acting crowd*, which remains popular today and can be found in military and police manuals on crowd control (McPhail 1991). Blumer's model has five steps (see Figure 14.1):

1. Exciting event
2. Milling
3. A common object of attention
4. Common impulses
5. Collective behavior

According to Blumer, people who are experiencing social unrest feel uneasy about the future. They are searching for something but do not have a clear idea of what that is. In this state, they are vulnerable to rumors, are highly suggestible, and may act erratically. If an exciting event occurs when people are feeling this way, the situation is ripe for collective behavior. Individuals who become preoccupied with the exciting event yield control of their personal behavior to the event and contribute to the formation of an acting crowd. At this point, milling occurs. People stand or walk around, talking about the exciting event. Milling is a form of circular reaction. As people talk about the exciting event, they respond to and reinforce one another's behavior. Eventually this leads to collective excitement, a more intense form of milling. In the fourth step, people focus on one feature of the exciting event. Under the influence of social contagion, they are now ready to act. Collective behavior is the final step in Blumer's model.

As his description of collective behavior shows, Blumer agreed with Le Bon that individuals are transformed by the crowd (McPhail 1991). In some cases, acting crowds participate in admirable causes. But acting crowds also participate in aggressive and violent forms of collective behavior such as lynchings, protests, and riots.

Convergence Theory

Convergence theory offers another explanation for collective behavior. According to this perspective, people are drawn to crowds because they

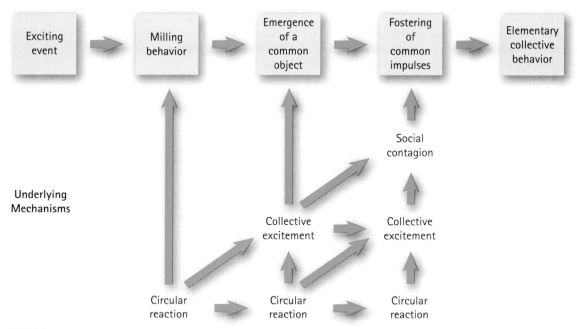

FIGURE 14.1

Herbert Blumer's Model of Social Unrest

Source: McPhail 1991, 11.

share similar attitudes, feelings, and predispositions to act in certain ways. A collective mind does not emerge as a result of contagion. Individuals share common attitudes and beliefs before they even come together. A demonstration in Chicago in 1968 called the Days of Rage provides a good example. Gary Marx and Douglas McAdam (1994) described it this way:

> This was a nationally publicized protest against the Vietnam War and domestic problems called to coincide with the Democratic National Convention. It was sponsored by Students for a Democratic Society. The demonstration was advertised as likely to be confrontational and violent. Persons wanting to nonviolently demonstrate were more likely to stay away than were persons seeking violent confrontation. Not surprisingly, there was considerable violence on the part of both protestors and police—people came to Chicago expecting a confrontation. (43)

Emergent Norm Theory

The idea that the madding crowd transforms individuals and produces a collective mind was challenged by twentieth-century social psychologists who argued that the social interaction of individuals in a crowd shaped the development of emergent norms (McPhail 1991). Muzafer Sherif, whose autokinetic experiments showed how norms develop in unusual situations (see Chapter 12), exerted a clear influence on Ralph Turner and Lewis Killian, who subsequently developed the **emergent norm theory** of collective behavior. These sociologists rejected the assumption that crowds acted in unanimous agreement. Instead, they argued that individuals in a crowd do not necessarily share the same attitudes or feelings and may have different motives for participating in collective behavior.

One of the first questions that Turner and Killian addressed in their theory was "How do crowds form?" They concluded that people come together in response to an unusual situation or problem. Preexisting social groups assist in the formation of collectivities by initiating communication between people. Rumors, which develop in response to unusual situations, play an important role in the development of collective behavior. Questions about what is happening, uncertainties about reality, and ideas about what should be done are proposed by individuals who are motivated to participate in collective behavior for different reasons (Turner and Killian 1987; McPhail 1991).

Turner and Killian (1987, 31) identified five distinct types of participants in collective behavior based on their motivations:

Ego-involved: Individuals who feel a strong personal involvement or commitment to an extraordinary event

Concerned: Individuals who are responsive to the emergent norms that indicate the necessary and appropriate action but feel less committed than the ego-involved to take immediate action

Insecure: Individuals who gain satisfaction from participating in collective behavior, regardless of the issue, perhaps to gain a sense of power

Curious: Individuals who are initially motivated by curiosity to an exciting event

Exploiters: Individuals who have no interest in the issue but take advantage of the opportunity to gain something from the event—looters in riots and instigators of racial tensions, for example

A second question that Turner and Killian addressed was "What do participants do in a crowd?" In answering this question, they first considered the traits common to all crowds: uncertainty, permissiveness, lack of social constraints, urgency, heightened suggestibility, and common mood (see Figure 14.2). Building on the conclusions that Sherif drew from his experiments with the autokinetic effect, they then argued that people turn to

one another for ideas about how to respond to an unusual situation. Figure 14.2 shows the interaction of various components of their model. Uncertainty and urgency influence the milling process as participants seek to find out what is happening, what should be done, and who should act first. The diverse motives of individual participants interact through the keynoting process, which influences an emergent norm and the definition of the situation. The interaction among all of these relationships leads to collective behavior.

SOCIAL MOVEMENTS

Although the Civil War and the end of slavery in the United States offered hope for justice and equal treatment for all Americans, debates over segregation and discrimination raged on for more than one hundred years. In 1896 the U.S. Supreme Court gave its approval to segregation when it upheld the "separate but equal" doctrine in *Plessy v. Ferguson.* In 1905, W. E. B. Du Bois along with other members of the Niagara Movement demanded that discriminatory laws based on race be abolished. And in 1941 a labor leader by the name of A. Philip Randolph threatened to organize a massive march on Washington if President Roosevelt did not ban job discrimination in the government and war industries.

Up until World War II, the dominant response of minorities to injustice was one of adaptation (Farley 2000). In the 1940s and the 1950s, legal efforts to bring about change resulted in some remarkable victories, including the 1954 Brown decision, which overturned the "separate but equal" principle. A year later, the action of one black woman in Montgomery, Alabama, marked the transition from adaptive responses to active protests. Rosa Parks was arrested for violating the city's segregation ordinance for refusing to give up her seat on a bus to a white man. This event led to successful desegregation of the city's bus system. Dr. Martin Luther King, Jr., who took a primary role in this campaign, became the leader of the nonviolent phase of the civil rights movement.

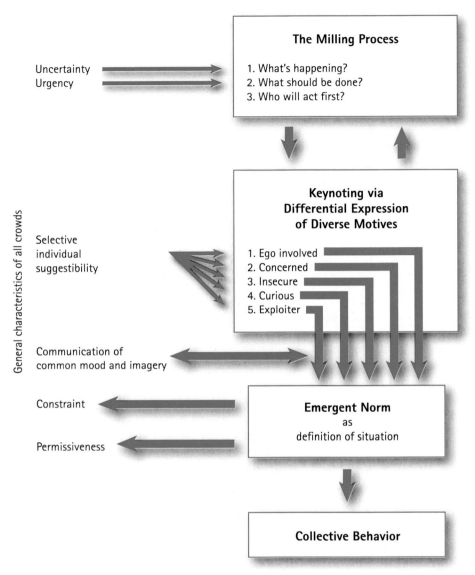

FIGURE 14.2

The Emergent Norm Model

Source: McPhail 1991, 79; based on Turner and Killian 1987.

After King's assassination in 1968, the civil rights movement moved into a second phase that led to a wave of violent rebellions across the United States (Farley 2000). The leaders of this phase included angry young men who encouraged violence to achieve the goals of the civil rights movement. Expressions like "black power" and "black consciousness" reflected the militant nature of this phase.

The civil rights movement did not end prejudice or discrimination, but it did result in gains for

The U.S. civil rights movement brought social change that was long overdue. But it was a difficult struggle. Determined activists often met resistance from law enforcement, who used fire hoses to control crowds of protesters.

minorities in education and employment. And laws enacted since the 1960s have increased the political participation of minorities and the number of elected positions won by them.

A chronology of the civil rights movement in the United States shows the kind of determination it takes to bring about social change (see Table 14.2). It also provides a blueprint for the kind of organized activities that contribute to a successful **social movement**. This fight for justice involved many kinds of collective behavior, including protests, marches, and sit-ins. It also required the cooperative efforts of leaders and followers.

In the United States, important social movements have included efforts to abolish slavery, ban alcohol, protest war, and promote feminism, environmentalism, and civil rights (Oberschall 1993; Vago 1999). The American Revolution itself was a social movement. U.S. history is full of examples. But the 1960s is recognized as a unique period in U.S. history, a time when social movements flourished. What is a social movement? And what makes it a unique form of collective behavior?

Herbert Blumer (1951b; 199) defined social movements as "collective enterprises to establish a new order of life." Turner and Killian (1987) saw them as organized and sustained attempts by ordinary people to either bring about or stop social change (see also Goodwin and Jasper 2003). A number of other features distinguish modern conceptualizations of social movements (Wilson 1973; Zurcher and Snow 1981; Turner and Killian 1987; Benford 1992; Snow and Oliver 1995). They tend to last longer than other forms of collective behavior, involve a greater degree of organization and structured leadership, and actively mobilize resources that are needed to achieve change-oriented goals. Finally, since most social movements are dedicated to bringing about justice, their actions have political ramifications.

In pursuit of their goals, social movements may involve all kinds of collective behavior, including protests, strikes, riots, crowds, rumors, and propaganda. In some cases, they also involve fads and fashions. Consider the music, fashions, hairstyles, and language of the 1960s, all reflective of

TABLE 14.2	A CHRONOLOGY OF THE U.S. CIVIL RIGHTS MOVEMENT

1896: Supreme Court upholds "separate but equal" doctrine in *Plessy* v. *Ferguson*

1905: W. E. B. Du Bois and others form the Niagara Movement, demanding abolition of racially discriminatory laws

1909: The National Association for the Advancement of Colored People (NAACP) is formed

1941: Labor Leader A. Philip Randolph threatens massive march on Washington; President Roosevelt orders the end of racial discrimination in war industries and government

1948: President Truman ends segregation in the armed forces

1954: Supreme Court, in *Brown* v. *Board of Education of Topeka,* rules that segregated public schools are unconstitutional

1955: Emmett Till is lynched in Mississippi; Rosa Parks is arrested for violating the bus segregation ordinance in Montgomery, Alabama; the Montgomery bus boycott begins

1956: Supreme Court rules that segregation on public buses is unconstitutional

1957: Southern Christian Leadership Conference (SCLC) is formed with Martin Luther King Jr. as president; President Eisenhower sends paratroopers to Little Rock, Arkansas, to enforce school integration

1960: Sit-ins at segregated lunch counters begin in Greensboro, North Carolina, Nashville, Tennessee, and elsewhere; student activists form the Student Nonviolent Coordinating Committee (SNCC, pronounced "snick")

1961: "Freedom Riders" expose illegal segregation in bus terminals

1963: Major demonstrations are begun by the SCLC in Birmingham, Alabama, to protest segregation; Medgar Evers, head of the Mississippi NAACP, is assassinated; the March on Washington attracts hundreds of thousands of demonstrators to Washington, DC; four black girls are killed by a bomb at Birmingham's Sixteenth Street Baptist Church

1964: Hundreds of white college students participate in Freedom Summer, a Mississippi voter registration project; three civil rights workers are murdered near Philadelphia, Mississippi; the Civil Rights Act of 1964, banning discrimination in voting and pubic accommodations, is passed; the Mississippi Freedom Democratic Party challenges the state's all-white delegation to the Democratic National Convention in Atlantic City, NJ; Martin Luther King Jr. receives the Nobel Peace Prize

1965: Malcolm X is assassinated in New York City; police brutally attack a planned march in Selma, Alabama; a massive march takes place from Selma to Montgomery after a U.S. District Court rules that protestors have the right to march; President Johnson signs the Voting Rights Bill into law; riot in the Watts section of Los Angeles is the largest race riot in U.S. history up to that time

1966: SNCC leader Stokely Carmichael popularizes the slogan "Black Power"; the Black Panther Party is formed in Oakland, CA; riots occur in major cities continuing through 1967; SNCC votes to exclude white members

1968: Martin Luther King Jr. is assassinated in Memphis; riots occur in more than 100 cities; Richard Nixon is elected president

Source: Blumberg 2003, 16.

the so-called youth movement. Fads and fashions can serve as symbols of a social movement, giving it a unique identity that bolsters the solidarity of its followers (Goodwin and Jasper 2003).

Social movements are often considered a relatively modern form of collective behavior. But Turner and Killian (1987) suggest a relatively long

history, citing the Crusades (1096–1270) as an early example. In fact, history shows us many instances of human beings joining together to protest injustices or to bring about some kind of social change. To emphasize the similarities between social movements, Turner and Killian compare the Crusades to the civil rights movement in the United States (see Box 14.5). But they also recognize significant differences. Others have recognized the similarities and differences in social movements by classifying them on the basis of salient characteristics (Blumer 1939/1969; Aberle 1966; Cameron 1966).

David Aberle (1966) classified social movements along two dimensions: the *locus* of the desired change—individuals or some supra-individual system—and the *amount* of change sought. According to Aberle, a supra-individual system could be "the economic order, the technological order, the political order, the law, a total society or culture, the world, or indeed the cosmos" (316). And the amount of change could be partial or total. These two dimensions produce four types of social movements: transformative movements, reformative social movements, redemptive movements, and alternative movements (see Figure 14.3).

Transformative social movements represent the most dramatic form of social change possible. They target everyone in society (supra-individual) and seek total change. Revolutions that fit into this category include those that have taken place in the United States, France, Russia, China, and Cuba. The Nazi movement in the 1930s fits into this category. And so do millenarian movements. **Reformative social movements** seek partial change in supra-individual systems. Examples include the women's suffrage, child labor law, and environmental movements. **Redemptive social movements** target individuals for total change.

BOX 14.5   THE CRUSADES AND THE CIVIL RIGHTS MOVEMENT

In the year 1096, in the square before the cathedral at Clermont, Pope Urban II issued his call for a crusade to free the Christian Holy Land from domination by the Muslims. Within a short time, all of Europe was in a state of unprecedented excitement and feverish activity.

The Crusades

For several months after the Council of Clermont, France and Germany presented a singular spectacle. The pious, the fanatic, the needy, the dissolute, the young and the old, even women and children, and the halt and lame, enrolled themselves by hundreds. In every village the clergy were busied in keeping up the excitement, promising eternal rewards to those who assumed the red cross, and fulminating the most awful denunciations against all the worldly-minded who refused or even hesitated. . . . All those who had property of any description rushed to the mart to change it into hard cash. Lands and houses could be had for a quarter of their value, while arms and accoutrements of war rose in the same proportion. . . . During the spring and summer of this year (1096) the roads teemed with crusaders, all hastening to the towns and villages appointed as the rendezvous of the district. Some were on horseback, some in carts, and some came down the rivers in boats and rafts, bringing their wives and children, all eager to go to Jerusalem. Very few knew where Jerusalem was. Some thought it fifty miles away, and others imagined that it was but a month's journey; while at sight of every town or castle the children exclaimed, "Is that Jerusalem? Is that the city?" (Turner and Killian 1987, 1–2)

Nearly a thousand years later, in the United States, hundreds of "crusaders" converged at the call of a modern spiritual leader, Martin Luther King Jr., to march the 50 miles from Selma to Montgomery, Alabama.

The Selma March

In a growing stream, the marchers assembled in Selma. The men, women, and children who followed King into the streets and into jail all through the campaign were ready to walk again. And outsiders flocked to his call; clerics and nuns, pert coeds and hot-eyed student rebels; VIPs like the U.N.'s Ralph Bunche and anonymous farmhands from the southwest Alabama cattle, corn and cotton country. A blind man came from Atlanta, a one-legged man from Saginaw, Michigan. An Episcopal minister from Minneapolis got plane fare from a parishioner and took the gift to be a sign from God that he should make the pilgrimage. And a little Selma Negro girl tagged along "for freedom and justice and so the troopers can't hit us no more." (Turner and Killian 1987, 2)

Source: Turner, Ralph H., Killian, Lewis M., *Collective Behavior*, 3rd Edition. ©1987. Reprinted by permission of Pearson Education, Inc., Upper Saddle River, NJ.

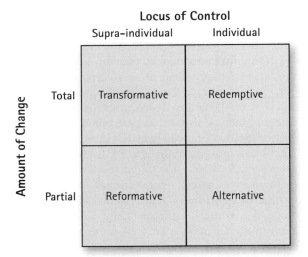

Locus of Control

FIGURE 14.3

Aberle's Typology of Social Movements

Source: Aberle 1966, 316.

Fundamentalist Christian groups that seek to convert new members through the experience of being "born again" fit this type. And **alternative social movements** seek partial change in the behavior of individuals. Early-twentieth-century temperance movements, which attempted to solve problems of alcohol abuse, are of this type.

Although some social movements fit neatly into one of these four classes, others are not pure types and may show characteristics of the others (Aberle 1966). In addition, the classification of a social movement can change over time. For example, if an alternative movement fails to change the behavior of individuals, it might attempt to change the laws. In that case, it would be reclassified as a reformative movement. According to Aberle, social movements commonly shift from one type to another. And some successful social movements even become part of the mainstream.

SOCIAL MOVEMENT THEORIES

Social movement theories grapple with challenging questions (Goodwin and Jasper 2003). What

prompts social movements? Why do they arise at a particular place and time? Who joins a social movement? Who remains committed and who quits? How are social movements organized? And what determines their success or failure? Let us take a look at the theories that have attempted to answer these questions.

Mass Society Theory

According to William Kornhauser's (1959) **mass society theory**, social movements occur in mass societies—industrial societies that involve bureaucratic organizational structures that create an impersonal society. Such societies lack social groups that provide people with a sense of belonging to the community, leaving individuals feeling "alienated, anxious, and marginal." Social movements provide individuals with "substitute communities" that provide them with a sense of belonging (Marx and McAdam 1994, 80). In fact, people who feel a strong need to belong may seek out a social movement for the opportunity it provides for affiliation (Kornhauser 1959).

Relative Deprivation Theory

Another explanation of social movements suggests that frustration plays a role in this specific form of collective behavior (Gurney and Tierney 1982; Marx and McAdam 1994). Rooted in Dollard's frustration-aggression theory (see Chapter 10), **relative deprivation theory** proposes that perceptions of relative deprivation contribute to frustration, which is released through participation in a social movement. Consider what happens. People experience disappointment and frustration when their expectations for a better life are not met. They see a gap between what they think they deserve and what they actually have, a condition of relative deprivation (Gurr 1970). People may believe that they deserve a better income, more political freedom, more respect, or a sense of belonging. When they feel deprived, especially compared to other people, this produces "an underlying state of . . . psychological tension that is relieved by [social movement] participation (Gurney and Tierney 1982, 36).

Alexis de Tocqueville (1856/1955) aptly described how relative deprivation could contribute to social movements in his explanation of the French Revolution. As he pointed out, German peasants endured worse conditions than French peasants did. Why, then, did they not revolt like the French? According to Tocqueville, because they did not experience relative deprivation (see Box 10.2). Unlike the French, they had not witnessed any improvements. Having no basis of comparison for the feudal system that they had always known, they did not experience relative deprivation.

Relative deprivation takes a variety of forms. Tocqueville described a condition known as *rising expectations*. Social psychologists argue that this kind of relative deprivation explains the rise of the civil rights movement in the United States. They point out that the strong postwar economy and early civil rights victories—such as the outlawing of school segregation—caused black Americans to expect conditions in their lives to improve significantly.

And President Johnson's War on Poverty offered hope to the destitute. But these expectations turned to disappointment when white Americans resisted the court's desegregation ruling and when the nation's attention turned to the Vietnam War. The riots that erupted in cities across the United States from 1964 to 1968 have been attributed to black Americans' feelings of relative deprivation (Sears and McConahay 1973). The perception that other groups were making faster gains than they were created hostility and conflict.

James C. Davies (1962) envisioned this particular pattern of rising expectations, gains, and then setbacks as a graph on which the pattern resembles an inverted J (see Figure 14.4). The gains that are made in the beginning contribute to and parallel rising expectations. However, as people's expectations continue to rise, the actual conditions begin to deteriorate. In some cases, authorities may reverse the direction of the gains, taking back freedoms or rights. J-curve relative deprivation can explain a number of social movements, including the revolutions in France, Russia, and Iran. As Davies

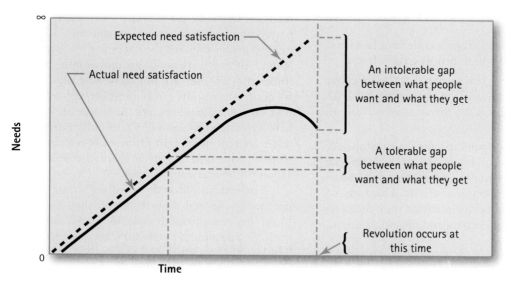

FIGURE 14.4

Davies's J Curve of Relative Deprivation

Source: Davies 1962, 6.

points out, the actual conditions are less important than the perceptions of the people who feel deprived.

The Value-Added Perspective

Adopting what he called the **value-added perspective**, Neil Smelser (1962) proposed that six conditions exist when collective behavior occurs: structural conduciveness, structural strain, a generalized belief, a precipitating factor, the mobilization of individuals for action, and social control. These six conditions can exist at any time, but collective behavior is likely to happen when they occur in precisely that order.

1. *Structural conduciveness* refers to a state of readiness. The social structure of society must be organized to allow or facilitate collective behavior.

2. *Structural strain* occurs when perceptions of relative deprivation develop and when people recognize that problems exist.

3. A *generalized belief* develops when people recognize what the problems are and develop solutions for them.

4. *Precipitating factors* trigger collective behavior. Dramatic events often produce this effect.

5. *Mobilization for action* means that the first four conditions necessary for collective behavior have been met and the group is now ready to act.

6. *Social control* operates to contain or stop collective behavior. The police or military can attempt to control crowd behavior or to completely crush a social movement. The authorities may seek to control a riot, but their actions can also exacerbate and prolong it.

Smelser's value-added perspective provides a way of recognizing the conditions that are likely to lead to collective behavior. In contrast to earlier theories, which focused on the irrational impulses of crowds, it identifies and explains the social factors that contribute to collective behavior.

Resource Mobilization Theory

Early theories of social movements focused on shared grievances and generalized beliefs as the most important factors in explaining the emergence of a social movement (McCarthy and Zald 1973, 1977). Critics of these theories recognize that grievances play a part in social movements, and they are willing to grant that discontent in any society can garner enough support for collective action (Marx and McAdam 1994; McCarthy and Zald 1973, 1977). But they point out that strain or discontent alone does not explain the emergence of social movements. Indeed, social movements develop at certain times in specific locations. What determines the timing and place? McCarthy and Zald (1973, 1977) argue that it ultimately depends on the political and economic resources that are available to the movement. These resources include money, leadership, supporters, media access, office space, and equipment.

McCarthy and Zald (1973, 1977) identify three key differences between traditional theories and **resource mobilization theory**. The first difference involves the support base of a social movement. Traditional theories claim that an aggrieved population supports a social movement. This aggrieved group supplies the necessary resources and labor. Although outside groups might provide some support, they are not viewed as key players. In contrast, resource mobilization theory holds that social movements are not necessarily propelled by the grievances of a particular group. And other sources of support come from *conscience constituents* who may not even share the underlying values of the social movement.

The second difference involves strategies and tactics. Traditional theories argue that leaders of social movements attempt to exert influence through bargaining, persuasion, and even violence. The specific strategies and tactics they choose depend on past experiences with officials, ideology, and the effectiveness of past efforts. Resource mobilization theory also accepts the importance of strategies and tactics in interacting with authorities. But it also recognizes specific strategic tasks, including "mobilizing supporters," "neutralizing and/or transforming mass and elite publics into sympathizers," and "achieving change in targets" (McCarthy and Zald 2003, 172). Decisions regarding tactics are influenced by considerations about the kinds of conflicts they may create.

The third difference between traditional theories and resource mobilization theory involves their perspectives on the role played by the larger society. Whereas traditional theories consider the hostility or tolerance of society toward social movements, resource mobilization theory focuses on how society provides the infrastructure for social movements.

According to resource mobilization theory, social movements flourish during economically prosperous periods (Marx and McAdam 1994). People are more willing to contribute money to causes when they have the resources to do so. This may even stimulate the formation of formal organizations that are specifically designed to raise money for these causes. A strong economy also encourages collective action because it improves the financial condition of society's disadvantaged. Marx and McAdam claim that this occurs both directly and indirectly—through higher employment rates and well-funded social programs.

The Self-Concept and Social Movements

Robert White (1993, 63) reported the comments that a veteran of the Provisional Irish Republican Army expressed in 1984:

> [The English] ruled Ireland with a mailed fist, literally. A grasp of iron and nobody stepped out of line. And it's only natural that a people are going to breed at some stage someone who says, "I am not going to take that." Now what does that make him? Does that make him a rabble rouser? Does it make him a trouble maker? It ought to. I mean, obviously if he stands up and hits back it makes him a combatant. And it makes him, therefore, eventually a rabble rouser and a murderer and a terrorist. And if that's what a terrorist is, I want to be a terrorist.

Who joins or supports a social movement? Who remains, and who drops out? The answers to these questions have changed over time. Early research on social movements was influenced by scholars' attitudes toward the people who participated in this form of collective behavior. In fact, until the 1960s, social movements frightened the scholars who studied them (Goodwin and Jasper 2003). Goodwin and Jasper captured the feelings and attitudes of scholars who studied social movements:

> They saw them as dangerous mobs who acted irrationally, blindly following demagogues who sprang up in their midst. . . . Most elites, including university professors, had little sympathy for them. Crowds were thought to whip up emotions that made people do things they otherwise would not do, would not want to do, and should not do. They transformed people into unthinking automatons, according to scholars of the time. The last hurrah of this line of thinking was in the 1950s, as scholars analyzed the Nazis in the same way they had crowds: as people who were fooled by their leaders, whom they followed blindly and stupidly. (5)

The civil rights movement in the United States changed these kinds of preconceived notions about social movements. This time, well-educated and privileged people recognized that the demands of this social movement were justified and long overdue (Goodwin and Jasper 2003) (see Box 14.6). Goodwin and Jasper also note that "it was hard to dismiss civil rights demonstrators as misguided, immature, or irrational" (5). This led scholars to take a different approach to the study of social movements.

One of the most recent approaches in social movement theories proposes that these explanations must involve the self-concept (Stryker, Owens, and White 2000). This, however, will be no easy task. Variations in the way that social psychologists conceptualize the self or identity present a huge challenge. Consider the difference between individual identities and collective identities. *Individual identities* define the self as a particular sort of person, and they represent that part of

BOX 14.6	THE CIVIL RIGHTS AND REASONS: KING'S LETTER FROM JAIL

In 1963, Martin Luther King Jr. brought a campaign of nonviolence and passive resistance to Birmingham, Alabama, where racial segregation and discrimination were pervasive. During protest demonstrations, hundreds were arrested. King chose to go to jail rather than to obey a court order to end the demonstrations. While in solitary confinement, he responded to a letter written to him by eight leading clergymen. They had asked him to call off the demonstrations and to rely instead on negotiations and the courts. King spent Easter weekend drafting his response.

Letter from Birmingham City Jail

While confined here in the Birmingham City Jail, I came across your recent statement calling our present activities "unwise and untimely." . . .

I think I should give the reason for my being in Birmingham, since you have been influenced by the argument of "outsiders coming in." . . . I am here, along with several members of my staff, because we were invited here. I am here because I have basic organizational ties here. Beyond this, I am in Birmingham because injustice is here. Just as the 8th century prophets left their little villages and carried their "thus saith the Lord" far beyond the boundaries of their home town, and just as the Apostle Paul left his little village of Tarsus and carried the gospel of Jesus Christ to practically every hamlet and city of the Graeco-Roman world, I too am compelled to carry the gospel of freedom beyond my particular home town. . . . Injustice anywhere is a threat to justice everywhere. . . .

You deplore the demonstrations that are presently taking place in Birmingham. But I am sorry that your statement did not express a similar concern for the conditions that brought the demonstrations into being. I am sure that each of you would want to go beyond the superficial social analyst who looks merely at effects, and does not grapple with underlying causes. I would not hesitate to say that it is unfortunate that so-called

demonstrations are taking place in Birmingham at this time, but I would say in more emphatic terms that it is even more unfortunate that the white power structure of this city left the Negro community with no other alternative.

In any nonviolent campaign there are four basic steps: 1) collection of the facts to determine whether injustices are alive; 2) negotiation; 3) self-purification; and 4) direct action. We have gone through all of these steps in Birmingham. There can be no gainsaying of the fact that racial injustice engulfs this community. Birmingham is probably the most thoroughly segregated city in the United States. Its ugly record of police brutality is known in every section of this country. Its unjust treatment of Negroes in the courts is a notorious reality. There have been more unsolved bombings of Negro homes and churches in Birmingham than any city in this nation. These are the hard, brutal, and unbelievable facts. . . .

We know through painful experience that freedom is never voluntarily given by the oppressor; it must be demanded by the oppressed. Frankly I have never yet engaged in a direct action movement that was "well timed," according to the timetable of those who have not suffered unduly from the disease of segregation. For years now I have heard the word "Wait!" It rings in the ear of every Negro with a piercing familiarity. This "wait" has almost always meant "never." It has been a tranquilizing Thalidomide, relieving the emotional stress for a moment, only to give birth to an ill-formed infant of frustration. We must come to see with the distinguished jurist of yesterday that "justice too long delayed is justice denied." We have waited for more than 340 years for our constitutional and God-given rights. The nations of Asia and Africa are moving with jet-like speed toward the goal of political independence, and we still creep at horse and buggy pace toward the gaining of a cup of coffee at a lunch counter. . . .

Source: King 1963/2000, 569–570.

---

the self-concept alone (Thoits and Virshup 1995). In contrast, *collective identities* involve individuals' identifications with a group or category. Neither can be ignored in a social movement theory.

This conceptual difference illustrates a manageable difficulty. It is minor when you consider

the multitude of ways that social psychologists view the self-concept. A short list of terms used to refer to this concept highlights the magnitude of the problem: *self-concept, identity, personal identity, social identity, self,* and *collective identity.* To this list, we might add a number of related concepts, such as *self-esteem, identity salience, self-efficacy,* and *self-actualization.* Defining these terms would show significant differences in social psychologists' conceptualizations of the self-concept.

Solving these problems will take time. But the IRA warrior's quotation at the start of this section drives home the need for this new approach. Not only do participants consider the injustices that motivate them to join a social movement, but they also consider the question *Who am I?* As this particular example shows, the answers are bound to provide valuable insights.

SUMMARY

1. Collective behavior refers to a wide variety of behaviors, including disaster behavior, panics, fashions, fads, crazes, riots, and public opinion. These different kinds of collective behavior have a number of characteristics in common. The behavior is unexpected and emerges as a response to a common stimulus. It does not conform to social norms but is characterized by modified norms that may conflict with dominant norms. And the behavior can spread quickly.

2. Lynch mobs, rioting crowds, and curious spectators represent the most common form of collective behavior—the crowd, a temporary gathering of people in close proximity who share a common focus of attention and who exert a mutual influence on one another. A crowd is not a social grouping. Herbert Blumer identified four types of crowds: a casual crowd, a conventional crowd, an expressive crowd, and an acting crowd.

3. Communication plays a central role in collective behavior. In some cases, it can create panic or mass hysteria. The mass media play a central role in the transmission of other kinds of information that are also considered collective behavior: rumors, gossip, urban legends, and public opinion.

4. Propaganda refers to intentional attempts to influence mass audiences through techniques that involve spoken, written, or visual representations. The perception that mass audiences were easy to manipulate caused alarm over the potentially damaging influence of propaganda and led to the creation of the Institute for Propaganda Analysis (IPA) in 1937. The IPA identified seven common devices or tools that propagandists use.

5. Charles Mackay compiled the earliest historical descriptions of collective behavior. About fifty years later, Gustave Le Bon offered the first scientific explanation of the "madness of crowds." According to Le Bon, the transformation that affected individuals in a crowd developed under particular conditions. One of those conditions was the loss of personal responsibility that resulted from the anonymity of a crowd.

6. In 1921, Robert Park and Ernest Burgess coined the term *collective behavior.* Herbert Blumer later wove their basic ideas together in his model of the acting crowd. His version of collective behavior remains popular today and is the basis of manuals on crowd control.

7. Convergence theory argues that people are drawn to crowds because they share similar attitudes, feelings, and predispositions to act in certain ways. This theory rejects the idea that a collective mind emerges as a result of contagion.

8. Ralph Turner and Lewis Killian developed the emergent norm theory, which argues that individuals in a crowd do not necessarily share the same attitudes or feelings and have different motives for participating in collective behavior.

9. Blumer defined social movements as "collective enterprises to establish a new order of life." Turner and Killian saw them as organized and sustained attempts by ordinary people to either bring about or stop social change. Social movements involve all kinds of collective behavior, including protests, riots, and propaganda.

10. David Aberle identified four types of social movements: transformative, reformative, redemptive,

and alternative movements. Some movements are of more than one type.

11. According to mass society theory, social movements provide individuals with "substitute communities" that provide them with a sense of belonging. People who feel a strong need to belong may seek out a social movement for the opportunity it provides for affiliation.

12. Relative deprivation theory suggests that frustration plays a role in collective behavior. Perceptions of relative deprivation contribute to frustration, which is released through participation in a social movement.

13. According to the value-added perspective of social movements, six conditions exist when collective behavior occurs: structural conduciveness, structural strain, a generalized belief, precipitating factors, mobilization for action, and social control.

14. According to resource mobilization theory, strain or discontent in society alone does not explain the emergence of social movements. Ultimately, the emergence of a social movement depends on the political and economic resources that are available to the movement.

15. Who joins or supports a social movement? Who remains, and who drops out? The answers to these questions may be found in a new approach to explaining social movements, which emphasizes the importance of the self-concept.

KEY TERMS

Collective behavior   398
Casual crowd   399
Conventional crowd   400
Expressive crowd   400
Acting crowd   400
Panic   400
Fashions   401
Fads   402
Craze   403

Rumor   404
Urban legends   405
Public opinion   405
Public   405
Propaganda   406
Contagion theory   411
Convergence theory   411
Emergent norm theory   412
Social movement   415

Transformative social movement   417
Reformative social movement   417
Redemptive social movement   417
Alternative social movement   418
Mass society theory   418
Relative deprivation theory   418
Value-added perspective   420
Resource mobilization theory   420

CRITICAL REVIEW QUESTIONS

1. Find an editorial cartoon that illustrates propaganda. What particular strategy of propaganda does it illustrate?

2. Use resource mobilization theory to analyze Al Qaeda as a social movement.

3. What characteristics of collective behavior and social movements explain why it is difficult to predict a revolution?

Glossary

Accommodation A cognitive process that involves the modification of an existing schema to process new information.

Acting crowd A crowd that consists of individuals who are organized to achieve a clear goal.

Actor-observer bias The tendency of actors to explain their own actions in terms of situational factors, while observers tend to explain actors' behaviors in terms of stable dispositions.

Adaptational perspective A life course perspective that emphasizes the process of adult socialization.

Additive task A task that makes a group's successful performance dependent on the sum of individual efforts.

Adjustment function The idea that attitudes help people satisfy their needs, reach a goal, or avoid an undesirable outcome.

Adult socialization The process of learning and adapting to adult roles.

Affective component The component of an attitude that refers to a person's emotions or feelings toward a particular attitude object.

Agape An altruistic love style that is selfless and giving.

Age norms Social norms or expectations that define what individuals should do at certain ages.

Agents of socialization People, groups, and institutions that influence the growth and development of new members of society.

Age statuses Positions in society that are defined by one's age.

Aggression Any kind of behavior that seeks to injure another person either physically or psychologically.

Alternative social movement A social movement that seeks partial change in the behavior of individuals.

Altruism An unselfish regard for the welfare of others with no expectation of benefiting in any way.

Anonymity Result of steps taken to protect the identity of subjects who participate in a study.

Anxious/ambivalent attachment The kind of attachment seen in children who show great distress when they are separated from a caregiver and then anger upon that person's return.

Assimilation A cognitive process that involves the use of an existing schema to classify new information.

Attachment theory A theory that the ability to develop healthy adult relationships is affected by the kind of attachment that develops between a child and a caregiver during infancy.

Attitude A tendency to evaluate a person, object, or idea with some degree of approval or disapproval.

Attribution The process by which we come to understand who other people are, based on their behavior.

Authoritarian personality A set of personality traits that is linked to bias against members of out-groups.

Avoidant attachment The kind of attachment seen in children who appear indifferent to or detached from their caregivers.

Balance theory A theory that explains interpersonal relationships in terms of the positive or negative relationships (consistency) among attitudes and people.

Behavioral component The component of an attitude that refers to a person's actions with respect to an attitude object.

Behavioral intentions Intentions to act in a certain way that are influenced by an individual's attitude toward a behavior and by his perception of what others think he ought to do.

Behaviorism A theoretical perspective that emphasizes the idea that explanations of human development should be based not on unconscious motives or cognitive processes but rather on observations of overt behavior.

Belief in a just world The belief that people deserve what they get in life, good or bad.

Brainstorming technique A problem-solving strategy that encourages group members to contribute ideas spontaneously.

Bystander effect The observation that as the number of bystanders increases, our own sense of personal responsibility decreases.

Casual crowd A crowd that consists of individuals who are aware of others but interact with them only briefly and with little emotional involvement.

Category-based expectations Expectations about individuals' behaviors based on the categories to which they are assigned.

Catharsis The idea that alleviating bottled-up emotions can reduce the likelihood of committing future acts of aggression.

Classical conditioning A learning process that involves the pairing of a neutral stimulus with a stimulus that naturally elicits a response so that the neutral stimulus eventually elicits that response.

Cognition Knowledge, opinions, or beliefs.

Cognitive component The component of an attitude that refers to the thoughts that people have about an attitude object.

Cognitive consistency The idea that people prefer agreement in their attitudes.

Cognitive dissonance A state of psychological discomfort that occurs when people recognize that their cognitions are inconsistent.

Cognitive neoassociation model A theory that when people feel bad, they tend to be angry and aggressive.

Cohort All people who are born in a particular period of time, move through the life course together, and experience historical events at about the same age.

Collective behavior Unexpected behavior that emerges as a response to a common stimulus and may involve modified norms that conflict with dominant norms.

Commitment A component of love that involves the short-term decision to love someone and the long-term commitment to maintain that love.

Common Rule Ethical guidelines for conducting scientific research that are designed to protect human subjects from harm.

Companionate marriage Marriage based on the values of friendship and equality.

Comparison level The outcome that a person believes he or she deserves from a particular relationship.

Comparison level for alternatives A comparison of the outcome that an individual might derive from another relationship to the outcome from a current relationship.

Compliance A behavioral response to social influence that reflects an outward yielding to group pressure without producing changes in a person's privately accepted beliefs or attitudes.

Concepts General ideas that capture the similarities among specific things or processes.

Concordance The degree of similarity between different types of twins.

Confidentiality A guarantee to subjects who participate in a study that any information they provide will be kept private.

Conflict-habituated marriage Marriage characterized by tension and conflict largely kept under control.

Conformity A behavioral response to social influence that leads a person to yield to group pressure.

Conjunctive task A task that makes a group's successful performance dependent on the weakest member of the team.

Conscious The part of the mind that is experienced as immediate awareness.

Consensus The extent to which most people respond to a particular entity.

Conservation The idea that the amount of a substance stays the same even though its appearance may change.

Consistency The extent to which an individual responds to a particular entity in the same way over time and on different occasions.

Contact theory The theory that contact between members of different groups can reduce prejudice when they have equal status, intimate contact, institutional support, and cooperative interdependence.

Contagion theory An explanation of behavior that proposes that people gathered in a crowd lose a sense of individuality and are susceptible to contagious feelings and ideas.

Contingency theory of leadership The belief that personal style and the particular situation determines a leader's effectiveness.

Control group The group in an experiment that is not exposed to the independent variable and is then compared to the experimental group.

Conventional crowd A crowd that consists of individuals who recognize a set of conventional norms and interact in a fairly structured situation.

Convergence theory A theory of collective behavior that proposes that people are drawn to crowds because they share similar attitudes, feelings, and predispositions to act in certain ways.

Correspondent inferences The use of different kinds of information to draw conclusions about the specific traits or dispositions of an actor.

Craze An extreme version of a fad.

Cultural routines Taken-for-granted patterns of behavior that provide children with a sense of belonging.

Debriefing Fully informing subjects about the real purpose of a research study after they have participated.

Defensive attributional bias A distorted explanation for the cause of something that allows individuals to feel that they can control what happens to them.

Definition of a situation A perception of the way things are based on socially constructed meanings.

Dehumanization The process of portraying an enemy as subhuman and lacking individuality.

Dependent variable The variable that a researcher measures in an experiment to determine whether it was influenced by the introduction of the independent variable.

Descriptive self-disclosure A form of self-disclosure in which people talk about the facts of their lives.

Developmental perspective A life course perspective that focuses on how individuals grow over a period of time.

Devitalized marriage Marriage that is initially intimate and loving but deteriorates over time, causing resentment and disillusionment.

Diffusion of responsibility The tendency for bystanders to feel less personal responsibility for helping when other bystanders are present.

Discounting principle The idea that the cause of an effect is discounted if other plausible causes could have exerted an influence.

Discrimination A learning process that leads people to distinguish various stimuli.

Disjunctive task A task that makes a group's successful performance dependent on the strongest member of the team.

Displacement The tendency for people to direct their aggression toward a safe target rather than the real source of their frustration.

Dispositional identities Characteristics and behavioral tendencies that constitute an individual's identity.

Distinctiveness The extent to which an individual's reaction to a particular entity sets it apart from his or her reactions to other entities.

Distraction-conflict theory The theory that an audience produces arousal in someone who is performing a task because it divides his or her attention between the audience and the task.

Distributive justice The idea that the rewards and costs of each person in a relationship will be proportional.

Door-in-the-face technique A compliance strategy that operates on the idea that people are more likely to agree to a small request after they have refused a large request.

Dramaturgical school of thought A theoretical perspective that views people as actors whose everyday lives involve specific roles that are intricately bound to the roles of others.

Dyad A group consisting of two people.

Ego The conscious, rational part of the personality that emerges when a child discovers that the id cannot always be satisfied immediately.

Ego-defensive function The idea that attitudes can protect a person's ego or self-image.

Egoism The idea that self-interest motivates all human behavior.

Electra complex Freud's term for the female version of the Oedipus complex.

Emergent norm theory A theory that individuals who participate in collective behavior are influenced by a norm that arises out of an unusual situation.

Empathy An emotional response that is oriented toward another person and involves concern for that person's welfare.

Equilibration A fluctuation between assimilation and accommodation that occurs when disequilibrium is caused by rapid cognitive change.

Equilibrium A comfortable or steady state that results from the balancing of the processes of assimilation and accommodation.

Equity theory A theoretical perspective that argues that a relationship is felt to be fair when one person's outcomes and contributions equal the other person's outcomes and contributions.

Eros   A love style that is passionate, involving powerful physical attraction.

Ethnographies   Detailed descriptions of the events and statements made by people observed in field research.

Evaluation apprehension   The effect of arousal caused by people's awareness that others are judging them.

Evaluative self-disclosure   A form of self-disclosure in which people talk about their feelings or personal opinions.

Excitation transfer theory   A theory that physiological arousal at one point in time can influence an aggressive response later.

Exosystem   An interrelationship between two or more settings that affect individuals who are not active participants in those settings.

Expectation states theory   A theory that members of a group form expectations at its first meeting about the likely contributions of individuals to the group's goals.

Experimental group   The group in an experiment that is exposed to the independent variable.

Experimental realism   An attempt to fully involve a subject in a believable experiment by reducing the artificial nature of the experimental situation.

Experimental research   A research method that is designed to measure the effect of an independent variable on a dependent variable under tightly controlled conditions.

Expressive crowd   A crowd that consists of individuals who assemble for an event that is designed to allow them to release their emotions.

Expressive (socioemotional) leaders   Leaders who try to keep groups together by promoting unity and harmony.

External validity   The extent to which research findings can be generalized to other settings and populations.

Extinction   The disappearance of a learned response.

Extraneous variable   An unspecified factor that exerts an effect on a dependent variable in an experiment.

Fads   Manifestations of collective behavior that involve something particularly unusual or novel, spread quickly, and then disappear.

Family of orientation   The family into which individuals are born.

Family of procreation   The family that individuals create through marriage.

Fashions   Items such as clothing and accessories that enjoy popularity for a short period of time.

Field experiment   An experiment that takes place in a natural setting.

Filter theory   A theory that claims that people sift through successive levels of criteria in search of a marital partner.

Foot-in-the-door technique   A compliance strategy that operates on the idea that someone is more likely to agree to a large favor if you can get the person to do a small favor first.

Frustration   Interference with the achievement of a goal that prevents a person from enjoying an expected reward.

Frustration-aggression theory   A theory that frustration, blocking the achievement of a goal, precipitates an aggressive response.

Fundamental attribution error   The tendency to emphasize dispositions as the causes of other people's behaviors and to ignore situational factors as causes.

Game stage   In Mead's theory of symbolic interaction, the completing stage of the self.

Gatekeeper   A person who has the power to grant or deny researchers access to groups or situations they want to study.

Generalized other   A representation of an individual's internalization of society's rules.

Great-person theory of leadership   A theory that individuals who possess certain personality traits are likely to emerge as leaders irrespective of the situation.

Group-based social hierarchy   A hierarchy that is defined by the social power, prestige, and privilege possessed by individuals by virtue of their ascribed memberships in particular groups.

Group cohesiveness   The property of a group that binds members together.

Group norms   Shared expectations about how group members ought to behave.

Group polarization   The tendency for groups to shift decisions in an extreme direction toward the initial opinions of group members.

Group position model A theory that prejudice involves the classification of people into racial categories.

Group selection An evolutionary theory that argues that groups consisting of cooperative members are more likely to survive and pass on their genes than groups composed of selfish members.

Groupthink A faulty decision-making process that leads cohesive in-groups to seek concurrence, thereby preventing consideration of information or opinions that might cause conflict.

Guttman scale A measurement instrument that represents a hierarchy of attitudes, ranging from the least extreme to the most extreme.

Habits Learned associations between external stimuli and observable responses.

Hawthorne effect An experimental result that is produced by subjects' awareness of being observed, not by the introduction of an independent variable.

Hierarchichal classification The ability to sort and classify objects into classes and subclasses.

Historical time The influence that historical periods or circumstances exert on the life course.

Homogamy The tendency to meet, date, and marry someone who is similar in age, social class, race, education, religion, and other important characteristics.

Hostile aggression Aggression that involves an impulsive emotional response that aims to injure a person.

Hypothesis A tentative statement about the relationship between two or more variables.

I The impulsive, spontaneous component of the self.

Id The part of the personality that is the source of biological drives and desires that demand immediate and continual satisfaction.

Identification The process of accepting the attitudes, values, and beliefs of someone we like or admire.

Identity salience The level of importance attached to a particular identity.

Ideological asymmetry A subtle kind of influence that either reinforces or weakens the social hierarchy by legitimizing ideologies.

Illusory correlation The perception of a link between two variables when in fact no relationship exists.

Imaginary audience A distorted image characteristic of adolescence that makes teenagers feel that they are the focus of others' attention.

Impression management The attempt to present oneself as one wishes to be viewed by others.

Independent variable The variable that is manipulated in an experiment to determine whether it has an effect on another (dependent) variable.

Induced compliance A cognitive dissonance research design that shows how people react when they are persuaded to behave in a way that is inconsistent with a privately held attitude.

Informational social influence A form of group influence that operates on people's need to be right.

Informed consent A subject's agreement to participate in a study after researchers have informed him or her about the research, including all possible risks.

In-group The group to which an individual feels he or she belongs.

In-group bias The tendency to view one's own group as superior to other groups, which are judged according to in-group standards.

Institutional review board A committee formed by universities and research institutions to ensure that subjects' rights are protected.

Instrumental aggression Aggression that aims to achieve a particular goal.

Instrumental leaders Task-oriented leaders who seek to help groups achieve particular goals.

Insufficient justification A cognitive dissonance research design that shows how people react when they are given a small incentive to deviate from a privately held attitude.

Internalization The process of accepting externally imposed rules as one's own internalized standards.

Internal validity The degree to which a theoretical concept fits a researcher's empirical measurement of that concept.

Intersubjectivity The process by which two individuals, who undertake a joint task from two different perspectives and understandings, arrive at a common understanding.

Intimacy The closeness and affectionate feelings of connection that people experience in relationships.

Jigsaw classroom A strategy for reducing prejudice in schools that involves the cooperative learning of small groups of racially mixed students.

Kin selection An evolutionary theory that focuses on the survival of the individual's gene pool as an explanation for altruism.

Knowledge function The idea that attitudes help organize information and provide frames of reference for understanding other people.

Laboratory experiment An experiment that takes place in a highly controlled situation.

Learned helplessness A defeatist attitude that results from the belief that a negative outcome is due to internal, stable factors.

Legitimizing myths Attitudes, values, beliefs, stereotypes, and ideologies that justify the social practices of a particular social system.

Life course The progression of an individual through a sequence of socially defined roles over the course of his or her lifetime.

Likert scale An instrument with a multiple-choice format that measures a favorable or unfavorable attitude toward a subject of interest.

Locus of control The inclination to attribute the causes of events to either oneself or to the environment.

Looking-glass self A process by which we view ourselves from the imaginary stance of others.

Lowballing A compliance strategy that involves the principles of consistency and commitment.

Ludus A love style that is playful, casual, and carefree.

Macrosystem The outermost circle in Bronfenbrenner's socialization model, which refers to the broad ideology, customs, and laws of an individual's culture, subculture, or social class.

Mania A love style that is characterized by intense jealousy, possessiveness, and an obsessive preoccupation with the lover.

Mass media All of the ways used to spread cultural knowledge to large audiences, including books, magazines, newspapers, television, and movies.

Mass society theory A theory that social movements provide individuals in mass societies with "substitute communities" that give them a sense of belonging.

Me The component of the self that represents the self as the object and gives direction to an act.

Mere exposure The idea that liking or attraction for someone or something increases with greater exposure.

Mesosystem The interrelationships among two or more settings that influence the development of a child.

Microsystem The innermost structure in Bronfenbrenner's socialization model, which involves an individual's activities, roles, and interpersonal relationships.

Multiple personality Mead's term for an illness characterized by two separate "me's" and "I's" that produce two separate selves.

Multiple selves The idea that an individual has many social selves or different relationships with various people.

Mundane realism The extent to which an experimental situation resembles a real-life situation or experience.

Naturalistic observation (field research) A research method that involves the observation of human behavior as it occurs in a natural setting.

Negative state relief model A theory that the decision to help others is influenced by whether people believe that helping others will alleviate their own suffering.

Noncommon effects The differing effects of an actor's behavior.

Normative-crisis perspective A life course perspective that views adult development as a sequence of tasks that must be accomplished in a particular order.

Normative social influence A form of group influence that operates on people's desire to be liked.

Norm of reciprocity A social norm that says we should return to others what they have given to us in some equivalent form.

Norm of responsibility A social norm that says we should help people who are dependent on us.

Obedience A behavioral response to social influence that leads a person to follow a command or a direct order.

Oedipus complex Freud's term for the anxiety that results from a young boy's sexual desire for his mother, which is accompanied by the fear that his father will punish him for this desire.

Operant conditioning A learning process that involves the shaping of behavior by its consequences.

Operationalization The process of translating abstract concepts into concrete, measurable variables.

Out-group A group to which an individual does not feel he or she belongs.

Out-group favoritism A form of deference that operates when subordinate group members favor members of the dominant group over their own.

Out-group homogeneity bias The tendency to minimize the differences among members of other groups.

Overjustification The tendency to focus on an external incentive for a particular behavior rather than on an internal reward.

Panic A form of collective behavior that results when a group views a situation as threatening.

Participant observation A qualitative research method in which researchers play active roles in the situations that they are studying.

Passion A component of love that consists of romantic feelings and desires resulting from physical attraction.

Passive-congenial marriage Marriage that begins with low expectations that are based on practical considerations.

Peer culture A stable set of activities or routines, values, and concerns that develop from the interaction of peers.

Perceived behavioral control A person's perception of how easy or difficult it is to perform a behavior.

Personal fable A distorted image that gives teenagers an exaggerated sense of self-importance.

Persuasive arguments perspective An explanation for group polarization, which claims that individuals are influenced during group discussions by ideas that support their own initial position as well as by new ideas that they had not considered.

Planned behavior model A modified version of the reasoned action model that includes a person's perception of how easy or difficult it is to perform a behavior.

Play stage The stage in Mead's theory of symbolic interactionism in which a child takes the role of specific people and imagines the world from their perspectives.

Population The total group of people of research interest.

Postdecision cognitive dissonance Dissonance created in the decision-making process that leads individuals to increase liking for the chosen alternative and to decrease liking for what they did not choose.

Posttesting The last stage in an experiment when the effect of the independent variable is measured and compared to measurements taken in the pretest.

Power The ability to dominate a relationship by controlling the receipt of rewards.

Pragma A love style characterized by a practical approach to love.

Preconscious The part of the mind that contains memories that can be readily accessed and transferred to the conscious level.

Prejudice Negative attitudes held about members of certain groups that are based on membership in those groups.

Preparatory stage The stage in Mead's theory of symbolic interactionism in which a child simply imitates the behavior of others.

Pretesting A stage in an experiment when measurements are taken that will be compared to the results obtained after the introduction of the independent variable.

Primacy effect The tendency to give greater weight to early information in the formation of impressions.

Primary group A small group of people whose relationships are intimate and lasting.

Primary socialization The process by which individuals acquire the knowledge and learn the norms and roles of their society in preparation for adulthood.

Principle of consistency An individual's need to be consistent in thoughts and actions.

Principle of equity The idea that people expect to get as much out of a relationship as they put into it.

Principle of least interest The idea that the person who has the least interest in continuing a relationship gains control.

Principle of reciprocity A social norm that says if someone does you a favor, you should repay it in kind.

Principle of scarcity The tendency to assign greater value to an item simply because it is rare or will not be available for long.

Private speech Speech directed at oneself that allows individuals to be both the subject and object of their own behaviors.

Projection A process that allows individuals to eliminate their own undesirable traits by criticizing others for possessing them.

Propaganda A form of collective behavior that involves intentional attempts to influence mass audiences through techniques employing spoken, written, or visual representations.

Prosocial behavior Helping behavior that benefits other people.

Protestant ethic Weber's concept of a pattern of traits associated with the rise of capitalism in the West, including hard work, temperance and moderation, and the rejection of worldly comforts.

Public People who share opinions on a variety of social issues.

Public opinion A form of collective behavior consisting of the attitudes that the public holds on issues.

Random assignment A procedure for assigning subjects to experimental or control groups to make sure that any differences between the groups are due only to chance.

Realistic conflict theory A theory that prejudice is a consequence of groups' competition for scarce resources and power.

Reasoned action model A theory that explains the psychological processes that link people's attitudes to their behavior.

Recency effect The tendency to give greater weight to later information in the formation of impressions.

Reciprocal altruism An evolutionary theory that suggests that helping in the short run increases the probability that our genes will be protected in the future.

Redemptive social movement A social movement that targets individuals for total change.

Reformative social movement A social movement that seeks partial change in the structure of society.

Rejection-then-retreat technique A form of the door-in-the-face technique that is viewed as a process involving the norm of reciprocity.

Relationship-oriented leaders Leaders who pay attention to the feelings of group members and how those affect relationships with other group members.

Relative deprivation The perception that one's condition is worse than that of others, who serve as a basis for comparison.

Relative deprivation theory A theory that frustration, which occurs when people's expectations for a better life are not met, can lead to participation in a social movement.

Reliability The extent to which research measurements show consistent results.

Rescue marriage Marriage that provides partners with comfort for past unhappiness.

Resocialization The process by which individuals unlearn past attitudes, values, and behaviors and replace them with new ones.

Resource mobilization theory A theory that social movements develop at certain times and in specific locations depending on the political and economic resources that are available to the movement.

Reversibility The idea that the shape or appearance of something that has been changed can return to its original form.

Risky shift The observation that groups are more likely than individuals to take higher risks in making decisions.

Rites of passage Formal ceremonies that signify important life transitions, including weddings, religious confirmation, and funerals.

Role identities The social categories, group memberships, and social roles that define one's identity.

Romantic marriage Marriage characterized primarily by a passionate sexual relationship and partners' beliefs that they were destined to be together.

Rumor Unsubstantiated information that spreads informally, most often by word of mouth.

Sample A set of representative subjects selected in a way that allows researchers to draw inferences about the population under study.

Scaffolding Adjustments that teachers make in assisting students who are attempting to solve a problem.

Scapegoat A target onto which aggression is displaced.

Schema A cognitive structure that individuals use to identify and process information.

Scientific approach A systematic attempt to gather and analyze data for the purpose of understanding human behavior.

Secondary group A large group of people who interact in an impersonal way on a temporary basis to achieve a particular goal.

Secure attachment A healthy kind of attachment that develops between a child and caregiver that builds trust through interactions that meet the child's needs.

Selective exposure The tendency to seek out or pay attention to information that suggests that we hold the correct attitudes.

Self-concept An awareness of who one is.

Self-debilitation The self-destructive behavior of subordinate group members, whose response to negative stereotypes results in a self-fulfilling prophecy.

Self-disclosure A conversation in which people reveal personal information about themselves to others.

Self-efficacy An individual's belief about his or her ability to bring about a desired outcome.

Self-esteem An individual's evaluation of his or her self-worth.

Self-fulfilling prophecy A false definition of a situation that contributes to an expected outcome by influencing the behavior of the individuals involved.

Self-identities Descriptions of the traits that people associate with their self-concept.

Selflessness An unselfish regard for the welfare of others.

Self-perception theory A theory that claims that people draw inferences about their attitudes from observations of their own behavior.

Self-serving bias The tendency to take credit for our successes but to blame our failures on someone or something else.

Semantic differential scale A measurement instrument that evaluates an attitude object by checking a point along a continuum that stretches between a pair of adjectives that are opposite in meaning.

Seriation The ability to order items along a quantitative dimension such as height or weight.

Significant others Important people who exert a strong influence on children during the development of the self.

Social change The transformation of culture and society over time.

Social comparison Comparing oneself to others in order to develop a sense of one's identity.

Social comparison perspective An explanation for group polarization that claims that people are motivated to evaluate their own opinions by comparing them to those of others.

Social control An attempt to regulate human behavior that involves various strategies for producing conformity to social norms.

Social desirability A bias caused by people's consideration of what will make them look good.

Social dilemma Situations that involve choices between self-interest and collective interest.

Social Distance Scale An instrument that was designed to measure attitudes toward various racial or nationality groups.

Social dominance orientation A psychological component in social dominance theory that reflects the influence of one's group status, gender, socialization, and temperament.

Social dominance theory A theory that prejudice involves a group-based social hierarchy, which is maintained by a number of social processes.

Social exchange theory A theory of interpersonal relationships that views people as rational bookkeepers who assess the costs and benefits of a particular relationship.

Social facilitation The tendency to perform better on simple tasks but to do worse on difficult ones when others are present.

Social group Two or more people who interact with one another, have a common identity, and feel a sense of unity.

Social identity The part of an individual's self-concept that is derived from an awareness of one's membership in a particular social group and influences self-esteem.

Social identity theory The theory that an individual's self-esteem can be reinforced by identification with an in-group when the individual believes that the in-group is superior to other groups (out-groups).

Social impact theory The theory that a group's size, strength, and immediacy are the most important factors influencing an individual's conformity to the group.

Social influence   The exercise of power by a person or group to produce changes in an individual's thoughts, feelings, or behaviors.

Socialization   The process by which individuals learn the values, norms, beliefs, and roles of their society. This process also involves the development of a self-concept or identity.

Social learning theory   A theory that people learn behaviors by observing models.

Social loafing   The tendency for members of a group to put less effort into a task when individual contributions cannot be evaluated.

Socially defined time   Social norms or expectations that define what individuals should do at certain ages.

Social movement   An organized and sustained attempt to either bring about or stop social change.

Social norms   Rules that define what is expected in order to belong to a group or society.

Social penetration theory   A theory that explains how close relationships develop through a process of self-disclosure.

Social psychology   The scientific study of the relationship between the individual and society that focuses on the way that our thoughts, feelings, and behaviors are influenced by other people.

Social reality   A subjective determination of how other people view the world, including their opinions, beliefs, and attitudes.

Status system   A group structure that reflects the distribution of power among group members.

Stereotype   A generalized belief about members of a certain group that ignores the distinct traits of individual members of the group.

Storge   An affectionate form of love that typically develops between siblings and friends.

Superego   The part of the personality that represents the internalized moral values of one's society.

Survey research   A research method that involves the collection of data from a representative sample of subjects by means of questionnaires.

Symbolic interactionism   A theory that focuses on the development of the self as a product of social interaction that involves the acquisition of shared meanings.

Task-oriented leaders   Leaders who focus on the group's goal.

Theory   A general explanation of the relationships among a set of variables.

Threat-to-self-esteem model   A theory that people may reject assistance when it conflicts with internalized norms that influence their feelings of self-worth.

Thurstone scale   An instrument that includes a variety of statements along an evaluative continuum that measures the degree of favorability or unfavorability about a particular subject of interest.

Total marriage   Marriage in which the partners' lives are fully enmeshed, in work or play.

Traditional marriage   Marriage characterized by a clear-cut division of roles and responsibilities.

Transformative social movement   A social movement that targets everyone in a society and seeks a total change in that society.

Triad   A group consisting of three people.

Triangulation   The use of more than one research method to compare the findings on a particular topic of interest.

Twenty Statements Test   An instrument developed by Kuhn to measure an individual's self-concept.

Ultimate attribution error   The tendency to ignore situational explanations for the behavior of members of a particular group and to focus instead on dispositional traits that characterize all members of that particular group.

Unconscious   The part of the mind that contains ideas and motivations that are beyond an individual's awareness.

Urban legends   A form of collective behavior involving modern morality tales that happen to anonymous others.

Value-added perspective   A theory that six conditions exist when collective behavior occurs.

Value-expressive function   The idea that attitudes reflect cherished beliefs and values that are central to our self-image.

Variables   Concepts that vary over space and time.

Vital marriage   Marriage in which the partners are intensely bound together through shared values and the desire to be together.

Zone of proximal development   The gap between what a child can do independently and what he or she can do with a teacher's assistance.

References

Abelson, R. P. 1972. "Are Attitudes Necessary?" In *Attitudes, Conflicts, and Social Change*, ed. B. T. King and E. McGinnies. New York: Academic Press.

Aberle, D. 1966. *The Peyote Religion Among the Navaho*. Chicago: Aldine.

Aderman, D. 1972. "Elation, Depression, and Helping Behavior." *Journal of Personality and Social Psychology* 24: 91–101.

Adorno, T. W., E. Frenkel-Brunswik, D. J. Levinson, and R. N. Sanford. 1950. *The Authoritarian Personality*. New York: Harper & Row.

Ahammer, I. M., and J. P. Murray. 1979. "Kindness in the Kindergarten: The Relative Influence of Role Playing and Prosocial Television in Facilitating Altruism." *International Journal of Behavioral Development* 2: 133–157.

Ainsworth, M. D. S. 1979. "Infant-Mother Attachment." *American Psychologist* 34: 932–937.

Ajzen, I. 1985. "From Intentions to Actions: A Theory of Planned Behavior." In *Action-Control: From Cognitions to Behaviors*, ed. J. Kuhland and J. Beckman. Heidelberg, Germany: Springer.

Ajzen, I. 1987. "Attitudes, Traits, and Actions: Dispositional Prediction of Behavior in Personality and Social Psychology." In *Advances in Experimental Social Psychology* (vol. 20), ed. L. Berkowitz. San Diego, CA: Academic Press.

Ajzen, I. 1988. *Attitudes, Personality, and Behavior*. Chicago: Dorsey.

Ajzen, I. 1991. "The Theory of Planned Behavior." *Organizational Behavior and Human Decision Processes* 50: 179–211.

Ajzen, I., and M. Fishbein. 1980. *Understanding Attitudes and Predicting Social Behavior*. Englewood Cliffs, NJ: Prentice Hall.

Allan, S. 1999. *News Culture*. Philadelphia: Open University Press.

Allen, V. L., and D. A. Wilder. 1975. "Categorization, Belief Similarity, and Intergroup Discrimination." *Journal of Personality and Social Psychology* 32: 971–977.

Allison, S. T., J. K. Beggan, and E. H. Midgley. 1996. "The Quest for 'Similar Instances' and 'Simultaneous Possibilities': Metaphors in Social Dilemma Research." *Journal of Personality and Social Psychology* 71: 479–497.

Allport, F. H. 1920. "The Influence of the Group upon Association and Thought." *Journal of Experimental Psychology* 3: 159–182.

Allport, F. H. 1924. *Social Psychology*. Boston: Houghton Mifflin.

Allport, G. W. 1935. "Attitudes." In *Handbook of Social Psychology*, ed. C. Murchison. Worcester, MA: Clark University Press.

Allport, G. W. 1979. *The Nature of Prejudice*. Reading, MA: Addison-Wesley.

Allport, G. W. 1985. "The Historical Background of Social Psychology." In *The Handbook of Social Psychology* (3rd ed., vol. 1), ed. G. Lindzey and E. Aronson. New York: Random House.

Altemeyer, B. 1988. *Enemies of Freedom: Understanding Right-Wing Authoritarianism*. San Francisco: Jossey-Bass.

Altman, I., and D. A. Taylor. 1973. *Social Penetration: The Development of Interpersonal Relationships*. New York: Holt, Rinehart and Winston.

Amato, P. R. 1983. "Helping Behavior in Urban and Rural Environments: Field Studies Based on a Taxonomic Organization of Helping Episodes." *Journal of Personality and Social Psychology* 45: 571–586.

Amir, Y. 1969. "Contact Hypothesis in Ethnic Relations." *Psychological Bulletin* 71: 319–342.

Anderson, C. A. 1989. "Temperature and Aggression: Ubiquitous Effects of Heat on Occurrence of Human Violence." *Psychological Bulletin* 106: 74–96.

Anderson, C. A., and D. C. Anderson. 1984. "Ambient Temperature and Violent Crime: Tests of the Linear and Curvilinear Hypotheses." *Journal of Personality and Social Psychology* 46: 91–97.

Anderson, C. A., and K. B. Anderson. 1998. "Temperature and Aggression: Paradox, Controversy, and a (Fairly) Clear Picture." In *Human Aggression: Theories, Research, and Implications for Social Policy*, ed. R. G. Geen and E. I. Donnerstein. San Diego: Academic Press.

Anderson, C. A., K. B. Anderson, and W. Deuser. 1996. "Examining an Affective Aggression Framework: Weapon and Temperature Effects on Aggressive Thoughts, Affect, and Attitudes." *Personality and Social Psychology Bulletin* 22: 366–376.

Anderson, C. A., K. B. Anderson, N. Dorr, K. M. Deneve, and M. Flanagan. 2000. "Temperature and Aggression." In *Advances in Experimental Social Psychology*, ed. M. P. Zanna. San Diego: Academic Press.

Anderson, N. H. 1968. "Likableness Rating of 555 Personality-Trait Words." *Journal of Personality and Social Psychology* 9, no. 3: 272–279.

Archer, R. L. 1979. "Role of Personality and the Social Situation." In *Self-Disclosure*, ed. G. J. Chelune. San Francisco: Jossey-Bass.

Arliss, L. P. 1991. *Gender Communication*. Englewood Cliffs, NJ: Prentice Hall.

Aronson. E. 1997. "The Theory of Cognitive Dissonance: The Evolution and Vicissitudes of an Idea." In *The Message of Social Psychology: Perspectives on Mind in Society*, ed. C. McGarty and S. A. Haslam. Cambridge, MA: Blackwell.

Aronson, E. 1999. "Stateways Can Change Folkways." In *Hatred, Bigotry, and Prejudice: Definitions, Causes and Solutions*, ed. R. M. Baird and S. E. Rosenbaum. New York: Prometheus Books.

Aronson, E., M. Brewer, and J. M. Carlsmith. 1985. "Experimentation in Social Psychology." In *The Handbook of Social Psychology* (3rd ed., vol. 1), ed. G. Lindzey and E. Aronson. New York: Random House.

Aronson, E., and D. Bridgeman. 1979. "Jigsaw Groups and the Desegregated Classroom: In Pursuit of Common Goals." *Personality and Social Psychology Bulletin* 5: 438–446.

Aronson, E., and A. Gonzalez. 1988. "Desegregation, Jigsaw, and the Mexican-American Experience." In *Towards the Elimination of Racism: Profiles in Controversy*, ed. P. A. Katz and D. Taylor. New York: Plenum.

Aronson, E., and S. Patnoe. 1997. *Cooperation in the Classroom: The Jigsaw Method*. New York: Longman.

Aronson, E., C. Stephan, J. Sikes, N. Blaney, and M. Snapp. 1978. *The Jigsaw Classroom*. Beverly Hills, CA: Sage.

Asch, S. 1946. "Forming Impressions on Personality." *Journal of Abnormal and Social Psychology* 41: 258–290.

Asch, S. E. 1955. "Opinions and Social Pressure." *Scientific American* 193: 31–35.

Babbie, E. 1995. *The Practice of Social Research* (7th ed.). Belmont, CA: Wadsworth.

Bach, G. R., and P. Wyden. 1970. *The Intimate Enemy: How to Fight Fair in Love and Marriage*. New York: Avon Books.

Bachrach, S., and A. Kassof. 2001. *Flight and Rescue*. Washington, DC: United States Holocaust Memorial Museum.

Baldwin, M. S., J. P. R. Keelan, B. Fehr, V. Enns, and E. Koh-Rangarajoo. 1996. "Social-Cognitive Conceptualization of Attachment Working Models: Availability and Accessibility Effects." *Journal of Personality and Social Psychology* 71: 94–109.

Bales, R. F. 1950. *Interaction Process Analysis: A Method for the Study of Small Groups*. Reading, MA: Addison-Wesley.

Bales, R. F. 1953. "The Equilibrium Problem in Small Groups." In *Working Papers in the Theory of Action*, ed. T. Parsons, R. F. Bales, and E. A. Shils. Glencoe, IL: Free Press.

Bandura, A. 1965a. "Influence of Models' Reinforcement Contingencies on the Acquisition of Imitative Responses." *Journal of Personality and Social Psychology* 1: 589–595.

Bandura, A. 1965b. "Vicarious Processes: A Case of No-Trial Learning." In *Advances in Experimental Social Psychology* (vol. 2), ed. L. Berkowitz. New York: Academic Press.

Bandura, A. 1973. *Aggression: A Social Learning Analysis*. Englewood Cliffs, NJ: Prentice Hall.

Bandura, A. 1977. *Social Learning Theory*. Englewood Cliffs, NJ: Prentice Hall.

Bandura, A. 1983. "Psychological Mechanisms of Aggression." In *Aggression: Theoretical and Empirical Reviews* (vol. 1), ed. R. G. Geen and E. I. Donnerstein. New York: Academic Press.

Bandura, A. 1986. *Social Foundation of Thought and Action: A Social Cognitive Theory*. Englewood Cliffs, NJ: Prentice Hall.

Bandura, A. 1989. "Social Cognitive Theory." In *Annals of Child Development* (vol. 6.), ed. R. Vasta. Greenwich, CT: JAI Press.

Bandura, A. 1992. "Perceived Self-Efficacy in Cognitive Development and Functioning." *Educational Psychologist* 28: 117–148.

Bandura, A., D. Ross, and S. A. Ross. 1961. "Transmission of Aggression Through Imitation of Aggressive Models." *Journal of Abnormal and Social Psychology* 63: 575–582.

Bandura, A., D. Ross, and S. A. Ross. 1963. "Vicarious Reinforcement and Imitative Learning." *Journal of Abnormal and Social Psychology* 67: 601–607.

Banner, L. W. 1983. *American Beauty*. Chicago: University of Chicago Press.

Barchas, P. R., and M. H. Fisek. 1984. "Hierarchical Differentiation in Newly Formed Groups of Rhesus and Humans." In *Essays Toward a Sociophysiological Perspective*, ed. P. R. Barchas. Westport, CT: Greenwood Press.

Barkan, S. E. 1997. *Criminology: A Sociological Understanding*. Upper Saddle River, NJ: Prentice Hall.

Barker, R., T. Dembo, and K. Lewin. 1941. "Frustration and Aggression: An Experiment with Young Children." *University of Iowa Studies in Child Welfare* 18: 1–314.

Baron, J., and J. G. Miller. 2000. "Limiting the Scope of Moral Obligations to Help: A Cross-Cultural Investigation." *Journal of Cross-Cultural Psychology* 31: 703–725.

Baron, R. A. 1971. "Reducing the Influence of an Aggressive Model: The Restraining Effects of Discrepant Modeling Cues." *Journal of Personality and Social Psychology* 20: 140–145.

Baron, R. A. 1983a. "The Control of Human Aggression: An Optimistic Overview." *Journal of Social and Clinical Psychology* 1: 97–119.

Baron, R. A. 1983b. "The Control of Human Aggression: A Strategy Based on Incompatible Responses."

In *Aggression: Theoretical and Empirical Reviews* (vol. 2), ed. R. G. Geen and E. I. Donnerstein. New York: Academic Press.

Baron, R. A. 1986. "Distraction-Conflict Theory: Progress and Problems." In *Advances in Experimental Social Psychology* (vol. 19), ed. L. Berkowitz. Orlando, FL: Academic Press.

Baron, R. A. 1993. "Reducing Aggression and Conflict: The Incompatible Response Approach, or Why People Who Feel Good Usually Won't Be Bad." In *The Undaunted Psychologist: Adventures in Research*, ed. C. G. Brannigan and M. R. Merrens. Philadelphia: Temple University Press.

Baron, R. A., and C. R. Kepner. 1970. "Model's Behavior and Attraction Toward the Model as Determinants of Adult Aggressive Behavior." *Journal of Personality and Social Psychology* 14: 335–344.

Baron, R. A., and V. M. Ransberger. 1978. "Ambient Temperature and the Occurrence of Collective Violence: The 'Long, Hot Summer' Revisited." *Journal of Personality and Social Psychology* 36: 351–360.

Baron, R. A., and D. R. Richardson. 1994. *Human Aggression.* New York: Plenum Press.

Barratt, E. S., and J. H. Patton. 1983. "Impulsivity: Cognitive, Behavioral, and Psychophysiological Correlates." In *Biological Bases of Sensation Seeking, Impulsivity, and Anxiety*, ed. M. Zuckerman. Hillsdale, NJ: Erlbaum.

Barsam, R. M. 1992. *Nonfiction Film: A Critical History.* Bloomington: Indiana University Press.

Bar-Tal, D., and A. Raviv. 1982. "A Cognitive-Learning Model of Helping Behavior Development: Possible Implications and Applications." In *The Development of Prosocial Behavior*, ed. N. Eisenberg. New York: Academic Press.

Bar-Tal, D., R. Sharabany, and A. Raviv. 1982. "Cognitive Basis of the Development of Altruistic Behavior." In *Cooperation and Helping Behavior: Theories and Research*, ed. V. J. Derlega and J. Grzelak. New York: Academic Press.

Bartholomew, K., and L. Horowitz. 1991. "Attachment Styles Among Young Adults: A Test of a Four-Category Model." *Journal of Personality and Social Psychology* 61: 226–244.

Bass, B. M. 1990. *Bass and Stogdill's Handbook of Leadership: Theory, Research, and Managerial Applications* (3rd ed.). New York: Free Press.

Bass, B. M. 1997. "Does the Transactional-Transformational Leadership Paradigm Transcend Organizational and National Boundaries?" *American Psychologist* 52: 130–139.

Bassili, J. N., and A. Provencal. 1988. "Perceiving Minorities: A Factor-Analytic Approach." *Personality and Social Psychology Bulletin* 14: 5–15.

Batson, C. D. 1991. *The Altruism Question: Toward a Social-Psychological Answer.* Hillsdale, NJ: Erlbaum.

Batson, C. D. 2001. "Addressing the Altruism Question Experimentally." In *Altruism and Altruistic Love: Science, Philosophy, and Religion in Dialogue*, ed. S. G. Post, L. B. Underwood, J. P. Schloss, and W. B. Hurlbut. New York: Oxford University Press.

Batson, C. D., N. Ahmad, S. Yin, S. J. Bedell, J. W. Johnson, C. M. Templin, and A. Whiteside. 1999. "Two Threats to the Common Good: Self-Interested Egoism and Empathy-Induced Altruism." *Personality and Social Psychology Bulletin* 25: 3–16.

Batson, C. D., M. H. Bolen, J. A. Cross, and H. E. Neuringer-Benefiel. 1986. "Where Is the Altruism in the Altruistic Personality?" *Journal of Personality and Social Psychology* 50: 212–220.

Batson, C. D., P. J. Cochran, M. F. Biederman, J. L. Blosser, M. J. Ryan, and B. Vogt. 1978. "Failure to Help When in a Hurry: Callousness or Conflict?" *Personality and Social Psychology Bulletin* 4: 97–101.

Batson, C. D., and J. S. Coke. 1981. "Empathy: A Source of Altruistic Motivation for Helping?" In *Altruism and Helping Behavior*, ed. J. P. Rushton and R. M. Sorrentino. Hillsdale, NJ: Erlbaum.

Batson, C. D., B. D. Duncan, P. Ackerman, T. Buckley, and K. Birch. 1981. "Is Empathic Emotion a Source of Altruistic Motivation?" *Journal of Personality and Social Psychology* 40: 290–302.

Batson, C. D., J. Fultz, and P. A. Schoenrade. 1987. "Distress and Empathy: Two Qualitatively Distinct Vicarious Emotions with Different Motivational Consequences." *Journal of Personality* 55: 19–40.

Batson, C. D., T. R. Klein, L. Highberger, and L. L. Shaw. 1995. "Immorality from Empathy-Induced Altruism: When Compassion and Justice Conflict." *Journal of Personality and Social Psychology* 68: 1042–1058.

Batson, C. D., and K. C. Oleson. 1991. "Current Status of the Empathy-Altruism Hypothesis." In *Review of Personality and Social Psychology.* Vol. 12, *Prosocial Behavior*, ed. M. S. Clark. Newbury Park, CA: Sage.

Batson, C. D., F. O'Quinn, J. Fultz, N. Vanderplas, and A. M. Isen. 1983. "Influence of Self-Reported Distress and Empathy on Egoistic Versus Altruistic Motivation to Help." *Journal of Personality and Social Psychology* 45: 706–718.

Batson, C. D., K. Sager, E. Garst, M. Kang, K. Rubchinsky, and K. Dawson. 1997. "Is Empathy-Induced Helping Due to Self-Other Merging?" *Journal of Personality and Social Psychology* 73: 495–509.

Baumeister, R. F., and M. R. Leary. 1995. "The Need to Belong: Desire for Interpersonal Attachments as a Fundamental Human Motivation." *Psychological Bulletin* 117: 497–529.

Baumeister, R. F., and S. R. Wotman. 1992. *Breaking Hearts: The Two Sides of Unrequited Love.* New York: Guilford Press.

Beck, S. B., C. I. Ward-Hull, and P. M. McLear. 1976. "Variables Related to Women's Somatic Preferences of the Male and Female Body." *Journal of Personality and Social Psychology* 34: 1200–1210.

Becker, H. S. 1960. "Notes on the Concept of Commitment." *American Journal of Sociology.* 66: 32–40.

Becker, H. S. 1964. "Personal Change in Adult Life." *Sociometry* 27: 40–53.

Becker, H. S., B. Geer, E. C. Hughes, and A. L. Strauss. 1961. *Boys in White: Student Culture in Medical School.* Chicago: University of Chicago Press.

Beilin, H. 1992. "Piaget's Enduring Contribution to Developmental Psychology." *Developmental Psychology* 28: 191–204.

Bell, P. A. 1980. "Effects of Heat, Noise, and Provocation on Retaliatory Evaluative Behavior." *Journal of Social Psychology* 110: 97–100.

Bellah, R. N., R. Madsen, W. Sullivan, A. Swidler, and S. Tipton. 1985. *Habits of the Heart: Individualism and Commitment in American Life.* Los Angeles: University of California Press.

Bem, D. J. 1967. "Self-Perception: An Alternative Interpretation of Cognitive Dissonance Phenomena." *Psychological Review* 74: 183–200.

Bem, D. J. 1972. "Self-Perception Theory." In *Advances in Experimental Social Psychology* (vol. 6), ed. L. Berkowitz. San Diego: Academic Press.

Bem, D. J., and H. K. McConnell. 1970. "Testing the Self-Perception Explanation of Dissonance Phenomena: On the Salience of Premanipulation Attitudes." *Journal of Personality and Social Psychology* 14: 23–31.

Benedict, R. 1934. *Patterns of Culture.* Boston: Houghton Mifflin.

Benford, R. D. 1992. "Social Movements." In *Encyclopedia of Sociology* (vol. 4), ed. E. F. Borgatta and M. Borgatta. New York: Macmillan.

Bengtson, B. L., M. N. Reedy, and C. Gordon. 1985. "Aging and Self-Conceptions: Personality Processes and Social Contexts." In *Handbook of the Psychology of Aging*, ed. J. E. Birren and K. W. Schaie. New York: Van Nostrand Reinhold.

Bennett, W. J., ed. 1993. *The Book of Virtues.* New York: Simon & Schuster.

Benokraitis, N. V. 2005. *Marriages and Families: Changes, Choices, and Constraints.* Upper Saddle River, NJ: Prentice Hall.

Berger, J., S. J. Rosenholtz, and M. Zelditch. 1980. "Status Organizing Processes." *Annual Review of Sociology* 6: 479–508.

Berger, J., D. G. Wagner, and M. Zelditch. 1985. "Expectation States Theory: Review and Assessment." In *Status, Rewards, and Influence*, ed. J. Berger and M. Zelditch. San Francisco: Jossey-Bass.

Berger, P. L., and T. Luckman. 1966. *The Social Construction of Reality.* New York: Anchor Books.

Berk, L. E. 2000. *Child Development.* Needham Heights, MA: Allyn & Bacon.

Berkowitz, L. 1962. *Aggression: A Social Psychological Analysis.* New York: McGraw-Hill.

Berkowitz, L. 1965. "Some Aspects of Observed Aggression." *Journal of Personality and Social Psychology* 2: 359–369.

Berkowitz, L. 1969. "The Frustration-Aggression Hypothesis Revisited." In *Roots of Aggression*, ed. L. Berkowitz. New York: Atherton Press.

Berkowitz, L. 1972. "Social Norms, Feelings, and Other Factors Affecting Helping and Altruism." In *Advances in Experimental Social Psychology* (vol. 6), ed. L. Berkowitz. New York: Academic Press.

Berkowitz, L. 1974. "Some Determinants of Impulsive Aggression: Role of Mediated Associations with Reinforcements for Aggression." *Psychological Review* 81: 165–176.

Berkowitz, L. 1981. "How Guns Control Us." *Psychology Today*, June, pp. 11–12.

Berkowitz, L. 1984. "Some Effects of Thoughts on Anti- and Prosocial Influences of Media Events: A Cognitive-Neoassociation Analysis." *Psychological Bulletin* 95: 410–427.

Berkowitz, L. 1987. "Mood, Self-Awareness, and Willingness to Help." *Journal of Personality and Social Psychology* 52: 721–729.

Berkowitz, L. 1989. "Frustration-Aggression Hypothesis: Examination and Reformulation." *Psychological Bulletin* 106: 59–73.

Berkowitz, L. 1993. *Aggression: Its Causes, Consequences, and Control.* New York: McGraw-Hill.

Berkowitz, L., and L. R. Daniels. 1964. "Affecting the Salience of the Social Responsibility Norm: Effect of Past Help on the Responses to Dependency Relationships." *Journal of Abnormal and Social Psychology* 68: 275–281.

Berkowitz, L., and R. G. Geen. 1966. "Film Violence and the Cue Properties of Available Targets." *Journal of Personality and Social Psychology* 3: 525–530.

Berkowitz, L., and A. Le Page. 1967. "Weapons as Aggression-Eliciting Stimuli." *Journal of Personality and Social Psychology* 7: 202–207.

Beroff, J., E. Douvan, and R. Julka. 1981. *The Inner American: A Self-Portrait from 1957–1976.* New York: Basic Books.

Berscheid, E. 1983. "Emotion." In *Close Relationships*, ed. H. H. Kelley, E. Berscheid, A. Christensen, J. H. Harvey, T. L. Huston, G. Levinger, E. McClintock, L. A. Peplau, and D. R. Peterson. New York: Freeman.

Berscheid, E., K. K. Dion, E. Walster, and G. W. Walster. 1971. "Physical Attractiveness and Dating Choice: A Test of the Matching Hypothesis." *Journal of Experimental Social Psychology* 7: 173–189.

Berscheid, E., and E. Walster. 1974. "Physical Attractiveness." In *Advances in Experimental Social Psychology* (vol. 7), ed. L. Berkowitz. New York: Academic Press.

Berscheid, E., and E. Walster. 1978. *Interpersonal Attraction*. Reading, MA: Addison-Wesley.

Blackwell, D. L. 1998. "Marital Homogamy in the United States: The Influence of Individual and Paternal Education." *Social Science Research* 27: 159–188.

Blake, R., and W. Dennis. 1943. "The Development of Stereotypes Concerning the Negro." *Journal of Abnormal and Social Psychology* 38: 525–531.

Blau, P. M. 1964. *Exchange and Power in Social Life*. New York: Wiley.

Block, J. J. 1983. "Differential Premises Arising from Differential Socialization of the Sexes: Some Conjectures." *Child Development* 54: 1335–1354.

Block, J. R., and H. Yuker. 1992. *Can You Believe Your Eyes?* New York: Brunner/Mazel.

Blumberg, R. L. 2003. "The Civil Rights Movement." In *The Social Movement Reader: Cases and Concepts*, ed. J. Goodwin and J. M. Jasper. Malden, MA: Blackwell.

Blumer, H. 1948. "Public Opinion and Public Opinion Polling." *American Sociological Review* 13: 542–549.

Blumer, H. 1951a. "The Field of Collective Behavior." In *Principles of Sociology*, ed. A. M. Lee. New York: Barnes & Noble.

Blumer, H. 1951b. "Social Movements." In *Principles of Sociology*, ed. A. M. Lee. New York: Barnes & Noble.

Blumer, H. 1958. "Race Prejudice as a Sense of Group Position." *Pacific Sociological Review* 1: 3–7.

Blumer, H. 1969. "Collective Behavior." In *Principles of Sociology* (3rd ed.), ed. A. M. Lee. New York: Barnes & Noble. Originally published 1939.

Bobo, L. D. 1999. "Prejudice as Group Position: Microfoundations of a Sociological Approach to Racism and Race Relations." *Journal of Social Issues* 55: 445–472.

Bobo, L. D., and E. B. Garcia. 1992. *The Chippewa Indian Treaty Rights Survey: A Preliminary Report* (Working Paper No. 9). Madison, WI: The Robert M. LaFollette Institute of Public Affairs, University of Wisconsin.

Bobo, L. D., and V. L. Hutchings. 1996. "Perceptions of Racial Group Competition: Extending Blumer's Theory of Group Position to a Multiracial Social Context." *American Sociological Review* 61: 951–972.

Bogardus, E. S. 1925. "Measuring Social Distance." *Journal of Applied Sociology* 9: 299–308.

Bolig, R., P. J. Stein, and P. C. McHenry. 1984. "The Self-Advertisement Approach to Dating: Male-Female Differences." *Family Relations* 22: 587–592.

Bond, C. F., Jr., and L. J. Titus. 1983. "Social Facilitation: A Meta-Analysis of 241 Studies." *Psychological Bulletin* 94: 264–292.

Bond, M. H. 1988. "Finding Universal Dimensions of Individual Variation in Multicultural Studies of Values: The Rokeach and Chinese Value Surveys." *Journal of Personality and Social Psychology* 55: 1009–1015.

Bond, R., and P. B. Smith. 1996. "Culture and Conformity: A Meta-Analysis of Studies Using Asch's Line Judgment Task." *Psychological Bulletin* 119: 111–137.

Bontempo, R., S. Lobel, and H. Triandis. 1990. "Compliance and Value Internalization in Brazil and the U.S. *Journal of Cross-Cultural Psychology* 21: 201–213.

Borden, R. J., R. Bowen, and S. P. Taylor. 1971. "Shock Setting Behavior as a Function of Physical Attack and Extrinsic Reward." *Perceptual and Motor Skills* 33: 563–568.

Borden, R. J., and S. P. Taylor. 1976. "Pennies for Pain: A Note on Instrumental Aggression Toward a Pacifist by Vanquished, Victorious, and Evenly Matched Opponents." *Victimology* 1: 154–157.

Bornstein, R. F. 1989. "Exposure and Affect: Overview and Meta-Analysis of Research, 1968–1987." *Psychological Bulletin* 106: 265–289.

Bornstein, R. F., D. R. Leone, and D. J. Galley. 1987. "The Generalizability of Subliminal Mere Exposure Effects: Influence of Stimuli Perceived Without Awareness on Social Behavior." *Journal of Personality and Social Psychology* 53: 1070–1079.

Bossard, J. H. S. 1932. "Residential Propinquity as a Factor in Marriage Selection." *American Journal of Sociology* 38: 219–224.

Bouchner, G. 1999. "Pop Beat." *Los Angeles Times*, August 7, p. 1.

Bowen, E., ed. 1968. *This Fabulous Century, 1870–1900*. New York: Time-Life Books.

Bowen, E., ed. 1969a. *This Fabulous Century, 1910–1920*. New York: Time-Life Books.

Bowen, E., ed. 1969b. *This Fabulous Century, 1920–1930*. New York: Time-Life Books.

Bowen, E., ed. 1970. *This Fabulous Century, 1960–1970*. New York: Time-Life Books.

Bower, G. H., K. P. Monteiro, and S. G. Gilligan. 1978. "Emotional Mood as a Context for Learning and Recall." *Journal of Verbal Learning and Verbal Behavior* 17: 573–585.

Bowlby, J. 1951. *Maternal Care and Mental Health.* World Health Organization Monograph no. 2. Geneva: World Health Organization.

Bowlby, J. 1969. *Attachment and Loss.* Vol. 1, *Attachment.* New York: Basic Books.

Bowlby, J. 1980. *Attachment and Loss.* Vol. 3, *Loss.* New York: Basic Books.

Bowlby, J. 1988. *A Secure Base, Parent-Child Attachment, and Healthy Human Development.* New York: Basic Books.

Bowles, S., and H. Gintis. 1976. *Schooling in Capitalist America: Educational Reform and the Contradictions of Economic Life.* New York: Basic Books.

Brauer, M., C. M. Judd, and M. D. Gliner. 1995. "The Effects of Repeated Expressions on Attitude Polarization During Group Discussions." *Journal of Personality and Social Psychology* 68: 1014–1029.

Brehm, J. W. 1956. "Post-Decision Changes in Desirability of Alternatives." *Journal of Abnormal and Social Psychology* 52: 384–389.

Brehm, J. W. 1966. *A Theory of Psychological Reactance.* New York: Academic Press.

Brehm, S. S., and J. W. Brehm. 1981. *Psychological Reactance.* New York: Academic Press.

Brennan, K. A., and P. R. Shaver. 1995. "Dimensions of Adult Attachment, Affect Regulation, and Romantic Relationship Functioning." *Personality and Social Psychology Bulletin* 21: 267–283.

Brewer, M. B. 1979. "In-Group Bias in the Minimal Inter-Group Situation: A Cognitive-Motivational Analysis." *Psychological Bulletin* 86: 307–324.

Brewer, M. B., and R. J. Brown. 1998. "Intergroup Relations." *The Handbook of Social Psychology* (4th ed), ed. D. T. Gilbert, S. T. Fiske, and G. Lindzey. New York: McGraw-Hill.

Brim, O. G., Jr. 1966. "Socialization Through the Life Cycle." In *Socialization After Childhood: Two Essays,* by O. G. Brim Jr. and S. Wheeler. New York: Wiley.

Brim, O. G., Jr., and C. D. Ryff. 1980. "On the Properties of the Life Events." In *Life-Span Development and Behavior* (vol. 3), ed. P. B. Baltes and O. G. Brim Jr. New York: Academic Press.

Brockner, J., and J. Z. Rubin. 1985. *Entrapment in Escalating Conflicts: A Social Psychological Analysis.* New York: Springer-Verlag.

Bronfenbrenner, U. 1979. *The Ecology of Human Development.* Cambridge, MA: Harvard University Press.

Bronfenbrenner, U. 1993. "The Ecology of Cognitive Development: Research Models and Fugitive Findings." In *Development in Context,* ed. R. H. Wozniak and K. W. Fisher. Hillsdale, NJ: Erlbaum.

Brown, A., and J. Campione. 1994. "Guided Discovery in a Community of Learners." In *Classroom Lessons: Integrating Cognitive Theory and Classroom Practice,* ed. K. McGilly. Cambridge, MA: MIT Press.

Brown, R. 1965. *Social Psychology.* Glencoe, IL: Free Press.

Brown, R. 1974. "Further Comment on the Risky Shift." *American Psychologist* 29: 468–470.

Bruner, J. S. 1983. "The Acquisition of Pragmatic Commitments." In *The Transition from Prelinguistic to Linguistic Communication,* ed. R. M. Golinkoff. Hillsdale, NJ: Erlbaum.

Bruner, J. S., and V. Sherwood. 1976. "Peekaboo and the Learning of Rule Structure." In *Play: Its Role in Development and Evolution,* ed. J. S. Bruner, A. Jolly, and K. Sylva. New York: Basic Books.

Bryan, J. H., and M. A. Test. 1967. "Models and Helping: Naturalistic Studies in Aiding Behavior." *Journal of Personality and Social Psychology* 6: 400–407.

Buchwald, A. 1979. "Why Can't Blacks Agree on Everything?" *Eugene Register-Guard,* October 28, p. 23.

Budd, L. J. 1956. "Altruism Arrives in America." *American Quarterly* 8: 40–52.

Budescu, D. V., and I. Erev, eds. 1999. *Games and Human Behavior: Essays in Honor of Amnon Rapoport.* Mahwah, NJ: Erlbaum.

Budman, S. H., S. Soldz, A. Demby, M. Davis, and J. Merry. 1993. "What Is Cohesiveness? An Empirical Examination." *Small Group Research* 24: 199–216.

Burgess, E., and P. Wallin. 1953. *Engagement and Marriage.* Philadelphia: Lippincott.

Burns, J. M. 1978. *Leadership.* New York: Harper Torchbooks.

Burnstein, E. 1982. "Persuasion as Argument Processing." In *Group Decision Making,* ed. H. Brandstatter, J. H. Davis, and G. Stocker-Kreichgauer. London: Academic Press.

Burnstein, E., and K. Sentis. 1981. "Attitude Polarization in Groups." In *Cognitive Responses in Persuasion,* ed. R. E. Petty, T. M. Ostrom, and T. C. Brock. Hillsdale, NJ: Erlbaum.

Burnstein, E., and A. Vinokur. 1977. "Persuasive Argumentation and Social Comparison as Determinants of Attitude Polarization." *Journal of Experimental Social Psychology* 13: 315–332.

Burr, W. R. 1973. *Theory Construction and the Sociology of the Family.* New York: Wiley.

Buss, A. H. 1961. *The Psychology of Aggression.* New York: Wiley.

Buss, A. H. 1971. "Aggression Pays." In *The Control of Aggression and Violence,* ed. J. L. Singer. New York: Academic Press.

Buss, A. H., and M. Perry. 1992. "The Aggression Questionnaire." *Journal of Personality and Social Psychology* 63: 452–459.

Buss, D. M., et al. 1990. "International Preferences in Selecting Mates: A Study of 37 Cultures." *Journal of Cross-Cultural Psychology* 21(March): 5–47.

Byrne, D. 1971. *The Attraction Paradigm.* New York: Academic Press.

Cain, L. D. 1964. "Life Course and Social Structure." In *Handbook of Modern Sociology*, ed. R. E. L. Faris. Chicago: Rand McNally.

Cairns, R. B. 1979. *Social Development: The Origins and Plasticity of Interchanges.* San Francisco: Freeman.

Cairns, R. B. 1998. "The Making of Developmental Psychology." In *Handbook of Child Psychology* (5th ed., vol. 1), ed. W. Damon and R. M. Lerner. New York: Wiley.

Camacho, L. M., and Paulus, P. B. 1995. "The Role of Social Anxiousness in Group Brainstorming." *Journal of Personality and Social Psychology* 68: 1071–1080.

Cameron, W. B. 1966. *Modern Social Movements: A Sociological Outline.* New York: Random House.

Campbell, A., P. E. Converse, W. E. Miller, and D. E. Stokes. 1960. *The American Voter.* New York: Wiley.

Campbell, D. T. 1963. "Social Attitudes and Other Acquired Behavioral Dispositions." In *Psychology: A Study of a Science* (vol. 6), ed. S. Coch. New York: McGraw-Hill.

Campbell, J. D., and P. J. Fairey. 1989. "Informational and Normative Routes to Conformity: The Effect of Faction Size as a Function of Norm Extremity and Attention to the Stimulus." *Journal of Personality and Social Psychology* 57: 457–468.

Canada, G. 1995. *Fist Stick Knife Gun: A Personal History of Violence in America.* Boston: Beacon Press.

Cantril, H. 1941. *The Psychology of Social Movements.* New York: Wiley.

Caplow, T. 1984. "Rule Enforcement Without Visible Means: Christmas Giving in Middletown." *American Journal of Sociology* 89: 1306–1323.

Caporael, L. R., and M. B. Brewer, eds. 1991. "Issues in Evolutionary Psychology." *Journal of Social Issues* 47(3).

Capozza, D., and R. Brown. 2000. *Social Identity Processes.* Thousand Oaks, CA: Sage.

Capra, F. 1972. *The Name Above the Title.* New York: Bantam Books.

Carey, G. 1994. "Genetics and Violence." In *Understanding and Preventing Violence: Biobehavioral Influences* (vol. 2), ed. A. J. Reiss, Jr., K. A. Miczek, and J. A. Roth. Washington, D.C.: National Academy Press.

Carlsmith, J. M., and A. E. Gross. 1969. "Some Effects of Guilt on Compliance." *Journal of Personality and Social Psychology* 11: 232–239.

Carlsmith, J. M., and C. A. Anderson. 1979. "Ambient Temperature and the Occurrence of Collective Violence: A New Analysis." *Journal of Personality and Social Psychology* 37: 337–344.

Carlson, M., and N. Miller. 1987. "Explanation of the Relation Between Negative Mood and Helping." *Psychological Bulletin* 102: 91–108.

Carlson, M., A. Marcus-Newhall, and N. Miller. 1990. "Effects of Situational Aggression Cues: A Quantitative Review." *Journal of Personality and Social Psychology* 58: 622–633.

Carnevale, P. J., D. G. Pruitt, and P. I. Carrington. 1982. "Effects of Future Dependence, Liking, and Repeated Requests for Help on Helping Behavior." *Social Psychology Quarterly* 45: 9–14.

Charney, I. 1974. "Marital Love and Hate." In *Violence in the Family*, ed. S. K. Steinmetz and M. A. Straus. New York: Dodd, Mead.

Charon, J. M. 2004. *Symbolic Interactionism: An Introduction, an Interpretation, an Integration.* Upper Saddle River, NJ: Prentice Hall.

Chavez, S. 2002. "A Rescuer's Tale: Fight, Then Flight." *Los Angeles Times*, April 22, p. A1.

Chemers, M. M., C. B. Watson, and S. T. May. 2000. "Dispositional Affect and Leadership Effectiveness: A Comparison of Self-Esteem, Optimism, and Efficacy." *Personality and Social Psychology Bulletin* 26: 267–277.

Chen, S. C. 1937. "Social Modification of the Activity of Ants in Nest-Building." *Physiological Zoology* 10: 420–436.

Cherlin, A. J. 1999. *Public and Private Families.* New York: McGraw-Hill.

Choo, P., T. Levine, and E. Hatfield. 1996. "Gender, Love Schemas, and Reactions to Romantic Break-Ups." *Journal of Social Behavior and Personality* 5: 143–160.

Christiansen, K. O. 1977. "A Preliminary Study of Criminality Among Twins." In *Biological Bases of Criminal Behavior*, ed. S. A. Mednick and K. O. Christiansen. New York: Gardner Press.

Chugani, H. T., M. E. Behen, F. Nagy, O. Muzik, and D. C. Chugani. 1998. "Local Brain Functional Activity Following Early Social Deprivation: A Study of Postinstitutionalized Romanian Orphans." *Annals of Neurology* 44: 555.

Cialdini, R. B. 1993. *Influence: Science and Practice* (3rd ed.). New York: HarperCollins.

Cialdini, R. B., R. J. Borden, A. Thorne, M. R. Walker, S. Freeman, and L. R. Sloan. 1976. "Basking in Reflected Glory: Three (Football) Field Studies." *Journal of Personality and Social Psychology* 34: 366–375.

Cialdini, R. B., B. L. Darby, and J. E. Vincent. 1973. "Transgression and Altruism: A Case for Hedonism." *Journal of Experimental Social Psychology* 9: 502–516.

Cialdini, R. B., and D. T. Kenrick. 1976. "Altruism as Hedonism: A Social Development Perspective on the Relationship of Negative Mood State and Helping." *Journal of Personality and Social Psychology* 34: 907–914.

Cialdini, R. B., D. T. Kenrick, and D. J. Baumann. 1982. "Effects of Mood on Prosocial Behavior in Children and Adults." In *The Development of Prosocial Behavior*, ed. N. Eisenberg. New York: Academic Press.

Cialdini, R. B., M. Schaller, D. Houlihan, K. Arps, J. Fultz, and K. A. Beaman. 1987. "Empathy-Based Helping: Is It Selflessly or Selfishly Motivated?" *Journal of Personality and Social Psychology* 52: 749–758.

Cialdini, R. B., and M. R. Trost. 1998. "Social Influence: Social Norms, Conformity, and Compliance." In *Handbook of Social Psychology* (vol. 2), ed. D. T. Gilbert, S. T. Fiske, and G. Lindzey. New York: McGraw-Hill.

Cialdini, R. B., J. E. Vincent, S. K. Lewis, J. Catalan, D. Wheeler, and B. L. Darby. 1975. "A Reciprocal Concessions Procedure for Inducing Compliance: The Door-in-the-Face Technique." *Journal of Personality and Social Psychology* 31: 206–215.

Clark, M. L., and M. Ayers. 1993. "Friendship Expectations and Friendship Evaluations: Reciprocity and Gender Effects." *Youth and Society* 24: 299–313.

Clarke, A. C. 1952. "An Examination of the Operation of Residual Propinquity as a Factor in Mate Selection." *American Sociological Review* 27: 17–22.

Clausen, J. A. 1986. *The Life Course: A Sociological Perspective*. Englewood Cliffs, NJ: Prentice Hall.

Clausen, J. A. 1995. *American Lives: Looking Back at the Children of the Great Depression*. Berkeley: University of California Press.

Cohen, E. D., ed. 1992. *Philosophical Issues in Journalism*. New York: Oxford University Press.

Cohn, E. G. 1993. "The Prediction of Police Calls for Service: The Influence of Weather and Temporal Variables on Rape and Domestic Violence." *Environmental Psychology* 13: 71–83.

Cohn, T. S. 1953. "The Relation of the F-Scale to a Response to Answer Positively." *American Psychologist* 8: 335.

Colby, A., and L. Kohlberg. 1987. *The Measurement of Moral Judgment*. Vol. 1, *Theoretical Foundations and Research Validation*. Cambridge: Cambridge University Press.

Cole, W. G. 1959. *Sex and Love in the Bible*. New York: Association Press.

Collins, N. L., and L. C. Miller. 1994. "Self-Disclosure and Liking: A Meta-Analytic Review." *Psychological Bulletin* 116: 457–475.

Comstock, G., and E. Scharrer. 1999. *Television, What's On, Who's Watching, and What It Means*. San Diego: Academic Press.

Comte, A. 1973. *System of Positive Polity*. New York: Ben Franklin. Originally published 1851–1854.

Cooley, C. H. 1909. *Social Organization*. New York: Scribner.

Cooley, C. H. 1970. *Human Nature and the Social Order*. New York: Schocken Books. Originally published 1902.

Corsaro, W. A. 1979a. "Young Children's Conception of Status and Role." *Sociology of Education* 52: 46–59.

Corsaro, W. A. 1979b. "'We're Friends, Right?': Children's Use of Access Rituals in a Nursery School." *Language in Society* 8: 315–336.

Corsaro, W. A. 1981. "Entering the Child's World: Research Strategies for Field Entry and Data Collection in a Preschool Setting." In *Ethnography and Language in Educational Settings*, ed. J. L. Green and C. Wallat. Norwood, NJ: Ablex.

Corsaro, W. A. 1985. *Friendship and Peer Culture in Early Years*. Norwood, NJ: Ablex.

Corsaro, W. A. 1988. "Routines in the Peer Culture of American and Italian Nursery School Children." *Sociology of Education* 61: 1–14.

Corsaro, W. A. 1992. "Interpretive Reproduction in Children's Peer Cultures." *Social Psychology Quarterly* 55: 160–177.

Corsaro, W. A. 1997. *The Sociology of Childhood*. Thousand Oaks, CA: Pine Forge Press.

Corsaro, W. A., and D. Eder. 1995. "Development and Socialization of Children and Adolescents." In *Sociological Perspectives on Social Psychology*, ed. K. S. Cook, G. A. Fine, and J. S. House. Needham Heights, MA: Allyn & Bacon.

Corsaro, W. A., and T. A. Rizzo. 1988. "Discussion and Friendship: Socialization Processes in the Peer Culture of Italian Nursery School Children." *American Sociological Review* 53: 879–894.

Coser, L. A. 1977. *Masters of Sociological Thought: Ideas in Historical and Social Context*. New York: Harcourt Brace Jovanovich.

Cotton, J. L. 1986. "Ambient Temperature and Violent Crime." *Journal of Applied Social Psychology* 16: 786–801.

Cottrell, N. B. 1972. "Social Facilitation." In *Experimental Social Psychology*, ed. C. G. McClintock. New York: Holt, Rinehart and Winston.

Cottrell, N. B., D. L. Wack, G. J. Sekerak, and R. M. Rittle. 1968. "Social Facilitation of Dominant Responses by the Presence of an Audience and the Mere Presence of Others." *Journal of Personality and Social Psychology* 9: 245–250.

Craig, G. J., and, D. Baucum. 2002. *Human Development* (9th ed.).

Upper Saddle River, NJ: Prentice Hall.

Crano, W. 1994. "Context, Comparison, and Change: Methodological and Theoretical Contributions to a Theory of Minority (and Majority) Influence." In *Minority Influence*, ed. S. Moscovici, A. Mucchi-Faina, and A. Maass. Chicago: Nelson-Hall.

Croteau, D., and W. Hoynes. 2003. *Media/Society: Industries, Images, and Audiences* (3rd ed.). Thousand Oaks, CA: Pine Forge Press.

Cuber, J., and P. Haroff. 1965. *Sex and the Significant Americans*. Baltimore: Penguin.

Cunningham, J. D. 1981. "Self-Disclosure Intimacy: Sex, Sex-of-Target, Cross-National, and Generational Differences." *Personality and Social Psychology Bulletin* 7: 314–319.

Cunningham, M. R. 1979. "Weather, Mood, and Helping Behavior: Quasi-Experiments with the Sunshine Samaritan." *Journal of Personality and Social Psychology* 37: 1947–1956.

Cunningham, M. R. 1986. "Measuring the Physical in Physical Attractiveness: Quasi-Experiments on the Sociobiology of Female Facial Beauty." *Journal of Personality and Social Psychology* 50: 925–935.

Cunningham, M. R., A. P. Barbee, and C. L. Pike. 1990. "What Do Women Want? Facial Metric Assessment of Multiple Motives in the Perception of Male Facial Physical Attractiveness." *Journal of Personality and Social Psychology* 59: 61–72.

Dabbs, J. M., Jr., with M. G. Dabbs. 2000. *Heroes, Rogues, and Lovers: Testosterone and Behavior*. New York: McGraw-Hill.

Dabbs, J. M., Jr., T. S. Carr, R. L. Frady, and J. K. Riad. 1995. "Testosterone, Crime, and Misbehavior Among 692 Male Prison Inmates." *Personality and Individual Differences* 18: 627–633.

Dabbs, J. M., Jr., R. L. Frady, T. S. Carr, and N. F. Besch. 1987. "Saliva Testosterone and Criminal Violence in Young Adult Prison Inmates." *Psychosomatic Medicine* 49: 174–182.

Dabbs, J. M., Jr., M. F. Hargrove, and C. Heusel. 1996. "Testosterone Differences Among College Fraternities: Well-Behaved vs. Rambunctious." *Personality and Individual Differences* 20: 157–161.

Dabbs, J. M., Jr., and R. Morris. 1990. "Testosterone, Social Class, and Antisocial Behavior in a Sample of 4,462 Men." *Psychological Science* 1: 209–211.

Dabbs, J. M., Jr., R. B. Ruback, R. L. Frady, C. H. Hopper, and D. D. Sgoutas. 1988. "Saliva Testosterone and Criminal Violence Among Women." *Personality and Individual Differences* 9: 269–275.

Dalgard, O. S., and E. Kringlen. 1978. "Criminal Behavior in Twins." In *Crime in Society*, ed. L. D. Savitz and N. Johnston. New York: Wiley.

Darley, J. M., and C. D. Batson. 1973. "From Jerusalem to Jericho: A Study of Situational and Dispositional Variables in Helping Behavior." *Journal of Personality and Social Psychology* 27: 100–108.

Darley, J. M., and B. Latané. 1968. "Bystander Intervention in Emergencies: Diffusion of Responsibility." *Journal of Personality and Social Psychology* 8: 377–383.

Darwin, C. 1859. *On the Origin of Species*. London: Murray.

Darwin, C. 1871. *The Descent of Man and Selection in Relation to Sex*. London: Murray.

Davies, J. C. 1962. "Toward a Theory of Revolution." *American Sociological Review* 27: 5–19.

Davis, K. 1940. "Extreme Social Isolation of a Child." *American Journal of Sociology* 45: 554–565.

Davis, K. 1947. "Final Note on a Case of Extreme Social Isolation." *American Journal of Sociology* 52: 432–437.

Davis, K. 1949. *Human Society*. New York: Macmillan.

Davis, M. H. 1994. *Empathy: A Social Psychological Approach*. Dubuque, IA: Brown/Benchmark.

Dawes, R. M. 1991. "Social Dilemmas, Economic Self-Interest, and Evolutionary Theory." In *Frontiers of Mathematical Psychology: Essays in Honor of Clyde Coombs*, ed. D. R. Brown and J. E. Keith Smith. New York: Springer-Verlag.

Demos, J. 1986. *Past, Present, and Personal: The Family and the Life Course in American History*. New York: Oxford University Press.

Dennis, W. 1973. *Children of the Creche*. New York: Appleton-Century-Crofts.

Derlega, V. J., S. Metts, S. Petronio, and S. T. Margulis. 1993. *Self-Disclosure*. Newbury Park, CA: Sage.

Desportes, J. P., and J. M. Lemaine. 1988. "The Sizes of Human Groups: An Analysis of Their Distributions." In *Environmental Social Psychology*, ed. D. Canter, J. C. Jesuino, L. Soczka, and G. M. Stephenson. Dordrecht, Netherlands: Kluwer.

Deutsch, M. 1973. *The Resolution of Conflict: Constructive and Destructive Processes*. New Haven, CT: Yale University Press.

Deutsch, M., and M. E. Collins. 1951. *Interracial Housing: A Psychological Evaluation of a Social Experiment*. Minneapolis: University of Minnesota Press.

Deutsch, M., and R. M. Krauss. 1960. "The Effect of Threat upon Interpersonal Bargaining." *Journal of Abnormal and Social Psychology* 61: 181–189.

Deutsch, M., and R. M. Krauss. 1962. "Studies of Interpersonal Bargaining." *Journal of Conflict Resolution* 6: 52–76.

Dewey, J. 1922. *Human Nature and Conduct*. New York: Modern Library.

Diehl, M., and W. Stroebe. 1991. "Productivity Loss in Idea-Generating Groups: Tracking Down the Blocking Effect." *Journal of Personality and Social Psychology* 61: 392–403.

Dion, K. K. 1985. "Socialization in Adulthood." In *The Handbook of Social Psychology* (3rd ed.), ed. L. Gardner and E. Aronson. New York: Random House.

Dion, K. K., and K. L. Dion. 1988. "Romantic Love: Individual and Cultural Perspectives." In *The Psychology of Love*, ed. R. J. Sternberg and J. L. Barnes. New Haven, CT: Yale University Press.

Dion, K. L. 1979. "Intergroup Conflict and Intragroup Cohesiveness." In *The Social Psychology of Intergroup Relations*, ed. W. G. Austin and S. Worchel. Pacific Grove, CA: Brooks/Cole.

Dion, K. L. 2000. "Group Cohesion: from 'Fields of Forces' to Multidimensional Construct." *Group Dynamics* 4: 7–26.

Doll, J., and I. Ajzen. 1992. "Accessibility and Stability of Predictors in the Theory of Planned Behavior." *Journal of Personality and Social Psychology* 63: 754–765.

Dollard, J., L. W. Doob, N. E. Miller, O. H. Mowrer, and R. R. Sears. 1939. *Frustration and Aggression.* New Haven, CT: Yale University Press.

Donnerstein, E. I., and J. Hallam. 1978. "Facilitating Effects of Erotica on Aggression Against Women." *Journal of Personality and Social Psychology* 36: 1270–1277.

Donnerstein, E. I., and M. Donnerstein. 1976. "Research in the Control of Interracial Aggression." In *Perspectives on Aggression*, ed. R. G. Geen and E. C. O'Neal. New York: Academic Press.

Donnerstein, E. I., and D. W. Wilson. 1976. "The Effects of Noise and Perceived Control upon Ongoing and Subsequent Aggressive Behavior." *Journal of Personality and Social Psychology* 34: 774–781.

Doob, L. W. 1947. "The Behavior of Attitudes." *Psychological Review* 54: 135–156.

Dorman, M. 2002. "The Killing of Kitty Genovese." *Newsday*, March 13, p. B2.

Dornbusch, S. M. 1955. "The Military Academy as an Assimilating Institution." *Social Forces* 33: 316–321.

Doty, R. M., B. E. Peterson, and D. G. Winter 1991. "Threat and Authoritarianism in the United States, 1978–1987." *Journal of Personality and Social Psychology* 61: 629–640.

Dreben, E. K., S. T. Fiske, and R. Hastie. 1979. "The Independence of Evaluative and Item Information: Impression and Recall Order Effects in Behavior-Based Impression Formation." *Journal of Personality and Social Psychology* 37: 1758–1768.

Dugatkin, L. 1999. *Cheating Monkeys and Citizen Bees.* Cambridge, MA: Harvard University Press.

Dumont, L. 1965. "The Modern Conception of the Individual: Notes on Its Genesis." *Contributions to Indian Sociology* 66: 13–61.

Dumont, L. 1970. *Homo Hierarchicus.* Chicago: University of Chicago Press.

Durkheim, É. 1897. *Suicide.* New York: Free Press.

Durkheim, É. 1898. *The Rules of Sociological Method.* New York: Free Press.

Durkheim, É. 1964. *The Division of Labor in Society.* New York: Free Press. Originally published 1893.

Durkheim, É. 1965. *The Elementary Forms of the Religious Life.* Trans. J. W. Swain. New York: Free Press.

Duval, S., and R. A. Wicklund. 1973. "Effects of Objective Self-Awareness on Attribution of Causality." *Journal of Experimental Social Psychology* 9: 17–31.

Duvall, E. M. 1971. *Family Development* (4th ed.). Philadelphia: Lippincott.

Dweck, C. S. 1975. "The Role of Expectations and Attributions in the Alleviation of Learned Helplessness." *Journal of Personality and Social Psychology* 31: 674–685.

Dwyer, J. 1999. "Bullets Flew After Fall—Report." *Daily News*, April 1, p. 5.

Dyer, W. W. 2002. *Wisdom of the Ages: 60 Days to Enlightenment.* New York: HarperCollins.

Eagly, A. H. 1992. "Uneven Progress: Social Psychology and the Study of Attitudes." *Journal of Personality and Social Psychology* 63: 693–710.

Eagly, A. H., and S. Chaiken. 1993. *The Psychology of Attitudes.* Fort Worth, TX: Harcourt Brace Jovanovich.

Eder, D. 1988. "Building Cohesion Through Collaborative Narration." *Social Psychology Quarterly* 51: 225–235.

Eder, D., C. C. Evans, and S. Parker. 1995. *School Talk: Gender and Adolescent Culture.* New Brunswick, NJ: Rutgers University Press.

Ehrlich, H. J. 1973. *The Social Psychology of Prejudice.* New York: Wiley Interscience.

Eibl-Eibesfeldt, I. 1989. *Human Ethology.* Hawthorne, NY: Aldine de Gruyter.

Einstein, A. 1933. "Why War? Letter to Professor Freud." Geneva: International Institute of Intellectual Cooperation, League of Nations.

Einstein, A. 1988. "The Einstein-Freud Correspondence (1931–1932)." In *Einstein on War.* New York: Random House.

Eisenberg, N. 1982. "The Development of Reasoning Regarding Prosocial Behavior." In *The Development of Prosocial Behavior*, ed. N. Eisenberg. New York: Academic Press.

Eisenberg, N. 1986. *Altruistic Emotion, Cognition, and Behavior.* Hillsdale, NJ: Erlbaum.

Eisenstadt, S. N. 1956. *From Generation to Generation: Age Groups and Social Structure.* Glencoe, IL: Free Press.

Elder, G. H., Jr. 1974. *Children of the Great Depression: Social Change in Life Experience.* Chicago: University of Chicago Press.

Elder, G. H., Jr. 1975. "Age Differentiation in the Life Course." *Annual Review of Sociology* 1: 165–190.

Elder, G. H., Jr. 1995. "The Life Course Paradigm: Social Change and Individual Development." In *Examining Lives in Context: Perspectives on the Ecology of Human Development*, ed. P. Moen, G. H. Elder Jr., and K. Lüscher. Washington, DC: American Psychological Association.

Elder, G. H., Jr. 1998. "The Life Course as Developmental Theory." *Child Development* 69: 1–12.

Elder, G. H., Jr. 2003. "The Life Course in Time and Place." In *Social Dynamics of the Life Course*, ed. W. R. Heinz and V. W. Marshall. Hawthorne, NY: Aldine de Gruyter.

Elder, G. H., Jr., and M. K. Johnson. 2003. "The Life Course and Aging: Challenges, Lessons, and New Directions." In *Invitation to the Life Course: Toward a New Understanding of Later Life*, ed. R. Settersten. Amityville, NY: Baywood.

Elder, G. H., Jr., J. Modell, and R. D. Parke. 1993. "Studying Children in a Changing World." In *Children in Time and Place: Developmental and Historical Insights*, ed. G. H. Elder Jr., J. Modell, and R. D. Parke. Cambridge: Cambridge University Press.

Elder, G. H., Jr., and A. O'Rand. 1995. "Adult Lives in a Changing Society." In *Social Psychology: Sociological Perspectives*, ed. K. Cook, G. A. Fine, and J. S. House. Needham Heights, MA: Allyn & Bacon.

Elder, G. H., Jr., and R. Rockwell. 1976. "Marital Timing in Women's Life Patterns." *Journal of Family History* 1: 34–53.

Elkin, F., and G. Handel. 1984. *The Child and Society: The Process of Socialization.* New York: Random House.

Elkind, D. 1962. "Quantity Conceptions in College Students." *Journal of Social Psychology* 57: 459–465.

Elkind, D. 1994. *A Sympathetic Understanding of the Child: Birth to Sixteen* (3rd ed.). Needham Heights, MA: Allyn & Bacon.

Elkind, D., and R. Bowen. 1979. "Imaginary Audience Behavior in Children and Adolescence." *Developmental Psychology* 15: 33–44.

Ellis, L. 1982. "Genetics and Criminal Behavior." *Criminology* 20: 43–66.

Ellul, J. 1966. *Propaganda: The Foundations of Men's Attitudes.* New York: Knopf.

Emery, R. E. 1982. "Interparent Conflict and the Children of Discord and Divorce." *Psychological Bulletin* 92: 310–330.

Engel, E. 2002. *A Dab of Dickens and a Touch of Twain.* New York: Pocket Books.

Erber, R. 1991. "Affective and Semantic Priming: Effects of Mood on Category Accessibility and Inference." *Journal of Experimental Social Psychology* 27: 480–498.

Erikson, E. H. 1995. "The Human Life Cycle." In *Erik H. Erikson: A Way of Looking at Things*, ed. S. Schlein. New York: Norton.

Eron, L. D. 1980. "Prescription for Reduction of Aggression." *American Psychologist* 35: 244–252.

Eron, L. D. 1982. "Parent-Child Interaction, Television Violence, and Aggression of Children." *American Psychologist* 37: 197–211.

Eron, L. D., L. R. Huesmann, M. M. Lefkowitz, and L. O. Walder. 1972. "Does Television Violence Cause Aggression?" *American Psychologist* 27: 253–263.

Everson, W. K. 1971. *The Triumph of the Will—The Documentary Tradition: From Nanook to Woodstock*, ed. L. Jacobs. New York: Hopkins & Blake.

Farley, J. E. 2000. *Majority-Minority Relations.* Upper Saddle River, NJ: Prentice Hall.

Fazio, R. H., M. P. Zanna, and J. Cooper. 1977. "Dissonance and Self-Perception: An Integrative View of Each Theory's Proper Domain of Application." *Journal of Experimental Social Psychology* 13: 464–479.

Feagin, J. R., and C. B. Feagin. 2003. *Racial and Ethnic Relations.* Upper Saddle River, NJ: Prentice Hall.

Feeney, J. A. 1996. "Attachment, Caregiving, and Marital Satisfaction." *Personal Relationships* 3: 401–416.

Feeney, J. A., and P. Noller. 1990. "Attachment Style as a Predictor of Adult Romantic Relationships." *Journal of Personality and Social Psychology* 58: 281–291.

Feeney, J. A., and P. Noller. 1996. *Adult Attachment.* Thousand Oaks, CA: Sage.

Fein, E., and S. Schneider. 1995. *The Rules: Time-Tested Secrets for Capturing the Heart of Mr. Right.* New York: Warner Books.

Feshbach, S. 1964. "The Function of Aggression and the Regulation of Aggressive Drive." *Psychological Review* 71: 257–272.

Feshbach, S., and R. D. Singer. 1971. *Television and Aggression.* San Francisco: Jossey-Bass.

Festinger, L. 1954. "A Theory of Social Comparison Processes." *Human Relations* 7: 117–140.

Festinger, L. 1957. *A Theory of Cognitive Dissonance.* Stanford, CA: Stanford University Press.

Festinger, L. 1964. "Behavioral Support for Opinion Change." *Public Opinion Quarterly* 28: 404–417.

Festinger, L., and J. M. Carlsmith. 1959. "Cognitive Consequences of Forced Compliance." *Journal of Abnormal and Social Psychology* 58: 203–210.

Festinger, L., S. Schacter, and K. Back. 1950. *Social Pressures in Informal Groups: A Study of a Housing Community*. New York: Harper Bros.

Festinger, L., H. W. Riecken, and S. Schacter. 1956. *When Prophecy Fails*. Minneapolis: University of Minnesota Press.

Fiedler, F. 1967. *A Theory of Leadership Effectiveness*. New York: McGraw-Hill.

Fiedler, K. 2000. "Illusory Correlations: A Simple Associative Algorithm Provides a Convergent Account of Seemingly Divergent Paradigms." *Review of General Psychology* 4: 25–58.

Fischer, K., T. J. Schoeneman, and D. W. Rubanowitz. 1987. "Attributions in the Advice Columns: II. The Dimensionality of Actors' and Observers' Explanations for Interpersonal Problems." *Personality and Social Psychology Bulletin* 13: 458–466.

Fischer, W. F. 1963. "Sharing in Preschool Children as a Function of Amount and Type of Reinforcement." *Genetic Psychology Monographs* 68: 215–245.

Fishbein, M., and I. Ajzen. 1974. "Attitudes and Opinions." *Annual Review of Psychology* 23: 487–544.

Fishbein, M., and I. Ajzen. 1975. *Belief, Attitude, Intention, and Behavior: An Introduction to Theory and Research*. Reading, MA: Addison-Wesley.

Fisher, J. D., A. Nadler, and B. M. De Paulo, eds. 1983. *New Directions in Helping: Recipient Reactions to Aid*. New York: Academic Press.

Fisher, J. D., A. Nadler, and S. Whitcher-Alagna. 1982. "Recipient Reactions to Aid." *Psychological Bulletin* 81: 27–54.

Fleming, D. 1967. "Attitude: The History of a Concept." In *Perspectives in American History* (vol. 1), ed. D. Fleming and B. Bailyn. Cambridge, MA: Charles Warren Center for Studies in American History.

Forgas, J. P., and S. Moylan. 1987. "After the Movies: The Effects of Mood on Social Judgments." *Personality and Social Psychology Bulletin* 13: 467–477.

Forsyth, D. R. 2000. "One Hundred Years of Group Research: Introduction to the Special Issue." *Group Dynamics* 4: 3–6.

Fraley, R. C., and P. R. Shaver. 1998. "Airport Separations: A Naturalistic Study of Adult Attachment Dynamics in Separating Couples." *Journal of Personality and Social Psychology* 75: 1198–1212.

Freedman, J. L. 1984. "Effect of Television Violence on Aggressiveness." *Psychological Bulletin* 96: 227–246.

Freedman, J. L. 1986. "Television Violence and Aggression: A Rejoinder." *Psychological Bulletin* 100: 372–378.

Freedman, J. L., and S. Fraser. 1966. "Compliance Without Pressure: The Foot-in-the-Door Technique." *Journal of Personality and Social Psychology* 4: 195–202.

Freud, A., and D. Burlingham. 1973. *Infants Without Families: Reports on the Hampstead Nurseries, 1939–1945*. New York: International Universities Press.

Freud, S. 1910. "Five Lectures on Psychoanalysis." In *The Standard Edition of the Complete Psychological Works of Sigmund Freud* (vol. 11), ed. J. Strachey. London: Hogarth.

Freud, S. 1962. *Civilization and Its Discontents*. Trans. J. Strachey. New York: Norton. Originally published 1930.

Freud, S. 1999. *The Interpretation of Dreams*. Trans. J. Crick, ed. R. Robertson. Oxford: Oxford University Press. Originally published 1899.

Frey, D. 1986. "Recent Research on Selective Exposure to Information." In *Advances in Experimental Social Psychology* (vol. 19), ed. L. Berkowitz. New York: Academic Press.

Frey, D., and R. A. Wicklund. 1978. "A Clarification of Selective Exposure: The Impact of Choice." *Journal of Experimental Social Psychology* 14: 132–139.

Friedrich, L. K., and A. H. Stein. 1973. "Aggressive and Prosocial Television Programs and the Natural Behavior of Preschool Children." *Monographs of the Society for Research in Child Development* 38 (Serial No. 151).

Friedrich, L. K., and A. H. Stein. 1975. "Prosocial Television and Young Children: The Effects of Verbal Labeling and Role Playing on Learning and Behavior." *Child Development* 46: 27–38.

Friedrich-Cofer, L., and A. C. Huston. 1986. "Television Violence and Aggression: The Debate Continues." *Psychological Bulletin* 100: 364–371.

Friedrich-Cofer, L. K., A. C. Huston-Stein, D. M. Kipnis, E. J. Susman, and A. S. Clewett. 1979. "Environmental Enhancement of Prosocial Television Content: Effects of Interpersonal Behavior, Imaginative Play, and Self-Regulation in a Natural Setting." *Developmental Psychology* 15: 637–646.

Gallup Poll. 1997. Poll conducted December 5.

Gallup Poll. 1999. "Media Portrayals of Violence Seen by Many as Causes of Real-Life Violence." http:www.gallup.com.

Gallup Poll. 2000a. Poll conducted February 28.

Gallup Poll. 2000b. Poll conducted May 5.

Gallup Poll. 2000c. Poll conducted November 26–27.

Galton, F. 1879. "Composite Portraits, Made by Combining Those of Many Different Persons in a Single Resultant Figure." *Journal of the Anthropological Institute* 8: 132–144.

Gangestad, S. W., and R. Thornhill. 1997. "Human Sexual Selection and Developmental Stability." In

Evolutionary Social Psychology, ed. J. A. Simpson and D. T. Kenrick. Mahwah, NJ: Erlbaum.

Gangestad, S. W., R. Thornhill, and R. A. Yeo. 1994. "Facial Attractiveness, Developmental Stability, and Fluctuating Asymmetry." *Ethnology and Sociobiology* 15: 73–85.

Gans, H. 1962. *Urban Villagers*. Glencoe, IL: Free Press.

Gans, H. 1980. *Deciding What's News: A Study of CBS Evening News, NBC Nightly News, Newsweek, and Time*. New York: Vintage Books.

Garcia-Coll, C. T., and H. A. Vazquez-Garcia. 1995. "Developmental Processes and Their Influence on Interethnic and Intercultural Relations." In *Toward a Common Destiny: Improving Race and Ethnic Relations in America*, ed. W. D. Hawley and A. W. Jackson. San Francisco: Jossey-Bass.

Gastorf, J. W., J. Suls, and G. S. Sanders. 1980. "Type A Coronary-Prone Behavior Pattern and Social Facilitation." *Journal of Personality and Social Psychology* 8: 773–780.

Gay, P. 1984. *The Bourgeois Experience: Victoria to Freud* (vol. 1). New York: Oxford University Press.

Gecas, V. 1981. "Contexts of Socialization." In *Social Psychology: Sociological Perspectives*, ed. M. Rosenberg and R. Turner. New York: Basic Books.

Gecas, V. 1989. "The Social Psychology of Self-Efficacy." *Annual Review of Sociology* 15: 1291–1316.

Gecas, V. 1992. "Socialization." In *Encyclopedia of Sociology*, ed. E. F. Borgatta and M. Borgatta. New York: Macmillan.

Gecas, V., and P. J. Burke. 1995. "Self and Identity." In *Sociological Perspectives on Social Psychology*, ed. K. S. Cook, G. A. Fine, and J. S. House. Needham Heights, MA: Allyn & Bacon.

Geen, R. G., and L. Berkowitz. 1966. "Name-Mediated Aggressive Cue Properties." *Journal of Personality* 34: 456–465.

Geen, R. G., and Donnerstein, E. I. 1998. *Human Aggression*. San Diego: Academic Press.

Geen, R. G., and E. C. O'Neal. 1969. "Activation of Cue-Elicited Aggression by General Arousal." *Journal of Personality and Social Psychology* 11: 289–292.

Geen, R. G., and D. Stonner. 1971. "Effects of Aggressiveness Habit Strength on Behavior in the Presence of Aggression-Related Stimuli." *Journal of Personality and Social Psychology* 17: 149–153.

Geen, R. G., D. Stonner, and G. L. Shope. 1975. "The Facilitation of Aggression by Aggression: Evidence Against the Catharsis Hypothesis." *Journal of Personality and Social Psychology* 31: 721–726.

Gelles, R. J. 1987. *The Violent Home*. Newbury Park, CA: Sage.

Gentry, W. D. 1970. "Effects of Frustration, Attack, and Prior Aggressive Training on Overt Aggression and Vascular Processes." *Journal of Personality and Social Psychology* 16: 718–725.

Gerard, H. B., R. A. Wilhelmy, and E. S. Conolley. 1968. "Conformity and Group Size." *Journal of Personality and Social Psychology* 8: 79–82.

Gergen, K. J., S. J. Morse, and K. A. Bode. 1974. "Overpaid or Overworked? Cognitive and Behavioral Reactions to Inequitable Rewards." *Journal of Applied Social Psychology* 4: 53–58.

Gilbert, G. M. 1951. "Stereotype Persistence and Change Among College Students." *Journal of Abnormal and Social Psychology* 46: 245–254.

Gilovich, T., V. H. Medvec, and S. Chen. 1995. "Commission, Omission, and Dissonance Reduction: Coping with Regret in the 'Monty Hall' Problem." *Personality and Social Psychology Bulletin* 21: 182–190.

Glaser, B., and A. Strauss. 1967. *The Discovery of Grounded Theory*. Chicago: Aldine.

Goffman, E. 1952. "On Cooling the Mark Out: Some Aspect of Adaptation to Failure." *Psychiatry* 15: 451–463.

Goffman, E. 1959. *The Presentation of Self in Everyday Life*. New York: Anchor-Doubleday.

Goffman, E. 1961. *Asylums*. New York: Anchor-Doubleday.

Goffman, E. 1963. *Notes on the Management of Spoiled Identity*. Englewood Cliffs, NJ: Prentice Hall.

Gold, R. L. 1969. "Roles in Sociological Field Observation." In *Issues in Participant Observation*, ed. G. J. McCall and J. L. Simmons. Reading, MA: Addison-Wesley.

Goldstein, J. H., and R. L. Arms. 1971. "Effects of Observing Athletic Contests on Hostility." *Sociometry* 34: 83–90.

Goleman, D. 1984. "Order Found in Development of Emotions." *New York Times*, June 19, p. C1.

Goleman, D. 1995. "For Man and Beast, Language of Love Shares Many Traits." *New York Times*, February 14, p. C1.

Gonzales, M. H., J. M. Davis, G. L. Loney, C. K. Lukens, and C. M. Jughans. 1983. "Interactional Approach to Interpersonal Attraction." *Journal of Personality and Social Psychology* 44: 1192–1197.

Goodman, W. 1990. "Slowly Killing Romania's Children." *New York Times*, October 5, p. C38.

Good Morning America. 1997. "Parenting: The First Years Last Forever." April 21.

Goodwin, J., and J. M. Jasper, eds. 2003. *The Social Movements Reader: Cases and Concepts*. Malden, MA: Blackwell.

Goranson, R., and L. Berkowitz. 1966. "Reciprocity and Responsibility Reactions to Prior Help." *Journal of Personality and Social Psychology* 3: 227–232.

Gordon, L. V. 1960. *Survey of Interpersonal Values*. Chicago: Science Research Association.

Gottman, J. M. 1999. *The Seven Principles for Making Marriage Work*. New York: Three Rivers Press.

Gould, R. L. 1972. "The Phases of Adult Life: A Study in Developmental Psychology." *American Journal of Psychiatry* 129: 521–531.

Gould, R. L. 1978. *Transformations: Growth and Change in Adult Life*. New York: Simon & Schuster.

Gouldner, A. W. 1960. "The Norm of Reciprocity: A Preliminary Statement." *American Sociological Review* 25: 161–178.

Grammer, K., and R. Thornhill. 1994. "Human (*Homo sapiens*) Facial Attractiveness and Sexual Selection: The Role of Symmetry and Averageness." *Journal of Comparative Psychology* 108: 233–242.

Green, B. F. 1954. "Attitude Measurement." In *Handbook of Social Psychology* (vol. 1), ed. G. Lindzey. Reading, MA: Addison-Wesley.

Green, J. A. 1972. "Attitudinal and Situational Determinants of Intended Behavior Toward Blacks." *Journal of Personality and Social Psychology* 22: 13–17.

Greenberg, M. S., and S. P. Shapiro. 1971. "Indebtedness: An Adverse Effect of Asking for and Receiving Help." *Sociometry* 34: 290–301.

Greenspoon, J. 1955. "The Reinforcing Effect of Two Spoken Sounds on the Frequency of Two Responses." *American Journal of Psychology* 68: 409–416.

Griffin, E., and G. G. Sparks. 1990. "Friends Forever: A Longitudinal Exploration of Intimacy in Same-Sex Friends and Platonic Pairs." *Journal of Social and Personal Relationships* 7: 29–46.

Griffith, J., and J. Greenlees. 1993. "Group Cohesion and Unit Versus Individual Deployment of U.S. Army Reservists in Operation Desert Storm." *Psychological Reports* 73: 272–274.

Griffitt, W., and R. Veitch. 1971. "Hot and Crowded: Influences of Population Density and Temperature on Interpersonal Affective Behavior." *Journal of Personality and Social Psychology* 17: 92–98.

Grush, J. E. 1976. "Attitude Formation and Mere Exposure Phenomena: A Nonartifactual Explanation of Empirical Findings." *Journal of Personality and Social Psychology* 33: 281–290.

Guardagno, R. E., T. Asher, L. J. Demaine, and R. B. Cialdini. 2001. "When Saying Yes Leads to Saying No: Preference in Consistency and the Reverse Foot-in-the-Door Effect." *Personality and Social Psychology Bulletin* 27: 859–867.

Guerin, B. 1986. "Mere Presence Effects in Humans: A Review." *Journal of Experimental Social Psychology* 22: 38–77.

Gunaratna, R. 2002. *Inside Al Qaeda: Global Network of Terror*. New York: Columbia University Press.

Gurney, J. N., and K. T. Tierney. 1982. "Relative Deprivation and Social Movements: A Critical Look at Twenty Years of Theory and Research." *Sociological Quarterly* 23: 33–47.

Gurr, T. R. 1970. *Why Men Rebel*. Princeton, NJ: Princeton University Press.

Guttman, L. 1944. "A Basis for Scaling Qualitative Data." *American Sociological Review* 9: 139–150.

Hallie, P. P. 1971. "Justification and Rebellion." In *Sanctions for Evil*, ed. N. Sanford and C. Comstock. San Francisco: Jossey-Bass.

Hamilton, D. L. 1981. "Illusory Correlation as a Basis for Stereotyping." In *Cognitive Processes in Stereotyping and Intergroup Behavior*, ed. D. L. Hamilton. Hillsdale, NJ: Erlbaum.

Hamilton, D. L., and R. K. Gifford. 1976. "Illusory Correlation in Interpersonal Perception: A Cognitive Basis of Stereotypic Judgments." *Journal of Experimental Social Psychology* 12: 392–407.

Hamilton, D. L., S. Stroessner, and D. Mackie. 1993. "The Influence of Affect on Stereotyping: The Case of Illusory Correlations. In *Affect, Cognition, and Stereotyping: Interactive Processes in Group Perception*. San Diego: Academic Press.

Hamilton, W. D. 1964. "The Genetic Evolution of Social Behavior." *Journal of Theoretical Biology* 7: 1–52.

Hammer, R. 1971. *The Court-Martial of Lt. Calley*. New York: Coward, McCann, and Geoghegan.

Hammersley, M., and P. Atkinson. 1990. *Ethnography: Principles in Practice*. New York: Routledge.

Handlin, O. 1963. "Review of 20th Anniversary Edition of *An American Dilemma*." *New York Times Book Review*, April 21, p. 1.

Haney, W. C., W. C. Banks, and P. G. Zimbardo. 1973. "Interpersonal Dynamics in a Simulated Prison." *International Journal of Criminology* 1: 69–97.

Hardin, B. 1968. "The Tragedy of the Commons." *Science* 162: 1243–1248.

Harkins, S. G., and J. M. Jackson. 1985. "The Role of Evaluation in Eliminating Social Loafing." *Personality and Social Psychology Bulletin* 11: 457–465.

Harragan, B. L. 1977. *Games Mother Never Taught You*. New York: Warner Books.

Harries, K. D., and S. J. Stadler. 1988. "Heat and Violence: New Findings from Dallas Field Data, 1980–1981." *Journal of Applied Social Psychology* 18: 129–138.

Harrison, A. A., and M. M. Connors. 1984. "Groups in Exotic Environments." In *Advances in Experimental Social Psychology* (vol. 8), ed. L. Berkowitz. Orlando, FL: Academic Press.

Hart, B. 1991. "Input Frequency and Children's First Words." *First Language* 11: 289–300.

Haslam, S. A., C. McGarty, and P. Brown. 1996. "The Search for Differentiated Meaning Is a Precursor to Illusory Correlation." *Personality and Social Psychology Bulletin* 22: 611–619.

Hatfield, E., and R. Rapson. 1996. *Love and Sex: Cross-Cultural Perspectives.* Needham Heights, MA: Allyn & Bacon.

Havighurst, R. J. 1953. *Human Development and Education.* New York: Longman.

Havighurst, R. J. 1972. *Developmental Tasks and Education* (3rd ed.). New York: McKay.

Hazan, C., and P. R. Shaver. 1987. "Romantic Love Conceptualized as an Attachment Process." *Journal of Personality and Social Psychology* 52: 511–524.

Hazan, C., and P. R. Shaver. 1994. "Attachment as an Organizing Framework for Research on Close Relationships." *Psychological Inquiry* 5: 1–22.

Hearold, S. 1986. "A Synthesis of 1043 Effects of Television on Social Behavior." In *Public Communications and Behavior* (vol. 1), ed. G. Comstock. New York: Academic Press.

Heider, F. 1944. "Social Perception and Phenomenal Causality." *Psychological Review* 51: 358–374.

Heider, F. 1946. "Attitudes and Cognitive Organization." *Journal of Psychology* 21: 107–112.

Heider, F. 1958. *The Psychology of Interpersonal Relations.* New York: Wiley.

Heinz, W. R., and V. W. Marshall, eds. 2003. *Social Dynamics of the Life Course.* Hawthorne, NY: Aldine de Gruyter.

Hepworth, J. T., and S. G. West. 1988. "Lynchings and the Economy: A Time-Series Reanalysis of Hovland and Sears." *Journal of Personality and Social Psychology* 55: 239–247.

Hersh, S. S. 1970. *My Lai 4: A Report on the Massacre and Its Aftermath.* New York: Vintage Books.

Hibbert, C. 2000. *Queen Victoria.* New York: Basic Books.

Hiebert, R. E., and S. J. Gibbons. 2000. *Exploring Mass Media for a Changing World.* Mahwah, NJ: Erlbaum.

Hill, C., T. Z. Rubin, and L. A. Peplau. 1976. "Breakups Before Marriage: The End of 103 Affairs." *Journal of Social Issues* 32: 147–168.

Ho, R. K. K. 1994. "America Has Become a Factory for Film Violence." *Cleveland Plain Dealer,* December 14, p. 11B.

Hobbes, T. 1904. *Leviathan.* Cambridge: Cambridge University Press. Originally published 1651.

Hobhouse, L. T. 1906. *Morals in Evolution: A Study in Comparative Ethics.* London: Chapman & Hall.

Hochschild, A. R. 2003. *The Second Shift: Working Parents and the Revolution at Home.* New York: Viking/ Penguin. Originally published 1989.

Hogan, R., G. J. Curphy, and J. Hogan. 1994. "What We Know About Leadership Effectiveness and Personality." *American Psychologist* 49: 493–504.

Hogg, M. A. 1987. "Social Identity and Group Cohesiveness." In *Rediscovering the Social Group: A Self-Categorization Theory,* ed. J. C. Turner, M. A. Hogg, P. J. Oakes, S. D. Reicher, and M. Wetherell. Oxford: Blackwell.

Hogg, M. A., and D. J. Terry. 2001. *Social Identity Processes in Organizational Contexts.* Ann Arbor, MI: Sheridan Books.

Hokanson, J. E. 1970. "Psychophysiological Evaluation of the Catharsis Hypothesis." In *The Dynamics of Aggression,* ed. E. I. Megargee and J. A. Hokanson. New York: Harper & Row.

Holahan, C. J. 1977. "Effects of Urban Size and Heterogeneity on Judged Appropriateness of Altruistic Responses: Situational vs. Subject Variables." *Sociometry* 40: 378–382.

Hollander, E. P. 1985. "Leadership and Power." In *Handbook of Social Psychology* (3rd ed., vol. 2), ed. G. Lindzey and E. Aronson. New York: McGraw-Hill.

Hollin, C. R. 1989. *Psychology and Crime.* London: Routledge.

Holmes, T. H., and R. H. Rahe. 1967. "The Social Readjustment Rating Scale." *Journal of Psychosomatic Research* 11: 213–218.

Holtz, R., and N. Miller. 1985. "Assumed Similarity and Opinion Certainty." *Journal of Personality and Social Psychology* 48: 890–898.

Homans, G. C. 1950. *The Human Group.* New York: Harcourt, Brace, & World.

Homans, G. C. 1961. *Social Behavior: Its Elementary Forms.* New York: Harcourt, Brace, & World.

Homans, G. C. 1976. "Commentary." In *Advances in Experimental Social Psychology* (vol. 9), ed. L. Berkowitz and E. Walster. New York: Academic Press.

Hovland, C. I., and R. R. Sears. 1940. "Minor Studies in Aggression: Correlation of Lynchings with Economic Indices." *Journal of Psychology* 9: 301–310.

Hovland, C. I., A. A. Lumsdaine, and F. D. Sheffield. 1949. *Studies in Social Psychology During World War II* (vol. 3). Princeton, NJ: Princeton University Press.

Howard, J. 1970. *Please Touch: A Guided Tour of the Human Potential Movement.* New York: Dell.

Huesmann, L. R. 1982. "Television Violence and Aggressive Behavior." In *Television and Behavior: Ten Years of Scientific Progress and Implications for the Eighties.* Vol. 2, *Technical Reviews,* ed. D. Pearl, L. Bouthilet, and J. Lazar. Washington, DC: National Institute of Mental Health.

Huesmann, L. R., L. D. Eron, M. M. Lefkowitz, and L. O. Walder. 1984. "The Stability of Aggression over Time and Generation." *Developmental Psychology* 20: 1120–1134.

Huesmann, L. R., K. Lagerspetz, and L. D. Eron. 1984. "Intervening Variables in the TV Violence-Aggression Relation: Evidence from Two Countries." *Developmental Psychology* 20: 746–775.

Huff, D. 1954. *How to Lie with Statistics.* New York: Norton.

Huffman, D. A. 1971. "Impossible Objects as Nonsense Sentences." In *Machine Intelligence*, ed. B. Meltzer and D. Michie. Edinburgh: Edinburgh University Press.

Huston, T. L. 1973. "Ambiguity of Acceptance, Social Desirability, and Dating Choice." *Journal of Experimental Social Psychology* 9: 32–42.

Inhelder, B., and Piaget, J. 1958. *The Growth of Logical Thinking from Childhood to Adolescence.* Trans. A. Parsons and S. Pilgram. New York: Basic Books.

Insko, C. A. 1965. "Verbal Reinforcement of Attitude." *Journal of Personality and Social Psychology* 2: 621–623.

Insko, C. A., and J. Schopler. 1998. "Differential Trust of Groups and Individuals." In *Intergroup Cognition and Intergroup Behavior*, ed. C. Sedikides and J. Schopler. Mahwah, NJ: Erlbaum.

Isen, A. M. 1970. "Success, Failure, Attention, and Reactions to Others: The Warm Glow of Success." *Journal of Personality and Social Psychology* 15: 294–301.

Isen, A. M., M. Clark, and M. Schwartz. 1976. "Duration of the Effect of Good Mood on Helping: 'Footprints on the Sands of Time.'" *Journal of Personality and Social Psychology* 34: 385–393.

Isen, A. M., N. Horn, and D. L. Rosenhan. 1973. "Effects of Success and Failure on Children's Generosity." *Journal of Personality and Social Psychology* 27: 239–247.

Isen, A. M., and P. F. Levin. 1972. "The Effect of Feeling Good on Helping: Cookies and Kindness." *Journal of Personality and Social Psychology* 34: 385–393.

Isen, A. M., T. E. Shalker, M. Clark, and L. Karp. 1978. "Affect, Accessibility of Material in Memory, and Behavior: A Cognitive Loop." *Journal of Personality and Social Psychology* 36: 1–12.

Isen, A. M., and S. F. Simonds. 1978. "The Effect of Feeling Good on a Helping Task That Is Incompatible with Good Mood." *Social Psychology Quarterly* 41: 346–349.

Isenberg, D. J. 1986. "Group Polarization: A Critical Review and Meta-Analysis." *Journal of Personality and Social Psychology* 50: 1141–1151.

Jaccard, J. 1979. "Personality and Behavioral Prediction: An Analysis of Behavioral Criterion Measures." In *Methods for Studying Person-Situation Interaction*, ed. L. Kahle and D. Fiske. San Francisco: Jossey-Bass.

Jackall, R. 1995. *Propaganda.* London: Macmillan.

Jackson, D. Z. 2000. "Injustice, American-Style." *Boston Globe*, March 1, p. A15.

James, J. A. 1951. "A Preliminary Study of the Size Determinant in Small Group Interaction." *American Sociological Review* 16: 474–477.

James, W. 1890. *The Principles of Psychology.* New York: Holt.

James, W. 1992. *Writings, 1878–1899.* New York: Literary Classics.

Janis, I. L. 1971. "Groupthink." *Psychology Today*, November, pp. 43–46.

Janis, I. L. 1982. *Groupthink: Psychological Studies of Policy Decisions and Fiascos* (2nd ed.). Boston: Houghton Mifflin.

Jankowski, M. S. 1991. *Islands in the Street.* Berkeley: University of California Press.

Johnson, C., and B. Mullen. 1994. "Evidence for the Accessibility of Paired Distinctiveness in Distinctiveness-Based Illusory Correlation in Stereotyping." *Personality and Social Psychology Bulletin* 20: 65–70.

Jones, E. E., and K. Davis. 1965. "From Acts to Dispositions: The Attribution Process in Person Perception." In *Advances in Experimental Social Psychology* (vol. 2), ed. L. Berkowitz. New York: Academic Press.

Jones, E. E., and V. A. Harris. 1967. "The Attribution of Attitudes." *Journal of Experimental Psychology* 3: 1–24.

Jones, E. E., and D. McGillis. 1976. "Correspondent Inferences and the Attribution Cube: A Comparative Reappraisal." In *New Directions in Attribution Research* (vol. 1), ed. J. H. Harvey, W. J. Ickes, and R. F. Kidd. Hillsdale, NJ: Erlbaum.

Jones, E. E., and R. E. Nisbett. 1971. *The Actor and the Observer: Divergent Perceptions of the Causes of Behavior.* Morristown, NJ: General Learning Press.

Jones, E. E., L. Rock, K. G. Shaver, G. R. Goethals, and L. M. Ward. 1968. "Pattern and Performance and Ability Attribution: An Unexpected Primacy Effect." *Journal of Personality and Social Psychology* 10: 317–340.

Jones, J. T., and J. D. Cunningham. 1996. "Attachment Styles and Other Predictors of Relationship Satisfaction in Dating Couples." *Personal Relationships* 3: 387–399.

Josephson, W. D. 1987. "Television Violence and Children's Aggression: Testing the Priming, Social Script, and Disinhibition Prediction." *Journal of Personality and Social Psychology* 53: 882–890.

Jourard, S. M. 1971. *The Transparent Self* (2nd ed.). New York: Van Nostrand Reinhold.

Jourard, S. M., and P. Lasakow. 1958. "Some Factors in Self-Disclosure." *Journal of Abnormal and Social Psychology* 56: 91–98.

Judd, C. M., C. S. Ryan, and B. Park. 1991. "Accuracy in the Judgment of

In-Group and Out-Group Variability." *Journal of Personality and Social Psychology* 61: 366–379.

Kaczmarek, P., B. Backlund, and P. Biemer. 1990. "The Dynamics of Ending a Romantic Relationship: An Empirical Assessment of Grief in College Students." *Journal of College Student Development* 31: 319–324.

Kakar, S. 1978. *The Inner World: A Psychoanalytic Study of Childhood and Society in India*. Oxford: Oxford University Press.

Kaler, S. R., and B. J. Freeman. 1994. "Analysis of Environmental Deprivation: Cognitive and Social Development in Romanian Orphans." *Journal of Child Psychology and Psychiatry* 35: 769–781.

Kalmijn, J. 1998. "Intermarriage and Homogamy: Causes, Patterns, Trends." *Annual Review of Sociology* 24: 395–421.

Kaplan, K. J., I. J. Firestone, R. Degnore, and M. Morre. 1974. "Gradients of Attraction as a Function of Disclosure Probe Intimacy and Setting Formality: On Distinguishing Attitude Oscillation from Attitude Change—Study One." *Journal of Personality and Social Psychology* 30: 638–646.

Kaplan, M. F. 1987. "The Influencing Process in Group Decision Making." In *Review of Personality and Social Psychology* (vol. 8), ed. C. Hendrick. Newbury Park, CA: Sage.

Kaplan, P. S. 2000. *A Child's Odyssey: Child and Adolescent Development*. Belmont, CA: Wadsworth.

Karau, S. J., and K. D. Williams. 1993. "Social Loafing: A Meta-Analytic Review and Theoretical Integration." *Journal of Personality and Social Psychology* 65: 681–706.

Karau, S. J., and Williams, K. D. 2001. "Understanding Individual Motivation in Groups: The Collective Effort Model." In *Groups at Work: Theory and Research*, ed. M. E. Turner. Mahwah, NJ: Erlbaum.

Karlins, M., T. L. Coffman, and G. Walters. 1969. "On the Fading of Social Stereotypes: Studies in Three Generations of College Students." *Journal of Personality and Social Psychology* 13: 1–16.

Kassin, S. 1998. *Psychology*. Upper Saddle River, NJ: Prentice Hall.

Katz, A. M., and R. Hill. 1958. "Residential Propinquity and Marital Selection: A Review of Theory, Method, and Fact." *Marriage and Family Living* 20: 237–335.

Katz, D. 1960. "The Functional Approach to the Study of Attitudes." *Public Opinion Quarterly* 24: 163–204.

Katz, D., and K. Braly. 1933. "Racial Stereotypes of One Hundred College Students." *Journal of Abnormal Psychology* 42: 280–290.

Keating, C. F. 1985. "Gender and the Physiognomy of Dominance and Attractiveness." *Social Psychology Quarterly* 48: 61–70.

Keating, D. 1979. "Adolescent Thinking." In *Handbook of Adolescent Psychology*, ed. J. Adelson. New York: Wiley.

Keelan, J. P. R., K. K. Dion, and K. L. Dion. 1998. "Attachment Style and Relationship Satisfaction: Test of a Self-Disclosure Explanation." *Canadian Journal of Behavioural Science* 30: 24–35.

Keen, S. 1986. *Faces of the Enemy*. San Francisco: HarperSanFrancisco.

Keller, H. 1980. *The Story of My Life*. Mahwah, NJ: Watermill Press. Originally published in 1902.

Kelley, H. H. 1951. "Communication in Experimentally Created Hierarchies." *Human Relations* 4: 39–56.

Kelley, H. H. 1967. "Attribution Theory in Social Psychology." In *Nebraska Symposium on Motivation* 15: 192–238.

Kelley, H. H. 1971. *Attribution in Social Interaction*. Morristown, NJ: General Learning Press.

Kelley, H. H., and J. W. Thibaut. 1978. *Interpersonal Relations: A Theory of Interdependence*. New York: Wiley.

Kelman, H. 1961. "Processes of Opinion Change." *Public Opinion Quarterly* 25: 57–58.

Kelman, H., and V. L. Hamilton. 1989. *Crimes of Obedience: Toward a Social Psychology of Authority and Responsibility*. New Haven, CT: Yale University Press.

Kenny, T. 1990. "Mission of Mercy Begins to Save Romanian Children." *USA Today*, July 12, p. 7A.

Kenrick, D. T., D. J. Baumann, and R. B. Cialdini. 1979. "A Step in the Socialization of Altruism as Hedonism: Effects of Negative Mood on Children's Generosity Under Public and Private Conditions." *Journal of Personality and Social Psychology* 37: 747–755.

Kerckhoff, C., and K. E. Davis. 1962. "Value Consensus and Need Complementarity in Mate Selection." *American Sociological Review* 27: 295–303.

Kerr, N. L., and S. E. Bruun. 1981. "Ringelmann Revisited: Alternative Explanations for the Social Loafing Effect." *Personality and Social Psychology Bulletin* 7: 224–231.

Kerr, N. L., and C. M. Kaufman-Gilliland. 1994. "Communication, Commitment, and Cooperation in Social Dilemmas." *Journal of Personality and Social Psychology* 66: 513–529.

Kerr, P. 1983. "Officials Warn Public of Frauds by Phone." *New York Times*, May 14, p. 12.

Kidd, R. F., and Marshall, L. 1982. "Self-Reflection, Mood, and Helpful Behavior." *Journal of Research in Personality* 16: 319–334.

Kilgannon, C. 2001. "The *Times* Will Publish Personal Ads." *New York Times*, March 31, p. B6.

King, J. 2002. *Hate Crime: The Story of a Dragging in Jasper, Texas*. New York: Pantheon Books.

King, M. L., Jr. 2000. "Letter from Birmingham City Jail." In *The American Reader: Words That Moved a Nation*, ed. D. Ravitch. New York: HarperCollins. Originally published 1963.

Kirschenbaum, A. 1974. "A Cog in the Wheel: The Defense of 'Obedience to Superior Orders' in Jewish Law." *Israel Yearbook on Human Rights* 4: 168–193.

Kirscht, J. P., and R. C. Dillehay. 1967. *Dimensions of Authoritarianism: A Review of Research and Theory*. Lexington: University of Kentucky Press.

Kleinfield, N. R. 2001. "U.S. Attacked." *New York Times*, September 12, pp. A1, A7.

Klenke, K. 1996. *Women and Leadership: A Contextual Perspective*. New York: Springer.

Klimek, D. 1979. *Beneath Mate Selection in Marriage: The Unconscious Motives in Human Pairing*. New York: Van Nostrand Reinhold.

Knox, D., and C. Schacht. 2000. *Choices in Relationships*. Belmont, CA: Wadsworth/Thomson Learning.

Knox, D., L. Gibson, M. E. Zusman, and C. Gallmeier. 1997. "Why College Student Relationships End." *College Student Journal* 31: 449–452.

Knox, R. E., and J. A. Inkster. 1968. "Postdecision Dissonance at Post-Time." *Journal of Personality and Social Psychology* 8: 319–323.

Kogan, N., and M. A. Wallach. 1964. *Risk-Taking: A Study in Cognition and Personality*. New York: Holt.

Kohlberg, L. 1963. "A Development of Children's Orientations Toward a Moral Order: I. Sequence in the Development of Moral Thought." *Vita Humana* 6: 11–33.

Kohlberg, L. 1969. "Stage and Sequence: The Cognitive Developmental Approach to Socialization." In *Handbook of Socialization Theory and Research*, ed. D. A. Goslin. Chicago: Rand McNally.

Kohlberg, L. 1984. *Essays on Moral Development*. Vol. 2, *The Psychology of Moral Development*. San Francisco: HarperSanFrancisco.

Kohlberg, L., and R. Mayer. 1972. "Development as the Aim of Education." *Harvard Educational Review* 42: 449–496.

Kohn, M. L. 1959. "Social Class and Parental Values." *American Journal of Sociology* 64: 337–351.

Kohn, M. L. 1969. *Class and Conformity: A Study in Values*. Homewood, IL: Dorsey.

Kohn, M. L., and C. Schooler. 1983. *Work and Personality: An Inquiry into the Impact of Social Stratification*. Norwood, NJ: Ablex.

Kornhauser, W. 1959. *The Politics of Mass Society*. New York: Free Press.

Koski, L. R., and P. R. Shaver. 1997. "Attachment and Relationship Satisfaction Across the Lifespan." In *Satisfaction in Close Relationships*, ed. R. J. Sternberg and M. Hojjat. New York: Guilford Press.

Kozulin, A. 1999. *Vygotsky's Psychology: A Biography of Ideas*. Cambridge, MA: Harvard University Press.

Kramer, B. M. 1949. "The Dimensions of Prejudice." *Journal of Psychology* 24: 389–451.

Kraus, S. J. 1995. "Attitudes and the Prediction of Behavior: A Meta-Analysis of the Empirical Literature." *Personality and Social Psychology Bulletin* 21: 58–75.

Kravitz, D. A., and B. Martin. 1986. "Ringelmann Rediscovered: The Original Article." *Journal of Personality and Social Psychology* 50: 936–941.

Krebs, D., and Adinolfi, A. A. 1975. "Physical Attractiveness, Social Relations, and Personality Style." *Journal of Personality and Social Psychology* 31: 245–253.

Krebs, D., and D. T. Miller. 1985. "Altruism and Aggression." In *Handbook of Social Psychology* (3rd ed., vol. 2), ed. G. Lindzey and E. Aronson. New York: Random House.

Kruttschnitt, C., L. Heath, and D. A. Ward. 1986. "Family Violence, Television Viewing Habits, and Adolescent Experiences Related to Violent Criminal Behavior." *Criminology* 24: 235–267.

Kuhn, D., N. Langer, L. Kohlberg, and N. Hann. 1977. "The Development of Formal Operations in Logical and Moral Judgment." *Genetic Psychology Monographs* 95: 97–188.

Kuhn, M. H. 1960. "Self-Attitudes by Age, Sex, and Professional Training." *Sociological Quarterly* 1: 39–55.

Kunz, P. R., and M. Woolcott. 1976. "Season's Greetings: From My Status to Yours." *Social Science Research* 5: 269–278.

Landers, A. 1996. *The Best of Ann Landers: Her Favorite Letters of All Time*. New York: Ballantine.

Langlois, J. H., and L. A. Roggman. 1990. "Attractive Faces Are Only Average." *Psychological Science* 1: 115–121.

Langlois, J. H., L. A. Roggman, R. J. Casey, J. M. Ritter, L. A. Rieser-Danner, and V. Y. Jenkins. 1987. "Infant Preferences for Attractive Faces: Rudiments of a Stereotype?" *Developmental Psychology* 23: 363–369.

Langlois, J. H., L. A. Roggman, and L. Musselman. 1994. "What Is Average and What Is Not Average About Attractive Faces?" *Psychological Science* 5: 214–220.

La Piere, R. T. 1934. "Attitudes Versus Actions." *Social Forces* 13: 230–237.

Latané, B. 1981. "The Psychology of Social Impact." *American Psychologist* 36: 343–356.

Latané, B., and J. M. Darley. 1970. *The Unresponsive Bystander: Why Doesn't He Help?* New York: Appleton-Century-Crofts.

Latané, B., and S. Nida. 1981. "Ten Years of Research on Group Size and Helping." *Psychological Bulletin* 89: 308–324.

Latané, B., K. Williams, and S. Harkins. 1979. "Many Hands Make Light Work: The Causes and Consequences of Social Loafing." *Journal of Personality and Social Psychology* 37: 822–832.

Laumann, E. O., J. H. Gagnon, R. T. Michael, and S. Michaels. 1994. *The Social Organization of Sexuality: Sexual Practices in the United States.* Chicago: University of Chicago Press.

Laurenceau, J. P., L. F. Barrett, and P. R. Pietromonaco. 1998. "Intimacy as an Interpersonal Process: The Importance of Self-Disclosure and Perceived Partner Responsiveness in Interpersonal Exchanges." *Journal of Personality and Social Psychology* 74: 1238–1251.

Lavee, Y., and D. H. Olson. 1993. "Seven Types of Marriage: Empirical Typology Based on Research." *Journal of Marriage and Family Therapy* 19: 325–340.

Lawler, E. J. 1992. "Affective Attachments to Nested Groups: A Choice-Process Theory." *American Sociological Review* 57: 327–339.

Le Bon, Gustave. 1960. *The Crowd: A Study of the Popular Mind.* New York: Viking. Originally published 1895.

Lee, J. A. 1988. "Love-Styles." In *The Psychology of Love*, ed. R. J. Sternberg and M. L. Barnes. New Haven, CT: Yale University Press.

Leffler, A., D. L. Gillespie, and J. C. Conaty. 1982. "The Effects of Status Differentiation on Nonverbal Behavior." *Social Psychology Quarterly* 45: 153–161.

Lerner, M. J. 1980. *The Belief in a Just World: A Fundamental Delusion.* New York: Plenum Press.

Lerner, R. M. 1986. *Concepts and Theories of Human Development* (2nd ed.). New York: Random House.

Leslie, L. A., T. L. Huston, and M. P. Johnson. 1986. "Parental Reactions to Dating Relationships: Do They Make a Difference?" *Journal of Marriage and the Family* 48: 57–66.

Levine, J. M., and R. L. Moreland. 1998. "Small Groups." In *Handbook of Social Psychology* (4th ed.), ed. D. T. Gilbert, S. T. Fiske, and G. Lindzey. New York: McGraw-Hill.

Levine, J. M., and L. Thompson. 1996. "Intragroup Conflict." In *Social Psychology: Handbook of Basic Principles*, ed. E. T. Higgins and A. W. Kruglanski. New York: Guilford Press.

Levine, R., S. Sato, T. Hashomoto, and J. Verman. 1995. "Love and Marriage in Eleven Cultures." *Journal of Cross-Cultural Psychology* 26: 554–571.

Le Vine, R. A., and D. T. Campbell. 1972. *Ethnocentrism: Theories of Conflict, Ethnic Attitudes, and Group Behavior.* New York: Wiley.

Levine, R. V., T. S. Martinez, G. Brase, and K. Sorenson. 1994. "Helping in 36 U.S. Cities." *Journal of Personality and Social Psychology* 67: 69–82.

Levinson, D. 1978. *The Seasons of a Man's Life.* New York: Ballantine.

Levinson, D. 1996. *The Seasons of a Woman's Life.* New York: Ballantine.

Lewin, K. 1947. "Group Decision and Social Change." In *Readings in Social Psychology*, ed. T. M. Newcomb and E. L. Hartley. New York: Holt.

Lewin, K., R. Lippitt, and R. K. White. 1939. "Patterns of Aggressive Behavior in Experimentally Created 'Social Climates.'" *Journal of Social Psychology* 10: 271–299.

Leyens, J. P., L. Camino, R. D. Parke, and L. Berkowitz. 1975. "Effects of Movie Violence on Aggression in a Field Setting as a Function of Group Dominance and Cohesion." *Journal of Personality and Social Psychology* 32: 346–360.

Liebow, E. 1967. *Talley's Corner: A Study of Negro Streetcorner Men.* Boston: Little, Brown.

Likert, R. 1932. "A Technique for the Measurement of Attitudes." *Archives of Psychology* 140: 5–53.

Lindsey, L. L. 1997. *Gender Roles: A Sociological Perspective.* Upper Saddle River, NJ: Prentice Hall.

Linville, P. W., and G. W. Fischer. 1993. "Exemplar and Abstraction Models of Perceived Group Variability and Stereotypicality." *Social Cognition* 11: 92–125.

Lippman, W. 1991. *Public Opinion.* New Brunswick, NJ: Transaction. Originally published 1922.

Livermore, B. 1993. "The Lessons of Love." *Psychology Today*, March-April, pp. 30–39, 80.

Livingston, J. 1996. *Crime and Criminology.* Upper Saddle River, NJ: Prentice Hall.

Locke, J. 1913. *Some Thoughts Concerning Education.* London: Cambridge University Press. Originally published 1693.

Lofland, J. 1984. *Analyzing Social Settings.* Belmont, CA: Wadsworth.

Lofland, J. 1985. *Protest: Studies of Collective Behavior and Social Movements.* New Brunswick, NJ: Transaction.

London, P. 1970. "The Rescuers: Motivational Hypotheses About Christians Who Saved Jews from the Nazis." In *Altruism and Helping Behavior*, ed. J. Macaulay and L. Berkowitz. New York: Academic Press.

Longfellow, H. W. 1955. "A Psalm of Life." In *The World's Best-Loved Poems*, ed. J. G. Lawson. New York: Harper Bros.

Longmore, M. A., W. D. Manning, and P. C. Giordano. 2001. "Preadolescent Parenting Strategies and Teens' Dating and Sexual Initiation: A Longitudinal Analysis." *Journal of Marriage and Family* 63: 322–335.

Lorenz, K. 1966. *On Aggression.* New York: Harcourt, Brace, & World.

Lorenz, K. 1974. *Civilized Man's Eight Deadly Sins.* New York: Harcourt Brace Jovanovich.

Lortie, D. C. 1959. "Laymen to Lawmen: Law School, Careers, and Professional Socialization." *Harvard Educational Review* 29: 352–369.

Los Angeles Times. 1999. "Arson, Rioting Mar the Close of Woodstock '99 Rock Festival." July 27, p. 2.

Lott, A. J., and B. E. Lott. 1965. "Group Cohesiveness as Interpersonal Attraction: A Review of Relationships with Antecedent and Consequent Variables." *Psychological Bulletin* 64: 259–309.

Luchins, A. S. 1957. "Experimental Attempts to Minimize the Impact of First Impressions." In *The Order of Presentation in Persuasion*, ed. C. I. Hovland. New Haven, CT: Yale University Press.

Lukes, S. 1973. *Individualism.* Oxford: Blackwell.

Maass, A., S. G. West, and R. B. Cialdini. 1987. "Minority Influence and Conversion." In *Group Processes*, ed. C. Hendrick. Newbury Park, CA: Sage.

MacArthur, J. R. 1992. *Second Front: Censorship and Propaganda in the Gulf War.* Berkeley: University of California Press.

Mackay, C. 1841. *Memories of Extraordinary Popular Delusions and the Madness of Crowds.* London: Office of the National Illustrated Library.

Mackie, D. M., L. I. Worth, and A. G. Asuncion. 1990. "Processing of Persuasive In-Group Messages." *Journal of Personality and Social Psychology* 58: 812–822.

Maddox, G. L., and J. Wiley. 1976. "Scope, Concepts, and Methods in the Study of Aging." In *Handbook of Aging and the Social Sciences*, ed. R. H. Binstock and E. Shanas. New York: Van Nostrand Reinhold.

Mainemer, H., L. C. Gilman, and E. W. Ames. 1998. "Parenting Stress in Families Adopting Children from Romanian Orphanages." *Journal of Family Issues* 19: 164–180.

Mannheim, K. 1952. "The Problem of Generations." In *Essays on the Sociology of Knowledge*, ed. D. Kecskemeti. London: Routledge.

Mark, V. H., and F. R. Ervin. 1970. *Violence and the Brain.* New York: Harper & Row.

Marshall, V. W. 1983. "Generations, Age Groups and Cohorts: Conceptual Distinctions." *Canadian Journal on Aging* 2(2): 51–61.

Marshall, V. W., and M. M. Mueller. 2003. "Theoretical Roots of the Life-Course Perspective." In *Social Dynamics of the Life Course*, ed. W. Heinz and V. W. Marshall. Hawthorne, NY: Aldine de Gruyter.

Marx, G. T., and D. McAdam. 1994. *Collective Behavior and Social Movements: Process and Structure.* Upper Saddle River, NJ: Prentice Hall.

Mathews, J. 2000. "Father's Complaints Shut Down Research; Agencies Act on Privacy Concerns." *Washington Post*, January 12, p. B7.

Mayer, J. D., Y. N. Gaschke, D. L. Braverman, and T. W. Evans. 1992. "Mood-Congruent Judgment Is a General Effect." *Journal of Personality and Social Psychology* 63: 119–132.

Mayo, E. 1966. *Human Problems of an Industrial Civilization.* New York: Viking.

McAlary, M. 1997. "Mark of a Murderer." *Esquire*, September, pp. 88–95, 154.

McCarthy, J., and M. N. Zald. 1973. *The Trend of Social Movements in America: Professionalization and Resource Mobilization.* Morristown, NJ: General Learning Press.

McCarthy, J., and M. N. Zald. 1977. "Resource Mobilization and Social Movements: A Partial Theory." *American Journal of Sociology* 82: 1212–1241.

McCarthy, J., and M. N. Zald. 2003. "Social Movement Organizations." In *The Social Movements Reader: Cases and Concepts*, ed. J. Goodwin and J. M. Jasper. Malden, MA: Blackwell.

McCauley, C. R., and M. E. Segal. 1987. "Social Psychology of Terrorist Groups." In *Group Processes and Intergroup Relations: Review of Personality and Social Psychology* (vol. 9), ed. C. Hendrick. Newbury Park, CA: Sage.

McConnell, A. R., J. M. Leibold, and S. J. Sherman. 1997. "Within-Target Illusory Correlations and the Formation of Context-Dependent Attitudes." *Journal of Personality and Social Psychology* 73: 675–686.

McCormick, N. B., and C. J. Jesser. 1983. "The Courtship Game: Power in the Sexual Encounter." In *Changing Boundaries: Gender Roles and Sexual Behavior*, ed. E. R. Allgeier and N. B. McCormick. Palo Alto, CA: Mayfield.

McDougall, W. 1908. *An Introduction to Social Psychology.* Boston: Luce.

McGrath, J. E., H. Arrow, and J. L. Berdahl. 2000. "The Study of Groups: Past, Present, and Future." *Personality and Social Psychology Review* 4: 95–105.

McGuire, W. J. 1968. "Personality and Susceptibility to Social Influence." In *Handbook of Personality Theory and Research*, ed. E. F. Borgatta and W. W. Lambert. Chicago: Rand McNally.

McGuire, W. J. 1985. "Attitudes and Attitude Change." In *Handbook of Social Psychology* (3rd ed., vol. 2), ed. G. Lindzey and E. Aronson. New York: Random House.

McKinney, J. C. 1966. *Constructive Typology and Social Theory.* New York: Appleton-Century-Crofts.

McMillen, D. L., and J. B. Austin. 1971. "Effect of Positive Feedback on Compliance Following Transgression." *Psychonomic Science* 24: 59–61.

McPhail, C. 1991. *The Myth of the Madding Crowd.* Hawthorne, NY: Aldine de Gruyter.

McPhail, C. 1994. "The Dark Side of Purpose in Riots: Individual and Collective Violence." *Sociological Quarterly* 35 (January): i–xx.

Mead, G. H. 1925. "The Genesis of the Self and Social Control." *International Journal of Ethics* 35: 251–277.

Mead, G. H. 1934. *Mind, Self, and Society: From the Standpoint of a Social Behaviorist*, ed. C. W. Morris. Chicago: University of Chicago Press.

Mednick, S. A., W. F. Gabrielli Jr., and B. Hutchings. 1983. "Genetic Influences in Criminal Behavior: Evidence from an Adoption Cohort." In *Prospective Studies of Crime and Delinquency*, ed. K. T. Van Dusen and S. A. Mednick. Boston: Kluwer-Nijhoff.

Mednick, S. A., W. F. Gabrielli Jr., and B. Hutchings. 1987. "Genetic Factors in the Etiology of Criminal Behavior." In *The Causes of Crime: New Biological Approaches*, ed. S. A. Mednick, T. E. Moffitt, and S. A. Stack. New York: Cambridge University Press.

Meltzer, B. N. 1972. *The Social Psychology of George Herbert Mead*. Kalamazoo: Center for Sociological Research, Western Michigan University.

Menschel, R. 2002. *Markets, Mobs, and Mayhem*. Hoboken, NJ: Wiley.

Merton, R. K. 1948. "The Self-Fulfilling Prophecy." *Antioch Review* 8: 193–210.

Merton, R. K. 1949. "Discrimination and the American Creed." In *Discrimination and National Welfare*, ed. R. MacIver. New York: Harper Bros.

Meyers, A. S. 2000. "A Look at . . . Informed Consent: A Lot of Rules, Too Many Exceptions." *Washington Post*, January 30, p. B3.

Michaels, J. W., J. M. Blommel, R. M. Brocato, R. A. Linkous, and J. S. Rowe. 1982. "Social Facilitation and Inhibition in a Natural Setting." *Replications in Social Psychology* 2: 21–24.

Mickelson, K. D., R. C. Kessler, and P. R. Shaver. 1997. "Adult Attachment in a Nationally Representative Sample." *Journal of Personality and Social Psychology* 73: 1092–1106.

Midlarsky, E., and J. H. Bryan. 1972. "Affect Expressions and Children's Imitative Altruism." *Journal of Experimental Research in Personality*.

Midlarsky, E., J. H. Bryan, and P. Brickman. 1973. "Aversive Approval: Interactive Effects of Modeling and Reinforcement on Altruistic Behavior." *Child Development* 44: 321–328.

Mielenz, C. C. 1979. "Non-Prejudiced Caucasian Parents and Attitudes of Their Children Toward Negroes." *Journal of Negro Education* 48: 84–91.

Mikulincer, J., and V. Florian. 1996. "Emotional Reactions to Interpersonal Losses over the Life Span: An Attachment Theoretical Perspective." In *Handbook of Emotion, Adult Development, and Aging*, ed. C. Magai and S. H. McFadden. San Diego: Academic Press.

Milavsky, J. R., R. Kessler, H. Stipp, and W. S. Rubens. 1982. "Television and Aggression: Results of a Panel Study." In *Television and Behavior: Ten Years of Scientific Progress and Implications for the Eighties*. Vol. 2, *Technical Reviews*, ed. D. Pearl, L. Bouthilet, and J. Lazar. Rockville, MD: National Institute of Mental Health.

Milgram, S. 1961. "Nationality and Conformity." *Scientific American* 205(6): 45–51.

Milgram, S. 1965. "Some Conditions of Obedience and Disobedience to Authority." *Human Relations* 18: 57–76.

Milgram, S. 1970. "The Experience of Living in Cities." *Science* 167: 1461–1468.

Milgram, S. 1974. *Obedience to Authority*. New York: Harper & Row.

Milgram, S., L. Bickman, and L. Berkowitz. 1969. "Note on the Drawing Power of Crowds of Different Size." *Journal of Personality and Social Psychology* 13: 79–82.

Mill, J. S. 1859. *On Liberty*. London: Parker.

Miller, J. G. 1984. "Culture and the Development of Everyday Social Explanation." *Journal of Personality and Social Psychology* 46: 961–978.

Miller, J. G. 1994. "Cultural Diversity in the Morality of Caring: Individually Oriented Versus Duty-Based Interpersonal Moral Codes." *Cross-Cultural Research* 28: 3–39.

Miller, J. G., D. M. Bersoff, and R. L. Harwood. 1990. "Perceptions of Social Responsibilities in India and in the United States: Moral Imperatives or Personal Decisions?" *Journal of Personality and Social Psychology* 58: 33–47.

Miller, L. C., J. H. Berg, and R. L. Archer. 1983. "Openers: Individuals Who Elicit Intimate Self-Disclosure." *Journal of Personality and Social Psychology* 44: 1234–1244.

Mills, C. W. 1959. *The Sociological Imagination*. New York: Oxford University Press.

Mills, R. S. L., and Grusec, J. E. 1989. "Cognitive, Affective, and Behavioral Consequences of Praising Altruism." *Merrill-Palmer Quarterly* 35: 299–326.

Minow, N., and C. Le May. 1995. *Abandoned in the Wasteland: Children, Television, and the First Amendment*. New York: Hill & Wang.

Mita, T. H., M. Dermer, and J. Knight. 1977. "Reversed Facial Images and the Mere-Exposure Hypothesis." *Journal of Personality and Social Psychology* 35: 597–601.

Modell, J., F. Furstenberg Jr., and T. Hershberg. 1976. "Social Change and Transitions to Adulthood in Historical Perspective." *Journal of Family History* 1: 7–32.

Molloy, J. T. 1975/1988. *Dress for Success.* New York: Wyden.

Molloy, J. T. 1981. *New Dress for Success.* New York: Wyden.

Moore, D. W. 1997. "AIDS Issue Fades Among Americans." *Gallup Poll*, October 17. http://www.gallup.com.

Moscovici, S. 1980. "Toward a Theory of Conversion Behavior." In *Advances in Experimental Social Psychology* (vol. 13), ed. L. Berkowitz. New York: Academic Press.

Moscovici, S. 1994. "Three Concepts: Minority, Conflict, and Behavioral Style." In *Minority Influence*, ed. S. Moscovici, A. Mucchi-Faina, and A. Maass. Chicago: Nelson-Hall.

Moscovici, S., E. Lage, and M. Naffrechoux. 1969. "Influences of a Consistent Minority on the Responses of a Majority in a Color Perception Task." *Sociometry* 32: 365–380.

Moscovici, S., and M. Zavalloni. 1969. "The Group as a Polarizer of Attitudes." *Journal of Personality and Social Psychology* 12: 124–135.

Moss, M. K., and R. A. Page. 1972. "Reinforcement and Helping Behavior." *Journal of Applied Social Psychology* 2: 360–371.

Moyer, K. E. 1976. *The Psychobiology of Aggression.* New York: Harper & Row.

Moyers, W. 1982. "World War II: The Propaganda Battle." In *A Walk Through the Twentieth Century.* Narr. Bill Moyers. Public Broadcasting System.

Mucchi-Faina, A., A. Maass, and C. Volpato. 1991. "Social Influence: The Case of Originality." *European Journal of Social Psychology* 21: 183–197.

Muhammad, L. 1996. "Exhausting Philosophy: Beliefs, Both Flip and Profound, Find Their Way to Bumper Stickers." *Louisville Courier-Journal*, August 19, p. 1D.

Mullen, B., and C. Copper. 1994. "The Relation Between Group Cohesiveness and Performance: An Integration." *Psychological Bulletin* 115: 210–227.

Mullen, B., and C. Johnson. 1995. "Cognitive Representation in Ethnophaulisms and Illusory Correlation in Stereotyping." *Personality and Social Psychology Bulletin* 21: 420–433.

Mullen, B., C. Johnson, and E. Salas. 1991. "Productivity Loss in Brainstorming Groups: A Meta-Analytic Interpretation." *Basic and Applied Social Psychology* 12: 3–24.

Murphy, P. L., and C. T. Miller. 1997. "Postdecisional Dissonance and the Commodified Self-Concept: A Cross-Cultural Examination." *Personality and Social Psychology Bulletin* 23: 50–62.

Myers, D. G. 1978. "Polarizing Effects of Social Comparison." *Journal of Experimental Social Psychology* 14: 554–563.

Myrdal, G. 1944. *An American Dilemma: The Negro Problem and Modern Democracy.* New York: Harper Bros.

Nelson, R. A. 1996. *A Chronology and Glossary of Propaganda in the United States.* Westport, CT: Greenwood Press.

Nemeth, C. J. 1994. "The Value of Minority Dissent." In *Minority Influence*, ed. S. Moscovici, A. Mucchi-Faina, and A. Maass. Chicago: Nelson-Hall.

Nemeth, C. J., and J. Wachtler. 1983. "Creative Problem Solving as a Result of Majority Versus Minority Influence." *European Journal of Social Psychology* 13, 45–55.

Neugarten, B. L. 1969. "Continuities and Discontinuities of Psychological Issues into Adult Life." *Human Development* 12: 121–130.

Neugarten, B. L. 1970. "Dynamics of Transition of Middle Age to Old Age." *Journal of Geriatric Psychiatry* 4: 71–87.

Newcomb, T. 1953. "An Approach to the Study of Communicative Acts." *Psychological Review* 60: 393–404.

Newson, J., and Newson, E. 1975. "Intersubjectivity and the Transmission of Culture: On the Social Origins of Symbolic Functioning." *Bulletin of the British Psychological Society* 28: 437–446.

Newsweek. 1997. "Your Child." Special edition. Spring-Summer.

Newsweek. 2000. "Your Child." Special edition. Fall-Winter.

New York Times. 1999. "Quotation of the Day." July 27, p. A2.

New York Times. 2002. "India: Panic and Death After Monster Reports." August 20, p. A8.

Northrop, C. E. 1990. "How Good Samaritan Laws Do and Don't Protect You." *Nursing* 20(2): 50–51.

Nuwer, H. 1999. *Wrongs of Passage: Fraternities, Sororities, Hazing, and Binge Drinking.* Bloomington: Indiana University Press.

Oakes, W. F. 1967. "Verbal Operant Conditioning, Intertrial Activity, and the Extended Interview." *Journal of Personality and Social Psychology* 6: 198–202.

Oberschall, A. 1993. *Social Movements: Ideologies, Interests, and Identities.* New Brunswick, NJ: Transaction.

O'Flaherty, W., and Derrett, J., eds. 1978. *The Concept of Duty in South Asia.* Delhi, India: Vikas.

Oliner, S. P., and P. M. Oliner. 1988. *The Altruistic Personality: Rescuers of Jews in Nazi Europe.* New York: Free Press.

Osborn, A. F. 1963. *Applied Imagination* (3rd ed). New York: Scribner.

Osgood, C. E., G. J. Suci, and P. H. Tannenbaum. 1957. *The Measurement of Meaning.* Urbana: University of Illinois Press.

Oskamp, S. 1991. *Attitudes and Opinions.* Englewood Cliffs, NJ: Prentice Hall.

Overton, W. F. 1984. "World Views and Their Influence on Psychological Theory and Research: Kuhn-Lakotes-Lunden." In *Child Development and Behavior* (vol. 18), ed. H. W. Reese. New York: Academic Press.

Owen, W. F. 1985. "Metaphor Analysis of Cohesiveness in Small Discussion Groups." *Small Group Behavior* 16: 415–424.

Page, C. 2000. "Diallo Debacle Shows System Failure." *Buffalo News*, March 3, p. 3C.

Paik, H., and G. Comstock. 1994. "The Effects of Television Violence on Antisocial Behavior: A Meta-Analysis." *Communication Research* 21: 516–546.

Pankratz, S. 2000. "Research Alert! Lessons from the UIC Shutdown." In *The Spark*. Thousand Oaks, CA: Pine Forge Press.

Parish, T. S., and R. S. Fleetwood. 1975. "Amount of Conditioning and Subsequent Change in Racial Attitudes of Children." *Perceptual and Motor Skills* 40: 79–86.

Park, B., and M. Rothbart. 1982. "Perception of Out-Group Homogeneity and Levels of Social Categorization: Memory for the Subordinate Attributes of In-Group and Out-Group Members." *Journal of Personality and Social Psychology* 42: 1051–1068.

Park, B., C. S. Ryan, and C. M. Judd. 1992. "Role of Meaningful Subgroups in Explaining Differences in Perceived Variability for In-Groups and Out-Groups." *Journal of Personality and Social Psychology* 63: 553–567.

Park, R. E., and E. W. Burgess. 1921. *Introduction to the Science of Sociology*. Chicago: University of Chicago Press.

Parke, R. D., L. Berkowitz, J. P. Leyens, S. G. West, and R. J. Sebastian. 1977. "Some Effects of Violent and Nonviolent Movies on the Behavior of Juvenile Delinquents." In *Advances in Experimental Social Psychology* (vol. 10), ed. L. Berkowitz. New York: Academic Press.

Parlee, M. B. 1979. "The Friendship Bond." *Psychology Today*, October, pp. 43–45.

Parshall, G. 1994. "Words with Attitude." *U.S. News and World Report*, June 27, pp. 61–67.

Patterson, P., and L. Wilkins. 2002. *Media Ethics: Issues and Cases*. New York: McGraw-Hill.

Paulus, P. B., and V. R. Brown. 2003. "Enhancing Ideational Creativity in Groups: Lessons from Research on Brainstorming." In *Group Creativity*, ed. P. B. Paulus and B. A. Nijstad. New York: Oxford University Press.

Paulus, P. B., V. R. Brown, and A. H. Ortega. 1997. "Group Creativity." In *Social Creativity* (vol. 2), ed. R. E. Purser and A. Montuori. Cresskill, NJ: Hampton.

Paulus, P. B., M. T. Dzindolet, G. Poletes, and L. M. Comacho. 1993. "Perception of Performance in Group Brainstorming: The Illusion of Group Productivity." *Personality and Social Psychology Bulletin* 19: 78–89.

Paulus, P. B., T. S. Larey, and M. T. Dzindolet. 2000. "Creativity in Groups and Teams." In *Groups at Work: Advances in Theory and Research*, ed. M. E. Turner. Hillsdale, NJ: Erlbaum.

Paulus, P. B., T. S. Larey, and A. H. Ortega. 1995. "Performance and Perceptions of Brainstormers in an Organizational Setting." *Basic and Applied Social Psychology* 17: 249–265.

Pavlov, I. P. 1910. *The Work of the Digestive Glands* (2nd ed.). Trans. W. H. Thompson. London: Griffin.

Pavlov, I. P. 1927. *Conditional Reflexes: An Investigation of the Physiological Activity of the Cerebral Cortex*. London: Oxford University Press.

Pearlman, J. 1999. "At Full Blast." *Sports Illustrated*, December 23, pp. 1–5.

Pegalis, L. J., D. R. Shaffer, D. G. Bazzini, and K. Greenier. 1994. "On the Ability to Elicit Self-Disclosure: Are There Gender-Based and Contextual Limitations on the Opener Effect?" *Personality and Social Psychology Bulletin* 20: 412–420.

Perper, T., and V. S. Fox. 1980a. "Flirtation and Pickup Patterns in Bars." Paper presented at the meeting of the Eastern Conference on Reproductive Behavior, New York, June.

Perper, T., and V. S. Fox. 1980b. "Flirtation Behavior in Public Settings." Paper presented at the meeting of the Eastern Region of the Society for the Scientific Study of Sex, Philadelphia, April.

Perret, D. I., K. A. May, and S. Yoshikawa. 1994. "Facial Shape and Judgements of Female Attractiveness." *Nature* 368: 239–242.

Pessin, J. 1933. "The Comparative Effects of Social and Mechanical Stimulation on Memorizing." *American Journal of Psychology* 45: 263–270.

Pettigrew, T. F. 1979. "The Ultimate Attribution Error: Extending Allport's Cognitive Analysis of Prejudice." *Personality and Social Psychology Bulletin* 5: 461–476.

Phillips, S. T., and R. C. Ziller. 1997. "Toward a Theory and Measure of the Nature of Nonprejudice." *Journal of Personality and Social Psychology* 72: 420–434.

Piaget, J. 1926. *The Language and Thought of the Child*. New York: Harcourt, Brace.

Piaget, J. 1950. *The Psychology of Intelligence*. London: Routledge.

Piaget, J. 1952. *The Origins of Intelligence in Children*. Trans. M. Cook. New York: International Universities Press.

Piaget, J. 1967. *Six Psychological Studies*. New York: Vintage Books.

Piliavin, J. A., and H. W. Charng. 1990. "Altruism: A Review of Recent Theory and Research." *Annual Review of Sociology* 16: 27–65.

Piper, W. E., M. Marrache, R. La Croix, A. M. Richardsen, and B. D. Jones. 1983. "Cohesion as a Basic Bond in Groups." *Human Relations* 36: 93–108.

Pliner, P. 1982. "The Effects of Mere Exposure on Liking for Edible Substances." *Appetite* 3: 283–290.

Popenoe, D. 2000. *Sociology* (11th ed.). Upper Saddle River, NJ: Prentice Hall.

Potter, W. J. 1998. *Media Literacy.* Thousand Oaks, CA: Sage.

Powell, C. L. 1999. "Colin Powell Remembers Father Always Stood Tall." *Chicago Sun-Times*, June 20, p. 35.

Pratto, F., J. H. Liu, S. Levin, J. Sidanius, M. Shih, H. Bachrach, and P. Hegarty. 2000. "Social Dominance Orientation and the Legitimization of Inequality Across Cultures." *Journal of Cross-Cultural Psychology* 31: 369–409.

Pratto, F., J. Sidanius, L. M. Stallworth, and B. F. Malle. 1994. "Social Dominance Orientation: A Personality Variable Predicting Social and Political Attitudes." *Journal of Personality and Social Psychology* 67: 741–763.

Prothro, E. T. 1952. "Ethnocentrism and Anti-Negro Attitudes in the Deep South." *Journal of Abnormal and Social Psychology* 47: 105–108.

Provence, S. A., and R. C. Lipton. 1962. *Infants in Institutions.* New York: International Universities Press.

Pruitt, D. G. 1998. "Social Conflict." In *The Handbook of Social Psychology* (4th ed., vol. 2), ed. D. T. Gilbert, S. T. Fiske, and G. Lindzey. New York: McGraw-Hill.

Putnam, R. D. 2000. *Bowling Alone.* New York: Simon & Schuster.

Psychology Today. 2000. "Are Freud's Dreams Coming True?" January/February, pp. 50–78.

Qian, Z., and S. H. Preston. 1993. "Changes in American Marriage, 1972–1987: Availability and Forces of Attraction by Age and Education." *American Sociological Review* 58: 482–495.

Rafter, N. H. 1992. "Criminal Anthropology in the United States." *Criminology* 30: 525–545.

Rajecki, D. W., S. B. Bledsoe, and J. L. Rasmussen. 1991. "Successful Personal Ads: Gender Differences and Similarities in Offers, Stipulations, and Outcomes." *Basic and Applied Social Psychology* 12: 457–469.

Rajecki, D. W., R. F. Kidd, and B. Ivins. 1976. "Social Facilitation in Chickens: A Different Level of Analysis." *Journal of Experimental Social Psychology* 12: 233–246.

Ray, J. J. 1980. "Authoritarianism in California 30 Years Later—with Some Cross-Cultural Comparisons." *Journal of Social Psychology* 111: 9–17.

Regan, D. T., M. Williams, and S. Sparling. 1972. "Voluntary Expiation of Guilt: A Field Replication." *Journal of Personality and Social Psychology* 24: 42–45.

Regan, D. T., and M. Kilduff. 1988. "Optimism About Elections: Dissonance Reduction at the Ballot Box." *Political Psychology* 9: 101–107.

Reifman, A. S., R. P. Larrick, and S. Fein. 1991. "Temper and Temperature on the Diamond: The Heat-Aggression Relationship in Major League Baseball." *Personality and Social Psychology Bulletin* 17: 580–585.

Reis, H. T., J. Nezlek, and L. Wheeler. 1980. "Physical Attractiveness in Social Interaction." *Journal of Personality and Social Psychology* 38: 604–617.

Reis, H. T., L. Wheeler, N. Spiegel, M. H. Kernis, J. Nezlek, and

M. Perri. 1982. "Physical Attractiveness in Social Interaction: II. Why Does Appearance Affect Social Experience?" *Journal of Personality and Social Psychology* 43: 979–996.

Richert, J. P. 1974. "The Impact of Ethnicity on the Perception of Heroes and Historical Symbols." *Canadian Review of Sociology and Anthropology* 11: 156–163.

Ridgeway, C. L. 1982. "Status in Groups: The Importance of Motivation." *American Sociological Review* 47: 76–88.

Ridgeway, C. L. 1991. "The Social Construction of Status Value: Gender and Other Nominal Characteristics." *Social Forces* 70: 367–386.

Riley, M. W. 1973. "Aging and Cohort Succession: Interpretations and Misinterpretations." *Public Opinion Quarterly* 37: 35–49.

Riley, M. W. 1979. "Introduction: Life-Course Perspectives." In *Aging from Birth to Death*, ed. M. W. Riley. Boulder, CO: Westview Press.

Ringelmann, M. 1913. "Recherches sur les moteurs animés: Travail de l'homme." *Annales de l'Institut National Agronomique* (Series 2) 12: 1–40.

Ripley, A. 2002. "Behind the Killer Smiles." *Time*, November 4, pp. 34–41.

Roane, K. R. 2000. "The Verdict: Not Guilty." *U.S. News and World Report*, March 6, p. 30.

Roberts, A. 2000. "Focus: A Tale of Two Princes." *London Sunday Telegraph*, June 11, p. 18.

Robertson, I. 1987. *Sociology* (3rd ed.). New York: Worth.

Robertson, R. 2000. "Are Freud's Dreams Coming True? At Age 100 Freud's *Interpretation of Dreams* Enjoys a New Awakening." *Psychology Today*, January-February, pp 50–52.

Robinson, D. 1976. "Fashions in Shaving and Trimming of the Beard: The Men of the *Illustrated London*

News, 1842–1972." *American Journal of Sociology* 81: 133–141.

Robinson, D. T., and J. W. Balkwell. 1995. "Density, Transitivity, and Diffuse Status in Task-Oriented Groups." *Social Psychology Quarterly* 58: 241–254.

Robinson, J. P., P. R. Shaver, and L. S. Wrightsman, eds. 1991. *Measures of Social Psychological Attitudes.* Vol. 1, *Measures of Personality and Social Psychological Attitudes.* New York: Academic Press.

Rodgers, J. E. 1999. "Flirting Fascination." *Psychology Today,* January-February, pp. 36–41, 64–70.

Roeper, R. 2001. *Urban Legends.* Franklin Lakes, NJ: New Page Books.

Roethlisberger, F. J. 1949. *Management and Morale.* Cambridge, MA: Harvard University Press.

Roethlisberger, F. J., and W. J. Dickson. 1939. *Management and the Worker.* Cambridge, MA: Harvard University Press.

Rogoff, B. 1990. *Apprenticeship in Thinking: Cognitive Development in Social Context.* New York: Oxford University Press.

Rogoff, B. 1998. "Cognition as a Collaborative Process." In *Handbook of Child Psychology,* gen. ed. W. Damon. Vol. 2, *Cognition, Language, and Perceptual Development,* ed. D. Kuhn and R. S. Siegler. New York: Wiley.

Rogoff, B., J. Mistry, A. Goncu, and C. Mosier. 1993. "Guided Participation in Cultural Activity by Toddlers and Caregivers." *Monographs of the Society for Research in Child Development* 58(8, Serial No. 236).

Rosenberg, D. 1992. "Good Samaritan Engineers." *Technology Review* 95(7): 18.

Rosenberg, L. A. 1961. "Group Size, Prior Experience, and Conformity." *Journal of Abnormal and Social Psychology* 63: 436–437.

Rosenberg, M. 1965. *Society and the Adolescent Self-Image.* Princeton, NJ: Princeton University Press.

Rosenberg, M. 1979. *Conceiving the Self.* New York: Basic Books.

Rosenhan, D. L. 1970. "The Natural Socialization of Altruistic Autonomy." In *Altruism and Helping Behavior,* ed. J. Macaulay and L. Berkowitz. New York: Academic Press.

Rosenhan, D., B. Underwood, and B. Moore. 1974. "Affect Moderates Self-Gratification and Altruism." *Journal of Personality and Social Psychology* 30: 546–552.

Rosenthal, R. 1971. "Teacher Expectations." In *Psychology and the Educational Process,* ed. G. S. Lesser. Glenview, IL: Scott, Foresman.

Rosenthal, R., and L. Jacobson. 1968. *Pygmalion in the Classroom: Teacher Expectation and Pupils' Intellectual Development.* New York: Holt, Rinehart and Winston.

Rosnow, R. L. 1991. "Inside Rumor: A Personal Journey." *American Psychologist* 46: 484–496.

Rosnow, R. L., and G. Fine. 1976. *Rumor and Gossip: The Social Psychology of Hearsay.* New York: Elsevier.

Ross, E. A. 1908. *Social Psychology: An Outline and Source Book.* New York: Macmillan.

Ross, L. 1977. "The Intuitive Psychologist and His Shortcomings: Distortions in the Attribution Process." In *Advances in Experimental Social Psychology* (Vol. 10), ed. L. Berkowitz. New York: Academic Press.

Rotenberg, K. J., and N. Chase. 1992. "Development of the Reciprocity of Self-Disclosure." *Journal of Genetic Psychology* 153: 75–86.

Rotter, J. B. 1966. "Generalized Expectancies for Internal Versus External Control of Reinforcement." *Psychological Monographs* 80(1, Whole No. 609).

Rotter, J. B. 1971. "External Control and Internal Control." *Psychology Today,* May, pp. 37–42, 58–59.

Rotton, J., and J. Frey. 1985. "Air Pollution, Weather, and Violent Crimes: Concomitant Time-Series Analysis of Archival Data." *Journal of Personality and Social Psychology* 49: 1207–1220.

Rotundo, E. A. 1993. *American Manhood: Transformations in Masculinity from the Revolution to the Modern Era.* New York: Basic Books.

Rousseau, J.-J. 1955. *Émile.* New York: Dutton. Originally published 1762.

Rousseau, J. J. 1968. *The Social Contract.* New York: Penguin. Originally published 1762.

Rowe, D. C. 1985. "Sibling Interaction and Self-Reported Delinquent Behavior: A Study of 265 Twin Pairs." *Criminology* 23: 223–240.

Rowe, D. C. 1986. "Genetic and Environmental Components of Antisocial Behavior: A Study of 265 Twin Pairs." *Criminology* 24: 513–532.

Rowe, D. C., and D. W. Osgood. 1984. "Heredity and Sociological Theories of Delinquency: A Reconsideration." *American Sociological Review* 49: 526–540.

Rubin, Z. 1970. "Measurement of Love." *Journal of Personality and Social Psychology* 16: 265–273.

Rubin, Z., and L. A. Peplau. 1973. "Belief in a Just World and Reactions to Another's Lot: A Study of Participants in the National Draft Lottery." *Journal of Social Issues* 29(4): 73–93.

Rubin, Z., and L. A. Peplau. 1975. "Who Believes in a Just World?" *Journal of Social Issues* 31: 65–89.

Rubin, Z., C. T. Hill, L. A. Peplau, and C. Dunkel-Schetter. 1980. "Self-Disclosure in Dating Couples: Sex Roles and the Ethic of Openness." *Journal of Marriage and the Family* 42: 305–317.

Ruder, M. K., and D. L. Gill. 1982. "Immediate Effects of Win-Loss on Perceptions of Cohesion in Intramural and Intercollegiate Volleyball Teams." *Journal of Sport Psychology* 4: 227–234.

Rule, B. G., B. R. Taylor, and A. R. Dobbs. 1987. "Priming Effects of Heat on Aggressive Thoughts." *Social Cognition* 5: 131–143.

Rushton, J. P. 1975. "Generosity in Children: Immediate and Long-Term Effects of Modeling, Preaching, and Moral Judgment." *Journal of Personality and Social Psychology* 31: 459–466.

Rushton, J. P. 1989. "Genetic Similarity, Human Altruism, and Group Selection." *Behavioral and Brain Science* 12: 503–518.

Russell, D. 1978. "Leave It to the Merry Prankster, the Artful Dodger, and the Body Puncher." *TV Guide*, December 16, pp. 39–44.

Rutter, M., and the English and Romanian Adoptees Study Team. 1998. "Developmental Catch-Up, and Deficit, Following Adoption After Severe Global Early Privation." *Journal of Child Psychology and Psychiatry* 39: 465–476.

Ryan, J., and W. M. Wentworth. 1999. *Media and Society: The Production of Culture in the Mass Media.* Needham Heights, MA: Allyn & Bacon.

Ryan, W. 1971. *Blaming the Victim.* New York: Pantheon.

Saegert, S. C., W. C. Swap, and R. B. Zajonc. 1973. "Exposure, Context, and Interpersonal Attraction." *Journal of Personality and Social Psychology* 25: 234–242.

Safire, W. 1990. "On Language: The Mood of 'Tude." *New York Times*, November 25, sec. 6, p. 18.

Safire, W. 1999. "The Loyalty Mystery." *New York Times*, January 11, 1999, p. A17.

Salovey, P., J. D. Mayer, and D. L. Rosenhan. 1991. "Mood and Helping: Mood as a Motivator of Helping and Helping as a Regulator of Mood." *Review of Personality and Social Psychology* 12: 215–237.

Sanders, G. S., R. S. Baron, and D. L. Moore. 1978. "Distraction and Social Comparison as Mediators of Social Facilitation Effects." *Journal of Experimental Social Psychology* 14: 291–303.

Sawyer, A. G. 1981. "Repetition, Cognitive Responses, and Persuasion." In *Cognitive Responses in Persuasion*, ed. R. E. Petty, T. M. Ostrom, and T. C. Brock. Hillsdale, NJ: Erlbaum.

Sawyer, K., and E. Pianin. 2003. "Report Blames Flawed NASA Culture for Tragedy." *Washington Post*, August 27, p. A1.

Sawyer, K., and R. J. Smith. 2003. "NASA's Culture of Certainty: Debate Was Muffled on Risks to Shuttle." *Washington Post*, March 2, p. A1.

Schacter, S., and J. E. Singer. 1962. "Cognitive, Social, and Physiological Determinants of Emotional States." *Psychological Review* 69: 379–399.

Schoeneman, T. J., and D. E. Rubanowitz. 1985. "Attributions in the Advice Columns: Actors, Observers, Causes, and Reasons." *Personality and Social Psychology Bulletin* 11: 315–325.

Schopenhauer, A. 2000. *Parerga and Paralipomena: Short Philosophical Essays* (vol. 1). Trans. E. F. J. Payne. Oxford: Clarendon Press.

Schreiber, F. R. 1973. *Sybil.* New York: Warner Books.

Schroeder, D. A., L. A. Penner, J. F. Dovidio, and J. A. Piliavin. 1995. *The Psychology of Helping and Altruism: Problems and Puzzles.* New York: McGraw-Hill.

Schuman, H. 1972. "Attitudes Versus Actions Versus Attitudes Versus Attitudes." *Public Opinion Quarterly* 36: 347–354.

Schuman, H. 1995. "Attitudes, Beliefs, and Behavior." In *Sociological Perspectives on Social Psychology*, ed. K. S. Cook, G. A. Fine, and J. S. House. Needham Heights, MA: Allyn & Bacon.

Schuman, H., C. Steeh, L. D. Bobo, and M. Krysan. 1997. *Racial Attitudes in America: Trends and Interpretations.* Cambridge, MA: Harvard University Press.

Schuman, H., and M. P. Johnson. 1976. "Attitudes and Behavior." *Annual Review of Sociology* 2: 161–207.

Schuman, H., and S. Presser. 1995. *Questions and Answers in Attitude Surveys.* Newbury Park, CA: Sage.

Schwartz, M. A., and B. M. Scott. 1997. *Marriages and Families.* Upper Saddle River, NJ: Prentice Hall.

Schwartz, S. H. 1975. "The Justice of Need and the Activation of Humanitarian Norms." *Journal of Social Issues* 31: 111–136.

Scott, W. A. 1965. *Values and Organizations: A Study of Fraternities and Sororities.* Chicago: Rand McNally.

Sears, D. O., and J. B. McConahay. 1973. *The Politics of Violence: The New Urban Blacks and the Watts Riot.* Boston: Houghton Mifflin.

Sears, D. O., and R. E. Whitney. 1973. *Political Persuasion.* Morristown, NJ: General Learning Press.

Segaloff, N. 2001. *The Everything Tall Tales, Legends, and Outrageous Lies Book.* Holbrook, MA: Adams Media.

Seligman, M. E. P. 1975. *Helpless: On Depression, Development, and Death.* San Francisco: Freeman.

Selznick, G. J., and S. Steinberg. 1969. *The Tenacity of Prejudice: Anti-Semitism in Contemporary America.* New York: Harper & Row.

Seta, C. E., and J. J. Seta. 1995. "When Audience Presence Is Enjoyable: The Influences of Audience Awareness of Prior Success on Performance and Task Interest." *Basic and Applied Social Psychology* 16: 95–108.

Seta, J. J. 1982. "The Impact of Comparison Processes on Coactors' Task Performance." *Journal of Personality and Social Psychology* 42: 281–291.

Settersten, R. A., Jr. 1999. *Lives in Time and Place: The Problems and Promises of Developmental Science.* Amityville, NY: Baywood.

Settle, T. 1993. "Fitness and Altruism: Traps for the Unwary Bystander and Biologist Alike." *Biology and Philosophy* 8: 61–84.

Shackelford, T. K., and R. J. Larsen. 1997. "Facial Asymmetry as an Indicator of Psychological, Emotional, and Physiological Distress." *Journal of Personality and Social Psychology* 72: 456–466.

Shaffer, D. R. 2000. *Social and Personality Development.* Belmont, CA: Wadsworth.

Shaffer, D. R., L. J. Pegalis, and D. G. Bazzini. 1996. "When Boy Meets Girls (Revisited): Gender, Gender-Role Orientation, and Prospect of Future Interaction as Determinants of Self-Disclosure Among Same- and Opposite-Sex Acquaintances." *Personality and Social Psychology Bulletin* 22: 495–506.

Sharp, F. C. 1928. *Ethics.* New York: Century.

Shaver, P. R., C. Hazan, and D. Bradshaw. 1988. "Love as Attachment." In *The Psychology of Love,* ed. R. J. Sternberg and M. L. Barnes. New Haven, CT: Yale University Press.

Shavitt, S., D. M. Sanbonmatsu, S. Smittipatana, and S. S. Posavac. 1999. "Broadening the Conditions for Illusory Correlation Formation: Implications for Judging Minority Groups." *Basic and Applied Social Psychology* 21: 263–279.

Shaw, G. B. 1916. *Pygmalion.* London: Constable.

Shaw, M. E., and P. R. Costanzo. 1970. *Theories of Social Psychology.* New York: McGraw-Hill.

Sherif, M. 1935. "A Study of Some Social Factors in Perception." *Archives of Psychology* 27(187): 5–59.

Sherif, M. 1936. *The Psychology of Social Norms.* New York: Harper Bros.

Sherif, M. 1966. *In Common Predicament: Social Psychology of Intergroup Conflict and Cooperation.* Boston: Houghton Mifflin.

Sherif, M., and C. W. Sherif. 1969. *Social Psychology.* New York: Harper & Row.

Sherif, M., O. J. Harvey, J. White, W. Hood, and C. W. Sherif. 1961. *Intergroup Conflict and Cooperation: The Robber's Cave Experiment.* Norman: University of Oklahoma, Institute of Intergroup Relations.

Shermer, M. 2004. *The Science of Good and Evil: Why People Cheat, Gossip, Care, Share, and Follow the Golden Rule.* New York: Times Books.

Shoemaker, P. J., and S. D. Reese. 1996. *Mediating the Message: Theories of Influence on Mass Media Content* (2nd ed.). White Plains, NY: Longman.

Short, R. E. 1990. *Sex, Love, or Infatuation.* Minneapolis, MN: Augsburg.

Sibicky, M. E., D. A. Schroeder, and J. F. Dovidio. 1995. "Empathy and Helping: Considering the Consequences of Intervention." *Basic and Applied Social Psychology* 16: 435–453.

Sidanius, J., and F. Pratto. 1999. *Social Dominance.* New York: Cambridge University Press.

Sidanius, J., F. Pratto, and L. D. Bobo. 1994. "Social Dominance Orientation and the Political Psychology of Gender: A Case of Invariance?" *Journal of Personality and Social Psychology* 67: 998–1011.

Sidanius, J., F. Pratto, and L. D. Bobo. 1996. "Racism, Conservatism, Affirmative Action, and Intellectual Sophistication: A Matter of Principled Conservatism or Group Dominance?" *Journal of Personality and Social Psychology* 70: 476–490.

Siebenaler, J. B., and D. K. Caldwell. 1956. "Cooperation Among Adult Dolphins." *Journal of Mammalogy* 37: 410–414.

Simmel, G. 1964. *The Sociology of Georg Simmel,* trans. and ed. K. H. Wolff. Glencoe, IL: Free Press. Originally published 1905.

Simmel, G. 1964. "The Metropolis and Mental Life." In *The Sociology of Georg Simmel,* ed. L. Wolff. New York: Free Press. Originally published 1905.

Simmel, G. 1971. "Fashion." In *Georg Simmel: On Individuality and Social Forms,* ed. D. N. Levine. Chicago: University of Chicago Press. Originally published 1904.

Simmons, R. G. 1991. "Presidential Address on Altruism and Sociology." *Sociological Quarterly* 32: 1–22.

Simmons, R. G., S. D. Klein, and R. L. Simmons. 1977. *The Gift of Life: The Effect of Organ Transplantation on Individual Family and Societal Dynamics.* New Brunswick, NJ: Transaction.

Simonton, D. K. 1987. *Why Presidents Succeed: A Political Psychology of Leadership.* New Haven, CT: Yale University Press.

Simpson, G. E., and J. M. Yinger. 1985. *Racial and Cultural Minorities: An Analysis of Prejudice and Discrimination.* New York: Plenum.

Simpson, J. A. 1987. "The Dissolution of Romantic Relationships: Factors Involved in Relationship Stability and Emotional Distress." *Journal of Personality and Social Psychology* 53: 683–692.

Simpson, J. A., W. S. Rholes, and J. S. Nelligan. 1992. "Support Seeking and Support Giving within Couples in an Anxiety-Provoking Situation: The Role of Attachment Styles." *Journal of Personality and Social Psychology* 62: 434–446.

Simpson, J. A., W. S. Rholes, and D. Phillips. 1996. "Conflict in Close Relationships: An Attachment Perspective." *Journal of Personality and Social Psychology* 71: 899–914.

Singer, J. L., and D. G. Singer. 1981. *Television, Imagination, and Aggression: A Study of Preschoolers.* Hillsdale, NJ: Erlbaum.

Singer, J. L., D. G. Singer, and W. S. Rapaczynski. 1984. "Family Patterns and Television Viewing as Predictors of Children's Beliefs and Aggression." *Journal of Communication* 34: 73–89.

Singh, D. 1993. "Adaptive Significance of Female Physical Attractiveness: Role of Waist-to-Hip Ratio." *Journal of Personality and Social Psychology* 65: 293–307.

Singh, D. 1995a. "Female Health, Attractiveness, and Desirability for Relationships: Role of Breast Asymmetry and Waist-to-Hip Ratio." *Ethology and Sociobiology* 16: 465–481.

Singh, D. 1995b. "Female Judgment of Male Attractiveness and Desirability for Relationships: Role of Waist-to-Hip Ratio and Financial Status." *Journal of Personality and Social Psychology* 69: 1089–1101.

Singh, D., and R. K. Young. 1995. "Body Weight, Waist-to-Hip Ratio, Breasts, and Hips: Role in Judgments of Female Attractiveness and Desirability for Relationships." *Ethology and Sociobiology* 16: 483–507.

Skinner, B. F. 1938. *The Behavior of Organisms.* New York: Appleton.

Skinner, B. F. 1948. *Walden Two.* Englewood Cliffs, NJ: Prentice Hall.

Skvoretz, J. 1988. "Models of Participation in Status-Differentiated Groups." *Social Psychology Quarterly* 51: 43–57.

Smalley, S., and M. Miller. 2002. "'Dear Policeman, I Am God.'" *Newsweek*, October 21, pp. 24–32.

Smelser, N. J. 1962. *Theory of Collective Behavior.* Glencoe, IL: Free Press.

Smith, A. 1999. *The Theory of Moral Sentiments.* Washington, DC: Regnery. Originally published 1759.

Smith, T. 1987. "That Which We Call Welfare by Any Other Name Would Smell Sweeter: An Analysis of the Impact of Question Wording on Response Patterns." *Public Opinion Quarterly* 51: 404–421.

Smith, T. W. 1981. "Can We Have Confidence in Confidence? Revisited." In *Measurement of Subjective Phenomena*, ed. D. F. Johnston. Washington, DC: U.S. Government Printing Office.

Snow, D. A., and P. E. Oliver. 1995. "Social Movements and Collective Behavior." In *Sociological Perspectives on Social Psychology*, ed. K. S. Cook, G. A. Fine, and J. S. House. Needham Heights, MA: Allyn & Bacon.

Snow, D. A., and C. L. Phillips. 1982. "The Changing Self-Orientations of College Students: From Institution to Impulse." *Social Science Quarterly* 63: 462–476.

Snyder, M. 1978. "When Belief Creates Reality: The Self-Fulfilling Impact of First Impressions on Social Interaction." In *Experiencing Social Psychology*, ed. A. M. Pines and C. Maslach. New York: Knopf.

Snyder, M., and D. Kendzierski. 1982. "Acting on One's Attitudes: Procedures for Linking Attitudes and Behavior." *Journal of Experimental Social Psychology* 18: 165–183.

Sorokin, P. A. 1948. *The Reconstruction of Humanity.* Boston: Beacon Press.

Sorokin, P. A. 1950a. *Altruistic Love.* Boston: Beacon Press.

Sorokin, P. A. 1950b. *Explorations in Altruistic Love and Behavior.* Boston: Beacon Press.

Sorokin, P. A. 1954. *Forms and Techniques of Altruistic and Spiritual Growth.* Boston: Beacon Press.

Spence, J. T., R. Helmreich, and J. Stapp. 1973. "A Short Version of the Attitudes Toward Women Scale (AWS)." *Bulletin of the Psychonomic Society* 2: 219–220.

Sprafkin, J. N., R. M. Liebert, and R. W. Poulos. 1975. "Effects of Prosocial Televised Example on Children's Helping." *Journal of Experimental Child Psychology* 20: 119–126.

Sprecher, S., and D. Felmlee. 1993. "Conflict, Love, and Other Relationship Dimensions for Individuals in Dissolving, Stable, and Growing Premarital Relationships." *Free Inquiry in Creative Sociology* 21: 115–125.

Stack, C. B. 1974. *All Our Kin.* New York: Harper & Row.

Stamp, G. H. 1994. "The Appropriation of the Parental Role Through Communication During the Transition to Parenthood." *Communication Monographs* 61: 89–112.

Staub, E. 1978. *Positive Social Behavior and Morality.* Vol. 1, *Social and Personal Influences.* New York: Academic Press.

Staub, E. 1979. *Positive Social Behavior and Morality:* Vol. 2, *Socialization and Development.* New York: Academic Press.

Stauber, J., and S. Rampton. 1995. *Toxic Sludge Is Good for You! Lies, Damn Lies, and the Public Relations Industry.* Monroe, ME: Common Courage Press.

Steblay, N. M. 1987. "Helping Behavior in Rural and Urban Environments: A Meta-Analysis." *Psychological Bulletin* 102: 346–356.

Stein, A. H., and L. K. Friedrich. 1975. "The Impact of Television on Children and Youth." In *Review of Child Development Research*, ed. E. M. Hetherington. Chicago: University of Chicago Press.

Stein, L. B., and S. L. Brodsky. 1995. "When Infants Wail: Frustration and Gender as Variables in Distress Disclosure." *Journal of General Psychology* 122: 19–27.

Steinmetz, S. K. 1977. *The Cycle of Violence: Assertive, Aggressive, and Abusive Family Interaction.* New York: Praeger.

Steinmetz, S. K., and M. A. Straus. eds. 1974. *Violence in the Family*. New York: Dodd, Mead.

Sternberg, R. J. 1988a. *The Triangle of Love*. New York: Basic Books.

Sternberg, R. J. 1988b. "Triangulating Love." In *The Psychology of Love*, ed. R. J. Sternberg and M. L. Barnes. New Haven, CT: Yale University Press.

Sternberg, R. J., and M. L. Barnes, eds. 1988. *The Psychology of Love*. New Haven, CT: Yale University Press.

Sternberg, R. J., and S. Grajek. 1984. "The Nature of Love." *Journal of Personality and Social Psychology* 47: 312–329.

Stevenson, H. W. 1992. "Learning from Asian Schools." *Scientific American*, December, pp. 70–75.

Stevenson, H. W., and S.-Y. Lee. 1990. "Contexts of Achievement: A Study of American, Chinese, and Japanese Children." *Monographs of the Society for Research in Child Development* 221 (1–2).

Stevenson, H. W., and J. W. Stigler. 1992. *The Learning Gap: Why Our Schools Are Failing and What We Can Learn from Japanese and Chinese Education*. New York: Summit Books.

Stiles, W. B., P. L. Shuster, and J. A. Harrigan. 1992. "Disclosure and Anxiety: A Test of the Fever Model." *Journal of Personality and Social Psychology* 63: 980–988.

Stokes, J. P. 1983. "Components of Group Cohesion: Inter-Member Attraction, Instrumental Value, and Risk Taking." *Small Group Behavior* 14: 163–173.

Stoner, J. A. F. 1961. "A Comparison of Individual and Group Decisions Involving Risk." Unpublished master's thesis, Massachusetts Institute of Technology.

Storms, M. 1973. "Video Tape and the Attribution Process: Reversing Actor's and Observer's Points of View." *Journal of Personality and Social Psychology* 27: 166–175.

Storr, A. 1968. *Human Aggression*. New York: Atheneum.

Stouffer, S. A., E. A. Suchman, L. C. De Vinney, S. A. Star, and R. M. Williams Jr. 1949. *The American Soldier: Adjustment During Army Life* (vol. 1). Princeton, NJ: Princeton University Press.

Strasser, T. 1981. *The Wave: The Classroom Experiment That Went Too Far*. New York: Dell.

Straus, M. A. 1974. "Leveling, Civility, and Violence in the Family." *Journal of Marriage and the Family* 36: 12–29.

Straus, M. A., R. J. Gelles, and S. K. Steinmetz. 1980. *Behind Closed Doors: Violence in the American Family*. Garden City, NY: Anchor-Doubleday.

Strauss, N. 1999. "'69 or '99, a Rock Festival Is a Combustible Mix." *New York Times*, August 8, sec. 2, p. 1.

Stroebe, W., and M. Diehl. 1994. "Why Groups Are Less Effective than Their Members: On Productivity Losses in Idea-Generating Groups." In *European Review of Social Psychology* (vol. 5), ed. W. Stroebe and M. Hewstone. Chichester, England: Wiley.

Stroebe, W., M. Diehl, and G. Abakoumkin. 1992. "The Illusion of Group Effectivity." *Personality and Social Psychology Bulletin* 18: 643–650.

Stroebe, W., C. A. Insko, V. D. Thompson, and B. D. Layton. 1971. "Effects of Physical Attractiveness, Attitude Similarity, and Sex on Various Aspects of Interpersonal Attraction." *Journal of Personality and Social Psychology* 18: 79–96.

Stryker, S. 2002. *Symbolic Interactionism: A Social Structural Version*. Caldwell, NJ: Blackburn Press.

Stryker, S. 1987. "Identity Theory: Developments and Extensions." In *Self and Identity: Psychosocial Perspectives*, ed. K. Yardley and T. Honess. New York: Wiley.

Stryker, S. 2000. "Identity Competition: Key to Differential Social Movement Participation?" In *Self, Identity, and Social Movements*, ed. S. Stryker, T. J. Owens, and R. W. White. Minneapolis: University of Minnesota Press.

Stryker, S., and R. Serpe. 1982. "Towards a Theory of Family Influence in the Socialization of Children." In *Research in Sociology of Education and Socialization* (Vol. 4), ed. A. Kerckhoff. Greenwich, CT: JAI Press.

Stryker, S., T. J. Owens, and R. W. White, eds. 2000. *Self, Identity, and Social Movements*. Minneapolis: University of Minnesota Press.

Sumner, W. G. 1960. *Folkways*. New York: Mentor Books.

Sweeney, P. D., and K. L. Gruber. 1984. "Selective Exposure: Voter Information Preferences and the Watergate Affair." *Journal of Personality and Social Psychology* 46: 1208–1221.

Tajfel, H. 1981. *Human Groups and Social Categories: Studies in Social Psychology*. Cambridge: Cambridge University Press.

Tajfel, H. 1982a. *Social Identity and Intergroup Relations*. Cambridge: Cambridge University Press.

Tajfel, H. 1982b. "Social Psychology of Intergroup Relations." *Annual Review of Psychology* 33: 1–39.

Tajfel, H., and M. G. Billig. 1974. "Familiarity and Categorization in Intergroup Behavior." *Journal of Experimental Social Psychology* 10: 159–170.

Tajfel, H., M. G. Billig, R. P. Bundy, and C. Flament. 1971. "Social Categorization and Intergroup Behavior." *European Journal of Social Psychology* 1: 149–178.

Tajfel, H., and J. C. Turner. 1979. "An Integrative Theory of Intergroup Conflict." In *The Social Psychology of Intergroup Relations*, W. G. Austin and S. Worchel. Monterey, CA: Brooks/Cole.

Tannen, D. 1990. *You Just Don't Understand: Women and Men in Conversation.* New York: Ballantine Books.

Tannen, D. 1998. *The Argument Culture: Moving from Debate to Dialogue.* New York: Random House.

Taylor, G. 1990. "Good Samaritans Kick." *National Law Journal* 12 (44): 2.

Taylor, L. 1984. *Born to Crime: The Genetic Causes of Criminal Behavior.* Westport, CT: Greenwood Press.

Teger, A. I. 1980. *Too Much Invested to Quit.* New York: Pergamon Press.

Terborg, J. R., C. H. Castore, and J. A. De Ninno. 1976. "A Longitudinal Field Investigation of the Impact of Group Composition on Group Performance and Cohesion." *Journal of Personality and Social Psychology* 34: 782–790.

Teske, R. H. C., Jr., and M. H. Hazlett. 1985. "A Scale for the Measurement of Attitudes Toward Handgun Control." *Journal of Criminal Justice* 13: 373–379.

't Hart, P. 1991. "Groupthink, Risk-Taking, and Recklessness: Quality of Process and Outcome in Policy Decision Making." *Politics and the Individual* 1: 67–90.

Thibaut, J. W., and H. H. Kelley. 1959a. *Interpersonal Relations: A Theory of Interdependence.* New York: Wiley.

Thibaut, J. W., and H. H. Kelley. 1959b. *The Social Psychology of Groups.* New York: Wiley.

Thoits, P. A., and L. K. Virshup. 1995. "*Me*'s and *We*'s: Forms and Functions of Social Identities." In *Self and Identity: Fundamental Issues,* ed. R. D. Ashmore and L. Jussim. New York: Oxford University Press.

Thomas, E. 1996. "The End of the Road." *Newsweek,* April 15, p. 36.

Thomas, R. M. 2000. *Comparing Theories of Child Development.* Belmont, CA: Wadsworth.

Thomas, W. I., and D. Thomas. 1928. *The Child in America.* New York: Knopf.

Thomas, W. I., and F. Znaniecki. 1918. *The Polish Peasant in Europe and America.* Chicago: University of Chicago Press.

Thorndike, E. L. 1898. *Animal Intelligence.* New York: Macmillan.

Thorne, Barrie. 1997. *Gender Play: Girls and Boys in School.* New Brunswick, NJ: Rutgers University Press.

Thurstone, L. L. 1928. "Attitudes Can Be Measured." *American Journal of Sociology* 33: 529–554.

Thurstone, L. L. 1946. "Comment." *American Journal of Sociology* 52: 39–40.

Tickle-Degen, L., and R. Rosenthal. 1987. "Group Rapport and Nonverbal Behavior." In *Review of Personality and Social Psychology* (vol. 9), ed. C. Hendrick. Newbury Park, CA: Sage.

Time. 1997. "How a Child's Brain Develops." Special report. February 3.

Tocqueville, A. de. 1955. *The Old Regime and the French Revolution,* trans. S. Gilbert. Garden City, NY: Anchor-Doubleday. Originally published 1856.

Tolson, J. 1999. "The Bible of Dreams Turns 100: A Century On, Freud Still Influential." *U.S. News and World Report,* November 8, p. 79.

Tönnies, F. 1988. *Community and Society.* New Brunswick, NJ: Transaction. Originally published 1887.

Tressider, M. 1997. *The Secret Language of Love.* San Francisco: Chronicle Books.

Triandis, H. C. 1971. *Attitude and Attitude Change.* New York: Wiley.

Triandis, H. C., R. Bontempo, M. J. Villareal, M. Asai, and N. Lucca. 1988. "Individualism and Collectivism: Cross-Cultural Perspectives on Self-Ingroup Relationships." *Journal of Personality and Social Psychology* 54: 323–338.

Trinkhaus, J. 1994. "Wearing Baseball-Type Caps: An Informal Look." *Psychological Reports* 74: 585–587.

Triplett, N. 1898. "The Dynamogenic Factors in Pace Making and Competition." *American Journal of Psychology* 9: 507–533.

Trivers, R. L. 1971. "The Evolution of Reciprocal Altruism." *Quarterly Review of Biology* 46: 35–57.

Trotter, R. J. 1992. "The Three Faces of Love." In *Marriage and Family in a Changing Society,* ed. J. M. Henslin. New York: Free Press.

Tucker, A. W. 1955. "Game Theory and Programming." Department of Mathematics, The Oklahoma Agricultural and Mechanical College, Stillwater. (Mimeographed.)

Turner, J. C. 1978. "Social Categorization and Social Discrimination in the Minimal Group Paradigm." In *Differentiation Between Social Groups: Studies in the Social Psychology of Intergroup Relations,* ed. H. Tajfel. London: Academic Press.

Turner, J. C. 1987. *Rediscovering the Social Group: A Self-Categorization Theory.* New York: Blackwell.

Turner, J. H. 1978. *The Structure of Sociological Theory.* Homewood, IL: Dorsey Press.

Turner, R. H., and L. M. Killian. 1987. *Collective Behavior* (3rd ed.). Englewood Cliffs, NJ: Prentice Hall.

Uhlenberg, P., and S. Miner. 1995. "Life Course and Aging: A Cohort Perspective." In *Handbook of Aging and the Social Sciences* (4th ed.), ed. R. H. Binstock and L. K. George. San Diego: Academic Press.

Vago, S. 1999. *Social Change* (4th ed.). Upper Saddle River, NJ: Prentice Hall.

Valenstein, E. S. 1986. *Great and Desperate Cures: The Rise and Decline of Psychosurgery and Other Radical Treatments for Mental Illness.* New York: Basic Books.

Van Dusen, K. T., S. A. Mednick, W. F. Gabrielli Jr., and B. Hutchings.

1983. "Social Class and Crime: Genetics and Environment." In *Prospective Studies of Crime and Delinquency*, ed. K. T. Van Dusen and S. A. Mednick. Boston: Kluwer-Nijhoff.

van Gennep, A. 1960. *The Rites of Passage*, trans. M. B. Visedom and G. L. Caffe. Chicago: University of Chicago Press. Originally published 1910.

Van Manen, K. J., and S. K. Whitbourne. 1997. "Psychosocial Development and Life Events in Adulthood." *Psychology and Aging* 12: 239–246.

Van Sant, P. 1991. "Report Updates Living Conditions for Romanian Orphans." *CBS Evening News*, July 26.

Veblen, T. 1930. *The Theory of the Leisure Class*. New York: Modern Library. Originally published 1911.

Verplanck, W. S. 1955. "The Control of the Content of Conversation: Reinforcement of Statements of Opinion." *Journal of Abnormal and Social Psychology* 51: 668–676.

Vidmar, N., and M. Rokeach. 1974. "Archie Bunker's Bigotry: A Study in Selective Perception and Exposure." *Journal of Communication* 24: 36–47.

Vold, G., and T. Bernard. 1986. *Theoretical Criminology* (3rd ed.). New York: Oxford University Press.

Volpato, C., A. Maass, A. Mucchi-Faina, and E. Vitti. 1990. "Minority Influence and Social Categorization." *European Journal of Social Psychology* 20: 119–132.

von Hecker, U. 1993. "On Memory Effects of Heiderian Balance: A Code Hypothesis and an Inconsistency Hypothesis." *Journal of Experimental Social Psychology* 29: 358–386.

Vygotsky, L. S. 1962. *Thought and Language*, trans. E. Hanfmann and B. Vakar. Cambridge, MA: MIT Press. Originally published 1934.

Vygotsky, L. S. 1978. *Mind in Society: The Development of Higher Psychological Processes*, ed. M. Cole, V. John-Steiner, S. Scribner, and E. Souberman. Cambridge, MA: Harvard University Press. Originally published 1930, 1933, 1935.

Wadsworth, B. J. 1979. *Piaget's Theory of Cognitive Development*. New York: Longman.

Wagner, J. A. 1995. "Studies of Individualism-Collectivism: Effects on Cooperation in Groups." *Academy of Management Review* 38: 152–172.

Wald, M. L. 2003. "Shuttle Flights May Resume Before NASA Culture Changes." *New York Times*, August 8, p. A15.

Waldman, A. 2000. "District Attorney Defends Handling of the Diallo Case." *New York Times*, p. A1.

Walker, I., and M. Crogan. 1998. "Academic Performance, Prejudice, and the Jigsaw Classroom: New Pieces to the Puzzle." *Journal of Community and Applied Social Psychology* 8: 381–393.

Wallace, R. A., and A. Wolf. 1999. *Contemporary Sociological Theory: Expanding the Classical Tradition*. Upper Saddle River, NJ: Prentice Hall.

Wallace, W. 1971. *The Logic of Science in Sociology*. Chicago: Aldine-Atherton.

Waller, W. 1937. "The Rating and Dating Complex." *American Sociological Review* 2: 727–734.

Wallerstein, J. S., and S. Blakeslee. 1995. *The Good Marriage: How and Why Love Lasts*. Boston: Houghton Mifflin.

Walster, E., E. Aronson, D. Abrahams, and L. Rottman. 1966. "Importance of Physical Attractiveness in Dating Behavior." *Journal of Personality and Social Psychology* 4: 508–516.

Walster, E., E. Berscheid, and G. W. Walster. 1973. "New Directions in Equity Research." *Journal of Personality and Social Psychology* 25: 151–176.

Walster, E., and G. W. Walster. 1969. "The Matching Hypothesis." *Journal of Personality and Social Psychology* 6: 248–253.

Walster E., G. W. Walster, and E. Berscheid. 1978. *Equity: Theory and Research*. Needham Heights, MA: Allyn & Bacon.

Walters, G. D. 1992. "A Meta-Analysis of the Gene-Crime Relationship." *Criminology* 30: 595–613.

Walters, G. D., and T. W. White. 1989. "Heredity and Crime: Bad Genes or Bad Research?" *Criminology* 27: 455–485.

Ward, O. 1990. "Romanian Orphans Suffer Despite Aid: Lack of Trained Staff Is Endangering Lives." *Toronto Star*, July 14, p. A3.

Ware, C. F. 1935. *Greenwich Village*. Boston: Houghton Mifflin.

Washington Post/ABC News. 2000. Poll conducted November 27.

Watson, J. B. 1913. "Psychology as the Behaviorist Views It." *Psychological Review* 20: 158–177.

Watson, J. B. 1925. *Behaviorism*. New York: Norton.

Weber, M. 1930. *The Protestant Ethic and the Spirit of Capitalism*, trans. T. Parsons. New York: Scribner.

Weber, M. 1977. "Politics as a Vocation." In *From Max Weber: Essays in Sociology*, ed. and trans. H. Gerth and C. W. Mills. New York: Oxford University Press.

Webster, N. 1824. *The American Spelling Book*. Bedford, MA: Applewood. Originally published 1788.

Wegener, D. T., and R. E. Petty. 1994. "Mood Management Across Affective States: The Hedonic Contingency Hypothesis." *Journal of Personality and Social Psychology* 66: 1034–1048.

Wegener, D. T., R. E. Petty, and D. J. Klein. 1994. "Effects of Mood on High Elaboration Attitude Change: The Mediating Role of Likelihood Judgments." *European Journal of Social Psychology* 24: 25–44.

Weigel, R., and L. Newman. 1976. "Increasing Attitude-Behavior Correspondence by Broadening the Scope of the Behavioral Measure." *Journal of Personality and Social Psychology* 30: 793–802.

Weiner, B. 1986. *An Attributional Theory of Motivation and Emotion.* New York: Springer-Verlag.

Weiner, B., I. Freize, A. Kukla, L. Reed, B. Rest, and R. M. Rosenbaum. 1971. *Perceiving the Causes of Success and Failure.* Morristown, NJ: General Learning Press.

Weiss, R. F. 1968. "An Extension of Hullian Learning Theory to Persuasive Communication." In *Psychological Foundations of Attitudes,* ed. A. G. Greenwald, T. C. Brock, and T. M. Ostrom. New York: Academic Press.

Wertsch, J. V., and P. Tulviste. 1992. "L. S. Vygotsky and Contemporary Developmental Psychology." *Developmental Psychology* 28: 548–558.

Whitbourne, S. K. 1986. *The Me I Know: A Study of Adult Development.* New York: Springer-Verlag.

Whitbourne, S. K., and J. B. Ebmeyer. 1990. *Identity and Intimacy in Marriage: A Study of Couples.* New York: Springer-Verlag.

White, R. W. 1993. *Provisional Irish Republicans.* Westport, CT: Greenwood Press.

Whitehead, B. D., and D. Popenoe. 2001. "The State of Our Unions: The Social Health of Marriage in America, 2001." *National Marriage Project,* http://www.marriage.rutgers.edu.

Whiting, J. W. M., R. Kluckhohn, and A. Anthony. 1958. "The Function of Male Initiation Ceremonies at Puberty." In *Readings in Social Psychology,* ed. E. E. Maccoby, T. M. Newcomb, and E. L. Hartley. New York: Holt.

Whitley, B. E., Jr. 1999. "Right-Wing Authoritarianism, Social Dominance Orientation, and Prejudice."

Journal of Personality and Social Psychology 77: 126–134.

Whitney, K., L. M. Sagrestano, and C. Maslach. 1994. "Establishing the Social Impact of Individuation." *Journal of Personality and Social Psychology* 66: 1140–1153.

Whyte, W. F. 1943. *Street Corner Society: The Social Structure of an Italian Slum.* Chicago: University of Chicago Press.

Whyte, W. H., Jr. 1956. *The Organization Man.* New York: Simon & Schuster.

Wicker, A. 1969. "Attitude Versus Actions: The Relationship of Verbal and Overt Behavioral Responses to Attitude Objects." *Journal of Social Issues* 25(4): 41–78.

Wicker, T. 1975. *A Time to Die.* New York: Quadrangle/Times Books.

Widom, C. S. 1989. "The Intergenerational Transmission of Violence." In *Pathways to Criminal Violence,* ed. N. A. Weiner and M. E. Wolfgang. Newbury Park, CA: Sage.

Wiggins, J. S., N. Wiggins, and J. C. Conger. 1968. "Correlates of Heterosexual Somatic Preference." *Journal of Personality and Social Psychology* 10: 82–90.

Wilder, D. A. 1986. "Social Categorization: Implications for Creation and Reduction of Intergroup Bias." In *Advances in Experimental Social Psychology* (vol. 19), ed. L. Berkowitz. New York: Academic Press.

Will, G. F. 1990. *Men at Work: The Craft of Baseball.* New York: Harper Perennial.

Williams, M. R., and M. D. Cooper. 2002. *Power Persuasion: Moving an Ancient Art into the Media Age.* Greenwood, IN: Educational Video Group.

Williams, R. M., Jr. 1984. "Field Observations and Surveys in Combat Zones." *Social Psychology Quarterly* 47: 186–192.

Williamson, J. B., D. A. Karp, J. R. Dalphin, and P. S. Gray. 1982. *The*

Research Craft: An Introduction to Research Methods (2nd ed.) Reading, MA: Addison-Wesley.

Wilson, C. C., II, and F. Gutierrez. 1995. *Race, Multiculturalism, and the Media: From Mass to Class Communication.* Thousand Oaks, CA: Sage.

Wilson, C. C., II, F. Gutierrez, and L. M. Chao. 2003. *Racism, Sexism, and the Media: The Rise of Class Communication in Multicultural America.* Thousand Oaks, CA: Sage.

Wilson, D. S. 1992. "On the Relationship Between Evolutionary and Psychological Definitions of Altruism and Selfishness." *Biology and Philosophy* 7: 61–88.

Wilson, E. O. 1996. *In Search of Nature.* Washington, DC: Island Press.

Wilson, J. Q. 1973. *Political Organizations.* New York: Basic Books.

Wilson, W. J. 1995. "Jobless Ghettos and the Social Outcome of Youngsters." In *Examining Lives in Context: Perspectives on the Ecology of Human Development,* ed. P. Moen, G. H. Elder Jr., and K. Lüscher. Washington, DC: American Psychological Association.

Wirth, L. 1938. "Urbanism as a Way of Life." *American Journal of Sociology* 44: 1–24.

Wolfe, C., and S. Spencer. 1996. "Stereotypes and Prejudice: Their Overt and Subtle Influence in the Classroom." *American Behavioral Scientist* 40: 176–185.

Wood, D. J. 1989. "Social Interaction as Tutoring." In *Interaction in Human Development,* ed. M. H. Bornstein and J. S. Bruner. Hillsdale, NJ: Erlbaum.

Wood, G. S. 1991. *The Radicalism of the American Revolution.* New York: Vintage Books.

Wood, M. R., and L. A. Zurcher Jr. 1988. "The Development of a Postmodern Self: A Computer-Assisted Comparative Analysis of Personal Documents." Westport, CT: Greenwood Press.

Wood, W., F. Y. Wong, and J. G. Chachere. 1991. "Effects of Media Violence on Viewers' Aggression in Unconstrained Social Interaction." *Psychological Bulletin* 109: 371–383.

Wood, W., S. Lundgren, J. A. Ouellette, S. Busceme, and T. Blackstone. 1994. "Minority Influence: A Meta-Analytic Review of Social Influence Processes." *Psychological Bulletin* 115: 323–345.

Word, C. O., M. P. Zanna, and J. Cooper. 1974. "The Nonverbal Mediation of Self-Fulfilling Prophecies in Interracial Interaction." *Journal of Experimental Social Psychology* 10: 109–120.

Worringham, C. F., and D. M. Messick. 1983. "Social Facilitation of Running: An Unobtrusive Study." *Journal of Social Psychology* 121: 23–29.

Wortman, C. B., P. Addesman, E. Herman, and R. Greenberg. 1976. "Self-Disclosure: An Attributional Perspective." *Journal of Personality and Social Psychology* 33: 184–191.

Yamagishi, T. 1995. "Social Dilemmas." In *Sociological Social Psychology*, ed. K. S. Cook, G. A. Fine, and J. S. House. Needham Heights, MA: Allyn & Bacon.

Zajonc, R. B. 1965. "Social Facilitation." *Science* 149: 269–274.

Zajonc, R. B. 1968. "Attitudinal Effects of Mere Exposure." *Journal of Personality and Social Psychology* 9(Suppl. 2, pt. 2): 1–29.

Zajonc, R. B., A. Heingartner, and E. M. Herman. 1969. "Social Enhancement and Impairment of Performance in the Cockroach." *Journal of Personality and Social Psychology* 13: 83–92.

Zajonc, R. B., and S. M. Sales. 1966. "Social Facilitation of Dominant and Subordinate Responses." *Journal of Experimental Social Psychology* 2: 160–168.

Zanna, M. P., and R. H. Fazio. 1982. "The Attitude-Behavior Relation: Moving Toward a Third Generation of Research." In *Consistency in Social Behavior: The Ontario Symposium* (vol. 2), ed. M. P. Zanna, E. T. Higgins, and C. P. Herman. Hillsdale, NJ: Erlbaum.

Zanna, M. P., C. A. Kiesler, and P. A. Pilkonis. 1970. "Positive and Negative Attitudinal Affect Established by Classical Conditioning." *Journal of Personality and Social Psychology* 14: 321–328.

Zebrowitz-McArthur, L. A. 1988. "Person Perception in Cross-Cultural Perspective." In *The Cross-Cultural Challenge to Social Psychology*, ed. M. H. Bond. Newbury Park, CA: Sage.

Zellinger, D. A., H. Fromkin, D. E. Speller, and C. A. Kohn. 1974. *A Commodity Theory Analysis of the Effects of Age Restrictions on Pornographic Materials*. Lafayette, IN: Purdue University, Institute for Research in the Behavioral, Economic and Management Sciences.

Zillmann, D. 1971. "Excitation Transfer in Communication-Mediated Aggressive Behavior." *Journal of Experimental Social Psychology* 7: 419–434.

Zillmann, D. 1983. "Transfer of Excitation in Emotional Behavior." In *Social Psychophysiology*, ed. J. T. Cacioppo and R. E. Petty. New York: Guilford Press.

Zillmann, D., A. H. Katcher, and B. Milavsky. 1972. "Excitation Transfer from Physical Exercise to Subsequent Aggressive Behavior." *Journal of Experimental Social Psychology* 8: 247–259.

Zimbardo, P. G. 1972. "Pathology of Imprisonment." *Society* 9(4): 4–8.

Zimbardo, P. G., C. Haney, W. C. Banks, and D. A. Jaffe. 1973. "Pirandellian Prison: The Mind Is a Formidable Jailer." *New York Times Magazine*, April 8, pp. 38–60.

Zimmerman, B. J. 1983. "Social Learning; A Contextualist Account of Cognitive Functioning." In *Recent Advances in Cognitive-Developmental Theory*, ed. C. J. Brainerd. New York: Springer-Verlag.

Zoglin, R. 1996. "Blaming the Victim." *Newsweek*, November 4, p. 48.

Zuber, J. A., H. W. Crott, and J. Werner. 1992. "Choice Shift and Group Polarization: An Analysis of the Status of Arguments and Social Decision Schemes." *Journal of Personality and Social Psychology* 62: 50–61.

Zurcher, L. A., Jr. 1977. *The Mutable Self*. Beverly Hills, CA: Sage.

Zurcher, L. A., Jr., and D. A. Snow. 1981. "Collective Behavior: Social Movements." In *Social Psychology: Sociological Perspectives*, ed. M. Rosenberg and R. Turner. New York: Basic Books.

Credits

Unless otherwise indicated, page numbers refer to photos.

Chapter 1 Page 2: © Tom & Dee Ann McCarthy/CORBIS/Bettmann; page 6: © Rob Lewine Photography/CORBIS; page 7: Courtesy of the Library of Congress; page 9: © DOHERTY/OBSERVER DISPATCH/CORBIS SYGMA; page 10: T.L. Baker. 1988. *Doing Social Research*. New York: McGraw-Hill; page 15: © Jeffrey Greenberg/Photo Researchers, Inc.; page 19: © Jeff Greenberg/The Image Works; page 22: © Bojan Brecelj/CORBIS.

Chapter 2 Page 32: © Jose Luis Pelaez, Inc./CORBIS; page 36: © Roger Ressmeyer/CORBIS; page 41: © Royalty-Free/CORBIS; page 42, Table 2.2: From Wadsworth, Barry, *Piaget's Theory of Cognitive and Affective Development*, 2/e Published by Allyn & Bacon, Boston, MA. Copyright © 1979 by Pearson Education. Adapted by permission of the author; page 44, Fig. 2.1: From Berk, Laura E. *Child Development*, 5/e. Published by Allyn & Bacon, Boston, MA Copyright © 2000 by Pearson Education. Reprinted by permission of the publisher; page 50: © LWA-JDC/CORBIS; page 59, Table 2.4: Bandura, A. 1971. *Social Learning Theory*. Morristown, NJ: General Learning Press; page 64: © Ariel Skelley/CORBIS; page 67, Box 2.3: Andrew Roberts, "Focus: The Tale of Two Princes,"*Sunday Telegraph*, June 11, 2000. Copyright © 2000. Reprinted by permission.

Chapter 3 Page 70: © Bill Aron/Photo Edit; page 75, Box 3.1: Arnold van Gennep, *The Rites of Passage*, 138–139. Copyright © 1960. Reprinted by permission of The University of Chicago Press; page 76: © Nathan Benn/CORBIS; page 80, Table 3.1: From *International Encyclopedia of the Social Sciences*, by Macmillan © 1968, Macmillan. Reprinted by permission of the Gale Group; page 82: © A. Ramey/Photo Edit; page 85, Fig. 3.1: From *The Seasons of a Man's Life* by Daniel Levinson, Copyright © 1978 by Daniel J. Levinson. Used by permission of Alfred A. Knopf, a division of Random House, Inc. and Sll/Sterling Lord: Literistic, Inc.; page 90, Box 3.3: "Joey's Problem: Nancy and Evan Holt," from *The Second Shift* by Arlie Hochschild and Ann Machung, copyright © 1989, 2003 by Arlie Hochschild. Used by permission of Viking Penguin, a division of Penguin Group (USA) Inc.; page 92, Table 3.4: Reprinted with the permission of The Free Press, a Division of Simon & Schuster Adult Publishing Group, from *American Lives: Looking Back at the Children of the Great Depression* by John A. Clausen. Copyright © 1993 by John A. Clausen. All rights reserved; page 95: © Annie Griffiths Belt/CORBIS; page 96, Box 3-5: Cited in Erving Goffman, 1961. *Asylums*. New York: Random House. Originally published in Sanford M. Dornbusch, "The Military Academy as an Assimilating Institution," *Social Forces*, XXXIII, 1955, p. 317.

Chapter 4 Page 103, top left: © Larry Williams/CORBIS; page 103, bottom left: © LWA-Dann Tardif/CORBIS; page 103, right: © Karen Huntt/CORBIS; page 111: © Charles Gupton/CORBIS; page 113, Box 4.4: Courtesy of The Morris Rosenberg Foundation; page 117: © Michael Newman/Photo Edit.

Chapter 5 Page 122: © Matt A. Brown/NewSport/Corbis; page 127, left: © Brooks Kraft/CORBIS; page 127, right: © DENVER POST/KENT MEIREIS/CORBIS SYGMA; page 128, Fig. 5.2: Jones and Davis, "From Acts to Dispositions: The Attribution Process in Person Perception." In L. Berkowitz, *Advances in Experimental Social Psychology*, Vol. 2, 1965, p. 222. Copyright © 1965, with permission from Elsevier; page 133, Fig. 5.5: From *An Attributional Theory of Motivation and Emotion* by Bernard Weiner. Copyright © 1986. Reprinted by permission; page 134, Box 5.2: H. W. Stevenson and Shin-Ying Lee. 1990. "Contexts of Achievement: A Study of American Chinese, and Japanese Children." *Monographs of the Society for Research in Child Development*, No. 221, 55, nos. 1-2; page 136, Fig. 5.6: H. W. Stevenson and Shin-Ying Lee. 1990. "Contexts of Achievement: A Study of American Chinese, and Japanese Children." *Monographs of the Society for Research in Child Development*, No. 221, 55, nos. 1-2; page 138, Box 5.3: By permission of Estelle P. Lederer Trust and Creators Syndicate, Inc.; page 138, Table 5.1: Jones and Harris, 1967, "The Attribution of Attitudes," *Journal of Experimental Psychology* 3: 1–24. Copyright 1967, by permission from Elsevier; page 140: AP/Wide World Photos; pages 142-143, Box 5.4: From Rubin and Peplau (1975) "Who Believes in a Just World?" *Journal of Social Issues* 31:3, pages 69–70. © 1975. Reprinted by permission of Blackwell Publishing, Ltd.; page 144, Box 5.5: "Test Your Image IQ" from *New Dress for Success* by John Molloy. Copyright © 1988 by John T. Molloy. By permission of Warner Books, Inc.; page 147, left: © NOVASTOCK/Photo Edit; page 147, right: © Myrleen Ferguson Cate/Photo Edit.

Chapter 6 Page 150: © Marjorie Farrell/The Image Works; page 153, Box 6.1: Excerpt from "On Language: The Mood of 'Tude" by William Safire, *The New York Times* November 25, 1990. Copyright 1990 by the New York Times Company. Reprinted by permission; page 157, Table 6.2: From Janet T. Spence. "A Short Version of the Attitudes Toward Women Scale." (AWS) *Bulletin of the Psychonomic Society, Inc.*, Vol. 2, pp. 219–220. Reprinted by permission of the Psychonomic Society; page 157, Table 6.3: Reprinted from *Journal of Criminal Justice*, Vol. 13, 1985, page 375. Copyright 1985 with permission from Elsevier; page 158, Table 6.4: From *Psychology of Attitudes* 1st edition by Eagly. © 1993. Reprinted with permission of Wadsworth, a division of Thomson Learning: www.

thomsonrights.com. Fax 800-730-2215; page 159: © Reuters/ CORBIS; page 161, quote: Safire, "Essay: The Loyalty Mystery" by William Safire. *The New York Times* January 11, 1999; page 161: © Mark Peterson/CORBIS; page 162, Table 6.5: Katz, "The Functional Approach to the Study of Attitudes," *Public Opinion Quarterly* 24: 192. Copyright © 1960. Reprinted by permission of Oxford University Press, UK; page 166, Table 6.6: From *Psychology of Attitudes* 1st edition by Eagly. © 1993. Reprinted with permission of Wadsworth, a division of Thomson Learning: www.thomsonrights.com. Fax 800-730-2215; page 168: © David Young-Wolff/Photo Edit; page 174, Fig. 6.4: © 2000 The Gallup Organization; page 177, Fig. 6.6: I. Ajzen (1987). "Attitudes, Traits, and Actions. Dispositional Prediction of Behavior in Personality and Social Psychology." In L. Berkowitz, ed. *Advances in Experimental Social Psychology*, Vol. 20. Copyright 1987 with permission from Elsevier.

Chapter 7 Page 180: © Jon Feingersh/CORBIS; page 187, Fig. 7.2: Reprinted from *The Organization Man* by William H. Whyte. Copyright © 1956. Reprinted by permission of The University of Pennsylvania Press; page 191, left: © Bettmann/ CORBIS; page 191, right: Underwood & Underwood/ CORBIS; page 192, Fig. 7.3: "Measuring the Physical in Physical Attractiveness: Quasi-Experiments on the Sociobiology of Female Facial Beauty." *Journal of Personality and Social Psychology* Figure 1, page 928. Copyright © 1986 by the American Psychological Association. Reproduced by permission; page 193, four photos: Dr. Judith Langlois; page 198, Table 7.2: From *The Psychology of Love* by R. J. Steinberg and M. L. Barnes. Copyright © 1988. Reprinted by permission of Yale University Press; page 199: © Ariel Skelley/CORBIS; page 208, Box 7.5: From *The Rules: Time Tested Secrets for Capturing the Heart of Mr. Right* by Ellen Fein. Copyright © 1995 by Ellen Fein and Sherrie Schneider. By permission of Warner Books, Inc. All rights reserved. To purchase copies of this book, please call 1-800-759-0190; page 209, Box 7.6: Reprinted with the permission of The Free Press, a Division of Simon & Schuster Adult Publishing Group, from *The Sociology of Georg Simmel*, translated and edited by Kurt H. Woolf. Copyright © 1950 by The Free Press. Copyright renewed 1978 by The Free Press. All rights reserved; page 210, Fig. 7.4: N. B. McCormick and C. J. Jesser. 1983. "The Courtship Game: Power in the Sexual Encounter." In *Changing Boundaries: Gender Roles and Sexual Behavior*, ed. E. R. Allgeier and N. B. McCormick. Palo Alto, CA: Mayfield.

Chapter 8 Page 214: © Claudia Kunin/CORBIS; page 219, excerpt: *The Holy Bible*, International Version, 1988, p. 1307. Grand Rapids, MI: Zondervan Publishing House; page 219, Table 8.1: Zick Rubin, "Measure of Love," *Journal of Personality and Social Psychology*, Vol.16, No.2, page 67. © 1969, 1970 by Zick Rubin. Reprinted by permission of the author; page 220, left: © Ant Strack/CORBIS; page 220, center: Jose Luis Pelaez, Inc./CORBIS; page 220, right: © Steve Prezant/ CORBIS; page 222, Table 8.2: Short, "Distinguishing Love

and Infatuation" from *Sex, Love and Romance*. Copyright © 2004. Reprinted by permission of Frederick Fell Publishers; page 224: © Ariel Skelley/CORBIS; page 225, Fig. 8.1: From *The Psychology of Love* by R. J. Steinberg and M. L. Barnes. Copyright 1988. Reprinted by permission of Yale University Press; page 226, Table 8.3: Levine, "Love and Marriage in Eleven Cultures," *Journal of Cross Cultural Psychology*. Copyright © 1995. Reprinted by permission of Sage Publications, Inc.; page 227, Table 8.4: Buss et al., "International Preferences in Selecting Mates: A Study of 37 Cultures," *Journal of Cross Cultural Psychology*. Copyright © 1990. Reprinted by permission of Sage Publications, Inc.; page 230, Box 8.2: Short, "Should You Marry?" from *Sex, Love and Romance*. Copyright © 2004. Reprinted by permission of Frederick Fell Publishers; page 233, Table 8.5: Benokraitis, Nijole V. *Marriages and Families: Changes, Choices, and Constraints*, 3rd Edition, © 1999. Reprinted by permission of Pearson Education, Inc., Upper Saddle River, NJ; page 234: © Cassy Cohen/Photo Edit; page 235, Box 8.4: From *The Good Marriage* by Judith S. Wallerstein and Sandra Blakeslee. Copyright © 1995 by Judith S. Wallerstein and Sandra Blakeslee. Reprinted by permission of Houghton Mifflin Company and Carol Mann Agency. All rights reserved; page 236, Table 8.6: Knox et al., "Why College Student Relationships End," *College Student Journal* 3:45 (1997). Reprinted by permission; page 238: © Royalty-Free/CORBIS.

Chapter 9 Page 240: © David Young-Wolff/CORBIS; page 243, Box 9.1: Reprinted with the permission of Simon & Schuster Adult Publishing Group, from *The Book of Virtues* by William J. Bennett. Copyright © 1993 by William J. Bennett. All rights reserved; page 244, left: © CORBIS SYGMA; page 244, top right: © Hulton-Duetsch Collection/CORBIS; page 244, bottom right: © Reuters/CORBIS; page 246, Fig. 9.1: Batson et al., "Distress and Empathy: Two Qualitatively Distinct Vicarious Emotions with Different Motivational Consequences." *Journal of Personality* 55. Copyright 1987. Reprinted by permission of Blackwell Publishing; page 247, Box 9.3: M.H. Davis. 1994. *Empathy: A Social Psychological Approach*. Dubuque, IA: Brown/Benchmark; page 250, Table 9.2: Adapted with the permission of The Free Press, a Division of Simon & Schuster Adult Publishing Group, from *Cheating Monkeys and Citizen Bees* by Lee Dugatkin. Copyright © 1999 by Lee Dugatkin. All rights reserved; page 255: © Robert Brenner/Photo Edit; page 258, Table 9.3: Robert Levine et al. "Helping in 36 US Cities." *Journal of Personality and Social Psychology* 67: Table 1, p. 72. Copyright © 1994 by the American Psychological Association. Reprinted by permission; page 262: © Viviane Moos/CORBIS; page 266, Table 9.4: Joan Miller, "Perceptions of Social Responsibilities in India and the US: Moral Imperatives or Personal Decisions?" *Journal of Personality and Social Psychology* 58. Copyright 1990 by the American Psychological Association. Adapted by permission; page 267, Table 9.5: Reprinted with permission from *Journal of Applied*

Fig. 13.2: B. Latane (1981). "The Psychology of Social Impact." *American Psychologist.* Copyright © 1981 by the American Psychological Association. Adapted by permission; page 385, Table 13.1: From Janis, Irving L., *Groupthink: Psychological Studies of Policy Decisions and Fiascos, Second Edition.* Copyright © 1982 by Houghton Mifflin Company. Adapted with permission. Adapted with the permission of The Free Press, a Division of Simon & Schuster Adult Publishing Group, from *Decision Making: A Psychological Analysis of Conflict, Choice, and Commitment* by Irving Janis and Leon Mann. Copyright © 1977 by The Free Press. All rights reserved; page 387: © Reuters/CORBIS; page 388, Box 13.3: From *Risk Taking* 1st edition by KOGAN. © 1964. Reprinted with permission of Wadsworth, a division of Thomson Learning: www.thomson rights.com. Fax 800-730-2215; page 390: Getty Images, Inc.; page 393, Table 13.2: Deutsch et al., "Studies of Interpersonal Bargaining," *Journal of Conflict Resolution.* Copyright © 1962. Reprinted by permission of Sage Publications, Inc.

Chapter 14 Page 396: © Olivier Coret/In Visu/CORBIS; page 399, Table 14.1: Clark McPhail, *The Myth of the Madding Crowd.* Copyright © 1991. Reprinted by permission of Transaction Publishers; page 401, Box 14.1: "World Briefing Asia: Panic and Death After Monster Reports." *The New York Times,* August 20, 2002. Copyright © 2002. Reprinted by permission of Reuters; page 402, left: © CORBIS; page 402, center:

© Bettmann/CORBIS; page 402, right: © Bettmann/CORBIS; page 405, Box 14.3: From *The Everything Tall Tales, Legends, and Outrageous Lies Book.* Copyright © 2001, Adams Media Corporation. Used by permission of Adams Media. All rights reserved; page 406, Box 14.4: Introduction from *Toxic Sludge Is Good for You* by Mark Dowie. Copyright © 1995. Reprinted by permission of Common Courage Press; page 407: © CORBIS; page 410: © Bernd Obermann/CORBIS; page 412, Fig. 14.1: Clark McPhail, *The Myth of the Madding Crowd.* Copyright © 1991. Reprinted by permission of Transaction Publishers; page 414, Fig. 14.2: Clark McPhail, *The Myth of the Madding Crowd.* Copyright © 1991. Reprinted by permission of Transaction Publishers; page 415: © Bettmann/CORBIS; page 416, Table 14.2: Rhoda Blumberg, "The Civil Rights Movement" in Goodwin et al., *The Social Movement Reader: Cases and Concepts.* Copyright 2003. Reprinted by permission of Blackwell Publishing; page 417, Box 14.5: Turner, Ralph, Killian, Lewis M., *Collective Behavior,* 3rd Edition, © 1987. Reprinted by permission of Pearson Education, Inc.; page 418, Fig. 14.3: D. F. Aberle, *The Peyote Religion among the Navaho.* Copyright © 1966. Reprinted by permission of The University of Chicago Press; page 422, Box 14.6: Reprinted by arrangement with the Estate of Martin Luther King, Jr., c/o Writers House as agent for the proprietor. New York, NY. Copyright © Martin Luther King., Jr., copyright renewed 1991 Coretta Scott King.

Author Index

Subject Index